Critical Issues in American Religious History

A Reader

Critical Issues in American Religious History

A Reader

Robert R. Mathisen

A Markham Press Fund Publication from
Baylor University Press
Waco, Texas

Library of Congress Cataloging-in-Publication Data

Critical issues in American religious history : a reader / [edited by]
Robert R. Mathisen.
    p. cm.
Includes bibliographical references.
  ISBN 0-918954-79-7 (pbk. : alk. paper)
  1. United States—Church history. I. Mathisen, Robert R.
BR515 .C75 2001
277.3—dc21

                        2001002819

This volume is the thirty-seventh
published by the Markham Press
Fund of Baylor University Press,
established in memory of Dr. L. N.
and Princess Finch Markham of
Longview, Texas, by their daughters,
Mrs. R. Matt Dawson of Waco,
Texas, and Mrs. B. Reid Clanton of
Longview, Texas.

Printed in the United States of
America on acid-free paper.

Contents

Contents

83   Chapter 3
The Era of the Great Awakening

Issue: *What was the meaning of the Great Awakening?*

Documents
1. An Essay for Reviving Religion, 1733
2 Thoughts on the Revival of Religion, 1742
3. Seasonable Thoughts on the State of Religion, 1743
4. "What a Vile Creature I Am," 1744
5. The Testimony of Harvard College Against George Whitefield, 1744
6. The Millennium, 1758

Essays
CEDRIC COWING. "The Great Awakening: Revelation and Reason" in *The Great Awakening and The American Revolution: Colonial Thought in the 18th Century* (1971).

DAVID S. LOVEJOY. "The Great Awakening as Subversion and Conspiracy" in *Religious Enthusiasm in the New World* (1985).

Contents

Contents

Contents

Contents

Contents

Contents

Contents

Contents

Contents

Contents

Foreword

Students need to read documents, but reading documents in a vacuum breeds confusion. Students need to read the authoritative interpretations of established scholars, but reading only such interpretations sucks the humanity, the unpredictability, and much of the fun out of doing history. So the obvious solution for introducing students to the warp as well as the woof of history is to present a carefully chosen combination of documents and interpretation. Yet coming up with such a combination is a lot easier said than done.

For this book, which examines "critical issues in American religious history," the job is done very well. The first trick for this kind of book is making sure that the "critical issues" chosen are truly important and that they can be illuminated by a combination of historians' essays and documents from the appropriate periods. On this score endless debate is possible. Why not consider slavery in the colonial period instead of the nineteenth century? Why treat religion and science in confrontation after the Civil War but neglect the remarkably harmonious uses of religion and science for many of the decades before the Civil War? Why feature fundamentalism versus modernism, which exercised only a part of America's Protestants, but not Protestantism versus Roman Catholicism, an antagonism that goes way back and that exercised almost every generation of Americans until the very recent past (if, indeed, it does still not exercise great numbers of American believers)? Why say this book is about "America" but include nothing on Canada and Mexico?

An answer to these questions, some of which are more pressing than others, might go like this: In the first instance, an introductory textbook has to be under 20,000 pages long, and if an editor stuck in something substantial about every important question concerning religious history in only the United States, that is about how long the book would be. In the second instance, however, the issues that are spotlighted here have in fact been the focus of much attention, they have engaged public debate by common people as well as academic debate by scholars, and they have all been better studied in recent years by fresh discoveries of interesting documents. This would be a good answer. Professor Mathisen's judgments about what have been the big issues in American religion can be relied upon. Some of his choices, like the antebellum West and America as empire-builder, are especially useful for expanding the traditional, but also parochial, renditions. Mathisen does not have a God-like ability to judge significance, but if readers pay serious attention to the subjects he has selected as critical issues, they will learn a very great deal about a lot of interesting history.

But what about the specific selections for the individual critical issues? Again, someone who has worked in the field for some time could maybe come up with a completely different table of contents. Yet here as well, Professor Mathisen's stack up very well against alternatives. Take the chapter on the Civil War. In just a few pages, we hear a sober word on slavery from Abraham Lincoln more than five years before the shooting started, two pious letters from the Confederates, the unrivaled public theory of Lincoln's Second Inaugural Address from 1865, the Rev. Henry Ward Beecher's much less weighty address a month later, and then a first-hand account of revivals in the Confederate army. These documents are followed by substantial studies from three of the leading historians of religion in that terrible war—and the proportion among those three articles is correct too, for there has been almost twice as much good scholarship on religion in the South as on religion in the North. The result is a unit that, while it, of course, does not say everything that can be said about the topic, nonetheless communicates important things about the complex, tangible, lived reality of what actually happened.

The choices for the other critical issues are just as defensible. Together they make up a very useful introduction to the subject. There is also enough here to give so-called experts in the field a lot to ponder as well.

Mark A. Noll
Professor of History
Wheaton College

Preface

"[History shows] the Necessity of a *Publick Religion,* from its usefulness to the Publick; the Advantage of a Religious Character among private Persons, the Mischiefs of Superstition, & c. and the excellency of the CHRISTIAN RELIGION above all others antient or modern."

—Benjamin Franklin

Writing in 1749 in a plan for educating the young people of Pennsylvania, Benjamin Franklin was certain of the practical utility of religion. Some time later he observed that most persons "have need of the motives of religion to restrain them from vice, to support their virtue, and retain them in the practice of it till it becomes habitual."

More than two centuries later historian Henry F. May drew the attention of his readers to the place of religion in America's past. "The recovery of American religious history," he claimed, "has restored a knowledge of the mode, even the language, in which most Americans, during most of American history, did their thinking about human nature and destiny."

The link between the words of the eighteenth-century statesman and the twentieth-century historian is at the heart of this volume. For on many occasions Americans as a religious people have experienced tension and indecision as they have wrestled with a variety of critical issues that crossed their paths. How to implement their religious creeds and ideals in an ever-changing society is recorded, as May noted, in the language of the people as they have sought to articulate their identity and destiny.

The issues discussed in this work are deemed critical because they illustrate four interrelated dimensions of religious tension in America's religious experience. (See the illustration on the next page.) The first is American civilization's ongoing grappling with the relationship between the secular and the sacred. The people of America continue to experience the discomfort of what noted historian George Marsden refers to as the "paradoxically curious mix of the religious and

American Religion in Tension

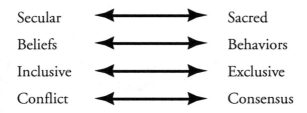

Secular	Sacred
Beliefs	Behaviors
Inclusive	Exclusive
Conflict	Consensus

the secular." From the colonial period to the present, partisans on both sides have drawn their lines in the sand, only to discover that the shifting winds of modernization have eroded the lines, forcing the creation of new ones.

A second shade of meaning suggested by the title is the contradictory manner in which Americans have applied their religious beliefs to their behavior. Numerous critical issues have arisen in America's past which illustrate Jewish scholar Will Herberg's contention that Americans make a distinction between professed religion and "operative religion"—that religion by which Americans actually live. Franklin was correct in noting that religion has restrained Americans from vice, but at times it has also supported vice, as with slavery, which nearly consumed the nation over a century ago.

The increasing pluralism of the American culture produces the title's third implied dimension. How inclusive (and, therefore, exclusive) would the great American tent of religion be? As modern church historian Sydney Ahlstrom has noted, "The most fundamental divisions in America's religious life are a direct inheritance from the Old World." How would America deal with its inheritance? The critical issue of inclusiveness for American religion has posed questions such as, Shall women be ordained? Shall a Roman Catholic be elected president? For these and other questions, American religionists have long experienced the uncertainty of their religious pluralism.

The issue of conflict and consensus illustrates the fourth and final nuance signified by the title of this work. What historian of modern Christianity Martin Marty refers to as the centrifugal and centripetal forces within American religion have been present since the beginning of our nation. They have intensified, however, in the past century, as he eloquently describes in the second volume of his modern American religion series (The Noise of Conflict, 1919-1941), *in which religious strife is the keynote, and in the third volume*

(Under God, Indivisible, 1941-1960), *in which consensus predominates. The ongoing tension over the issue of exclusiveness and inclusiveness has quite naturally resulted in periods of conflict and consensus.*

The issues identified as critical in this volume serve as windows through which to view America on its religious pilgrimage. Some issues examined here were specific to particular periods and places, while others touch cultural nerves that extend through much of the nation's past. Each of the voices heard in the documents and essays articulates some facet of religion in America—the institution in this nation that Frenchman Alexis de Tocqueville considered to be the most important of all.

Critical Issues in American Religious History

A Reader

Chapter 1

Interpreting Religion in America

"For the study and understanding of American culture, the recovery of American religious history may well be the most important achievement of the last thirty years." Writing these words in 1964, the eminent historian Henry F. May recognized that *"even for those students of American culture who do not find religious thought and practice intrinsically interesting, knowledge of religious history has become a necessity."* May asserted that *"the recovery of American religious history has restored a knowledge of the mode, even the language, in which most Americans, during most of American history, did their thinking about human nature and destiny."*

About ten years after May wrote these words, Sydney E. Ahlstrom stated that *"the moral and spiritual development of the American people is one of the most intensely relevant subjects on the face of the earth."* In arguing this, he noted that as the major current in American religious history, Christianity consists of many substreams which contribute to *"the radical diversity of American religious movements."* Furthermore, he posited that any interpretation of religion in America must be broadened to include secular convictions and movements, some of which endangered the very survival of the churches. Clearly, Ahlstrom's history of the American people is a history of a people facing numerous critical issues.

With the more recent rise of postmodern thought, however, several questions concerning present attention to religion in America need to be asked. Is knowledge of religious history as necessary now as it was for May in 1964? If it is, how can it be made a relevant part of Americans' thought and behavior? If it is not, what has replaced it in the national culture? How do the tensions in American religion both reflect and produce tension in the broader American culture? Historians of American religious history continue to wrestle with questions such as these.

Essays

In the first essay, Henry F. May, professor emeritus of history at the University of California, Berkeley, explains why the recovery of American religious history during the middle third of the twentieth century took place, and then suggests the meaning of the recovery for the next generation. Martin E. Marty of the University of Chicago describes in the second essay how and why American religion made a perceptible shift away from becoming more secular and less influential in American life during the second half of the twentieth century. In the third essay, Warren A. Nord of the University of North Carolina reports on his study of the place given to religion in high school textbooks and reflects on what this says about how religion is interpreted in America.

The Recovery of American Religious History

HENRY F. MAY

SOURCE: Henry F. May, "The Recovery of American Religious History." *American Historical Review,* LXX (1964), 79-92. Reprinted with permission.

For the study and understanding of American culture, the recovery of American religious history may well be the most important achievement of the last thirty years. A vast and crucial area of American experience has been rescued from neglect and misunderstanding. Puritanism, Edwardsian Calvinism, revivalism, liberalism, modernism, and the social gospel have all been brought down out of the attic and put back in the historical front parlor. Out of monographic research on these and other topics, it begins to be possible to build a convincing synthesis, a synthesis independent of political history, though never unrelated to it.[1]

Even for those students of American culture who do not find religious thought and practice intrinsically interesting, knowledge of religious history has become a necessity. This is most obviously the case for those interested in American intellectual history. In the first place, the recovery of American religious history has restored a knowledge of the mode, even the language, in which most Americans, during most of American history, did their thinking about human nature and destiny. In the second place, the recovery has necessitated, though it has not yet really affected, a reorganization. Obviously the categories of V. L. Parrington, once so satisfactory, will no longer work. One cannot, for instance, oppose "French" liberalism to Calvinist conservatism as the poles between which to classify both political and religious thought in the early national period. What is one to do with orthodox clergy who supported the American and for long defended the French Revolution, with Whig conservatives who were Unitarians, or with doctrinally conservative Presbyterians who took the side of Jackson in politics? There are too many exceptions: they destroy instead of proving the rules. Nor can one talk any longer, without important qualifications, about an "American faith" in which optimism about man is inescapably linked to democracy. To insist on such a link, one has to rule out of the American democratic tradition not only such "belletristic" aberrants as Henry James, Hawthorne, Poe, and Melville, not only such political exceptions as Calhoun or Henry Adams, but also John Adams and Madison, which is difficult, and both Lincoln and Mark Twain, which is downright impossible.[2] To summarize the central American tradition has become a far more difficult task than it once was, and a far more interesting one.

Restoring a language and shaking up a set of categories are not the only changes wrought in intellectual history by the recovery of religious history. By analogy the work of religious historians illuminates two major perennial problems of the American intellectual historian. The first of these is the relation of American to European thought. Obviously American church history cannot be studied without reference to the Reformation, and thus to European thought since (or perhaps before) the patristic period. Yet, as Tocqueville, Schaff, and Bryce saw and as lesser European commentators have often not understood, American religion cannot be forced into European categories. Like many other kinds of American experience, religious experience serves both as link and barrier between the continents.

The other problem of intellectual history illuminated by the example of religious history is the even more difficult one of the relation between ideas and institutions. For this the history of American Protestantism, with its long effort to institutionalize successive religious impulses, offers also some highly interesting suggestions.[3]

That part of literary history which lies closest to intellectual history has been transformed with it, or even before it.[4] At an opposite pole in American studies, the analysis of American class structure has been enriched. Sociologists must study church history and even theology. Simple lines between denominations will no longer do; to locate someone in American society it is necessary to say what *kind* of a Baptist or Presbyterian he is, and where, in religious and other terms, he comes from.[5] Historians of our two greatest political crises have revived a religious interpretation of each.[6] Theorists of American foreign policy—including some theorists not far removed from the scene of action—frequently invoke kinds of thought that were originally theological.[7]

Of the several meanings intended by the title of this article most historians will, I think, readily admit the fact of an increased emphasis on religious history. Many have also observed—whether or not they have approved—the emergence of a more sympathetic assessment of American religious experience. Here consensus stops; historians disagree about the causes of these related changes. Part of the disagreement is inevitably ideological; part arises from the complexity of the subject. In American historiography, as in American religion, categories shift and change. Yet categories are necessary, and a look back at major names and dates suggests a few.

The recovery of American religious history really began in the 1930's. In the twenties, nineteenth-century "scientific" history was being challenged by the brilliant agnostic relativism of Becker, the fervent progressivism of Parrington, and the somewhat selective determinism of Beard.[8] "Puritanism," and the larger religious tradition loosely associated with it, was under heavy attack inside and outside historical circles. Harold Stearns explained in 1922 that there was no article on religion in his *Civilization in the United States* because he could find no one interested in the topic.[9] This was a Menckenesque exaggeration, but it was true that American religion, aside from the dramatic forays of the fundamentalists, did not look very interesting. The dominant liberal Protestantism was reaching the end of a long, ignominious, and unsuccessful effort to accommodate its teaching at any cost to the ultrasecular culture of the day.[10]

Seminary historians played their parts in this effort at accommodation, trying hard to follow the lead of the dominant university historians. Most of them, attempting to be neutral and "scientific," produced factual monographs limited by denominational lines. The two best-known general histories of American religion written during the period, those by H. K. Rowe (1924) and W. W. Sweet (1930), followed the lead of standard secular interpretation. Rowe emphasized the growth of liberalism and religious freedom, Sweet, the frontier. Both works were respectable; neither was highly original.[11]

In the thirties, when the recovery began, a student who wanted a treatment of American religious history with some feeling for theology had to go back beyond the twenties to such books as F. H. Foster's *Genetic History of New England Theology* (Chicago, 1907) or Leonard Bacon's *History of American Christianity* (New York, 1897). If he wanted to investigate religious experience, he invariably started with William James's unique and curious classic of 1902. Only for the topic of religion and social class—a topic that interested him greatly—did he have a first-rate recent work, H. Richard Niebuhr's *Social Sources of Denominationalism* (New York, 1929), which applied to American religion the insights of Max Weber and Ernst Troeltsch.

In this atmosphere, the recovery of American religious history was begun by the only people in a position to undertake it, the immensely energetic secular scholars of the day. To men schooled in objective examination of, as nearly as possible, *all* the data, religion was too big to be ignored in the flippant manner of a Harold Stearns. Herbert Schneider, who occupied a chair of religion at Columbia University, treated the American religious past with much learning.[12] At the end of the period Ralph Henry Gabriel in *The Course of American Democratic Thought* (New York, 1940) gave religion a much more active constituent role in intellectual history than had Parrington, though he too discussed religious ideas without much theological analysis.[13]

The best-informed and most influential student of American social history was A. M. Schlesinger, who says with great candor in his recent autobiography that the central questions of religious thought have never held much interest for him.[14] Accepting nonetheless readily the importance of religion for most Americans in the past, Schlesinger directed toward this field the efforts of many students, all of whom did their best to penetrate its obscure shadows with the clear light of objective research. In an influential essay of 1932,[15] Schlesinger himself applied to religious history the insight that was shortly to inform his *Rise of the City*. In the neglected period of the late nineteenth century, he said, American religion had undergone a series of highly important reactions: to Darwinism, higher criticism, comparative religion, and, most important of all, to the challenge of the city.

Commenting much later on this essay and its influence, one of the current group of able seminary historians finds its insight useful and important even from his own very different point of view.[16] Nevertheless, says this later critic, Schlesinger's description of the church transforming itself in response to the urban challenge, like Sweet's description of the church reacting to the frontier, makes the role of the church too passive and neglects inner changes not entirely determined by these external pressures. Whatever the merits of this criticism and the now widespread view it implies, the rescue of religious history was largely begun, as it had to be, from a secular point of view not unlike that of Schlesinger.

Though secular and academic historians dominated this stage of the recovery until after World War II, two quite different tendencies of the thirties foreshadowed a challenge to this domination. The first was the expansion and reorientation of the study of American literature. Still full of the revolts and rejections of the twenties, but discontented with the simple categories of the past and only partly satisfied with the Marxist stereotypes of the present, many of the best young students were fascinated by the complexities, doubts, and inner struggles of writers like Melville, Hawthorne, and James. Nothing, they found, could be farther from the truth than the facile dictum of Howells, still faithfully echoed in very recent years, that American literature dealt characteristically with the surface, "smiling aspects of life." Sometimes venturing beyond American literature into one of the new programs in American studies, students coming from literature departments encountered (more often than history graduate students of this period) the infinitely complex world of recent historical thought, from Mannheim to Whitehead or Collingwood. Admiring complexity and uncompromising intellectual struggle, some of them discovered a new field: theology. To literary intellectuals of the thirties, theology was approachable partly because it seemed to have so little to do with religion, especially the religion of the First Methodist Church in the generic home town.

In the study of religious thought in American literature or culture, students of this kind found gifted mentors. One was F. O. Matthiessen, immensely attractive as a scholar and leader to this generation, and far more passionately interested than most of his students in the relation between social radicalism and religious commitment.[17] Even more important for the systematic study of American religious thought was Perry Miller. In 1928, consciously defying the advice of his own teachers and the Menckenian prejudices of the times, Miller had begun his gigantic excavation of Puritanism.[18] In many ways a product of the alienated and tormented twenties, an atheist and something of a radical, Miller yet went to work to rescue Puritan and Calvinist thought with a relish for all its paradoxes and tensions, and with a zeal, sometimes with a polemic intensity, comparable almost to that of Edwards himself. Surely the result of his labor, deepening the history of the American mind in a chronological sense as well as others, must be one of the most enduring as well as one of the strangest monuments of the radical thirties.

The other development that began in the 1930's to suggest the rise of a new kind of religious history was the turn toward neo-orthodoxy within Protestantism itself. Like Edwards and many other American religious figures, Reinhold Niebuhr, the central American figure in this diverse movement, drew heavily on contemporary European thought. But, again like Edwards and many other prophets, he started by reacting to the smug society he encountered around him. It was not Auschwitz or Hiroshima, but Detroit in the twenties that started Niebuhr on the road away from accommodation and optimism and toward a belief in a world under judgment.[19] Thus there is something in common between Niebuhr's rejections and those of contemporary literary critics, though very little that is common in their respective affirmations.

Two very different works in American religious history reflected a neo-orthodox emphasis in this period of beginnings. The first was Joseph Haroutunian's study of American Calvinist theology, *Piety vs. Moralism* (New York, 1932). Only a book written, like this one, from a neo-orthodox point of view could at this moment have restored meaning to the long-neglected family fights of New England divines, distinguishing in their thought between the new and the merely orthodox. The other historical work that reflected the new theological tendency was H. Richard Niebuhr's *The Kingdom of God in America*, eventually to become one of the most influential books in the whole field. In his introduction, Niebuhr criticized his own much-admired *Social Sources of Denominationalism*. A sociological approach like that of the earlier book, he now said, "helped to explain why the religious stream flowed in these particular channels'" but failed to "account for the force of the stream itself."[20] American Christianity should be treated not as a series of institutions but as a prophetic movement, never completely embodied in any institutional forms, liable to decay but capable of perennial self-renewal. This deeply Protestant view of church history was to influence many of the ablest religious historians of the next period. Shorn of some of its religious meaning, Niebuhr's suggestion was usable by historians of other kinds of ideas and institutions.[21] Might not his idea of a cycle of reform, organization, decline, and renewal illuminate the fate of many kinds of ideas in a fluid and energetic society? One might suggest progressive education, temperance, conservation—almost any American movement, perhaps including political democracy itself—as test cases.

In the period since the Second World War, the period of fruition that succeeded this one of preparation, all the influences already active continued to operate. Social historians, among them students of both Schlesingers, of Oscar Handlin, of Richard Hofstadter, and others, continued to deal with the history of American religion from a largely secular point of view. A flood of monographs continued to analyze American literature in more and more specifically religious terms. The influence of neo-orthodoxy, spreading like other major movements in American thought from a small center ever more widely, affected historical writing on all sorts of subjects. The clear and acknowledged influence of Reinhold Niebuhr on Arthur Schlesinger, Jr., C. Vann Woodward, and George F. Kennan suggests the dimensions of this periphery.[22]

Three new influences must be added to the list. The first is the development of a new kind of intellectual history, or, more accurately, the revival of an old one. The new intellectual history places more emphasis on the analysis of ideas and less on description of their social antecedents.[23] Needed and overdue, this tendency may sometimes have gone too far, detaching one part of human experience from another in a somewhat mechanical manner, and talking too simply about the influence of one book an another. In any case, much of the new intellectual history has avoided the opposite error of treating ideas, religious ideas included, as simple responses to clearly identifiable stimuli.

The second postwar development that affected religious history came from an opposite quarter and was perhaps complementary. Sociologists and social historians, among them David Riesman and Oscar Handlin, developed a new kind of analysis and criticism of American society, emphasizing the search for identity among the pressures of a plural, yet sometimes conformist society. To some students of American religion, this suggested a new interpretation of the past and present role of religious groups.[24]

The third new influence, pervasive and complex, was the religious revival of the 1950's. The nature and even the existence of this revival have been endlessly debated. Was there any connection between such phenomena as swelling church statistics, highly successful traditional revivalism, best-selling and sugary "peace-of-mind" manuals, semiofficial association of God with American foreign policy, and gingerly, reluctant inquiry into the religious turn of "intellectuals" carried out by the editors of the *Partisan Review?* Could any of these have any connection with the devastating disjunctions of Karl Barth or the tragic view of history propounded by Reinhold Niebuhr? Was this really a revival of religion, or only a search for identity on the part of third generation immigrants or other-directed exurbanites?

At least three aspects of this complex phenomenon must be taken into consideration for our present purposes. First was the new realization of American religion's numerical growth, both short-term and long-term. According to widely cited reports, more than 60 per cent of the population were now church members, as opposed to 5 per cent in 1776 and 35 per cent in 1900. How far to accept either the accuracy or the implications of these figures was a complex question. Yet it was clear that one could no longer talk about American religion as something that used to be important. At least according to the most concrete indexes—numbers, buildings, and money—it was a spectacular success. One exaggerated but suggestive interpretation said that rapid growth had from the beginning determined the whole nature of American Protestantism. The American churches were not branches of European Christendom, but new churches, with the good and bad characteristics of new churches everywhere.[25]

A second element of the revival was the continuing vitalization of theology. One historian had this to say:

One must go back to the sixteenth century to find an era of equal theological fertility and creativeness. In America it is at least a century and a half since theologians held a position of such importance in our national thought. Now that John Dewey is dead there is in the United States scarcely a single philosopher of public eminence who is confronting the traditional "problems of man" as comprehensively as are at least a half-dozen theologians.[26]

Often the theological renaissance and the popular growth seemed opposed rather than complementary; no one criticized so harshly the easy, amorphous popular "faith in faith" as those who had for some time been demanding faith in something more specific and difficult. Yet some highly sophisticated historians of religion concluded that this revival, with its depths and shallows, its center and periphery, was not altogether different from revivals in the past.[27]

A third fact about this revival, which did seem to differentiate it somewhat from its predecessors, was the complexity of its effect on American intellectuals. As with some of the earlier revivals, a great many intellectuals remained hostile to this one in all its aspects. Others, including poets, novelists, and a few historians, stood fundamentally within it. A large number, however, and the most important group for our present purposes, belonged in neither of these opposing camps. As Sydney Ahlstrom put it, "curiosity about religion" penetrated intellectual circles far beyond the ranks of the committed. This "curiosity" might "lead a person merely to taste some popular book, to take up the study of some religious poet, or to dedicate himself to a lifetime vocation of religious research."[28] In the middle of the twentieth century, that is, not everyone could find himself at home either among believers or militant secularists.

The consequences of these diverse changes were themselves diverse. The first was a new understanding of the nature of the mainstream of American religious history. In the thirties, many students of American religion had understandably admired Puritanism and Edwardsian Calvinism and disliked revivalism. Now it seemed clear that (as Miller's own work had indicated) both Covenant Theology and Consistent Calvinism had been brilliant, heroic, but unsuccessful attempts to channel the turbulent flood of American religious energy. The mainstream, for better or worse, had been revivalistic, emotional, even somewhat pragmatic. Faced with the task of evangelizing an unchurched continent, of combatting not only infidelity but barbarism, first on the frontier and then in the cities, the American churches had indeed compromised theological differences. So far had this process gone that they had almost lost their distinctive task and message. But when adaptation had gone too far, self-criticism had restored some balance, in the early eighteenth century, in the late nineteenth century, again in the mid-twentieth century.

Obviously this reorientation owed much to the past insights of Sweet, Schlesinger, and Richard Niebuhr. It owed much also to the new investigation of revivalism by such lay historians as W. G. McLoughlin, Jr., and Bernard Weisberger.[29] Still more important, however, were the insights of Timothy Smith, himself a minister, and the seminary historians Sidney Mead and Winthrop S. Hudson. All these saw the past tasks of American religion as men who had a more than academic concern with its present pastoral duties. And all looked at revivals from the midst of a period of revival.

Smith found much of the vitality of American nineteenth-century religion in the perfectionist tradition. It was the belief in the possibility of perfect holiness, he argued, that furnished the energy for many reform crusades. Somewhat more complex in their loyalties, Mead and Hudson emphasized both the failures and successes of the revivalist tradition, failures and successes inseparable from those of American culture.[30]

The second consequence of the new religious surge owed more to the theological renaissance than to the popular increase. This was the demand on the part of a number of the seminary historians for a new kind of church history, emancipated from the long subservience to "positivist lay historians." With varying degrees of fervor, a number of manifestoes including more than one presidential address to the American Society of Church History called for a separate "church history." This must be the history of the church eternal, invisible, and universal; it must indeed be a narration of the continuing work of the Holy Spirit on earth.[31]

To the more extreme of these statements, lay historians and even some of the more moderate "church" historians themselves could raise several objections. In the first place, it seemed strange for Protestants to be quite so confident about the exact operation of the Holy Spirit or its limits. Was not church history, by some of the definitions now suggested, history itself? If so, could one be quite certain to whom it was given to understand it?[32] Second, on quite a different level, the demand for a separation from "positivist lay historians" seemed sometimes to ignore the fact that historians so described had done much of the research on which any interpretation of the American religious past, from any point of view, had to depend.[33] Third, this same demand for sharp separation seemed to ignore the nature of the current revival. Despite the great either-or's of some of its theologians, its effect had been to blur, not to sharpen the line between believers and nonbelievers, among historians as elsewhere. To draw a line between believing "church historians" and "positivist lay historians" had become impossible. Examples of both could be found, but one could also point to historians who combined impeccable secular academic credentials with seminary training, ministerial experience, or explicit religious affiliation. Many others had been touched to one degree or another by the revival of "interest in religion," and some who had not could hardly be called "positivists." The nature of the current religious situation had made religious classification of historians impossible. No one could say with precision where, in religious terms, the best new writing was coming from.

It is a little easier to say where the best work in religious history was *not* coming from. The groups that recently seem to have contributed least are opposites: atheists and Roman Catholics. No one in the recent period has examined American religion with the scholarly love-hatred of H. L. Mencken at his best. An explanation is suggested by Martin Marty's sketch of the history of the American infidel.[34]

By the early twentieth century the commitments of American Protestantism had become so amorphous that there was nothing left to hate. Perhaps one of the tests of the depth of neo-orthodoxy is the question whether it will produce a neoatheism.

Since the 1955 bombshell of Monsignor John Tracy Ellis, Catholic intellectuals have been discussing the failure of American Catholicism to participate proportionally in American intellectual life in general. Some of them have also suggested that American Catholic history in particular has been slighted, and especially the history of the recent period of rapid Catholic increase.[35] Undoubtedly the social explanations suggested by Ellis, arising from the immigrant past of the American church, contain part of the answer. But some other suggestions have more relevance for our present purpose. One Catholic writer blames Catholic "formalism," "the tendency to see the world as 'finished' and all things in it as obvious in their essence and meaning," and also Catholic "Authoritarianism," of which one result is "the illusion of a neat universe in which nothing eludes the conceptions of a searching mind."[36] Still another suggests that the failure arises partly from the great difficulty, for American Catholics, especially since the crisis ending with Leo XIII's letter on Americanism, of carrying on a searching dialogue with non-Catholic American culture.[37]

These descriptions of Catholic difficulties seem relevant to some of the conclusions of this article. A point of view that has proved extremely fruitful both for Protestant and for nonreligious American historians (and for many who lie, as we have seen, between these two categories) is that suggested by Richard Niebuhr. From this point of view, religious impulses are never fully embodied in religious institutions, and the unity to be found in American church history must be found in a cycle of renewal and decline. Obviously, it would be impossible for a Catholic historian of Catholicism to take exactly this point of view. It may be that in this period of new openings, an analogous point of view may be found from which American Catholics can look freshly at their own church, and at American religious history in general.

A partly relevant parallel is offered by American Jewish history. Though historians of American Judaism, like their Catholic colleagues, have bewailed the slowness of development in their field, the problem seems almost opposite.[38] Much of the American Jewish history that has appeared in answer to such complaints deals successfully—not without internal friction and dispute—with exactly the problem so difficult for Catholics: the adjustment of an old and international religion to a Protestant or post-Protestant national culture. Where historians of American Judaism have been less successful, according to some critics, is in dealing with belief and doctrine. This may well arise from the comparatively nondoctrinal character of Judaism itself. Again, perhaps some variant of the approach that has proved fruitful for Protestantism may further illuminate the history of Judaism in America. If so, it will demand both an understanding of the religious stream and a knowledge of its secular channels.

The recovery of American religious history has been the work of thoroughly secular academic historians and also of believers, so far usually believers in some kind of Protestantism. The recent revival of religion has restored something of a balance between these two groups, and thereby it has greatly benefited American religious history. It has done this by restoring depth and variety rather than dogmatism. In America at least, most good history, whether of religion or anything else, has been written by people who are respectful of data, imaginative in dealing with many kinds of experience, and open to new insights—even incomplete and shifting insights. History written by those who confidently describe a single grand design, whether providential, evolutionary, or economic, sometimes impresses, but seems not to endure. Many, though not all, of the best recent historians of American religion do indeed believe that there is purpose in history. Of those who do believe this, few if any suppose that they understand this purpose in any detail. In dealing with the religious past, it is not ordinarily those "interested in religion" who sound dogmatic and defensive today, but rather the more rigid of the behaviorists, Freudians, and economic determinists.

Religious history, in any of the possible meanings of this term, is by no means sweeping all before it, any more than is religion itself. Rather, the revival of both has brought American history back into the great dialogue between secular and religious thought. It is to this dialogue, after all, that American culture itself owes much of its vigor and complexity.

Endnotes

*Mr. May, Margaret Byrne Professor of American History, University of California, Berkeley, read an earlier version of this article at a meeting of the American Studies Association, Pacific Coast Branch, at Fresno, California, in 1959. He wrote *Protestant Churches and Industrial America* (New York, 1949).

[1]Such a synthesis is not yet published. Most of the important contributions to the recovery have as yet been monographic or critical. Students have, however, been provided with a superb bibliography, a first-rate atlas, and one of the most illuminating of source collections: Nelson R. Burr, *Critical Bibliography of Religion in America* (2 vols., Princeton, N.J., 1957); Edwin S. Gaustad, *Historical Atlas of Religion in America* (New York, 1962); H. Shelton Smith *et al., American Christianity: An Historical Interpretation with Representative Documents* (2 vols., New York, 1960). The Burr bibliography makes it unnecessary, as it would in any case be impossible, to mention all the significant works in any category discussed in this article.

[2]Henry Nash Smith, *Mark Twain, The Development of a Writer* (Cambridge, Mass., 1962), seems to have the last word on the much-argued question of Clemens' pessimism. A recent contribution to the large and growing literature on Lincoln's complex religious views is William J. Wolf, *The Almost Chosen People* (New York, 1959). Though the mature views of the two men are in many ways opposite, I think it legitimate to call both post-Calvinist.

[3]See below, pages 85-86.

[4]See below, pages 84-85, and also the section, "Religion and Literature," in Burr, *Critical Bibliography*, II, 847-953.

[5]A good short list of works on "Church and Class" by sociologists and historians will be found *ibid.*, 606-10. An example of effective use, by a historian, of religious categories for social analysis is Lee Benson, *The Concept of Jacksonian Democracy: New York as a Test Case* (Princeton, N.J., 1961), esp. 186-207.

[6]A religious interpretation of the Revolution is reasserted by Carl Bridenbaugh, *Mitre and Sceptre: Transatlantic Faiths, Ideas, Personalities, and Politics, 1689-1775* (New York, 1962). A religious, or partly religious explanation of the Civil War seems to me to rest on two assertions: that serious and intractable moral conflicts were important in causing the war and that in nineteenth-century America such conflicts were peculiarly difficult to avoid or compromise because of the dominance of evangelical Protestantism in both sections. The importance of the moral conflict is implied by much though not all recent writing on slavery and anti-slavery, and directly argued in the well-known articles of 1946 and 1949 by Bernard DeVoto and A.M. Schlesinger, Jr. (Bernard DeVoto, "The Easy Chair," *Harper's*, CXCII [Feb., Mar. 1946], 123-26, 234-37; A.M. Schlesinger, Jr., "The Causes of the Civil War: A Note on Historical Sentimentalism," *Partisan Review*, XVI [Sept. 1949], 969-81.) The distinct importance of religion in sharpening the conflict is forcefully argued, with respect to the South, by Charles G. Sellers, Jr., "The Travail of Slavery," in *The Southerner as American*, ed. *id.* (Chapel Hill, N.C., 1960), 40-71.

[7]McGeorge Bundy calls Reinhold Niebuhr "probably the most influential single mind in the development of American attitudes which combine moral purpose with a sense of political reality," though he is not uncritical of Niebuhr. (McGeorge Bundy, "Foreign Policy: From Innocence to Engagement," in *Paths of American Thought*, ed. Arthur M. Schlesinger, Jr., and Morton White [Boston, 1963], 293-308).

[8]In an interesting article tracing schools of American intellectual history, Robert Alan Skotheim suggests that the school of historians dominant in the twenties and afterward tended to regard some ideas as determined by the socioeconomic environment, and others as possessing autonomous causal importance. Religious ideas, to which men of this school were generally unsympathetic, were usually in the first of these categories, while scientific ideas and proposals for social reform tended to be placed in the second. On the other hand, says Skotheim, come later writers including Perry Miller seemed to make religious thought autonomous and causative, and to treat opposing secular currents as environmental in origin. (Robert Alan Skotheim, "The Writing of American Histories of Ideas: Two Traditions in the xxth Century," *Journal of the*

History of Ideas, XXV [Apr.-June 1964], 257-78.)

[9]*Civilization in the United States*, ed. Harold Stearns (New York, 1922), v-vi.

[10]For excellent accounts of American religion in this period, see Robert T. Handy, "The American Religious Depression, 1925-1935," *Church History*, XXIX (Mar. 1960), 3-16, and Winthrop S. Hudson, *The Great Tradition of the American Churches* (New York, 1953), 195-225.

[11]The foregoing paragraph and some other parts of this article owe much to the illuminating essay "Church History" by George Huntston Williams in *Protestant Thought in the Twentieth Century*, ed. Arnold S. Nash (New York, 1941), 147-78.

[12]Herbert Schneider, *The Puritan Mind* (New York, 1930). In his later *History of American Philosophy* (New York, 1946) Schneider himself generously criticized this early work in the light of Perry Miller's later research. (See pages 28, 29.)

[13]Skotheim points out that Gabriel treated American religion with great respect even in essays published in the mid-twenties. Gabriel's interpretation of American intellectual history seems to me to belong neither to the dominant secular and environmentalist movement, nor to the later countermovement to which Skotheim assigns it, but to have some characteristics of both. (Skotheim, "Writing of American Histories of Ideas," 275-77.)

[14]A.M. Schlesinger, *In Retrospect: The History of a Historian* (New York, 1963), 193.

[15]*Id.*, "A Critical Period in American Religion, 1875-1900," *Proceedings of the Massachusetts Historical Society*, LXIV (1930-32), 523-47.

[16]Robert T. Handy, "The Protestant Quest for a Christian America, 1830-1930," *Church History*, XXII (Mar. 1953), 10.

[17]See *F.O. Matthiessen 1902-1950: A Collective Portrait*, ed. Paul M. Sweezy and Leo Huberman (New York, 1950).

[18]See Miller's introduction to the paperback edition of his *Orthodox in Massachusetts* (Boston, 1959), xvii. Other scholars, some of them preceding Miller, played some part in the reassessment both of the Puritans and of Edwards, but I believe few would deny him the major role in this enterprise.

[19]See Reinhold Niebuhr, *Leaves from the Notebook of a Tamed Cynic* (New York, 1930); June Bingham, *Courage to Change, An Introduction to the Life and Thought of Reinhold Niebuhr* (New York, 1961), 129-39.

[20]H. Richard Niebuhr, *The Kingdom of God in America* (New York, 1937), vii.

[21]This is suggested by John Higham, "American Intellectual History: A Critical Appraisal," *American Quarterly*, XIII (No. 2, 1961), 232.

[22]See Schlesinger, "Causes of the Civil War"; C. Vann Woodward, "The Irony of

Southern History," *Journal of Southern History*, XIX (Feb. 1953), 3-19; George F. Kennan, *Russia and the West under Lenin and Stalin* (Boston, 1961), *passim*. The more direct influence of neo-orthodoxy on the writing of European history, especially religious history, is excellently analyzed by E. Harris Harbison, "The 'Meaning of History' and the Writing of History," *Church History*, XXI (June 1952), 197-207.

23Two articles by John Higham reflect the development discussed here. In "Intellectual History and Its Neighbors," *Journal of the History of Ideas*, XV (June 1954), 339-47, he distinguishes between "internal" and "external" intellectual history in a neutral manner. In "American Intellectual History: A Critical Appraisal," he seems to come down on the side of more internal analysis and specifically relates this tendency to the recent rise of American religious history. The same tendency is discussed in detail by Skotheim, who finds that by 1950 both the older and the newer historians were turning away from environmentalism and toward a somewhat more autonomous treatment of ideas. Skotheim attributes this change in large part to the failure of relativism to prove adequate in the political crisis of the 1940's. This analysis seems to me sound except that the change referred to was under way in some quarters before that crisis. (Skotheim, "Writing of American Histories of Ideas," 277-78.)

24See, for instance, Will Herberg's acute and influential *Protestant-Catholic-Jew* (Garden City, N.Y., 1955).

25Franklin H. Littell, *From State Church to Pluralism* (New York, 1962). For the percentage figures, see *Yearbook of the American Churches*, 1963 ed. (New York, 1963), 276, and 1933 ed. (New York, 1933), 99. As the editors of these compilations point out, criteria of membership vary drastically from church to church and period to period. Probably the statistics of the recent growth are more acceptable than the older ones. S.M. Lipset argues plausibly that American religion has experienced a "continuous boom" from the beginning rather than a specially sharp recent increase. (S.M. Lipset, *The First New Nation* [New York, 1963], 144-47.)

26Sydney Ahlstrom, "The Levels of Religious Revival," *Confluence*, IV (Apr. 1955), 41.

27A generally hostile assessment of the popular revival can be found in Martin Marty, *The New Shape of American Religion* (New York, 1959), and a still harsher one is A. Roy Eckhardt, *The Surge of Piety in America* (New York, 1958). A more balanced treatment, in my opinion, is Ahlstrom's "Levels of Religious Revival." The revival of the fifties is related to earlier revivals in Timothy L. Smith, "Historic Waves of Religious Interest in America," *Annals of the American Academy of Political and Social Science*, CCCXXXII (Nov. 1960), 9-19.

28Sydney Ahlstrom, "Theology and the Present-Day Revival," *ibid.*, 27.

[29]William G. McLoughlin, Jr., *Modern Revivalism: Charles Grandison Finney to Billy Graham* (New York, 1950); Bernard A. Weisberger, *They Gathered at the River* (Boston, 1958).

[30]Timothy Smith, *Revivalism and Social Reform,* (New York, 1957); Winthrop S. Hudson, *The Great Tradition of the American Churches* (New York, 1953); Sidney Mead, *The Lively Experiment* (New York, 1963). Most of the essays in the last book had been published in the fifties, though some of their direction had been suggested earlier in Mead's *Nathaniel William Taylor* (Chicago, 1942).

[31]Most of these essays are cited in Winthrop S. Hudson, "Shifting Trends in Church History, " *Journal of Bible and Religion,* XXVIII (Apr. 1960), 235-38. For another list, see the section on "Religious Historiography" in Burr, *Critical Bibliography,* I. 22-27.

[32]Something like this question is raised from the point of view of a church historian in the excellent article by William A. Clebsch, "A New Historiography of American Religion," *Historical Magazine of the Protestant Episcopal Church,* XXXII (Sept. 1963), 225-57. Arthur S. Link argues eloquently that from the point of view of "Biblical faith," there is no such thing as Christian history as distinguished from other history. (Arthur Link, "The Historian's Vocation," *Theology Today,* XIX [Apr. 1963], 75-89.)

[33]In the exuberance of the moment even Sydney Mead, sometimes criticized for his moderation by other "church" historians, said that it was no longer necessary to pay homage to "the rather presumptuous occupants of university chairs of secular history," or to orient church history according to "the unpredictable and transient interpretive vagaries" or these men. In 1963, however, he called for a much wider interpretation of the meaning of church history than these earlier statements suggested and condemned the tendency to widen the breach between religious and secular historians. (Sidney Mead, "Prof. [*sic*] Sweet's 'Religion and Culture in America,'" [review article], *Church History,* XXII [Mar.1953], 33-49, and "Church History Explained," *ibid.,* XXXII [Mar. 1963], 3-31.)

[34]Martin Marty, *The Infidel: Freethought and American Religion* (Cleveland, 1961).

[35]John Tracy Ellis, "The American Catholic and the Intellectual Life," reprinted in *The Catholic Church U. S. A.,* ed. Louis J. Putz (Chicago, 1956), 315-57; Henry J. Browne, "American Catholic History: A Progress Report, Research and Study," *Church History,* XXVI (Dec. 1957), 373.

[36]Thomas F. O'Dea, *American Catholic Dilemma: An Inquiry into the Intellectual Life* (New York, 1958), 156, 158.

[37]Walter J. Ong, "The Intellectual Frontier," in *Catholic Church,* ed. Putz, 394-415.

[38]Oscar Handlin, "New Paths in American Jewish History," *Commentary*, VII (Apr. 1949), 388-93; Moses Rischin, *An Inventory of American Jewish History* (Cambridge, Mass., 1954).

Rediscovery: Discerning Religious America
MARTIN E. MARTY

SOURCE: From *Religion and Republic* by Martin E. Marty. Copyright © 1987 by Martin E. Marty. Reprinted by permission of Beacon Press, Boston.

For a great many years until mid-twentieth century, religion in the United States gave every indication of becoming increasingly secular, institutionalized, and less influential in American life. Yet the years since then have brought unanticipated changes in the relationship between religion and culture, and as a result, academic theorists have sought—and developed—fresh theories to account for these surprising cultural shifts.

First, contrary to expectations, religion is very much in evidence, which means that the secular paradigm and prophecy that had dominated Western academic thought have come to be questioned. Second, rather than being contained within formal institutions, religion has unmistakably and increasingly diffused throughout the culture, and has assumed highly particular forms in the private lives of citizens. Third, traditional religion has not fallen away, as expected, but has survived and staged an impressive comeback, establishing itself firmly and enduringly in large subcultures.

Before exploring these shifts, three important points must be made. The first is that continuity—especially with regard to religiosity and secularity, the social locations of religion, and the durability of traditional faiths, in the face of change—has long been a fundamental feature of American religious culture. Though academic theorists have often overlooked it, it has not gone entirely unnoticed. The "consensus historians" of the 1950s, for example, took note of it, and by minimizing the stresses and strains of American life, accented the "givenness," the stable threads of American religion. Halfway through the period, historically informed sociologists, while impressed with the changes taking place, were able to keep their balance in the face of such change. In 1963 Seymour Martin Lipset, for example, in *The First New Nation* used the observations of both foreign visitors and American chroniclers to show that all-pervasive religion had characterized American culture through the years. While trying to do justice to the persistent secularity born of American pluralism—a secularity that manifests itself in the practical American temper—and the moral, as opposed to the transcendental, motif in much American faith, Lipset saw that voluntaryism was the source of religious strength. American citizens *chose* to be religious because they were free not to be; religious organizations survived because they had to compete for loyalty.

Second, academics trained in the sociology of knowledge—theorists in theology, religious studies, and humanistic or social scientific disciplines—were tuned in to certain of the more subtle shifts in American culture. They saw that most of those living *in* the culture have fewer options for their lives than is generally realized, fewer tools for analysis, and many motives for resisting change. John Murray Cuddihy recognized that some core-culture analysts were theorists writing "from within the eye of the hurricane of modernization, where all [was] calm and intelligible." He knew that "for the underclass below, as for the ethnic outside, modernization [was] a trauma." In their humble dwellings, they had neither the peace nor the time to reflect on possible alternative courses: the wind was coming their way, and they had to put up the sandbags, move on, or be destroyed.

Another way to put this is to caricature American society in terms borrowed from the comics and playpen; such an exercise leads to interesting results:

> Society can be diagramed in a shape more or less like Al Capp's cartoon creation the Shmoo. The Shmoo's motion is largely in its head. A broad middle and a leaden bottom keep it earthbound. The child's roly-poly toy, all beaming and motion-filled in the face, is ungraspably broad in the middle, and burdened by weights so that it lands right side up when buffeted, and quickly comes to rest.

The academic specialist naturally notices exaggerated tilts of the head among elites; mass communicators consistently report on all signs of novelty and sensation. Thus, when late in the sixties, for example, the offspring of certain professors, mass media communications, and middle-class suburbanites took up astrology and began to express a belief in omens, the media at once exploited this "occult explosion," while theologians and social thinkers felt called upon to come up with fresh theories about neo-religiosity or transcendence. In fact, the number of the new devotees did not significantly alter the proportion of the population that had always believed in such phenomena. The body of the societal shmoo—or the weighted portion of the cultural roly-poly—had barely moved. Both head and body merit observation; theories drawn from observing only one are inevitably vulnerable.

Proof of religious continuity in American life can be found in many ways, not least in the polling data. Thus, for example, in a poll taken in 1962 as compared with one in 1965, the data seemed to show a widespread, if shallow, *revival* of religion, followed immediately by a sort of *revolution* in religion. There were "startling indications of change and . . . more puzzling indications of non-change."

> Some . . . recalling the drama of the last dozen years, may look for more in these polls than they will deliver. Often . . . readers may have "felt in their bones" that epochal change in the world of science and the mass media or education will have induced epochal change in one or another of the sectors of the churches' lives. They will consult the statistics of those sectors and find a relatively undramatic change in percentages from 1952 to 1965.

Polls today show that continuity persisting. This is not to say that there have not also been certain quite sudden documentable and dramatic changes. Attendance at mass and other religious observances, for example, fell off significantly after Vatican II, when true voluntaryism hit Roman Catholicism. Mainline Protestant and Jewish organizations have shown a continuing decline in their relative place among denominations, though it must be noted that this follows a trend as old as the one that began with the Methodist and Baptist revivals around 1800, when Episcopalians, Congregationalists, and Presbyterians began to lose primacy. The fundamentalist, Pentecostal, and evangelical churches have clearly gained in visibility, morale, and strength; their code words have become a part of American culture. Recent Gallup polls, for example, have found Americans more ready than ever to identify themselves as "born again." Yet such shifts tend to occur within the borders of an "all-pervasive religiousness" and a concurrent and "persistent secularity."

It is essential to think of these issues in a context that takes account also of generations—our third point. Two or more must always coexist. If there are two generations of Americans with different religious experiences, there are as well two generations of academic theorists with quite different outlooks. A generational shift appears to separate the period from roughly the end of World War II (or the beginning of the Eisenhower era) through the mid-sixties, from the late sixties into the 1980s. Still, the concept "generation" cannot be taken too literally in the biological sense, or too narrowly in the cultural sense. Robert Wohl in *The Generation of 1914* shows how the generational approach to self-understanding may confine and mislead if it is the only norm used for measuring cultural possibility. In trying to grasp something as elusive as culture, however, the generational handle can be quite valuable. José Ortega y Gasset saw this; he defined culture as

> only the interpretation which man gives to his life, the series of more or less satisfying solutions he finds in order to meet the problems and necessities of life, as well those which belong to the material order as the so-called spiritual ones. . . . [Culture is] the conception of the world or the universe which serves as the plan, riskily elaborated by man, for orienting himself among things, for coping with his life, and finding a direction amid the chaos of his situation.

These interpretations, these "more or less satisfying solutions," tend to appear along generational lines. Ortega was almost certainly too mechanical in his idea that cultural generations occurred fifteen years apart; he was more subtle when he recognized that several generations of coevals are alive at the same time. Those who have undergone a similar set of experiences at decisive stages in their life-careers tend to develop common outlooks. This is as true of those within the culture who endow with meaning both their fortune and their suffering—the religious—as it is of those who recognize and label the cultural change they perceive. The latter belong also to the *Zeitgeist*, perhaps more than many of them realize. If their particular task is to analyze and understand their culture, they sometimes extrapolate on the basis of what they see emerging, inevitably prophesying futures that do not always unfold as they predicted. This is most obvious in the paradigm shifts that they experience or initiate. I use the term *paradigm* here to mean both the "disciplinary matrix . . . the entire constellation of beliefs, values, techniques, and so on shared by the members of a given community" *and* the "exemplars," those "concrete puzzle-solutions that, employed as models or examples, can replace explicit rules as a basis for the solution of the remaining puzzles of normal science. . . ."

The Diffusion of Religion

Humanists, social scientists, and theologians, it appears, are as susceptible to fads as other mortals. In the second of the generations, they saw religiousness everywhere, for by 1970, religion was "in." Scholars who at one time could account for its signs merely by saying that religiousness was an underclass phenomenon, or that it belonged on the ethnic margins of society, could no longer do so. Too many of their own children were caught up in cults and the occult. The Beautiful People were "into" an alphabet of phenomena, from astrology to Zen. Middle-class Catholics and Episcopalians were "speaking in tongues" in pentecostal enclaves. Certainly, the fervent evangelical culture could not be classified as "marginal" when successive presidents—Ford, Carter, Reagan—openly claimed membership in it. All this occurred, paradoxically, while a moderate, but still marked, decline in support of mainline religious institutions was so clearly taking place.

The cultural turn that was evident among elites, and the durable, but newly visible, "pervasive religiousness" in the broad culture, found theorists with explanations in hand. Some employed a neo-Marxist view that saw religion as the "opiate" for the failed "revolution" of the late sixties. Freudian observations about the need for new illusions, Sartrean suggestions of bad faith as evasions of reality, or Weberian notions about how authentic and deeply held religious views could alter the social and cultural environment were used by others. None need concern us here. Instead, our focus will be the fundamental shift in paradigms; here "modernity," which could include diffused religions, replaced—or at least challenged—"secularity," which had to explain religion away. This occurred, first, when scholars redefined religion and saw it diffused in culture; and second, when they amplified the model of what it is to be human in culture. For the redefinition of religion, the notion of modernity as differentiation was rescued from Talcott Parsons's macrotheory. Cuddihy summarized well the "differentiated modernity" motif:

> Differentiation is the cutting edge of the modernization process, sundering cruelly what tradition had joined. It . . . separates church from state (the Catholic trauma), ethnicity from religion (the Jewish trauma). . . . Differentiation slices through ancient primordial ties and identities, leaving crisis and "wholeness-hunger" in its wake.

To this, Robert N. Bellah added the idea of diffusion, a motif he retrieved from oft-discredited evolutionary models. Bellah defined evolution as

> a process of increasing differentiation and complexity of organization that endows the organism, social system, or whatever the unit in question may be with greater capacity to adapt to its environment, so that it is in some sense more autonomous relative to its environment than were its less complex ancestors.

Bellah tracked this definition through five stages, toward "post-modern religion," where it was "precisely the characteristic of the new situation that the great problem of religion, . . . the symbolization of man's relation to the ultimate conditions of his existence, is no longer the monopoly of any groups explicitly labeled religious." Religion, it appears, is diffused throughout the culture, difficult to grasp or observe. It has become a private affair, its fate no longer tied to organizations and institutions. Thus it had only been *apparently* paradoxical to observe that in the earlier generation religious institutions prospered while they shrouded a deeper secularization, yet in the second generation they languished while religion itself thrived.

We can summarize the change in religious definition in the phrase "from Thwackum to Geertz." Sidney E. Mead, historian and polemicist, looked back on the cultural laggards who had confined religion to institutions, and called them sectarians, temple-ists, or Thwackumites, after Henry Fielding's Parson Thwackum:

> When I mention religion I mean the Christian religion; and not only the Christian religion, but the Protestant religion; and not only the Protestant religion, but the Church of England. And when I mean honor, I mean that mode of Divine grace which is not only consistent with, but dependent upon, this religion; and is consistent with and dependent upon no other.

Although Mead, like Bellah, believed that religion extended beyond churches and synagogues into civil or republican faiths, Luckmann, and others, saw it as diffused to the point where it had become "invisible" in private life. "Religious institutions," he wrote, "are not universal," but the very "social processes that lead to the formation of Self [are] fundamentally religious." Thus a new note was introduced into cultural anthropology in the West: the means that people use to transcend their mere biological nature, and all the symbolization and socialization that are part of these means, are inherently religious. In that sense, religion is universal and inescapable; it is, furthermore, incapable of disappearing.

Expansive new definitions of religion began to appear. The most widely accepted one, that of Clifford Geertz, defined religion as (1) a system of symbols that act to (2) establish powerful, pervasive, and long-lasting moods and motivations in men, by (3) formulating conceptions of a general order of existence, and (4) clothing these conceptions with such an aura of factuality, that (5) the moods and motivations seem uniquely realistic.

Suddenly, the problem of definition became, "Where does religion *stop?*" If everything is religious, is then nothing religious? Obviously, superhuman beings or forces, as well as belief, dogma, and institutions, have no place in Geertz's definition. It points clearly, however, to the diffusion of "pervasive religiousness" in culture, even at those times when sacred institutions are enduring a crisis of legitimacy. This protean religion is ubiquitously available; it can be found in self-help books on airport newsstands, on television, in therapy groups, in university classes that deal with religion, or in the private search of lonely metaphysical windowshoppers and spiritual shoplifters as they put together individual world views.

In Geertzian terms, scholars whom the Vatican Secretariat for Non-Believers gathered periodically to study "the culture of unbelief" found only "cultures of *other*-belief." But true unbelief or pure-form secularization was found only rarely, least of all in America.

Yet broad definitions of religion often met with protest, as, for example, when the U.S. Supreme Court called secular humanism a matter of "ultimate concern," and thus, in Paul Tillich's version, a religion. Theologian Julian N. Hartt, fully aware of Buddhism and Taoism, sounded provincially Western when he tried to provide limits: "We ought to say that a man is not really religious unless he feels that some power is bearing down on him, unless, that is, he believes he must do something about divine powers who have done something about him." James Gustafson wanted to reserve the word *religious* for that "dimension of experience (in which not all persons consciously share) that senses a relationship to an ultimate power that sustains and stands over against humans in the world." Anthropologist Melford Spiro agreed; the symbol system required the inclusion of "superhuman" forces or powers. Yet even these confinements, moving religion, as they did, far beyond Thwackumism, allowed for its extremely wide diffusion in American culture. American religion thus seeped into the cultural cracks and barnacles itself to nonreligious phenomena.

The shift from the secular paradigm to religion as all-pervasive forced theorists, perhaps *enabled* them, to look for dimensions they had at another time ignored. Certain social scientists were able to confirm trends in their earlier work. Daniel Bell began to speak up for the values of the sacred and the transcendent. Philip Rieff awaited the recovery of the sacred after the triumph of the therapeutic. Scholarly definitions of *the sacred* were perhaps not what ministers, priests, and rabbis had in mind when they spoke of God. Humanistic thinkers, however, have often been in advance of theological thinkers; in this case, certainly, for avant-garde theologians who had accepted the secular paradigm now had to account for the survival of the sacred. The counterculture, the Age of Aquarius, the Jesus People, all had come and gone, leaving as their marks new evidence that humans seemed to be durably religious.

The new danger now is that the persistent secularity of American culture will be forgotten. The nation is as pluralist as ever, and in the operative aspects of its national life—in the university, the marketplace, or the legislature—American remains secular, with no single transcendent symbol to live by. Unless theorists and theologians reckon with *both* all-pervasive religiousness *and* persistent secularity, they will again be left stranded with each cultural shift, in search of theories to match their perceptions. The double paradigm will no doubt diminish the audaciousness of certain prophecies and projections: bold predictions of the purely secular city or a thoroughly sacral culture are obviously highly dramatic. But these predictions are as likely to be wrong as right, as the human record in general, and the recent American generational shift in particular, show.

At the end of the first of our generations, I argued that *"a preferable alternative seems to be the religio-secular model of indeterminacy, open to infinite transformations and toward the development of new kinds of consciousness."* Admittedly, then as now, "the coinage 'religio-secular' to characterize the past, the present, and the tendency of American society, is not very fortunate, but we have not heard more elegant alternatives." But it is a historically accurate model, one that is evident in very many cultures—from Greco-Roman through Enlightenment to recent American— and both more true to what Wilfred Sellers has called "the manifest image of man," and richer for projecting the probable path of culture.

Resurgent Antimodern Religion

Through the two generations when secularism reigned, one large subculture resisted its sway. It included Hassidic and other mystical or orthodox movements in Judaism; numbers of American-born "sects" like the Latter-Day Saints, Jehovah's Witnesses, and Adventists; Pentecostal and charismatic movements in conventional Christianity; traditionalist Catholicism, to a lesser extent; and to a greater one, evangelical and fundamentalist Protestantism. That subculture is now resurgent. In 1980 it could claim the loyalty of all three major presidential candidates, along with entertainers and entrepreneurs, athletes and beauty queens. Obviously, such a subculture can hardly be described as marginal.

Its recent gains come in substantial measure from the selective use of secular techniques and modern technology; it is characterized by certain signs of secular "worldliness" and modern "diffusion." Yet these appear to be inadequate to account for the survival and strength of this steadfastly antimodern force. If religion elsewhere in the culture is so diffuse, why is it here so organized? If most religious institutions have become "refined" and civil, why are these so belligerent and aggressive? If a good deal of religiosity dissolves into the culture, why does this variety remain lumpish, unwilling to be filtered?

Cuddihy's concept of "dedifferentiating" and "demodernizing" cultural elements points to an embracing theory. Modernity meant differentiation and diffusion; if carried too far, they could leave a "wholeness-hunger" in their wake that only antimodernity could address. But Cuddihy was no determinist: modernity was not an inevitable culminating stage of evolution. One could choose to go behind it or beyond it.

Demodernization, from Marx to Mao, is dedifferentiation. . . . Inward assent to the disciplines of differentiation, the practice of its rites, may be viewed as the *paideia* of the West. "Ideology" is the name we give to the various resistance movements mounted to stem the onslaught of the differentiation process. Essentially these movements are demodernizing, dedifferentiating, rebarbative.

This "old-time" religion never really disappeared; packaged in modern forms and transmitted through sophisticated media, it came back with a vengeance during the second of the two generations. In its Catholic form, it survived in various traditionalist movements or in its selective support for certain of the more conservative policies of Pope John Paul II. Among Jews, it became a charismatic movement, attracting those who had a predilection for Hassidic or mystical forms of Judaism, as well as those whose faith encompassed biblical claims to the land of Israel. Among the elites in mainline Protestant denominations, it took form in movements of "lay concern" against liberal theology, and in opposition to liturgical revision.

The most interesting and apparently most durable of these phenomena by far was the Protestant fundamentalist resurgence. Threatened with extinction around 1925 after the Scopes trial, fundamentalists went underground. There they endured, learned modern techniques, and worked their way back to cultural visibility. Calling themselves evangelicals, the moderates among them gathered power through the benign ministry of Billy Graham in the 1950s and after. Fundamentalism was eclipsed by the secular theology, liberal civil rights and antiwar movements, the civil religion of the New Frontier, and Vatican II, but only momentarily, for it came back to new vogue—and with new force—during the late sixties.

By the early seventies the evidence was in: conservative churches clearly were growing, and overly modernized mainline ones just as obviously declining. In an apparently secular and certainly diffusive religious America, the "strong" churches were paradoxically prospering, perhaps precisely because they were antimodern—absolutist, fanatic, conformist, highly committed to the group, rigidly disciplined, and zealous to proselytize. They were, in short, uncivil.

But it was not long before much of the new conservatism had become civil and moved into the cultural mainstream. In 1974 then-conservative congressman John B. Anderson pointed out signs of the times at a meeting of the National Association of Evangelicals in Boston, signs so obvious that one needed no opinion poll to confirm them:

It was [the liberals] who denied the supernatural acts of God, conforming the gospel to the canons of modern science. . . . It was *they* who were the friends of those in positions of political power. *They* were the "beautiful people," and *we*—you will recall—were the "kooks." We were regarded as rural, reactionary, illiterate fundamentalists who just didn't know better.

Well, things have changed. Now *they* are the "kooks"—and we are the "beautiful people." *Our* prayer breakfasts are so popular that only those with engraved invitations are allowed to attend. *Our* evangelists have the ready ear of those in positions of highest authority. *Our* churches are growing, and theirs are withering. . . . *They* are tired, worn-out nineteenth century liberals trying to repair the pieces of an optimism shattered by world wars, race riots, population explosion, and the specter of worldwide famine. *We* always knew that things would get worse before the Lord came again.

The media, in their extensive coverage of the Protestant New Christian Right and the pressure it can bring to bear so effectively on vulnerable "public" institutions—schools, legislatures, broadcasters, and others—have been accused of focusing disproportionately on a not fully representative front. Yet by doing so, they draw attention to the groups' more militant counterparts around the world, the tribalisms that Harold Isaacs spoke of:

We are experiencing on a massively universal scale a convulsive ingathering of people in their numberless groupings of kinds—tribal, racial, linguistic, religious, national. It is a great clustering into separatenesses that will, it is thought, improve, assure, or extend each group's power or place, or keep it safe or safer from the power, threat, or hostility of others.

Wary as Americans must be of analogies to social movements elsewhere, they are yet mindful of the acute versions of tribal fundamentalisms in Hindu-Muslim subcontinental conflicts in Asia, in Tribal Africa, in Jewish-Muslim rationales behind struggles in the Middle East, or Protestant-Catholic versions in Northern Ireland. These elements in world politics, vivid and startling as they obviously are, might reasonably be expected to lead social theorists and theologians to conclude that these fundamental tribalisms are the only portent in America's cultural future. But if the polity holds, Americans are not likely to jettison their traditions of pluralism and civility, and in doing so, yield entirely to one or another of the contenders. These forces by now have perhaps brought into the fold all those in the culture for whom the fundamentalist message rings clear and true—though without, of course, having exhausted all of the uses to which well-organized minorities can be put. Furthermore, they will undoubtedly stimulate backlashing and counterorganizing coalitions. Finally, by making too much of them, we may overlook the creative apathy of much of the public, which, by ignoring them, usually outlasts them.

There are, however, good reasons for taking the extreme Right seriously. Much of its power comes from Lipset's voluntaryism. Just as volunaryism once helped assure the life of strong denominations, this American response to the separation of church and state has now proved to be an effective instrument for rallying the demodernizers. Mainline religions—Catholic, Jewish, and Protestant—have become so bureaucratized, so remote from the aspirations of their adherents, that they are ineffective. But because the Right depends upon constant voluntary financial support and response to direct mail, it keeps in constant touch with its constituents, has its finger, so to speak, on their pulse.

In many ways the new traditionalisms—or newly visible old traditionalisms with new glosses—illustrate the antimodern or demodernizing impulse. First, they are frankly nostalgic, longing for that simpler, ordered, homogeneous world that once satisfied the "wholeness-hunger" of individuals, subcultures, and the larger culture, that prepluralist world in which Catholics dominated Christendom, Jews were at home in shtetl or ghetto, and Protestants ran the American empire. Second, they attract those discontented with the chaos of pluralism, the hallmark of modernity. Just as Marx and Mao accomplished dedifferentiation by ideologies that coerced the masses, these new voluntaryists look to both legal instruments and persuasion to overcome the Babel of voices that cancel one another out. Third, they are intolerant of the pluralist society's moral anomie, its apparent inability to generate positive values for common action.

These themes are grounded in others. One is a hunger for authority. A century ago, in a similarly erosive situation, absolutes could be found in Roman Catholic claims of papal infallibility and Protestant appeals to biblical truth. Now, in a similar and more intense crisis, infallibility and inerrancy have again become symbols of potent absolutisms.

The newly assertive forces are not, however, merely content to exact intellectual fidelity to absolute propositions. The craving for experience is part of a larger "wholeness-hunger." In its compromise with secular, dissected religion, modern religiosity ministered to this hunger only passively. Yet modernity creates great pressure for the individual in culture who is seeking meaning for all of life, including the experiential dimensions. That is why so many of the new movements include glossolalia, or tongue-speaking, fervent devotional movements, and the like.

Finally, in what may appear to be a paradox—since it cancels out the aims of these parties to shape more than their own subculture, to have their way, that is, in much of the society around them—the Protestant Right tends to be explicitly premillennial. In their reading of history, the world will worsen in anticipation of the end of history and the Second Coming of Christ, who will restore all order and beauty. Why, then, bother to reform American if it is soon to pass away?

Here one must point to an adaptation of the older millennialisms. Present-day propagators of the vision take care not to set the date for the Second Coming. There is time for enjoyment of the world God gave, even if he will soon cause it to burn. Authors of bestsellers on impending Armageddon regularly and unabashedly flaunt Rolls-Royces, or plow their royalties into long-term real estate investments. On evangelistic television we see a frankly hedonistic side to the new Christian Right. And America, though not here to stay, has, of course, been elected by God to train evangelists to rescue individuals before the end. Humanism and pluralism will only deflect it from its mission. In this regard, the new premillennialism matches Marxist and other eschatologies, since it gives its adherents a sense that they alone know exactly where history is going.

In all these respects, the movements show that neither simple diffusion nor any single style of rationality or experience is acceptable to everyone in a pluralist culture. These forces attract people wary of what Robert Lifton calls the "protean" personality style, favoring, rather, the "constrictive" style. The protean satisfies "wholeness-hunger" with nibbles from many cuisines; the constrictive type favors spiritual home-cooking, in great gulps.

Here are Cuddihy's people in the path of the hurricane of modernization. They do not all reside in humble dwellings; many of them are moving into higher social classes. The outsider has the perspective to make relative judgments on the many versions of religious traditionalisms, but those inside either lack such a perspective, or if they do not, perhaps set aside the problem because of other satisfactions in sharing a particular vision.

It may be that the traditionalisms may soon be bought off by the danegeld that is abundant in American life. They may, in the process of enlarging their subculture and winning some points, find themselves joining the mainline, and in doing so, bartering away their own particularity. To William McLoughlin, a historian of the revivalism from which the movements draw strength, they represent a partly permanent feature of American life, but also—and here, drawing on Anthony F. C. Wallace's "revitalization" theory—a passing stage. After a "period of individual stress" when an old cultural synthesis breaks up, there is a second "period of cultural distortion" before a new orientation takes shape. These prospering groups are part of this second stage. In that phase, a "nativist or traditionalist movement" arises, wherein older generational leaders, decrying the ecclesiastical and civil systems, call for a return to the ways of the fathers, the old-time religion.

In a risky scenario for the early 1990s, McLoughlin expected a new consensus to emerge. It would thrust into leadership a U.S. president committed to the kind of fundamental restructuring that followed previous American awakenings—in 1776, 1830, and 1932. The new vision, he thought, would "not come from Marxism or the Orient but from our own cultural past." Revitalization and reorientation are by definition syncretic; this combination would fuse some "softer" elements with more formal inherited Judeo-Christian and civil covenants. Some political analysts contended that in the 1980s such restructuring was beginning, though it appeared to be doing so without the "softness" McLoughlin envisioned.

McLoughlin's scenario, like so many others, presumes that there will be some sort of national consensus. Robert Heilbroner, in a script that foresees the collapse of the present American polity and ethos, agrees, but thinks it would be an imposed one. Although this looks very much like demodernization—presaging as it does the rise of a coercive state religion, a deification of the state itself, and the minimizing of pluralism—Heilbroner remains sanguine, believing that some sort of congenial socialist pattern will emerge. The record of the American past, however, suggests that if this kind of mild Maoism were to appear, something called "Christian republicanism" would more likely be the nominal ideology to cover the adjustment to a new approved social contract.

We are left now with a many-layered culture. Legally, at base, and in many parts of the ethos, America is a secular, nonreligious culture; in practice, a pluralistic one. But that culture houses an impressive number of religious institutions that attract the loyalties of three out of five citizens, and the weekly participation of two out of five—and are likely to continue to do so indefinitely. Over these is a layer of particled religion, whose institutions count for less and which may take the form of private support. Some would put the whole complex in a container called "civil" or "public" religion, the consensus that presumably holds America together. Meanwhile, as we await a *new* consensus, traditionalist religion thrives. Through it all, a paradigm that seems ambivalent and equivocal, combining as it does both religious and secular elements, does justice to the viscous aspects of American cultural life.

The rediscovery of American religion implies a long tradition . . . For the present, at the very least, informed Americans are learning that their university, communication, literary, governmental, and intellectual elites overlook the dynamism of religion at their peril. In the emerging generation, during what appears to be a major cultural restructuring that goes from the nation's capital to its most remote precincts, to misperceive the role of religion, in what Ortega called the effort "to meet the problems and necessities of life, as well as those which belong to the material order as the so-called spiritual ones," will be more foolish than ever before.

History Texts *and*
Why is There So Little Religion in the Textbooks ?
WARREN A. NORD

SOURCE: From *Religion and American Education: Rethinking a National Dilemma* by Warren A. Nord. Copyright © 1995 by the University of North Carolina Press. Used by permission of the publisher.

It has been claimed that (conscientious) students are likely to have read more than thirty thousand pages of textbook prose by the time they have finished high school; perhaps 75 percent of school classwork and 90 percent of homework focus on textbooks. Needless to say, we are not likely to remember many of the dates and battles, the facts and formulas, the ideas and theories, that fill those pages. This does not mean we have not been deeply influenced by textbooks, however. Frances Fitzgerald suggests that what "sticks to the memory" is "not any particular series of facts but an atmosphere, an impression, a tone. And this impression may be all the more influential just because one cannot remember the facts and arguments that created it." What we believe about the world is typically not the result of carefully constructed arguments based on hard evidence and careful reasoning but impressions gained more or less unconsciously from a meshing of schooling and life experiences, and our understanding of some aspects of life—of history, for example—is likely to be gained almost entirely from a few courses in school, from a few textbooks. The responsibility of textbook authors and publishers, Fitzgerald suggests, is "awesome, for, as is not true of trade publishers, the audiences for their products are huge, impressionable, and captive."

As we saw [earlier] religion had all but disappeared from textbooks by the end of the nineteenth century. To locate it in contemporary textbooks we must consult texts that chart old traditions and, for the most part, distant lands. I will demonstrate this in graphic detail by way of a review of high school textbooks in a variety of subjects. (I will have a little to say about college and elementary school texts as well.) And why is religion absent from the texts? A part of the reason is, no doubt, that religion is controversial; textbook publishers, eager to maximize profits, exile it to safe and distant places. But I trust that it will come as no surprise at this point in the book that there is a more fundamental reason: textbook authors and publishers are sufficiently secular that religion is no longer considered relevant enough, or sufficiently likely to be true, to have anything other than a historical role to play in the stories textbooks tell.

History Texts

In 1989 and 1992 I reviewed forty-two high school textbooks in American and world history, economics, home economics, biology, physics, and physical science, which are approved for use in North Carolina schools. (North Carolina uses the standard textbooks of the major publishers, so there is no reason to believe that they are in any way peculiar.) My primary questions were, What do students learn about religion in those social studies and science courses where a case might be made for the relevance of religion? To what extent is religion treated uniformly in textbooks? Is there a cumulative effect of the way religion is treated?

Only the history texts dealt with religion in any significant way, and they mentioned it a good deal. Nonetheless, over the past decade a half-dozen studies by individuals and organizations have concluded that the texts are highly inadequate in conveying an understanding of the place of religion in history. The historian Timothy Smith has written that the thirteen high school American history texts he reviewed fell "far below the standard of American historical scholarship by ignoring or distorting the place of religion in American history. Where they do mention religious forces, the facts to which they allude are so incomplete or so warped that they deny students access to what the great majority of historical scholars think is true." People for the American Way, a liberal, separationist organization established, in large part, to counter the influence of the Religious Right, was led to an unanticipated conclusion in its study of American history textbooks: "These texts simply do not treat religion as a significant element in American life—it is not portrayed as an integrated part of the American value system or as something that is important to individual Americans. . . . When religion is mentioned, it is just that—mentioned. In particular, most books give the impression that America suddenly turned into a secular state after the Civil War." That the texts are inadequate is a matter of consensus. The extent and nature of their shortcomings are more controversial.

In his study of world history texts Paul Gagnon points out that the moral principles of Judaism and Christianity "lie at the heart of most subsequent world ideologies, even those determinedly anti-religious. . . .Yet the basic ideas of Judaism and Christianity are all but ignored in some of these texts and only feebly suggested in the rest." In the four North Carolina world histories, all of Jewish and Christian history up to the Middle Ages is handled, on average, in six pages, while sixty pages are typically given to Greece and Rome. The texts give twice as much space to ancient Egypt as they do to ancient Israel, and three of the four give more space to Sumeria. None of the world histories provide students the Ten Commandments or mention the central claim of Christianity—that Jesus was God incarnate. (Jesus typically receives about four paragraphs, or less than half the space one text gives Eleanor of Aquitaine and another gives Joseph Stalin.) The texts typically provide a relatively liberal view of early Judaism and Christianity, emphasizing monotheism, justice, and love; they downplay or completely ignore sin, salvation, damnation, the millennium, cosmology, and faith.

The treatments of Islam and non-Western religions are marginally better in one respect. The texts give them about the same amount of space—two or three pages—given Judaism and Christianity, but as the total number of pages on Islamic, Indian, and Chinese civilizations is considerably less than that devoted to Western civilization, a somewhat higher proportion of them deal with religion; hence religion may seem to be a more important part of those civilizations.

The closer we get to the modern West, the more religion disappears, and the few references for the years after 1800 are there for their political or social significance. So, for example, the texts briefly discuss Islamic fundamentalism and the Iranian revolution, the confrontation of Hindus and Muslims in the partition of India, the creation of Israel and the wars that followed, a religious conflict in Ireland. Anti-Semitism, the Dreyfuss Affair, and the Holocaust receive several paragraphs in each of the books.

What is most obviously missing is any account of the intellectual, theological, or denominational development of religion after the Reformation. None of the texts say anything about higher criticism, the development of liberal theology, or (non-Islamic) fundamentalist responses to religious liberalism and modernity. None of them mention any post-1800 theologian or religious thinker. (A pope is mentioned here and there for political reasons.) The secularization of the modern world, one of the great themes of modern history, is ignored—though each of the books says something about the conflict of religion with Darwinism (albeit it a single sentence in two of the four books). None discuss the spiritual crisis of the modern world so much in evidence in the arts, as well as in religion (though one text does devote two paragraphs to religion as part of the modern "search for stability").

The American history texts contain just enough about Native American religions—a sentence here, a paragraph there—to mystify students completely. There will typically be several paragraphs on Spanish missions. Each of the five texts contains a section of from three to seven pages on the Puritans and Pilgrims, but this is a little misleading, for only a few paragraphs in those sections deal with anything explicitly religious, and even then it is almost always "church-state" relations that are discussed. Roger Williams, Anne Hutchinson, the Quakers, and the development of religious toleration in the eighteenth century are discussed briefly. Three of the five texts provide short accounts of the Great Awakening, and two mention Deism.

Four of the texts have sections, ranging from three paragraphs to six pages, on religion in the early nineteenth century, usually covering the Transcendentalists, the Mormons, and the revivals of the Second Great Awakening, but after the Civil War religion becomes largely invisible. None of the texts mentions the split between Protestant liberalism and fundamentalism at the beginning of the twentieth century. Only one text mentions the Social Gospel; none mentions the watershed Scopes Trial. Two of the texts relate Martin Luther King's views on nonviolence and human rights to his religious convictions, but the role of black churches in the civil rights movement is not discussed. Only two of the texts mention the rise of the Religious Right in the 1970s. No other religious topic receives more than a sentence.

One text gives more space to farming in the colonies than it does to religion; another gives more pages to cowboys and cattle drives at the end of the nineteenth century than to all of post-1800 religion. The American histories devote, on average, about 1 percent of their space to matters having anything to do with religion after 1800. In his study of the American history texts, Paul Vitz correctly concluded that none of them "acknowledges, much less emphasizes, the great religious energy and creativity of the United States."

More important than the particular religious topics discussed or not discussed, and the relative amount of space they receive, is the worldview within which the historian works. Obviously, historians must be selective. In spite of their length (the world histories average 785 pages, the American histories 850 pages) much must be left out. What is included and what is excluded? Political and social history receive far and away the most emphasis, while the texts make scant mention of intellectual and cultural history of literature, science, art, education, philosophy, or religion. The world histories contain relatively more about culture generally, and religion in particular, than do the American histories, but this is largely because they treat cultures that are more distant historically and geographically; as they approach the modern West, cultural history tends to disappear there too. When religion is mentioned in any of the texts, it is almost always for its relevance to political and social events and movements. This assumption—that the history we want our children to learn is political and social, rather than cultural, intellectual, or religious—is rich with significance.

But the problem cuts deeper. Whatever stories the historian chooses to tell are open to various interpretations; they are understood differently from within different worldviews. Consider the following passage from one of the world history texts:

Because the Egyptians feared the Hebrews, they made them slaves. The Hebrew leader Moses led the Hebrews from Egypt to Palestine. Under the rule of their early kings—Saul, David, and Solomon—the Hebrew nation prospered. . . .

King Solomon died about 900 B.C. Then Palestine split into two kingdoms. The Kingdom of Israel was formed in the north. The Kingdom of Judah was formed in the south. The Kingdom of Israel lasted for 250 years. Then it was destroyed by the Assyrians. The kingdom of Judah lasted for 400 years. However, during much of its history it was part of other empires.

Authors of textbooks often attempt to tiptoe gingerly around events with religious significance, leaving questions about causes and meaning aside. Still, the author of the above passage does not quite succeed: was it Moses who led the Israelites out of bondage or God? According to Scripture, "when Pharaoh let the people go, God did not guide them by the road towards the Philistines. . . . God made them go round by way of the wilderness towards the Red Sea . . . . And all the time the Lord went before them, by day a pillar of cloud to guide them on their journey, by night a pillar of fire." What are the facts? For many religious conservatives it is a *fact* that God led the Israelites out of Egypt, and even on the liberal account, there is likely to be a religious meaning to the scriptural passage that is missing from the textbook account. Moreover, according to Scripture it was God who made Israel a great nation, and it was God who raised up the Assyrians and Babylonians to punish Israel for its sins. Now in these last cases the textbook author has not overtly contradicted the scriptural account; he has not said God didn't raise up the Assyrians and Babylonians. Still, he has left out what is most important to the scriptural version: the role of God in shaping history. The meaning of the scriptural story is completely lost in the textbook; it becomes, in effect, a different story. History is not, after all, a simple chronicle of events: it provides explanations of events that have a certain significance and meaning.

Clearly the author is not treating religion as people within that religious tradition would treat it. The author has chosen to tell the story from a secular rather than a religious frame of reference; he is telling us that what is important, indeed what is true, is a sequence of secular, political events with no obvious significance, and he makes no effort to explore the inner, religious dynamic of the scriptural account.

A few paragraphs later in the same text a student would read this statement: "The holy writings of the Hebrews included the Ten Commandments and the Old Testament." Wrong. The holy writings of Christians include the Old Testament, but there is no Old Testament for ancient Hebrews (or modern Jews) because they have no New Testament. This is not just a minor matter of names, for to understand the Hebrew Scriptures as the Old Testament is to interpret it as referring prophetically to the coming of Christ.

Thus the textbook author has, within several paragraphs, managed to retell the story of the ancient Hebrews first from within the worldview of a modern, secular historian, and second, using the language of Christianity rather than Judaism. Whose story is it? From within what worldview should it be written?

Or, to bring the story a little closer to our times, we have seen that nineteenth-century schoolbooks often put Abraham Lincoln's life into the perspective of God's purposes in history. In fact, most Americans, and most of the central actors in the Civil War (certainly Lincoln and Jefferson Davis, for example) understood that war as part of the working out of God's purposes, yet none of the American histories I reviewed mentioned—much less adopted—that interpretation of events or reflected on the spiritual significance of the Civil War for the meaning of America. In its chapter on the years 1860-65 the most popular text included sections on Native Americans, women, the National Banking Act of 1863, agricultural expansion, and the growth of railroads, as well as the Civil War, but ventured not a single comment about the religious beliefs of anyone or the religious significance of the war.

Everyone agrees that the texts slight religion, but the deeper questions are about causality and meaning. Textbook authors inevitably operate from within a worldview, a set of philosophical commitments which define for them what is important, what can and cannot count as a fact, what justifies claims about the meaning of events. Modern historians employ a secular, often scientific, methodology that allows no room for miracles, divine providence, or religious accounts of the meaning of historical change. It may very well be that modern, secular ways of understanding history are more reasonable than religious ways of understanding it. That is not the issue. My point is simply that religious and modern secular ways of understanding history are fundamentally different, and religious understandings of history are not found in the textbooks.

Judaism, Christianity, and Islam all understand history in terms of God's purposes. Whether or not one interprets such talk literally (as conservatives do) or mythically (as liberals do), there is an irreducible religious meaning to history that cannot be captured in fully secular language. Yet none of the books provide any sense of what that meaning might be. Indeed, none of the texts I reviewed were self-consciously reflective about the *meaning* of history at all. Paul Gagnon writes that none of the world history texts he reviewed "defines what history is, how it is written, what its strengths and weaknesses may be, how it relates to the student's life and other studies, or what connection it could have with preparing thoughtful and informed citizens." Only three of the nine North Carolina texts say anything about the nature or value of history, and two of these discussions are but a single page. They include no mention of religious interpretations of history. . . .

Why Is There So Little Religion in the Textbooks?

It is often argued that religion is kept out of public school textbooks because it is too controversial, and there is undoubtedly something to this. As Frances Fitzgerald explains it, the textbook industry is not large; public schools spend less than 1 percent of their budgets on textbooks. Hence publishers can't afford to have more than one or two of their texts on the market at the same time. Consequently, she claims, "all of them try to compete for the center of the market, designing their books not to please anyone in particular but to be acceptable to as many people as possible. The word "controversial" is as deeply feared by textbook publishers as it is coveted by trade book publishers.

So it has always been. In an effort to appeal to as wide an audience as possible, an 1844 advertisement for *McGuffey's Eclectic Fourth Reader* announced: "No *sectarian* matter has been admitted into this work." The publisher explained: "It has been submitted to the inspection of highly intelligent clergymen and teachers of the various Protestant and Catholic denominations, and nothing has been inserted, except with their united approbation."

Tony Podesta, a past president of People for the American Way, has written that the "real explanation of the inadequate coverage of religion in US history texts is . . . [that] textbook publishers are still afraid of offending anyone, from moral majoritarians to civil libertarians." Jeffrey Pasley has suggested that "textbook publishers aren't ideologues, but merely salesmen eager to please." Herbert Adams, president and CEO of Laidlaw Brothers, has said that "people are afraid that if they allude to religion, they'll get into a controversy over separation of church and state. The assumption is if you put religion in a book, it won't sell." The result, Joan Delfattore argues, is that "the textbook development process in America has less to do with educating a nation than with selling a product." Thou shalt not offend that ye may profit.

In 1990 California considered adopting a new series of social studies books published by Houghton Mifflin which included a great deal more about religion than other texts—enough more so that everyone could find something objectionable. At the adoption hearings, Christian fundamentalists testified that various passages demeaned them. Atheists felt their views had not been represented. Jews argued that Judaism was treated primarily as an antecedent to Christianity. "This is not a threat," one Muslim spokesmen said, "but if our demands are not met, we will withdraw our children from school and mount lawsuits." At one point, police had to be called into the hearings to restore order. Gilbert Sewall commented in the *Social Studies Review:* "It is not hard to guess the chilling message these California carnivals are sending to other publishers."

Nonetheless, the books were adopted and are now used in most California school systems; indeed, the Houghton Mifflin series was the only series adopted by the state. As much of a liability as controversy is, it need not rule a book out—at least if the people who make the decisions have the wherewithal to resist some public unhappiness. Indeed, it is clear that most textbooks contain a good deal of controversial material—it is just not controversial to the relevant textbook commissions or educational bureaucracies. Evolution has returned to most biology books although it is still controversial, and feminism and multiculturalism seem to have won the day in readers and social studies texts. That is, a (relatively) liberal educational establishment has been able to ensure that controversy will not keep their issues and themes out of texts.

Stephen Bates has shown how this works in fascinating detail. In the mid-1980s fundamentalist parents sought to have their children excused from using the Holt reading series required in the Hawkins County, Tennessee, public schools. As 2,261 pages of internal Holt files subpoenaed for the resulting court case showed, the Holt readers had come under considerable criticism from both the Left and the Right. What is striking is the extent to which the Holt editors bent over backward to respond to the concerns of the Left and their almost total resistance to the concerns of the Right. For example, they devised elaborate schemes for counting characters in stories and faces in pictures to ensure that women and minorities were adequately represented (at least 50 percent must be women), and they sometimes changed the sex of characters in stories to make their quotas; they required that women and blacks not be described or pictured in stereotypical roles; sexist language (for example, "manmade," "workmanlike," "statesman") was eliminated from the texts. In a 1981 speech Holt editor Barbara Theobald denounced conservative pressure groups as "censors" of the kind one finds in "totalitarian societies." But at the "other end of the spectrum," she went on to say, "we have other groups . . . who seek to improve our educational institutions and textbooks in a positive manner." As Bates reports it, for Theobald "critics who wanted schoolbooks to feature more women were 'positive pressure groups,' whereas those who wanted fewer women were 'censors.'"

The most impressive evidence that controversy is not a sufficient explanation for the absence of religion is to be found on college campuses. Given academic freedom and insulation of faculty from public pressures, controversy can add to the value of book. But college biology, economics, and psychology texts and courses are not likely to be any more sensitive to religion than high school texts. Although there is no doubt more room in college for the idiosyncratic professor and text, texts in these subjects are as secular as are the high school texts. Controversy is not the heart of the matter.

There is another explanation for secular textbooks: they are written by secular intellectuals and published by secular publishers, both of whom are committed to spreading secular ways of understanding the world. This explanation comes in two forms. The more wild-eyed of the televangelists speak darkly of a conspiracy of secular humanists. This is nonsense. Paul Vitz, no liberal, says in his study of textbooks that "there is no evidence of any kind of conscious conspiracy operating to censor textbooks." But, Vitz goes on to say, there is "a very widespread secular and liberal mindset" that "pervades the leadership in the world of education (and textbook publishing) and a secular and liberal bias is its inevitable consequence." There is something to this.

Ever since the seventeenth century scholars in virtually all fields have come more and more to reject religious ways of understanding the world for those provided by modern science and social science. In the scholarly world—the world of most textbook authors and publishers—religion is marked off from respectable pursuits by an intellectual wall of separation, and most scholars never set foot on holy ground. Indeed, secular ways of thinking are so deeply embedded in the academic disciplines that religious alternatives simply cannot be taken seriously. The argument is not that scholars are atheists (though, no doubt, intellectuals are among the least religious of modern folk); it is that the conventional wisdom of their disciplines leaves no philosophical room for religious claims and arguments. At best, most modern scholarship relegates religion to the private world of faith—and often assigns it to the realm of superstition. That is, religion is left out of the texts precisely because it is *not* controversial; it is so uncontroversial that it need not be considered.

Of course, it is not just the intellectuals among us who are secularized. As I argued in chapter 1, we all live our lives in a public world which is largely secular. In fact, we have become so secular that most of us completely fail to miss religion in the textbooks.

Over the last three hundred years, business, law, politics, psychology, medicine, and education have all been secularized. We allow students to earn high school diplomas and undergraduate, graduate, and professional degrees without taking a single course in religion or discussing religion in whatever courses are required. We assume that everything worth knowing about every field of study can be learned without learning anything about religion.

Militant secularists (or atheists) are rare creatures among textbook authors as well as within the general public, and secularization proceeds nicely without them. Capitalism and consumerism, pluralism, nationalism, individualism, science, and technology divert our attention from the life of the spirit, undercut traditional religion, refocus our interests, provide us with new ways of thinking about the world, and, in the process, secularize us. Religion occupies but a small part of our time, and it influences few of our decisions. Exorcisms are rare, and the church no longer regulates the economy. This being the case, psychologists and economists can write textbooks about our (essentially) secular world without having to say very much about religion. Religion simply has not played nearly so much of a role in our public life in the last two or three hundred years as it once did.

There are, then, three different reasons why the textbooks have become secular. First, religion *is* increasingly irrelevant in our public, secular world. Second, intellectuals do not take religion seriously; it doesn't fit into the categories of their respective disciplines. Yet, third, religion possesses considerable vitality within our culture. Many people believe it is neither irrelevant nor a superstition. Hence religion continues to be the source of much controversy and of considerable danger to publishers.

Conclusions

There have been incremental improvements in the latest editions of at least a few social studies and history textbooks—due, in part at least, to the textbook studies of the late 1980s—and the new national standards for teaching American and world history give significantly more attention to religion than do the textbooks, though they continue to slight theology and do not even raise the question of using religious categories for interpreting history. . . . As far as I can tell, however, texts in disciplines other than history and social studies have shown no greater sensitivity to religion.

What continues to be missing in all the texts, however, is any sensitivity to contemporary religious ways of interpreting the subject at hand. If religion is mentioned more (here and there), the governing philosophical assumptions that shape the kinds of explanations offered in the texts remain entirely secular. It is tremendously important to keep in mind that textbooks don't just teach subjects, they initiate students into intellectual disciplines; they don't just teach facts, they teach ways of thinking about the world.

There *is* something like a coherent worldview, a loosely structured set of philosophical commitments, which underlie and give shape to the texts—at least those texts I reviewed. No doubt not every author buys into it completely, and it is not typically taught self-consciously as a worldview by the authors—in part, at least, because it is so much a part of the intellectual air we breathe daily. The philosophical commitments that define this worldview are the same commitments that support and make sense of the dominant cultural and intellectual institutions of modernity: the knowledge we acquire in the present is more valuable than the wisdom of the past; our task is to free ourselves from the dead hand of tradition and superstition; we are no longer born into communities bound together in webs of (natural) social obligations; we are individuals first and foremost; human relationships are essentially contractual; the idea of the public good is problematic and is dissolved into the relative satisfaction of individuals and interest groups; reason is "deconstructed" into its scientific or narrowly utilitarian components, and though it may be competent to tell us about the facts, it is no longer competent to render judgment concerning moral matters; values are matters of personal choice or social convention; pluralism is assumed and defended—and then often confused with relativism; nature was long ago desacralized, and there is no purpose to be discovered in its processes; science and social science provide us with our only true knowledge of the world. By implication, religion is irrelevant to understanding the world.

Questions for Reflection and Discussion

1. Identify several secular and religious influences discussed by Henry May which prompted the recovery of American religious history during the middle of the twentieth century.

2. How does Martin Marty account for the diffusion of religion in the American culture in the last quarter of the twentieth century?

3. How does Warren Nord account for the lack of religion in public school textbooks?

4. Explain how each of the three writers reflects on the interaction and tension between the secular and the sacred.

5. Describe how the three essays interpret the place of religion in American culture.

Additional Readings

Ahlstrom, Sydney, E. *A Religious History of the American People*. New Haven: Yale University Press, 1972.

Albanese, Catherine. *America: Religions and Religion*. 3rd ed. Belmont, CA: Wadsworth Publishing Co., 1998.

Bloom, Harold. *The American Religion: The Emergence of the Post-Christian Nation*. New York: Simon and Schuster, 1992.

Conkin, Paul. *American Originals: Homemade Varieties of Christianity*. Chapel Hill: University of North Carolina Press. 1992.

Finke, Roger, and Rodney Stark. *The Churching of America, 1776-1990: Winners and Losers in Our Religious Economy*. New Brunswick: Rutgers University Press, 1992.

Gaustad, Edwin S. *A Religious History of America*. New revised edition. San Francisco: HarperCollins, 1990.

Gleason, Philip. *Keeping the Faith: American Catholicism, Past and Present*. Notre Dame: University of Notre Dame Press, 1987.

Hackett, David, ed. *Religion and American Culture*. New York: Routledge, 1995.

Handy, Robert T. *A Christian America: Protestant Hopes and Historical Realities*. New York: Oxford University Press, 1984.

Marsden, George. *Religion and American Culture*. San Diego: Harcourt Brace Jovanovich, Publishers, 1990.

Marty, Martin E. *Modern American Religion*. 3 vols. Chicago: The University of Chicago Press, 1986-96.

_____. *Pilgrims in Their Own Land: 500 Years of Religion in America*. Boston: Little, Brown and Company, 1984.

McDannell, Colleen. *Material Christianity: Religion and Popular Culture in America*. New Haven: Yale University Press, 1995.

McNamara, Patrick H., ed. *Religion American Style*. New York: Harper and Row, Publishers, 1974.

Moore, R. Laurence. *Selling God: American Religion in the Marketplace of Culture*. New York: Oxford University Press, 1994.

Mulder, John M., and John F. Wilson, eds. *Religion in American History: Interpretive Essays*. Englewood Cliffs: Prentice-Hall, Inc., 1978.

Noll, Mark, Nathan Hatch, and George Marsden. *The Search for Christian America*. Reprint ed. Colorado Springs, Co: Helmers Howard Publishers, 1989.

Ruether, Rosemary Radford, and Rosemary Skinner Keller, eds. *Women and Religion in America*. 3 vols. San Francisco: Harper and Row, Publishers, 1981-86.

Sachar, Howard M. *A History of the Jews in America.* New York: Knopf, 1992.

Sernett, Milton C., ed. *Afro-American Religious History: A Documentary Witness.* Durham: Duke University Press, 1985.

Stout, Harry, and Darryl Hart. *New Directions in American Religious History.* New York: Oxford University Press, 1997.

Weisenfeld, Judith, and Richard Newman, eds. *This Far by Faith: Readings in African-American Women's Religious Biography.* New York: Routledge, 1995.

Williams, Peter W. *Popular Religion in America: Symbolic Change and the Modernization Process.* Urbana: University of Illinois Press, 1989.

Chapter 2

Religion in Early America

Issue

How inclusive would religion be in early America?

Variety and dissent characterized the American religious scene almost from the beginning of European transplantation to the New World. Soon after his arrival in Virginia, John Rolfe declared that "Almighty God . . . hath opened the gate and led me by the hand that I might plainly see and discern the safe paths wherein to tread." Only a few years later in 1619 the Virginia legislature initiated the process that would make the Church of England the publicly supported and officially established church in Virginia.

Over the next several decades, hundreds of miles to the north, the New England Way took shape, first in the colony of Massachusetts, then in Connecticut, and later in New Hampshire. Unlike with Virginia's Anglicanism, in New England, London did not superintend the enterprise or approve the clergy or doctrine. Hence, a religious diversity was planted in America by the middle of the seventeenth century.

Variety in early America's religious experience resulted largely from the numerous doors opened to the religiously oppressed of Europe. From Germany's Palatinate, refugees relocated along the Hudson River Valley in New York. Savannah, Georgia, was settled by Lutherans fleeing persecution in Salzburg, Austria. Then, too, like a magnet, vacant spaces of early America attracted many who yielded to the tendency to become their own religious masters, as with the Quakers in Pennsylvania who implemented William Penn's "Holy Experiment."

The religious diversity of early America did not produce a religious tolerance spread evenly among the settlers. To the contrary, examples of religious diversity resulting from the lack of religious tolerance were not rare in the first century and a half of the American odyssey. The frequent grinding of the gears in the religious machines of early America attest to the struggles of the people over the question of how inclusive religion among the settlers would, and should, be.

And complicating the dynamic of religious diversity in early America was the ever-present racial diversity. How did the early settlers' beliefs in freedom and equality translate into religious behavior? What evidence is there that the knitting together of religious diversity and racial diversity intensified the cultural conflict of early America? How did women influence the role of religion in early America?

Documents

Though some of the first English settlements in America were the result of Protestant dissenters, soon thereafter Catholics also made their way across the Atlantic. The first document is Father Pierre Baird's initial response to his contact with Native Americans in the New World. In the second selection, Father Andrew White, who ministered to the Jesuit mission in Maryland, recounts the celebrating of the mass in 1634, the first such occasion in America. Fearful of papal plots and imperialism, only seven years later the colony of Virginia made clear its anti-Catholic sentiment in a statement barring Catholics from political office and also from any proselytizing activities. The third document spells out these limitations on Catholics in Virginia. In the fourth document, Quaker leader William Penn challenges his followers in 1669 to imitate the example of the first century Bereans who displayed great courage in the face of strong opposition. That Quakers in the New World endured their own opposition is described in the fifth document, which records the 1677 trial of Quaker leader Margaret Brewster, charged with violating Massachusetts' law requiring an oath of fidelity. The Reverend Francis Le Jau of the Society for the Propagation of the Gospel tells in the final selection of slave conversions on the Carolina frontier.

1. A French View of Native Americans, 1611
SOURCE: D. B. Quinn, ed., *New American World* (New York: Arno Press and Hector Bye, 1979) IV, 392-94.

And now you have had, my Reverend Father, an account of our voyage, of what happened in it, and before it, and since our arrival at this settlement. It now remains to tell you that the conversion of this country, to the Gospel, and of these people to civilization, is not a small undertaking nor free from great difficulties; for, in the first place, if we consider the country, it is only a forest, without other conveniences of life than those which will be brought from France, and what in time may be obtained from the soil after it has been cultivated. The nation is savage, wandering and full of bad habits; the people few and isolated. They are, I say, savage, haunting the woods, ignorant, lawless and rude: they are wanderers, with nothing to attach them to a place, neither homes nor relationship, neither possessions nor love of country; as a people they have bad habits, are extremely lazy, gluttonous, profane, treacherous, cruel in their revenge, and given up to all kinds of lewdness, men and women alike, the men having several wives and abandoning them to others, and the women only serving them as slaves, whom they strike and beat unmercifully, and who dare not complain; and after being half killed, if it so please the murderer, they must laugh and caress him.

With all these vices, they are exceedingly vainglorious: they think they are better, more valiant and more ingenious than the French; and, what is difficult to believe, richer than we are. They consider themselves, I say, braver than we are, boasting that they have killed Basques and Malouins, and that they do a great deal of harm to the ships, and that no one has ever resented it, insinuating that it was from a lack of courage. They consider themselves better than the French; "For," they say, "you are always fighting and quarreling among yourselves; we live peaceably. You are envious and are all the time slandering each other; you are thieves and deceivers: you are covetous, and are neither generous nor kind; as for us, if we have a morsel of bread we share it with our neighbor."

They are saying these and like things continually, seeing the above-mentioned imperfections in some of us, and flattering themselves that some of their own people do not have them so conspicuously, not realizing that they all have much greater vices, and that the better part of our people do not have even these defects, they conclude generally that they are superior to all christians. It is self-love that blinds them, and the evil one who leads them on, no more nor less than in our France, we see those who have deviated from the faith holding themselves higher and boasting of being better than the catholics, because in some of them they see many faults; considering neither the virtues of the other catholics, nor their own still greater imperfections; wishing to have, like Cyclops, only a single eye, and to fix that one upon the vices of a few catholics, never upon the virtues of the others, nor upon themselves, unless it be for the purpose of self-deception.

Also they [the savages] consider themselves more ingenious, inasmuch as they see us admire some of their productions as the work of people so rude and ignorant; lacking intelligence, they bestow very little admiration upon what we show them, although much more worthy of being admired. Hence they regard themselves as much richer than we are, although they are poor and wretched in the extreme. . . .

All these things, added to the difficulty of acquiring the language, the time that must be consumed, the expenses that must be incurred, the great distress, toil and poverty that must be endured, fully proclaim the greatness of this enterprise and the difficulties which beset it. Yet many things encourage me to continue in it. . . .

In conclusion, we hope in time to make them susceptible of receiving the doctrines of the faith and of the christian and catholic religion, and later, to penetrate farther into the regions beyond, which they say are more populous and better cultivated. We base this hope upon Divine goodness and mercy, upon the zeal and fervent charity of all good people who earnestly desire the kingdom of God, particularly upon the holy prayers of Your Reverence and of our Reverend Fathers and very dear Brothers, to whom we most affectionately commend ourselves.

From Port Royal, New France, this tenth day of June, one thousand six hundred and eleven.

[Signed:] PIERRE BAIRD

2. English America's First Mass, 1634

SOURCE: *Relatio Itineris in Marylandiam, Or, Narrative of a Voyage to Maryland* (Baltimore: Maryland Historical Society, 1844), 30-33.

At length, sailing from this place, we reached the *cape*, which they call *Point Comfort*, in Virginia, on the 27th of February, full of apprehension, lest the English inhabitants, who were much displeased at our settling, should be plotting something against us. Nevertheless the letters we carried from the King, and from the high treasurer of England, served to allay their anger, and to procure those things which would afterwards be useful to us. For the Governor of Virginia hoped, that by this kindness toward us, he would more easily recover from the Royal treasury a large sum of money which was due him. They only told us that a rumor prevailed, that six ships were coming to reduce everything under the power of the Spaniards, and that for this reason, all the natives were in arms; this we afterwards found to be true. Yet I fear the rumor had its origin with the English.

After being kindly treated for eight or nine days, we set sail on the third of March, and entering the Chesapeak Bay, we turned our course to the north to reach the *Potomeack* River. The Chesopeacke Bay, ten leagues (30 Italian miles) wide, flows gently between its shores: it is four, five and six fathoms deep, and abounds in fish when the season is favorable; you will scarcely find a more beautiful body of water. Yet it yields the palm to the Potomeack River, which we named after St. Gregory.

Having now arrived at the wished-for country, we allotted names according to circumstances. And indeed the Promontory, which is toward the south, we consecrated with the name of St. Gregory (now Smith Point,) naming the northern one (now Point Lookout) St. Michael's, in honor of all the angels. Never have I beheld a larger or more beautiful river. The Thames seems a mere rivulet in comparison with it; it is not disfigured with any swamps, but has firm land on each side. Fine groves of trees appear, not choked with briers or bushes and undergrowth, but growing at intervals as if planted by the hand of man, so that you can drive a four-horse carriage, wherever you choose, through the midst of the trees. Just at the mouth of the river, we observed the natives in arms. That night, fires blazed through the whole country, and since they had never seen such a large ship, messengers were sent in all directions, who reported that a *Canoe*, like an island had come with as many men as there were trees in the woods. We went on, however, to Herons' Islands, so called from the immense numbers of these birds. The first island we came to, [we called] St. Clement's Island, and as it has a sloping shore, there is no way of getting to it except by wading. Here the women, who had left the ship, to do the washing, upset the boat and came near being drowned, losing also a large part of my linen clothes, no small loss in these parts.

This island abounds in cedar and sassafras trees, and flowers and herbs, for making all kinds of salads, and it also produces a wild nut tree, which bears a very hard walnut with a thick shell and a small but very delicious kernel. Since, however, the island contains only four hundred acres, we saw that it would not afford room enough for the new settlement. Yet we looked for a suitable place to build only a Fort (perhaps on the island itself) to keep off strangers, and to protect the trade of the river and our boundaries; for this was the narrowest crossing-place on the river.

On the day of *the Annunciation of the Most Holy Virgin* Mary in the year 1634, we celebrated the mass for the first time, on this island. This had never been done before in this part of the world. After we had completed the sacrifice, we took upon our shoulders a great cross, which we had hewn out of a tree, and advancing in order to the appointed place, with the assistance of the Governor and his associates and the other Catholics, we erected a trophy to Christ the Saviour, humbly reciting, on our bended knees, the Litanies of the Sacred Cross, with great emotion.

3. Anti-Catholicism, 1641
SOURCE: Francis X. Curran, S.J., ed., *Catholics in Colonial Law* (Chicago: Loyola University Press 1963), 22.

It is enacted by the authority aforesaid, that according to a Statute made in the third year of the reign of our sovereign Lord King James, of blessed memory, no popist [sic] recusant shall at any time hereafter exercise the place or places of secretary, counsellor, register, commissioner, surveyor or sheriff, or any other public place, but be utterly disabled for the same;

And further, be it enacted by the authority aforesaid, that none shall be admitted into any of the aforesaid offices or places before he or they have taken the oaths of supremacy and allegiance. And if any person or persons whatsoever shall by any sinister or secret means contrive to himself any of the aforesaid places, or any other public office whatsoever, and refuse to take the aforesaid oaths, he or they so convicted before any assembly shall be dismissed of his said office, and for his offense herein, forfeit a thousand pounds weight of tobacco, to be disposed of by the next grand assembly after conviction.

And it is enacted by the authority aforesaid that the statutes in force against popish recusants be duly executed in the government; and that it shall not be lawful, under the penalty aforesaid, for any popish priest that shall hereafter arrive here to remain above five days, after warning given for his departure by the governor or commander of that place where he or they shall be, if wind and weather hinder not his departure; this act to be in force after ten days from the publication here at James City.

4. Pennsylvania and the Quakers, 1669

SOURCE: *The Select Works of William Penn*, 4th ed. (London: William Phillips, 1825), I, 225-26.

TO THE NOBLE BEREANS OF THIS AGE

When our dear Lord Jesus Christ, the blessed author of the Christian religion, first sent forth his disciples, to proclaim the happy approach of the heavenly kingdom, among several other things that he gave them in charge, it pleased him to make this one of their instructions; "Into whatsoever city or town ye shall enter, enquire who in it is worthy;" foreseeing the ill use unworthy persons would make of that message, and with what unweariness the implacable pharisee, and subtle scribe, would endeavour to pervert the right way of the Lord, and thereby prejudice the simple against the reception of that excellent testimony.

This being the case of the people called Quakers, who above every tribe of men are most maliciously represented, bitterly envied, and furiously oppugned by many of the scribes and pharisees of our time, for as impious wretches as those of that time reputed our blessed Saviour and his constant followers to be; it becometh us, in a condition so desperate, to provide ourselves with some worthy readers, men that dare trust their reason above reports, and be impartial in an age as biassed as this we live in; whose determinations shall not wait upon the sentence of ignorance nor interest, but a sincere and punctual examination of the matter.

And since there are none recorded in sacred writ, on whom the Holy Ghost conferred so honourable a character, but the Bereans of that age (for that they both searched after truth impartially, and when they found it, embraced it readily, for which they were entitled noble); therefore it is that to you, the offspring of that worthy stock, and noble Bereans of our age, I, in behalf of the so much calumniated abettors of the cause of truth, chose to dedicate this defence of our holy profession from the injurious practices of a sort of men, who, not unlike to the Jews of Thessalonica, that, envying the prosperity of the gospel among your ancestors, made it their business to stir up the multitude against the zealous promoters of it. And no matter what it be, provided they can but obtain their end of fixing an odium upon the Quakers: they do not only boldly condemn what they esteem worst in us (how deservedly we will not now say) but insinuate what is best to be criminal.

The sobriety of our lives, they call a cheat for custom; and our incessant preachings and holy living, a decoy to advance our party: if we say nothing to them when they interrogate us, it is sullenness or inability; if we say something to them, it is impertinency, or equivocation. We must not believe as we do believe, but as they would have us believe, which they are sure to make obnoxious enough, that they may the more securely inveigh against us. Nor must our writings mean what we say we mean by them, but what they will have them to mean, lest they should want proofs for their charges. It was our very case that put David upon that complaint, "Every day they wrest my words: all their thoughts are against me for evil." But to David's God we commit our slandered cause, and to you the Bereans of our age.

Degenerate not from the example of your progenitors; if you do, you are no longer true Bereans, and to such we inscribe this work: if you do not, we may assure ourselves of the justice of a fair enquiry and an equal judgment.

The God and Father of our Lord Jesus Christ augment your desire after truth, give you clearer discerning of the truth, and enable you both more readily to receive, and with greater resolution to maintain the truth. I am

A christian Quaker, and your christian friend,

WILLIAM PENN.

5. The Trial of Margaret Brewster, 1677

SOURCE: Nathaniel B. Shurtleff, Ed., *Records of the Governor and Company of the Massachusetts Bay in New England* V *1674-1686,* 60, 154-155.

Clerk. Margaret Brewster.

M.B. Here.

Clerk. *Are you the Woman?*

M.B. Yes, I am the Woman.

Governour. *Read her* Mittimus.

The *Mittimus* was read.

Governour, to the People. *What have you to lay to her Charge?*

Constable. *If this be the Woman, I don't know; for she was then in the Shape of a Devil: I thought her Hair had been a Perriwig, but it was her own Hair.* The Constable said more, but so faintly and low as not to be understood.

Gov. *You hear your Accusation.*

M.B. I do not hear it.

Gov. *Are you the Woman that came into Mr. Thatcher's Meetinghouse with your Hair fruzled, and dressed in the Shape of a Devil?*

M.B. I am the Woman that came into Priest *Thatcher's* House of Worship with my Hair about my Shoulders, Ashes upon my Head, my Face coloured black, and Sackcloth upon my upper Garments.

Gov. *You own yourself to be the Woman.*

M.B. Yea, I do.

Gov. *What made you come so?*

M.B. I came in Obedience to the Lord.

Gov. *The Lord! The Lord never sent you, for you came like a Devil, and in the Shape of a Devil incarnate.*

M.B. Noble Governour! Thy Name is spread in other Parts of the World for a moderate Man, now I desire thee and thy Assistants to hear me with Patience, that I may give an Account of my so coming among you.

Gov. *Too moderate for such as you: But go on.*

M.B. The Lord God of Heaven and Earth, the Maker and Creator of all Mankind, laid this Service upon me more than three Years ago to visit this bloody Town of *Boston.*

Here some spake to the Governour to stop her from speaking any more; but the Governour said, *Let her go on.*

M.B. And when the appointed Time drew near, the Lord pleased to visit me with Sickness, before I could clearly give up this Service, and as I may say, I was raised as one from the Dead, and came from my sick Bed to visit the bloody Town of *Boston,* and to bear a living Testimony for the God of my Life, and go as a Sign among you; and as I gave up to this Service, my Sickness went away. It is said the Prophet *Jonah* was three Days in the Whale's Belly, but I could compare my condition to nothing, but as if I had been in the Belly of Hell for many Weeks, and I think I mayso say for some Months, until I gave up to this Service; and now if you be suffered to take away my Life, I am very well contented.

Gov. *You shall escape with your Life.*

Simon Broadstreet. *You are a Blasphemer.*

M.B. I have not blasphemed.

S. Broadstreet. *I cannot believe what you say to be true.*

M.B. Canst thou not believe? Well, I am sorry thou canst not believe.

Gov. *Are you a married Woman?*

M.B. I am.

Gov. *Did your Husband give Consent to your Coming?*

M.B. Yea, he did.

Gov. *Have you any Thing to shew under his Hand?*

M.B. He gave his Consent before many Witnesses in *Barbadoes,* and said, *He did believe this Service was of God,* and he durst not withstand it, but was willing to give me up to this Service, as many in *Barbadoes* can witness; and now, if you be suffered to take away my Life, I can now lay down my Head in Peace, for I have thus far done what the Lord required at my Hands, and am clear of the Blood of all People in this Place, so far as I know; and the Desire of my Soul is, that it may be with this Town as it was with *Nineveh* of old, for when the Lord sent his Prophet *Jonah* to cry against *Nineveh,* it is said, *They put on Sackcloth, and covered their Heads with Ashes, and repented and the Lord withdrew his judgments for forty Years:* And my Soul cries to the Lord that this People may repent, that the Lord may spare them yet forty Years: For it was in true Obedience to the Lord, and in Love to your Souls, that I was made to come as a Sign amongst you, for I feel that in my Heart at this Moment, that I could even give up my Life to be sacrificed for the Good of your Souls. I have nothing but Love in my Heart to the worst of my Enemies here in this Town.

Gov. *Hold, hold Woman, you run too fast.* Silence in the Court.

M.B. Governour! I desire thee to hear me a little, for I have something to say in Behalf of my Friends in this Place: I desire thee and thine Assistants to put an End to these cruel Laws that you have made to prosecute my Friends for meeting together to worship the True and Living God. Oh Governour! I cannot but press thee again and again, to put an End to these cruel Laws that you have made to fetch my Friends from their peaceable Meetings, and keep them three Days in the House of Correction, and then whip them for worshipping the True and Living God: Governour! Let me intreat thee to put an End to these Laws, for the Desire of my Soul is, that you may act for God, and then would you prosper, but if you act against the Lord and his blessed Truth, you will assuredly come to nothing, the Mouth of the Lord hath spoken it; for if you will draw your Swords against the Lord and his People, the Lord will assuredly draw his Sword against you; for there never was any Weapon formed against God and his blessed Truth that ever prospered: It's my Testimony for the Lord God of my Life.

Gov. *Hold Woman.* Call *Lydia Wright.*

Clerk. *Call* Lydia Wright of Long-Island

L. Wright. Here.

Gov. *Are you one of the Women that came in with this Woman into Mr. Thatcher's Meeting-house to disturb him at his Worship?*

L.W. I was; but I disturbed none, for I came in peaceably, and spake not a Word to Man, Woman, or Child.

Gov. *What came you for then?*

L.W. Have you not made a Law that we should come to your Meeting? For we were peaceably met together at our own Meeting-house, and some of your Constables came in, and haled some of our Friends out, and said, *This is not a Place for you to worship God in.* Then we asked him, *Where we should worship God?* Then they said, *We must come to your publick Worship.* And upon the First-day following I had something upon my Heart to come to your publick Worship, when we came in peaceably, and spake not a Word, yet we were haled to Prison, and there have been kept near a Month.

S. Broadstreet. *Did you come there to hear the Word?*

L.W. If the Word of God was there, I was ready to hear it.

Gov. *Did your Parents give Consent you should come thither?*

L.W. Yes, my Mother did.

Gov. *Shew it.*

L.W. If you will stay till I can send Home, I will engage to get from under my Mother's Hand, that she gave her Consent.

Juggins, a Magistrate, said, *You are led by the Spirit of the Devil, to ramble up and down the Country, like Whores and Rogues a Caterwawling.*

L.W. Such Words do not become those who call themselves *Christians,* for they that sit to judge for God in Matters of Conscience, ought to be sober and serious, for Sobriety becomes the People of God, for these are a weighty and ponderous People.

Gov. *Do you own this Woman?*

L.W. I own her, and have Unity with her, and I do believe so have all the faithful Servants of the Lord, for I know the Power and Presence of the Lord was with us.

Juggins. *You are mistaken: You do not know the Power of God; you are led by the Spirit and Light within you, which is of the Devil: There is but one God, and you do not worship the God which we worship.*

L. W. I believe thou speaketh Truth, for if you worshipped that God which we worship, you would not persecute his People, for we worship the God Of *Abraham, Isaac,* and *Jacob,* and the same God that *Daniel* worshipped.

So they cried, *Take her away.*

Then *Mary Miles* was called.

Clerk. *Mary Miles* of *Black-point.*

M.M. I am here.

Gov. *Do you live at* Black-point?

M.M. Nay: My former Living was there, but my outward Living is now at *Salem,* when I am at Home.

Gov. *Are you a married Woman?*

M.M. Nay, I am not married.

Gov. *Did you come into Mr. Thatcher's Meeting-house with this Woman that had a black Face?*

M.M. Yea, I did.

Gov. *What was the Cause?*

M.M. My Freedom was in the Lord, and in Obedience to his Will, and the Unity of his Spirit, I came.

Gov. *So, so, then you had Unity with her, it seems, but you had not Communion with her, for you had not a black Face.*

M.M. I had good Unity with her, and do believe, and witness, and bear my Testimony for the Lord, that it was his Work and Service that she went in; therefore I had Unity and Fellowship with her, and the Lord in his due Time will reveal and manifest his own Work.

Gov. *Hold your Tongue, you prating Housewife; you are led by the Spirit of the Devil to run about the Country a wandering, like Whores and Rogues.*

M.M. They that are led by the Spirit of God deny the Works of the Devil: The Earth is the Lord's and the Fulness thereof; and he can command his Servants to go wheresoever he pleaseth to send them; and none can hinder his Power, for it is unlimited.

Cryer. *Take them away, and carry them to Prison.*

M.M. Yea, I am made willing to go to Prison, and to Death, if it were required of me to seal the Testimony of *Jesus* with my blood, as some of my Friends and Brethren have done, whose Blood you have shed, which cries to the Lord for Vengeance, and the Cry will not cease till Vengeance come upon you.

Then *Barbara Bowers* was called.

Margaret Brewster answered, *Barbara Bowers* was not concerned with us in this Service.

Gov. *Let us hear what she says.*

B. Bowers. I was in the Meeting-house, but did not go in with them. Then they were all carried to Prison again, and about an Hour after brought again into the Court, when the Governour being present, the Clerk read the Sentence as follows, viz.

Margaret Brewster, *You are to have your Clothes stript off to the Middle, and to be tide to a Cat's Tail at the* South *Meeting-house, and to be drawn through the Town, and to receive twenty Stripes upon your naked Body.*

M.B. The Will of the Lord be done: I am contented.

The Clerk proceeded, saying, Lydia Wright *and* Mary Miles, *You are to be tied to the Cart's Tail also.* Barbara Bowers, *You are to be tied also.*

M. Brewster. I told the Court before, that *Barbara* was not concerned with us in the Service, and therefore I desire you may remit her Sentence; for I knew not of her Coming with us, neither did I see her with us, til we came into the Common-Goal: Therefore I desire she may not suffer.

Gov. *Take her away.*

Goaler. *I am loath to pull you.*

M.B. I will go without pulling, and go as chearfully as *Daniel* went to the Lion's Den, for the God of *Daniel* is with me; and the God of *Abraham, Isaac,* and *Jacob,* goes along with me: The same God that was with the three Children in the fiery Furnace goes with me now; and I am glad that I am worthy to be a Sufferer in this bloody Town, and to be numbered amongst my dearly and well-beloved Brethren and Sisters, that sealed their Testimonies with their Blood.

So they were carried to Prison again, this being the Seventh-day of the Week; and on the Fifth-day following, the Sentence was executed.

6. Slave Conversion on the Carolina Frontier, 1709

SOURCE: *The Carolina Chronicle of Dr. Francis Le Jau, 1706-1717.* Edited by Frank W. Klingberg (Berkeley: University of California Press, 1956), 60-61.

[October 20, 1709] As for the Spiritual State of my Parish this is the Account I can give of it for the present.

The extent of it is 20 Miles in length, and from 7 to 14 in breadth. Number of families 80, of the Church of England. Dissenting families 7, if so many, I find but 4 very strict. Baptised this half year past a Marryed Woman and 17 Children. Actual Communicants in all about 50: Constant Communicants every two Months near 30, among whom are two Negroes.

Since I came I baptised in all 2 Adults & 47 Children. Our Congregation is generally of about 100 Persons, sometimes more, several that were inclinable to some of the dissenting partys shew themselves pritty constant among us, and I do what possible to edify them and give them satisfaction in their doubts. On Sunday next I design God willing to baptise two very sensible and honest Negro Men whom I have kept upon tryal these two Years. Several others have spoken to me also; I do nothing too hastily in that respect. I instruct them and must have the consent of their Masters with a good Testimony and proof of their honest life and sober Conversation: Some Masters in my parish are very well satisfyed with my Proceedings in that respect: others do not seem to be so; yet they have given over opposing my design openly; it is to be hoped the good Example of the one will have an influence over the others. I must do the Justice to my Parishioners that tho' many Young Gentlemen are Masters of Great Estates, they and almost all the heads of all our Neighbouring families are an Example of Sobriety, honest & Zeal for the Service of the Church to all the province.

To remove all pretence from the Adult Slaves I shall baptise of their being free upon that Account, I have thought fit to require first their consent to this following declaration *You declare in the Presence of God and before this Congregation that you do not ask for the holy baptism out of any design to ffree yourself from the Duty and Obedience you owe to your Master while you live, but meerly for the good of Your Soul and to partake of the Graces and Blessings promised to the Members of the Church of Jesus Christ.* One of the most Scandalous and common Crimes of our Slaves is their perpetual Changing of Wives and husbands, which occasions great disorders: I also tell them whom I baptise, *The Christian Religion dos not allow plurality of Wives, nor any changing of them: You promise truly to keep to the Wife you now have till Death dos part you.* I[t] has been Customary among them to have their ffeasts, dances, and merry Meetings upon the Lord's day, that practice is pretty well over in this Parish, but not absolutely: I tell them that present themselves to be admitted to Baptism, they must promise they'l spend no more the Lord's day in idleness, and if they do I'l cut them off from the Comunion.

These I most humbly Submit to the judgment of my Superiors whose Commands and instructions I will follow while I live: I see with an incredible joy the fervor of several of those poor Slaves. Our free Indians our Neighbours come to see me, I admire the sense they have of Justice, and their patience; they have no Ambition; as for their sense of God, their Notions are obscure indeed, but when we take pains to Converse with them, in a jargon they are able to understand: We perceive their Souls are fit Materials which may be easily polish't, they agree with me about the duty of praying, & doing the good & eschewing the evil. The late Colonel Moore and our present Governor have in a great measure put a Stop to their perpetual murdering one another which some of them cannot to this day cannot conceive to be evil. Some of them to whom the Devil has formerly appeared, as they coldly declared to myself, say that evil Spirit never incites them to any thing more than hatred, revenge, and Murder of those that offend them.

I am told still that if anything opposes the publishing of the Gospel among the Indians it shall be the manner how our Indian Trade is carryed on, chiefly the fomenting of War among them for our people to get Slaves. I am so told in general but know no particulars; but it is too true interest has a great power here and dos occasion injustices too visibly to my great sorrow, and thro' misfortune I see no remedy but to be patient and pray and labour as much as I am able in the place I am sent to. . . .

Essays

The three essays below address the critical issue of religious freedom and opportunity in early America. Black women's interactions with religious forces in colonial America are surveyed by Lillian Ashcraft Webb of Clark Atlanta University (Georgia) in the first essay. In the second essay, Francis D. Cogliano,

Senior Lecturer in American History at LaSainte Union College in Great Britain, traces the rise of anti-Catholicism in sixteenth century England and its subsequent impact on seventeenth- and eighteenth-century New England. Mary Maples Dunn of Radcliffe College describes in the final essay the gender differentiation that developed with respect to religion among early colonial Puritan Congregationalism and Quakerism. Taken together, these three statements illustrate the challenges of matching religious behavior with religious belief.

Black Women and Religion in the Colonial Period
LILLIAN ASHCRAFT WEBB

SOURCE: Excerpts from *Women and Religion in America, volume 2, The Colonial and Revolutionary Periods* by Rosemary Radford Ruether. Copyright © 1983 by Rosemary R. Ruether and Rosemary S. Keller. Reprinted by permission of HarperCollins Publishers, Inc.

Black women, brought as slaves to North America in the seventeenth and eighteenth centuries, responded to conditions of servitude from perspectives of their West African cultural heritage. It is important, therefore, to understand this African background when assessing black women's interactions with religious forces in colonial America, particularly in English Protestant territories.

African Background
In most West African tribes, women were persons in their own right, with responsibilities and privileges not always based on their husbands' and fathers' patriarchal powers. Women controlled marketplaces, and their economic monopoly provided them with leverage for autonomous activity and with opportunities for leadership experiences.

In religious ceremonies, for example, women frequently were priests and leaders of cults. They sometimes maintained secret societies of their own. Whatever was the extent of West African women's participation in society beyond the marketplace and the immediate residential compound, it was based on realities of their economic initiative and contribution. These helped refine and solidify communal sharing and group identification.

Traditional religious systems permeated all facets of life in Africa, blurring distinctions between sacred and secular. Religious laws regulated sexual relationships, marriage rituals and responsibilities, and ceremonies of passage through puberty. They prescribed women's activities during pregnancy and shortly after childbirth, regulated dietary habits, and provided for lifetime continuance of sexual and other physical and psychological nurture. Religious beliefs and practices primarily were localized tribally and were inherited from ancestors, but several tribes often shared similar elements and patterns of beliefs, practices, and rituals.

European Reactions

European Christians had inherited strict monogamous views on sexuality. Believing themselves to have a monopoly on virtue and right-living, they curiously devoured licentious travel narratives about life in Africa. People in Africa, unlike their European contemporaries, practiced pragmatic approaches to human sexuality such as arranging for the fulfillment of sexual needs "in absentia" when spouses were deceased or otherwise away. Some tribes adhered to a system of levirate—a widow's being inherited by her brother-in-law. This insured that: (1) widows would have "continuity" in "mating with the deceased husband," and (2) the children of the deceased would have the presence of a father figure and an assured share in the deceased father's inheritance. Several societies with disproportionately high female populations assured virtually all women benefits of marriage through polygamy. (Polyandry was of negligible dimensions by the sixteenth century in Africa.) Such institutional practices as these offended Western Christian sensibilities, and explorers fueled European ethnocentrism by circulating narratives that described Africans as savages.

Religious fervor that had only smoldered in sixteenth-century Europe caught ablaze in the seventeenth century, and the African narratives had an especially disquieting effect upon English settlers in the American wildernesses.

> The age was driven by the twin spirits of adventure and control . . . [with] voyages of discovery overseas . . . [and] inward voyages of [self-]discovery. . . . [Within] this charged atmosphere of self-discovery . . . Englishmen . . . used peoples overseas as social mirrors . . . and . . . they were especially inclined to discover attributes in . . . [those] they called savages which they found first but could not speak of in themselves.

Although Winthrop Jordan made this statement to describe English religious zealots, it remains valid when applied to other seventeenth-century Euro-Americans.

The most probable frontal attack upon populations introduced into a male-oriented and -dominated society is that of denigrating the image of the "conquered" people's males. From that assault there follows aspersions upon the women. Europeans looked at blacks through stereotypes and not as human beings with individual strengths and weaknesses in character.

Prior to the importation of African women, settlers already had begun differentiating among character types when assigning work to European female servants. Because of their own Christian piety, their acceptance of rumors that Africans were savage, and their need for cheap labor, colonists arbitrarily presumed that every black woman was "nasty" and "beastly." Consequently, the colonial mind was set early in the seventeenth century to be insensitive to individual black character or sex when assigning work.

Seventeenth-Century Black Experiences

African women's initial experiences with the "churched" in North America was one of exclusion from church membership. The Anglican-dominated legislature in Virginia, for example, enacted a law that distinguished between servants. European servants were designated "Christian," and African laborers were referred to as "Negro servants" (implying that they were non-Christian). Colonists underscored the distinction by neglecting to bring "Negro servants" into the Christian church, sometimes legislating against black church attendance and discouraging black conversions. Settlers took these steps in an effort to protect their property (their black servants) since they were uncertain that Christianized servants could be held in bondage.

Ever since the Diet of Worms (1521), "the notion half-lurking . . . was that baptism and consequent conversion to Christianity affected the freedom of a slave." This posed a problem, but on the surface it seemed easily resolved. If masters did not teach Africans to be Christians, they could "justly" enslave them for the purpose of Christianizing them at some future, undesignated time. That way pious masters were less disturbed in their consciences, believing they had complied with the letter of the Diet and with the spirit of English Common Law by bringing Africans into geographical proximity to Christianity. One clergyman's extrapolation was representative of that generation's thinking; according to him, "perpetual bondage among Christians made useful servants of savages."

Whenever colonists introduced Christianity to Africans, black women quickly played a prominent role. Many already had Spanish Christian names when imported (Angela, for example). This indicated, according to one social scientist, that a number of Africans previously had been baptized. More recently, though, Murray Heller (editor of a study of black names) concluded to the contrary: "It appears . . . that whether or not baptism was involved, whites tended to supply their black slaves, to a great extent, with biblical and Christian names." The second, recorded Spanish-christened woman imported to North America from Africa was Isabella. Her "brush" with Christianity is among the earliest written accounts mentioning an African woman. She arrived on the first shipment of African "servants" to dock at a North American port. (Anthony—also spelled variously—whom she later married, was also on that vessel, which sailed into Jamestown in 1619.)

A brief entry (1624-1625) in parish church records mentions: "Anthony, negro, Isabell, a negro, and William, her child, baptized." Whether or not this was a family baptism into Christianity is, unclear. Probably William only was ceremonially baptized as the first child born to African parents in North America. St. George Tucker noted in his dissertation on slavery that whether baptized or not, Negroes were uniformly reported as infidels.

Before African women were imported to America, adultery and rape were legally punishable by death and fornication by whipping. The legislation charged local church parishes with publishing and enforcing that code. It is doubtful that the law ever was applied to curb the raping of black women by white men. Whipping was a common form of punishment during the colonial period, but local church parishes seemed less reluctant to whip black women than white men for sexual offenses. A point of reference is the 1640 Sweet case in which the white man (Sweet) was found guilty of getting a black woman servant pregnant. She was whipped, and he was sentenced to public penance. The close association between church officials and unfair penal enforcements is not likely to have gone unobserved by black women, even those most recently arrived from Africa.

Massachusetts, though close on the heels of Virginia in practicing and instituting slavery, was the first recorded English colony to accept an adult of African ancestry into full fellowship among Christians. John Winthrop recorded in his memoirs that a black woman, after having proven her "true godliness" over many years, was baptized and communed into the Puritan congregation in 1641. Black conversion to Christianity in North American colonies was token and generally without positive impact upon white attitudes towards Africans.

By 1660, Massachusetts, Virginia, and other English colonies already established at that time had taken steps to make slavery a legal, self-perpetuating institution. Intending to settle the question of whether or not converted slaves should be freed, Virginia passed legislation in 1662 which stated that children would inherit their mothers' social statuses—not their religious conditions. Still not certain that Christians could be enslaved, for there was no English positive law to that effect, Virginia enacted legislation which prohibited a slave's status from being altered because he or she was baptized.

The Church of England kept its distance while these disincentives to Christian conversion were imposed on African slaves. Their avaricious owners jealously guarded slave property against the potentially enlightening influences of Christian teachings. Eventually, an evangelizing unit was organized—the Council for Foreign Plantations—for the purpose of converting Africans and Indians. After 1660, the restored crown tried to centralize English authority. In 1661, 1680, and 1682, the crown urged royal colonies to support the council as it introduced ministers who would specialize in the work of converting Negroes and Indians to Christianity.

Not even Quakers, however, expressed full awareness of the evils of slavery, although the system was crystallizing into an ominous institution by the mid-seventeenth century. Though Fox and other Quakers showed concern over the plight of slaves, they accepted slavery as a *fait accompli* and encouraged those of their faith to give slaves religious instruction and to take slaves to meetings. In 1672, Virginia and other colonies enacted stalemating legislation that forbade Negro attendance at Quaker meetings.

Black women more frequently were identified as converts than black men. Before the turn of the eighteenth century, "free" black women were motivated to join churches. Ginney Bess was one of the first identified by name to take her child for baptism. Her action, in 1683, probably indicates that she had been baptized at a time previous to presenting her child for this sacrament. Reasons for joining churches were numerous. DuBois (and, more recently, Alex Haley) conjectured that African women usually made the initial breakthrough to "accept" Christianity, hoping their conversion would benefit them and their families. Masters of slaves commented that the birth of children (those born in America) motivated black women to embrace Christianity.

Sometimes women as well as men sought asylum from harsh masters in Catholic Florida under the guise of being anxious for baptism and religious instruction. Spanish Florida was a refuge for the alert and enterprising from nearby colonies.

"Witchcraft mania" spread throughout the Christian world during the seventeenth century. Congregationalists, believing "powers of the devil could be executed by human witches," seemed particularly prone to this witchcraft mania, and it assumed noticeable proportions beginning in 1647 in Connecticut and climaxing in 1692 at Salem. A black woman servant named Marja was one of its first victims. Marja was accused of conspiring with two men to burn down a building in Roxbury, Massachusetts. She alone was executed by burning at the stake because she did "not . . . have 'the feare of God before her eyes' [and her actions were] 'instigated by the divil.'" Her punishment was unusually harsh and of the genre mostly reserved for those thought to be devil-possessed. The severity of the punishment was an apparent indication that paranoia had set into the colony, that social instability prevailed there, and that a mind-set fixed on impending "spiritual" doom abounded.

In Salem, the epidemic was related to the failure of Puritans to put forth a concerted effort to Christianize African people. It was compounded by a decline in old-fashioned piety and by conflicting social interests. A major character in the Salem hysteria was a half-Indian, half-African slave woman named Tituba, whom the town's pastor had imported from Barbados. As she worked to complete household chores, Tituba unraveled tales about witches, demons, and ghosts, holding the pastor's daughter and other teenage girls in rapt attention. Soon the impressionable girls began to experiment with fortune-telling. Feeling guilty about their activities, the girls began to believe themselves to be punished for being "tools of the devil." They imagined themselves the victims of witchcraft and pointed accusing fingers at townsfolk, setting off a panic. The hysteria ended with trials, during which twenty residents were executed. One hundred fifty others, including Tituba and another Negro servant, Mary Black, were jailed. Both were later released, and Tituba was sold to pay for her jail expenses. Her quick confession "exorcised" the evil spirits from her body and saved her life. "Clemency" for Tituba suggests that the real source of the furor was elsewhere. It lends credence to recent interpretations which indicate that no small amount of the confusion was touched off by conflicting class interests and religious tensions in the Puritan town.

Eighteenth-Century Black Experiences

In the wake of the Salem trials, a group of slaves in Massachusetts requested (in 1693) that Cotton Mather organize them into a body for weekly religious instruction and worship. Only in 1701 did leadership within the Church of England form a united drive to evangelize and teach among slaves. This missionary band was called the Society for the Propagation of the Gospel (SPG). The SPG operated out of London and was financially independent of local church parishes. As a result, the SPG bypassed usual problems that individual pastors often had encountered and took its preachments more successfully into slave communities. The SPG appointed some 30 missionaries and catechists to preach and teach a gospel with emphasis on morality and ritual. Although the SPG owned slaves in its early years and took the position that emancipation was not a mandatory result of conversion, settlers were suspicious that the intentions of the society were to initiate the first step toward freedom for black slaves.

The SPG was not intentionally sexist in its conversion program. But it did make special appeal to males and provided an all-male leadership role model. Moreover, missionaries and catechists sometimes directed lessons in reading and writing to particularly apt male youths, grooming them to become teachers (tutors) among other black slaves. Many women and girls, nevertheless, were numbered among SPG missionaries' acclaimed converts.

Missionaries soon became aware of African cultural retentions among slaves. Discussion of this problem took place in missionary reports to the SPG headquarters in London about, for example, polygamous tendencies, male separations from women who either could not or had not given birth as a result of their mating, and the women's frequent changing of "husbands." These reports revealed the cultural parochialism typical among Anglican clergy. Their consternation, however, inspired legislation to "regularize" marriage procedures and to control immorality among slaves. The clergy complained that white settlers were poor exemplars of moral virtue.

White women in New York City tried to alleviate social repression against women of African ancestry. Much of this repression was caused by the colonist's belief that African women could not become productive or responsible for their behavior outside of slavery. These white women reflected the influence of Enlightenment thought, which stressed possibilities for improving the social environment—both people and institutions.

In 1712, the white women opened a school to "train" black women, hoping they would be socially responsible and assimilable. Alleged "Negro plots" to burn down the city and massacre white colonists fueled fear and renewed urgency to restrict their social mobility. These apparently brought about the demise of the 1712 school movement, but several other schools for Negro women were opened in 1740 and later in the century.

The Great Awakenings, which highlighted American sectarianism and fragmented Anglican SPG activity around mid-century, also gave Africans/Afro-Americans an opportunity for virtually unrestricted participation in Christianity in North America for the first time. During the religious ferment and widespread conversion experiences, white antislavery sentiment and black assertiveness intensified. In 1743, for example, a black woman and her husband sued a white man for trespassing upon her character. They made clear their understanding that a Christian woman's (including a black woman's) moral reputation should not be impugned without legal challenge. The suit also indicated the extent to which Christian puritanism had seeped into the black community, causing the ostracism of reputedly immoral black folk.

Popular Great Awakening evangelists, such as George Whitefield, commented on the enthusiasm with which Negroes, particularly women, received the gospel and its messengers. John Wesley, himself an antislavery advocate, noted in his Diary that the first Negroes that he baptized into Methodism were two women slaves. Yet sentiment against slave conversions still abounded, and circuit riders had to urge owners to send slaves to religious instruction and to worship. Quakers and other anti-slavery groups increased their proclamations and other active challenges to the institution of slavery.

The best-known black Christian writer in the prerevolution decade was Phillis Wheatley. Her writings suggest that she had been accepted into membership in Boston's Old South Meeting House before 1769 when her pastor, Reverend Sewall, died. By the time she was eighteen (1772), Miss Wheatley showed herself to be a fully converted, zealous Congregationalist. Her writings, when analyzed from the perspective of one's conversion, indicate that Phillis rejoiced in the psychological succor of her Christian faith and had little awareness of her African background. In this respect, hers was not a singular reaction, even among slaves. Missionaries of the period said of slave converts, "They will ever bless God for their knowing good things which they knew not before [their enslavement]." Phillis's letters—rather than her poems, which have been overly politicized by biographers—demonstrate her responsiveness to Christian conversion.

In other ways, black women who came of age under the tutelage of American colonial evangelistic and missionary zeal, claimed rights to creative religious action. Katherine Ferguson, organizer of the first Sabbath school for children in New York City, is one example. In her early years, Katy's mistress was a Christian woman who permitted the young slave girl to attend church services. This early involvement probably accounted in part for Miss Ferguson's later religious devotion and charitable efforts as much as her having been purchased by a sympathetic friend when she was sixteen. Although she herself never learned to read or write, she helped to make such learning available to children from the poorhouse without regard to race or color. Having been separated from her own mother at the age of eight, she expressed an affinity for reaching out to children from destitute backgrounds, to neglected youths and unwed mothers. Her "work contributed to the development of free secular education for the poor. For this reason, her name is noted among those considered pioneer educators in America. . . . In tribute to Katy and in recognition of her early contributions, a home for unwed mothers— the Katy Ferguson Home—in New York was named in her honor." Wives and women converts of pioneering black preachers and church pastors were among the more obscure missionaries and charitable workers at the turn of the century.

Ironically, the century closed with discordant tones from the ranks of Quakerism. Several black women applied for membership into that faith. They were subjected to prolonged monthly, quarterly, and annual meetings where their applications were scrutinized, tabled, and kept in committee for months before the women eventually were admitted. It is possible that they never would have been admitted, except that they were mulattos.

Sarah Johnson, who died in 1845 after a life that spanned more than a century, is an example of the black Christian of this period. The poignancy of black women's religious experiences in North American colonies is summarized in the black pastor's eulogizing at her funeral. In a manner characteristic of Christian clergy, her African Methodist Episcopal pastor referred continuously to what was commendable that he had observed in her outward behavior. . . .

Exposing the Idolatry of the Romish Church: Anti-popery and Colonial New England
FRANCIS D. COGLIANO

SOURCE: Francis D. Cogliano, *No King, No Popery: Anti-Catholicism in Revolutionary New England* (Westport, CT: Greenwood Press, 1996), 5-18. Copyright © 1996 by Francis D. Cogliano. Reprinted with permission of Greenwood Publishing Group, Inc. All rights reserved.

I

By the mid-eighteenth century it was impossible for Englishmen in Britain or America to divorce anti-popery from their notion of what it was to be English. The anti-Catholic tradition that the colonists brought with them to the New World can be traced at least as far back as 1563 when the Protestant martyrologist John Foxe published the first English edition of his *Actes and Monuments*. Commonly called *The Book of Martyrs,* Foxe's book chronicled in brutal, graphic detail the suffering and torture allegedly inflicted upon Protestants by Catholics. Although the architect of Catholic oppression was ultimately the pope, Foxe paid careful attention to the actions of his supposed minions, the kings of France and Spain. Foxe also paid particular attention to the fate of Protestants persecuted during the reign of Mary Tudor. It is to Foxe that Queen Mary owes her reputation as "Bloody Mary." Foxe did more than simply chronicle Catholic atrocities. He also laid the groundwork for the marriage of Protestantism to the concept of what it was to be English. Queen Mary was nefarious not only for her persecutions, but because she had wed the Catholic king of Spain, thereby endangering the Protestant succession in England. *The Book of Martyrs* demonstrated that tyranny came from abroad: Versailles, Madrid, and ultimately the Vatican, from which the pope attempted to control the world. Conversely, freedom resided wherever true Englishmen and women lived. By definition a true Englishman was a Protestant.

Foxe depicted England as a uniquely Protestant nation and the English people as the chosen people of God. From the *Actes and Monuments* readers learned that true Englishmen were Protestants and that Catholics were bloodthirsty zealots who served foreign despots and would stop at nothing to extirpate Protestantism. *The Book of Martyrs* is one of the earliest expressions of a cultural formula that became a commonplace in the Anglo-American world during the seventeenth and eighteenth centuries: to be English was to be Protestant, to be Protestant was to be free, therefore Englishmen were by nature free men. The association between Protestantism and the vaunted "liberties of Englishmen" was a close one for Englishmen in England and in the colonies.

The influence of Foxe's *Book of Martyrs* should not be underestimated. It went through many editions and held a prominent place in English Protestant churches well into the nineteenth century. In many Anglican churches the *Book of Martyrs* had a place next to the Bible on the altar. Readings from the *Actes and Monuments* were also made part of the liturgy in some parishes. By the seventeenth century the message of the *Book of Martyrs* had filtered throughout English society. In England, Protestantism became wed to the notion of being a good Englishman. Catholicism, or popery, was antithetical to the survival of England and had to be countered.

Foxe's book was popular because it resonated so strongly among the people of sixteenth- and seventeenth-century England. The Englishman or woman born in 1550 could easily recall the Marian persecutions, the rising of the Catholic northern earls against Queen Elizabeth in 1570, the attempt by the Spanish to conquer England in 1588, as well as the 1605 Gunpowder Plot of Guy Fawkes and a small band of Catholic conspirators who attempted to assassinate King James I and destroy Parliament. The struggle between Spain and England in the early modern period gave rise to a potent variant of English anti-popery which was oriented against the Iberian power. According to this "Black Legend," the Spanish were the most powerful and ruthless of papists. They were especially bent upon conquering England and subjecting the English to their infamous Inquisition. The image of captured English sailors enslaved on Spanish galleys was particularly powerful and common in the sixteenth century. The frequent conflicts between Spain and England made the fear and hatred of Spain and things Spanish a common element of English nationalism. Each of these incidents reinforced the theme of Foxe's *Book of Martyrs:* Catholics were forever scheming to return England to Rome, and they would stop at nothing to achieve their goal, including regicide.

Ironically, the only British regicides of the seventeenth century were Protestants who killed a king they suspected of harboring popish sympathies. Only when the English fear of things Catholic and the belief that popery and tyranny were synonymous are taken into account, can the political upheavals of seventeenth-century England be properly understood. For example, Charles I was widely suspect, in part, because his wife was a French Catholic and because his archbishop had introduced "popish" innovations into the Anglican church. Questions about Charles' alleged Catholicism helped make his overthrow and execution justifiable in the minds of many Protestants. After the Stuart Restoration, the fear of resurgent Catholicism became more pronounced. Protestants even suspected that the great London fire of 1666 was the work of Catholic saboteurs. In 1679 a wave of anti-Catholic paranoia swept the country in the wake of the so called "Popish Plot" of Catholics to take over the country. Charles II, like his father, was widely suspected of being a crypto-Catholic. His brother and successor, James II, was a practicing Catholic. The prospect of a Catholic succession after the birth of his son in 1685 was the primary cause of the Glorious Revolution. Forevermore the Stuarts were linked in the popular mind with popery and tyranny. They reinforced their place as a treacherous Catholic dynasty during the two eighteenth-century attempts by the Stuart Pretenders to seize the throne and overturn the Catholic succession.

Anti-Catholicism permeated English culture by the end of the seventeenth century. It found expression not only in Foxe's *Actes and Monuments* but in the streets of England as well. David Cressy has demonstrated that a "Protestant calendar" existed in Elizabethan and Stuart England that gave the people ample opportunity to commemorate important days in the English Protestant year. For example, the English regularly celebrated Guy Fawkes Day (Gunpowder Treason Day) with the ringing of bells and the burning of bonfires. Each year Englishmen honored the anniversary of Queen Elizabeth's accession (November 17) in a similar manner. By the end of the seventeenth-century, public demonstrations in England frequently included the burning of the pope and the devil in effigy.

Popular anti-popery remained a feature of English life during the eighteenth century. In 1715 and 1745 angry Protestant crowds attacked Catholics during the attempts of the Stuart Pretenders to seize the throne. Crowds burned the pope in effigy on Gunpowder Treason Day as well as in more spontaneous demonstrations such as the street fights between Whigs and Tories in 1715. Popular celebrations with an anti-papal theme occurred whenever Britain defeated one of her Catholic foes. Crowds gathered to salute Vice-Admiral Edward Vernon and to celebrate his triumph over the Spanish at Porto Bello in 1739. Similar celebrations greeted the news of the fall of Louisbourg in 1745 and the capture of Quebec in 1759. The potency and persistence of popular anti-Catholicism became apparent in 1780 when thousands of Londoners participated in the Gordon Riots which were sparked by a parliamentary act to repeal anti-Catholic legislation.

English settlers brought the English anti-papal tradition to New England during the seventeenth century. Foxe's *Book of Martyrs* was a commonly owned book in seventeenth-century Massachusetts. The town of Concord owned a copy which it made available to interested townsmen. Adaptations of Foxe's stories appeared in children's books. New Englanders embraced the Protestant calendar of early modern England. During the seventeenth century, New Englanders occasionally celebrated Guy Fawkes Day. The people of colonial New England also embraced the political and patriotic aspects of anti-popery. For them the opposition to Catholicism and their loyalty as Englishmen and women were one and the same.

During the eighteenth century, New England anti-popery, while similar to its English cousin, developed along its own lines according to local circumstances. While popery threatened the liberties of New Englanders, they feared the Catholic Indians of Canada and their French sponsors more than Spanish galleys. Until the end of the Seven Years' War, anti-popery remained a potent force in New England life. The New England variant of anti-popery would play an important role in the coming of the American Revolution.

II

In 1750 Judge Paul Dudley of the Massachusetts Supreme Court of Judicature, a prominent colonist, died at age seventy five. Dudley willed to his alma mater, Harvard College (Dudley received his A.B. from Harvard in 1690 and his A.M. in 1693), £133.6.8 to endow a series of four lectures to be given annually at the college. According to Dudley's will, the third lecture should be devoted toward "exposing the Idolatry of the Romish church, their tyranny, usurpations and other crying wickedness, in their high places; and finally that the church of Rome is that mystical Babylon, that man of sin, that Apostate church spoken of in the New Testament." Dudley's will reflected three of the most important criticisms of the Catholic Church among eighteenth-century New Englanders: the beliefs that the Catholic Church was idolatrous, tyrannical, and represented the Antichrist of the Book of Revelation.

One of the most consistent criticisms of the Catholic Church among eighteenth-century New Englanders was its idolatry. Pierre Berault, a former Jesuit who had become a Protestant and wrote an exposé of his former faith, declared: "That it is flat Idolatry to worship God in any Image is expressed and manifested by the Children of Israel when they made the Golden Calf to be a representation of God." Berault concluded, "The Idolatry of Rome is as gross and wicked as theirs was." The author of an anonymous catechism published in 1746 explained in no uncertain terms the view that New England Protestants took toward Catholic idolatry: "it is not lawful to make Images of God; nor to direct our Worship to an Image or to give religious Worship to any Creature." To do so would be an expression of superstition, not faith. The author continued, "It were innumerable to account the many vain Fopperies in their Devotions, which they place Religion in; As the tooth of St. Christopher, the Hair of St. Peter's Beard." The Catholic attachment to religious relics was unacceptable idolatry and superstition in the eyes of New England's Protestants.

The idolatrous nature of Catholicism was more than the alleged hair and teeth of long-dead saints. In Protestant eyes, idolatry lay at the very heart of the Catholic liturgy. The outspoken pastor of Boston's West Church, Jonathan Mayhew, devoted the 1765 Dudleian Lecture to the subject on May 8, 1765. In a sermon titled *Popish Idolatry*, Mayhew attacked the doctrine of transubstantiation and the eucharist as the chief forms of idolatry in the Catholic Church: "The host is often carried in procession with great solemnity: and those who are but casually present when it passes are obliged to kneel down in an act of worship to God; unless perhaps, they will run the risque of the inquisition, or of being knocked on the head by the devout rabble that attend it." Mayhew went on to allege that the very absurdity of transubstantiation was proof that it was an idolatrous belief. In so doing, Mayhew attacked the very heart of the Catholic liturgy, and the most important tenets of the Catholic faith.

New Englanders believed that the Catholic clergy promoted idolatry in order to keep the laity in a state of scriptural and spiritual ignorance. A former priest explained popish bigotry as the product of "blind faith in what the preachers and

Priests tell them; and next to this, that it is not allowed to them to read scriptures, nor books of controversy about religion." In the 1777 Dudleian Lecture, Edward Wigglesworth criticized the Catholic Church for "setting up oral traditions as of equal authority with sacred Scriptures, [which] has opened the door for the admission of doctrines and precepts into that church, subversive to those delivered by Christ and his Apostles." To eighteenth-century New Englanders, ignorance of the scripture was a certain invitation to eternal damnation in the eyes of God. Scriptural illiteracy led to anti-Christian idolatry, which in turn made it impossible for individuals to enjoy God's saving grace. In their attitudes toward scripture, Catholics were the antithesis of New Englanders. . . .

New Englanders believed that the Catholic clergy promoted idolatry in order to keep the laity ignorant of the spiritual truths of scripture. In this manner Catholics were denied salvation and were easily controlled by priests. Anti-Catholic writers devoted extensive space to decrying the power and influence of the Catholic clergy. Antonio Gavin, a former Jesuit, described the Catholic clergy as "wolves in sheep's clothing, that devour [the laity], and put them in the way of damnation." Three attributes dominate the descriptions of the clergy in eighteenth-century literature: carnality, greed, and cruelty.

Perhaps the most popular literary portrayal of Catholic priests in colonial New England was that of the priest as lecher. It was a common belief that all Catholic priests took advantage of their positions to gratify their sexual desires. New Englanders believed that the origins of popish carnality lay in church doctrine. They held that priestly celibacy was unnatural and impossible. According to *A Protestant's Resolution:* "The Popish doctrine forbidding [priests] to marry, is a devilish and wicked Doctrine. . . it leads to much Leudness and Villainy, as Fornication, Adultery, Incest, Sodomy, Murder & c." New Englanders had an apparently insatiable appetite for tales of popish carnality. While such accounts probably more accurately reflect the prurient interests of colonial New Englanders than the indiscretions of the eighteenth-century Catholic clergy, the belief that the clergy consisted of adulterous, immoral lechers whose first priority was to gratify their own depraved desires was widespread in colonial New England. . . .

Clerical extortion undermined the desire of the laity to work hard and earn money at all. Colonial New Englanders routinely characterized Catholic countries as havens not only of tyranny but its byproducts, sloth and corruption. Reverend Samuel Cooper, of the prestigious Brattle Church in Boston, declared with reference to Catholic Italy, "we cannot wonder to see the Idleness prevail in those Countries where Tyranny riots upon the Fruits of honest diligence." When the clergy robbed the benighted laity of their money, they also took their economic initiative and industriousness. To colonial New Englanders, who prided themselves on their hard work, Catholic indolence was as odious as Catholic idolatry.

The Catholic clergy was more than greedy and lascivious in New England eyes; they were also inhumanely cruel, especially to Protestants. According to Antonio Gavin, "The Roman Catholics with the Pope say ... that no man can be saved out of their communion, and so they reckon enemies of their faith all those that are of a different opinion. And we may be sure that the Protestants . . . are their irreconcilable enemies." Priests taught Catholics that they were not required nor expected to show mercy to heretics. The subtitle to a pamphlet entitled *Popish Cruelty Displayed* is testimony to the connection between the clergy and persecution in the minds of New Englanders:

> Being a full and true Account of the Bloody and Hellish Massacre in Ireland, Perpetrated by the Instigation of the Jesuits, Priests, and Fryars, who were the chief Promoters of those Horrible Murthers, unheard of Cruelties, barbarous Villainies and inhuman Practices, executed by the Irish Papists upon the English Protestants in the Year 1641.

According to this pamphlet the Catholic clergy instigated the alleged massacres of 1641 by providing eucharist to the Irish "upon the condition they should neither spare, Man, Woman, nor Child of the Protestants. . . . They openly professed, that they held it as lawful to kill a Protestant as to kill a Dog." Colonial New Englanders had little problem believing that Catholic priests were the authors of such massacres when they looked to the north and saw the results of Jesuit influence among the Native Americans of Canada who occasionally raided the New England frontier.

The ultimate engine of popish cruelty was the infamous Court of Inquisition employed to root out heresy in Catholic countries. According to Samuel Cooper, "the inhumanity of her court of inquisition is not to be equaled among the most barbarous nations, nor by any court erected by the gravest tyrant." The Inquisition was especially galling to New Englanders because it existed to forbid free expression, especially in matters of religion. In 1750 Jonathan Mayhew declared, "God be thanked, one may in any part of the British Dominions, speak freely . . . without being in danger either of the bastille or the inquisition." According to former Inquisitor Antonio Gavin, "the Inquisitors have a despotic power to command every living soul; and no excuse is to be given, nor contradiction to made to their orders, nay the people have not liberty to speak nor complain." The methods of the Inquisition were enough to make the blood of the staunchest Protestants curdle. Gavin described an oven with a large pan in it, a wheel "covered on both sides with thick boards . . . all the circumference of the wheel set with sharp rasors," and a pit full of serpents and toads. According to Gavin:

> The dry pan and gradual fire are for the use of Hereticks, and those that oppose the Holy Father's will and pleasure, for they are put all naked and alive into the pan, and the cover of it being locked up, the executioner begins to put in the oven a small fire, and by degrees he augmenteth it till the body is burnt into ashes. The second is designed for those that speak against the Pope and the Holy Fathers, and they are put within the wheel, and the door being locked, the executioner turns the

wheel till the person is dead. And the third is for those who contemn the images, and refuse to give the due respect and veneration to ecclesiastical persons, for they are thrown into the pit, & there they become food of the serpents and toads.

For a people well versed in Foxe's *Book of Martyrs,* such behavior from Catholic clergymen, while frightening, was certainly not surprising.

New Englanders so feared and hated the Catholic clergy that they took legal action to insure that they would not have to suffer the presence of Catholic clerics in their midst. With the exception of James II's brief reign, Catholics were denied religious freedom in all the New England colonies. Massachusetts adopted the strongest measures to prevent the presence of Catholicism within its borders. In 1647 the Great and General Court, "taking into consideration the great wars, combustions and divisions which are this day in Europe, and at the same are observed to be raised chiefly by the secret underminings and solicitations of those of the Jesuitical order," adopted a law banishing all Catholic clergymen from Massachusetts. Any priests found in Massachusetts who had once been banished, were to be executed. Massachusetts lawmakers reenacted the law on June 17, 1700, against "divers Jesuits, priests, and popish missionaries" not for instigating trouble in Europe but "who by their subtile insinuations industriously labor to debauch, seduce and withdraw the Indians from their due obedience to his majesty." The 1700 law reflects the specific New England context for the fear of Catholicism as the eighteenth century began. Rather than focus on the threat popery posed to the Protestant succession in Britain, New Englanders were more concerned about the activities of the popish missionaries who threatened them from Canada. The anti-priest law of 1700 remained in force until the American Revolution.

New Englanders primarily feared the Catholic clergy as the agents of popish oppression. Exposing "the tyranny, usurpations and other crying wickedness in their high places," was the second heading in Judge Dudley's bequest against popery. In New England eyes, the Catholic clergy were part of a vast hierarchy that oppressed lay people, stifled free discourse, and hampered free trade. At the head of this hierarchy was the pope, an omnipotent, bloodthirsty bigot who would stop at nothing to extirpate Protestantism.

For eighteenth-century New Englanders, well versed as they were in English history, popery and tyranny were synonymous. Jonathan Mayhew declared: "we ought in reason and prudence to detest the church of Rome, in the same degree that we prize freedom. Her laws, more arbitrary than those of Draco, are, in effect, like his, all written in blood. Popery and liberty are incompatible; at irreconcilable enmity with each other." Tyranny was the corollary of popery. Conversely, liberty was the corollary of Protestantism. Just as there could be no reconciliation between Protestantism and tyranny, there could be no compromise between popery and liberty.

New Englanders believed that Catholics were part of a vast international conspiracy to seek world domination. They believed that Catholics owed their loyalty first and foremost to that conspiracy and its head, the pope. They held that the pope used his religious influence to maintain his tyrannical grip. Because they owed their allegiance to the pope, Catholics could not be trusted with any civil power in Protestant countries. Englishmen cited this belief as a justification for their anti-Catholic laws. New Englanders readily concurred. In 1772 the freeholders of Boston voted that Catholics should be excluded from voting because "those they call hereticks may be destroyed without mercy; beside their recognizing the Pope in so absolute a manner, in subversion of the Government leading directly to the worst anarchy and confusion, civil discord, war, and bloodshed." A subject could not have two masters, and, since the pope required blind and absolute obedience, Catholics could not be trusted with civil power.

The papal threat concerned more than religion. The freedom of humanity was at stake in the battle between Catholicism and Protestantism. Jonathan Mayhew explained:

> Our controversy with her [the Catholic Church] is not merely a religious one . . .
> but a defense of our laws, liberties and civil rights as men, in opposition to the
> proud claims and encroachments of ecclesiastical persons, who under the pretext of
> religion, and saving men's souls, would engross all power and property to themselves and reduce us to the most abject slavery.

Such a view fostered a manichean outlook toward Catholicism and Catholics among New Englanders. They believed there could be no compromise between popish tyranny and Protestant liberty.

III

At no time was anti-papal feeling higher than during the last great conflict between the French and the English in North America, the French and Indian War (1754-63). New Englanders participated in the conflict in extraordinary numbers. For them the conflict was an anti-papal crusade. As Sylvanus Conant, the pastor at Middleborough, Massachusetts, told the militia of the town on April 6, 1759, "our Enemies in the present bloody Controversy are no less Enemies to God, to Religion, Liberty, and the pure Worship of the Gospel than to us." Samuel Bird assured a group of soldiers, "you are to fight for King George, the best of Kings, against proud Lewis; . . . you are to draw the Sword in the Cause of King JESUS, the King of Kings, in the Defence of his Subjects: against the Emissaries and Incendiaries of Hell and Rome." Such conclusions were a natural consequence of an anti-papal perspective which recognized no room for compromise between popery and Protestantism.

The anxiety of New Englanders was very great in the early years of the conflict when the French enjoyed repeated successes on the battlefield. The prospect of French victory terrified New Englanders. Jonathan Mayhew described the dreadful consequences of French victory in the Massachusetts election sermon he delivered on May 29, 1754. The annual election sermon was probably the single most important sermon delivered throughout the year, for the minister had the collective ear of the political and clerical leaders of the colony. Mayhew made the most of his opportunity.

According to Mayhew, if the French defeated the English, tyranny would triumph over liberty and evil over good. The minister described a chilling vision of New England after a French victory.

> Do I behold them spreading desolation thro' the land! Do I see the slaves of Louis with their Indian allies dispossessing the freeborn subjects of King George of the inheritance received from their forefathers? . . . Do I see this godly patrimony ravished from them by those who never knew what property was, except by seizing that of others for an insatiable Lord!

Mayhew struck a nerve in all New Englanders with such a vision. The prospect of Catholic slaves and Indians ravishing the property of free-born English Protestants was the worst nightmare of colonial New Englanders. The minister skillfully described a conquered New England where the French had conquered not only the people but their history. How, after all, could New Englanders stand by and see their patrimony stolen from them by popish slaves? To do so would be to lose all that the settlers of New England had achieved.

True Christianity was at stake in the conflict. Mayhew described the religious life of post-conquest New England:

> Do I see Christianity banished for popery! The Bible for the mass-book! The oracles of truth, for fabulous legends! Do I see the sacred edifices erected here to the honour of the true God and his Son . . . laid in ruins themselves! Instead of a train of Christ's faithful, laborious ministers, do I behold an herd of lazy monks, and Jesuits, and exorcists and inquisitors!

If the French were not defeated, Mayhew warned, "liberty, property, religion, happiness" would be "changed, or rather transubstantiated into slavery, poverty, superstition, wretchedness." Mayhew's election sermon is a masterpiece of anti-papal propaganda. The minister cleverly and effectively drew a contrast between a Protestant and a Catholic New England to demonstrate to his fellow Yankees what was at stake in the conflict with France. Mayhew's sermon is the most famous of hundreds of similar sermons delivered throughout New England in the early years of the war.

New England anxiety turned to cautious optimism in 1758, when, for the second time in thirteen years, an Anglo-American expedition captured Louisbourg. Revitalized by the ministry of William Pitt, the English captured Quebec in September 1759. In 1760 they captured Montreal. When the Treaty of Paris was signed in 1763, the British had won the war and driven the French from North America.

Nathaniel Appleton explained the victory in true New England fashion, "as Canada was the only Province of Roman Catholicks in these Northern Parts of America, so God has now made himself known by [the] awful Judgements which he has executed upon Them." Though it might enjoy some early success, popery could not triumph because God would not permit it.

The conquest of Canada became one of the highlights in the triumphal story of Protestantism in New England. In a style reminiscent of Mayhew, Eli Forbes described his post-war vision of Canada as a Protestant utopia.

> Canada is subdued-how pleasing the sound . . . Methinks I see Towns enlarged, Settlements increased and this howling wilderness become a fruitful Field, which the Lord hath blessed; and to complete the scene, I see Churches rise out of the Superstitions of Roman Bigotry and flourish in Every Christian Grace, and divine Ornament, where has been the seat of Satan and Indian Idolatry.

Freed from the shackles of popery, Canada would flourish under Protestantism just as New England had. Where popery hindered industry, Protestantism encouraged it. Protestant enlightenment would supplant popish ignorance. Above all, exclaimed Nathaniel Appleton, "Romish corrupt Principles [would] be extirpated so as never to have Root again in this new World!" In the twelve years between the Peace of Paris and the fighting in Lexington, concern over Catholicism in Canada would be a major preoccupation in New England.

IV

The various elements of colonial New England anti-popery combined to form what I have called the anti-papal persuasion. This was a coherent intellectual system with an internal logic which helped define colonial New England culture. The system was greater than the sum of its parts. As an intellectual system, anti-popery was cyclical: Protestants were free because they had the intellectual freedom to read scripture; in turn, their intellectual freedom permitted their religious and political freedom; religious and political freedom produced economic initiative and drive which produced economic prosperity—the emblem of a free society; prosperity allowed the freedom and education to study scripture. Popery promoted a contrary cycle: Catholics were denied access to scripture, therefore they were ignorant; ignorance, in turn, made them easy dupes for tyrants, secular and religious, thus the church hierarchy was able to steal the wealth of its laity; therefore Catholics were mired in poverty and ignorance which cost them their freedom and their souls.

The image of Catholicism that prevailed in colonial New England was a nightmarish inversion of all that New Englanders held dear. Catholics embodied all the vices and weaknesses that New Englanders abhorred and were determined to avoid. They were licentious, ignorant, lazy, and illiterate. They had no self-control. They did not control their property. They did not exercise their own judgment in matters of politics or religion. Rather, Catholics were controlled by a domineering, scheming, grasping hierarchy headed by the pope who was in league with Satan. The papal world was a caricature of all that colonial New Englanders detested and feared.

In defining their foes, anti-popery also helped New Englanders define themselves. In decrying the characteristics of Catholicism, New Englanders defined themselves as sober, industrious, literate, and, above all, free. The comparison with Catholicism is significant for it gave New Englanders an important yardstick by which they could measure their own society. They were able to reach the conclusion that they were "God's New English Israel" when they compared their society to the decadent corruption and oppression they saw in France, Spain, and Italy.

Anti-popery provided the people of eighteenth-century New England with a sense of control and order in an uncertain and dangerous world. Since the majority of colonial New Englanders were nominally Calvinists of various stripes, most would not presume to claim control over the destiny of their souls. However, by comparison with Catholics, they exercised remarkable autonomy over their lives and property in this world. In politics they enjoyed local control of their governments, unlike Catholics who were ruled by tyrants at the beck and call of the pope in Rome. In religious matters, their ministers were answerable to their congregations in stark contrast to the Roman hierarchy. New Englanders did not pay tithes to support an indolent, lascivious, unprincipled, clergy. There were no priests in New England to ravish its virtuous Protestant maidens or to rob its freemen of their hard-earned patrimony.

Anti-papal values bound colonial New Englanders together despite their pronounced economic, political, religious, and intellectual divisions. The anti-papal persuasion muted social divisions by appealing to common cultural values. The pervasiveness of the anti-papal persuasion and the vital social role it played in eighteenth-century New England are most apparent in Boston's commemoration of Guy Fawkes Day.

Saints and Sisters: Congregational and Quaker Women in the Early Colonial Period

MARY MAPLES DUNN

SOURCE: Mary Maples Dunn. "Saints and Sisters: Congregational and Quaker Women in the Early Colonial Period." *American Quarterly* 30, 5 (1978), 582-601. © The American Studies Association. Reprinted by permission of the Johns Hopkins University Press.

It is frequently observed in Christian societies that the women go to church. The implication is that the church, or even religion, is in some way more necessary to women than to men, although women are submissive to the men who dominate the priesthoods. But how and why this gender differentiation develops in respect to religion is imperfectly understood; we are not certain that it is inherent in Christianity itself; we do not know why it becomes part of a social-religious order, what functions it might have in that society, nor what conditions produce the dichotomy. American experience in the seventeenth and early eighteenth centuries offers the historian two Protestant cases to investigate and contrast, the Puritan Congregationalists and the Quakers. Puritans and Quakers pursued different routes to settlement in America, with different results for women.

The religious intensity and excitement in England prior to and during the Civil War gave rise to both Puritanism and Quakerism, and provided a background in which a rethinking of Christian doctrine was taking place and church governance and church-state relationships were being questioned. This fluid situation was particularly important to women. The Protestant dismissal of the cult of Mary and of the nunneries opened up questions about the position of women, both in society and in the structure of the church, and destroyed the most powerful female religious symbol and role model. The result was a period of intense religious activity in which Puritan and Quaker women in America took part. Indeed, removal to America may have been particularly invigorating to the Protestant women who took part in these religious migrations, because of the sense shared by both men and women that they were free from traditional restraints. But in Puritan Congregationalism, despite the vigor and enthusiasm of the first-generation women, women were disciplined to accept male authority, socialized to submission, and accustomed to filling the churches. Amongst Quakers we discover religious experience and church governance more equally shared by women and men.

There were at least three factors that determined these different outcomes for women in the "City on a Hill" and the "Holy Experiment." First, it was necessary to the development of a predominantly female piety that there be some objectives of the society that required female piety, and at least to some extent excused it in men. Second, scripture had to be interpreted in a way that asserted female inferiority. Therefore, the interests of those who had the power to formulate doctrine and interpret the word of God were determinants of the female role. The third factor is related to the second. Those who had the power to exert discipline over women had power to socialize them in the church.

The Puritan development precedes the Quaker one. The first generation of Puritan immigrants to America were not yet sectarians; they were groping their way toward a form of church governance which would be free from the evils of episcopacy. The godly, both inside and outside the ministry, were making their way toward a doctrinal position that would explain their sense of communion with God. The lines between lay and clerical authority were blurred. Puritans certainly brought in their baggage a sense of the inferiority of women; but belief in female equality before the Lord also made it uncertain what role women would play in a new religious order.

The fundamental statement of female inferiority was, of course, found in Genesis. Eve, the first to listen to Satan and the seducer of Adam, brought to women a heavy share of original sin; and to Adam, to man, the message that he should have known better than to listen to woman. Woman in this case was also a vehicle for Satan, not able to see through his wiles, wanting in intellect, needing protection. Genesis 3:16 imposed the correction and punishment: "Unto the woman he said, I will greatly increase thy sorrows, & thy conceptions. In sorrow shalt thou bring forth children, and thy desire shall be subject to thine husband, and he shall rule over thee." The Calvinist sense of original sin was powerful, and it was unlikely that Puritans could ever reject the notion that God required submission of women.

The traditional Christian rules which might govern the place and conduct of a woman in the church, and the authorities she should seek in matters of doctrine, were asserted for Puritans by St. Paul. Paul was widely accepted as authority by those who wished to recapitulate in their own time the primitive Christian church, and he was therefore important to New World Puritans. Paul seemed to make his position clear in his letters to the Corinthians and, later, to Timothy and Titus. In I Cor. 14:34-35 he said, "Let your women keep silence in the Churches: for it is not permitted unto them to speak: but they ought to be subject, as also the Law saith. And if they will learn any thing, let them ask their husbands at home: for it is a shame for a woman to speak in the Church." It was not possible to construe this injunction narrowly as to time and place, that is, only to Corinth, since the Apostle was equally specific in the later letter to Timothy (I Tim. 2:11-12), "Let the women learn in silence with all subjection. I permit not a woman to teach, neither to usurp authority over the man, but to be in silence."

Paul apparently derived these rules from the customs with which he was familiar; he may have asserted them at first only for Corinth, and later reaffirmed them in the realization that the end of human time was not, after all, at hand. This could account for the fact that in other ways Paul had a more liberating message for women. In Titus 2:3-4, older women were given a teaching function: "teachers of honest things, they may instruct the young women to be sober minded, that they love their husbands, that they love their children." Paul also insisted that women were to share equally in the benefits of the new order. He wrote to the Galatians (3:28), "There is neither Jew nor Grecian: there is neither bond nor free: there is neither male nor female: for you are all one in Christ Jesus." Furthermore, even in the first letter to the Corinthians there is some confusion, since he said in I Cor. 11:3-5, "But I will that you know, that Christ is the head of every man: & the man is the woman's head: and God is Christ's head. Every man praying or prophecying having any thing on his head, dishonoreth his head. But every woman that prayeth or prophecieth bareheaded, dishonoreth her head: for it is even one very thing, as though she were shaven." The implication of inferiority is clear; but so is the possibility of speaking in the church, and the ancient Biblical tradition of women prophets receives recognition.

The people of New England could, if they wanted, find in Paul a situation parallel to their own: a radical spiritual message of equality in tension with social custom. It was not certain how the tension between these two views of women would be resolved in New England, and in this situation (which may have obtained at all times and on all frontiers in the Christian religion) many women engaged themselves in both experiments in church governance and in the discussion of doctrine. A few of them made their marks.

Women shared fully in the excitement that creation of a new religious settlement produced, and they responded to the challenge with intelligence, vigor, and enthusiasm. The covenanted or gathered church was a source of a feeling of equality. Women also tried to control doctrines in many areas, including those relating specifically to women. Unfortunately, heresy trials constitute much of the evidence that women tried to assert themselves. This is unfortunate because those charged with heresy were considered extremists whom the Puritans rejected and because these women were more apt to perish than to publish. Their trial records are our only evidence of their doctrinal positions, and those records were written by male opponents. Nevertheless, they are ample testimony that women were neither silent nor submissive.

Anne Hutchinson is the most famous of these women, because the doctrine that she, John Cotton, and their followers tried to bring to general acceptance in Boston would have changed profoundly the thrust of the Massachusetts experiment. Hutchinson and the Antinomians rejected the doctrine of sanctification or the "Covenant of Works" (the idea that outward behavior or a righteous life was a sign of justification or redemption of one's soul by Christ). Their own doctrine, or "Covenant of Grace," insisted that redemption came only through the gift of grace. Hutchinson's own knowledge of this was her sense of direct communion with the Holy Spirit. In the Antinomian view, the Covenant of Works had a deadening effect on the spiritual life of the community because it encouraged too much scrutiny of behavior and led to formalism or legalism in establishing rules of behavior which, consistently observed, would prepare for or offer evidence of election by God to sainthood. The Antinomians acquired a following that threatened a breakdown in Massachusetts' ideological unity, an overturning of the authority of law and therefore of social discipline, and a real revolution in the norms for Christian (Puritan) behavior. It was possible for a woman to share in the leadership of such a movement because the Covenant of Grace could free her from restraints emanating from a rigid application of the rules of a Covenant of Works.

The story of Hutchinson's trial and defeat is too well known to need retelling here. However, it is worth pointing out again that she was a tough woman, intelligent and learned, determined to remake the church. She had remarkable vigor and a charisma that might have changed the course of Massachusetts history had she been a man. It was clear that her judges, particularly John Winthrop, thought she headed a "potent party" and was a formidable enemy. They were determined to get rid of her. She was a good match for them in all theological discussions, and over and over again in the trial they were forced to revert to the issue of women speaking and teaching. Hutchinson insisted that she worked within the Pauline rules; her judges were sure she did not.

At the heart of their disagreement was the fact that Hutchinson applied Paul in a positive way to her situation, while her judges were determined to stick to the reading most restricting for women. For example, she maintained that in the large meetings held in her house to discuss sermons, she could speak because this was private, that is, not in the church; that she could, as an older woman, teach younger women; that she could, when asked, teach and counsel men in private. But she also declared a right to public utterance in exercising a gift of prophesy, for which she found Biblical precedent. Her judges decided that the age of prophesy was over. Finally, ". . .to justify this her disordered course, she said she walked by the rule of the Apostle, Gal. which she called *the rule of the new creature. . . .*" [italics added], that is, Gal. 3:28 "there is neither male nor female: for you are all one in Christ Jesus." Hutchinson insisted, then, in applying the broadest possible definition of Christian responsibility to women's roles in religion. Because she argued in the context of a situation which seemed to her judges to be threatening to the Puritan establishment, they were not able to consider the problem dispassionately, and the judgment against her was the most important decision Puritans made about women's place in the formulation of doctrines. . . .

However, some evidence of aggressive females and a church seemingly more open to the formulation of less limiting policies for women is found in the note-book or diary of John Fiske (1637-1675), a clergyman of Wenham. In this church, in which the pastor always referred to his congregation as "the brethren and sis-ters," and usually fully identified women (that is, he used both the father's and husband's names and the woman's Christian name), there was brisk debate in the 1640s over female membership. It was argued first that women themselves had publicly to relate their religious experiences and their sense of election, if the church were to judge their fitness for membership. Therefore the act of qualification seemed to require women to speak in church. The diary noted that in some churches men, elders or ministers, were reading the women's statements, on the grounds that women should keep silent; and Wenham produced scriptural examples of female prophets to justify female public speaking of this kind. The case was similar to the one made by Anne Hutchinson.

Secondly, Wenham church decided that women were not automatically trans-ferred from one church to another when their husbands moved, and it badgered the Salem church to get individual dismissions for women. The issue appears to have been pushed by one Joan White, who also took an active role in church governance; she spoke in church meetings and made motions which the congrega-tion acted upon. In her relation, she said that she "was brought up in a poore Ignorant place," and although she came to New England because she believed good people came there, she was "for a long space of time living far in ye woods, from the means; and reading on Rom. 10, Faith commeth by hearing; put her affections onward ye desire of ye means." In short, she wanted to get out of the woods and into a church, and was enjoying every minute of it. Wenham, too, had to face the difficulty of an "unnatural birth." In 1646 John Fiske examined a still-born child who might have been judged a monster, but Fiske proved a careful observer. In the presence of female witnesses, he performed a partial autopsy, de-cided that the child was basically normal, and cleared the mother.

Wenham church gives us a number of aggressive women, behaving independently, taking an active role in church governance, and being taken seriously. Then in late 1655, Fiske and a number of his followers moved from Wenham to Chelmsford, where they started a new church. In establishing local practices, they concluded in early 1656, "this day agrrd [sic] by ye church yt ye officer should repeate & declare ye Relation of ye wo: to ye church." In the following decade fewer and fewer women appear in Fiske's pages, and in Chelmsford as in almost all churches, women were referred to as "wife of"; first names generally went unrecorded. Women lost not only voice, but also identity. Furthermore, the experience in Chelmsford was not unique. By 1660, in all of the church records examined for this study, silence had been enjoined on women in the matter of the relation. Silence also prevented them from having a voice in cases of discipline. Judgment was in the hands of men, and more and more the minister instructed the brethren in their voting. Women seem to have been disciplined in numbers out of proportion to their share of congregational populations, and their offenses were increasingly connected with social behavior, not with heresy. What had happened?

Certainly women continued to respond positively to the church, far more so than the men. Scattered admissions data for 28 Congregational churches (18 from Massachusetts and 10 from Connecticut) show a steady growth in the proportion of female admissions. In the 1630s and 1640s male and female admissions were fairly equal, but a shift began in the 1650s, and after 1660 female admissions exceed male. . . .

Before 1660 women probably joined the church in numbers somewhat out of proportion to their part of the total population. However, by 1640 women may have accounted for as much as 40 percent of the population and by 1660, at least in Massachusetts, the sex ratio would have narrowed still further. In any case, the more important point to be developed is women's preponderance in the church population, even after their attempts to share in governance were defeated and male membership shrank.

The best explanation for this phenomenon may come from the anthropologists, who have suggested that all societies tend to esteem male roles more than female ones; and that there is a universal tendency to make what the man does a matter of public importance, what the woman does a domestic matter, carrying less status. New England allows us to add another dimension to these statements: when a society as a whole suffers from a serious conflict in its goals, it can *use* gender role differences to resolve that conflict. It can do this by assigning one set of goals to men, and another to women. This guarantees that those goals which are feminine will become domestic issues and command less social importance. The men can ignore them and apply themselves to male goals.

The Puritans had not been long in New England before the ministry began to murmur about some decline in piety. When it became clear that they would not be called home to England in triumph, men turned to building a permanent civil society. Historians have long tried both to explain the Puritans' loss of a sense of mission and to discover how they handled their guilt. But it is possible that what was seen as a "declension" was only a loss of *male* piety, that Puritans adopted more stringent gender role differences, and turned their church into a feminine institution. In this church, passive females, ruled over by ministers, would personify Christian virtue. One stage in defusing goal conflict, then, was female dominance in number in the church; it is well known that such organizations lose value when they lose male members.

A number of issues are important in understanding the religious terms of the decline in male admissions. Some ministers understood (where historians have failed) that there were still many *people* joining the church; the problem was that there were fewer men. But they did not seem to comprehend that policies which they and the elders espoused would have the effect of discouraging male admissions. This was because their thrust in church governance was to reduce the role played by lay men, just as the role of women had been reduced.

Ministers had responded to the Antinomian crisis by resisting *all* claims to lay prophetic power, since it had produced extreme criticism of ministers during the crisis, and in general threatened the ministers' status in the church. This was much contested in the 1630s and '40s, but accepted by the 1660s, with the inevitable result that the lay contribution to the making of the church in New England was reduced. The issues of tests for membership and authority of the ministers over the congregations were also resolved in ways that led to expectations of male passivity.

Ministers wanted control over the vote and voice of the congregations. The Synod of 1637 opposed the practice of asking questions after sermons and lectures, an opposition certainly created by the Antinomians. The Cambridge Platform further decreased the laymen's right to speak (it required permission from the elders) or to participate in discipline cases; and in the 1640s the ministers took on a kind of veto power in church deliberations. Many ministers also wanted to relax the requirement, adopted in the 1630s, that full membership depend in part on a satisfactory account of conversion. They believed that an increase in membership would follow such relaxation, and the Half-Way Covenant of 1660 was a step in that direction. Later we find the suggestion that men who wanted full membership be allowed the women's "privilege"; that is, that they be excused from speaking, and allow the ministers to report their relations for them. The causes and means by which such positions were reached were complex, but the effect was to enjoin silence on the men, to lose the egalitarianism inherent in a company of saints, and to create a ministerial elite. No doubt this was easier to achieve when the majority of the devout were women. . . .

Women after 1660 could find great reinforcement in religion for the female image most of them had always accepted, and which coincided with their traditional place in the family. To be a good woman was to be a good Christian. But to be a good man was to be a good citizen, active, competitive, self-confident. The women were given, and accepted, the task of preservation of as many values of the Christian community as could be discovered in the family. Only for women did religion and social goals maintain a close correlation. Puritan women, then, subscribed to a Christian role developed out of male needs to pursue social goals no longer validated by religion, out of ministerial determination to control doctrine and governance. They accepted it because of the defeat and discipline of female dissenters, because of the correlation between female socialization into family roles and their place in the church. Perhaps a new role was created, too: as members of the church, women became the keepers of the covenant and protectors of the idea of mission. Put historically, women accepted the burdens of the past, and men the burdens of the future. Put politically, gender differentiation could in this way be seen as a stage in the separation of church and state.

Quaker women were not so bound by either scripture or society as Puritan women. When Pennsylvania was founded in 1682, and Quakers found themselves in control of an important settlement, the sect had already come through its experimental stage and had resolved most major questions of doctrine and of church governance as they applied to women. Quakers were persecuted before 1682, but not directly because of the role women played in the group. Policies in respect to women never threatened the society as a whole, and women had the support of the leaders of the Quaker movement. Both George Fox and Margaret Fell championed female equality and ministries and the inclusion of women in the governance of the Society. William Penn was committed to a policy of religious toleration, and religious unity was never a goal, even in Pennsylvania, as it had been in Massachusetts at the time of the Antinomian crisis. Moreover, Quakers early began to accept their identity as a "peculiar" people who marked themselves as social deviants by such characteristics as their speech, "hat honor" principle, and refusal to take oaths.

Quakers, in common with other radical sects of seventeenth-century England, but unlike New England Puritans after the Antinomian crisis, believed in spiritual rebirth, direct inspiration by the Divine Light, and lay ministries. All three of these doctrinal positions were important to women. Friends insisted on the possibility of being reborn in the spirit, and on an informing, indwelling Divine Light. Sex bias had no place in this conversion experience; there was nothing inherent in the female to prevent her spiritual rebirth, to hinder the work of the Divine Light. As Fox put it, in an interesting variation of Paul's message to the Galatians, "Ye are all one *man* in Christ Jesus [italics added]."

Puritans, more ambivalent, believed in spiritual equality, too, but they did not make room for women in the ministry or church governance and did not allow revision of scriptural prescriptions for female behavior. But through emphasis on the Divine Light, viewed as a continuing revelation, Friends could ignore ancient limitations on women by claiming that the new Light could, at a minimum, serve as a guide to understanding earlier revelations. This was crucial to defining the female role. For example, the curse laid on women in Genesis, which was seen by Puritans as the fundament of inferiority and submission, was reinterpreted by Fox, who considered the spiritual regeneration of the converted as a triumph over this curse. His opinion was that, before the Fall, men and women were equal; after their rebirth, this equality returns: "For man and woman were helpsmeet, in the image of God and in Righteousness and holiness, in the dominion before they fell;

but, after the Fall, in the transgression, the man was to rule over his wife. But in the restoration by Christ into the image of God and His righteousness and holiness again, in that they are helpsmeet, man and woman, as they were before the Fall." We have statements by women, too, emphasizing the curse and woman's role in redemption. Women could address each other as "you that are of the true Seed of the promise of God in the beginning, that was to bruise the Serpent's head." The emphasis here is not on guilt or original sin but on regeneration and triumph.

Nor did Fox or the female Friends of the formative generation accept the restrictions that St. Paul laid on the women of Corinth and Puritans laid on the women of New England. The Quakers dismissed these rules as not pertaining to the regenerate, or to those in whom Christ dwells. As Fox put it, "and may not the spirit of Christ speak in the Female as well as in the Male? is he then to be limited?" Fell was certain that Paul spoke to Corinth alone, or to certain women only. On the issue of learning from their husbands, she pointed out that not all women marry; and in fact it was acceptable to Quakers that some women stay single. George Keith used as a text the woman from Samaria (John 4:28-30) who proclaimed Christ without a university education. Quakers produced other Biblical evidence, too, to prove that women often played active and prophetic roles: Miriam, Hannah, Mary Magdalen, Susannah, Mary, and Martha were only a few of their cloud of witnesses. This was an important doctrinal position for women, but also for all Quakers, who simply took their protest against an ordained ministry as authorities on revelation to its logical conclusion. In fact, having exposed and solved for themselves contradictions in Christian messages to women, Friends proceeded to go their own way. Fox's first disciple was probably a woman, and if Fox was the father of Quakerism, Fell was its mother.

The first and most notable way in which Quaker women acted upon their dispensation and through the spirit within was to engage in the lay ministry; through this ministry, they could influence doctrine. A woman first pursued an internal commitment to a public ministry. She had to be convinced of the presence of Christ within and that He spoke through her. She might be uncertain and need support and encouragement from other Friends. When her work as a public exponent of the truth was established she might then believe herself called to carry that truth abroad. In the early years of the Society, these missions were designed to proselytize; later, as the Friends became more withdrawn, they were intended to help keep strong the faith. Of the first 59 publishers of the truth who came to America from 1656 to 1663, nearly half (26) were women; of these, only four were traveling in ministry with their husbands. Many of these women exhibited enormous courage and bravery in the face of the frequently hostile environment and establishments. Mary Dyer may have been unusual in courting death in Massachusetts, but she was not unusual in her determination to spread the Quakers' message. The later ministry, in which women were equally active, could also take them far afield, although they travelled to established meetings to maintain a high level of religious experience. All of these women had the support of their own meetings and were heard with respect at others.

The other area in which Quaker women engaged most actively was the women's meetings, and here we find them playing a part in church governance, the discipline of women, and the control of membership. Some historians have assumed that women's meetings were established to give women enough authority to keep them happy but not enough to make them powerful. The records of women's meetings do convey a sense of lesser bodies, with relatively little money, not given the quasi-judicial function which men's meetings had in dealing with controversy. However, Fox was concerned about the role of women, and his message to them was unconventional; and the Fell women, Margaret and her daughter Sarah, had a great deal to do with the formation of early women's meetings and saw them as an instrument for the expansion of woman's role.

This is not to say that all Friends agreed; a minority of males attacked the establishment of women's meetings, and believed in male superiority. The Wilkinson-Story schism was in part the result of some men's objections to the founding of women's meetings, and there was opposition to the principle of equality throughout the colonial period. However, men's meetings sometimes helped to assert the authority of the women's meetings. The Narragansett, Rhode Island, Men's Meeting was once asked to sign certificates of dismissal for women who were moving from one meeting to another, dismissals which had already been signed by the women's meeting. They replied that this would "degrade" the women's meeting, and stated their belief that "both male & female are all one in Christ Jesus."

The Quaker meeting structure was complicated. As it developed in Pennsylvania, there was a local weekly meeting for worship and local preparative meetings, or business meetings which got ready for the monthly meeting. The monthly meetings were also business meetings, made up of representatives (sometimes called overseers) from several weekly meetings which formed a small geographic cluster within a county. Quarterly meetings were county based; and the Philadelphia yearly meeting was colony-wide, although it met in Burlington in alternate years until 1760. All of the meetings for business had separate meetings for men and women, except the Select Meeting (or meeting for ministers and elders) which also had yearly, quarterly, and monthly components. This was set up by the yearly meeting in 1714, but not until 1740 was there a requirement that women be included as elders as well as ministers. Thus women were included in every part of the Friends' meeting structure and hierarchy.

The first women's monthly meetings were formed in 1681, on the advice of a yearly meeting held in Burlington, which decided that, as Friends were becoming more numerous, it was necessary to establish a woman's monthly meeting "for the better management of the discipline and other affairs of the church more proper to be inspected by their sex." It is possible to watch through the records of monthly meetings the slow growth of organization and organizational skills at these "grass roots" levels. At first the women simply recorded the fact that they met, but soon they began to see what business they should undertake. They disciplined women who behaved questionably, or who were not attending meeting, and began to collect money to distribute to the poor. They appointed representatives to the quarterly and yearly meetings and decided who might go out on public ministries. Not all of these women's meetings were assertive; some seemed to defer to the men. The Bucks Quarterly Women's Meeting, for example, was uneasy about contributing to the yearly meeting without seeking consent from the men. Other meetings took pleasure in vigorous decision making, and in meetings with stable memberships, such as Chester, one finds older women, like Grace Lloyd, year after year accepting responsibility for female behavior and participation in quarterly and yearly meetings. They must have been influential in socializing young women to an active role. . . .

We can conclude that Quaker women played a more forceful role in the Society of Friends than Puritan women did in the Congregational church. Quaker doctrine provided for a reinterpretation of scriptural prescriptions of female inferiority and submission; Puritans reaffirmed both Genesis and St. Paul. Quaker women, through the Divine Light and their lay ministry, maintained an important position for themselves in the formulation of doctrine; Puritan women were defeated in their attempts to influence doctrine. Quaker women had their own place in church governance, disciplined themselves, and shared control of membership; Puritan women were disciplined to silence, and socialized to accept moral responsibility for the continuation of a Christian community.

The Quakers may have developed an active and workable role for women, but they did not have a major influence on the American Protestant view of women. Never in the mainstream of American religious life, Friends did not retain their dominance in politics or culture even in Pennsylvania, and in the course of the eighteenth century they became more and more introspective, exclusive, and "peculiar." In the face of rigorous discipline numbers decreased, but the religious commitment of those who remained was enhanced. Quaker women, pious and active, may eventually have had some influence on American women as moral custodians; but women of other sects did not learn from the Friends what they needed to know to change their position in the church.

The Puritans, on the other hand, *were* the mainstream of American religious life, and the congregational way, which marked the politics and culture of New England in such distinctive ways, had a far-reaching influence. Friends may have demonstrated the best that the religious revolution of the seventeenth century could do for women; but it was the Puritan mode of female piety and submission to ministerial authority that was to dominate both pew and pulpit in America.

Questions for Reflection and Discussion

1. According to Lillian Ashcraft Webb, how were black women treated differently by several religious groups in the colonial period?

2. To what factors does Francis Cogliano attribute anti-popery in colonial New England?

3. What accounts for the contrasting experiences of Congregational and Quaker women in the early colonial period according to Mary Maples Dunn?

4. How is the tension between inclusion and exclusion illustrated by the religious experiences of Americans in the early period?

5. Does this chapter on religion in early America reflect conflict or consensus?

6. Is there any evidence of a gap between people's religious beliefs and their behaviors in America's colonial experience?

Additional Readings

Bercovitch, Sacvan. *The American Jeremiad*. Madison: University of Wisconsin Press, 1978.

Bonomi, Patricia U. *Under the Cope of Heaven: Religion, Society, and Politics in Colonial American*. New York: Oxford University Press, 1986.

Bowden, Henry Walker. *American Indians and Christian Missions: Studies in Cultural Conflict*. Chicago: University of Chicago Press, 1981.

Bridenbaugh, Carl. *Mitre and Sceptre: Transatlantic Faiths, Ideas, Personalities, and Politics, 1689-1775*. New York: Oxford University Press, 1962.

Butler, Jon. "Magic, Astrology, and the Early American Religious Heritage." *American Historical Review* 84 (1979): 317-346.

Davidson, James West. *The Logic of Millennial Thought: Eighteenth Century New England*. New Haven: Yale University Press, 1977.

Ellis, John Tracy. *Catholics in Colonial America*. Baltimore: Helicon Press. 1965.

Glazer, Nathan. *American Judaism*. Chicago: University of Chicago Press, 1972.

Greer, Allan. *The Jesuit Relations: Natives and Missionaries in Seventeenth-Century North America*. New York: St. Martin's Press, 2000.

Knight, Janice. *Orthodoxies in Massachusetts: Rereading American Puritanism*. Cambridge: Harvard University Press, 1994.

McLoughlin, William. *Cherokees and Missionaries, 1789-1839*. Norman: University of Oklahoma Press, 1995.

Miller, Perry. *The New England Mind: From Colony to Province*. Boston: Beacon Press, 1953.

Scherer, Lester B. *Slavery and the Negro Churches in Early America, 1619-1819*. Grand Rapids, Mich.: William B. Eerdmans, 1975.

Solberg, Winton U. *Redeem the Time: The Puritan Sabbath in Early America*. Cambridge, Mass.: Harvard University Press, 1977.

Stout, Harry S. *The New England Soul: Preaching and Religious Culture in Colonial New England.* New York: Oxford University Press, 1986.

Terrell, John U. *The Arrow and the Cross: A History of the American Indians and the Missionaries.* Santa Barbara, CA: Capra Press, 1979.

Vaughan, Alden T. *The New England Frontier: Puritans and Indians, 1620-1675.* Boston: Little, Brown and Company, 1969.

Woloch, Nancy. *Women and the American Experience.* New York: Knopf, 1985.

Chapter 3

Few events in American history have produced so many conflicting perceptions and seemingly irreconcilable interpretations as the series of religious revivals in the late 1730s and early 1740s known as the Great Awakening. To revivalists like Jonathan Edwards, the Awakening was "an extraordinary and mighty Work of God's Special Grace." Its fruits

The Era of the Great Awakening

Issue

What was the meaning of the Great Awakening?

included the transformation of society and the saving of individual souls. "When once the Spirit of God began to be so wonderfully poured out in a general way through the Town [Northampton]," he wrote, "People had soon done with their old Quarrels, Backbitings, and Intermeddling with other men's Matters."

Among Edwards's antagonists, however, the Awakening was something quite different—a confusion that produced "enthusiastic Heat" and "Commotion in the Passions." Not only did it fail to reform hearts and minds, but, wrote Charles Chauncy, a Boston cleric, "Tis not evident to me that Persons . . . have a better Understanding of Religion, a better Government of their Passions, a more Christian love to their Neighbour, or that they are more decent and regular in their Devotions toward God."

For all the verbal sparring between Edwards, Chauncy, and many clergy and laypersons of their time, more recently the larger question has been raised as to the historical reality of the phenomenon now labeled "the Great Awakening." In 1982, Jon Butler caught the attention of colonial historians with his suggestion that the Awakening was an "interpretive fiction," conceived by the minister-scholar Joseph Tracy, who first used the term "Great Awakening" in his 1841 publication by that title. Tracy produced his work, Butler contends, to support America's nineteenth-century revivals, particularly the "Second Awakening" then in process.

In his *Inventing the "Great Awakening"* (1999), Frank Lambert pursues the argument that the Great Awakening is an historical invention, started by the revivalists and anti-revivalists, and continued by later evangelicals for their own designs. Whether the Awakening is to be understood as a series of scattered religious revivals, occurring primarily in New England and New Jersey, or, as presented by historians of the past several decades, "the first unifying event of the colonial experience, the origins of the American evangelical tradition, and a major source of revolutionary antiauthoritarian and republican rhetoric," will continue to be debated. Is it important to determine if there really was "a Great Awakening"? Why is this debate critical to understanding the place of religion in colonial America and even later? How and why did the Great Awakening produce both conflict and consensus?

Documents

Numerous voices during the mid-eighteenth century discussed the nature and meaning of the Great Awakening. In the first selection, preacher Samuel Wigglesworth laments in 1733 that the glory of New England's past has vanished as the tolerance for evil has increased; therefore he extends an urgent call for the reviving of religion. Among the foremost antagonists who expressed their opinions about the influence and significance of the Awakening were Jonathan Edwards and Charles Chauncy. In the early 1740s they exchanged written volleys from which the excerpts in documents two and three were taken. The fourth document is taken from Reverend Thomas Prince's funeral sermon for his daughter, Deborah, who died in 1744. His revival accounts and this funeral sermon advertised the Awakening's successes and contributed to its "invention." That same year the Old Lights of Harvard College responded to New Light George Whitefield's denunciation of Harvard for its lapsed spiritual condition. The fifth selection is from their retort. In the final document, evangelical Joseph Bellamy encourages pious Americans who began to ask in the 1750s if the millennium promised by Edwards would ever arrive, and calls upon them to hasten the much-anticipated establishment of God's kingdom on earth.

1. An Essay for Reviving Religion, 1733

SOURCE: Samuel Wigglesworth, *An Essay for Reviving Religion. A Sermon Delivered . . . May 30th. MDCCXXXIII. Being the Anniversary for the Election . . .* (Boston, 1733), 22–26, 30–31.

It is a Truth, that we have a *goodly exterior Form of Religion;* Our *Doctrine, Worship and Sacraments* are *Orthodox, Scriptural* and *Divine.* There is an external Honour paid to the *Sabbath;* and a professed Veneration for Christ's *Ambassadors* for the sake of their Lord. We set up and maintain the *Publick Worship* of God, and the Voice of the Multitude saying, *Let us go into the House of the Lord*, is yet heard in our Land.

Moreover *Practical Religion* is not quite extirpated among us, and there are, it is to be hoped, a considerable number of serious and vigorous Christians in our Churches, whose *Piety* is acknowledged and respected by their Neighbours, whilst Living; and their *Memories* preserved for it when deceased. Whilst on the other hand, the *prophane and wicked Person* is generally abhor'd; and the more deformed Vices seek the retreats of Darkness to hide their detestable heads.

And yet with what sorrow must we speak, that these things are but the *Remains* of what we *Once* might show; the shadow of past and vanish'd Glory! . . .

If the *Fear of the Lord* be to *Hate Evil*, as *Prov. 8.13*. Then it is to be feared that our *Religion runs low*, and but little of this Fear is in us: Inasmuch as we find our selves stained with so many most odious Vices, especially *Uncleanness, Drunkenness, Theft, Covetousness, Violence, Malice, Strife*, and others: Which tho', as 'twas said before, they be look'd upon with dishonour, yet multitudes are found who are not ashamed to commit them; and where such *Iniquities abound*, may we not infer that *the Love of many waxeth cold?*

Again, How *Weak is the Testimony that is born by our Good Men against those Transgressions!* Ought not holy Ones when they *Behold the Transgressor, to be grieved!* Will they not hate the things which God hates, and express a suitable indignation at the presumption of the Wicked, and the affronts which they put upon the Majesty of Heaven? *Reproving*, and bringing them to *Punishment?* If therefore our *Professors of Religion* think *Open Prophaneness* unworthy of their Wrath: If our *Ministers of Religion* are sparing to bear their publick Testimony against it; and when also the *Ministers of Justice* are too Complaisant to the Sons of Wickedness, to Execute the wholesome Laws of the Province upon them; unto how low an ebb is our Goodness come! . . .

We bless God that we see our Land from time to time cleansed from *Innocent Blood* by the Blood of the Murderer, & other abominable Wickednesses receiving their due Recompense: But it would compleat our Joy if many other Crimes which we think also deserving to be *punish'd by the Judges* were more severely animadverted upon; That so *All Iniquity may stop its mouth*. And would our *Courts of Judicature* please to frown upon those *Litigious* Persons, who make uneasy Work for them, and disturb the repose of their Neighbours; they would do a Work acceptable to God & Man; and Religion would escape the wounds which it daily receives from strife & envy. . . .

2. Thoughts on the Revival of Religion, 1742
SOURCE: Sereno E. Dwight, ed., *The Works of President Edwards with a Memoir of His Life* (1830).

God has made as it were two worlds here below, two great habitable continents, far separated one from the other: The latter is as it were now but newly created; it has been, till of late, wholly the possession of Satan, the church of God having never been in it, as it has been in the other continent, from the beginning of the world. This new world is probably now discovered, that the new and most glorious state of God's church on earth might commence there; that God might in it begin a new world in a spiritual respect, when he creates the *new heavens* and *new earth*.

God has already put that honour upon the other continent, that Christ was born there literally, and there made the "purchase of redemption." So, as Providence observes a kind of equal distribution of things, it is not unlikely that the great spiritual birth of Christ, and the most glorious "application of redemption," is to begin in this. . . .

The other continent hath slain Christ, and has from age to age shed the blood of saints and martyrs of Jesus, and has often been as it were, deluged with the church's blood.— God has, therefore, probably reserved the honor of building the glorious temple to the daughter that has not shed so much blood, when those times of the peace, prosperity and glory of the church, typified by the reign of Solomon, shall commence. . . .

The old continent has been the source and original of mankind in several respects. The first parents of mankind dwelt there; and there dwelt Noah and his sons; there the second Adam was born, and crucified, and raised again: And it is probable that, in some measure to balance these things, the most glorious renovation of the world shall originate from the new continent, and the church of God in that respect be from hence. And so it is probable that will come to pass in spirituals, which has taken place in temporals, with respect to America: that whereas, till of late, the world was supplied with its silver, and gold, and earthly treasures from the old continent, now it is supplied chiefly from the new; so the course of things in spiritual respects will be in like manner turned.—And it is worthy to be noted, that America was discovered about the time of the reformation, or but little before: Which reformation was the first thing that God did towards the glorious renovation of the world, after it had sunk into the depths of darkness and ruin, under the great anti-christian apostasy. So that, as soon as this new world stands forth in view, God presently goes about doing some great thing in order to make way for the introduction of the church's latter-day glory—which is to have its first seat in, and is to take its rise from that new world.

It is agreeable to God's manner, when he accomplishes any glorious work in the world, in order to introduce a new and more excellent state of his church, to begin where no foundation had been already laid, that the power of God might be the more conspicuous; that the work might appear to be entirely God's, and be more manifestly a creation out of nothing. . . . When God is about to turn the earth into a paradise, he does not begin his work where there is some good growth already, but in the wilderness, where nothing grows, and nothing is to be seen but dry sand and barren rocks; that the light may shine out of darkness, the world be replenished from emptiness, and the earth watered by springs from a droughty desert: agreeable to many prophecies of scripture. . . . Now as when God is about to do some great work for his church, his manner is to begin at the lower end; so, when he is about to renew the whole habitable earth, it is probable that he will begin in this utmost, meanest, youngest and weakest part of it, where the church of God has been planted last of all: and so the first shall be last, and the last first: and that will be fulfilled in an eminent manner in Isa. xxiv.19. "From the uttermost part of the earth have we heard songs, even glory to the righteous. . . ."

. . . And if we may suppose that this glorious work of God shall begin in any part of America, I think, if we consider the circumstances of the settlement of New-England, it must needs appear the most likely, of all American colonies, to be the place whence this work shall principally take its rise. And, if these things be so, it gives more abundant reason to hope that what is now seen in America, and especially in New-England, may prove the dawn of that glorious day; and the very uncommon and wonderful circumstances and events of this work, seem to me strongly to argue that God intends it as the beginning or forerunner of something vastly great.

I have thus long insisted on this point, because, if these things are so, it greatly manifests how much it behoves us to encourage and promote this work, and how dangerous it will be to forbear so doing. It is very dangerous for God's professing people to lie still, and not to come to the help of the Lord, whenever he remarkably pours out his Spirit, to carry on the work of redemption in the application of it; but above all, when he comes forth to introduce that happy day of God's power and salvation, so often spoken of. . . .

3. Seasonable Thoughts on the State of Religion, 1743

SOURCE: Charles Chauncy, *Seasonable Thoughts on the State of Religion in New England* (Boston, 1743).

'This true, we read of the coming on of a *glorious State* of Things in the LAST DAYS: Nor will the *Vision fail.*—We may rely upon it, the Prophesies, foretelling the Glory of the REDEEMER'S *Kingdom* will have their Accomplishment to the making this Earth of *Paradise,* in Compare with what it now is. But for the *particular Time* when this will be, it *is not for us to know it, the Father having put it in his own Power.* And whoever pretend to such Knowledge, they are wise above what is written; and tho' they may think they know much, they really know nothing as to this Matter.

It may be suggested, that "the Work of GOD'S SPIRIT that is so extraordinary and wonderful, is the *dawning,* or at least, a *Prelude* of that *glorious Work of god,* so often foretold in Scripture, which, in the Progress and Issue of it, shall renew the whole world." But what are such Suggestions, but the Fruit of Imagination? Or at best, uncertain Conjecture? And can any good End be answered in endeavoring, upon Evidence absolutely precarious, to instill into the minds of people a Notion of the *millennium* State, as what is now going to be introduced; yea, and of AMERICA, as that Part of the World, which is pointed out in the *Revelations* of GOD for the Place, where this glorious Scene of Things, "will, probably, first begin?" How often, at other Times, and in other Places, has the Conceit been propagated among People, as if the Prophecies touching the Kingdom of CHRIST, in the *latter Days*, were NOW to receive their Accomplishment? And what has been the Effect, but their running wild? So it was in GERMANY, in the Beginning of the Reformation. The *extraordinary* and wonderful Things in that Day, were look'd upon by the Men then thought to be most under the SPIRIT'S *immediate Direction*, as "the Dawning of that glorious Work of GOD, which should renew the whole World"; and the Imagination of the Multitude being fired with this Notion, they were soon persuaded, that the Saints were now to reign on Earth, and the Dominion to be given into their Hands: And it was under the Influence of this vain Conceit (in which they were strengthened by *Visions, Raptures, and Revelations*) that they took up Arms against the lawful *Authority*, and were destroy'd, at one Time and another, to the Number of an HUNDRED THOUSAND. . . .

And 'tis well know, that this same Pretence of the near Approach of the MILLENNIUM, the promised Kingdom of the MESSIAH, was the *Foundation-Error of the French Prophets,* and those in their Way, no longer ago than the Beginning of this Century: And so infatuated were they at last, as to publish it to the World, that the glorious Times they spake of, *would be manifest over the whole Earth, within the Term of three years.* And what Set of Men have ever yet appear'd in the Christian World, whose Imaginations have been thorowly warmed, but they have, at length, wrought themselves up to a *full Assurance*, that NOW was the Time for the Accomplishment of the Scriptures, and the Creation of the *new Heavens*, and the *new Earth*? No one Thing have they more unitedly concurred in, to their own shameful Disappointment, and the doing unspeakable Damage to the Interest of Religion.— A sufficient Warning, one would think, to keep Men modest; and restrain them from Endeavors to lead People into a Belief of that, of which they have no sufficient *Evidence;* and in which, they may be deceived by their vain *Imaginations,* as Hundreds and Thousands have been before them.

There are unquestionably many Prophesies concerning CHRIST, and the *Glory of his Kingdom,* still to be fulfilled; and it may be of good Service to labor to beget in People a Faith in these Things; or, if they have Faith, to quicken and strengthen it: But is can answer no good End to lead People into the Belief of any *particular* Time, as the Time *appointed* of GOD for the Accomplishment of these Purposes of his Mercy; because this is one of those Matters, his Wisdom had thought fit to keep conceal'd from the Knowledge of Man. Our own Faith therefore upon this Head can be founded only on *Conjecture;* and as 'tis only the like *blind Faith* we can convey to others, we should be cautious, lest their Conduct should be agreeable to their Faith. When they have imbib'd from us the Thought, as if the glorious Things, spoken of in Scripture, were to come forward in their Day, they will be apt (as has often been the Case) to be impatient, and from their *Officiousness* in tendering their Help where it is not needed, to disserve the Interest of the Redeemer.

4. "What a Vile Creature I Am," 1744

SOURCE: [Thomas Prince], *Christian History* (Boston, 1744, 1745), 20, 21-29, 31.

And this brings me to the known Occasion of this Discourse, *the Death of my Dear and eldest Daughter.* . . .

It was on Dec. 23, 1723, when He Gave her to me. . . . As she grew up, he was pleas'd to restrain her from youthful Vanities, to make her serious, and move her to study the BIBLE and the best of Authors both of History and Divinity: Among the latter of which, Dr. *Watts* and Mrs. *Row's* Writing were very agreeable and familiar to Her. The SPIRIT OF GOD was also pleas'd to work on her heart by, Dr. *Sewall's* Ministry, for whom she had a high Esteem, and by other Means of Grace: Especially when she came to be about Fourteen Years of Age, 'convincing and humbling her (as in a Paper of hers she represents it) of all her Sins both Original and Actual, of their Greatness and Heinousness, and of her Need of a SAVIOUR: enabling her, as she hoped, to repent of her Sins and forsake them; to look on CHRIST as a compleat Redeemer; to renounce her own Righteousness, and depend on his only; and making her willing to accept Him as offer'd in the Gospel, as her Prophet, Priest and King, to instruct, intercede for and rule over Her.'

Upon this she was desirous of Renewing her covenant in Publick, and coming up to all his Ordinances: But Apprehensions of her own Unworthiness and Fears of Eating and Drinking Judgment to herself, discourag'd and prevented her; till July 18, 1739, when she narrowly escaped being drowned. . . .

Being affected with this great Danger and Deliverance, she seem'd to be further awakened and stirred up to her Duty of Devoting Herself to her DIVINE PRESERVER, of walking in all his Commandments, and living to his Glory. And in consequence of this, at her own Motion, she was on Lordsday the 5th of the following Month, Propounded; and the 19th Publickly Gave Herself to GOD in Covenant, and came into full Communion with us.

When Mr. *Whitefield* came and preached in the Fall of the Year ensuing; she, with Multitudes of Others, was excited to a livelier View of Eternity, to a greater Care of her immortal Soul, to a stricter Search into Herself, and a more earnest Labour after vital Piety and the Power of Godliness, and to make them more the Business of her Life. And now such Experimental and Searching Writers as Mr. *Shepherd* of Cambridge, Mr. *William Guthry* of Scotland, Mr. *Flavel* and *Mead* of England, Mr. *Stoddard* of North-Hampton and Mr. *Mather* of Windsor in New-England, &c, were more diligently read and highly valued.

She now suspected all her former Experiences; that her Heart remain'd unrenewed, and that she had not rightly received CHRIST: until Dec. 13, 1740: When on a Day of Private Prayer and Fasting, those Divine Passages were set home with surprizing and overcoming Power on her distressed soul in *Mat.* viii, *Mark* i, and *Luke* v. And there came a Leper to Him, full of Leprosy, who seeing JESUS, fell on his face and besought Him, saying, 'Lord if Thou WILT, Thou CANST make me clean:' And JESUS moved with Compassion, put forth his Hand, and touched Him, and saith unto Him," I WILL!—Be Thou clean!" And as soon as He had spoken, immediately, the Leprosy departed from Him, and He was cleansed. With those Passages of Grace, there came into her such a sweet and raised View both of the *Power, Willingness* and *Will* of this DEAR REDEEMER, to cleanse her from the Leprosy of Sin and save Her; as to satisfy her of it, and draw her to him in such a Manner as she never felt before. And she told her younger Sister, that if ever she rightly embraced the SAVIOUR and was converted; she thought it was at that happy Season. Tho' this I never knew 'till since her Funeral; it being one of her Infirmities to be too reserved.

Mr. *Tennent's* Searching Preaching raised in Her, as in many Others, a great and constant Jealousy of being Deceived: And upon every spiritual Declension, a cloud of Darkness overwhelm'd her and inclin'd her to judge she was. His insisting also that without *sanctifying Grace*, our BLESSED SAVIOUR gives none a *Right* to Partake at his Table, occasioned her much Perplexity. For from thence she argued; that unless she *knew* she had *sanctifying Grace*, she cou'd not *know* she had a *Right*: And to Partake without *knowing* she had a *Right*, would be not to Partake in *Faith*, but in *Presumption*, and this she had no Right to do. And hence, when Doubts of her State of Grace arose, she dare not Participate; but only attended with Desire, and I believe with deep Regret and Self-abasement. So though her Jealousies and Fears were troublesome; I am apt to think they were useful; not only to make her Look more into and see herself, and make her more broken, humble, and careful, but also excite her Prayers and Labours after livelier Degrees of Grace and the clearer Evidence of it. . . .

But I now come to her *Sickness*.

On *Tuesday, May 29* she was seized on a sudden with a slow Fever; And upon going up to her Chamber drop'd a Word, as if she should never come down alive.

From the Beginning she was much more apprehensive of *Danger* than any else: And though concerned about her Soul; yet complained of her Stupidity, Hardness of Heart, blindness of Mind, Impenitence and Unbelief; censuring and condemning herself of all Good, denying she had any sanctifying Grace, but judging she had been deceiving Herself with the counterfeit Resemblance of it. . . . And though I reasoned with her about her *former Experience,* yet all in vain. 'O Dear Father, (said she) you have better Apprehension of me than you should have: You don't know what a vile Creature I am: I have dreadfully apostatized from CHRIST, have grown exceeding negligent of religious Duties, and was returning to the World again.' I told her, we did not perceive it; that I could not see those Decays she spoke of, to be inconsistent with a regenerate State, though they were Matter of deep Abasement, and she should have a Care she denied not the gracious Work of GOD within Her. . . .

I told Her CHRIST as a compassionate Saviour had revealed Hell to us on Purpose, that we might be afraid of it, and by the Fear be mov'd to fly to him to save us from it; and this must therefore be a dutiful Compliance with his gracious Purpose; that this Kindness in discovering Hell, with his Concern and willingness to save us from it, is a Part of his Amiableness, for which we ought to love and embrace him; though we should indeed be excited also with the higher Motives of *his Personal Excellancies:* . . .

I also argued from her Love to the house and Word of GOD, and to his People and Ministers; from her peculiar Love to Those whom she apprehended to be most eminent for vital Piety; especially those ministers who most laid open the Hypocrisy of the Hearts of Men, who made the Hypocrites and Formalists the most uneasy, and were most zealous for the power of Godliness: . . .

I then chang'd the Tenor of my discoursing from Day to Day. And *supposing she were not converted*, represented her Case as indeed very dreadful, but not as desperate: And at several Times, as she was through grievous Illness able to bear, endeavoured to set before her the infinite Fountain of Mercy and Grace in GOD; how this Fountain is open, free, and eternally overflowing; how He thereby glorifies every Person in the Godhead, both FATHER, SON and SPIRIT, and how he would be so far from loosing any Glory, that he would glorify more of his Perfections in Forgiving and Saving her, than in Rejecting and Damning her. I endeavour'd also to set before her the wondrous Piety, Condescension, Offices, Humiliation, Sufferings, Sacrifice, Righteousness, Merits, Exaltation, Glory, Power, Grace, Calls and Promises of CHRIST: how touched with a fellow-Feeling of her Infirmities and Miseries; how tenderly compassionate; how open his Arms; how earnestly inviting and intreating; how ready to receive her; bestow his Righteousness on her, intercede for and reconcile her to the HOLY GOD: . . .

[But on her deathbed, she finally spoke a "new Language."] *O I love the* LORD JESUS *with all my Heart! I see such an Amiableness, such an* AMIABLENESS *in Him; I prize Him above a thousand Words! And the Delights and Pleasures of the World are nothing to* HIM! I ask'd her, If she could now Resign Herself to his arms? She replied—*O Yes! I Believe in Him! I rejoice in Him! And I rejoice in all the Agonies I have borne! And tell the young People of it:* Tell such a one, and such a one, and such a one, and all the Society, for the strengthening of their Faith and their Encouragement to go on! Tell such a one, Not to mind the Vanities of the World, but seek to make her Hope stronger Tell such a one, To live nearer to God, and live nearer to Him: Tell such a one, Not to be so careful about worldly Matters, but to be more careful after CHRIST and Grace. And having deliver'd the like pithy pertinent and pathetick Messages for 5 others. I then ask'd her—'Well, my dear Child! What have you to say to me?' *O Sir*, said she, *that you may be more fervent in your Ministry, and in exhorting and expostulating with Sinners!*

5. The Testimony of Harvard College Against George Whitefield, 1744

SOURCE: *The Testimony of the President, Professors, Tutors and Hebrew Instructor of Harvard College in Cambridge Against the Reverend Mr. George Whitefield, and his Conduct* (Boston, 1744), 3-5.

In regard to the Danger which we apprehend the People and Churches of this Land are in, on the Account of the Rev. Mr. *George Whitefield*, we have tho't ourselves oblig'd to bear our Testimony, in this public Manner, against him and his

Way of Preaching, as tending very much to the Detriment of Religion and the entire Destruction of the Order of these Churches of Christ, which our Fathers have taken such Care and Pains to settle, as by the Platform, according to which the Discipline of the Churches of *New England* is regulated: And we do therefore hereby declare, That we look upon his going about, in an Itinerant Way, especially as he hath so much of an enthusiastic Turn, utterly inconsistent with the Peace and Order, if not the very Being of these Churches of Christ.

And now, inasmuch as by a certain Faculty he hath of raising the Passions, he hath been the Means of rousing many from their Stupidity, and setting them on thinking, whereby some may have been made really better, on which Account the People, many of them, are strongly attach'd to him (tho' it is most evident, that he hath not any superior Talent at instructing the Mind, or shewing the Force and Energy of those Arguments for a religious Life, which are directed to in the everlasting Gospel). Therefore, that the people who are thus attach'd to him, may not take up an unreasonable Prejudice against this our testimony, we think it very proper to give some Reasons for it, which we shall offer, respecting the Man himself, and then his Way and Manner of Preaching.

First, as to the Man himself, whom we look upon as an Enthusiast, a censorious, uncharitable Person, and a Deluder of the People; which Things, if we can make out, all reasonable Men will doubtless excuse us, tho' some such, thro' a fastinating Curiosity, may still continue their Attachment to him.

First then, we charge him, with *Enthusiasm*. Now that we may speak clearly upon this Head, we mean by an *Enthusiast*, one that acts, either according to Dreams, or some sudden Impulses and Impressions upon his Mind, which he fondly imagines to be from the Spirit of God, perswading and inclining him thereby to such and such Actions, tho' he hath no Proof that such Perswasions or Impressions are from the holy Spirit: For the perceiving a strong Impression upon our Minds, or a violent Inclination to do any Action, is a very different Thing from perceiving such Impressions to be from the Spirit of God moving upon the Heart: For our strong Faith and Belief, that such a Motion on the Mind comes from God, can never be any Proof of it; and if such Impulses and Impressions be not agreeable to our Reason, or to the Revelation of the Mind of God to us, in his Word, nothing can be more dangerous than conducting ourselves according to them; for otherwise, if we judge not of them by these Rules, they may as well be the Suggestions of the evil Spirit: And in what Condition must that People be, who stand ready to be led by a Man that conducts himself according to his Dreams, or some ridiculous and unaccountable Impulses and Impressions on his Mind? . . .

6. The Millennium, 1758

SOURCE: Joseph Bellamy, *Works*, I, excerpted from 495-516.

. . . Surely it is infinitely unbecoming the followers of Him who is *King of kings and Lord of lords*, to turn aside to earthly pursuits, or to sink down in unmanly discouragements, or to give way to sloth and effeminacy, when there is so much to be done, and the glorious day is coming on. How should those who handle the pen of the writer, exert themselves to explain and vindicate divine truths, and paint the Christian religion in all its native glories! How should the pulpit be animated, from sabbath to sabbath, with sermons full of knowledge and light, full of spirit and life, full of zeal for God, and love to men, and tender pity to infatuated sinners! Christ loves to have his ministers faithful, whether the wicked will hear or not. And let pious parents be unwearied in their prayers for, and instructions of their children, and never faint under any discouragements; as knowing, that Christ is exalted to give repentance and remission of sins, and can do it for whom he will. Bring your children and friends, with all their spiritual diseases, and lay them at his feet; as once they did their sick, when this kind Saviour dwelt on earth. Let pious persons of every age, and in every capacity, awake from sleep, and arise from the dead, and live and act worthy their glorious character and high expectations; and in their several stations exert themselves to the utmost to promote the Redeemer's glorious cause. Let this age do their share, as David, although the temple was not to be built in his day, yet exerted himself to lay up materials for that magnificent edifice, on which his heart was intently set; as knowing, that in his son's day it would be set up in all its glory. So let us rise up, and with the greatest alacrity contribute our utmost towards this building, this living temple, this temple all made of lively stones, of stones alive, in which God is to dwell, and which will infinitely exceed in glory the temple of Solomon, that was built of dead timber and lifeless stones. And let this be our daily prayer, and answer to which we may be assured of, whatever other requests are denied us, *our Father which art in heaven, &c. for thine is the kingdom, the power, and the glory, for ever.* AMEN.

Essays

The three essays reprinted below address the range of social, political, and religious conflict and unrest that accompanied the Great Awakening. The first, by Cedric Cowing of the University of Hawaii, Manoa, describes the conflicting emphases between emotion and reason in the lives of theologians, evangelists, and pewsitters. Consequences of the Revival are given special attention. Some of the tensions between belief and behavior of Awakening leaders are given close examination by David S. Lovejoy of the University of Wisconsin in the second essay. In the final essay, Martha T. Blauvelt of The College of Saint Benedict in Saint Joseph, Minnesota, and Rosemary Skinner Keller of Union Theological Seminary show that the widespread exclusion of women from the mainstream of American society did not preclude their inclusion in Awakening activities, though a fuller expansion of women's evangelical role was delayed until the nineteenth century.

The Great Awakening: Revelation and Reason
CEDRIC COWING

SOURCE: From *The Great Awakening and the American Revolution: Colonial Thought in the 18th Century* by Cedric Cowing. Pp. 67-69, 70-74. Copyright © 1971 by Rand McNally and Company. Reprinted with permission of the author.

Effects of the Revival

The very characteristics of the Great Awakening that the Old Lights found distasteful had a profound and as yet unmeasured effect on American intellectual and political life. In most places, the Calvinistic emphasis on Terrors of the Law was important in attracting male converts. It appealed to the "middle aged" men who had a rising concern for life after death and had not heard before—during the barren period of the early 18th century—the full exposition of Calvinistic federal theology. The conundrums of Calvinism were also a challenge to young men dealing with an abstract system for the first time. While fear for their souls dominated both groups, there were those analytical and skeptical enough to be more angry than afraid. These particular "children of wrath" were angry that God could be so unjust, so unreasonable and inhuman as to impute Adam's sin to all mankind and predestine the vast majority to hell. This anger heightened the suggestibility of many stable men who were not neurotic, exceptionally intelligent, or easily scared.

Gilbert Tennent was the epitome of the New Light in his ability to arouse fear and anger and bring on sudden convictions. Like Jonathan Edwards—who could be as effective on occasion—Tennent relied heavily on direct address and made no agreeable gestures to diffuse the impression of his words. The relentless manner of such preachers in presenting astringent doctrines affected not only those of choleric and melancholic temperament, who were more easily stirred, but often reached the sanguine and phlegmatic men as well. And when the latter were "re-born," they were not likely to fall away.

The initial power of evangelical Calvinism came from stressing God's sovereignty and the Terrors of the Law, without exploring certain implications. Presented in the right way, the authoritarian idea of God's sovereignty could appear equalitarian. All men were worms dependent on God's mercy, incapable of understanding life's higher meaning. Even the Saints might be fooling themselves, and further introspection might reveal hypocrisy. The proud and the complacent as well as the overtly sinful were in danger. No one was secure. God's sovereignty could be a reminder to the *nouveaux riches,* the upwardly mobile who were forgetting Him, and this aspect could gain approval from pious and less self-confident common folk. At the same time, it could comfort members of old families of the Elect who felt their status threatened by impious climbers.

Beginning a sermon with the Terrors was a prerequisite for evangelical pastors. Aroused by fear and anger, listeners were made ready for the "good news." Of course the clergy alternated it with other themes and adjusted the severity to the audience. Jonathan Edwards was unusually terrifying when he preached "Sinners in the Hands of an Angry God" at Enfield in 1741 because he knew the congregation there bad become loose and indolent. A delicate proportion was involved; the Terrors had to last long enough to stir the most secure, but not so long as to bring mass insanity or suicide. Ministers who moved too soon from this theme to God's mercy failed to reach many souls. Edwards seldom made this mistake. Of all God's doctrines he believed sovereignty the most blessed. He wrote: "But the most awful truths of God's word ought not to be withheld from public congregations, because it may happen that some melancholic persons in Christendom exceedingly abuse the awful things contained in the scripture, to their own wounding."

Preaching that was merely an emotional assault on the brain was not enough; the preacher also had to provide an escape from the induced stress. Hellfire was presented solely as the result of rejecting the offer of eternal salvation won by faith. Emotionally disrupted by this threat, then rescued from everlasting torment by a total change of heart, the convert was now in a state to be helped by emphasizing the complementary gospel of love. The punishment for backsliding from a state of grace was always in mind; but once conversion had taken place, love rather than further fear could be used to consolidate the gain. John Wesley described the right method as beginning with the preaching of the law "in the strongest, the closest, the most searching manner possible. After more and more persons are convinced of sin, we may mix more and more of the gospel, in order to beget faith, to raise into the spiritual life those whom the law has slain.". . .

There would seem to be a definite relationship between males, Terrors of the Law, and sudden experiences. A psychologist in his study of college and seminary students in the 1920s, distinguished 143 instances of sudden conviction; he labelled them "Definite Crisis" cases. Of these, three-fourths were men, although in his general sample, only a third were male. He also demonstrated a strong link between type of theology and Definite Crisis experiences. Those who had heard "stern theology," namely preaching of the Terrors of the Law, were *more than five times* as likely to have a Definite Crisis as those who had heard only "moderate theology." This suggests that the New Light emphasis on the Terrors was apt to "convict" more men than women and to do it more suddenly.

Is a Definite Crisis to be preferred to the gradual or temporary emotional stimulus experiences because it leads to a more profound and permanent change? Does it have greater political and social consequences than the others? Modern scholars disagree but evangelists have always said yes, Jehovah's Witnesses, among the most involved in this field today, have learned to expect—like other direct salesmen—an early decision to "close with Jesus" or no decision at all. Eighteenth century awakeners explicitly favored the crises although professing sympathy for those who suffered prolonged anxiety and indecision. Jonathan Edwards believed that the immediacy of spoken words and not the memory of them were most likely to prick the heart and that great terrors led to sudden light and joy. Samuel Buell thought that the more powerful the conviction, the sooner the relief. After a lifetime of evangelism, John Wesley affirmed that sudden effects seemed to be the most enduring. Early in this century, America's most distinguished psychologist of religion reached the same conclusion. In his *Varieties of Religious Experience,* William James wrote, "As a matter of fact, all the more striking instances of conversion, . . . *have* been permanent."

The emphasis on "the Word," spoken and written, provided some check on mysticism and promoted literacy and rationality. Edwards liked converts who had "seen" passages from scripture and felt joy afterward. Whitefield said he clung to the scriptures because beyond them were only illusions.

Modern religious educators, offended by the aggressive and vulgar tactics of many Fundamentalist revivalists, have deplored Definite Crisis cases. They have associated such phenomena with religious illiteracy, backwoods ignorance, and susceptibility to hysteria. These educators admit that crises are apt to occur among the unchurched after puberty and urge the early Christian training of children as insurance against such emotional excesses. Their disapproval is rationalistic and aesthetic, but it also rests on the belief that crisis conversions in our own time are superficial and impermanent.

The British psychiatrist, William Sargant, provides strong endorsement of Definite Crisis experiences, however. He emphasizes the therapeutic value of total collapse and argues that the potential for reformation is greatest among those who have been completely overcome. When the cerebral apparatus short-circuits to save itself from unbearable stress and the victim slumps into a coma-tose state, a *tabula rasa* condition follows. It may be three or four months before the patient's pre-collapse habits and thoughts are fully restored. If, in the in-terim, the patient is systematically reconditioned, he may well be transformed for life; he may be "born again." On this ground Sargant admires Jonathan Edwards' techniques and praises as psychologically sound the elaborate follow-up system of John Wesley and the Methodists, particularly their stress on "classes" and self-criticism to maintain morale and discipline among the converts and weed out hypocrites in the crucial retraining period.

There were many physical and mental collapses in the Great Awakening. Charles Chauncy referred frequently and deprecatingly to the "swooning" and the "struck." Jonathan Parsons of Lyme saw several stout men fall "as if a cannon ball had been discharged." David Hall of Sutton, a sympathizer, believed that the New Lights were encouraging too much crying and falling down.

It should be remembered at this point that the New Lights were not seeking sudden conversions alone, but sudden convictions followed at appropriate inter-vals by definite, datable conversion experiences. The interval between conviction and conversion could vary considerably, depending upon the temperament of the individual. Two weeks was too short; two years was too long; two months was an optimum. It would be a misrepresentation of the New Lights not to emphasize this, because the period of anxiety was important. The minister could use the signs, stages and behavior of this interim to corroborate the testimony offered by the convert later; and the pastors were cautious, in the 18th century, resisting pressure to telescope these days of concern and trial. In the revivals of the 19th century, when conversion followed conviction closely, the cases of abiding change seem to have been fewer.

The impact of the Great Awakening on learning was profound although it is still not fully understood; only some of the immediate aspects will be indicated here. When the joy and relief of sudden conversion subsided, most converts felt a strong sense of obligation, at first to God and then to the community at large. They were receptive and educable; young male converts were eager to become ministers and begin proselytizing. Respectable New Light clergy offered their pastoral studies as "schools of the prophets" to train these neophytes. The young men hungered for instruction, not only by hearing the Word in extra lectures, but also by reading good books. In addition to the scriptures, they sought out the solid works of Puritanism: Ames, Baxter, Flavel, Hooker, Shepard, Cotton, Willard, Mather, and Stoddard. The majority of the authors were colonial divines of the 17th century; studying their works was more effective than the jeremiad had ever been in reinforcing ideas of special destiny and separation from Europe, and in fostering incipient nationalism.

In Britain, many of the converts of Whitefield and Wesley were motivated to learn to read and write, but in the northern colonies where people were already literate—except for the Indians and Negroes—the energies and discipline released by the New Light were the inspiration needed to master abstract religious material. In comprehending theological as well as devotional printed matter, the emotions aided the development of cognitive skills. The novices in focusing on the stages of conversion were studying a process analogous to the still mysterious secular sequence of gathering data, altering hypotheses, and somehow relying upon intuition to synthesize the conclusions. This type of thinking would have a more general utility later. The Great Awakening induced a grass roots intellectualism that ultimately spread in every direction, from belief in God's sovereignty all the way to agnosticism.

There is ample testimony that community morals improved markedly after large-scale conversion. Reformations were common and religious talk was everywhere. The saved even displayed affection for people they had formerly hated. There is no way to measure how long such effects lasted, but the revivalists, of course, believed that their ministers, like Jonathan Edwards, were so careful in admitting newcomers to communion that few backslid. New Lights describe the awakened as animated by a new principle, pursuing their daily life with a new confidence, satisfaction, and purpose.

At the same time, the Church of England received refugees from the emotionalism of the revival. Rectors boasted of the high quality of families joining their flocks and the general Anglican immunity to the New Light.

The Awakening accentuated divisions and produced schisms in the Reformed churches. In New England the opposers were dubbed Old Lights. In the Middle Colonies, both the Dutch Reformed and the Presbyterians split into Old Sides and New Sides. The factions created earlier by Frelinghuysen and the Tennents were thus confirmed and revealed openly. In the ensuing competition for churches and believers, the evangelical New Siders proved to have a big advantage in youth and numbers.

Separation was one inevitable result of the revival. In cases where a conservative minister failed to respond to his awakened parishioners, they sometimes seceded, gathering the true believers into a new congregation. The separatists justified themselves by asserting the Cambridge Platform and trying to operate independently and democratically. In Connecticut, because of the religious establishment created by the Saybrook Platform, they ran into legal trouble. The separated churches could not get tax revenues and had to support themselves at the same time their members were still compelled to contribute taxes to the established churches. The Connecticut laws had the effect of reinforcing a natural tendency of many separatists to organize as Baptists in order to take advantage of the legal toleration afforded that sect in the colony. Separatism was marked in sparsely settled eastern Connecticut and in Plymouth Colony.

The Great Awakening may have added as many as fifty thousand church members and 150 new churches to New England; and the composition of the flocks was altered significantly. In the quiet era before the revival the churches had catered to women and to men of affairs. The Awakening brought into the churches a variety of new men—rural, youthful, middle-aged, phlegmatic, unchurched, Indian, Negro—and some of Pilgrim stock. In churches following the halfway plan, many became communicants and some "owned the covenant." This influx of males guided by the New Light resulted in increased power of the church in the community since in virtually all the congregations, only men could vote.

The majority of the clerical elite found the New Light satisfying and incidentally useful in regaining some of the clerical power that had ebbed away. Many of ministerial lineage, although quakerish in their own piety, identified with the New Light party, and encouraged or sympathized with the strong responses of the unchurched and the backsliders. This respected group aided the Awakening, believing that it was, by and large, in the tradition of mid-17th century Puritanism and the founding fathers. It accepted as allies the many converts who became New Light pastors. The newcomers were activists ready to work among the unchurched and on the frontier. They were different from the elite in at least two ways: they were not the sons of clergymen and they had graduated from college in their twenties, not in their teens. Yet these evangelical parvenus complemented the older, genteel ministers. Together, the two elements in the New Light ministry consolidated the newly pious among the Calvinistic population in the northern colonies.

The Great Awakening, after its initial phase, divided the colonies along rather sharp lines. To assert, however, that the upper classes of the towns were anti-revival, and the yeomen of the countryside were eager for the "good news" is an oversimplification. It is perhaps more accurate to agree with Jonathan Edwards that the inclination toward the New Light was a matter of "sensibility," a quality unevenly distributed in the community. The old stock of clerical lineage and the yeomen evidently had more of it than the rationalistic men in-between who had come to town to make their fortunes.

The Great Awakening as Subversion and Conspiracy

DAVID S. LOVEJOY

SOURCE: Reprinted by permission of the publisher from *Religious Enthusiasm in the New World* by David S. Lovejoy, pp. 195-201, 206-7, 208-10, 213-14, Cambridge, MA: Harvard University Press, Copyright © 1985 by the President and Fellows of Harvard College.

A widespread reason for opposition to the Great Awakening was the belief that it posed a threat to social and political stability, besides undermining orthodox religion. According to opponents, the enthusiasm of religious radicals was subversive of established institutions, and one had only to look at the course of history since the Reformation for evidence of the troubles it had caused in the past. To these opponents the Revival was openly vulnerable to such criticism, for its revivalists were a clear and present danger to society at large, as well as to the well being of Church and State.

Books, tracts, sermons, letters, and newspapers condemned the "New Way" and spoke of the ignorant, the rabble, the "admiring Vulgar," and Negroes, all of whom revival ministers and exhorters aroused and made restless and kept from their callings. Virginia Anglicans accused Samuel Davies of *"holding forth* on working days," contrary to the "religion of labour," and causing Virginians to neglect their duties in providing for their families. Davies certainly did not increase his popularity in either Williamsburg or London when he replied that his people spent less than half as many working days listening to him hold forth on the "Word of Life" as Anglicans were "obliged to keep holy according to their calendar." Davies's quip made little impression; not long afterwards the Virginia governor and council intervened in support of orthodoxy and by proclamation prohibited "all Itinerant Preachers whether New Light men, Moravians or Methodists" from preaching or holding meetings. Connecticut's government claimed that James Davenport's wild behavior had a "natural tendency to disturb and destroy the peace and order" of the colony. In response to these disturbing tendencies in this "Land of steady habit," the legislature, like Virginia's, put a stop to traveling preachers through severe laws to protect the good people of the colony and shelter the established Church.

That the "peace and order" of the American colonies generally were disrupted by the Awakening there can be no doubt. Itinerant preachers and lay exhorters provoked "Ministers against Ministers," church against church; they upset ecclesiastical harmony, tending to schism, confusion, and disorder. A telescoping of the conversion process and a mindless play upon the emotions of its victims distorted theology and misrepresented God's relationship to man. But the "wandering Spirit" of enthusiasm also set husbands against wives, children against parents, servants against masters; it made a shambles of that reverence traditionally due the "Aged and Honourable," precisely what had been said in both England and the colonies about George Fox and his Quakers. When George Whitefield preached from colony to colony, day laborers threw down their tools and mechanics shut up their shops to follow him, shirking their responsibilities and abandoning their families. The same was true of Gilbert Tennent. If only he could be persuaded to release the "Strollers" who tagged along after him and let them get back to their looms and lasts, their packs and grubbing hoes, the world might return to peace and quiet and an orderly face of affairs. Enthusiasm, charged Charles Chauncy of Boston in a tone reminiscent of the seventeenth century, always filled the church with confusion and the state with disorder. The boys at Harvard, despite all the holy talk, said another critic, received nothing but enthusiasm from Whitefield and Tennent, along with large doses of pride and a "Contempt of their Betters."

Enthusiasm harbored radical behavior which also challenged custom and convention, obedience and morality. The heart when brimful of Christ's Spirit often found itself perfect and sinless and free from control and discipline. To some in whom the Spirit dwelt this meant sexual license, and the Awakening had its share, recalling the immorality of the Anabaptists and Ranters and other antinomian perfectionists. Enthusiasm, wherever it appeared, supposedly betrayed strong tendencies to promiscuity and communal marriage; it tended to destroy property, Chauncy claimed, and not least "to make all things common, *wives* as well as *goods.*"

Jonathan Edwards several times warned of what he called a "counterfeit of love" to which the "wildest enthusiasts" were vulnerable. Love and affection within an isolated group often became indistinguishable from mere attraction between the sexes, which easily degenerated into the gross and criminal. The early Gnostics suffered this kind of decline, as did the Family of Love, and no doubt, Edwards suggested, it was this decay of affection which led to the community of women we hear so much about among several of the sects. The practice of "mutual embraces" and "holy kisses" could only turn "Christian love into unclean and brutish lust." Right there in Northampton, Massachusetts, at the height of the Awakening, Edwards saw the risk of unchaperoned young people in mixed company meeting for religious services. Although at the moment the youngsters' minds were taken up with a "sense of divine things," this would wear off sooner or later and offer plenty of opportunities to "consort together in couples for other than religious purposes." Who knows, soon some might attend such meetings merely for the sake of "company-keeping."

This all seems pretty chaste; it appears that Edwards was unnecessarily alarmed. But the history of enthusiasm, at least, warned him about "future dangers" set up by the Devil. Revival enthusiasm grew in some places to perfectionism and antinomianism, as it had countless times before. There were several instances of putting away wives and taking up with more fitting soul mates, a reordering thought permissible, given the dispensations which accompanied sinlessness—in the style of French Prophets and the Dutartres' holy household in South Carolina. Pregnancy aggravated one such couple's live-in arrangement in Cumberland, Rhode Island, although the father of the young lady (already married) earlier had explained that he saw no harm in his daughter's home away from home since she and her spiritual companion always "lay with a Bible between them." A similar occurrence shocked the people of Canterbury, Connecticut, when it ended in the tragic poisoning of a cast-off wife and two children. An accompanying difficulty in both these cases and one other, according to Isaac Backus, was that the orthodox clergy blamed the scandals on Separatists like Backus, who, they preached, were notorious for schism and faction and the destruction of communities. Outbursts of enthusiasm were associated historically with subversion of convention and morality, let alone Church and State, and the Great Awakening of the 1740s was no exception.

Religion and Slavery

A universal complaint against enthusiasts was that they undermined society. But just as the Great Awakening had its indigenous causes, so too a peculiarly American brand of subversion emerged from it which tended to disturb established colonial customs such as the enslavement of blacks and prejudicial treatment of Indians.

Since slavery's beginnings in seventeenth-century Virginia, there had been a question in many colonists' minds about converting Africans to Christianity. Supposedly it was a godly duty to do so, just as it was to spread the gospel among the Indians. But there was some hesitation, even refusal, among slave owners, who never could be sure how black salvation would affect outright ownership, and many suspected the worst in reaction and revenge. Conversion might be interpreted as a step in the direction of equality with whites, which was an absurdity and incongruous with the whole institution of slavery. King Charles II had encouraged the English Church and the gospel in the New World as a demonstration of his regard for American souls, black as well as white. But he blasted as gross "impiety" the slave owners' habit of prohibiting baptism "out of a mistaken opinion" that it made slaves *"ipso facto* free."

Quakers were among the first to take notice of the religious needs of black slaves. Teaching the enthusiastic principles of Quakerism to anyone was bad enough, but teaching them to slaves was doubly subversive. Several extremist women spread their heretical beliefs among blacks in Virginia as early as 1661. Because of opposition to their meetings, Quakers in York County began holding them in out-of-the-way places to which they invited neighboring blacks. That the governor and the county authority were convinced that something more than religion was at stake in these clandestine assemblies is clear from the oaths of supremacy and allegiance demanded from likely disturbers of the peace. Mary Chisman, wife of a prominent planter and already a Quaker, attended these meetings with her slaves, for which the government stepped in and charged her husband to prevent her, their slaves, and other members of the family from such suspect activities.

The ubiquitous William Edmundson found blacks at Barbados receptive to, even eager for, nurture of the inward light—so much so, in fact, that whites became apprehensive. A suspicious Anglican priest confronted Edmundson, and, besides damning Quakers as usual for blasphemy and heresy, he accused Edmundson and them also of making blacks Christians, a condition which could only teach them to rebel and cut the throats of whites. As the government was about to seize Edmundson for fomenting rebellion, he first, in good Quaker fashion, called upon the governor, who echoed the accusations. He told him that the only way to keep blacks *from* cutting white throats was to make them loving Christians; if they did rebel, it would be owing to the whites' denying them a "Knowledge of God and Christ Jesus," besides keeping them hungry.

Quakers would not become outright abolitionists for three or more generations, but they were well prepared to share their light with blacks, and blamed whites for preventing it. In the 1670s Alice Curwen sounded very much as George Whitefield would in the 1740s when she taught what Christianity would do for the souls of blacks, besides making them better slaves and less likely to cut anyone's throat. But when Curwen and her missionary friends actually preached Quaker truths to enslaved Negroes in Barbados, white society smelled racial equality and bloody rebellion.

In South Carolina, where blacks outnumbered whites by the early eighteenth century, masters were adamant almost to a man against including them in the gospel promise. They claimed slaves grew worse for being Christians despite laws which plainly disassociated baptism from freedom. Assembling blacks for worship was foolhardy they believed; it would give slaves a sense of their strength and tempt them to rebel despite bloody consequences, particularly on isolated plantations. Anyway, religious instruction took precious time away from work and would cut deeply into profits, besides drawing slaves away from their own gardens from which many fed and clothed themselves, freeing planters from the expense of both. These were strong reasons for not encouraging religion, although the SPG missionaries reported that planters would never admit the selfishness of the arguments. Slave owners insisted instead that Negroes were a wicked and stubborn race and therefore could never become true Christians. Several years later Samuel Davies, who spent a good deal of time with Virginia slaves as a Presbyterian minister, sensed a real need on the part of some of them for religious instruction and worship to relieve their habitual uneasiness. The chief trouble was the masters' neglect of them, as if their condition necessarily deprived them of immortal souls. Still other slaves, he found, looked to religion and particularly baptism as a step toward equality, an urge Davies learned to discourage. Apprehension remained among whites, however, lest religious education and eventual baptism become dangerously disruptive; converted blacks, who looked forward to a heavenly kingdom, might take steps to inherit an earthly one as well.

George Whitefield was no crusader against slavery. In fact, he was so far from attacking slavery as an institution that in 1741 he agreed to testify before Parliament in support of it in Georgia and later lamented that the trustees had deprived the colony of slave labor these many years. What a flourishing place it might have been, he commented, and think of the white lives their efforts would have saved! As late as 1751, when slaves became legal in Georgia, he regretted not possessing them at Bethesda, his orphanage—for their own good, of course—where he might make them comfortable and breed into their posterity the blessings of the Lord.

The moral issue of slavery aside, Whitefield did preach a God who was no respecter of color; therefore, his sincere desire to include blacks in his promotion of God's grace made many South Carolinians uneasy and got him off to a bad start in their colony. No emancipator, Whitefield pushed for better treatment of Negroes, chiefly proper care of their souls. Early in his colonial career he charged planters throughout the South with abusing their slaves and keeping them ignorant of Christianity. This he did in a series of published letters, and it did him no good either with the powers that be in South Carolina or the Anglican Commissary, Alexander Garden, who was already suspicious of Awakeners purely on religious grounds. Garden publicly accused Whitefield of "enthusiasm and pride," and lumped him with all the fanatics he could think of, including the Ranters, the Quakers, and the notorious French Prophets, as a bad lot. He claimed Whitefield's letters incited insurrection among blacks, and for these reasons by themselves, let alone enthusiasm, Whitefield was suspect. To compound the uneasiness, Whitefield talked of establishing a Negro school in the colony, and he would have, too, he reported, had he found the time and proper schoolmasters. When word spread later that he intended to convert "Whitefield's Folly," his orphan house at Bethesda, Georgia, into a college, his esteem in the South suffered badly. Because climate and isolation dictated severely against it, such a proposal suggested that there were devious designs, "some Venial Views," a "particular Scheme" up his sleeve, and southern planters wanted none of it.

What Whitefield had no time for, Hugh Bryan, a devoted follower, tried hard to accomplish. The story of Bryan bears out the truth of a revealing contemporary charge against Whitefield: that he "unhinged many *good sort* of people." Bryan was a well-to-do Carolina planter, officeholder, and Presbyterian. With Whitefield's advice and the help of his wife and brother he resolved to establish a school for blacks on his own plantation. But several events occurred which cast some doubt on Bryan's usefulness to Whitefield's crusade. As a result of his conversion and a measure of his zeal, he boldly attacked the Anglican priests in South Carolina, claiming their churches woefully neglected Christian duty to the colonists there. Full of "Decrees and Cannons," wrote Bryan, the orthodox clergy persecuted Christ's faithful ministers—meaning revival preachers—for not conforming, while "they themselves break their cannons every Day." Whitefield beamed approval and helped to see Bryan's charges in pamphlet form through Peter Timothy's press at Charlestown in January 1741. This was too much for Commissary Garden, whose shoddy treatment of Whitefield was obvious in Bryan's transparent indictment. The Commissary slapped a libel suit on all three—author, printer, and reverend agent—which detained Whitefield in South Carolina for some time, where he played the martyr and indulged himself in a "scene of suffering," delighted to call it "persecution." Whitefield posted bond, but the affair soon blew over when an appeal to England eventually stopped the proceedings.

Meanwhile, Bryan's wife died, with a testimony to Whitefield on her lips. Whether her death unstrung Bryan or whether too much of Whitefield's enthusiasm rubbed off on him would be difficult to determine. Under guidance of the Spirit, Bryan soon began prophesying the fiery destruction of Charlestown by blacks and their violent escape from slavery to freedom. Rumors spread quickly that he was holding encampments in Saint Helena's parish surrounded by "all sorts of people," most of them blacks in large numbers, gathered under the pretext of worship. What is surprising is how calmly the government seemed to take these wild claims, particularly since they followed by less than three years the notorious Stono Rebellion in South Carolina, which was put down only after the killing of forty blacks and half as many whites. Still, lest the black majority get wind of Bryan's "enthusiastic Prophecies," the government issued a warrant for his arrest. By this time he had recanted, calling the whole thing a delusion of the Devil rather than the bidding of the Holy Spirit, and begged forgiveness. But before his abrupt change of mind, he had lived for a time barefoot in the wilderness where the Spirit bade him attempt several miracles, including a smiting of the river waters that they might divide and let him pass. Undaunted after a thorough soaking, he foretold his own immediate death, and when that fizzled, too, he was persuaded to go home and retire from the prophesying business, shamefully confessing his delusion.

Great Awakening revivalists were not protoabolitionists. But like Whitefield they prayed and preached for the conversion of black slaves, who, if they could not win freedom, might win salvation. Most Carolinians, however, were convinced that slavery and religion, most of all enthusiasm, did not mix. Although they blamed Whitefield for Bryan's ominous fanaticism, like their government they came eventually to take the crisis in stride, and before long got a good laugh out of the outrageous episode.

Not so funny was the case of Anne Le Bresseur, a "Widow Gentlewoman of considerable Fortune" and a "prime Disciple of Mr. Whitefield's." Mme. Le Bresseur had difficulty settling down in a Charlestown communion once Whitefield began preaching there, and not many weeks after Hugh Bryan confessed his delusion, she shot herself with a brace of pistols. Just before her death a couple of hours later, she made clear her absolute assurance of salvation and her longing to enter the "blessed mansions which she knew were prepared for her." Whitefield, indeed, "unhinged many *good sort* of people," besides a good many others. . . .

Moravians and Indians

War with Spain had heightened suspicions about the interrelatedness of the Great Awakening, slave revolt, and Catholic intrigue. During the war with France, which began in 1744, George Whitefield's revivalists, although still suspect, were joined by Count Ludwig Zinzendorf's Moravians, who doggedly strove to share their piety and enthusiasm with American Indians. We left a handful of United Brethren at the Forks of the Delaware, where they had purchased Nazareth from George Whitefield in 1740. As their numbers increased under the aegis of Count Zinzendorf, they went on to settle nearby Bethlehem and the surrounding countryside. Unlike the Labadists before them, who pretty much forgot an original intention to Christianize the Indians, the Moravians immediately seized the opportunity, and their missions, along with their music, have become historically two of their most memorable legacies. Bringing God to the Indians was not an easy task, as John Wesley had learned to his surprise in Georgia. Moravian missionaries, unlike the earlier Rosicrucians outside Philadelphia, were not an educated cadre but ordinary people—farmers, mechanics, and artisans—whose religious zeal, which had brought them to the colonies in the first place, was reflected in their devoted missionary work. They taught Christianity in German, sometimes through interpreters, and their only text was the Bible. Very few learned the Indian languages. . . .

American colonists were divided in their opinions about Moravians. In fact, they were not unanimous in the way they viewed the increasing German population. As early as 1727 the Pennsylvania Council discussed the influx of Germans and resolved to require of them an oath of allegiance in the future. Complaints centered around their burgeoning numbers, their ignorance of the English language and laws, and their settling in communities distinct from Pennsylvania's other colonists. All of these posed questions of security in a colonial society and set a lot of people thinking. The imminence of war intensified such feelings, as did factional politics, and Benjamin Franklin used the Germans for purposes of propaganda in both instances to their disadvantage. Still, their numbers increased, and by the time of the American Revolution there may have been as many as 150,000 colonists of German origin in British America.

Granted the Moravians were a tiny part of these; but not only were they Germans, or adopted Germans; they were pietists and enthusiasts. There was plenty of dissatisfaction with them on religious grounds alone. The Maryland Scot Dr. Alexander Hamilton, whose grand tour took him through several colonies in 1744, came across a number of Moravians in both New Jersey and the Hudson River Valley and dubbed them a "wild, fanatick sect." He resented their living in common, "men and women mixed," in great barns or houses where they sleep, eat, drink, and "preach and howl." It was all started by that "German enthusiast," Count Zinzendorf, and he and they, like all enthusiasts, thought their "religion of the Lamb" to be the only true religion. But maybe they were right, Hamilton concluded, insofar as some, no doubt, were "wolves in sheep's clothing."

George Whitefield disengaged himself from the Moravians in 1740 over their loose doctrine of election and the presumption of perfection, after a short honeymoon celebrated in London, Georgia, and at the Forks of the Delaware. Gilbert Tennent of Pennsylvania and New Jersey had counted largely on Moravians for the success of his revivals, but when the zeal of the Awakening slackened, he backed off, took a sober look at the damage enthusiasm and fanaticism had done to evangelical Protestantism, and turned on the Moravians as scapegoats, damning them as confused and deluded and dangerous. Whitefield believed Tennent was unnecessarily severe in his condemnation of the Brethren and suggested that maybe some of Tennent's own "wild fire" was mixed with the sacred zeal which came only from God. Both revivalists agreed, however, that Moravian beliefs were mistaken, although Whitefield described himself as more temperate in his criticism than Tennent; in fact, in a fit of messianism, he compared himself to Jesus, who "sees all the quarrels . . . of His children, and yet bears with, and loves them still"—even Moravians.

As if to deflect attention from his own extravagances, which he regretted, Gilbert Tennent in 1743 lit into the Moravians with a fury, sounding very much like

Charles Chauncy against New Lights in New England. He resented their endeavors to conceal real opinions and distrusted their pretensions to simplicity. He questioned the ancient history of the sect and suggested strongly that its "whole system" was of recent origin, framed in 1725 at Count Zinzendorf's home in Saxony. He scoffed at their beliefs in the assurance of salvation and "sinless perfection." Their authoritarianism in church and society, their regulation of marriage, their unhealthy grip on children, and surveillance of converts all impinged, he said, on religious and civil liberty. They were worse than the Labadists in their "Mixture of many Errors." To await the voice of the Lord, like Quakers, only encouraged enthusiasm, and Zinzendorf's insistence that the elders and ministers of the church spoke only what "Christ works in them" smacked of "Immediate Inspiration." Not to be subject to the law, as the Count described his ministers, was rank antinomianism. And on top of this, they scorned learning and slighted human reason. Their beliefs and carryings on, Tennent concluded, were "Nonsense, Contradictions, and mysterious Gibberish."

Charles Chauncy in Boston had little sympathy for either Gilbert Tennent or the Moravians. At the peak of the Awakening, Chauncy claimed Tennent had welcomed their swelling numbers and succeeded in confusing them as well as other victims of the Revival. Now that he had changed his mind, said Chauncy, becoming apprehensive "lest the Churches should be undone with a *Spirit of Enthusiasm,"* he cut himself off from the Moravians and then blamed them for all the trouble. By 1743 both Whitefield and Tennent, two of the Awakening's leading figures, had turned their backs on the United Brethren, and the issue ironically was enthusiasm. Evangelical piety could get out of hand, they now confessed; when it did, it easily spilled over into enthusiasm, as it had with the Moravians, and as such it was subversive of true religion. These German pietists, then, were suspicious characters, and true believers ought to be wary of their "Unreasonableness, anti-evangelical, and licentious Religion." There were probably many people besides Charles Chauncy who were convinced that the pot was calling the kettle black.

Suspect in religion by both Old and New Lights, Moravians became objects of even greater suspicion when war broke out with France in 1744. New Yorkers found all matter of reasons for driving their missionaries out of the colony. The government dragged several to Manhattan for questioning. By what right did they preach to the Indians without the governor's leave? Who called them to the ministry? Why did they refuse to take oaths of allegiance? Some of their answers hardly satisfied a colony government whose geography seemed to invite French invasion from the north and whose people believed it was imminent. It was the "Saviours pleasure he should be a Minister," claimed one, while another confessed guilelessly that he had no idea whether the Indians wanted teachers, but he did know "that all the Earth was to be Subject to the Lord," and so he did his part. Still another claimed his commission to preach came from the Moravians at Bethlehem, and all of them, of course, refused oaths as contrary to the principles of their church. Public resentment against foreign-speaking busybodies, who consorted with the

Indians in out-of-the-way places, led to claims against their land and tales of complicity with the French, even Jesuit relations. . . .

. . . By 1751, after unsuccessfully trying to borrow or rent an empty church from some of the Lutherans, they [Moravians] felt sufficiently at home to build their own and solicited the "Fatherly Care and Protection" of the governor. Parliament played a role in changing attitudes; after scrutiny of its policy toward Moravians, it encouraged more of them to settle in the colonies and eased their lot by exempting them from taking oaths and bearing arms—the result of plenty of *"intrigue* and snaky crookedness," according to reports in Philadelphia. The idea that they were sympathetic to France and the warring Indians faded during the early skirmishes of the Seven Years' War, when hostile Indians fell upon one of their Pennsylvania missions at Gnädenhut and killed most of the whites there. Benjamin Franklin changed his mind, too, particularly after a visit to Bethlehem in 1755, where he found them well armed and where they entertained him splendidly with a capital sermon, "good musick, the organ being accompanied with violins, hautboys, flutes, clarinets, etc" and straightforward answers to his prying questions about religious practices, living arrangements, and marriage customs. They were all "very kind to me," he later recorded in the *Autobiography.* Although he was well aware that their use of firearms, if only for defensive purposes, was really a compromise of religious principles, he approved of it and later congratulated them for their helpful contributions during the war with France. Times had changed. The Awakening had spent its momentum, and its enthusiasm dampened. Moravians were behaving more like ordinary colonists, arming and being warred upon, and winning the praise of Benjamin Franklin. No subversion there.

But New Yorkers had looked very differently upon revivalists and Moravians in the 1740s. With Whitefield loose, behaving like Jesus, attracting thousands of crazy-acting converts, encouraging Negroes north and south, threatening to educate and convert them, and doing all these things on the eve of a Negro revolt which tore the city apart during a war with Catholic Spain, no wonder the government of New York became suspicious. And then this same government believed it was subject to similar subversion when the Moravians, already friendly with Whitefield and sharing his enthusiasm, took over his Negro academy, settled it and the neighborhood with several hundred fanatical foreigners like themselves, and then sent out their most zealous devotees to build missions where they taught Jesus and antinomianism and Christian unity to the Indians. In so doing they ignored established authorities, local churches, colonial boundaries, acts of naturalizaton, racial barriers, and colony laws, to say nothing of orthodox Protestantism. And all this just as Britain went to war with France and fought part of it in the New World very close to home.

Bad enough was these enthusiasts' foolishness about grace and conversion, about the immanent Spirit of Christ. But enthusiasm was explosive when it threatened to stir up black slaves to rebellion and made half-baked Christians out of Indians during a French war, besides instilling in both all manner of notions contrary to the settled order of things and their proper places within a white society. Enthusiasm was not just subversive; it courted revolution, and it ought to be suppressed wherever it emerged.

Women and Revivalism:
The Puritan and Wesleyan Traditions
MARTHA T. BLAUVELT and ROSEMARY SKINNER KELLER

SOURCE: Excerpts from *Women and Religion in America*, volume 2, *The Colonial and Revolutionary Periods* by Rosemary Radford Ruether. Copyright © 1983 by Rosemary R. Ruether and Rosemary S. Keller. Reprinted by permission of HarperCollins Publishers, Inc.

The story of the Great Awakening and the origins of evangelicalism in early America has traditionally focused on two men, Jonathan Edwards and George Whitefield. Edwards revitalized Puritanism by restoring private experience to the center of religious faith, and Whitefield, as an Anglican follower of John Wesley, introduced American colonists to the Wesleyan strain of piety. Together, they made evangelicalism—the theological emphasis on conversion as essential to salvation—the dominant characteristic of eighteenth-century religion.

Yet however important Edwards and Whitefield were to religion, as men they are not entirely appropriate representatives of early American evangelicalism. Colonial revivalism was significant not only in bringing a great theologian and "field preacher" to prominence, but in expanding women's religious activities. That expansion was more dramatic in the Wesleyan tradition than in the Puritan, but in both cases evangelicalism was women's chief vehicle in enlarging their religious sphere.

[The following] explores how Puritan women, such as Sarah Goodhue, Deborah Prince, and Sarah Osborn—at first privately and tentatively, then publicly and more confidently—worked to spread the evangelical tenets of their faith. It shows women in the more activist Wesleyan tradition, such as Barbara Heck and Selina, Countess of Huntingdon, organizing Methodist societies, establishing chapels and seminaries for training Methodist preachers, directing missions, and performing many of the functions of evangelical ministers. The experience of the Spirit within enabled these women to pursue such activities despite the protests of male clerics who could not envision the radical implications of evangelicalism. In this sense colonial revivalism witnessed an awakening of women's power as well as of religion and prepared the way for women's much wider participation in evangelicalism in the nineteenth century.

Puritan Evangelicalism
Puritanism began as a "revival" in the sense that the movement sought to revitalize and purify English Protestantism. Yet, as Rosemary Keller has shown, the Anne Hutchinson affair and the related experience of women in other New England towns quickly curtailed Puritanism's radical implications for women. The Hutchinson affair had implications for men as well: it intensified clerical resent-

ment against all challenges to authority. Puritan emphasis on the "new birth" was not to mean the overthrow of external authority by anyone, male or female. Although laymen maintained their power in secular matters, by the 1650s they found themselves silenced within many churches: ministers prevented them from asking questions after sermons and lectures, participating in disciplinary cases, or relating their own spiritual experiences before the church. The Hutchinson affair thus limited laymen's power as well as women's. Throughout colonial history, male and female lay authority would rise and fall together, as male laity attempted to retrieve power from ministers and women tried to share it with laymen. For both sexes, that rise and fall coincided with periods of revival and declension.

As lay ecclesiastical authority declined, fewer and fewer men joined New England churches, and by the late seventeenth century females dominated church membership rolls. In any case, their life experience made women more likely than men to experience conversion. As historian Gerald Moran has shown, Puritan theology required the sinner to admit total helplessness, to give up all dependence on self. Upon marriage, New England women underwent just such an experience: submission to their husbands and the prospect of death in childbirth reminded them of their lowliness and weakness. Men, in contrast, gained authority through marriage and found it correspondingly difficult to experience the humiliation necessary to conversion. As a result, the vast majority of seventeenth-century Puritan converts were married women, such as Mrs. Elizabeth White.

During the late seventeenth century, Puritanism's evangelical tradition began to find expression in distinct religious revivals. The political difficulties and Indian threats of the 1670s and 1680s encouraged many New Englanders to turn to God. In these revivals, men increased their representation in Puritan churches, but women did not lose their numerical advantage. What part women played in these revivals is obscure: little is known about their origins and effects. But these revivals mark the beginning of a new period in Puritan evangelicalism: thereafter, certain New England towns experienced periodic revivals as each generation came of age. These local revivals provided a forum for female religious activity and would, in time, merge with the First Awakening.

The one minimal evangelical role open to women in the late seventeenth century was preaching within the private circle. Anticipating death in childbirth, Sarah Whipple Goodhue wrote a *Valedictory* in 1681 that illustrates the limited religious roles women then had. Goodhue spoke as an evangelist confident of her own election and authority; she urged her "Children, neighbours and friends" to "get a part and portion in the Lord Jesus Christ." It is clear . . . that female religious meetings did not totally disappear after Anne Hutchinson's banishment. What activities such "private Societ[ies]" engaged in is unclear, but given the sensitivity of ministers to male infringement on their authority, such meetings must have confined themselves to fairly innocuous matters. That they met at all, however, suggests that women had developed a means to activism and sisterhood.

During most of the seventeenth century, women received little public acknowledgment of their piety. Significantly, neither Sarah Goodhue's *Valedictory* nor Elizabeth White's conversion account were published until the eighteenth century. Beginning in the 1690s, however, such ministers as Cotton Mather began to praise female piety in funeral sermons and elegies. By 1730, 40 percent of New England's extant funeral sermons were about women. These sermons typically praised women who converted early, prayed and fasted, went to church faithfully, read the Scriptures, submitted to God's will, and managed their households well.

Puritan ministers accorded women this public attention for several reasons. First, they felt compelled to recognize a change in reality: that there were a great many pious women in New England—indeed, that more women than men were pious. As Mather observed, "Tho' both *Sexes,* be thro the Marvellous Providence of our God Born into the World, in pretty AEqual Numbers, yet, in the Female, there seem to be the Larger Numbers, of them that are *Born Again,* and brought into the Kingdom of God." In trying to explain this, Mather developed a new understanding of the fall and of women's nature. He interpreted Eve's seduction, which men had conventionally viewed as evidence of women's evil and weakness, as a blessing in disguise. The childbirth women experienced as Eve's punishment inclined them to religion: "the Dubious Hazards of their Lives in their Appointed Sorrows, drive them the more frequently, & the more fervently to commit themselves into the Hands of their Only Saviour." Mather used Eve to exalt woman rather than to debase her, and in so doing he vastly upgraded the image of both Eve and woman.

But ministers may well have meant to do more than acknowledge a statistical change in church membership. During the last half of the seventeenth century, church membership declined in proportion to New England's population. At the same time, those few church members were being drawn from the less socially significant part of the population, the female half. In eulogizing women, ministers tried in effect to enhance the worth of that portion of their constituency that showed continued growth. At the same time, ministers hoped to reach the coming generation, especially New England's sons, through women. In short, ministers praised women in order to retrieve clerical authority.

Although turn-of-the-century ministers granted women unprecedented public recognition, they did not accord them qualities superior to those of men, as they would do in the nineteenth century. The premise of eighteenth-century sermons was that male and female natures were equally depraved; women were more religious than men because their *experiences* were different, not their natures. Women, such sermons insisted, were as good as men, not better. But the fact that ministers had to argue spiritual equality, and the care with which they cited example upon example of female virtue, suggests that many New Englanders needed convincing. The frequent reprinting of English misogynist literature throughout the eighteenth century suggests that clergymen had to deal with a still popular image of woman as the seductive Eve. Such tracts as Edward Ward's *Female Policy Detected: or the Arts of a Designing Woman* countered sermons on "The Good Works of a Vertuous Woman" and left colonists with an ambivalent attitude toward women that persisted throughout the colonial period. The most important change between 1700 and the Revolution lay not in ideology, but in activity. And the movement that unleashed that activity was the First Awakening. . . .

The most important expression of that activism was the rise of lay power. Laity not only attacked unregenerate ministers, but took over their clerical functions as well. Convinced that piety rather than learning qualified ministers, laymen began to preach. This resurgence of male lay activism and the Awakening's fervor emboldened women too, permitting them to criticize ministers openly. It also allowed them to perform some clerical functions—always excepting preaching. While Sarah Goodhue had offered religious advice only to her "Children, neighbours and friends," the Awakening's female converts advised total strangers. And a few, such as Sarah Osborn of Newport, publicly displayed doctrinal knowledge in evangelical tracts; her *Nature, Certainty and Evidence of true Christianity* (1755) evinced an erudition equal to many ministers. Women had begun to speak for themselves and no longer relied on male ministers for posthumous praise. Women also founded prayer societies, which gave their activities an organized basis. Although the Awakening did not put ministers, laymen, and women on the same level, it at least expanded the functions of laymen and women and helped close the gap between laity and clergy.

In judging the unregenerate and in taking on clerical roles, women gained public religious functions. Before, their religious roles had been largely private: they gave spiritual advice within the home and experienced conversion "in the closet." But during the Awakening, conversion became a dramatic, public event. Women experienced "violent fits" and their cries might be heard far beyond the confines of their homes. As the revival rendered religiosity public and emotional, it drew women into the public sphere.

Women acted independently as well as publicly during the Awakening. Many believed that the Spirit within directed them to attack sinners, separate from established churches, and advise others on religion. A few women transferred this spiritual independence to everyday life. For example, when Hannah Harkum's anti-evangelical parents turned her out, she became a professional seamstress and developed the business acumen that made her an equal partner in her later marriage.

These changes in women's religious functions were important, but they should not be exaggerated. Though women may have left the private religious realm somewhat, they by no means attained the prominence of even minor male evangelists. Thomas Prince's *Christian History*, which publicized virtually every revival in the Awakening, scarcely mentions women. And while Whitefield periodically noted women's activities in his popular *Journals*, most of his entries concerned his own evangelical gifts. No woman during the Awakening achieved the fame of Anne Hutchinson in the seventeenth century. And women who acted publicly or independently often had to defend themselves. Sarah Osborn of Newport was a devout, middle-aged, married schoolteacher. When she allowed her *Nature, Certainty and Evidence of true Christianity* to be published, however, she felt obliged to include an apologetic note on the title page: "Tho this *Letter* was Wrote in great *privacy* from *one Friend* to *another*, yet on representing that by allowing it to be *Printed*, it would probably reach *to many others in the like afflicted case,* and by the Grace of God be *very helpful to them,* the *Writer* was at length prevailed on to suffer it—provided her Name and Place of abode remained concealed." Similarly, when in 1766 and 1767 Osborn found hundreds pressing into her home for weekly religious meetings, she felt compelled to defend her behavior in an eight-page letter to a male critic.

Wesleyan Evangelicalism

John Wesley was introduced to the ministry of evangelical women through his mother, Susannah, and particularly through an experience of hers similar to that of Sarah Osborn. Wesley's father, Samuel, a clergyman in the Church of England, was away from home for an extended meeting of the governing body of the church in 1712. Susannah wrote Samuel in defense of the prayer meetings that she held in their home on Sunday evenings, meetings that drew as many as two hundred people, so that many had to be turned away "for want of room to stand."

Refuting charges that she was diverting people from the Sunday morning service, Susannah explained her own spiritual awakening: "At last it came into my mind, Though I am not a man, nor a minister, yet if my heart were sincerely devoted to God, and I was inspired with a true zeal for His glory, I might do something more than I do. I thought I might pray more for them, and might speak to those with whom I converse with more warmth of affection." Susannah claimed that the power of the Holy Spirit had been given directly to her and that she was actively responding with her personal commitment to service.

John Wesley was so moved by his mother's account of her role as an evangelist that he included her letter in his journal on the day of her death. Introducing the letter, which Susannah had written to Samuel when John was only nine years old, he stated that "even she [as well as her father and grandfather, her husband, and her three sons] had been, in her measure and degree, a preacher of righteousness."

Susannah's experience raised an issue that would remain central for generations to come as women in the evangelical tradition continued to expand their ministries: how far could a proper woman extend her evangelical work into the public sphere? Susannah did not consider preaching sermons which she would write herself, but she questioned whether "because of my sex it is proper for me to present the prayers of the people of God." Clearly, the people had been responding eagerly to the active presence of God they experienced through her: "Last Sunday I would fain have dismissed them before prayers; but they begged so earnestly to stay, I durst not deny them."

While both Puritans and Wesleyans shared "generic marks of Evangelicalism," theological distinctions within the two traditions made Wesleyans, from the earliest days of the movement, more open than Puritans to the public ministries of women. These "generic marks" have been defined by Donald Mathews as belief that the Christian life is essentially a personal relationship with God in Christ, established through the direct action of the Holy Spirit, an action which elicits in the believer a profoundly emotional conversion experience. This existential crisis, the *New Birth,* as Evangelicals called it, ushers the convert into a life of holiness characterized by religious devotion, moral discipline, and missionary zeal.

The focal point of one's life, then, was conversion. New birth was preceded by a complete breakdown of personal pride and self-possession and resulted in a new life of disciplined holiness centered in devotion and service to God in Christ.

Both the Calvinistic and Arminian heritages of the evangelical movement stressed the primacy of God's grace as the context within which persons make decisions. However, Puritans, in the Calvinistic tradition, continued to emphasize that the individual's role in the work of salvation was one of personal passivity and that humans could do nothing to affect God's determination of who was chosen. Methodists, on the other hand, stressed freedom of the will from their Arminian roots and rejected the Calvinistic God who left the sinner without assurance of salvation all his life while demanding strict obedience to an impossible ethic. Methodist doctrine allowed for the real possibility of backsliding and offered an endless number of chances to receive God's grace. Wesley's followers endeavored to present God's sovereign grace and human free will not as a paradox, but as complementary parts of the conversion experience. In actual practice, the emphasis was resolved in favor of commonsense belief in the ability to repent and to commit one's self to Christ.

While such theological differences were real, the key distinction, according to Mathews, was the Puritan emphasis on the necessity of proper doctrinal identification and self-definition, in contrast to the Methodist belief that the fruits of the committed life were more important than prolonged efforts of self-definition. Methodists were concerned to be "out and about," reforming the nation and saving the world. The key ideological distinction was that the Puritans placed theological definition at the center while Methodists avoided it.

A logical implication for evangelical women in both the Puritan and the Wesleyan traditions was that the Holy Spirit was given indiscriminately to men and women alike and that the chosen ones could not be identified by human eyes. Evangelical Puritan women, however, spent more time and energy in discerning the fine points and justifications of their new life in Christ. The more activist emphasis in Methodism resulted in an affirmation of their witnesses, both private and public, based on the criterion that God was "owning their ministry," that God was using women as agents of salvation.

John Wesley affirmed the spiritual independence of women from the time of his earliest experiences in ministry. He spent only two years in America, on an unproductive evangelical mission to Georgia (1736-1738) during the same period in which Edwards's work in Northampton was causing the first stirrings of the Great Awakening in New England. In Georgia, Wesley became involved in a personal and pastoral relationship with Sophy Hopkey, which he bungled. Even so, significant dimensions of his attitude toward women were already emerging in these early days of his ministry. According to Alan Hayes, Wesley affirmed Hopkey's spiritual independence from her husband, counseling her that she must make her own decisions regarding observance of fasts and attendance at dawn services and discussion groups. Hopkey told Wesley that her husband did not approve of his directing her spiritual life and that she should only obey her husband. Wesley responded with this principle: "In things of an indifferent nature you cannot be too obedient to your husband, but if his will should be contrary to the will of God, you are to obey God rather than man."

His affirmation of the public ministry of women developed after Wesley returned to England where he worked closely with women in the Methodist movement throughout the latter half of the eighteenth century. His advocacy of women's public witness expanded as he observed their effectiveness in winning souls to Christ. As Earl Kent Brown's study shows, "Mr. Wesley's attitude began to liberalize under the impact of the evangelical success of several women friends. He was a pragmatist when it came to institutions through which the gospel was spread. What impressed him was that God was blessing the women's work with a harvest of souls .... God was 'owning' their ministry." While he never formally appointed a woman to the itinerating ministry, several women actually "traveled the connection," journeying hundreds and thousands of miles throughout England to bear witness and to preach to groups of all size. . . .

As was true of evangelical women in the Puritan tradition, most Wesleyan women still performed their spiritual functions within their own homes. The belief that piety was rooted in woman's nature, which was fostered by the Great Awakening, flowered in late eighteenth-century Wesleyanism. The religious influence of female followers on their husbands and children gave women in the colonies their first evangelical roles and became the most immediate influence on early nineteenth-century Wesleyan women as well. . . .

Conclusion

When compared to the activities of nineteenth-century evangelical women, the efforts of women in the First Awakening and in the early Wesleyan movement in America seem minor. Both Puritan and Wesleyan women ran prayer meetings, but most eighteenth-century women dared to pray only before members of their own sex. Sarah Osborn and Prudence Gough, who held "mixed" meetings in their own homes, were rare exceptions. Even then Osborn and Gough prayed only before boys and black men and were careful not to assume a position of superiority over any white men who attended. "Mixed" prayer meetings would not become common for another hundred years. And unlike the nineteenth-century prayer societies, these eighteenth-century meetings rarely stimulated local revivals; colonial revivals seem to have occurred only in response to male preaching. Eighteenth-century evangelicalism produced no equivalents of Maggie Van Cott, Phoebe Palmer, and Amanda Berry Smith, who would become renowned evangelists and lead revivals throughout the world in the next century through the sanction of Methodism and the Holiness movement.

Eighteenth-century female evangelism was so limited largely because of ideological restraints. Women lacked a "Cult of True Womanhood" to give them confidence in female moral superiority and to unite them in a holy sisterhood. Further, they were not yet able to appropriate the implications of the Declaration of Independence—that they, too, had been endowed by their Creator with certain unalienable rights through the birthright of equality.

Few people, regardless of sex, accepted women's right to religious authority. By the time of the First Awakening, the image of woman as Eve had faded, but was still strong enough to undermine female religious authority. The general social and political confusion that accompanied the Awakening made the prospect of a sexual reordering seem more frightening. And even the more positive views of women were no less limiting to female evangelicalism. Jonathan Edwards suggested the constraints of the more "enlightened" eighteenth-century view of women. Like Cotton Mather, Edwards did not attribute evil, seductive, Eve-like qualities to women, but he clearly expected women to continue Eve's subordination. Edwards allowed reason to men and affections to women, whom God had made "weaker, more soft and tender, more fearful, and more affectionate, as a fit object of [men's] generous protection and defense." This was a feminine ideal that notably lacked the vigor of Mather's "Amazons of Zion." When Edwards criticized women who were "rugged, daring and presumptuous," he denied them the characteristics that New Light Protestants demanded in their clergy. His definition of women, in effect, removed them from evangelical leadership and rendered them inconsequential. The most far-reaching of his views regarding women was that men were reasonable and women affectionate as a result of distinct differences in their natures determined by God. This argument became the primary justification for the separation of men's and women's functions into public and private spheres during the nineteenth century.

The Great Awakening caused few immediate changes in women's lives, but it set in motion trends that would expand women's evangelical role in the next century. Despite the furor over the Awakening's excesses, its success in increasing church membership irrevocably committed Calvinist denominations to evangelicalism. The revival became so important to church growth that, by the nineteenth century, many ministers were willing to allow women a major role in revival creation; the desire for revivals would overcome social conventions. The Awakening also affected women's place in American ideology by exalting "Heart." "Heart religion"—that religion grounded in the affections—was the eighteenth-century synonym for evangelicalism. In the 1600s, "Heart" had been associated with women in a largely negative way: men's rationality made them strong, while women's emotionalism made them at best weak and at worst seductively evil. However, the Awakening gave "Heart" both a positive connotation and a central place in American culture, laying the foundation for women's evangelical triumph in the nineteenth century.

A study of nineteenth-century evangelicalism indicates that the Wesleyan movement proved the most liberating religious tradition for women in all areas of religious expression—preaching, missionary and missionary society organizations, deaconess societies, and social reform. Yet one must not minimize the struggles with established authorities that accompanied women's entrance into these fields.

Anne Hutchinson had made the same claim to spiritual authority—that the Holy Spirit was given to her directly and personally—which the circle of "Women in Mr. Wesley's Methodism" made in eighteenth-century England. Their legacy was carried through Selina Hastings, who moved into a "career" in social reform in mid-life, and Barbara Heck who broke up a game of cards, threw the cards into the fire, and summoned her cousin with these words: "Philip, you must preach to us, or we shall all go to hell, and God will require our blood at your hands." Nineteenth-century evangelical women were distinguished because they held word and action in essential unity. Anne Hutchinson, Selina Hastings, and Barbara Heck were their spiritual foremothers.

Questions for Reflection and Discussion

1. How do the documents present a variety of opinions about the consequences of the Great Awakening?

2. How does Cedric Cowing describe the tension between revelation (sacred) and reason (secular) during the Great Awakening?

3. According to David Lovejoy, the Great Awakening acted as a subversive, conspiratorial force. What evidence does he provide in support of this argument?

4. Martha Blauvelt and Rosemary Skinner Keller contend that the Great Awakening worked to make evangelicalism more inclusive for women. On what do they base this contention?

5. Which of the four tensions in American religion was (were) present during the Great Awakening?

Additional Readings

Bumsted, J.M and John E. Van de Wetering. *What Must I Do to be Saved? The Great Awakening in Colonial America.* Hinsdale, IL: Dryden Press, 1976.

Bushman, Richard. *The Great Awakening: Documents on the Revival of Religion, 1740-1745.* Reprint ed. Chapel Hill: University of North Carolina Press, 1989.

Butler, Jon. "Enthusiasm Described and Decried: The Great Awakening as Interpretive Fiction." *Journal of American History* 69 (1982-83): 305-325.

Cowing, Cedric B. *The Great Awakening and the American Revolution: Colonial Thought in the 18th Century.* Chicago: Rand McNally, 1971.

Gaustad, Edwin A. *The Great Awakening in New England.* San Francisco: Harper and Row, 1957.

Gewehr, Wesley M. *The Great Awakening in Virginia, 1740-1790.* Durham, NC: Duke University Press, 1930.

Goen, Clarence C. *Revivalism and Separatism in New England: Congregationalists and Separate Baptists in the Great Awakening.* New Haven: Yale University Press, 1962.

Heimert, Alan E. *Religion and the American Mind from the Great Awakening to the Revolution.* Cambridge: Harvard University Press, 1966.

Heimert, Alan and Perry Miller, eds. *The Great Awakening: Documents Illustrating the Crisis and Its Consequences.* Indianapolis, IN: Bobbs-Merrill, 1967.

Lambert, Frank. *Inventing the "Great Awakening".* Princeton, NJ: Princeton University Press, 1999.

Lovejoy, David. *Religious Enthusiasm in the New World: Heresy to Revolution.* Cambridge: Harvard University Press, 1985.

Maxson, Charles H. *The Great Awakening in the Middle Colonies.* Magnolia, MA: Peter Smith, 1990.

Nissenbaum, Stephen. *The Great Awakening at Yale College.* Belmont, CA: Wadsworth Publishing Company, 1972.

Stout, Harry S. *The New England Soul: Preaching and Religious Culture in Colonial New England.* New York: Oxford University Press, 1986.

_____. *The Divine Dramatist: George Whitefield and the Rise of Modern Evangelicalism.* Grand Rapids, Mich.: William B. Eerdmans, 1991.

Chapter 4

Little did John Winthrop know that his reference to Puritan New England as "a city upon a hill" would set into motion forces that would eventually contribute to the birth of a new nation. "The Lord will be our God, and delight to dwell among us as His own people [as He did among Israel]," he opined, "and will command a blessing upon us in all our ways,

Religious America in the American Revolution

Issue

How religious was the American revolution?

so that we shall see much more of His wisdom, power, goodness, and truth, than formerly we have been acquainted with."

This identifying of the American colonies with Israel continued unbroken for the next century and a half. According to Charles Chauncy of Boston on the eve of the American Revolution, as the founding fathers of New England had been rescued by God from tyrannical England many years after God had saved his people from Egypt and delivered them to their Promised Land, so now New England had been relieved from the oppressive Stamp Act, even as the Jews had been protected from the destruction of Ahaseurus. To reassure his audience of this in 1770, he contended that "perhaps, there are no people, now dwelling on the face of the earth, who may, with greater pertinency, adopt the language of king David, and say, 'our fathers trusted in thee; they trusted, and thou didst deliver them.'"

The blending of the secular and the sacred, however, often produced conflict, not consensus, among religious people in America, even within families. In 1775, Charles Wesley, who along with his brother John, was in the midst of promoting Methodism on both sides of the Atlantic, wrote, "I am on neither side [of the conflict], and yet on both; on the side of New England and of Old. Private Christians are excused, exempted, privileged to take no part in civil troubles." Only a few months later, John asserted in a letter to Lord North, "Here all my prejudices are against the Americans; for I am an High Churchman, the son of an High Churchman, bred up from my childhood in the highest notions of *passive obedience and non-resistance." Contrary to John's sentiment, the Rev. Francis Asbury, the only English Methodist preacher not to leave the colonies during the Revolution, lamented the fact that Wesley "dipped into the politics of America."*

Strong religious influence existed on both sides of this critical issue from the conception through infancy of the new nation. Among the questions which persist to the present are, who were the rebels in the American Revolution, the colonists or the English? How "religious" was the Revolution? Did Americans' success in the war prove God was on their side?

Documents

The interplay between religion and politics during the era of the American Revolution was woven into the books and sermons of scores of preachers during the last half of the eighteenth century. A quarter century before the war for independence broke out, theological liberal Jonathan Mayhew argued it was unreasonable for any people to grant unlimited submission to a civil authority. The first document records his thoughts. In the second and third selections, the partisan British position is presented by two clerics during the decade before the outbreak of the war. The Rev. Jonathan Boucher, a native of England and loyal Anglican, viewed the independence movement as an "immense mischief," while John Wesley attempted to calm his friends in America and called upon them to "fear God and honor the King." In his 1776 Election Sermon, delivered on the eve of the signing of the Declaration of Independence, Samuel West enjoined his listeners to respect lawful magistrates but resist merciless tyrants. His appeal is presented in the fourth document. In the final selection, Congregational pastor and dedicated patriot Samuel Sherwood describes in 1776 his millennial expectations for America resulting from its revolutionary struggle against Babylon (England).

1. Discourse Concerning Unlimited Submission, 1750
SOURCE: Jonathan Mayhew, *The Discourse Concerning Unlimited Submission* (Boston, 1750).

If we calmly consider the nature of the thing itself, nothing can well be imagined more directly contrary to common sense than to suppose that millions of people should be subjected to the arbitrary, precarious pleasure of one single man (who has naturally no superiority over them in point of authority), so that their estates and everything that is valuable in life, and even their lives also, shall be absolutely at his disposal, if he happens to be wanton and capricious enough to demand them. What unprejudiced man can think that God made all to be thus subservient to the lawless pleasure and frenzy of one, so that it shall always be a sin to resist him! Nothing but the most plain and express revelation from heaven could make a sober impartial man believe such a monstrous, unaccountable doctrine, and indeed, the thing itself appears so shocking—so out of all proportion—that it may be questioned whether all the miracles that ever were wrought, could make it credible, that this doctrine really came from God. At present, there is not the least syllable in scripture which gives any countenance to it. The hereditary, indefeasible, divine right of kings, and the doctrine of non-resistance which is built upon the supposition of such a right, are altogether as fabulous and chimerical as transubstantiation or any of the most absurd reveries of ancient or modern visionaries. These notions are fetched neither from divine revelation nor human reason; and if they are derived from neither of those sources, it is not much matter from whence they come, or whither they go. Only it is a pity that such doctrines should be propagated in society, to raise factions and rebellions, as we see they have, in fact, been both in the last and in the present reign.

But then, if unlimited submission and passive obedience to the higher powers, in all possible cases, be not a duty, it will be asked, "How far are we obliged to submit? If we may innocently disobey and resist in some cases, why not in all? Where shall we stop? What is the measure of our duty? This doctrine tends to the total dissolution of civil government; and to introduce such scenes of wild anarchy and confusion as are more fatal to society than the worst of tyranny."

After this manner, some men object; and, indeed, this is the most plausible thing that can be said in favor of such an absolute submission as they plead for. But the worst (or rather the best) of it is that there is very little strength or solidity in it. For similar difficulties may be raised with respect to almost every duty of natural and revealed religion. To instance only in two, both of which are near akin, and indeed exactly parallel, to the case before us: it is unquestionably the duty of children to submit to their parents, and of servants to their masters. But no one asserts that it is their duty to obey and submit to them in all supposable cases; or universally a sin to resist them. Now does this tend to subvert the just authority of parents and masters? Or to introduce confusion and anarchy into private families? No. How then does the same principle tend to unhinge the government of that larger family, the body politic? We know, in general, that children and servants are obliged to obey their parents and masters respectively. We know also, with equal certainty, that they are not obliged to submit to them in all things, without exception, but may, in some cases reasonably, and therefore innocently, resist them. These principles are acknowledged upon all hands, whatever difficulty there may be in fixing the exact limits of submission. Now there is at least as much difficulty in stating the measure of duty in these two cases as in the case of rulers and subjects. So that this is really no objection, at least no reasonable one, against resistance to the higher powers. Or, if it is one, it will hold equally against resistance in the other cases mentioned. . . .

A people, really oppressed to a great degree by their sovereign, cannot well be insensible when they are so oppressed. And such a people (if I may allude to an ancient fable) have, like the hesperian fruit, a dragon for their protector and guardian. Nor would they have any reason to mourn if some Hercules should appear to dispatch him. For a nation thus abused to arise unanimously, and to resist their prince, even to the dethroning him, is not criminal, but a reasonable way of vindicating their liberties and just rights; it is making use of the means, and the only means, which God has put into their power, for mutual and self-defense. And it would be highly criminal in them not to make use of this means. It would be stupid tameness and unaccountable folly for whole nations to suffer one unreasonable, ambitious and cruel man to wanton and riot in their misery. And in such a case it would, of the two, be more rational to suppose that they that did not resist, than that they who did, would receive to themselves damnation.

2. Southern Anglican Loyalist, 1770

SOURCE: Jonathan Boucher, *Reminiscences of An American Loyalist, 1738-1789* . . . (Boston, 1925), excerpted from 130-36.

GENTLEMEN,

It is some proof of the sad state of the times that we, the writers of this Address, though of some note in our country, and well known to you, find it necessary to communicate our sentiments to you through the medium of a newspaper. Yet conscious that we are not less interested than yourselves in the issue of this unhappy dispute, and conscious also that we have an equal right to debate and determine how it shall be conducted, we claim your attention. And be not so unwise to yourselves and unjust to us as to vote our remarks to be undeserving your notice, merely because owing to the high hand with which a certain party have carried all their points, we convey them to you through a proscribed newspaper, and without the signature of our real names.

Sent originally as ye were to mediate between us and our parent State, even the few who appointed you could and did commission you only to examine into and ascertain our alleged grievances, and to point out the best means of obtaining redress. The single question before you, as a Congress, was, whether the Parliament of Great Britain can constitutionally lay internal taxes on her colonies; and if they cannot, whether the 3d. per lb. duty on tea be a tax or not. You have been pleased very summarily to *Resolve* that they cannot. But we wish to remind you that Resolves are not arguments; and we cannot but think it assuming somewhat too much of the air and consequence of legal and constitutional Assemblies, thus superciliously to obtrude *Resolves* upon us, without condescending to give us any of the reasons which we are to suppose influenced you to make them. And yet from all we see of these Resolves (of which we claim a right to judge, and to be governed by or not as we think we see reason) we are free to tell you we think them unwise, and also that in their operation they will be ruinous.

This is not said at random. They have already drawn down upon us, or soon will, all the horrors of a Civil War, the evils of which alone infinitely surpass all our other political grievances, even if those were as great as our patriots describe them.

And unless you can now, in this your second meeting, have the good sense, the virtue and the fortitude to make Resolves against your former Resolves; or the people in general have the uncommon merit to avow and defend, cost them what it may, their real sentiments as well as their real interests, all that remains for us to do is to protest against your counsels, and to withdraw ourselves if we can out of the reach of their effects.

That the people of America should be severed from Great Britain, even your fellow-Congressionalists from the North will not be hardy enough yet to avow; but that this will certainly follow from the measures you have been induced by them to adopt, is obvious to every man who is permitted yet to think for himself. But consider, we pray you, for a moment in what a case we are likely to be should such an event be permitted for our sins to take place. Wholly unable to defend ourselves, see ye not that after some few years of civil broils all the fair settlements in the middle and southern colonies will be seized on by our more enterprising and restless fellow-colonists of the North? At first and for a while perhaps they may be contented to be the Dutch of America, i.e. to be our carriers and fishmongers; for which no doubt, as their sensible historian has observed, they seem to be destined by their situation, soil, and climate: but had so sagacious an observer foreseen that a time might possibly come when all North America should be independent, he would, it is probable, have added to his other remark, that those his Northern brethren would then become also the Goths and Vandals of America. This is not a chimerical conjecture: the history of mankind proves that it is founded in truth and the nature of things. And should the reflection chance to make any such impression on you, as we humbly think it ought, we entreat you only to remember that you are—*from the Southern Provinces....*

We charge you then, as ye will answer it to your own consciences, and to Him who is the discerner of Consciences, to be on your guard how ye countenance any measures which may eventually lead, first to a separation from Great Britain, and afterwards to the subjugating these Southern colonies to those of the North. Common prudence recommends this caution, no less than common gratitude. Why should we tell you in what a forlorn and helpless plight we are, even amidst all this parade of military preparations, and how utterly unfit to meet in war one of the most powerful nations now upon earth? However convenient it may be to our self-dubbed patriots to conceal the nakedness of our land, it cannot be unknown either to you or us. Exceedingly different from the Northern colonies, we have within ourselves an enemy fully equal to all our strength. From this enemy that no insurrection has yet been raised, we should be thankful to the mild, quiet, and submissive spirits of the numerous body of people alluded to; thankful to the energy still left to our laws; thankful in no small degree to a good and a gracious King, who, were he, like ourselves, to take Cromwell's unhallowed politics for his pattern, might soon find very different employment for our cockaded gentry than that of insulting and ill-treating, as they are now permitted daily to do, unoffending and peaceful citizens; and above all thankful to a good Providence for hitherto preserving us from this most dreadful calamity. We have too an injured, a vindictive and a barbarian enemy on our frontiers who, on the slightest encouragement, would soon glut their savage passion for revenge by desolating our outlying settlements. How easy will it be for Great Britain, should we so far provoke her, or in her own self-defense, by means of the navigation of the Mississippi to supply them with arms, ammunition, and officers: and how without arms or ammunition for a single campaign, without discipline, officers, or pay, should we be prepared to repel their incursions? . . .

3. A Calm Address to Our American Colonies, 1775

SOURCE: John Wesley, *A Calm Address to Our American Colonies* (London, 1775).

The grand question which is now debated (and with warmth enough on both sides) is this, Has the English Parliament power to tax the American colonies?

In order to determine this, let us consider the nature of our Colonies. An English Colony is a number of persons to whom the King grants a charter, permitting them to settle in some far country as a corporation, enjoying such powers as the charter grants, to be administered in such a manner as the charter prescribes. As a corporation they make laws for themselves: but as a corporation subsisting by a grant from higher authority, to the control of that authority, they still continue subject.

Considering this, nothing can be more plain, than that the supreme power in England has a legal right of laying any tax upon them for any end beneficial to the whole empire.

But you object, "It is the privilege of a Freeman and Englishman to be taxed only by his own consent. And this consent is given for every man by his representative in parliament. But we have no representation in parliament. Therefore we ought not to be taxed thereby."

I answer, This argument proves too much. If the parliament cannot tax you, because you have no representation therein, for the same reason it can make no laws to bind you. If a freeman cannot be taxed without his own consent, neither can he be punished without it: for whatever holds with regard to taxation, holds with regard to all other laws. Therefore he who denies the English Parliament the power of taxation, denies it the right of making any laws at all. But this power over the Colonies you have never disputed: you have always admitted statutes, for the punishment of offenses, and for the preventing or redressing of inconveniences. And the reception of any law draws after it by a chain which cannot be broken, the necessity of admitting taxation.

But I object to the very foundation of your plea. That "every freeman is governed by laws to which he has consented," as confidently as it has been asserted, it is absolutely false. In wide-extended dominions, a very small part of the people are concerned in making laws. This, as all public business, must be done by delegation, the delegates are chosen by a select number. And those that are not electors, who are for the greater part, stand by, idle and helpless spectators.

The case of electors is little better. When they are near equally divided, almost half of them must be governed, not only without, but even against their own consent.

An how has any man consented to those laws, which were made before he was born? Our consent to these, may and to the laws now made even in England, is purely passive. And in every place, as all men are born the subjects of some state or other, so they are born, passively, as it were consenting to the laws of that state. Any other than this kind of consent, the condition of civil life does not allow. . . .

Brethren, open your eyes! Come to yourselves! Be no longer the dupes of designing men. I do not mean any of your countrymen in America: I doubt whether any of these are in the secret. The designing men, the Ahithophels are in England; those who have laid their scheme so deep, and covered it so well, that thousands who are ripening it, suspect nothing at all the matter. These well-meaning men, sincerely believing that they are serving their country, exclaim against grievances, which either never existed, or are aggravated above measure, and thereby inflame the people more and more, to the wish of those who are behind the scene. But be not you duped any longer: do not ruin yourselves for them that owe you no good will, that now employ you only for their own purposes, and in the end will give you no thanks. They love neither England nor America, but play one against the other, in subserviency to their grand design, of overturning the English government. Be warned in time. Stand and consider before it is too late; before you have entailed confusion and misery on your latest posterity. Have pity upon your mother country! Have pity upon your own! Have pity upon yourselves, upon your children, and upon all that are near and dear to you! Let us not bite and devour one of another, lest we be consumed one of another! O let us follow after peace! Let us put away our sins; the real ground of all our calamities! Which never will or can be thoroughly removed, till we fear God and honour the King.

4. 1776 Election Sermon
SOURCE: Samuel West, *A Sermon Preached Before the Honorable Council* (Boston, 1776).

[In I Peter 2:13, 14, we hear] "Submit yourselves to every ordinance of man,"—or as the words ought to be rendered from the Greek, submit yourselves to every human creation; or human constitution,—"for the Lord's sake, whether it be to the king, or unto governors,—for the punishment of evil-doers, and for the praise of them that do well." Here we see that the apostle asserts that magistrates are of human creation that is, that magistrates have no power or authority but what they derive from the people; that this power they are to exert for the punishment of evil-doers, and for the praise of them that do well.

The only reason assigned by the apostle why magistrates should be obeyed . . . is because they punish the wicked and encourage the good; it follows, that when they punish the virtuous we have a right to refuse yielding any submission to them; whenever they act contrary to the design of their institution, they forfeit their authority to govern the people, and the reason for submitting to them immediately ceases. . . . Hence we see that the apostle, instead of being a friend to tyranny . . . , turns out to be a strong advocate for the just rights of mankind.

David, the man after God's own heart, makes piety a necessary qualification in a ruler: "He that ruleth over men must be just, ruling in the fear of God."

To despise government, and to speak evil of dignitaries is represented in Scripture as one of the worst of characters; and it is an injunction of Moses, "Thou shalt not speak evil of the ruler . . ." Great mischief may ensue upon reviling the character of good rulers; for the unthinking herd of mankind are very apt to give ear to scandal, and when it falls upon men in power, it brings their authority into contempt, lessens their influence, and disheartens them from doing service.

But though I would recommend to all Christians to treat rulers with proper honor and respect, none can reasonably suppose that I mean that rulers ought to be flattered in their vices, or honored and caressed while they are seeking to undermine and ruin the state; for this would be wickedly betraying our just rights, and we should be guilty of our own destruction.

It is with a particular view to the present unhappy controversy . . . that I chose to discourse upon the nature and design of government . . . so that we stand firm in our opposition to tyranny, while at the same time we pay all proper obedience to our lawful magistrates; while we are contending for liberty, may we avoid running into licentiousness . . . I acknowledge that I have undertaken a difficult task; but, it appears to me, the present state of affairs loudly calls for such a discourse. Need I upon this occasion descend to particulars? Can any one be ignorant what the things are of which we complain? . . . And, after all this wanton exertion of arbitrary power, is there any man who is not fired with a noble indignation against such merciless tyrants. . . .

To conclude: While we are fighting for liberty, and striving against tyranny, let us remember to fight the good fight of faith, and earnestly seek to be delivered from that bondage of corruption which we are brought in to by sin, and that we may be made partakers of the glorious liberty of the sons and children of God: which may the Father of Mercies grant us all, through Jesus Christ. "AMEN."

5. The Church's Flight into the Wilderness, 1776
SOURCE: Samuel Sherwood, *The Church's Flight into the Wilderness* (New York: S. Loudon, 1776), 45-46, 48-50.

We may, in a peculiar manner, notice the kind dealings of God in his providence towards this branch of his church, that he has planted as a choice vine, in this once howling wilderness. He brought her as on eagles wings from the seat of oppression and persecution "to her own place," has, of his unmerited grace, bestowed liberties and privileges upon her, beyond what are enjoyed in any other part of the world. He has nourished and protected her from being carried away to destruction, when great floods of his wrath and vengeance have been poured forth after her. God has, in this American quarter of the globe, provided for the woman and her seed, a fixed and lasting settlement and habitation, and bestowed it upon her, to be her own property forever. . . .

As there still remains among us, a godly remnant that have not apostatized from God, not departed from the faith of the gospel; and as these prophecies on which we have been treating will, many of them, most probably have their fulfillment in this land; there are yet solid grounds of hope and encouragement for us, in this dark and gloomy day. Tho' we may, in God's righteous providence, be sorely rebuked and chastised for our woeful apostasies, declensions and backslidings, yet we have, I think, good reason to believe, from the prophesies, so far as we are able to understand them, and from the general plan of God's providence, so far as opened to view . . . that we shall not be wholly given up to desolation and ruin. It is not likely nor probable, that God will revoke the grant he made of this land to his church. His gifts as well as calling are without repentance. It does not appear probable that a persecuting, oppressive and tyrannical power will ever be permitted to rear up its head and horns in it, notwithstanding its present violent assaults and struggles. Liberty has been planted here; and the more it is attached, the more it grows and flourishes. The time is coming and hastening on, when Babylon the great shall fall to rise no more; when all wicked tyrants and oppressors shall be destroyed forever. These violent attacks upon the woman in the wilderness, may possibly be some of the last efforts and dying struggles of the man of sin. These commotions and convulsions in the British empire may be leading to the fulfillment of such prophecies as relate to his downfall and overthrow, and to the future glory and prosperity of Christ's church. It will soon be said and acknowledged, that the kingdoms of this world are become the kingdoms of our Lord, and of his Christ. The vials of God's wrath begin to be poured out on his enemies and adversaries; and there is falling on them a noisome and grievous sore. And to such as have shed the blood of saints and prophets, to them, blood will be given to drink; for they are worthy. And they will gnaw their tongues of falsehood and deceit, for pain; and have the cup of the wine of the fierceness of her wrath; and be rewarded double. The Lamb shall overcome them, for he is Lord of Lords, and King of Kings; and they that are with him are called, and chosen, and faithful. May the Lord shorten the days of tribulation, and appear in his glory, to build up Zion; that his knowledge might cover the earth, as the waters do the seas; that wars and tumults may cease thro' the world, and the wolf and the lamb lie down together, and nothing hurt or destroy throughout his holy mountain.

Essays

The mix of the sacred and secular during the revolutionary era is discussed in the three essays below. In the first, Nathan O. Hatch of the University of Notre Dame describes how the interplay between republican principles and tradi-

tional religion produced a way of thinking he calls "civil millennialism." Jon Butler of Yale University traces the relationship between government and Christianity in colonial political culture, and then discusses the importance of millennialist rhetoric in revolutionary society. Butler's comments appear in the second essay. In the final essay, Mark Noll of Wheaton College (Illinois) provides an analysis of the decisive role the American Revolution has played in the religious life of the United States.

Visions of a Republican Millennium:
An Ideology of Civil Religion in the New Nation
NATHAN O. HATCH

SOURCE: From *The Sacred Cause of Liberty: Republican Thought and the Millennium in Revolutionary New England* by Nathan O. Hatch. Copyright © 1977 by Yale University Press. Reprinted with permission.

> *And may we not view it, at least, as probable, that the expansion of republican forms of government will accompany that spreading of the gospel, in its power and purity, which the scripture prophecies represent as constituting the glory of the latter days?*
>
> John Mellen, 1797

The Second Great Awakening, like its namesake a generation removed, was driven by the compelling hope of clergymen that their labors would be instrumental in establishing the kingdom of God on earth. Unlike the sudden ebb of revivalism in the 1740s, however, this later wave of religious fervor sustained its momentum throughout the first half of the nineteenth century and swelled the tide of millennial anticipation throughout Protestant America. With reference to the many prophetic signs heralding the kingdom, Lyman Beecher captured the spirit characteristic of his age:

> Soon will the responsive song be heard from every nation, and kindred, and tongue and people, as the voice of a great multitude, and as the voice of many waters, and as the voice of mighty thunderings, saying, Alleluia, for the Lord God Omnipotent reigneth.

Contemporary historians have been fascinated with this theme as a way of understanding the pervasive identification of the destiny of the American republic with the course of redemptive history. Not only had the brightness of the new morning made clear the imminence of the kingdom; it had also suggested that America was to be "both the locus and instrument of the great consummation." This millennial persuasion, buoyant with the civil and religious ideals of the young republic, functioned as a primary idiom of that distinct form of evangelical civic piety that historians have called a "religion of the Republic" or an American civil religion. Whatever the exact contours of this tendency to attribute to the nation "purposive functions, universal and catholic in scope," historians have generally agreed that Protestantism in the Age of Jackson aligned national purpose so closely with religious conviction that gradually, in the words of John E. Smylie, "the nation emerged as the primary agent of God's meaningful activity in history."

It has been an intriguing but complicated task to explain how the kingdom of God and the virtuous republic became for Americans one and the same empire. While students have concurred that visions of a Christian America inspired and motivated American reformers, benevolent volunteers, and foreign missionaries, they have explained the genesis of civil religion in a variety of ways, three of which deserve attention. Some scholars have linked the nineteenth-century ideal of a Christian America to the unsettling pluralism of competing denominations. Others have found a plausible explanation in American fears that waves of social instability and religious confusion would engulf the young nation as they had the French republic. A third perspective has taken note of the ease with which American churches accommodated their message to an age of romantic nationalism. Either alone or in combination, these explanations have provided the most satisfying answers recently given to the question of how the idea of the millennial kingdom became so profoundly Americanized by the second quarter-century of national experience.

The most widely accepted of these attempts to unearth the foundations of civil religion has found them resting upon the bedrock of American denominationalism. According to Sidney Mead, the establishment of religious freedom in America did not undermine the ancient assumption that the well-being of society depended upon commonly shared religious beliefs. The resulting tension forced America's Protestant communions to relax their exclusive claims to truth and pressured them to admit that some "brooding higher unity" lay at the core of all their teachings. In such a context, where multiple religious institutions cancelled out each other's exclusive claims, Americans began to grope for a communal identity to which they could assign an ultimate and inclusive function. That institution was, or became, the nation. The emergence of denominationalism thus transformed traditional understandings of the church; the concept of a chosen nation replaced that of an ecclesiastical community of the redeemed. The nation developed "the soul of a church" because no American denomination could any longer make such a claim.

If the mosaic composition of American Protestantism has offered some scholars an explanation of how the republic was seen as a redemptive instrument, others have suggested that the vision of a Christian America expressed the anxieties of troubled ministers "asserting the unity of culture in pressing danger of fragmentation." In his highly influential article, "From the Covenant to the Revival," Perry Miller argued that although the new religious nationalism of the Second Great Awakening developed in some measure as a reaction to disestablishment, its more important source was the intense desire to preserve the Union from the centrifugal forces of skeptical rationalism and social anarchy. Confronted with disruptive internal confusion as well as the ideology of the French Revolution, a "volcano" which "threatened to sweep the United States into its fiery stream," ministers sought an alternate program for Christian solidarity. They found it in the revival and proclaimed its message in the form of a new romantic patriotism.

While these first two explanations of the origins of civil religion describe it as an attempt to reclaim certain cherished values of the past in the face of an unnerving present, the third locates its source in the surprising degree to which Protestantism was swept along by the reigning climate of opinion. The kingdom of God and the nation became virtually equated, according to this interpretation, because of the readiness of Protestants to adapt their message to the spirit of the age. In contrast to earlier days, when clergymen did not retreat from challenging social assumptions that were alien to their purposes, churchmen after 1800 fell into step with the prevailing attitudes of romantic optimism and national idealism. In outlining "the American Democratic Faith" over three decades ago, Ralph Henry Gabriel emphasized that most Protestants gave a hearty assent to the national credo despite its buoyant secular optimism. Other more recent students of this period have likewise seen civil religion as primarily an accommodation of religion to "the prevailing republican enthusiasm and the cult of progress." In an age of followers, they have argued, Americans produced no prophets to decry their pilgrimage en masse to the altar of romantic nationalism.

Although these three explanations of American civil religion on the surface show little similarity, their different melodies seem to be only improvisations of several themes common to them all. In the first place, they have viewed the substitution of nation for church as an unwanted or unnoticed result of expediency. Far from being the product of consistent reasoning, this substitution seemed to rationalize some other more pressing end—such as the creation of national solidarity—or to locate the point where churchmen adrift upon a democratic sea happened to strike land. Secondly, scholars have assumed that the "religion of the Republic" which emerged during the opening decades of the nineteenth century was a substantial departure from previous configurations of political religion. The same elements which resulted in the Second Great Awakening and the subsequent "Benevolent Empire" served as a catalyst which fused liberty and Christianity, the republic and the kingdom, in the minds of men like Lyman Beecher and Francis Wayland. Enforcing the idea that this civic piety was a phenomenon unique to the age of democratic evangelicalism is a third assumption that in the Federalist era New England orthodoxy and republicanism were mutually exclusive and antagonistic forms of thought. Many scholars have assumed that while clergymen of the 1790s dreamed of society's theocratic destiny, their hopes were the very antithesis of the republican ideas held by French Jacobins abroad and Democratic Republicans at home. In contrast to the evident wedding of biblical and republican themes which historians discern in Jacksonian America, they have pictured New England Christianity in the 1790s as locked in mortal combat with republican thought.

The focus of these assumptions, sharpened by a scholarly convention that separates the "Middle Period" from the era of the Revolution, has allowed discussion of the "religion of the Republic" to proceed with little reference to the interaction of Christian and republican themes during the last quarter of the eighteenth century. Among other things, the Second Great Awakening has become a starting point to understand the religious patriotism of nineteenth-century America. By contrast, this study gropes forward toward the Great Revival and finds in its New England phase, at least, a fitting culmination of an intellectual tradition shaped during the founding of the republic. Yankee ministers who watched the dawn of the new century did not stumble unawares upon the road of civil religion; they actively sought a way of assigning to the American republic a major role in the scheme of providential history because signposts had for two generations indicated to thoughtful clergymen that the highway leading to the kingdom followed definite political as well as religious principles. Their sense of American destiny followed an older tendency to join theological and republican concerns.

During the last half of the eighteenth century, the Great War for the Empire, the first two revolutions of modern times, the founding of a new republic, and the estrangement of Federalist New England from Jeffersonian America prompted and gave character to new directions in religious thought. Overriding civic concerns led New England ministers to recast the major strains of their traditional eschatology. By bringing to the heart of redemptive history the republican values of civil and religious liberty, ministers articulated a civic theology that gave a profoundly new religious significance to the function of man as citizen, to the principles governing the civil order, and to the role of nations in bringing on the millennium. While the acid bath of war corroded in great measure the bonds between church and state elsewhere in America, in New England it seemed to etch in bold relief a view of history which identified the aspirations of the church with the rise of republican liberty. This shift was occasioned by the tumult of war and political upheaval but its real historical import stems from the persisting strength of the new ideological alignment long after the winning of independence. Sustaining political values as religious priorities became habitual among ministers of the early republic; they anticipated a republican millennium.

New England ministers responded to the founding of the American republic with their own brand of dialectic theology. They were the first to admit that the church had taken a serious beating at the hands of the war's impiety and the victory's "infidelity." Gloomy New England prophets perceived a serious religious depression in America, whether or not one in fact occurred. Yet in remarkable contrast to the anxious tones of their jeremiads, ministers had never been more confident of the kingdom's advance. Millennial expectancy during the last two decades of the century rose to unparalleled heights, while the perceived state of the church experienced the opposite effect. This paradox easily could be understood if the clergy's hopes sprang from a conviction that the darkest part of the night immediately preceded the dawn. But such is hardly the case. At the exact moment, rather, that piety seemed at an all-time low, the clergy proclaimed that the advancing kingdom had delivered "the deadly shock to the last section of the Babylonish Image. . . . The stone braves all opposition and advances and strikes with redoubled strength the feet of the mighty image: It trembles, it reels to and fro, and threatens to fall."

With this and other graphic depictions of the disarray and retreat of antichristian forces, clergymen voiced their confidence that the divine armies were at the point of storming the very gates of hell. The question of how churchmen could rejoice in the unprecedented success of the kingdom while their own churches lay devastated by the enemy suggests a reordering of their allegiance from *ecclesia* to *polis*. It can be fully answered only by clarifying their republican eschatology.

While the political shock waves of the 1790s raised New England anxieties to unparalleled heights, Congregational ministers never complained that the shattering of order had dulled their ability to explain the inner logic of the political world. By the end of the century their explanations of American and European history had become clearly focused upon certain well-defined interpretations of prophetic Scripture. The most common of these came from Daniel chapter two, which describes Nebuchadnezzar's dream of a great and terrible image that crumbled "like the chaff of the summer threshing floors" before the force of a stone hurled against its feet of iron and clay. After destroying the image, this stone, described by the prophet as "cut out of the mountain without hands," developed into a great mountain that filled the whole earth. Numerous interpreters found in this text a fascinating correlation between the stone and the American Revolution; between the feet of iron and clay and the nations of Europe; and between the growing mountain and the American republic. The meanings attributed to these and other apocalyptic images, moreover, reveal the interlocking providential and republican ideologies so characteristic of New England ministers in the age of the American and French Revolutions.

New England churchmen were emphatic in celebrating the American Revolution as the central event in this republican eschatology. In reflecting on the first twenty years of his country's political experiment, John Cushing of Ashburnham, Massachusetts, suggested in 1796 that "the revolution in America, in a political view, will prove to be the stone cut out of the mountain without hands, which will fill the whole earth." In similar fashion the erratic David Austin took for granted that:

> *the political stone* which is now giving the deadly shock to the last section of the Babylonish Image . . . . was it not the weighty stone which we all helped to lift, during the introduction and progress of that political revolution through which we have just now passed?

Clergymen were equally forthright to explain their reason for viewing the Revolution as a critical "sign of the times." The American victory became theologically significant to these men because it animated the new nation with the principle of liberty, both civil and religious. The Revolution assumed this lofty role, Joseph Eckley said in 1792, because of the general discussion it "introduced on the subject of national politicks," raising hopes that the day would soon come "when mankind universally shall be free." Elias Lee, a Connecticut Baptist, likewise equated the stone of Daniel with the war against Britain because it had raised "the standard of liberty and republicanism" against the pride and power of monarchy. In this scheme, the structure of freedom that arose from the ashes of war clearly became "the base of the approaching building of God."

By thus aligning a scheme of providential history with republican thought, this widely shared perspective on the Revolution made the realization of liberal political goals essential to the approach of the kingdom. The prospect of sharing the political ideals of the Revolution with all mankind became, in this climate of opinion, not only the clergy's fondest hope but also a necessary prerequisite for spreading the Christian message. David Austin stated explicitly this recurring inference:

> It seems no unnatural conclusion from ancient prophecy, . . . that in order to usher in . . . the *latter-day-glory,* TWO GREAT REVOLUTIONS are to take place; the *first* outward and political; the *second* inward and spiritual.

The gospel was only compatible with political forms that stood on the sacred ground of liberty.

Charting providential history by the milestones of civil and religious liberty was hardly a novelty for clergymen of the Federalist period. The notion of civil millennialism first became prominent during the Anglo-French wars which took place between 1745 and 1760, and received its most popular defense in John Adams's essay *A Dissertation on the Canon and Feudal Law.* During the Revolutionary crisis such ideas became a conventional pattern of understanding in New England, as evidenced by Samuel Sherwood's comments in 1776:

> Liberty has been planted here; and the more it is attacked, the more it grows and flourishes. The time is coming and hastening on, when Babylon the great shall fall to rise no more; when all tyrants and oppressors shall be destroyed forever.

America's recovery of its civil and religious rights in the victory over Britain intensified the conviction. By the end of the century a republican eschatology seemed in retrospect to have fired the American Revolution. It remained firmly enshrined in popular thought and offered a model for the coming age:

> No sooner had the *twenty years* of our political operation built for us this political temple; than wisdom fell from God in respect to the millennial temple; . . . and whilst European nations behold on these western shores of the Atlantic, the temple of freedom, over which our confederation spreads its wings, they shall see how delightful a picture of the approaching millennial confederation it presents.

Operating within the same moral framework, Yankee clergymen identified the nations of Europe as primary expressions of antichristian darkness. Jeremy Belknap, like many of his colleagues, demanded that America remain outside the orbit of European influence. "I detest the thought," he declared, "that any rotten toe of Nebuchadnezzar's image . . . should ever exercise dominion over this country." In his mind the nations of Europe had demonstrated beyond question their character as the feet of iron and clay that would crumble before the stone. Antichrist had chosen these nations, led by Britain and France, to become, in the words of Nathan Strong, "the last stage of anti-Christian apostacy." Having grown up in an eschatological tradition that identified the forces of evil with the politics of tyranny, these interpreters in the 1790s quite naturally assumed that "in the language of prophecy, tyrannical governments, both civil and ecclesiastical, are represented by fierce and destroying beasts . . ." Just as the kingdom advanced by the rise of civil and religious liberty, so the legions of Satan retreated with the demise of the "machinery of papal, and anti-republican despotism."

Federalist clergymen were persuaded that Satan had shifted his primary base of operations from a false church to the governments of certain despotic nations. With remarkable consistency they reiterated the eschatology which Samuel Sherwood and Samuel West had proclaimed at the outbreak of the American Revolution. "Until of late," wrote David Austin in 1799, Protestant divines had all "united in applying" the image of Antichrist to "the papal power." This had obviously been an error, he continued, because the feet of Nebuchadnezzar's image were "formed of *iron and of clay; of kingly and of priestly power combined.*" Against both, he cried, "the stone is now striking." In a similar vein, David Osgood analyzed the weakness of the Pope in the eighteenth century and came to the following conclusions:

> The marks of the beast and of the dragon, so visible and manifest upon it in ancient times, were nearly obliterated. The mother of harlots had either become a reformed prostitute, or having passed the days of vigour and passion, was a mere withered form in the last stage of decrepitude, retaining only the shadow and skeleton of former times.

The power of Satan, instead, had shifted to:

> The several systems of tyranny and oppression, of cruelty and persecution, which have preceded the present era [and] are designated in this book by THE DRAGON, THE BEAST, THE FALSE PROPHET, BABYLON THE GREAT, THE MOTHER OF HARLOTS, and the like.

In the perspective of such preachers, Antichrist had taken up politics as the most devious scheme to thwart Providence and had mounted his attack primarily along national rather than ecclesiastical lines. The Devil, said Elias Lee is "always busy about civil affairs; and like all other corrupt politicians endeavoring to turn everything to his own advantage."

This view of a political Antichrist—the first novel eschatological interpretation of evil since the Reformation—developed remarkable strength because it could appropriate for its own purposes the earlier tradition. No less an antichristian symbol than before, the papacy now appeared in alliance with the more awesome legions of civil despotism. "The league or combination, formed between civil and religious monarchies," continued Elias Lee, "is a matter of fact, which none can deny. These are a proper match for each other." They have sometimes quarreled, he admitted, but "like a company of rakes in a tavern; who after a few contradictions and hard blows, drink a bowl, shake hands, and become good friends." History taught the convincing lesson that despotic governments always maintained a religion of the same character.

Yet the turmoil of French politics after the Revolution—what Freeman Parker called a "great apocalyptic earthquake"—convinced clergymen of the same lesson taught by the American Revolution: that tyrannical political power was easily the master of her ecclesiastical counterpart. On the first Sunday of the nineteenth century, Nathan Strong of Hartford assessed the signs of the times in a manner that was becoming commonplace in New England:

> The general train of events in the political world, hath been drying up the mystical Euphrates, or diminishing the power and influence of the Antichristian Babylon. Rome has become an insignificant name, and scarcely is a thunder left in her vatican. . . .

Yankees were struck by the "surprising rise of the French empire upon the ruins of papal Europe" and found it a direct fulfillment of the prophecy of Revelation 17: "The Beast [Napoleonic France] shall hate the Whore [the Roman Church] and shall make her desolate and naked, and shall eat her flesh and burn her with fire." A despotic nation clearly had subdued the ecclesiastical embodiment of evil and reconfirmed for those petrified by French infidelity that the cosmic struggle between good and evil had shifted to national governments and the political principles they embodied. The only proper match for a nation that combined tyrannies in state and church was a nation that defended itself by a union of "civil and religious republicanism, or in other words, civil and religious liberty."

The American republic came for very good reason to seem the primary agent of redemptive history. While a church might espouse Christian freedom, only a nation could preserve the civil liberty which was its prerequisite. The force of this logic seemed even greater when ministers considered the means necessary to initiate the kingdom. The conviction became common that republican liberty was essential not only to the free presentation of the gospel but also to its ready understanding by those who heard it. Gad Hitchcock suggested that while men enjoying liberty could be motivated by religion, those deprived of it "become stupid, and debased in spirit, indolent and groveling, indifferent to all valuable improvement, and hardly capable of any." Even if tyrannical governments began to grant that religious freedom which they had always opposed, servile minds might well continue to shut out the light of truth.

The logical outcome of giving such high priority to civil freedom was to identify the expansion of American republicanism with the growth of Daniel's mountain. John Mellen of Barnstable made the point explicit:

> And may we not view it, at least, as probable, that the expansion of republican forms of government will accompany that spreading of the gospel, in its power and purity, which the scripture prophecies represent as constituting the glory of the latter days?

Following the logic of their own eschatology, clergymen placed the American nation at the center of redemptive history. They knew that only a republic could "wake up and encourage the dormant flame of liberty in all quarters of the earth . . . and thereby open and prepare . . . minds for the more easy reception of the truth and grace of the gospel." . . .

A Revolutionary Millennium?

JON BUTLER

SOURCE: Reprinted by permission of the publisher from pp. 212-218 in *Awash in a Sea of Faith* by Jon Butler, Cambridge, MA: Harvard University Press, Copyright © 1990 by the President and Fellows of Harvard College.

The association of society and government with Christianity was traditional in colonial political culture. But the Revolution strengthened the demand to associate society with Christianity in several ways—by revealing the previously shallow foundations of the association, by stressing a particular form of "republicanism" in government and society, and by stimulating a strong sense of cultural optimism that fitted certain religious themes, particularly American millennialism.

Dark concerns about America's religious future extended far beyond the chaplains working in the army camps. The destruction of church buildings, the interruption of denominational organization, the occasional decline in congregations and membership, the shattering of the Anglican church, and the rise of secular pride in revolutionary accomplishments all weighed on American religious leaders. Even as the Revolution advanced, denominational leaders often bemoaned rather than celebrated America's moral fiber. In 1780 the Synod of Philadelphia expressed dismay at the "decay of vital Piety, the degeneracy of Manners, want of public Spirit and prevalence of Vice and Immorality." In the same year the Philadelphia Baptist Association received letters from congregations "complaining in general of great declension in religion and vital piety" and "of amazing prevailing stupidity."

Republican political ideology heightened concern for moral and religious foundations. Republican principles had enormous importance for American religion because, though they were often vague and elusive, they placed great authority in the very laypeople with whom the clergy had long struggled. The "public," for revolutionary-era theorists, seldom included women, enslaved or free Africans, or poor whites. Yet even with these omissions, republican theory gave sovereignty to a remarkably extensive citizenry. In England sovereignty lodged in a Parliament whose House of Lords contained bishops and a hereditary aristocracy and whose Commons was elected through a narrowly drawn franchise. In America, by contrast, sovereignty rested in an electorate as numerous as it was diverse. And though the American scheme was celebrated, it also gave rise to concern, even among its ardent defenders, about tumult and rabble.

Contemporaries agreed that a successful republican society and government, by definition, depended on "a virtuous people." This sentiment did not take root in a reborn Puritanism but in more modern eighteenth-century principles. Episcopal ministers like William White, Lutherans like Henry Melchoir Muhlenberg, Scottish-born Presbyterians like John Witherspoon, and Baptists like John Leland and Isaac Backus all equated republican longevity with widely inculcated moral virtue. The whole of society, not merely some of its parts, constituted the bedrock of the future. The contrast was particularly noticeable in Massachusetts. John Winthrop's Puritan society had been ordered by means of hierarchical responsibilities assigned among the people, "some highe and eminent in power and dignitie; others meane and in subjection." The 1780 Massachusetts constitution, however, rested order on a broader foundation: "The happiness of a people, and the good order and preservation of civil government, essentially depend upon piety, religion, and morality." It did not mention the "highe and eminent" or "others meane and in subjection."

Optimism fueled the new republic. In celebration of Washington's inauguration, Charles Wilson Peale fitted Grey's Ferry Bridge across the Delaware River with Roman arches proclaiming "The New Era." Artists of all kinds chose Washington as their subject. Academies trumpeted the arts as a vital instrument in the creation of an independent American culture. A host of publications—the *United States Magazine,* the *American Monitor,* the *Columbian Magazine,* the *American Museum*—commissioned new verse, rediscovered colonial literature, and transformed both into a national literary heritage.

Much of the postrevolutionary optimism was openly secular, not religious, and reflected the Founding Fathers' Enlightenment convictions. This was especially true of those whom Pauline Meier has called the "old revolutionaries." Franklin, Washington, Jefferson, Madison, and Hamilton all professed beliefs in the supernatural: they were not willing to risk identification as atheists. But their references to the supernatural were vague and ethereal, and their views of religion were far different from those of the Congregational, Baptist, Presbyterian, and Episcopalian clergymen who backed the Revolution. Franklin's god was a god of ethics and production, not theology and revelation. As for Christology, the old revolutionaries had even less to say. If Christ was divine, it was because his morals were true to the dignity of mankind rather than because they were divine. Christ took his place beside Socrates, Plato, and the Stoics, none of whom might be his equals but all of whom were moral compatriots nonetheless. Washington was utterly disinterested in theology, and nineteenth-century free-thinkers were not without warrant in claiming him as their own. South Carolina's Christopher Gadsden quoted Juvenal, Pope, and Plato (the *Laws*, not the *Republic*) rather than Milton and Christ. Even John Adams, the "Puritan" revolutionary, believed that the argument for Christ's deity was an "awful blasphemy," best discarded in a new, enlightened age.

Progressive conceptions of time rooted in a secular, rather than a supernatural, view of life underwrote much of the new American optimism. "The Muses have crossed the Atlantic," John Adams wrote. The Massachusetts *Centinel* described the result: "England was in the days of yore, the seat of philosophy . . . but now it is become the asylum of vagabonds and imposters." Thomas Paine's arrogantly titled *Common Sense* called for independence based on a belief in a nonsupernatural inevitability. Americans (and Britons too) had been thrust into independence despite themselves—"the *time hath found us*," Paine wrote. Their cultural maturation over the previous half century had sealed their fate—"We are not the little people now, which we were sixty years ago." Therefore, he continued, "it is repugnant to reason, to the universal order of things, to all examples from the former ages, to suppose, that this continent can longer remain subject to any external power." Like Machiavelli, who warned Florentine humanists about the difficulties of mastering Fortune, Paine warned Americans to seize the moment. "It might be difficult, if not impossible, to form the Continent into one government half a century hence . . . the *present time* is the *true time*."

American religious leaders responded vigorously to these frequently contradictory stimuli. Their most important responses attempted to absorb and redirect the secular optimism. However frustrating their army service, chaplains glossed over their camp failures when they moved back into their town pulpits. Between 1763 and 1799 they published hundreds of sermons given before militia and army units both before and after the war. The complications of army life dissipated as their printed words floated out across the literate landscape. Their readers could concentrate on the chaplains' messages, efforts that were now joined to increased numbers of other commemorative sermons. Some, like those given with almost universal occurrence on July 4, simultaneously celebrated victory and independence. Fast and thanksgiving day sermons continued and even increased. Everywhere a torrent of ministers' words proclaimed American independence and Christianity together.

If claims measured God's approval, the clergy put the new nation in good stead. Providential rhetoric fixed God's sovereignty over the Revolution. Some clergymen described the struggle in Manichean terms. Abraham Keteltas, the New York Presbyterian, termed it "the cause of heaven against hell." Elhanan Winchester, a South Carolina Baptist, described British actions as motivated by "Rome and Hell." Joel Barlow asserted in his epic poem of American destiny, *The Vision of Columbus*, that Heaven approved independence as much as it had guided America's discoverers—"America" meaning the old mainland British colonies, of course, not the whole of the Western Hemisphere. Timothy Dwight proclaimed that only Israel had "experienced more extraordinary interpositions of Providence."

Millennialist rhetoric predicting Christ's return to earth also expanded. Millennialism thrived on dramatic events, such as the episodic colonial revivals or the French and Indian War, and the Revolution proved an efficient incubator for yet another cycle. Providential rhetoric revealed God's approval of the Revolution, but millennialist rhetoric located it in sacred time. Thinking that Christ's second coming would occur in a specific historical setting, Ebenezer Baldwin, a Connecticut clergyman, thought that the Revolution was "preparing the way for this glorious event." Samuel West, a New Hampshire minister, described the Revolution as fulfilling Isaiah's millennialist predictions. Some clergymen went further and suggested that the Revolution was a precursor to the beginning of the millennnium and, perhaps, the "sixth vial" described in the Revelation, which would destroy the Antichrist when it was emptied and usher in Christ's reign.

Yet the very ubiquity of such predictions produced a bewildering variety of styles. No single millennialist vision emerged in the early national period. As Ruth Bloch has noted, proponents variously predicted the coming of true liberty and freedom, a rise in piety, American territorial expansion, and even freedom from hunger. Many propagandists hedged their predictions, just as their predecessors had done in the 1740s and 1750s. The few who provided definite dates for specific events usually developed different and sometimes exotic chronologies. As Americans experienced political, social, and economic setbacks after independence had been won, others turned to darker visions of the world and the new nation's place in it. New Hampshire's Samuel MacClintock warned against "luxury, and those other vices." New Jersey's Jacob Green foresaw "contentions, oppressions, and various calamities." New York's "Prophet Nathan" wrote that crop failure resulted from Americans' greed and disunity.

Despite, or perhaps because of, its inconsistencies, millennialist rhetoric performed important functions in revolutionary society. Above all, Christian millennialism played a significant role in rationalizing popular secular optimism, which it transformed more often than it confronted. Rather than make extensive critiques of secular optimism, millennialist propagandists offered a vision of optimistic progress that was made more understandable by Christian teleology. This progress took root not in man, whose imperfections were all too visible even amid the Revolution, but in God, whose perfection was highlighted by invisibility.

At the same time, apocalyptic thinking generally declined in the revolutionary period. "Millennialism" had previously always had two important components: the destruction of the world, which would precede Christ's return (the apocalypse), and Christ's return and his thousand-year reign (the millennium). Before the Revolution, Jonathan Edwards and other commentators were as much interested in the apocalypse as in the millennium. But the Revolution's success and the desire to increase Christian adherence suppressed apocalyptic digression while raising millennialist speculation. Apocalyptic speculations tended to be negative and even violent in tone. Millennialist speculations were usually hopeful and roseate. With the success of the Revolution, millennialism suited the American temperament better than apocalypticism did, and in this regard the Revolution profoundly shifted the colonial millennialist tradition. The Revolution was an event whose character and outcome seemed to have signaled the beginning of Christ's thousand-year reign, thus making the apocalypse either history or irrelevant.

Millennialism also had important political implications. Millennialist rhetoric secured an unwilling and often perplexed society to the Christian plow with the harness of Christian time. It demanded lay adherence in a society where the people were now sovereign. When New Englanders sought a unicameral legislature and an elected executive on the ground the "the voice of the people is the voice of God" (the view of the *New England Chronicle*), the rhetoric largely benefited the advancement of Christianity: a legislature that spoke for God should also listen to those who articulated Christian theology, morals, and ethics. . . .

The American Revolution and the Religious History of the United States
MARK NOLL

SOURCE: From *Christians in the American Revolution* by Mark Noll. Pp. 163-175. Copyright © 1977 by Christian University Press. Reprinted with permission of the author.

As the course of American history in the nineteenth and twentieth centuries owes its direction to more than the events occurring during the War for Independence, so American religious history owes its shape to influences other than Christian activities during this period alone. Successive waves of immigrants have brought religious patterns from European and Asian homelands that have had a far-reaching effect on the general nature of religious life in the United States. The wide open spaces of the continent's heartland and the loosely organized cultural institutions which characterized large sections of the country into the twentieth century also exerted a telling influence on the development of religion in America. And the growth of technology and urbanization since the last century has presented churchmen with novel problems for which solutions from the past are not adequate. Recognizing the importance of these and other factors does not, however, detract from the decisive role which late eighteenth-century American history played in the development of religious life in the United States. Nor does it lessen the impact which the Revolutionary mixture of politics and religion has had on the public history of the country. While the ideas and actions of Christians at the time of the American Revolution did not lock succeeding generations into the patterns of the Revolutionary generation, they did exert a profound influence on the subsequent religious life of the independent United States.

In the first and most important place, Christians in America continued to assume that God had singled out the American nation for special privileges and responsibilities. Even before the Revolution, the assumption that God favored the

English nation and its American colonies was widespread, but this conviction was reforged with new intensity in the violent crucible of events that saw the United States break its ties with the mother country. The growing belief that Europe had entered a period of decadence led to a corresponding conviction that God's children were concentrated particularly in America. When the events of the Revolution seemed to bear out this assumption, when it became clear, in Moses Mather's words, "that it is God that fighteth for us," belief in America's special place in God's esteem took even firmer hold on the masses of Christian Americans. Against all odds, God had prospered the valiant efforts of his colonial children as they struggled to throw off the immoral tyranny of their despotic masters.

The elaborate system of covenantal thought which had undergirded earlier expressions concerning God's care for the colonies was largely abandoned during the second half of the eighteenth century, but the essential dogma of the covenantal system — that the colonies stood in a special relationship to God— survived as an article of faith throughout the denominational spectrum. By 1800 the assertion that God dealt with the United States in a unique way was a commonplace. In New England, for example, the opponents and the adherents of the theological system developed by Jonathan Edwards both accepted this conviction. An anti-Edwardsean, Joseph Lathrop of West Springfield, Massachusetts, spoke in 1795 of "the blessings . . . with which a gracious providence has distinguished our happy lot." Another opponent of Edwards' thought, Moses Hemmenway of Wells, Maine, used the public observance of George Washington's death as an occasion to remind his listeners that God was still dealing with America by means of special chastisements and rewards. On the other side of the theological fence, the Edwardsean Cyprian Strong of Chatham, Connecticut, could proclaim in 1799 that "we enjoy privileges and blessings, which are not realized by any other nation on earth." And in 1801 the incumbent at Edwards' old preaching station in Stockbridge, Massachusetts, Stephen West, could pray "that Zion [i.e., America] may soon hear the voice, *Arise, shine, for thy light is come.*"

This conviction that God dealt singularly with America continued to hold sway into the nineteenth and twentieth centuries. The final disestablishment of Congregationalism during the first third of the nineteenth century and the irrevocable spread of denominationalism throughout America during the same period meant that the way in which God's special relationship with America was understood lacked the sharp focus it had had in Puritan New England. Nevertheless, the practice of America's "civil religion" continued to flourish, as was manifest particularly in that great outburst of Christian evangelism and social involvement marking the entire first half of the nineteenth century. To all who would listen in the great metropolises and in tiny prairie outposts, revivalists such as Charles G. Finney proclaimed the need for Christian conversion. Christian social reformers such as Lyman Beecher organized countless service agencies to encourage Christian practice in the country. Abolition, temperance, benevolence to orphans, sailors, and prostitutes, and societies to support missions, Sunday schools, and Christian literature were merely a fraction of the enterprises spawned in this era. Beneath the torrents of activity lay the conviction that had gained new consciousness during the Revolution — America's duty was to respond to the singular blessings which God had bestowed upon the nation. Although external circumstances were altered significantly during the nineteenth century and although the particular correlations of theological and socio-political attitudes characterizing the Revolutionary age broke down in that same period, patterns of response from that earlier day continued to define the ways in which Christians viewed the relationship of religion and society.

As in the Revolution, a crusading zeal continued to mark those believers who sought the social changes which they felt Christian principles demanded. The Christian Patriotism of John Devotion shared with the abolitionism of Samuel Hopkins an urgent fervency which tended to equate the attainment of a particular goal in society with the triumph of Christian righteousness. Christian reformers in later American history continued to approach social problems in this same way. The reforms for which Christians have struggled have been diverse—abolition, prohibition, the destruction of godless foreign foes, an end to American involvement in foreign wars—but the presupposition underlying the various campaigns has been the same: when this reform is accomplished, America will have fulfilled its destiny as a uniquely Christian nation. The sources of this crusading zeal in the history of American Christianity are many, but not the least of them was the example of militant Christian advocacy during the American War for Independence.

Millennial overtones have also persisted in the course of America's history, due at least in part to the thorough millennialism that marked such a large part of the religious reaction to the Revolution. The way in which America's ideals of freedom and justice have been championed in public discourse has encouraged the idea that perfect freedom and perfect justice might be obtainable through the concentrated efforts of those upon whom God has already bestowed a foretaste of these blessings. During the Revolution, Christians felt that a successful completion of the war might be the prelude to the visible appearance of the Kingdom of God on earth. In later American history the millennial vision lost its sharp theological definition, but nevertheless lived on. Whether paternalistically in concern for our little brown brothers (President William McKinley), idealistically in the struggle to make the world safe for democracy (Woodrow Wilson), or with utopian fervor in the pledge to fight any foe in the defense of freedom (John F. Kennedy), Americans have taken seriously the founding fathers' assertion that the United States represented a *novus ordo seclorum* (a new order for the ages). Even as the objects of reforming zeal have changed throughout American history, so has the precise makeup of America's millennial vision. Without an understanding of the intense millennialism of the Revolutionary period, however, later American ideals for its own character and its role in the world can never be fully understood.

In sum, the Revolutionary period provided an opportunity for a modified Puritan synthesis to retain its viability in America. No longer adhering to the express tenets of Puritanism, American Christians after the Revolution nevertheless worked to maintain personal religion and a comprehensive Christian community. At least partially as a result of the war, American society in general replaced the church as the locus of communal Christian values. Because it was so obvious during the Revolution that God was concerned with the entirety of the American experience instead of merely ecclesiastical expressions, the transition from Puritan Christianity to American Christianity was made smoothly. Since God had so manifestly blessed the national enterprise during the war, the deduction could be made that God took a special interest in the nation as such. Americans who have had only nominal contact with Christian churches, or perhaps none at all, have been only slightly less eager to adopt the assumptions concerning a unique salvific role for the United States in the history of the world. An accounting of the religious and political relationship at the time of the American Revolution helps to explain how the concept of a Christian America came to be shared so widely both by sincere believers and the nominally religious in the United States.

The discussion [here] has been mainly concerned with the effects which the admixture of religious and political ideology during the Revolution wrought upon public life in the United States. The Revolution was no less important in shaping the internal life of American churches. During the war, religion lent its weighty support to political and social values emanating from nonreligious sources. This same pattern continued after the end of the conflict. Where colonial Christians in 1700 derived much of their world view from strictly theological sources, American Christians in 1800 absorbed much of their basic outlook on life from the surrounding culture. The shift that we have noted in intellectual leadership from ministers to statesmen entailed a definite alteration in the relationship of Christianity and culture in America. In 1700 religion had been an "exporter" of ideas and behavior patterns to American society; by 1800 it was an "importer." The ideas by which men lived, which dictated the allotment of their time and energy, which shaped the way they approached conflicts in society, and from which they developed their systems of values, came increasingly from nonreligious sources as the eighteenth century wore on. While Christians in early colonial America were by no means immune to influences from secular sources, these influences were outnumbered and outweighed by the products of religious thought and experience. By contrast, although believers during the early history of the United States maintained active religious lives, the major practical influences shaping their perspective on life were no longer the products of religious thought. It is not that religious activity diminished in late eighteenth- and early nineteenth-century America, but rather that the nature of that religious activity came more and more to be influenced by ideas from outside the church. Jonathan Edwards, the last American religious thinker whose ideas have had a formative effect upon American culture, died in 1758. The most important influences upon the American mind after Edwards came from men like Jefferson, Hamilton, and Madison who were concerned with public affairs and whose debt to religious thought was minimal.

The practical upshot of this development was that the thought and activity of the American churches tended to follow the thought and activity of the American nation. The ideals which had been fought for in the Revolution or which lay embedded in the arguments for independence — the ideals enshrined in the great national documents produced from 1776 to 1789 — came also to be the ideals of the churches. The convictions that men had rights by nature, that the pursuit of personal happiness was one of these unalienable rights, that all men were essentially equal, that personal freedom was necessary for social well-being, and that a collective "people" had it within their power to establish justice or secure the blessings of liberty to themselves and their posterity became the dogmas not merely of the new nation but also of its churches. The fact that these national ideals resembled many of the ideals of earlier American Christianity eased the process by which the churches assimilated the American political creed.

One of the most obvious indications that American Christians were following the thinking arising out of the Revolution was the acceptance of voluntaristic denominations as the standard for ecclesiastical organization. To be sure, other important factors besides the Whig ideology of the Revolution went into the formation of the American denominational system. The new United States government lacked the means or the will to control the religious lives of its people, and the presence of so many different religious groups in the new country made some system of mutual toleration and respect a necessity. But Whig ideology also played a part in sanctioning a state of affairs which natural conditions had brought about. From the Revolution, Americans took strong ideas about the sanctity of natural rights and the dangers of governmental interference in personal affairs. What could be more natural than the right to construct a relationship with God on one's own terms? In keeping with the implications of this concept of freedom, American Christians came gradually to contend that no denomination could be inherently favored by law and that no law could interfere in the peaceable internal functions of the churches. This type of thinking strikes the twentieth-century American as commonplace, but in the eighteenth century, where the legal establishment of religion was the rule throughout the western world, American practice was truly innovative.

There were, moreover, influences from Whig ideology in the construction of the American denominational system. Political Whigs took it for granted that the people were capable of constructing their own political and social institutions. The idea of the social contract which influenced so much of eighteenth-century political theory presupposed this capacity as one of its unquestioned axioms. Although they were departing radically from earlier ecclesiastical patterns, American Christians under the influence of Whig thought also acted as if the creation, organization, and maintenance of church groups were human rights as intrinsic as the formation and direction of political institutions. In the Old World the church had been considered something given by God and regulated by his properly consecrated ministers. Except for a small dissenting fringe, European Christians into the nineteenth century did not entertain the idea that they were capable of creating churches and charting their courses. In America a different cast of mind prevailed; it was assumed that Christians had not only the right but also the duty to create ecclesiastical institutions as their own consciences demanded. This assumption produced both healthy and unhealthy effects: while it released the energy of count-less creative individuals for the widest possible variety of Christian expressions, it also tended to make the churches unduly subject to the whims of their creators. The stability and continuity, if also stagnation, which had attended the Old World idea of *the* church gave way to the energetic competitiveness, if also eccentricity, of the church*es* in the New World. The peculiar shape of denominational life in America owed much to the ideology of freedom championed so successfully in the Revolu-tionary period.

The ideas of the Revolution touched American theology no less than ecclesiology. The crass identification of Patriotism and Christianity was later extrapolated into the facile identification of America as a Christian country and United States citi-zens as Christians by cultural birthright. This identification, however, has not af-fected theological life in America as much as a subtler and more pervasive phenomenon—the basic shift away from a Calvinistic orientation in theology. Where the identification of all American citizens as Christian believers falls apart upon even superficial analysis, the movement away from Calvinism presents a more complicated picture. The influence of libertarian thought on American theology has been noted by historians of the United States, but the extent of its impact, as well as the exact role of the Revolution in exerting that influence, deserves closer attention.

A convenient way of describing the general shift in American theology over the last half of the eighteenth and the first half of the nineteenth centuries is to exam-ine the fate of the standard "five points" of Calvinism when confronted with the principles of the American Revolution. The first of the Calvinistic points, "total depravity," did not stand up well to the belief that individuals were inherently capable of shaping their own destinies. The earlier Puritans taught that human sinfulness prevented the unconverted person from performing any truly good deeds, including the act of turning from sin to God. Christians in the youthful United States continued to talk about the evil effects of sin, but they did not think that human evil deprived men of the power to determine their own religious or politi-cal destinies.

The concept of "unconditional election" also seemed to deny that men were fully capable of determining the course of their own lives. In the dominant colo-nial churches, the Calvinist teaching of election had maintained that it was God alone who, by an act of his sovereign will, called certain individuals to salvation. But if the establishment of a relationship with God was God's doing and not an individual's, it made a mockery of the conviction that each man had the inalien-able right to secure happiness as a result of his own efforts.

The anti-democratic tendency of the doctrine of election emerged even more clearly in the idea of a "limited atonement." The Calvinist believed that the efficacy of Christ's death and resurrection was restricted to those whom God elected to salvation. But since Americans believed that all men were created equal in political matters, it was difficult to believe that God would arbitrarily limit the effects of the work of Christ to only a few. The egalitarian strain emerging from the Revolution could make no sense of such a wanton infringement upon natural rights.

Further, the concept of "irresistible grace" seemed inimical to the Whig conviction that uncontrollable power was evil. To say, as the Edwardsean Calvinists did, that people became Christians apart from the self-determined choice of their own wills seemed dangerously close to asserting that God exercised the kind of irresponsible power against which the colonies had rebelled.

The last of the Calvinistic principles, the "perseverance of the saints," was usually retained by American Christians, but for a new reason. A believer was sustained in the faith not as a result of God's power but because of the continuing effect of his own choice for God. The believer possessed the sure hope of eternal life as a due right in consequence of his own decision to become a Christian.

Individual believers and various denominations participated in this movement away from Calvinism in different degrees. Indeed, the Calvinistic orientation persisted for a considerable time among some of the groups, such as the Presbyterians, who most ardently supported Whig thought. On the other hand, the denominations which grew most rapidly in the post-Revolutionary period, Baptists and Methodists, expressed their theology to a greater or lesser degree in the new forms. The influence of Whig ideology was certainly not the only impetus hastening the decline of Calvinism in America, but it played one of the most important roles in the process. The attention which the Revolution had called to the concept of freedom altered the definition of this idea that had prevailed in the largely Calvinistic colonies. Freedom in the Revolutionary generation came to mean primarily freedom *from* something—from tyranny, oppression, and the arbitrary exercise of power. Freedom in the earlier Calvinistic sense of the word had implied freedom *for* something—for fulfillment and hope, found only in being overmastered by God. The change was subtle, and it was obscured due to the fact that the single word "freedom" was used to express two related, but also contrasting, ideas. The crisis atmosphere of the Revolutionary period further obscured the two senses of "freedom" and greatly facilitated the process in the American churches by which the Whig idea of liberty came to replace the Calvinistic concept.

Just as it has been important to keep in mind the different Christian responses to the Revolution, so it is necessary to remember that these generalizations concerning the impact of the Revolution on later American religious history did not apply equally to all groups of Christians. In particular, minority groups outside of the English Puritan tradition were insulated from some of the ecclesiastical and theological changes brought about by Revolutionary thought. Groups such as the Lutherans or the Mennonites who retained the language and ecclesiastical practices of the Old World naturally tended to participate less actively in the trends and innovations characteristic of the American religious landscape. Even in the domain of religious minorities, however, the Revolutionary period witnessed patterns that have marked later American history.

The majority religious and cultural viewpoint—in the Revolutionary period, the mixture of libertarianism and Christianity—exerted weighty pressure on minority viewpoints to conform. While the Continental Congress and individual colonial legislatures did make provision for certain deviations from majority policy, the pacifists and Loyalists were still pressured culturally to conform to the Patriotic Whig position. Throughout American history a similar pressure, occasionally official but more often unofficial, has continued to encourage the assimilation of minority religious perspectives into the prevailing majority pattern. Only in recent years have historians made clear how intense were these pressures on Lutherans, Quakers, Dunkers, and other smaller religious groups to adopt the perspectives and practices of mainstream religious bodies. Partially as a result of this external pressure and partly as a product of the desires of those within the minority groups, denominations such as the Quakers and Moravians gradually relinquished some of the doctrinal and practical distinctions which set them apart from the Protestant bodies of Puritan heritage. The Revolutionary period was by no means the only epoch which saw this process at work, but it was one of particularly intense pressure to conform to the common American mold.

From the perspective of the minority groups themselves, it has taken supreme effort and many sacrifices to preserve distinctive traits that did not conform to the prevailing American patterns. Rather than compromise their loyalties to Great Britain, many Anglicans and a smattering of individuals from other denominations migrated to Canada or returned to England. Religious groups in later American history have also been forced into flight, either geographic or psychic, in order to preserve minority religious perspectives. For Mormons in mid-nineteenth-century America, escape to the barren West provided a means to preserve religious distinctives. For fundamentalists in the early twentieth century, withdrawal from the intellectual, scientific, and artistic mainstreams of American culture provided a psychic means to maintain deeply held beliefs. Little substantial similarity exists between pacifist Mennonites of rural Pennsylvania in the eighteenth century and either nineteenth-century Mormons or twentieth-century fundamentalists, but the formal similarity is striking: in each case withdrawal preserved the essentials of a religiosity unacceptable to the majority socio-religious point of view in the country. The behavior of religious minorities during the Revolution has served more as a model of escape for, rather than a direct influence upon, other hardpressed religious groups in the course of American history.

No history of the United States can claim our attention if it does not discuss the profound impact of the Revolutionary period on the future course of events in America. The ideas and actions which gave birth to a new nation or which emerged during that birth process constructed the foundation upon which subsequent American history has been built. Later men and women of ideas and actions have added distinctive personal touches to the edifice of American history, new ideas and patterns of behavior have altered its appearance significantly, and yet the foundation retains its fundamental importance.

In like manner, the religious history of the United States will never be adequately understood apart from a knowledge of Christian thought and behavior at the time of the Revolution. During this period believers were called upon to examine the elements of their religious heritages, and they responded by recasting many of them into new forms. For many believers the Revolution united religious beliefs and political principles into unified convictions about the proper nature of life as Christians and as American citizens. For a lesser number the Revolution called forth demanding sacrifices when personal convictions went against the grain of the Christian-Whig majority. The peculiarly American blending of religious, social, political, and cultural perspectives did not begin from scratch during the Revolution, but the period did encourage an interweaving of these various aspects of life. Throughout America's later history the relative strength of religious ideas vis-à-vis other forces in American culture has varied greatly, but the bond linking religion to all the other interests of life in society has never been broken.

Questions for Reflection and Discussion

1. Describe the interplay between religion and politics presented in the documents.

2. According to Nathan Hatch, how did the kingdom of God (sacred) and the virtuous republic (secular) become for Americans one and the same empire?

3. What religious and political implications of millennialism are identified by Jon Butler?

4. Discuss Mark Noll's analysis of the influence the American Republic had on the religious life of the independent United States.

5. How did the blending of the secular and the sacred in the American Revolution produce both conflict and consensus?

Additional Readings

Albanese, Catherine. *Sons of the Fathers: The Civil Religion of the American Revolution.* Philadelphia: Temple University Press, 1977.

Baldwin, Alice M. *The New England Clergy and the American Revolution.* New York: Frederick Ungar, 1958.

Bloch, Ruth H. "Religion and Ideological Change." In *Religion and American Politics: From the Colonial Period to the 1980s,* ed. Mark A. Noll, pp. 44-61. New York: Oxford University Press, 1990.

Bonomi, Patricia U. "Religious Dissent and the Case for American Exceptionalism." In *Religion in a Revolutionary Age,* ed. Ronald Hoffman and Peter J. Albert, pp. 31-51. Charlottesville: University of Virginia Press, 1994.

Cowing, Cedric B. The *Great Awakening and the American Revolution: Colonial Thought in the 18th Century.* Chicago: Rand McNally, 1971.

Greene, Jack P., and William G. McLoughlin. *Preachers and Politics: Two Essays on the Ori-*

gins of the American Revolution. Boston: American Antiquarian Society, 1977.

Griffin, Keith. *Revolution and Religion: The American Revolutionary War and the Reformed Clergy*. St. Paul, MN: Paragon House, 1994.

Hatch, Nathan O. *The Sacred Cause of Liberty: Republican Thought and the Millennium in Revolutionary New England*. New Haven: Yale University Press, 1977.

Kerber, Linda K. *Women of the Republic: Intellect and Ideology in Revolutionary America*. Chapel Hill: University of North Carolina Press, 1980.

McLoughlin, William G. "The American Revolution as a Religious Revival: 'The Millennium in One Country.'" *New England Quarterly* 40 (March 1967): 99-110.

May, Henry F. *Ideas, Faiths, and Feelings: Essays on American Intellectual and Religious History*. New York: Oxford University Press, 1982.

Noll, Mark A. *Christians in the American Revolution*. Grand Rapids: Christian University Press, 1977.

Phillips, Kevin. *The Cousins' Wars: Religion, Politics, and the Triumph of Anglo-America*. New York: Basic Books, 1999.

Tuveson, Ernest Lee. *Redeemer Nation: The Idea of America's Millennial Role*. Chicago: University of Chicago Press, 1968.

Valeri, Mark. "The New Divinity and the American Revolution." *William and Mary Quarterly* 3rd Series, 46 (October 1989): 741-769.

Chapter 5

American Religion in the Middle Period

Issue

What would be the role of religion in the early republic?

"I shall submit to your consideration . . . that our nation has been raised by Providence to exert an efficient instrumentality in this work of moral renovation," spoke moral reformer and revivalist Lyman Beecher. "The origin and history of our nation are indicative of some great design to be accomplished by it," he continued in his December 22, 1827, sermon. "Who can doubt that the spark which our forefathers struck will yet enlighten this entire continent? But when the light of such a hemisphere shall go up to heaven, it will throw its beams beyond the waves." He contended that ultimately "it will awaken desire, and hope, and effort, and produce revolutions and overturnings, until the world is free."

This vision Americans like Beecher held for their nation in the early republic of the middle period found expression in the writings of both religionists and secularists. About a year into the War of 1812, author and preacher Arthur Stansbury declared, "Our hope is not in our armies, it is not in our generals, it is not in our counsellors, it is not in our constitution: it is in this, that the Lord is long-suffering, and slow to wrath, and repenteth him of evil." Several months earlier a public debate was held in Baltimore on the topic "Can a Christian go to war and be justified by the Bible and his conscience?" Many Americans answered in the affirmative, and thereby began a new chapter in American civil religion.

Historian Nathan O. Hatch argues that the democratizing forces of the half century after the American Revolution "left as indelible an imprint upon the structures of American Christianity as it did upon those of political life." Clergy from different classes conflicted with each other to serve as spokesmen for the church. Yet, when new "outsider" groups, such as the Mormons, emerged from this conflict and tested the range of religious inclusiveness, they found it wanting. It was an age of religious populism not without conflict and boundaries.

Notwithstanding the religious chaos and crosscurrents of the early republic, Lyman Beecher's persuasion that America possessed "some great design to be accomplished" is matched by words written more recently. Historian Timothy Smith notes, "Men in all walks of life believed that the sovereign Holy Spirit was endowing the nation with resources sufficient to convert and civilize the globe, to purge human society of all its evils, and to usher in Christ's reign on earth." What were the roles of religion in the early republic, and did these roles operate in concert? What accounts for occasional discord? What were the critical issues for religion in the middle period? How did the sacred and secular manifest tension in the first half century of the new republic?

Documents

The documents below present a variety of roles for religion in the early republic. In the first selection, the founders of the American Bible Society believed their organization was essential in the dissemination of truth and the advancement of nationalism as people moved westward. Revivalist Charles G. Finney, in the second document, appeals to preachers and pewsitters to participate in national reform efforts to rid America of a variety of political and social evils. In the third selection, millennialist William Miller presents mathematical calculations in support of his prophecy of Christ's Second Coming to take place in 1843. He assumes a biblically literate readership prepared to accept biblical authority, a readership that was large in the 1830s and 1840s. The conflict between Jonathan Edwards and Charles Chauncy during the Great Awakening over the place of reason and emotion in revivalistic religion was echoed in the Second Awakening by revivalist Charles G. Finney and theologian John Williamson Nevin in their conflicting opinions regarding the use of the "anxious seat" (or "anxious bench"). Their discussions over the significance of feeling (emotion) and faith (doctrine), found in documents four and five, reflect the larger problem of convert recruitment in the West and on the frontier. In the final selection, Presbyterian minister and health reformer Sylvester Graham explains why defective diet was the source of America's antebellum problems. He believed adherence to his "Graham System" of vegetarianism and use of his graham bread would speed the arrival of the millennium in America.

1. Forming the American Bible Society, 1816

SOURCE: *Panoplist and Missionary Magazine*, XII (1816), 271-73.

Every person of observation has remarked that the times are pregnant with great events. The political world has undergone changes stupendous, unexpected, and calculated to inspire thoughtful men with the most boding anticipations.

That there are in reserve, occurrences of deep, of lasting, and of general interest, appears to be the common sentiment. Such a sentiment has not been excited without a cause, and does not exist without an object. The cause is to be sought in that Providence, which adapts, with wonderful exactitude, means to ends; and the object is too plain to be mistaken by those who carry a sense of religion into their speculations upon the present and the future condition of our afflicted race.

An excitement, as extraordinary as it is powerful, has roused the nations to the importance of spreading the knowledge of the one living and true God, as revealed in his Son, the Mediator between God and men, Christ Jesus. This excitement is the more worthy of notice, as it has followed a period of philosophy falsely so called, and has gone in the track of those very schemes which, under the imposing names of reason and liberality, were attempting to seduce mankind from all which can bless the life that is, or shed a cheering radiance on the life that is to come.

We hail the reaction, as auspicious to whatever is exquisite in human enjoyment, or precious to human hope. We would fly to the aid of all that is holy, against all that is profane; of the purest interest of the community, the family, and the individual, against the conspiracy of darkness, disaster and death—to help on the mighty work of Christian charity—to claim our place in the age of Bibles.

We have, indeed, the secondary praise, but still the praise, of treading in the footsteps of those who have set an example without a parallel—an example of the most unbounded benevolence and beneficence: and it cannot be to us a source of any pain, that it has been set by those who are of one blood with most of ourselves; and has been embodied in a form so noble and so Catholic, as *"The British and Foreign Bible Society."*

The impulse which that institution, ten thousand times more glorious than all that exploits of the sword, has given to the conscience of Europe, and to the slumbering hope of millions in the region and shadow of death, demonstrates to Christians of every country what they *cannot* do by insulated zeal; and what they *can* do by co-operation.

In the United States we want nothing but concert to perform achievements astonishing to ourselves, dismaying to the adversaries of truth and piety; and most encouraging to every evangelical effort, on the surface of the globe.

No spectacle can be so illustrious in itself, so touching to man, or so grateful to God, as a nation pouring forth its devotion, its talent, and its treasures, for that kingdom of the Savior which is righteousness and peace.

If there be a single measure which can overrule objection, subdue opposition, and command exertion, this is the measure. That all our voices, all our affections, all our hands, should be joined in the grand design of promoting "peace on earth and good will toward men"—that they should resist the advance of misery—should carry the light of instruction into the dominions of ignorance; and the balm of joy to the soul of anguish; and all this by diffusing the oracles of God—addresses to the understanding an argument which cannot be encountered; and to the heart an appeal which its holiest emotions rise up to second.

Under such impressions, and with such views, fathers, brethren, fellow-citizens, the *American Bible Society* has been formed. Local feelings, party prejudices, sectarian jealousies, are excluded by its very nature. Its members are leagued in that, and in that alone, which calls up every hallowed, and puts down every unhallowed, principle—the dissemination of the Scriptures in the received versions where they exist, and in the most faithful where they may be required. In such a work, whatever is dignified, kind, venerable, true, has ample scope: while sectarian littleness and rivalries can find no avenue of admission.

The only question is, whether an object of such undisputed magnitude can be best obtained by a national Society, or by independent associations in friendly understanding and correspondence.

Without entering into the details of this inquiry, we may be permitted to state, in a few words, our reasons of preference to a national Society supported by local Societies and by individuals throughout our country. Concentrated action is powerful action. The same powers, when applied by a common direction, will produce results impossible to their divided and partial exercise. A national object unites national feeling and concurrence. Unity of a great system combines energy of effect with economy of means. Accumulated intelligence interests and animates the public mind. And the Catholic efforts of a country, thus harmonized, give her a place in the moral convention of the world; and enable her to act directly upon the universal plans of happiness which are now pervading the nations.

It is true, that the prodigious territory of the United States—the increase of their population, which is gaining every day upon their moral cultivation—and the dreadful consequences which will ensue from a people's outgrowing the knowledge of eternal life; and reverting to a species of heathenism, which shall have all the address and profligacy of civilized society, without any religious control, present a sphere of action, which may for a long time employ and engross the cares of this Society, and of all the local Bible Societies of the land.

In the distinct anticipation of such an urgency, one of the main objects of the *American Bible Society,* is, not merely to provide a sufficiency of well printed and accurate editions of the Scriptures; but also to furnish great districts of the American continent with well executed Stereotype plates, for their cheap and extensive diffusion throughout regions which are now scantily supplied, at a discouraging expense; and which, nevertheless, open a wide and prepared field for the reception of revealed truth.

Yet, let it not be supposed, that geographical or political limits are to be the limits of the *American Bible Society.* That designation is meant to indicate, not the restrictions of their labor, but the source of its emanation. They will embrace, with thankfulness and pleasure, every opportunity of raying out, by means of the Bible, according to their ability, the light of life and immorality, to such parts of the world, as are destitute of the blessing, and are within their reach. In this high vocation, their ambition is to be fellow-workers with them who are fellow-workers with God. . . .

2. The Church Must Take Right Ground, 1835

SOURCE: Charles G. Finney, *Lectures on Revivals of Religion* (New York: Leavitt, Lord & Co., 1835).

I proceed to mention things *which ought to be done* to continue this great and glorious revival of religion, which has been in progress for the last ten years.

There should be great and deep repentings on the part of ministers. WE, my brethren, must humble *ourselves* before God. It will not do for us to suppose that it is enough to call on the *people* to repent. We must repent, we must take the lead in repentance, and then call on the churches to follow. . . .

The church must take right ground in regard to politics. Do not suppose, now, that I am going to preach a political sermon, or that I wish to have you join and get up a *Christian party* in politics. No, you must not believe that. But the time has come that Christians must vote for honest men, and take consistent ground in politics, or the Lord will curse them. They must be honest men themselves, and instead of voting for a man because he belongs to their party, bank or anti-bank, Jackson or anti-Jackson, they must find out whether he is honest and upright, and fit to be trusted. They must let the world see that the church will uphold no man in office who is known to be a knave, or an adulterer, or a Sabbath-breaker, or a gambler. Such is the spread of intelligence and the facility of communication in our country, that every man can know for whom he gives his vote. And if he will give his vote only for honest men, the country will be obliged to have upright rulers. All parties will be compelled to put up honest men as candidates. Christians have been exceedingly guilty in this matter. But the time has come when they must act differently, or God will curse the nation, and withdrew his Spirit. As on the subjects of slavery and temperance, so on this subject, the church must act right, or the country will be ruined. God cannot sustain this free and blessed country, which we love and pray for, unless the church will take right ground. Politics are a part of religion in such a country as this, and Christians must do their duty to the country as a part of their duty to God. It seems sometimes as if the foundations of the nation were becoming rotten: and Christians seem to act as if they thought God did not see what they do on politics. But I tell you, he does see it; and he will bless or curse this nation, according to the course they take. . . .

I believe the time has come, and although I am no prophet, I believe it will be found to have come, that the revival in the United States, will continue and prevail no further and faster than the church takes right ground upon this subject. The churches are God's witnesses. The fact is, that slavery is, preeminently, *the sin of the church.* It is the very fact that ministers and professors of religion of different denominations hold slaves, which sanctifies the whole abomination in the eyes of ungodly men. Who does not know that on the subject of temperance, every drunkard in the land will skulk behind some rum-selling deacon, or wine-drinking minister? It is the most common objection and refuge of the intemperate, and of moderate drinkers, that it is practiced by professors of religion. It is *this* that creates the imperious necessity for excluding traffickers in ardent spirit, and rum-drinkers, from the communion. Let the churches of all denominations speak out on the subject of temperance, let them close their doors against all who have anything to do with the death-dealing abomination, and the cause of temperance is triumphant. A few years would annihilate the traffic. Just so with slavery. . . .

The church must take right ground on the subject of temperance, and moral reform, and all the subjects of practical morality which come up for discussion from time to time.

There are those in the churches who are standing aloof from the subject of moral reform, and who are as much afraid to have anything said in the pulpit against lewdness, as if a thousand devils had got up into the pulpit. On this subject, the church need not expect to be permitted to take neutral ground. In the providence of God, it is up for discussion. The evils have been exhibited; the call has been made for reform. And what is to reform mankind but the truth? And who shall present the truth if not the church and the ministry? Away with the idea, that Christians can remain neutral, and yet enjoy the approbation and blessing of God.

In all such cases, the minister who holds his peace is counted among those on the other side. Everybody knows that it is so in a revival. It is not necessary for a person to rail out against the work. If he only keep still and take neutral ground, the enemies of the revival will all consider him as on their side. So on the subject of temperance. It is not needful that a person should rail at the cold-water society, in order to be on the best terms with drunkards and moderate drinkers. Only let him plead for the moderate use of wine, only let him continue to drink it as a luxury, and all the drunkards account him on their side. If he refuse to give his influence to the temperance cause, he is claimed, of course, by the other side, as a friend. On all these subjects, when they come up, the churches and ministers must take the right ground, and take it openly and stand to it, and carry it through, if they expect to enjoy the blessing of God in revivals. They must cast out from their communions such members, as, in contempt of the light that is shed upon them, continue to drink or traffic in ardent spirits.

There must be more done for all the great objects of Christian benevolence. There must be much greater effort for the cause of missions, and education, and the Bible, and all the other branches of religious enterprise, or the church will displease God. Look at it. Think of the mercies we have received, of the wealth, numbers, and prosperity of the church. Have we rendered unto God according to the benefits we have received, so as to show that the church is bountiful, and willing to give their money, and to work for God? No. Far from it. Have we multiplied our means and enlarged our plans, in proportion as the church has increased? Is God satisfied with what has been done, or has he reason to be? Such a revival as has been enjoyed by the churches of America for the last ten years! We ought to have done ten times as much as we have for missions, Bibles, education, tracts, free churches, and in all the ways designed to promote religion and save souls. If the churches do not wake up on this subject, and lay themselves out on a larger scale, they may expect that the revival in the United States will cease.

3. Millerites and Millennialism, 1836

SOURCE: William Miller, *Evidence from Scripture and History of the Second Coming of Christ about the Year 1843* (Boston: Moses A. Dow, 1841), 51, 53-54.

The time or length of the vision—the 2,300 days. What must we understand by days? In the prophecy of Daniel it is invariably to be reckoned years; for God hath so ordered the prophets to reckon days. Numb. xiv.34, "After the number of days in which ye searched the land, even forty days, each day for a year, shall you bear your iniquities, even forty years." Ezek. iv. 5, 6, "For I have laid upon thee the years of their iniquity, according to the number of the days, three hundred and ninety days; so shalt thou bear the iniquity of the house of Israel. And when thou hast accomplished them, lie again on thy right side, and thou shalt bear the iniquity of the house of Judah forty days; I have appointed thee each day for a year." In these passages we prove the command of God. We will also show that it was so called in the days of Jacob, when he served for Rachel, Gen. xxix. 27: "Fulfil her week (seven days) and we will give thee this also, for the service which thou shalt serve with me yet other seven years."

Nothing now remains to make it certain that our vision is to be so understood, but to prove that Daniel has followed this rule. This we will do, if your patience will hold out, and God permit. . . .

We shall again turn your attention to the Bible. Look at Ezra vii, 11-13: "Now this is the copy of the letter that the king, Artaxerxes, gave unto Ezra, the priest, the scribe, a scribe of the law of God: perfect peace, and at such a time. I make a decree that all they of the people of Israel, and of his priests and Levites in my realm, which are minded of their own free will to go up to Jerusalem, go with thee." This is the decree given when the walls of Jerusalem were built in troublous times. See, also, Neh. iv. 17-23. Ezra and Nehemiah being contemporary, see Neh. viii. 1. The decree to Ezra was given in the seventh year of Artaxerxes' reign, Ezra vii. 7, and that to Nehemiah in the twentieth year, Neh. ii, 1. Let any one examine the chronology, as given by Rollin or Josephus, from the seventh year of Artaxerxes to the twenty-second year of Tiberius Caesar, which was the year our Lord was crucified, and he will find it was four hundred and ninety years. The Bible chronology says that Ezra started to go up to Jerusalem on the 12th day of the first month, (see Ezra viii. 31,) 457 years before the birth of Christ; he being 33 when he died, added to 457, will make 490 years. Three of the evangelists tell us he was betrayed two days before the feast of the passover, and of course was the same day crucified. The passover was always kept on the 14th day of the first month forever, and Christ being crucified two days before, would make it on the 12th day, 490 years from the time Ezra left the river Ahava to go unto Jerusalem.

If this calculation is correct,—and I think no one can doubt it—then the seventy weeks was fulfilled to a day when our Savior suffered on the cross. Is not the seventy weeks fairly proved to have been fulfilled by years? And does not this prove that our vision and the 2300 days ought to be so reckoned? Yes, if these seventy weeks are a part of *the vision*. Does not the angel say plainly, I have come to show thee; therefore understand that matter, and consider the vision? Yes. Well, what can a man ask for more than plain positive testimony, and a cloud of circumstances agreeing with it?

But one thing still remains to be proved. When did the 2300 years begin? Did it begin with Nebuchadnezzar's dream? No. For if it had, it must have been fulfilled in the year A.D. 1697. Well, then, did it begin when the angel Gabriel came to instruct Daniel into the 70 weeks? No, for if then, it would have been finished in the year A.D. 1762. Let us begin it where the angel told us, from the going forth of the decree to build the walls of Jerusalem in troublous times, 457 years before Christ; take 457 from 2300, and it will leave A.D. 1843; or take 70 weeks of years, being 490 years, from 2300 years, and it will leave 1810 after Christ's death. Add his life, (because we begin to reckon our time at his birth,) which is 33 years, and we come to the same A.D. 1843.

4. Measures to Promote Revivals, 1835

SOURCE: Charles G. Finney, *Lectures on Revivals of Religion* (New York: Leavitt, Lord & Co., 1835).

In the present generation, many things have been introduced which have proved useful, but have been opposed on the ground *that they were innovations*. And as many are still unsettled in regard to them, I have thought it best to make some remarks concerning them. There are three things in particular, which have chiefly attracted remark, and therefore I shall speak of them. They are *Anxious Meetings, Protracted Meetings*, and the *Anxious Seat*. These are all opposed, and are called new measures. . . .

The Anxious Seat

By this I mean the appointment of some particular seat in the place of meeting, where the anxious may come and be addressed particularly, and be made subjects of prayer, and sometimes conversed with individually. Of late this measure has met with more opposition than any of the others. What is the great objection? I cannot see it. The *design* of the anxious seat is undoubtedly philosophical, and according to the laws of mind. It has two bearings:

1.   When a person is seriously troubled in mind, every body knows that there is a powerful tendency to try to keep it private that he is so, and it is a great thing to get the individual willing to have the fact known to others. And as soon as you can get him willing to make known his feelings, you have accomplished a great deal. When a person is borne down with a sense of his condition, if you can get him willing to have it known, if you can get him to break away from the chains of pride, you have gained an important point towards his conversion. This is agreeable to the philosophy of the human mind. How many thousands are there who will bless God to eternity, that when pressed by the truth they were ever brought to take this step, by which they threw off the idea that it was a dreadful thing to have any body know that they were serious about their souls.

2. Another bearing of the anxious seat, is to detect deception and delusion, and thus prevent false hopes. It has been opposed on this ground, that it was calculated to create delusion and false hopes. But this objection is unreasonable. The truth is the other way. Suppose I were preaching on the subject of Temperance, and that I should first show the evils of intemperance, and bring up the drunkard and his family, and show the various evils produced, till every heart is beating with emotion. Then I portray the great danger of *moderate drinking,* and show how it leads to intoxication and ruin, and there is no safety but in TOTAL ABSTINENCE, till a hundred hearts are ready to say, "I will never drink another drop of ardent spirit in the world; if I do, I shall expect to find a drunkard's grave." Now I stop short, and let the pledge be circulated, and every one that is fully resolved, is ready to sign it. But how many will begin to draw back and hesitate, when you begin to call on them to *sign a pledge* of total abstinence. One says to himself, "Shall I sign it, or not? I thought my mind was made up, but this signing a pledge *never* to drink again, I do not know about that." Thus you see that when a person is called upon to give a pledge, if he is found not to be decided, he makes it manifest that he was not sincere. That is, he never came to that resolution on the subject, which could be relied on to control his future life. Just so with the awakened sinner. Preach to him, and at the moment he thinks he is willing to do anything, he thinks he is determined to serve the Lord, but bring him to the test, call on him to do one thing, to take one step, that shall identify him with the people of God, or cross his pride—his pride comes up, and he refuses; his delusion is brought out, and he finds himself a lost sinner still; whereas, if you had not done it, he might have gone away flattering himself that he was a Christian. If you say to him, "There is the anxious seat, come out and avow your determination to be on the Lord's side," and if he is not willing to do so small a thing as that, then he is not willing to do *any thing,* and there he is, brought out before his own conscience. It uncovers the delusion of the human heart, and prevents a great many spurious conversions, by showing those who might otherwise imagine themselves willing to do any thing for Christ, that in fact they are willing to do *nothing.*

The church has always felt it necessary to have something of the kind to answer this very purpose. In the days of the apostles *baptism* answered this purpose. The gospel was preached to the people, and then all those who were willing to be on the side of Christ were called on to be *baptized.* It held the precise place that the anxious seat does now, as a public manifestation of their determination to be Christians. And in modern times, those who have been violently opposed to the anxious seat, have been obliged to adopt some substitute, or they could not get along in promoting a revival. Some have adopted the expedient of inviting the people who were anxious for their souls, to stay for conversation after the rest of the congregation had retired. But what is the difference? This is as much setting up a test as the other. Others, who would be much ashamed to employ the anxious seat, have asked those who have any feeling on the subject, to sit still in their seats when the rest retire. Others have called the anxious to retire into the lecture room. The object of all these is the same, and the principle is the same, to bring people out from the refuge of false shame. One man I heard of, who was very far gone in his opposition to new measures, in one of his meetings requested all those who were willing to submit to God, or desired to be made subjects of prayer, to signify it by leaning forward and putting their heads down upon the pew before them. Who does not see that this was a mere evasion of the anxious seat, and that it was designed to answer the purpose in its place, and he adopted this because he felt that something of the kind was important?

Now what objection is there against taking a particular seat, or rising up, or going into the lecture-room? They all mean the same thing, when properly conducted. And they are not novelties in principle at all. The thing has always been done in substance. In Joshua's day, he called on the people to decide what they would do, and they spoke right out, in the meeting, "We will serve the Lord; the Lord our God will we serve, and his voice will we obey."

5. The Anxious Bench, 1844

SOURCE: John Williamson Nevin, *The Anxious Bench* (Chambersburg, PA: German Reformed Church, 1844), excerpted from 15-17, 79-84.

It is true indeed, that throughout a large portion of the country the Anxious Bench, after having enjoyed a brief reputation, has fallen into discredit. It has been tried, and found wanting; and it might have been trusted that this experiment would be sufficient to drive it completely out of use. But unfortunately this has not been the case. Over a wide section of the land, we find it still holding its ground, without any regard to the disgrace with which it has been overtaken in the North and East. Peculiar circumstances have conspired to promote its credit, on this field.

It is within the range particularly of the German Churches, that a new life may be said to have been communicated latterly to the system of New Measures. No field is more interesting at this time, than that which is comprehended within these limits. A vast moral change is going forward upon it, involving consequences that no man can properly calculate. From various causes, a new feeling is at work everywhere on the subject of religion. As usual, the old struggles to maintain itself in opposition to the new, and a strong tendency to become extreme is created on both sides. The general mind unhappily has not been furnished thus far with proper protection and guidance, in the way of full religious teaching; and the result is that in these interesting circumstances it has become exposed more or less, at almost every point, to those wild fanatical influences, which in this country are sure to come in like a desolating flood wherever they can find room. Upstart sects have set themselves to take possession if possible of the entire field in this way, on the principle that the old organizations are corrupt and deserve to be destroyed. Their reliance of course in this work of reformation, is placed largely on New Measures! Thus a whole Babel of extravagance has been let loose upon the community, far and wide, in the name of religion, one sect vieing with another in the measure of its irregularities. In these circumstances, it has not been easy for the friends of earnest piety always in the regular churches, to abide by the ancient landmarks of truth and order. The temptation has been strong to fall in, at least to some extent, with the tide of fanaticism, as the only way of making war successfully on the dead formality that stared them in the face in one direction, and the only way of counteracting the proselyting zeal of these noisy sects in the other. . . . An inquiry into the merits of the Anxious Bench, and the system to which it belongs, is not only seasonable and fit in the circumstances of time, but loudly called for on every side. It is no small question, that is involved in the case. The bearing of it upon the interests of religion in the German Churches, is of fundamental and vital importance. A crisis has evidently been reached in the history of these Churches; and one of the most serious points involved in it, is precisely this question of New Measures. Let this system prevail and rule with permanent sway, and the result of the religious movement which is now in progress, will be something widely different from what it would have been under other auspices. The old regular organizations, if they continue to exist at all, will not be the same Churches. Their entire complexion and history, in time to come, will be shaped by the course of things with regard to this point. In this view, the march of New Measures at the present time, may well challenge our anxious and solemn regard. It is an interest of no common magnitude, portentous in its aspect, and pregnant with consequences of vast account. The system is moving forward in full strength, and putting forth its pretensions in the boldest style on all sides. Surely we have a right, and may well feel it a duty, in such a case, to institute an examination into its merits.

Nor is it any reason for silence in the case, that we may have suffered as yet comparatively little in our own denomination, from the use of New Measures. We may congratulate ourselves that we have been thus favored, and that the impression seems to be steadily growing that they ought not to be encouraged in our communion. Still, linked together as the German Churches are throughout the land, we have reason to be jealous here of influences, that must in the nature of the case act upon us from without. In such circumstances there is occasion, and at the same time room, for consideration. It might answer little purpose to interpose remonstrance or inquiry, if the rage for New Measures were fairly let loose, as a sweeping wind, within our borders. It were idle to bespeak attention from the rolling whirlwind. But with the whirlwind in full view, we may be exhorted reasonably to consider and stand back from its destructive path. We are not yet committed to the cause of New Measures, in any respect. We are still free to reject or embrace them, as the interests of the Church, on calm reflection, may be found to require. In such circumstances precisely, may it be counted in all respects proper to subject the system to a serious examination.

It has been sometimes intimated, that it is not safe to oppose and condemn the use of New Measures, because of their connections and purpose. Their relation to the cause of revivals, is supposed to invest them with a sort of sacred character, which the friends of religion should at least respect, even if they may not be able in all cases, to approve. The system has taken hold of the "horns of the altar," and it seems to some like sacrilege to fall upon it there, or to force it away from the purposes of justice to any other place. It is a serious thing, we are told, to find fault with any movement, that claims to be animated by the Spirit of God. By so doing, we render it questionable whether we have ourselves any proper sympathy with revivals, and furnish occasion to the world also to blaspheme and oppose everything of the kind. But this is tyrannical enough, to take for granted the main point in dispute, and then employ it as a consideration to repress inquiry or to silence objection. If New Measures can be shown to proceed from the Holy Ghost, or to be identified in any view with the cause of revivals, they may well demand our reverence and respect. If they can be shown even to be of *adiaphorous* character with regard to religion, harmless at least if not positively helpful to the Spirit's work, they may then put in a reasonable plea to be tolerated in silence, if not absolutely approved. But neither the one nor the other of these positions can be successfully maintained. It is a mere trick unworthy of the gospel, for any one to confound with the sacred idea of a revival, things that do not belong to it in truth at all, for the purpose of compelling a judgment in their favor. The very design of the inquiry now proposed, is to show that the Anxious Bench, and the system to which it belongs, have no claim to be considered either salutary or safe, in the service of religion. It is believed, that instead of promoting the cause of true vital godliness, they are adopted to hinder its progress. The whole system is considered to be full of peril, for the most precious interests of the Church. And why then should there be any reserve, in treating the subject with such freedom as it may seem to require? We may well feel indeed that the subject is solemn. All that relates to the interests of revivals, and the welfare of souls, is solemn; and it becomes us to approach it in a serious way. But this is no reason, why we should close our eyes against the truth, or refuse to call things by their proper names. This would be to trifle with sacred things truly. . . .

Notoriously, no conversions are more precarious and insecure than those of the Anxious Bench. They take place under such circumstances precisely, as should make them the object of earnest jealousy and distrust. The most ample evidence of their vanity, is presented on every side. And yet the patrons of the system are generally ready to endorse them, as though they carried the broad seal of heaven on their face. Of conversions in any other form, they can be sufficiently jealous. They think it well for the Church to use great caution, in the case of those who have been led quietly, under the ordinary means of grace to indulge the Christian hope. They shrink perhaps from the use of the Catechism altogether, lest they might seem to aim at a religion of merely human manufacture. But let the power of the Anxious Bench appear, and strange to tell, their caution is at once given to the winds. *This* they proclaim to be the finger of God. Here the work of religion is presumed at once to authenticate itself. With very little instruction, and almost no examination, all who can persuade themselves that they are converted, are at once hailed as brethren and sisters in Christ Jesus, and with as little delay as possible gathered into the full communion of the Church. And this is held to be building on the true foundation gold, silver and precious stones, while such as try to make christians in a different way are regarded as working mainly, almost as a matter of course, with wood, hay, and stubble. Wonderful infatuation! Stupendous inconsistency.

6. Human Aliment and the Wines of Scripture, 1855

SOURCE: Sylvester Graham, ed., *The Philosophy of Sacred History Considered in Relation to Human Aliment and the Wines of Scripture* (1855).

Having clearly and fully ascertained the true nature and character of God; the real nature and constitutional character, condition and relations of man; the primary purpose of God, in the creation and earthly existence of man; the great, paramount purpose of God, concerning man, in the economy of grace; and, in a general manner, the causes which render man, as a moral agent, incapable of being so acted on by the moral and spiritual power of God, as to be kept from sin with conscious freedom of choice and action, and which there by hinder the accomplishment of the great purposes of Divine benevolence, and prevent man's being brought into the spiritual kingdom of God, I now proceed to inquire more particularly,—

First, what effects the use of flesh as food, and of wine or alcoholic liquor of any kind, as a drink, have on the condition, character and actions of man, as a subject of the moral and spiritual government of God, with reference to the fulfillment of the great purposes of Divine benevolence, and,

Second, what are the bearings or teachings of the Bible, as a whole, in relation to these points: or, in other words, how far the Sacred Scriptures may, by accurate interpretation, be shown to be in harmony with the true revelations of God, in the volume of Nature.

It is evident that the first of these particular subjects of investigation, is mainly a question of natural Science, and as such, must be solved by the revelations of God in the volume of Nature. For, we have seen that, every law and principle, and property of Nature, is an institution of the Divine will,— that Nature is, in truth, the first great Volume of Divine Revelation, in which the deeply written will of God lies ever ready to be disclosed to the human mind by the true developments of science, and by accurate experience, —that the Revealed Word is but a Supplement to this first great Volume, and, in strictness, as a pure revelation, contains, principally, Divine instructions concerning moral and spiritual things, which Nature speaks not of, or but faintly implies, or dimly indicates; and that the truth of Nature and the true meaning of the Revealed Word, must be in harmony; and, consequently, it is impossible that the true meaning of the Revealed Word can, as a permanent law, be contrary to the laws of Nature. The truth of natural science, therefore, is the truth of God, and always comes with Divine authority to man:— and the Bible, as the revealed word of God, must, when accurately interpreted, be perfectly consistent with what is true in chemistry, and mineralogy, and botany, and zoology, and astronomy, and every other natural science. Yet the Bible was not given to teach us the natural sciences; and no correct philosopher thinks of going to the Bible to study these sciences. To ascertain what is true in these, he goes to the Volume of Nature as the primary and irreversible code of the omniscient and omnipotent Creator and Ruler of all things: And, in regard to his Bible, he is satisfied if he finds nothing in it, which is apparently incompatible with the demonstrations of natural science; and pleased if he finds it confirmed by scientific truth: knowing that the truth of Nature must stand, whether the apparent meaning of any particular portion of the Sacred Scriptures, agrees with it or not. He, therefore, who truly loves and reverences the Bible as the revealed word of God, will not be forward to introduce it into controversies of a scientific nature, and oppose his interpretations of it to the demonstrations of science, in such a manner as to make it appear that the Bible and the truths of natural science, are at variance: for he knows that this must only serve to invalidate his Bible, and not the truth of science. But, the true philosopher, who cordially and understandingly loves and reverences his Bible, will, as a scientific man, in all his investigations, and researches, pursue the truth for the truth's sake; and when he has fully ascertained the truth of science, if he finds any *apparent* want of agreement between this and his Bible, he will, with the spirit of truth still ruling his soul, honestly set about such an examination of the matter, as will enable him to show that the disagreement is only *apparent,* and that when accurately understood, the Bible perfectly harmonizes with scientific truth; or at least, that, the true meaning of the Revealed Word is not incompatible with the truth of natural science. . . .

But we shall lose much of the force of our argument if we do not continually keep in view the incontrovertible truth, that the health and happiness of the body of man is as truly a final cause of the gospel economy as the salvation of the soul; and that such is the compound nature and complicated structure of man, that the highest and best interests of the soul cannot be secured while the true interests of the body are violated or neglected: and therefore, the effects of intoxicating substances and of flesh-meat on the human body, in causing or aggravating the disorders and diseases which it suffers, and in producing is premature death, are fully to be taken into the account in the gospel view of the subject. And that we may the more accurately appreciate the extent of these evils, we should bear in mind that the same prophets who, speaking as they were moved by the Holy Spirit, foretold the coming of Christ and the introduction and effects of the gospel dispensation, clearly specified, among other legitimate results of the genuine operations of that dispensation, that the evil and rancorous passions of mankind should be subdued, and men should become peaceful and gentle, and kind and benevolent, and philanthropic and holy; and that all disease should be removed from among them, and human life should be greatly prolonged. These things, it is true, are generally supposed to refer more particularly to the Millennium. But what is the Millennium, other than that state of things on earth in which the gospel principles are fully understood and obeyed in the spirit?—for this would be the reign of Christ. And so perfectly is the gospel adapted to all the laws and conditions and relations of human nature, that it only needs to be thus universally understood and obeyed, to produce, as a natural and necessary consequence, all the blessings promised in the Millennium. And be assured, that until the gospel shall be regarded and obeyed as a scheme of divine benevolence, adapted to and embracing the whole nature of man, and aiming as really at the welfare of his body as of his soul, and as truly fitted and designed to secure his happiness in time as in eternity, the Millennium of our prayers and expectations will never be realized on earth.

Essays

The three essays reprinted here examine ways in which religion functioned in the early republic. The first, by Steven Mintz of the University of Houston, explains why many Americans in the early republic believed the United States was destined to take the initiative in promulgating Christian influence around the world and opposing all sorts of tyranny and injustice. In the second essay, Robert R. Mathisen of Western Baptist College (OR) describes the role Charles G. Finney played in the critical issue of appropriate "measures" or "means" used by evangelists of the early republic's Second Awakening. Gordon S. Wood of Brown University argues in the final essay that Mormonism was a product of both the religious chaos of the early republic and the complicated nature of early nineteenth-century American culture.

The Promise of the Millennium

STEVEN MINTZ

SOURCE: Mintz, Steven. *Moralists and Modernizers: America's Pre-Civil War Reformers.* pp. 16-24, 32-34, 35-38. © 1995 by The Johns Hopkins University Press. Reprinted with permission of The Johns Hopkins University Press.

Inscribed on the Great Seal of the United States are the Latin words *Novus ordo seclorum*—"a new order for the ages." The notion that the American Revolution inaugurated a new epoch in human history, a new era of virtue, justice, equality, and possibility, was widely shared by late-eighteenth-century and early-nineteenth-century Americans. The Revolution, declared Joseph Priestley, a chemist, an early Unitarian, and an immigrant from England, was nothing less than the harbinger of the millennium—the establishment of God's kingdom on earth. But this fervent optimism and sense of new possibilities was not confined to the religious. Many secular Americans also believed that the United States was the New Israel, destined to lead the world to universal peace and prosperity.

To be sure, millennial hopes were often mixed with fear and foreboding. Many early-nineteenth-century Americans felt a profound sense of peril—from irreligion, godlessness, greed, and anarchy. Nevertheless, the sense that a new age of human history had dawned helped unleash what Ralph Waldo Emerson called the "demon of reform," which flourished with such vigor in pre-Civil War America.

During the last years of the eighteenth century and the first years of the nineteenth, Americans of diverse backgrounds shared a conviction that the United States would lead the world toward Christ's millennial kingdom, a thousand years of " peace, purity, and felicity," as Timothy Dwight, later president of Yale College, declared in 1776. Inspired by the example of the revolutionaries who won American independence, by the philosophy of the Enlightenment, by the scientific and technological triumphs of the early Industrial Revolution, and, above all, by two critical trends in religious thought—religious liberalism and evangelical revivalism—many Americans believed that their country would take the lead in spreading Christian influence around the globe and combating all forms of tyranny and injustice.

Before the 1770s, millennial thought was often associated with passivity, apathy, and pessimism, as believers patiently awaited the destruction of a corrupt and evil world before the onset of a new era "when time shall be no more." But the success of the American Revolution, the rapid growth in church membership, and the quickening pace of technological and scientific progress stimulated a more hopeful and optimistic view: that the millennium would follow not a violent apocalypse or catastrophic conflagration, but successful efforts to defeat godlessness, irreligion, materialism, and selfishness and to establish a virtuous, just order on earth.

Unlike many present-day millennialists, who are deeply conservative in their economic and social views, profoundly skeptical of reform, and convinced that the millennium will arrive only after a bleak period of wars and natural disasters, their early-nineteenth-century counterparts tended to be much more hopeful. Their millennial vision contributed to a spirit of optimism, a sensitivity to human suffering, and a boundless faith in humanity's capacity to improve social institutions. The moral fervor, the expectancy, and the intense devotion to mission rooted in millennialist ideas inspired early-nineteenth-century efforts at reform and allowed different kinds of reformers to work together.

America's Revolutionary Heritage

One source of inspiration for reformers was the example of the patriots of the American Revolution who had risked their lives and honor to overcome tyranny and injustice. Pre-Civil War reformers pictured their efforts to abolish slavery or to improve the nation's educational system as attempts to realize the republican ideals enshrined in the Declaration of Independence. Proponents of women's rights, world peace, temperance, and abolition all drafted Declarations of Sentiments modeled on the wording of the Declaration of Independence. Workingmen's parties in New York and Philadelphia in the 1820s, abolitionists in 1830, and proponents of women's rights in 1848 each issued "Declarations of Sentiments" listing "a history of repeated injuries and usurpations" that justified their reforms. Convinced that the sacred principles of the Revolution had been corrupted, reformers sought to revive the Spirit of 1776 by exposing a host of abuses that contradicted the nation's revolutionary principles.

Early-nineteenth-century reformers saw their own crusades as the fulfillment of the political struggles begun during the Revolution. For America's pre-Civil War reformers, the nation's revolutionary heritage remained a standard for measuring present imperfections against a higher ideal.

The theory of natural rights embodied in the Declaration—the idea that "all men are created equal," that they were endowed with certain natural, essential, and inalienable rights—served as a powerful stimulus for reform. The principles of liberty and equality set forth in the Declaration led abolitionist William Lloyd Garrison to challenge the justice of the institution of slavery and encouraged suffragist Elizabeth Cady Stanton to press for equal rights for women.

It is not an accident that many of the nation's leading reformers were members of a specific generation—they were born between 1810 and 1820. Belonging to the new nation's second generation, and lacking any personal experience of the hardships and triumphs of the revolutionary era, these reformers felt an acute "belatedness"—that they had missed the sense of heroic mission and social solidarity experienced by the revolutionary generation. Also, at a time when many respectable careers for the young were becoming overcrowded, reform provided an outlet for intense personal energies and aspirations. For these women and men, reform offered a substitute cause—an opportunity to preserve a virtuous republic in the face of profound challenges: foreign immigration, intemperance, and rapid urban growth. And finally, many reformers were members of a transitional generation that had revolted against Calvinist religious orthodoxy, yet retained a deep sense of moral severity and dedication.

Nor was it accidental that the cause of reform had a particular attraction for residents of New England. Many New Englanders opposed America's second war of independence, the War of 1812, and, after the celebrated American victory in the Battle of New Orleans, found themselves stigmatized as traitors. For those New Englanders who had seen their political power collapse with the demise of the Federalist Party and who were dismayed by the growing separation of church and state, reform seemed a providential means of restoring order and morality to American society. Following the War of 1812, New England adopted a new stance toward the rest of the nation: many embarked on a missionary crusade to make their region's values the nation's.

Philosophy of the Enlightenment
Apart from the nation's revolutionary heritage, the roots of reform could also be found in Enlightenment philosophy. During the eighteenth century, French philosophes, Scottish moral philosophers, and such American thinkers as Benjamin Franklin and Thomas Jefferson developed a set of principles which had enormous importance for reform. One principle was that human beings were not innately sinful, but were basically good. Given a favorable environment, people's moral character would improve. A second principle was that poverty, disease, crime, and ignorance were not inevitable, but could be overcome by reform. By reshaping the environment, reformers could eliminate the causes of human misery. A central message of the Enlightenment was that the human condition was not inevitable; human action could alter it.

Perhaps the Enlightenment's most important contribution to reform was the view that all humanity was born equal in mental and moral capacities, and that environment and circumstance accounted for human differences. As a result, human beings were all entitled to equal respect, regardless of differences in their talents, wealth, and achievements.

The triumphs of eighteenth- and early-nineteenth-century science and technology contributed to a widespread faith in the capacity of human beings to improve society through the use of reason. The steam engine, gas-fueled lamps, potbellied stoves, and interchangeable parts were dramatic examples of humanity's expanding ability to make life better.

Another major intellectual source of the reform impulse was a philosophy imported from Scotland. Common sense realism, based on the psychological writings of philosophers Thomas Reid, Adam Smith, and Dugald Stewart, dominated academic curricula from about 1820 to 1870 and was quickly incorporated into the teachings of the nation's Protestant churches. This philosophy declared that the external world was much as it appeared and that to act properly each person need only follow the moral laws inscribed in one's conscience. Common sense philosophy seemed to offer a providential solution to bitter theological disputes. All theological issues, and even the Bible itself, were accessible to common sense, logic, and reason. Far from being a complicated and mysterious work, which only scholars and theologians could understand, the Bible was a text easily comprehended by almost everyone.

For liberals and conservatives alike, common sense philosophy offered a simple solution to the dislocations and upheavals of the age. Implanted within all people was a conscience—a small, steady voice that stood ready to guide them in the ways of virtue. But the conscience had to be properly nurtured and cultivated, since it constantly had to resist immorality and vice. Families, churches, schools, and moral reform societies would have to play a central role in shaping conscience.

Reform's Religious Roots

Of all the factors that stimulated the growth of reform, the main one was religion. Today, religion—especially the "fundamentalist" kinds of religion that dominated pre-Civil War America—is often conceived of as a conservative force. Social scientists often associate progress with secularization, that is, with the spread of education, technology, and scientific knowledge. And secularization, or the triumph of a scientific worldview, implies a falling away from religious belief. But in nineteenth-century America, as the United States rapidly "modernized," so church membership also increased. Religious commitment was of central importance in inspiring a wide range of reformers.

Almost all the leading reformers were devoutly religious men and women who wanted to deepen the nation's commitment to Christian principles. Proponents of temperance, abolition, and other reforms were convinced that drunkenness or slavery or other social evils were an affront not only to the country's republican values but to Christian morality.

During the eighteenth and early nineteenth centuries, religion was truly the seedbed of social protest and reform. It was no accident that America's first organized efforts to promote social change had religious roots. Among the Quakers in Pennsylvania the American reform impulse was born.

One of several radical religious sects that arose during the English civil wars in the mid-seventeenth century, the Quakers sought to live free from sin and from all enslaving creeds and institutions. They condemned war and refused to bear arms, take oaths, or bow or take off their hats to social superiors. Rejecting an educated, ordained ministry, such sacraments as baptism and the Lord's Supper, as well as a formal theology, the Quakers were "spiritualists" who believed that the Holy Spirit was present in every human heart, and that this "inward Christ" should guide each person's beliefs and actions.

Beginning in the 1670s, many Quakers migrated to the New World, particularly to Pennsylvania, Rhode Island, and the West Indies. Compared to other colonial religious sects, the Quakers were extraordinarily egalitarian. Embracing the idea that the Holy Spirit can speak through both women and men, Quaker women assumed prominent ministerial roles. The Friends rejected the notion that infants are born sinful and with an impaired capacity for reason, and so did not resort to corporal punishment of young children and permitted their offspring to participate in religious meetings from an early age. By the mid-eighteenth century, many Quakers had grown prosperous in trade and manufacturing, but the sect's increasing wealth produced a deep ambivalence. Prosperity and luxury were very much at odds with the traditional emphasis on plainness in speech, dress, and behavior.

During the Seven Years' War (1756-63), Quakers, particularly those living in Pennsylvania, divided over the question of whether or not to support the war effort. Many Quakers who opposed the war were subject to persecution for refusing to fight or to pay taxes. In response, Quaker pacifists sought to purify their sect and raise its moral standards. They reasserted the duty of the individual Quaker to confront social evil and relieve human suffering. As a result, a growing number of Quakers began to take active steps against poverty, the drinking of hard liquor, unjust Indian policies, and, above all, slavery. Between 1755 and 1776, the Society of Friends became the first organization in history to prohibit slaveholding, and Quakers founded the first societies to protest the institution.

In the future, Quakers would join reform movements in far higher numbers than their percentage in the nation's population would suggest. For example, perhaps three-quarters of all the members of antislavery societies formed before 1830 were members of the Society of Friends, and, according to one estimate, 40 percent of all female abolitionists and 19 percent of all pre-1830 feminists were Quaker women. In their desire to combat oppression and human suffering, their emphasis upon personal piety and individual commitment, and their staunch desire to lead the world toward the kingdom of God, the Quakers provided a moral example for later American reformers.

Religious Liberalism

Two significantly different trends in Protestant thought stimulated the rise of re-form activity: religious liberalism and evangelical revivalism. Religious liberalism was an emerging humanitarian form of religion that rejected the harsh Calvinist doctrines of original sin and predestination. Its preachers stressed the basic good-ness of human nature and each individual's capacity to follow the example of Christ by cultivating proper moral attitudes and behavior. Reason, intellectual freedom, and moral duty were the watchwords of the liberal Christian faith.

Religious liberals tended to reject literal interpretations of the Bible and instead emphasized the importance of reason in interpreting Scripture. They also rejected the orthodox boundaries of the Trinity and, denying the divinity of Jesus Christ, instead viewed him as a moral model whom all humanity should strive to emulate. Regarding God not as an angry and unpredictable Father but as an enlightened parent, liberals emphasized the possibility of salvation for all women and men. Arising partly in reaction against the fervent revivalism of the Great Awakening in the 1730s and 1740s, liberal Christianity sought to substitute reason for revela-tion. As Charles Chauncy, an early liberal minister put it in an essay entitled "Sea-sonal Thought on the State of Religion" (1734), "An enlightened Mind, and not raised Affections, ought always to be the guide of those who call themselves Men." But it was not until the early nineteenth century that religious liberalism would adopt clearly defined institutional forms: Unitarianism and Universalism.

William Ellery Channing (1780-1842) was America's leading exponent of reli-gious liberalism. Born in Newport, Rhode Island, and educated at Harvard, Channing served as minister of Federal Street Church in Boston for the last forty years of his life. In 1815, Channing played a major role in a bitter theological conflict that divided New England Congregationalists. During the "Unitarian Con-flict," theological conservatives, who emphasized predestination, human deprav-ity, and the infallibility of the Bible, fiercely clashed with liberals whose tenets were free will, the universal brotherhood of humanity, and human reason.

In Baltimore in 1819, Channing delivered a sermon entitled "Unitarian Chris-tianity," which proclaimed the principles of his faith and became the intellectual foundation for American Unitarianism. Emphasizing the importance of human reason in interpreting the Bible, Channing denied that there was a scriptural basis for the orthodox Calvinist beliefs in predestination and original sin. Instead, Channing stressed humanity's basic goodness and its capacity to affect personal salvation and described Christ as a model of moral perfection. In an essay entitled "The Perfect Life" (1831), Channing declared that the sole purpose of Christianity was "the perfection of human nature, the elevation of men into nobler beings." Channing's ideas stimulated many reformers to work toward improving the condi-tions of the physically handicapped, the criminal, the poor, and the enslaved.

Reluctant to found a new religious denomination, for fear that it would soon impose its own version of orthodoxy, he formed a conference of liberal Congrega-tional ministers in 1820, which was reorganized in 1825 as the American Unitar-ian Association. Adopting as its slogan "Deeds not creeds," the association stressed individual freedom of belief, a united world under a single God, the mortal nature of Jesus Christ, and the moral and ethical responsibilities of people toward their neighbors. Critics accused the new denomination of downplaying the foundations of religious faith—sin, divine passion, supernatural mystery, and the ecstasy of salvation. And wits mockingly declared that Unitarians, most of whom belonged to the commercial elite in eastern Massachusetts, were dedicated to "the Fatherhood of God, the Brotherhood of Man, and the Neighborhood of Boston." Yet few religious denominations exerted a stronger influence upon American intellectual life (through such figures as William Cullen Bryant, Henry Wadsworth Longfellow, James Russell Lowell, and Francis Parkman) or contributed as many prominent antebellum reformers, including Dorothea Dix, a crusader on behalf of the mentally ill; Samuel Gridley Howe, a staunch advocate for the blind; educational reformer Horace Mann; and Joseph Tuckerman, one of the nation's first advocates for the urban poor.

If Unitarianism drew its support largely from genteel, urban Boston, Universalism was its "lower-class" counterpart, with members in rural, economically marginal areas of New England, though it also gained influence in the Philadelphia area. Like the Unitarians, the Universalists rejected the central tenets of Calvinist orthodoxy, holding instead that God was a benevolent deity who would save all humankind (P.T. Barnum claimed that Universalism was the only religion that "really believes in success"). Sharing the Unitarians' optimistic view of human destiny and the innate goodness of human nature, the Universalists also downplayed theology and stressed conscience and benevolence. Like the Unitarians, the Universalists believed that Christians' fundamental duty was to demonstrate their piety through humanitarian and reformist endeavors.

The Second Great Awakening: The Revolt against Enlightened Religion

Another source of the reform impulse can be found in the enthusiastic revivals that swept the nation in the early nineteenth century. These revivals sought to awaken Americans to their need for religious rebirth and redemption. Highly emotional meetings were held by preachers in all sections of the country. So widespread were they in the early nineteenth century that they acquired a name, the "Second Great Awakening."

The Second Great Awakening had its symbolic beginning in a small frontier community in central Kentucky. This was one of the most remarkable events in American religious history. Between August 6 through August 12, 1801, thousands of people—perhaps as many as 25,000—gathered at Cane Ridge to fast and pray and take communion. This was the largest attendance at a religious revival in America up until this time, and it was a truly fantastic number. There were only 250,000 people in all of Kentucky, and Lexington, the state's largest city, only had 1,795 residents.

Cane Ridge became an instant legend. Never before had religious piety and fervor been so openly expressed or conversions so numerous. Early in 1801, only about 10 percent of all Kentuckians were formal members of a church; ministers complained about the pervasiveness of deism, rationalism, and religious indifference. Then, in the course of six months, in a series of religious revivals, at least 100,000 frontier Kentuckians, hungry for intense religious experience and eager for a sense of community, joined together in search of religious salvation.

There was not just one minister at Cane Ridge; there were more than a dozen. They came from many denominations: Presbyterian, Baptist, Methodist. There was at least one black minister. The people who attended the camp meeting came from all social classes and social groups; they included Kentucky's governor, prominent landowners, and college-educated ministers; many were young; and perhaps two-thirds were female.

Tales of the "physical exercises" that people experienced at Cane Ridge spread far and wide: weeping, shrieking, groaning, shouting, dancing, trembling, jerking, swooning. A minister named James Campbell left a vivid first-person description of the scene: "Sinners [were] dropping down on every hand, shrieking, groaning, crying for mercy, convoluted; professors praying, agonizing, fainting, falling down in distress."

The outpouring of religious feeling at Cane Ridge soon erupted across the entire country. In 1801 and 1802 revivals broke out in the Carolinas, Georgia, eastern Tennessee, Virginia, western Pennsylvania, and Ohio. Other revivals took place in New England, New Jersey, and New York. Within two years, dozens of ministers, missionaries, and itinerant preachers began organizing camp meetings. . . .

Religious Ferment

In 1783, Yale College's president, Ezra Stiles, predicted that three religious denominations—the Congregationalists, the Episcopalians, and the Presbyterians—would dominate the religious life of the new nation. His prediction proved to be entirely wrong. Stiles never imagined that a number of older denominations would quickly expand—notably, the Baptists, Catholics, and Methodists—and that a host of new denominations and movements would soon arise and radically reshape the religious landscape—adventists, perfectionists, primitivists, Christians, Disciples of Christ, Mormons, and separate African American churches.

During the late eighteenth and early nineteenth centuries, the Congregationalist and Episcopal churches grew relatively slowly. The number of Congregationalist churches rose from 750 in 1780 to 2,200 in 1860; the number of Episcopal congregations from 400 to 2,100. At the same time, other denominations—particularly the more pietistic and evangelical sects—expanded at a staggering pace. Baptists grew from approximately 400 congregations in 1780 to 12,150 in 1860; Lutherans from 225 to 2,100; Presbyterians from 500 to 6,400; Methodists from 50 in 1783 to 20,000 in 1860; Roman Catholics from 50 in 1780 to 2,500 in 1860. The African Methodist Episcopal church grew from 5 congregations in 1816 to more than 100 by 1850.

During the decades before the Civil War, America was a veritable "spiritual hothouse," a place of extraordinary religious ferment and enthusiasm. Many new religions and sects arose—among them, the Disciples of Christ, the Mormons, and the Shakers. An influx of foreign immigrants helped create ethnic and linguistic fissures in older churches, such as the Lutheran church and the Roman Catholic church. Older denominations splintered and fragmented, producing diverse forms of Presbyterianism (Old School, New School, Reformed, Associated) and many kinds of Baptist churches (General, Free Will, Regular, Separate). Lay members challenged established authority and demanded changes in ritual. In many churches, women suddenly assumed previously unheard-of roles.

It was a period of truly unprecedented innovation and experimentation in the realm of religion. At a time when religion was losing ground in Europe, America witnessed a remarkable outpouring of religious belief. According to one estimate, three-quarters of the American population in 1860 had a connection with a church. By 1860, the nation's churches reported having 26 million seats for the country's 31 million people.

Behind this explosion of religious enthusiasm and popular evangelicalism lay a broad cultural shift: a weakening of older structures of religious authority and a revolt against Calvinist notions of human depravity and a predestined elect. People sought new forms of religious fellowship, at camp meetings, urban prayer meetings, and Methodist "love feasts." In the increasingly fluid environment of early-nineteenth-century America, sects competed fiercely for members. Charismatic preachers, scorning pessimistic Calvinist views of human nature and recognizing people's ability to speed their own salvation, expressed exuberant confidence in their ability to save souls and promote revivals.

Three currents of popular religious thought exhibited particular vigor and intensity in antebellum America. The first, known as primitivism or restorationism, was a movement to recreate the practices of early New Testament Christianity and strip away ecclesiastical perversions and creeds. The second, millennialism or adventism, was a set of ideas connected with the second coming of Christ and the arrival of an era of earthly peace and the triumph of righteousness mentioned in the New Testament Book of Revelation. The third was the doctrine of holiness— a belief that moral and spiritual perfection and sinlessness were prerequisites for salvation. These intellectual currents contributed to the establishment of a number of new religious sects and denominations and greatly stimulated enthusiasm for personal piety, education, and social reform. . . .

Millennialism

Visions of the millennium—the return of Christ to earth and the arrival of a thousand years of universal peace and happiness—exerted enormous influence upon pre-Civil War America. Rooted in the books of Daniel and Revelation in the Bible, the millennial impulse took many different forms. Adventists believed that the literal second coming of Christ and the end of the world were at hand. Radical adventists often employed apocalyptic imagery—they expected the imminent destruction of the temporal world, and they predicted that the unrighteous would be purged in a holocaust that would engulf the earth and that the righteous would be resurrected. "Premillennialists" argued that Christ's second coming would precede his thousand-year reign on earth, which would culminate in the ultimate battle between good and evil at Armageddon. More common in antebellum America was an optimistic theological tradition known as "postmillennialism." This was the belief that Christ will return to earth only after the millennium—after clergy, missionaries, and reformers had defeated the forces of irreligion, evil, and vice and set the stage for the triumph of virtue and righteousness.

Antebellum America's millennial consciousness drew upon a variety of sources. In part, one basis was the long-standing view that Americans were, in Herman Melville's words, "the peculiar, chosen people, the Israel of our time," and that the millennium was destined to take place in America. The pace of scientific and technological innovation, the triumphs of the revivalists, and the strength of the nation's republican institutions further contributed to millennial fervor. The invention of the telegraph touched off a dramatic statement of millennialist hopes in *The Ladies' Repository*, a Methodist monthly, in 1850: "This noble invention is to be the means of extending civilization, republicanism, and Christianity over the earth. . . . Then will wrong and injustice be forever banished. Every yoke shall be broken, and the oppressed go free. Wars will cease from the earth. . . . Then shall come to pass the millennium."

Antebellum America spawned many religious sects and communitarian ventures that drew inspiration from their reading of the Book of Revelation. At utopian communities in Oneida, New York, and Zoar, Ohio, and in Shaker communities, men and women sought to live as if the millennium had already arrived. The desire to root out sin and set the stage for the millennium inspired countless missionaries to win the world for Christ. Millennialist visions also stimulated reform movements that attacked drinking, slavery, and other social evils. Millennialist imagery arose with particular intensity during the Civil War, when many Northerners believed that the conflict would cleanse the nation of sin and prepare the way for an age of righteousness. The North, in the words of Julia Ward Howe's "Battle Hymn of the Republic," had glimpsed "the glory of the coming of the Lord" and was fighting to purge the land of sin. Much as "Christ had died to make men holy," Northern soldiers were fighting to set men free.

Perhaps the most dramatic example of radical adventism in antebellum America involved a religious leader named William Miller (1782-1849), a farmer from Low Hampton, New York, who interpreted the Bible to pinpoint the return of Christ "around 1843." A native of Massachusetts, a veteran of the War of 1812, and a dabbler in deism, Miller underwent a dramatic conversion experience, after which he was baptized a Baptist and developed a method for computing the precise time of Christ's return. Joshua V. Himes, a Boston minister and a communications genius, popularized Miller's views in some five million pieces of literature. Tens of thousands of Americans prepared themselves for the imminent arrival of the millennium.

Miller initially predicted that the millennium would commence in March 1843. When his original prediction failed to come true, he first offered March 1844 as the date of Christ's return, and then October 22, 1844. It used to be said that many Millerites abandoned their jobs and property and gathered on hilltops to await the second coming. In fact, Miller's followers gathered at churches and prayed as the end of the world approached.

Although many were disillusioned after the failure of Miller's predictions, a number of the faithful remained convinced that the second coming was imminent. Some disappointed Millerites would follow the teachings of Ellen G. White, herself a Miller convert, which later formed the theological basis for Seventh-Day Adventism. Retaining the belief in the imminence of Christ's second coming, White advocated vegetarianism, forbade alcohol and tobacco, and criticized reliance on drugs and medicine. Other adventists would turn to the teaching of Charles Taze Russell, who believed that the millennium had already commenced but that its final consummation still lay in the future. Russell's successor, Joseph F. Rutherford, would draw upon Russell's teachings when he formed Jehovah's Witnesses in 1931.

Holiness Movements

The quest for holiness exerted a powerful attraction in pre-Civil War America. Many Protestants, mainly Methodist in background, were deeply troubled by the worldliness of established churches and struggled relentlessly to achieve John Wesley's ideal of perfect sanctification—a truly sinless Christian life, a life of purity and piety. Many others, particularly those converted in the revivals held by Charles Finney, sought feverishly to attain Finney's ideal of spiritual and moral perfection. To many individuals active in the pre-Civil War holiness movements, personal piety could be truly expressed only through acts of disinterested benevolence.

The central figure in the antebellum holiness movement was Phoebe Palmer, the daughter of English Methodist immigrants. In camp meetings, holiness revivals, home gatherings, and interdenominational prayer meetings, she converted thousands of Americans and Canadians with the message that salvation could be achieved through total submission to God's will. It was not necessary to wait for an emotional conversion experience; nor was it necessary to "struggle with the powers of darkness," she proclaimed in *The Way of Holiness* (1851). Salvation was immediately open to all who would consecrate themselves to God.

Women played a particularly active role in the holiness movement. Leaders were members of the laity, men and women who had an equal right to preach. It was assumed that both men and women could receive an infusion of the Holy Spirit and could testify in public to the experience of holiness. Above all, women were especially likely to engage in acts of practical benevolence, which demonstrated their obedience to God's law. Phoebe Palmer herself was a pioneer in urban philanthropy, establishing a mission in Five Points, New York City's most notorious slum, and dispensing assistance to inmates in New York's Tombs prison. . . .

Charles G. Finney

ROBERT R. MATHISEN

SOURCE: From *American Portraits: History through Biography*, Vol. 1, by Donald W. Whisenhunt. Pp. 211-14, 215-19. Copyright © 1993 by Kendall/Hunt Publishing Company. Reprinted with permission of the author.

The first half of the nineteenth century—the "middle period" of American history—has been and continues to be viewed by historians in a variety of ways. For some it is considered merely the postlude to the American Revolution and the prelude to the Civil War. For others it is seen as the Age of Jefferson and Jackson. Some writers have woven their story around the central theme of the growth of the democratic spirit, with the spread of political suffrage and the rise of the common man. Others argue that the key development of the period was the economic revolution which divided the American populace into distinct classes with conflicting social and political concerns.

However one wishes to define the American nation of 1800 to 1850, the student of American history cannot escape noticing that it was a time of social and intellectual challenges. Crosscurrents and antagonisms mounted between rich and poor, slave and free, saint and sinner. Each sought its own identity in the fluid nature of early nineteenth century society. Central to the contest between saint and sinner was the religious revival commonly known as the Second Great Awakening, which one historian describes as an organizing process that provided meaning and direction to people struggling with the social pressures of a nation moving into new economic, political, and geographic areas. At the heart of that process was the frontier evangelist known by many as the "father of the Second Great Awakening," Charles Grandison Finney. The place of Finney and the Second Awakening in the flow of social and intellectual challenges during the first half of the nineteenth century is a fascinating story.

In the years after the First Great Awakening of the 1740s, religious interest declined as the attention of the colonies was drawn in other directions. The French and Indian War (1754-1763) had a negative effect on all Americans, especially on their ideas of religion and morality. The Revolutionary War period brought a noticeable decline in church membership. Deism, introduced to the American colonies during the French and Indian War, became more popular among the educated elite along the East Coast. It taught that God revealed himself in nature and through reason, not through the Christian Scriptures or church tradition, as many Americans believed. More were inclined to take notice of these Americanized Enlightenment teachings when heroes of the Revolution such as Thomas Paine, Ethan Allen, and Thomas Jefferson embraced them and wrote their own endorsements in several books.

Along the rapidly expanding frontier of Ohio, Tennessee, Kentucky, Virginia, and the Carolinas following the Revolution, life was difficult and churches made little impact at first. The rush to the Ohio and Allegheny River valleys exceeded one million by 1803, at which time the frontier was extended even further with the addition of the Louisiana Purchase. The West was significantly different from the East, which still had its churches despite the rise of immorality and the threat of deism. There, where lawlessness seemed to be an apt description, there were no churches, and Christian ideas had not yet been introduced. The few circuit riders and missionaries who had been dispatched to the area found the task greater than their energies. The "new light" of the First Great Awakening which shone upon America through the preaching of Jonathan Edwards and George Whitefield was now barely a glimmer.

The new nation was poised for change as it entered the new century. Socially, a new egalitarianism was on the rise. It was in sharp contrast with the old hierarchical order of society inherited from Europe. Denominationally, new sects were appearing everywhere, as the old established churches were in retreat. Perhaps most significant was the philosophical conflict that arose between the First Great Awakening Calvinists, who stressed man's sinfulness and dependence on an all-knowing God, and new Enlightenment rationalists, such as the deists, who emphasized man's inborn goodness and dependence on one's own free will. The former placed mankind within the designs of a seemingly arbitrary God who chose some to be saved and others to be damned, while the latter saw man capable of choosing his own fate. Which one seemed to fit better the experiences of the American people who had taken destiny into their own hands in 1776 and roundly defeated the greatest empire in the world?

The answer to this question came in the form of the Second Great Awakening which spanned most of the first half of the nineteenth century. The American Revolution produced a continuing thirst for freedom, and the frontier of that period was the place to experience it. The religion of the frontier was to be a religion of voluntarism and charitable ("benevolent") participation. The breaking of ties between church and state produced by the Revolution created a new awakening of the people, who were now encouraged to use their own resources in meeting the challenges of an irreligious frontier. Through the birth of many agencies and organizations, through the establishing of numerous academies and schools, and through the arrival of a religious experience known as revivalism, the religious forces of the early nineteenth century constructed a potent counter-movement against religious indifference and hostility; and its thrust would leave its mark on the entire social and intellectual framework of the nation. . . .

Revivals were not new in the United States in 1800. They had marked the social upheavals of the First Great Awakening. Edwards and Whitefield were among the most powerful and influential revivalists of their day. There was a significant difference, however, between the revivals of the two awakenings that must be noted here. The theology of revivals in both Europe and in colonial New England held that awakenings would take place only at times of God's choosing. The logical conclusion derived from the Calvinist doctrine of election, the belief that God chose whom he would to receive His salvation from sin and condemnation, led most during the First Awakening simply to wait for God to let them know if they were among the elect. The individual had little or nothing to do with acquiring salvation. Revivals were the work of God, not man.

Between the two awakenings the theology of revivals went through an evolutionary change, so that by 1800 Rev. Timothy Dwight, president of Yale College, and grandson of Jonathan Edwards, was among those who in the early stages of the Second Awakening was "preaching down revival." In the language of revivalism, some now believed, as others had hinted earlier, that certain "measures" or "means" could be used by preachers and devout laity to bring the sinner to repentance and thereby produce revivals. More and more people came to believe they were free to choose salvation or reject it, a stance consistent with the twin emphases of voluntarism and participation, which characterized American society at the start of the nineteenth century.

While the use of "means" or "measures" was supported by Dwight and other preachers of the Second Awakening, such as Nathaniel Taylor and Lyman Beecher in his later years, it was the controversy created by Charles Finney's use of "new measures," specific evangelistic techniques that he found successful in enticing people to repentance, that placed him at the center of the Second Awakening. When he wrote in his *Lectures on Revivals of Religion* (1835) that "a revival is not a miracle, nor dependent on a miracle, in any sense. It is a purely philosophical result of the right use of the constituted means," the evolutionary process of the changing theology of revivalism was complete. Finney capped off what others before him had started. For this reason and other important influences he had on the revivalism of the first half of the nineteenth century, he gained the title of "father of the second awakening." . . .

The revivalist fame of Charles Finney rose from local to national in the years from 1825 to 1827 when he conducted even larger meetings in the New York towns of Western, Rome, Utica, Auburn, and Troy. As a result of his revival in Western in September 1825, eastern newspapers began to reprint stories from upstate New York papers about the revivals and the fledgling evangelist. As his fame increased, so did the controversies which surrounded him. The same newspapers which reported his revival activity printed caricatures of him as a "zealous fanatic." Other interested parties published tracts both attacking and defending his work. Unitarians, who rejected some of the traditional Christian teachings, were especially critical of Finney. They denounced his hell-fire preaching because it "frightened the feeble-minded" and caused them to "lose their sober sense and self command." His friends of the Oneida Presbytery came to his support, denouncing in turn those "enemies of the cross of Christ" who opposed the revivals.

While the early successes of Finney's revivalism in New York were no doubt due in part to his manners and methods, another element that worked in his favor were the socioeconomic conditions of that region of the state. With rapid industrial development, sparked by the completion of the Erie Canal in 1825, plus the arrival of scores of mills, small factories, packing houses, and distilleries, multitudes of migrants looking for their "promised land" settled in the areas near the canal. All this resulted in uncertainties created by change—change in land prices and ownership, population growth, class distinctions, and the end of isolation from the larger world.

As in all times of social upheaval, people then searched for certainties to carry them through. For many, one certainty was religion; in this case it was the enthusiastic variety provided by the Second Awakening preaching of Charles Finney. The area of New York west of the Hudson River Valley had already been labeled the "burnt-over district," due to the numerous scorchings it endured from several religious excitements even before Finney arrived. During the second quarter of the nineteenth century, for reasons still discussed among historians, this region of New York produced one agitation after another in both religion and politics. The birth of Mormonism, along with the rise of perfectionism, spiritualism, and millennialism, headed the list of religious enthusiasms, while the politics of the nation were affected by the anti-Masonic, Liberty, and Free Soil movements. This, then, was the social and cultural context in which Finney spoke the Word of the Lord during the Second Awakening.

If the greatness of a person is measured in part by the impact made in the lives of others, Finney deserves the designation of one historian who called him one of the most compelling persons in American religious history. Certainly he influenced those religious leaders who surrounded him, and in the process he changed the ways of revivalism. Unlike older evangelists who went it alone, Finney gathered a group of supporters who assisted him in the promotion of his work. On the local level it started with the formation of the Oneida Evangelical Association in 1826. This group even included his earlier theological antagonist, George Gale, who had remained Finney's close friend, and had by now come in line with the revivalist's theological views. Over the next few years the circle broadened to include others and eventually was dubbed the "holy band." This assembly of followers, many of whom were important Presbyterian and Congregationalist leaders in New York, rallied around Finney, defended him against his growing number of critics, and nudged their denominations toward the new kind of evangelism he employed. Some of them became famous in their own right, such as Theodore Weld who, after his conversion under the ministry of Finney, became one of the most important abolitionists in antebellum America.

Finney's revivals from 1827 to 1832 were the high point of his evangelistic career. He emerged as the recognized leader of the Second Great Awakening, having inherited the mantle of Timothy Dwight. The revivals during that period took him to the largest urban centers of the East, such as New York City, Philadelphia, Boston, and Rochester. For this he has been hailed as "the great innovator" of revivalism, for in moving the focus of protracted religious meetings from the rural areas of America to its growing urban centers, he was able to mobilize an entire community through the efforts of local volunteer workers. Prayer meetings were held at hours that farmers would have considered "unseasonable." The traditional practice of holding services at regularly scheduled times, such as Sunday and midweek, was replaced by special services each night for more hours than usual. The camp meeting, which was the soul of earlier Second Awakening days, evolved into the urban protracted meeting under his influence.

The amount of criticism leveled against him after the mid-1820s failed to slow down. Much of the new attack on him was due to the introduction of "new measures," based on his psychological theories of how the laws of the mind could be used to bring individuals and crowds to repentance. The measures included praying for people by name, permitting women to testify and pray publicly, and using an "anxious seat" where persons under conviction of sin would come of their own free will to make known their request for God's forgiveness. With a proper dose of excitement, a revivalist could use certain means to gain a response, Finney said, that a politician would use to draw attention to his candidacy or cause. Good preaching won souls and bad preaching did not. Good preaching had to be practical to reach the understanding of "the common people" and to elicit their response. The parallels drawn by some between Finney's modified Calvinist theology which emphasized the freedom of the individual to choose, and Andrew Jackson's "free will politics" of the common man, are understandable. The appeals made by both gained the responses sought.

Though the Second Great Awakening continued to at least the middle of the 1830s, Finney was forced to reduce his travels when he contracted cholera in 1832. Later he helped promote revivals in England in 1849-1850, and 1859-1860. In 1835 he began another phase of his life when he left the pastorate of the Chatham Street Chapel in New York City to accept an appointment as professor of theology at Oberlin College in Ohio. During his years as a revivalist he had preached a "socially relevant theology," one that would bring not only salvation to the individual, but bring the individual in contact with his neighbor and the evils of his society. His theology included the doctrine of Christian perfection, which did not call for the individual to live sinlessly perfect, but to live in total obedience to the law of a loving God. Borrowing the idea of "universal benevolence" from Jonathan Edwards, Finney held the vision of America as a nation ruled by the moral government of God—by its "laws of benevolence" that obligated every Christian to love both God and neighbor, and to rid society of its evils.

It is not surprising, then, to find that while Finney was teaching theology at Oberlin during the critical antebellum years, he was also practicing theology in much of America. A benevolent empire was to be erected in the nation, he reasoned, and Christians like himself were to be the builders. Historians over the past several decades have discovered that revivalistic religion and the quest for Christian perfection were at the very heart of the social reform movement which swept across the nation for about three decades before the Civil War. Rather than scorn earthly affairs, evangelists such as Finney played a key role in the widespread attack on a variety of obstacles hindering perfection. In doing so they prepared the way for the post-Civil war movement known as the social gospel.

Perhaps no hindrance loomed larger in the mind of the perfectionist in the 1830s than slavery. If the mounting national concern over this obstacle to freedom sounded, in the words of Thomas Jefferson, as a "fire bell in the night" in the early

1820s, a decade later its sound was more like an alarm. When a group of Finney's friends, including Theodore Weld and the Tappan brothers, made plans in the winter of 1832-1833 to organize an American antislavery society, they invited him to join them. Through what he identified as God's gradual revelation of moral truth to him, after some delay he took part in the organizing of the New York Anti-Slavery Society in December 1833. Soon thereafter he prohibited slaveholders and those involved in the slave traffic from communion in his New York church. His ongoing activity in the slavery controversy was one of moderation. During his years at Oberlin, which became a hotbed for abolitionist activity, Finney supported the movement but was careful not to be numbered among the "wild-eyed zealots" who often criticized him for what they considered cowardice on his part. He attempted to hold what he believed to be a sensible, biblical stance on the issue, and feared that any excessive, frenzied commotion by abolitionists—even Christian abolitionists—might hinder the results of revivalism, that itself would inevitably spread abolitionism peacefully. While revivalism and abolitionism were interrelated, he contended, the saving of souls must come first.

Any ambivalence present in Finney's attitude toward the proposed solutions to slavery did not carry over into his position on intemperate use of alcohol. Americans in the 1820s and 1830s drank immense amounts of spirits, mainly due to the availability of cheap corn and rye whisky distilled in the new frontier states of Tennessee and Kentucky. The founding of the American Temperance Union in 1826 marked the beginning of a national crusade against drunkenness. Some churches identified with the movement and made total abstinence a prerequisite for membership. During Finney's revival campaign in Rochester, New York, in 1830, he first made temperance a significant part of conversion. He feared that any resistance to the temperance movement would put a stop to revivals in the churches. Rather, churches should expel members who continued to drink or sell "ardent spirits." Moderation may have been Finney's answer to the slavery problem, but total abstinence was the only choice in solving the spirits problem.

A final obstacle to the building of the American benevolent empire to be considered here was the appalling plight of women in the nation, particularly in the city. This problem, which gained Finney's attention during his New York City pastorate, prompted him to deliver numerous sermons calling for the emancipation of women—a call consistent with the larger moral reform movement. With his encouragement, in 1834 the New York Female Moral Reform Society was organized in his church. Its goals included the distribution of goods to the poor, the search for jobs for the unemployed, the eradication of prostitution, and the provision of rights and equality for women.

The role of the Finneyites in the support of antebellum feminism did not stop there. A recent study by a woman historian argues that Finney's revivals were one of the primary reasons for the enfranchisement of women within the Christian community, raising them there to a level of equality. Finney's emphasis on the free moral agency of all human beings, male and female, provided the basis for his ideas of equality. Salvation was available to all, and all could (and should) participate equally in the activities of the church. He expected women to testify in the services, and he even encouraged women to preach, which his second wife did on a number of occasions. Some of his followers went on to call for, and gain, the ordination of women in some religious circles.

This support for full participation of women by Finney flowed into many areas of society. Women participated significantly in the antislavery movement. They founded moral reform societies and traveled through the Eastern states to recruit help for their causes. Many of the leaders in the antebellum women's rights movement had earlier been involved in the benevolent activities of the Finneyite reform societies.

Invariably historians speak of Charles Finney as both a revivalist and reformer in the same breath. While his years before Oberlin were devoted to revivalism, his time on the faculty of the school from 1835 to 1851 was given both to teaching and reform activity. That year he accepted the presidency of the yet young college with the stipulation that he would give general oversight to its mission and would be free to travel as he wished. Lydia, his wife for twenty-three years, had died in 1847. She had been a strong support for him and had provided a new role model for evangelical women. A year after Lydia's death, Finney married Mrs. Elizabeth Ford Atkinson, a widow of Rochester, New York, who had opened the Atkinson Female Seminary there a few years after his famed revival in that city. During their fifteen years of marriage, which ended in 1863 upon Elizabeth's death, she was a great help to him on his preaching campaigns which took him back to Boston, Rochester, and other sites of his revivals during the pre-Oberlin years. A year after Elizabeth's death, Finney, then seventy-two years old, married for the third time, to Rebecca Rayl, who was the assistant principal of the ladies' department at Oberlin. His final years before his death in 1875 were given largely to his campaigns against Freemasonry and to the writing of his memoirs.

For the impact he made in meeting the social and intellectual challenges of America during the first half of the nineteenth century, Finney was an immensely important person by any standard of measure. His revivals sparked the rising antislavery movement, taking it through the dark vale of abolitionism where even he feared to tread. As a religious revisionist, he advanced the thrust of modified Calvinism with its emphasis on the freedom of the individual to choose, thereby placing theology onto the pathway of a democratizing nation. And as a religious inventor, he fashioned the methods of high-pressure revivalism with his controversial "new measures." Neither American religion, nor the social and intellectual context within which it functioned, would ever be quite the same because of Charles G. Finney.

Evangelical America and Early Mormonism

GORDON S. WOOD

SOURCE: From Gordon S. Wood, "Evangelical America and Early Mormonism," *New York History* 61 (1980): 359-86. Copyright © 1980 by New York State Historical Association. Reprinted with permission.

It is one of the striking facts of American history that the American Revolution was led by men who were not very religious. At best the Founding Fathers only passively believed in organized Christianity and at worst they scorned and ridiculed it. Although few were outright deists, most, like David Ramsay, described the Christian church as "the best temple of reason." Washington was a frequent churchgoer, but he scarcely referred to God as anything but "the Great Disposer of events." Like the principal sources of their Whig liberalism—whether John Locke or the Commonwealth publicist "Cato"—they viewed religious enthusiasms as a kind of madness, the conceit "of a warmed or overweening brain." Jefferson's hatred of the clergy knew no bounds and he repeatedly denounced the "priestcraft" for converting Christianity into "an engine for enslaving mankind, . . . into a more contrivance to filch wealth and power to themselves." For Jefferson and his liberal colleagues sectarian Christianity was the enemy of most of what they valued—the free and dispassionate inquiry of reason into the workings of nature. As enlightened men they abhorred "that gloomy superstition disseminated by ignorant illiberal preachers" and looked forward to the day when "the phantom of darkness will be dispelled by the rays of science, and the bright charms of rising civilization." When Hamilton was asked why the members of the Philadelphia Convention had not mentioned God in the Constitution, he allegedly replied, speaking for many of this remarkable generation of American leaders, "we forgot."

By 1830, less than a half century later, it was no longer so easy to forget God. The Americans' world had been radically transformed. The Enlightenment seemed to be over, and evangelical Protestantism had seized control of much of the culture. The United States, said Tocqueville, had become the most thoroughly Christian nation in the world.

That year, 1830, was in fact a particularly notable one in the history of American religion. In that year the great preacher Charles G. Finney came to Rochester, New York, the fastest growing community in the United States, and launched a revival that eventually shook the nation. In that same year the Shakers had more members than at any other time of their history. In 1830 the religious fanatic Robert Matthews experienced the revelation that turned him into a wandering Jewish prophet predicting the imminent end of the world. At the same time, Alexander Campbell broke from the Baptists and began publication of the *Millennial Harbinger* in preparation for his momentous alliance with Barton Stone and the creation of the Disciples of Christ. And in that same crucial year, 1830, Joseph Smith published the *Book of Mormon*.

These remarkable religious events of 1830 were only some of the most obvious manifestations of a firestorm of evangelical enthusiasm that had been sweeping through American society for at least a generation. This movement—generally called the Second Great Awakening—was itself the expression of something bigger and more powerful than even religion. Evangelical revivalism, utopian communitarianism, millennial thinking, multitudes of dreams and visions by seekers, and the birth of new religions were in fact all responses to the great democratic changes taking place in America between the Revolution and the Age of Jackson. The remains of older eighteenth-century hierarchies fell away, and hundreds of thousands of common people were cut loose from all sorts of traditional bonds and found themselves freer, more independent, more unconstrained than ever before in their history. . . .

. . . This Second Great Awakening brought religion to the remotest areas of America, popularized religion as never before, and created a religious world unlike anything in Christendom. It was not just a continuation of the first Awakening of the mid-eighteenth century. It was more popular, more evangelical, more ecstatic, more personal, more secular, and more optimistic. It combined the past and present, communalism and individualism, folkways and enlightenment in odd and confusing ways. The sovereignty of Christ was reaffirmed, but people were given personal responsibility for their salvation as never before. Nearly everyone yearned for Christian unity, but never before or since was American Christendom so divided. For many the world was coming to an end, but at the same time everything in the here and now seemed possible. It was the time of greatest religious chaos and originality in American history. During this unique moment in annals of American religion, Mormonism was born.

At the time of the Revolution no one foresaw what would happen to American religion. Many of America's religious leaders, including the Calvinist clergy, endorsed the Revolution and its enlightened liberal impulses wholeheartedly. For most Protestant groups the great threat to religion came from the Church of England, and enlightened rationalists like Jefferson and Madison had little trouble in mobilizing Protestant dissenters against the established Anglican church. The Enlightenment's faith in liberty of conscience that justified this disestablishment of the Anglican church scarcely seemed dangerous to American religion. Even in Connecticut and Massachusetts, where religious establishments existed but were Puritan, not Anglican, Presbyterian and Congregational clergy invoked enlightened religious liberty against the dark twin forces of British civic and ecclesiastical tyranny without fear of subverting their own peculiar alliances between church and state. The Revolution and enlightened republicanism blended with evangelical Protestantism to promise all Americans, secular- and religious-minded alike, the moral regeneration the country needed. . . .

By the 1790s organized religion was in disarray. The Revolution had destroyed churches, interrupted ministerial training, and politicized people's thinking. The older established churches, now either dismantled or under attack, were unequipped to handle a rapidly growing and moving population. The proportion of college graduates entering the ministry fell off, and the number of church members declined drastically, with, it is estimated, scarcely one in twenty Americans being members of a church. At the same time the influence of enlightened liberalism was growing. It underlay the First Amendment and infected the thinking of gentlemen everywhere. It ate away the premises of Calvinism, indeed, of all orthodox Christian beliefs. It told people they were not sinful but naturally good, possessed of a moral sense or instinct, and that evil lay in the corrupt institutions of both church and state. For some enlightened gentlemen Christianity became simply the butt of dinner party jokes. Everywhere orthodox clergymen tried to reconcile their traditional beliefs with liberal rationalism and to make sense of what Jefferson called "the incomprehensible jargon of the Trinitarian arithmetic, that three are one, and one is three." This rational deism could not be confined to the drawing rooms of the gentry but even spilled into the streets. The anti-religious writings of Ethan Allen, Thomas Paine, Comte de Volney, and Elihu Palmer, reached out to new popular audiences and gave many ordinary people the sense that reason and nature were as important (and mysterious) as revelation and the supernatural. By the early nineteenth century, enlightened leaders like Jefferson and young John C. Calhoun were enthusiastically predicting that the whole country was rapidly on its way to becoming Unitarian.

All this accumulated evidence of religious apathy and growing rationalism has convinced many historians that the decade and a half following the Revolution were "the most irreligious period in American history," "the period of the lowest ebb-tide of vitality in the history of American Christianity." The early Republic has even been called "a heathen nation—one of the most needy mission fields in the world."

We are now only beginning to realize how misleading these common historical interpretations of popular infidelity and religious indifference in post-Revolutionary America are. The mass of American people had not lost their religiosity during the Enlightenment. Certainly the low proportion of church membership is no indication of popular religious apathy, not in America where church membership had long been a matter of an individual's conversion experience and not, as in the Old World, a matter of birth. To be sure, there were fierce expressions of popular hostility to the genteel clergy with their D.D.'s and other aristocratic pretensions. It was this egalitarian anti-clericalism rather than any widespread rejection of Christianity that lay behind the popular deism of these years. For most common people, Christianity remained the dominant means for explaining the world; all they wanted was for it to be adapted to their newly aroused and newly legitimated needs.

During the last quarter of the eighteenth century, powerful currents of popular evangelical feeling flowed beneath the refined and aristocratic surface of public life, awaiting only the developing democratic revolution to break through the rationalistic crust of the Enlightenment and to sweep over and transform the landscape of the country. Once ordinary people found that they could change traditional religion as completely as they were changing traditional politics, they had no need for deism or infidelity. By 1800 there was as little chance of all Americans becoming rational Unitarians as there was of their all becoming high-toned Federalists. Evangelical Christianity and the democracy of these years, the very democracy with which Jefferson rode to power and destroyed Federalism, emerged together and were interrelated.

This democracy and the popular evangelicism of the early nineteenth century were both products of a social disintegration unequalled in American history. All the old eighteenth-century aristocratic hierarchies, enfeebled and brittle to begin with, now collapsed under the impact of long developing demographic and economic forces. The population grew at phenomenal rates and spread itself over half a continent at speeds that astonished everyone. Between 1790 and 1820 New York's population quadrupled, and Kentucky's multiplied nearly eight times. People were on the move as never before, individuals sometimes uprooting themselves four or five or more times in a lifetime. Joseph Smith's father moved his family seven times in fourteen years. Ohio in a single decade grew from a virtual wilderness to become larger than most of the colonies had been at the time of the Revolution. This growth and movement of people combined with the spread of market economies to shatter all sorts of paternalistic social relationships and to excite the acquisitive impulses of countless individuals. Young people left their parents, women found new roles for themselves, servants stopped living in households, apprentices and journeymen grew apart from their masters and became employees, and numerous patrons and clients switched roles. In thousands of different ways connections that had held people together for centuries were strained and severed, and people were set loose in unprecedented numbers. . . .

By the early nineteenth century a radical and momentous transformation had taken place. Countless numbers of people involved in a simultaneous search for individual autonomy and for new forms of community experienced immense psychological shifts. While educated gentry formed new cosmopolitan connections, increasing numbers of common people found solace in the creation of new egalitarian and affective communities. From the Revolution on, all sorts of associations—from mutual aid societies to Freemasonry—arose to meet the needs of newly detached individuals; but most important for ordinary folk was the creation of unprecedented numbers of religious communities. The disintegration of older structures of authority released torrents of popular religiosity into public life. Visions, dreams, prophesyings, and new emotion-soaked religious seekings acquired a validity they had not earlier possessed. The evangelical pietism of ordinary people, sanctioned by the democratic revolution of these years, had come to affect the character of American culture in ways it had not at the time of the Revolution. It now became increasingly difficult for enlightened gentlemen to publicly dismiss religious enthusiasm as simply the superstitious fanaticism of the illiterate and lowborn. . . .

The result was an odd mixture of credulity and skepticism among people. Where everything was believable, everything could be doubted. All claims to expert knowledge were suspect, and people tended to mistrust, as George Tucker complained in 1827, anything outside of "the narrow limits of their own observation." Yet because people prided themselves on their shrewdness and believed they now understood so much, they could be easily impressed by what they did not understand. A few strange words like hieroglyphics spoken by a preacher or documentary patent displayed by a medicine seller could carry great credibility. In such an atmosphere, hoaxes of various kinds of quackery in all fields flourished.

Like the culture as a whole, religion was powerfully affected by these popularizing developments. Subterranean folk beliefs and fetishes emerged into the open and blended with traditional Christian practices to create a wildly spreading evangelical enthusiasm. Ordinary people cut off from traditional social relationships were freer than ever before to express publicly hitherto repressed or vulgar emotions. Thousands upon thousands became seekers looking for signs and prophets and for new explanations for the bewildering experiences of their lives. These marginal people came together without gentry leadership anywhere they could—in fields, barns, or homes—to lay hands on one another, to offer each other kisses of charity, to form new bonds of fellowship, to set loose their feelings both physically and vocally, and to Christianize a variety of folk rites. . . .

This genuine folk movement spawned hundreds and thousands of camp meetings and religious communities throughout the early Republic. By focusing on the most bizarre behavior of the revivals, like the "jerks" and "laughing jags," or on the most exotic expressions of the communalism, like the Shakers, we sometimes missed its popular strength and scope. It is obvious that this religious enthusiasm tapped long existing veins of folk culture, and many evangelical leaders had to struggle to keep the suddenly released popular passions under control. Some enthusiasts drew on folk yearnings that went back centuries and in the new free atmosphere of republican America saw the opportunity to establish long-desired utopian worlds in which all social distinctions were abolished, diet was restricted, and women and goods were shared. But for every such ascetic or licentious utopian community there were hundreds of other evangelical communities that clung, however tenuously, to one or another of the Old World religions. Presbyterian, Methodist, and Baptist evangelicals all participated in the Awakening and constituted its main force. Yet in the end, perhaps, our fascination with the unusual sects and prophets is not mistaken, for the radical enthusiasts and visionaries represented the advanced guard of this popular evangelical movement, with which they shared a common hostility to orthodox authority.

All of the evangelicals—from the Shakers to the Baptists—rejected in one degree or another the ways in which traditional society organized itself and assigned prestige. Thousands of ordinary people—farmers, bricklayers, millers, carpenters, petty businessmen of every sort, and their mothers, wives, and sisters—found in evangelicalism a counter-culture that condemned the conventional society and offered them alternative measures of social esteem. Being called by polite society "the scum of the earth, the filth of creation," these evangelicals made their fellowship, their conversion, experiences, and their peculiar folk rites their badges of respectability. They denounced the dissolute behavior they saw about them—the profanity, drinking, gambling, dancing, horseracing and other amusements shared by both the luxurious aristocracy at the top of the society and the unproductive rabble at the bottom. By condemning the vices of those above and below them, evangelicals struck out in both social directions at once and thereby began to acquire a nineteenth-century "middle-class" distinctiveness. . . .

From the disruptions and bewilderments of their lives many people could readily conclude that the world was on the verge of some great transformation—nothing less than the Second Coming of Christ and the Day of Judgment predicted in the

Bible. Millennialism of various kinds, both scholarly and popular, flourished in the turbulent decades following the Revolution and became the means by which many explained and justified the great social changes of the period. Although old and new millennial ideas mingled confusedly, some of the adventist beliefs in the early nineteenth century now assumed a character appropriate to the realities of a new improving American society. Older popular Christian beliefs in the millennium had usually assumed that Christ's coming would precede the establishment of a new kingdom of God. Christ's advent would be forewarned by signs and troubles, culminating in a horrible conflagration in which everything would be destroyed. Christ would then rule over the faithful in a New Jerusalem for a thousand years until the final Day of Judgment. Those who held such millennial beliefs generally saw the world as so corrupt and evil that only the sudden and catastrophic intervention of Christ could create the new world. But in the America of the early nineteenth century, such older cataclysmic interpretations of the millennium began to be replaced by newer ideas which pictured the Second Coming of Christ following, rather than preceding, the thousand years of glory and bliss. And such an approaching age of perfection seemed to be beginning in America itself. . . .

This, then, was the evangelical world out of which Mormonism arose. The Church of Jesus Christ of Latter-day Saints, for all its uniqueness, was very much a product of its time, but not in any simple or obvious way. Mormonism was undeniably the most original and persecuted religion of this period or of any period of American history. It defied as no other religion did both the orthodox culture and evangelical counter-culture. Yet at the same time it drew heavily on both these cultures. It combined within itself different tendencies of thought. From the outset it was a religion in tension, poised like a steel spring by the contradictory forces pulling within it.

Mormonism was both mystical and secular; restorationist and progressive; communitarian and individualistic; hierarchical and congregational; authoritarian and democratic; antinomian and arminian; anti-clerical and priestly; revelatory and empirical; utopian and practical; ecumenical and nationalist. Alexander Campbell was not exaggerating by much when he charged in 1831 that "this prophet Smith" had brought together in the Book of Mormon "every error and almost every truth discussed in New York for the last ten years." Mormonism set out to meet a wide variety of popular needs. It spoke, said John Greenleaf Whittier, "a language of hope and promise to weak, weary hearts, tossed and troubled, who have wandered from sect to sect, seeking in vain for the primal manifestations of the divine power."

Mormonism was a new religion, but it was not to be simply another denomination among the many others of America. The Church did not see itself as just another stage in the ongoing Protestant Reformation. It marked a new beginning in the Christian faith. Like the Disciples of Christ, with which it had much in common, Mormonism was to be "the only true and living church upon the face of the whole earth." But unlike the primitive gospelers, Mormonism did not seek to strip Christianity of its complexities and to ground itself in the literalism of the

Bible in order to have the broadest common basis of appeal. Instead, it added new complexities and institutions to Christianity, new rituals and beliefs, and new revelations and miracles. Most important, it added an extraordinary complement to the Scriptures. The Book of Mormon published in 1830 was undoubtedly the most distinctive and important force in establishing the new faith.

The Book of Mormon together with Joseph Smith's revelations gave to Mormonism a popular authoritative appeal that none of the other religions could match. Even the primitive gosplers' return to the simplicity of the New Testament had not ended their quarreling over interpreting the Scriptures. The Book of Mormon cut through these controversies and brought the Bible up-to-date. It was written in plain biblical style for plain people. It answered perplexing questions of theology, clarified obscure passages of the Bible, and carried its story into the New World. And it did all this with the assurance of divine authority. The Book of Mormon brought to the surface underlying currents of American folk thought that cannot be found in the learned pamphlets or public orations of the day. It reveals in fact just how limited and elitist our understanding of early nineteenth-century popular culture really is. The Book of Mormon is an extraordinary work of popular imagination and one of the greatest documents in American cultural history.

Its timing in 1830 was providential. It appeared at precisely the right moment in American history; much earlier or later and the Church might not have taken hold. The Book of Mormon would probably not have been published in the eighteenth century, in that still largely oral world of folk beliefs prior to the great democratic revolution that underlay the religious tumult of the early Republic. In the eighteenth century, Mormonism might have been too easily stifled and dismissed by the dominant enlightened gentry culture as just another enthusiastic folk superstition. Yet if Mormonism had emerged later, after the consolidation of authority and the spread of science in the middle decades of the nineteenth century, it might have had problems of verifying its texts and revelations. But during the early decades of the nineteenth century the time was ideally suited for the establishment of the new faith. The democratic revolution was at its height, all traditional authorities were in disarray, and visions and prophesying still had a powerful appeal for large numbers of people. A generation or so later it might have been necessary for Smith and his followers to get some university professors to authenticate the characters on the golden plates. But Martin Harris's failure to get such "professional" and "scientific" verification in the 1820s did not matter. After all, ordinary ploughmen had as much insight into such things as did college professors. . . .

It is not surprising that opponents of the new faith spent so much energy trying to discredit the origins of the new scripture, for it was precisely this kind of "surety," this concrete material evidence, that gave Joseph Smith's prophesying a legitimacy that the visions and predictions of the many other prophets of the day could not equal. The Book of Mormon nicely answered the warnings of the rational genteel world against "running into extremes, and making ourselves wise above what is written." It had a particular appeal for people emerging from a twilight folk world of dreams and superstitions and anxious to demonstrate their literacy and their enlightenment. Such a tangible document fit the popular belief that what was written was somehow truer and more authentic than what was spoken.

In other ways, too, Mormonism brought the folk past and enlightened modernity together. It sought to reconcile the ecstatic antinomian visions of people with the discipline of a hierarchical church. It drew upon the subjective emotionalism and individualism of revivalism and institutionalized them. Mormonism, in fact, can be understood as a popular version of the elitist churchly reaction to revivalism that began in the second and third decades of the nineteenth century. Just as High Church Episcopalians were looking back to the earliest days of their church for new apostolic authority, so too did Mormons appeal to ancient, pre-Reformation history as set forth in the Book of Mormon. Mormonism offered people the best of both the popular world of millenarian evangelicism and the respectable world of priestly churches. Almost overnight, Mormonism created an elaborate hierarchy, mysterious rituals, and a rich churchly tradition that reached back to apostolic times.

In dozens of different ways Mormonism blended the folk inclinations and religiosity of common people with the hardened churchly traditions and enlightened gentility of modern times. Like many other religious groups, the Mormons built a separate community of gathered saints, but at the same time they rejected the idea that they were just another sect representing a particular social fragment. They reversed America's separation of church and state and tried to reestablish the kind of well-knit commonwealth that John Winthrop had envisioned two hundred years earlier. Mormonism readily responded to the ancient popular yearnings for ascetic communal living and sharing, but at the same time, unlike Shakerism, it recognized the modern Americans' individualistic desires for property-owning. Since in the eyes of the gentry the Mormons were "the miserable Mormons," drawn from "the lowest and most ignorant walks of life," they, like other evangelicals, sought to establish among themselves new standards of respectability and prided themselves on what would become "middle-class" decorum and moral behavior. Mormonism answered the powerful anti-clerical, egalitarian feelings of people by erecting a church without a professional clergy and by making every man a priest.

Its theology, too, mingled supernatural folk wisdom with modern rationalism. It allied the deep lying popular emotionalism of the period with the Enlightenment's faith in useful knowledge and education. By drawing on the folk habit of identifying the physical and spiritual worlds, Mormonism gave God a more corporeal human character and at the same time made man more divine. Its beliefs fit the needs of lost, lonely people unsure of who they were and where they were going. It sought to counter the disruptive mobility of the times by strengthening the extended family. The baptism of the dead even reached across generations and recaptured for people the sense of ancestral continuity that modern rootlessness had destroyed. This practice, in fact, did for ordinary people what the formation of genealogical societies in the 1840s did for anxious elites. Mormonism recognized the uneasiness, the guilt, and the sinful feelings of people created by their social and geographical displacements, but at the same time it promised these people redemption through their own efforts. However much Mormonism harked back to ancient folkways, it was a religion designed for the future.

Like many other popular faiths of the period on both sides of the Atlantic, Mormonism was thoroughly millennialist. "We believe," wrote Smith, "in the literal gathering of Israel and in the restoration of the Ten Tribes. That Zion will be built upon this continent. That Christ will reign personally upon the earth, and that the earth will be renewed and receive its paradisiac glory." Again in its millennial ideas, as in so many other ways, early Mormonism combined disparate traditions. As scholars have noted, its belief in the Second Coming cannot be easily fitted into any single pattern of millennialism. Early Mormons followed the traditional belief in the corruption of the world and the imminence of Christ's arrival, and they searched the times for signs and omens of the cataclysmic event. At the same time, however, they shared in the more modern millennialist idea that the kingdom of God could be built in this world and that the everyday material benefits of progress were but the working out of God's purpose. Although other millenarians on both sides of the Atlantic emphasized the special role of their respective nations in the coming age of perfection, no American believers in Christ's Second Coming ever identified the New Jerusalem so particularly and so concretely with America as did the Mormons. Zion was literally to arise within the borders of the United States.

The identification between Mormonism and America was there at the beginning. No doubt it was and is a unique faith, but it is also uniquely American. It was born at a peculiar moment in the history of the United States, and it bears the marks of that birth. Only the culture of early nineteenth-century evangelical America could have produced it. And through it we can begin to understand the complicated nature of that culture.

Questions for Reflection and Discussion

1. Discuss the relation between the secular and the sacred provided by the documents.

2. Steven Mintz describes how the visions of the millennium exerted influence on America in the middle period. What conflicts did this produce in a young nation seeking a popular consensus?

3. Charles Finney is presented as a key figure of the Second Awakening by Robert Mathisen. How did this revival of sacred importance impact secular concerns of antebellum America?

4. How does Gordon Wood explain the rise of Mormonism out of the evangelical world?

5. Was the middle period a time of religious conflict or consensus? of inclusion or exclusion?

Additional Readings

Bodo, John R. *The Protestant Clergy and Public Issues, 1812-1848.* Princeton: Princeton

University Press, 1954.

Bruce, Dickson D., Jr. *And They All Sang Hallelujah: Plain Folk Camp-Meeting Religion, 1800-1845.* Knoxville: University of Tennessee Press, 1974.

Bushman, Richard L. *Joseph Smith and the Beginnings of Mormonism.* Urbana: University of Illinois Press, 1988.

Carwardine, Richard J. *Evangelicals and Politics in Antebellum America.* New Haven: Yale University Press, 1993.

Conkin, Paul K. *The Uneasy Center: Reformed Christianity in Antebellum America.* Chapel Hill: University of North Carolina Press, 1995.

Cross, Whitney, R. *The Burned-Over District: The Social and Intellectual History of Enthusiastic Religion in Western New York, 1800-1850.* Ithaca: Cornell University Press, 1950.

Doan, Ruth Alden. *The Miller Heresy, Millennialism, and American Culture.* Philadelphia: Temple University Press, 1987.

Foster, Charles I. *An Errand of Mercy: The Evangelical United Front, 1790-1837.* Chapel Hill: University of North Carolina Press, 1960.

Franchot, Jenny. *Roads to Rome: The Antebellum Protestant Encounter with Catholicism.* Berkeley: University of California Press, 1994.

Gribbin, William. *The Churches Militant: The War of 1812 and American Religion.* New Haven: Yale University Press, 1973.

Griffin, Clifford S. *Their Brothers' Keepers: Moral Stewardship in the United States, 1800-1865.* New Brunswick: Rutgers University Press, 1960.

Hambrick-Stowe, Charles. *Charles G. Finney and the Spirit of American Evangelicalism.* Grand Rapids, MI: Wm B. Eerdmans, 1996.

Hardesty, Nancy. *Your Daughters Shall Prophesy: Revivalism and Feminism in the Age of Finney.* Brooklyn, N.Y.: Carlson Publishing Co., 1991.

Hatch, Nathan O. *The Democratization of American Christianity.* New Haven: Yale University Press, 1989.

Lazerow, Jama. *Religion and the Working Class in Antebellum America.* Washington, D.C.: Smithsonian, 1995.

Loveland, Anne C. *Southern Evangelicals and the Social Order, 1800-1860.* Baton Rouge: Louisiana State University Press, 1980.

Shipps, Jan. *Mormonism: The Story of a New Religious Tradition.* Urbana: University of Illinois Press, 1985.

Smith, Timothy L. *Revivalism and Social Reform: American Protestantism on the Eve of the Civil War.* New York: Harper Torchbook, 1957.

Stein, Stephen. *The Shaker Experience in America.* New Haven: Yale University Press, 1992.

Chapter 6

As early as 1705, America was pictured as a garden—an unspoiled paradise. In his History and Present State of Virginia published that year, Robert Beverley laid the groundwork for a utopian vision of future opportunity that brought his successors westward during the antebellum era. "All the Countries . . . seated in or near the Latitude of Vir-

American Religion in the Antebellum Frontier West

Issue

How did the frontier West shape American religion?

ginia," he noted, "are esteem'd the Fruitfullest, and Pleasantest of all Clymates. . . . These are reckon'd the Gardens of the World. . . ." As one reads on, it appears Beverley struggles for the distinction between two garden metaphors: an untamed, primitive pre-fall Eden, and a tilled garden nurturing pastoral values.

Indeed, the myth of the garden continued to characterize the hopes and disillusionments of multitudes of Americans as they chased their dream of a paradisiacal destiny. For every Robert Beverley there were untold numbers like Kentuckian Moses Austin who lamented over irrational expectations: ". . . here is hundreds Travelling hundreds of Miles, they Know not for what Nor Whither, except its to Kentucky, passing land almost as good and easy obtain.d, the Proprietors of which would gladly give on any terms, but it will not do its not Kentuckey its not the Promis.d land its not the goodly inheratence the Land of Milk and Honey. And when arriv.d at this Heaven in Idea what do they find? A goodly land I will allow but to them forbiden Land. exausted and worn down with distress and disappointment. . . ."

The biblical imagery employed to describe the West—garden, paradise, promised land—continued into the first half of the nineteenth century and accents the findings of current scholars of the American frontier: The West is a place, process, and set of values. As a place, notes historian Patricia Nelson Limerick, "the American West was an important meeting point" where different races intersected. In antebellum America the frontier West was a place where white

*pioneers and Native Americans continued to intersect. The line between con-
sensus and conflict, and inclusion and exclusion, was usually drawn by the
circuit preacher, Bible society agent, or medical missionary. As a process, the
West produced a dynamic interplay between secular and sacred institutions,
resulting in long-lasting change for both. As a set of values, the West confronted
American religion with an array of critical issues. Did religious Americans have
a destiny manifested to them by a providential directive? Was the vast expanse of
the West an open invitation for religious diversity or an opportunity for building exclusive dominions? Was the mythic West still alive in 1860?*

Documents

*The interplay between the frontier West and American religion was vigorous
and dynamic during the middle decades of the nineteenth century. Methodist
circuit preacher James Gilruth recorded in 1834 the variety of activities he
performed while serving as Presiding Elder of the Detroit District within the
Ohio Methodist Conference. The first selection relates some of his experiences on
the rugged frontier. The conquest of the West brought farmers, trappers, and
missionaries in contact with Native Americans. In the second reading, Kentucky frontiersman Thomas Baldwin tells of the consolation his religious beliefs
brought to him after the deaths of his wife and three children at the hands of
Indians. Presbyterian missionaries Marcus and Narcissa Whitman endured the
difficult overland trek from the East Coast to the Oregon territory in 1836. The
third selection describes some of Narcissa's early impressions of the Indians among
whom they worked, along with an account of her duties. About ten years later
the Whitmans and a dozen companions were slain by Cayuse Indians. The
Society for the Promotion of Collegiate and Theological Education at the West
was founded in 1843 to promote the cause of Protestant church colleges on the
frontier. The rationale for these colleges and the challenges they faced from Roman Catholics are enumerated in the fourth reading. The decision of the Mormon leadership to escape prevailing oppression and move the nation westward
is announced in the fifth selection. America's claim to western regions put it in
conflict with European powers. In the final excerpt, former U.S. President John
Quincy Adams explains to his colleagues in the House of Representatives what
he believes are America's biblical and historical claims to Oregon in 1846.*

1. Methodist Circuit Preacher, 1834

SOURCE: W. W. Sweet, ed., *Religion on the American Frontier: The Methodists, 1783-1840* (New York: Cooper Square Publishers, 1964 [1946]), 370-71.

Tusd July 29. [1834] Rose at sunup—Spent the forepart of the day in sundry small matters—In the afternoon went to Wm Collens to git some hay—Taking My wife 2 smallest children suped at Br Mainards & returned home a little before sundown Day clear & pleasant to bed about 9.

   Wed July 30. Rose about sun rise—spent the morning till 10 in sundry small chores—tended the funeral of Mr Welshs infant—halled wood in the afternoon Day as yesterday—to bed about 10

   Thursd July 31. Rose about 6—Spent the day in aranging my papers money etc for Conferance (Giting my horse shod and making the necessary preparations)—counting tracts till $^1/_2$ past 10—Day as yesterday—to bed at 11—. . .

   Frid Aug 8 . . . Made arangement to set out on horseback for Ft Finley—Br Bibbins hors having become lame I set off alone about 9 uncouth like enough having 3 bed quilts & 5 lb cotten to carry beside great coat etc—I fed at Mr Sergants at the Big Spring—And in the afternoon rode to Finley & found My children well My daughter had been delivered of a child on the 4th of July but by the ignorent & bruital conduct of the Midwife the child was killed I spent the evening conversing with them on these & other matters till near 10—

   Sat Aug 9 . . . spent $^1/_2$ an hour assisting Frederik to catch a Raccoon that had come into his corn—And the rest of the morning in looking at his improvements & in conversation till about 8 A.M. when we all set off for campmeeting $2^1/_2$ miles distent—I preached with great liberty at 11 from John iii 5 & then called for Mourners a nomber presented themselves for the prayers of the righteous & it was said that two of them experienced peace. I preached again at 4 from Ps. cxix.1 with clearness and some power.—& again at candlelight from Matt xxii 39. with some power—In all my labour to day I was favoured with the attention of the people & the comfort of the spirit. At this I again called for Mourners some came and Prayer meeting continued for some time. Day hot with some thunder showers passing about—one of whom fill [fell] on us; accompanied by a pretty severe wind that broke down some timber very near the camp ground. To bed about 9. pretty tired.

2. Narrative of the Massacre of the Wife and Children of Thomas Baldwin, 1836

SOURCE: *Narrative of the Massacre . . . of the Wife & Children of Thomas Baldwin. . . .* (New York: Garland Publishing Co., 1977 [1836], 17-19.

It is the blessed religion which I would recommend as worthy to be cherished by all, that prepares their minds for all the events of this inconstant state, and instructs them in the nature of true happiness—afflictions will not then attack them by surprize, and will not therefore overwhelm them—they are not then overcome by disappointment, when that which is mortal dies;—they meet the changes in their lot without unmanly dejection—in the multitude of our sorrows in this world of misery, what but Religion can afford us consolation? It assures us that thro' all our disappointment and wo, there is a friend present with us, on whose affection, wisdom, power, and goodness, we can perfectly rely; and that an infinitely merciful and powerful Protector sustains us, guiding our erring footsteps, and strengthening our feeble spirits. He permits no afflictions to approach us but for some gracious and merciful purpose; to excite in us an earnest solicitude for our salvation, to reclaim us from error, or to subdue some favorite passion—subject to the control of this Almighty Guardian, all the trials of life are designed to establish our faith, to increase our humble dependence, to perfect our love and fortify our patience, and to make us meet for the inheritance of glory. So long as our Heavenly father is possessed of infinite wisdom to understand perfectly what is best for his children, and of infinite mercy to will all that he sees to be best for them, shall we not choose to have him do what he pleases? Dark are the ways of Providence while we are wrapt up in mortality—but, convinced there is a God, we must hope and believe, that all is right.

Although it has been my lot to drink deep of the cup of sorrow, yet I have never found my heart inclined to charge God foolishly—a gracious heart elevates nearer and nearer to God in affliction, and can justify him in his severest strokes, acknowledging them to be all just and holy—and hereby the soul may comfortably evidence to itself its own uprightness and sincere love to Him; yea, it hath been of singular use to some souls, to take right measures of their love to God in such trials; He that appointed the seasons of the year, appointed the seasons of our comfort in our relations; and as those seasons cannot be altered, no more can these;—all the course of Providence is guided by an unalterable decree; what falls out casually to our apprehension, yet falls out necessarily in respect to God's appointment—admit that he hath sorely afflicted us for our sins, by bereaving us by a sudden stroke of death of our nearest and dearest friends, yet there is no reason that we should be too much cast down under our severe afflictions, for it may be the fruits of his love to, and care of our souls, for to the afflicted he says, "whom I love, I rebuke and chasten."

That our greatest afflictions, so considered, many times prove our greatest blessings, is probably known by experience to many. It was my heavy afflictions, in being so suddenly and lamentably deprived of my family, that led me to prefer a life of retirement; and in that retirement from the busy scenes of the world, I was led to engage more seriously and earnestly in the perusal of the Holy Scriptures, whereby I was taught to seek a balm in that blessed RELIGION, that has never failed to sustain me in my most solitary moments; and by my own experience, I can assure all, the rich and the poor, the happy and the miserable, the healthy and the sick, in short, all descriptions of persons, whatever my be their station or their circumstances in this life, that they will experience infinite advantage in a religious retirement from the world; and while thus situated, whatever their troubles and afflictions may be, they ought to bear them without a murmur. A good man can never be miserable, who cheerfully submits to the will of Providence. To be truly happy in this world, we must manifest a quiet resignation to the will of an impartial God. If while we remain inhabitants of this "miserable world," we quietly submit to the will of, and exercise a true love to Him, we have great reason to believe that we shall hereafter be permitted to taste higher delights, and experience a degree of happiness that this frail world does not afford. As our prospects close not with this life, but are extended to the future, it is necessary that we should make provision for that also; none ought therefore to postpone the business of Religion, till night overtakes them—the night of death—when no man can work. Religion consoles the aching heart of the afflicted, and reconciles the unhappy to their misfortunes—the grieved parent who has burried his earthly comfort, his beloved partner and darling children, in the bosom of the valley, is comforted and cheered by the flattering persuasions of Religion—he is assured by it that if he lives faithful to Christ, he shall revisit his beloved friends in that blessed place where dwells every felicity, and an antidote for every care and painful sensation. To you, sir, and to all, I would then say, whatever may be your or their rank in life, if you wish to be happy in this world, and the secure a certainty of being infinitely more so in the world to come, I pray thee cherish RELIGION. That this may be the happy and final choice of all, is and ever shall be the prayer of their aged friend and well wisher,

THOMAS BALDWIN.

3. First White Women over the Rockies, 1837

SOURCE: C. M. Drury, ed., *First White Women over the Rockies* (Glendale, CA: Arthur H. Clark Co., 1963), I, 123-24, 125-26.

Wieletpoo [Waiilatpu] Jan 2 1837. Universal fast day. Through the kind Providence of God we are permitted to celebrate this day in heathen lands. It has been one of peculiar interest to us, so widely separated from kindred souls, alone, in the thick darkness of heathenism. We have just finished a separate room for ourselves with a stove in it, lent by Mr P for our use this winter. Thus I am spending my winter as comfortable as heart could wish, & have suffered less from excessive cold than in many winters previous in New York. Winters are not very severe here. Usually they have but little snow say there is more this winter now on the ground than they have had for many years previous & that the winter is nearly over. After a season of worship during which I felt great depressure of spirits, we visited the lodges. All seemed well pleased as I had not been to any of them before.

We are on the lands of the Old Chief Umtippe who with a lodge or two are now absent for a few days hunting deer. But a few of the Cayuses winter here. They appear to seperate in small companies, makes their cashes of provision in the fall & remain for the winter, & besides they are not well united. The young Chief Towerlooe is of another family & is more properly the ruling chief. He is Uncle to the Young Cayuse Halket now at Red River Mission whom we expect to return this fall & to whom the chieftainship belongs by inheritance. The Old Chief Umtippe has been a savage creature in his day. His heart is still the same, full of all manner of hypocracy deceit and guile. He is a mortal beggar as all Indians are. If you ask a favour of him, sometimes it is granted or not just as he feels, if granted it must be well paid for. A few days ago he took it into his head to require pay for teaching us the language & forbid his people from coming & talking with us for fear we should learn a few words of them. The Cayuses as well as the Nez Perces are very strict in attending to their worship which they have regularly every morning at day break & eve at twilight and once on the Sab. They sing & repeat a form of prayers very devoutly after which the Chief gives them a talk. The tunes & prayers were taught them by a Roman Catholic trader. Indeed their worship was commenced by him. As soon as we became settled we established a meeting among them on the Sab in our own house. Did not think it best to interfere with their worship but during the time had a family bible class & prayer meeting. Many are usually in to our family worship especially evenings, when we spend considerable time in teaching them to sing. About 12 or 14 boys come regularly every night & are delighted with it.

Sab Jan 29 Our meeting to day with the Indians was more interesting than usual. I find that as we succeed in their language in communicating the truth to them so as to obtain a knowledge of their views & feelings, my heart becomes more & more interested in them. They appear to have a partial knowledge of the leading truths of the Bible; of sin, so far as it extends to outward actions, but know [no] knowledge of the heart.

Feb 1st Husband has gone to Walla W to day & is not expected to return until tomorrow eve, & I am alone for the first time to sustain the family altar, in the midst of a room full of native youth & boys, who have come in to sing as usual. After worship several gathered close arround me as if anxious I should tell them some thing about the Bible. I had been reading the 12th chap of Acts, & with Richards help endeavoured to give them an account of Peter imprisonment &c, as well as I could. O that I had full possession of their language so that I could converse with them freely. . . .

March 6th Sab eve. To day our congregation has increased very considerably in consequence of the arrival of a party of Indians during the past week. A strong desire is manifest in them all to understand the truth & to be taught. Last eve our room was full of men & boys, who came every eve to learn and sing. The whole tribe both men women & children would like the same priviledge if our room was larger & my health would admit so much singing. Indeed I should not attempt to sing with them, were it not for the assistance my Husband renders. You will recollect when he was in Angelica he could not sing a single tune. Now he is able to sing several tunes & lead the school in them. This saves me a great deal hard singing. I have thought many times if the singers in my Fathers family could have the same priviledge or were here to assist me in this work how much good they could do. I was not aware that singing was a qualification of so much importance to a missionary. While I was at Vancouver one Indian woman came a great distance with her daughter as she said to hear me sing with the children. The boys have introduced all the tunes they can sing alone, into their morning & eve worship, which they sing very well. To be at a distance & hear them singing them, one would almost forget he was in a savage land.

March 30th Again I can speak of the goodness & mercy of the Lord to us in an especial manner. On the evening of my birthday March 14th we received a gift of a little Daughter a treasure invaluable. During the winter my health was very good, so as to be able to do my work. About a week before her birth I was afflicted with an inflamatory rash which confined me mostly to my room. After repeated bleeding it abated very considerably. I was sick but about two hours. She was born half past eight, so early in the evening that we all had time to get considerable rest that night.

4. The Need for Western Colleges, 1843

SOURCE: *The First Report of the Society for the Promotion of Collegiate and Theological Education at the West* (New York, 1844), 25-28.

The considerations advanced in my last article go to show, that Colleges are a necessity of every extensive community, marked by nature as a social unity. We are now to look at some reasons why they are peculiarly needed at the West. First, then, we find such a reason in the fact that Rome is at this time making unprecedented efforts to garrison this valley with her seminaries of education. She claims already to have within it between fifteen and twenty colleges and theological schools; and this number is rapidly increasing.

To these permanency is ensured by the steadfastness of her policy, the constancy of her receipts from Catholic Europe, yearly increasing under the stimulating reports of her missionaries, and by her exacting despotism, moral if nor ecclesiastic, over the earnings of her poor in this country. They are among the enduring formative forces in western society; and the causes which sustain them, will constantly add to their number. These institutions, together with numerous grades, under the conduct of their Jesuits and various religious orders, are offering (what professes to be) education almost as a gratuity, in many places in the West. Whatever other qualities her education may lack, we may be sure it will not want a subtle and intense proselytism, addressing not the reason but the senses, the taste, the imagination, and the passions; applying itself diversely to the fears of the timid, the enthusiasm of the ardent, the credulity of the simple, the affections of the young, and to that trashy sentiment and mawkish charity to which all principles are the same. Now the policy of Rome in playing upon all these elements through her educational enginery, is steadfast and profoundly sagacious. Her aim, in effect, is at the whole educational interest. The college is naturally the heart of the whole. The lower departments necessarily draw life from that. If Rome then grasps the college in the system of Western education, she virtually grasps the common school; she distills out the heart of the whole, if not a putrid superstition, at least that convert infidelity of which she is still more prolific. . . .

Another peculiar demand for colleges, may be found in the immense rapidity of our growth, and in the character of that growth, being a representative of almost every clime, opinion, sect, language, and social institute, not only of this country but of Christian Europe. Never was a more intense power of intellectual and moral fusion requisite to prevent the utter disorganization of society. Never was a people put to such a perilous proof of its power of assimilation, or required to incorporate with itself so rapidly such vast masses. We have in this fact, as well as in that of the Catholic aggression, dangers and trials put upon us, which our fathers never knew. Society here is new yet vast, and with all its forces in insulation or antagonism. Never was a community in more urgent need of those institutions, whose province it is profoundly to penetrate a people with a burning intelligence that shall fuse it into a unity with those great principles which are the organic life and binding forces of all society. . . .

The above exigencies of Western society cannot be met without colleges. I am far from undervaluing over [other?] movements of Christian philanthropy towards the country. I am most grateful for them. I bless God for his Word broadcast by the American Bible Society amid this people; I am thankful for the interest the American Tract Society are directing hitherward, and hail with pleasure all the living truth and hallowed thought brought by it into contact with the popular mind. The attitude and history of the American Home Missionary Society in relation to the West, fill my mind with a sentiment of moral sublimity, and give it rank among the noblest and most sagacious schemes in the records of Christian benevolence. It will stand in history invested, to a great extent, with the moral grandeur of a civilizer and evangelizer of a new empire. But these are far from excluding the scheme of colleges. The permanency of their benefits can be grounded only on a thorough and liberal popular enlightenment. The educational interest, then, must underlie them all. But the only way in which the East can lay a controlling grasp on this, is by the establishment among us of permanent educational institutions. In a population, one tenth at least of which cannot read, it is plain that education is an essential prerequisite to bringing a large class—and that most necessary to be reached—within the influence of truth through the press. And no system of foreign supply of ministers, teachers or educated men, can obviate the necessity of institutions that shall constantly send forth those that shall be the educators of this people, in the school, the pulpit, the legislature, and the various departments of social life. Artificial irrigation cannot take the place of living waters. We are grateful for streams from abroad, but we feel there is need of opening fountains of life in the bosom of the people itself. The supplies from abroad we cannot rely on long. They are every day becoming more inadequate in numbers, and must to some extent be deficient in adaptation to our wants; a deficiency that often for years, sometimes for life, shuts one out from the people.

The common exigencies, then, of every extensive society, require colleges within itself. The peculiar evils to which that of the West is exposed, obviously cannot be permanently and successfully met by other means. The question then recurs in every aspect of this subject, Will the East assist the West in establishing a Protestant system of home education, or will she leave her to grapple single-handed with Romanism, and the other peculiar dangers to which she is exposed, in addition to the necessities that cluster around every infant community, or will she attempt by palliatives addressed to the symptoms, to heal a disease seated in the heart? A dangerous malady is on the patient. The peril is imminent and requires promptitude. . . .

5. The Mormon Exodus Announced, October 8, 1845

SOURCE: B. H. Roberts, ed., *History of the Church of Jesus Christ of Latter-Day Saints* (Salt Lake City: Deseret Book Co, 2nd ed. rev., 1964), VII, 478-79, 480.

The exodus of the nation of the only true Israel from these United States to a far distant region of the west, where bigotry, intolerance and insatiable oppression lose their power over them—forms a new epoch, not only in the history of the church, but of this nation. And we hereby timely advise you to consider well, as the spirit may give you understanding, the various and momentous bearings of this great movement, and hear what the spirit saith unto you by this our epistle.

Jesus Christ was delivered up into the hands of the Jewish nation to save or condemn them, to be well or maltreated by them according to the determinate counsel and foreknowledge of God. And regard not that even in the light of a catastrophe wholly unlooked for. The spirit of prophecy has long since portrayed in the *Book of Mormon* what might be the conduct of this nation towards the Israel of the last days. The same spirit of prophecy that dwelt richly in the bosom of Joseph has time and again notified the counselors of this church of emergencies that might arise, of which this removal is one; and one too in which all the Latter-day Saints throughout the length and breadth of all the United States should have a thrilling and deliberate interest. The same evil that premeditated against Mordecai awaited equally all the families of his nation. If the authorities of this church cannot abide in peace within the pale of this nation, neither can those who implicitly hearken to their wholesome counsel. A word to the wise is sufficient. You all know and have doubtless felt for years the necessity of a removal provided the government [U.S.] should not be sufficiently protective to allow us to worship God according to the dictates of our own consciences, and of the omnipotent voice of eternal truth. . . . Wake up, wake up, dear brethren, we exhort you, from the Mississippi to the Atlantic, and from Canada to Florida, to the present glorious emergency in which the God of heaven has placed you to prove your faith by your works, preparatory to a rich endowment in the Temple of the Lord, and the obtaining of promises and deliverances, and glories for yourselves and your children and your dead. And we are well persuaded you will do these things, though we thus stir up your pure minds to remembrance. In so doing, the blessings of many, ready to perish like silent dew upon the grass, and the approbation of generations to come, and the hallowed joys of eternal life will rest upon you. And we can not but assure you in conclusion of our most joyful confidence, touching your union and implicit obedience to the counsel of the Great God through the Presidency of the saints. With these assurances and hopes concerning you, we bless you and supplicate the wisdom and furtherance of the Great Head of the Church upon your designs and efforts.

[Signed] BRIGHAM YOUNG, President.
Willard Richards, Clerk.

6. Justification by Scripture, 1846

SOURCE: Address before the U. S. House of Representatives, February 9, 1846.

. . . Sir, there has been so much said on the question of title in this case, that I believe it would be a waste of time for me to say anything more about it, unless I refer to a little book you have there upon your table, which you sometimes employ to administer a solemn oath to every member of this House to support the Constitution of the United States. If you have it, be so good to pass it to the Clerk, and I will ask him to read what I conceive to be the foundation of our title.

If the Clerk will be so good as to read the 26th, 27th, and 28th verses of the 1st chapter of Genesis, the committee will see what I consider to be the foundation of the title of the United States.

The Clerk read accordingly as follows:

"26. And God said, Let us make man in our image, after our likeness; and let them have dominion over the fish of the sea, and over the fowl of the air, and over the cattle, and over all the earth, and over every creeping thing that creepeth upon the earth.

"27. So God created man in his own image, in the image of God created he him: male and female created he them.

"28. And God blessed them, and God said unto them, Be fruitful and multiply, and replenish the earth, and subdue it; and have dominion over the fish of the sea, and over the fowl of the air, and over every living thing that moveth upon the earth."

That, sir (continued Mr. A), in my judgment, is the foundation not only of our title to the territory of Oregon, but the foundation of all human title to all human possessions. It is the foundation of the title by which you occupy that chair; it is the territory of Oregon; and we cannot do it without putting a close to any agreement which we have made with Great Britain that we will not occupy it.

And here I beg leave to repeat an idea that I have already expressed before, and that is, that there is a very great misapprehension of the real merits of this case founded on the misnomer which declares that convention to be a convention of joint occupation. It is a convention of non-occupation—a promise on the part of both parties that neither of the parties will occupy the territory for an indefinite space; first for ten years, then until the notice shall be given from one party to the other that the convention shall be terminated—that is to say, that the restriction, the fetter upon our hands shall be thrown off, which prevents occupation, and prevents the carrying into execution the law of God, which the Clerk has read from the Holy Scriptures. How, if this controversy in relation to the territory of

Oregon was with any other than a Christian nation, I could not cite that book. With the Chinese, and all nations who do not admit the canon of Scripture, it would be quite a different question. It would be a different question between us and the Indian savages, who occupy that country as far as there is any right of occupation, for they do not believe this book. I suppose the mass of this House believe this book. I see them go up and take their oath of office upon it; and many of the southern members kiss the book in token, I suppose, of their respect for it. It is between Christian nations that the foundation of title to land is laid in the first chapter of Genesis, and it is in this book that the title to jurisdiction, to eminent domain, to individual property, had its foundation—all of which flow from other sources subsequent to that which the Clerk read. . . .

Essays

The three essays below explore the reciprocal relationship between religion and the antebellum frontier West. In the first, T. Scott Miyakawa describes the influence of denominational western Dissenters on the institutions of the secular society, and in turn their effect on the Dissenters. In the second essay, Ferenc M. Szasz and Margaret Connell Szasz, both of the University of New Mexico, argue that the expanse of the immense territory of the West allowed for a variety of religious belief systems to flourish in an environment of tolerance and openness. Robert F. Berkhofer, Jr., of the University of California-Santa Cruz, contends, however, that little variety existed among Native American tribes as missionaries conformed the tribal peoples to the ways of the dominant culture at the expense of traditional native life.

The Heritage of the Popular Denominations

T. SCOTT MIYAKAWA

SOURCE: From *Protestants and Pioneers: Individualism and Conformity on the American Frontier* by T. Scott Miyakawa. Copyright © 1964 by the University of Chicago Press. Printed with permission.

In the first decades of the nineteenth century, the small struggling Dissenting sects grew rapidly to become the largest Protestant denominations in the West and in the United States as a whole. As it happened in the Old World, so too on the seaboard, the established churches and educated upper classes modified Dissent in the East. In the West, Dissent was freer to realize its potentialities. The Dissenting denominations were formed primarily to satisfy the religious aspirations of their followers. At the same time, however, they influenced the secular society and helped shape its institutions and in turn were affected by it. Indeed, even before their great expansion in the West, the Dissenting denominations had been in the forefront of the struggle for religious liberty and had helped to found what has become the

American pattern of organized religion, the coexistence, with mutual toleration, of many denominations and sects. The United States, as a number of observers have noted, has a new pattern of organized religion which differs from both the medieval and the Reformation churches. It involves both the unique values or beliefs of each denomination and the common body of values which all the major denominations share.

The first major thesis of the present study concerns the over-all organizational and social aspects of the popular denominations and their implications for western society. Contrary to popular tendency today to correlate the frontier with dissociated individuals, many western Dissenters were in fact conforming members of society and disciplined formal organizations with definite personal and social standards. . . . A corollary to this statement is that the popular denominations helped to create a western society experienced in using voluntary association to promote aims and mutual welfare not attainable by separate individuals. Dissent expected its members, however humble their circumstances, to assume responsibility for its activities and thus trained many in organizational leadership. The Dissenters then extended their experience with religious associations to secular organizations and to politics to realize additional objectives and to influence the government.

A concrete social contribution made by Dissent, as the result of a basic organizational purpose—the formation of a vital fellowship—was to provide a means for hitherto complete strangers, migrants on the frontier, to establish close personal relations quickly. Its discipline was avowedly aimed at encouraging its members and their families to maintain high standards of personal and social behavior and at preserving group unity. Anthropologists often define these explicit functions as manifest functions and the various unstated or implicit (and often unnoticed) services as latent functions. We have considered how the local members upheld the discipline by watching over one another, probing regularly into each person's conduct and feelings, and testifying on their spiritual condition. In conjunction with their beliefs and attitudes toward each other and toward the outside world, such practices could reduce certain anxieties and promote friendships, if not always unite the local church as a whole. Even when quarreling factions formed within a congregation, as among the Baptists during their great controversy, the members within the cliques were brought close together. Present-day stories about the frontier usually overlook this significant latent social function of the Dissenting organizations and discipline. This potentiality for fostering fellowship was perhaps another reason why the members accepted what to us may seem an onerous discipline. Together with the fellowship, we should mention other potential values many Dissenters found in their membership, such as the encouragement of devotion to their calling and the opportunities to improve such personal and social skills as speaking (both in public and in groups), reading, conducting meetings and committee sessions, and even some social etiquette. Perhaps these benefits might also be classified under informal adult education.

Besides fulfilling latent functions for individual migrants, Dissent also carried out many latent group functions. Settlers in early frontier society, lacking many traditional informal and formal legal agencies of control, had to take deliberate steps to maintain order and unity. The Dissenting fellowship, discipline, and church courts were well-suited to confront such a situation. The community could count on a solid core of disciplined citizens organized for religious purposes, it is true, but also latently able to wield collective as well as individual influence for peace and order. The popular denominations thus had a direct impact on the larger society and also exerted additional pressure as reference groups for many others in the community. Social scientists often define as reference groups those whose approval other individuals and groups seek. Obviously, reference groups may also set the standards which others follow on a single interest or over a wide range of behavior. Since non-members regularly attending western Presbyterian and Dissenting churches outnumbered the members severalfold, the Dissenting influence as reference groups was apparently greater than it seemed on the surface. The rapid rise of many members to economic and political prominence in the West would also have enhanced their prestige as reference groups.

The second main thesis of this study involves the more specific institutional and cultural traits of Dissent and their impact on western society: the popular denominations strengthened or were the source of many institutions and qualities, secular as well as religious, regarded as typically western and sometimes as characteristically American. In addition to its voluntary organizational features, equalitarianism, and faith in the common man, Dissent popularized the once peculiarly aristocratic Calvinistic system of calling, a heritage which the larger society later secularized into the idealization of the successful self-made man and his worldly achievements. The more controversial attitude of earlier Dissent included its suspicion of scholarship and art and its opposition to professionalism. With some notable exceptions, western popular denominations accepted or were ambivalent toward racism and slavery and, partly under revivalistic influence, long retained what some churchmen regarded as sectarian provincialism. . . .

. . . Within their organization, Dissenting denominations eliminated nearly all invidious distinctions, other than race, arising from accidents of birth and condition. They sought members among the humbler people and encouraged leadership from their ranks. Long before the Jacksonian movement, they opened all denominational offices to the many and infused their organizational life with new vigor. This democratic faith was an important reason for their strong opposition toward professional prerequisites to ordination. At the same time, it is evident that western popular denominations had learned to value formal organization, rules, and offices with definite responsibilities, though the Baptists had to go through a bitter struggle before the main movement could convince the antagonistic sectarians on the necessity for organization. The Baptist anti-mission controversy turned on the distinction between one form of sectarianism and the rising denominationalism more functionally attuned to the complex secular society. Dissenting procedures were democratic and often flexible but orderly, and they encouraged members to assume organizational responsibilities to enhance their rights. It is worth noting that Tocqueville, who was investigating among other things how American society with its individualism and equalitarianism could maintain order and avoid new despotism, stressed the role of voluntary associations. Such associations linked the citizens' private interests to their social responsibilities. Conversely, many members learned through participating in organizations how to be more effective in their personal lives.

Dissenters did not object to formal titles and offices which served functional purposes and did not exclude natural talent from any office it could hold. American Methodism created a formal episcopacy, which the British movement never did, and gave the bishops great authority but it fought attempts to require theological training for ordination. We may again reflect on that amusing interlude when some western circuit riders strongly opposed to theological seminaries wanted D.D. degrees automatically conferred on the itinerants when they became full elders. Here too, we see that under these circumstances the degrees would not have symbolized any barrier to unschooled but able men attaining office. In contrast to some Continental churches, for Dissent the officers and clergy did not constitute a privileged elite or separate order, but were basically fellow laymen entrusted with certain responsibilities for the common welfare. Their spiritual leadership determined their fitness to hold office, and holding office was not a right, as the Baptists among others made amply clear by electing their ministers annually. Once elected, the ministers and officers were responsible to the members and subject to lay criticism—at least in the members' view.

Since both Calvinism and Dissent emphasized the calling, it is difficult to distinguish their respective influences in implanting this system in western life. Initially in the West, even the Presbyterians had an almost sectarian attitude toward many cultural interests and defined the calling more narrowly than did the more urbane Old World Calvinists. Dissent was even narrower in its outlook and tended to restrict the calling, aside from the ministry, to economic or political activities. This "practical" approach to the calling substantially democratized, while it restricted, this once rather aristocratic ethic which had such profound consequences for both the religious and the secular life in the United States (as shown by Max Weber, H. R. Niebuhr, Talcott Parsons, and other authorities). This simplified system of calling apparently appealed to many struggling settlers who were also encouraged to raise their aspirations. European visitors were struck by the ceaseless working of Americans, even the well to do. As expected, Bishop Asbury set an example by his untiring labor and insistence that rest was for the next world. The Methodist Anning Owen aptly summarized the Dissenting and western Presbyterian ideal with his motto: "Work! work! work! this world is no place for rest."

Devotion to this-worldly duties, we should remember, originally expressed a religious ethic for other-worldly ends and was not a mundane preoccupation with materialism. Greed as such was always sinful. Strange as it may seem to us today, sectarian Dissent feared intellectual and cultural pursuits as potentially more dangerous distractions from the path to salvation than it feared business. Within a few years, the more secularized version of the calling came to value highly both personal achievement and rational productive industry alert to its opportunities, as distinct from purely exploitive ventures. Jacksonianism, as noted before, advanced these views politically when it praised the honest toil of a productive farmer or artisan or creative businessman, as opposed to the supposedly parasitical financial oligarchy. Later in the century, this emphasis on achievement strengthened the demand for competence which in turn increasingly meant professional training and higher standards. The system of calling was an integral component of the Calvinistic social and theocratic heritage, but at the same time was individualistic in holding each person responsible for his relations with God and serving Him through this-worldly duties. Dissent based its social control on its fellowship and discipline which included the public behavior and business practices of its communicants. Dissenters understood clearly that members would stray and consequently had created disciplinary institutions—a tradition contrary to some present day views that religion has little or nothing to do with business or practical affairs.

The western Dissenting stress on the calling would seem to contradict its persistent suspicion of scholarship and art. Opposition to cultural pursuits was originally a feature of the sectarian efforts to "withdraw" from the world, while the system of calling came from the Calvinistic ethic to enter, conquer, and transform that same world. More and more Dissenters acquired wealth and high political offices and their worldly successes were often attributed to devotion to calling. Yet, the popular denominations continue to oppose most efforts to establish professional standards, partly because they interpreted such attempts as undemocratic plots to prevent able but formally unschooled persons from realizing their potentialities. One tangible argument was that some wealthy conservatives, with no more intrinsic love for disinterested culture than the Dissenters and Jacksonians whom these conservatives disdained, tried to use criteria of excellence as weapons against the emerging democracy. The Dissenters, however, had a more basic, if perhaps unconscious, reason for fearing art and higher learning as potential distractions. Ambitious members were anxious to rise economically and politically as fast as possible and needed justification for all the labor and capital they put into their farms and businesses. Religious sanction elevated their work to a calling. If we oversimplify the complex interrelationships, we may also observe that Dissenting organization and calling helped to prepare the way for (was latently functional to) the industrialization of the Middle West later in the century. On the other hand, the suspicion of learning lingering in western popular denominations probably delayed (was latently dysfunctional to) the intellectual and theological efforts to understand this industrialization and urbanization and to reformulate their traditional practices to meet the new situation. As a result of this neglect, it is said, the popular denominations lost many workingclass members.

The popular denominational outlook was essentially what we would today consider middle class and not that of a traditional peasantry or radical revolutionaries. The Dissenters soon learned to appreciate elementary education and practical training as valuable for their callings. Before 1850, however, the majority could scarcely be expected to understand the extent to which religion and practical knowledge depended upon the Western (that is, Occidental) cultural heritage and its continuing development. While criticizing scholars and artists, Dissent unconsciously assumed their existence outside its membership and pragmatically utilized their contributions whenever convenient. Early western Dissent was more apt to understand democracy as eliminating intellectual standards than as providing better educational and cultural facilities open to all to train religious and civic leadership and to enrich the common life. Yet, in becoming the largest religious organizations in the American West and in the United States as a whole, the popular denominations had achieved new status. No longer a despised minority as they had been on the eighteenth-century seaboard, they had to assume more and more responsibility for secular culture as they increasingly had for western social and political welfare.

By the 1830's it is possible to detect the first modifications in the group sentiment, as distinct from the earlier personal views of a few cultured Dissenters. Thus, the Indiana Methodist Conference petition to the state legislature asking for a change in the Calvinistic monopoly of the state university contained some appreciative comments on learning, and the conference report recommending the founding of a college referred to the intrinsic value of higher education as well as to its importance in raising the quality of elementary education. At least a growing number of denominational leaders were ceasing to regard scholarship as an aristocratic plot to subvert democracy and beginning to see it as an opportunity which should be open to the people. Nevertheless, the persistent hostility to college-educated ministers shows how deeply imbedded this suspicion was. To some extent, the ambivalence toward learning survived longer among the western Dissenters than in eastern popular denominations because the new western communities did not have an influential elite to set rival standards that others could emulate. Instead, the Dissenters themselves were among the important reference groups.

According to Dr. Mecklin and other authorities, revivalism was not integral to Dissent, but it profoundly influenced the Dissenting denominations employing it. Western popular denominations considered the camp meetings and other spectacular revivalistic features as "extracurricular" activities outside the official denominational program, even if today some popular stories erroneously equate western religious life with revivalism. The major popular denominations used revivalism as a technique to win new converts and to quicken the fervor of their members, but in the process were thoroughly permeated with the revivalistic spirit. Western revivalism, in contrast to the later Finney and eastern reformistic revivalism, strengthened and prolonged emotionalism, equalitarianism, and hostility to scholarship, learned ministry, and broad civic outlook. Without assessing the views of the authorities on revivalism, we can still conclude from the Moravian experience that a sect could enjoy many cultural interests and from Quaker history that a sect could have broad humanitarian and social ethical concerns. Perhaps significantly, neither the Quakers nor the Moravians were directly involved in western revivalism. The Friends severely criticized it. The western Presbyterians did not acquire or reacquire their more churchly attitude toward cultural pursuits until many years after they had explicitly rejected western revivalism, as distinct from Finney and eastern reformistic revivalism with its direct interest in social welfare and education. The formal definition of a sect obviously depended more on empirical experiences than on its essential inner logic. The intense emotionalism and narrow outlook attributed to western revivalism actually ran counter (was dysfunctional) to the Dissenting system of calling with its stress on the sober, disciplined, and responsible members working in the community.

The growing sectarian rivalry multiplied the number of denominations coexisting in the West. At the same time, the early West experienced a less frequently mentioned development, that of many local Dissenting churches separating into two or more meetings instead of growing into larger units. Aside from such external factors as the desire to have the church close to home, the members could more easily maintain their active fellowship and discipline in small intimate meetings than in large ones. Since the communicants supported the regional, state, and national units of their denominations, this institutionalization into small local congregations helped at first to give Dissent its vitality and warm fellowship. However, later in the century when membership and community requirements changed, many towns were found to be without a single church large enough to provide such essential services as competent parish work, pastoral counseling, and religious education. We might also ask whether this sectarian rivalry and preference for small, like-minded groups would discourage the acceptance of persons with different interests. Each meeting could easily insist upon appreciably uniform views while it tolerated divergent opinions in other sects. If a member did not agree with his fellow communicants, he was likely to join another congregation of his denomination or possibly even another denomination. However vital the earlier fellowships, adherents would have had less experience in their church with "diversity within unity" than they might have had. Fortunately for western society, interdenominational and other organizations, among them political parties and civic associations, brought together the members of the various churches. The congenial, like-minded Dissenting fellowships may have been an important source of the conformity which some profess to find in many middle western communities.

Early nineteenth-century popular denominations institutionalized the prevailing racist patterns and subordinated the Negroes (and other non-Caucasians), to whom Dissent did not extend its equalitarianism. Race was an obvious basis for barring talent from high denominational offices when the Dissenters had eliminated almost all other invidious distinctions. So respectable was racism that no one attempted to conceal his prejudice. Except for groups like the Quakers, early western Dissent found it convenient to assert that pure religion had almost nothing to do with slavery or racism. In practice, the Dissenters had a double standard—the free Negroes and slaves were to accept the dualistic ethic that as long as the "Africans" could worship, they should not be concerned about their personal and social condition, while the Dissenters reserved for themselves the ethic of calling with its emphasis on worldly success and duty to change conditions. Western revivalism did not create the ancient dualistic view but did strengthen it by regarding conversion as a "spiritual" experience and the social environment, including discrimination and slavery under which members had to live, as belonging to the "material" or "sensual" realm with which religion was little concerned. In contrast to their eighteenth-century forbears who fought for religious principles, the early nineteenth-century Dissenters—again with such exceptions as the Quakers—did not seriously oppose secular laws infringing on the religious rights of the slaves. The British Baptist delegates in the 1830's felt impelled to remind their American hosts that the state laws against teaching slaves to read conflicted with the Baptist religious duty to study the Scriptures and that in denying offices to Negroes, American Baptists were contradicting their professed principles.

The Dissenting organization of small congenial meetings combined conveniently with sectarianism to justify the institutionalization of their prejudices against Negroes: the Negroes could form their own churches (under white control in the South) instead of worshiping with others. The still rankling troubles over race began when the Dissenters accepted the "white superiority" thesis. While we may wonder about Southerners like Bishop Capers who pioneered in the missions to the slaves and regarded Negroes as lacking some rational faculties, similar views prevailed widely among western Dissenters. Such well-meaning leaders as Peter Cartwright regularly referred to Negroes in terms which would be shocking today. These practices reveal how general was the often unconscious refusal to grant to the Negroes (and other non-Caucasians) even elementary consideration for their personal feelings and dignity. Many Dissenters who were opposed to slavery were at the same time prejudiced against its victims. Racism enabled them temporarily to blur the contradiction between Dissenting equalitarianism and their discrimination against Negroes—at the cost of further spreading this belief so highly dysfunctional to American democracy and corrosive to Dissenting ideals.

Finally, to return to the more general features of Dissenting control, we might ask about its discipline by peers, and not by authoritative officials. The experience was surely conducive to the development of voluntary associations and feeling of equality, but under some circumstances could it have also strengthened the conformistic rather than the individualistic heritage of the popular denominations? In Dissenting faith each member was directly responsible to God, and Dissent also expected each member to be responsible in his calling, both strongly individualistic emphases. On the other hand, the control by peer groups had conformistic tendencies by encouraging members to heed the views of their equals, especially in the smaller settlements during the period when the popular denominations were still suspicious of serious intellectual and artistic pursuits which might have provided alternative means of individual self-expression.

David Riesman and his associates have suggested in *The Lonely Crowd* that in the nineteenth century the dominant personality type was what they define as "inner directed," but in the twentieth century the proportion of "outer directed" characters is increasing. As a child, the inner directed person is trained to become a relatively self-disciplined adult and above all to have "generalized but nevertheless inescapably destined goals." Yet, we have seen that the popular denominations maintained group discipline over members throughout adult life, while denomination teaching encouraged the Dissenters (presumably good exemplars of inner direction) to strive strenuously in a calling toward group-approved goals. Their inner direction, in short, was partly (and only partly) conformity to peer control. Possibly, the proportion of outer directed personality was greater or the proportion of inner directed personality was less in the nineteenth century than it might appear in retrospect. . . .

Religion and Spirituality

FERENC M. SZASZ and MARGARET CONNELL SZASZ

SOURCE: "Religion and Spirituality" by Ferenc M. Szasz and Margaret Szasz, from *The Oxford History of the American West*, edited by Clyde A. Milner II et al., copyright © 1994 by Oxford University Press, Inc. Used by permission of Oxford University Press, Inc.

In the spring and summer of 1788, a number of eastern cities staged celebrations in honor of the new Constitution of the United States. The most impressive of these "federal processions" occurred in Philadelphia, where, on 4 July 1788, a crowd of about seventeen thousand watched five hundred people file past in a mammoth parade. According to the eyewitness Francis Hopkinson, the marchers grouped themselves by guild or profession, and eighty-fifth in line (after the lawyers but before the doctors) strolled "the clergy of the different Christian denominations, with the rabbi of the Jews, walking arm in arm." This public display of "charity and brotherly love" by Philadelphia's clergy proved a first, not only for America but probably for the entire world. It pointed to the fact that religion in the new federal Republic would play a vastly different role from anything that had gone before.

The clerics' optimism drew heavily from the political theory of James Madison, the American Enlightenment figure who thought most deeply about church-state relations. Acknowledging that a person's faith could never be determined by reason alone, Madison placed religious belief as the foremost of all natural rights. Since the state existed to protect these rights, it should never unnecessarily interfere with the realm of faith. The Philadelphia Convention of 1787 incorporated Madison's ideas into the Constitution; in 1791, these ideas formed the heart of the First Amendment. Unlike those nations with established churches, which included most of Europe, the United States would never develop any official church. Except for nineteenth-century denominational schools and missions among American Indians, no American church could rely on state support. Rather, each denomination *voluntarily* had to convince others that its position was the correct one. Almost every religious group accepted these boundaries. Each faith would set forth its position as best it could; "the people" would then choose their own religion.

The eminent twentieth-century theologian Paul Tillich once observed, "Religion is the substance of culture and culture the form of religion." Certainly this proved true for the trans-Mississippi West. The religious history of the West is all-embracing. It cannot be limited simply to kivas or churches, ceremonies or sermons, medicine men or clerics. Rather, western religion permeated the realms of politics, culture, and society. Perhaps the key to understanding religion in the West was the land. The vastness of this immense territory, with its many ecological subregions, provided a multitude of homes for native belief systems, as well as for the diverse faiths brought by European, African, and Asian immigrants. In the Great Plains, Rockies, Southwest, Plateau, Great Basin, and Pacific Coast regions, a variety of religious subcultures flourished. With a few notable exceptions, tolerance and openness characterized the world of western faiths. In the generations encompassed by our story, the West initiated a pattern of religious pluralism in American society—often without a culture-shaping mainstream—that anticipated many developments of the late twentieth century.

We begin with the 1840s, a pivotal decade for both the religious and the political fortunes of the nation. By this time, the main outlines of American religious history had been generally sketched out. The Roman Catholic church had become the nation's largest single denomination, a position it would sustain to the present day. With growth fueled largely by immigration, the church wrestled with multiethnic congregations and "foreign" image for over a century. The same stream of immigration brought over 250,000 German Jews, who soon scattered across the land. These Jews played vital entrepreneurial roles in the West, and some, such as the clothier Levi Strauss, rapidly rose to the realm of legend. In 1844, when the Latter-day Saints prophet Joseph Smith, Jr., died at the hands of an Illinois mob, the Saints numbered only about 14,000. The pundits of the day predicted their imminent collapse, but their subsequent move to the Great Basin region of Utah and Idaho gave the church new life. The mainline Protestant churches (Methodists, Baptists, Congregationalists, Presbyterians, Episcopalians, Lutherans) congratulated themselves that they had saved the trans-Appalachian region from "barbarism" through their "benevolent empire" of Bible, tract, Sunday school, and education societies. All were looking for new fields to conquer.

Simultaneously, in an era dominated by ideas of "manifest destiny," many Americans pushed across the Mississippi to claim Indian lands in Oregon country or Mexican California. Integral to this mass emigration, the Christian clergy joined the exodus in a race both to convert the Indians and retain the emigrating church members. During the antebellum era, the mainline Protestant denominations wielded the most influence in national affairs. Together, these groups composed what has been termed a "voluntary" religious establishment. While they disputed among themselves over theology and church polity, they agreed on essentials: Christianity had broken into "denominations," each of which had a distinct mission; Protestantism and democratic republicanism were forever intertwined; America had become God's "New Israel"; and the churches felt compelled to carry their mission to both whites and Indians *west* of the Mississippi.

The religious diversity that the European Americans brought west met an equal diversity among the indigenous faiths of the Native Americans. When the historian Robert F. Berkhofer, Jr., spoke of the "multiplicity of [the Indians'] specific histories," he referred primarily to their means of warfare, hunting, fishing, and social organization. But the Native Americans' varied ceremonial life and relationship to the supernatural shared a similar "multiplicity." Thus, in the nineteenth-century West, heterogeneous European-American religions interacted with equally heterogeneous native religions. The resulting blends, as seen in the Pueblo-Roman Catholic, Sioux-Episcopal, and Pima-Presbyterian amalgamations, proved unique in the history of American faith.

Long before the voyages of Columbus, American Indians had engaged in "religious borrowing and synthesis." Thus, when they began to graft European Christianity onto their own faiths, this was, as the anthropologist Robert Brightman has noted, "simply one more instance of a traditional receptivity to religious innovation." A major part of the history of native religion in the West is the story of its interaction with this imported Christianity.

From the 1760s, native groups of southern California had encountered the highly motivated Franciscans, who forced them into mission enclaves stretching from San Diego to San Francisco. The Franciscans retained their hold over thousands of native Californians until the Mexican government secularized the missions in the 1830s. In other regions of the Southwest, including present-day southern Arizona and parts of Texas, natives had also been influenced by Catholicism through missions founded in the late seventeenth and early eighteenth centuries. In the late 1500s, along the Rio Grande valley in what is now New Mexico, Tanoan and Keresan speakers, as well as the Zuni, had come under the control of these Hispanic Catholics, who occupied the region for eight decades—an era dominated by bitter church-state rivalry—before the natives drove them out in 1680. Don Diego de Vargas's *reconquista* of 1692 acknowledged native rights and marked the beginning of a rich blending of native ceremonies and worldview with those of Hispanic Catholicism, a blending that continues into the present. East of the Llano Estacado, crossed by Coronado in the 1540s, former Southeast Woodland tribes—Cherokees, Creeks, Choctaws, Chickasaws, and Seminoles—were settling in. Even before the era of removal forced their emigration, most of these groups had met Protestant missionaries. In general, the Christian messages were well received, especially by the Cherokees, whose leadership, epitomized by the mixed-blood John Ross, welcomed change and the incorporation of European ways. Christianity and traditional values blended among these Indians, historically known as the "Five Civilized Tribes," during their early decades in the Indian Territory.

Elsewhere in the West, however, native religions had remained beyond the thrust of Christian missionaries. In the Northwest Coast and Columbia River Plateau regions, Salishan, Sahaptian, Chinookian, and other linguistic groups had begun extensive cultural borrowing with the opening of the sea otter trade in the late eighteenth century, the startling visit of Lewis and Clark, and the intense international rivalry for beaver. Bargaining for iron pots, metal fishhooks, weapons, or the much desired blue beads had changed their cultures. They had incorporated the epithets of the Boston men into the Chinook trade jargon, and they had sharpened their shrewd trading skills in the vast exchange network that stretched east via the Nez Percés. Moreover, they had been weakened by European disease. But with the exception of a band of Catholic Iroquois, who settled among the Salishan-speaking Flatheads around 1820, and the quasireligious influence of the Hudson's Bay Company, this cultural borrowing had generally excluded Christianity. Not until the 1830s and 1840s, with the arrival of Oblate and Jesuit priests, plus missionaries from various Protestant denominations, did the Northwest Coast and Plateau people begin to address the many messages of Christianity. In the central Rockies, much of the Great Plains, and the western Great Basin, these missionaries arrived even later.

The Intertwining of Politics and Religion

In the mid-1840s, the Utes, Paiutes, and other natives living in the eastern Great Basin met one of the most unusual religious groups in nineteenth-century America. In no other area of the West were politics and religion more closely intertwined, for this region is forever linked with the saga of the Church of Jesus Christ of Latter-day Saints (the Mormons). Western Protestant-Catholic and Christian-Jewish tensions generally remained confined to harsh words and editorials. Only Mormon-Gentile (i.e., non-Mormon) relations crossed the line into mob violence. For many mid-nineteenth-century contemporaries, the Latter-day Saints pushed beyond the limits of America's famed religious toleration.

The story of the angel who led an upstate New York farm boy, Joseph Smith, Jr., to the buried golden plates on Hill Cumorah is well-known. Seated behind a curtain, Smith translated these plates to form *The Book of Mormon,* first printed in 1830. Read literally, *The Book of Mormon* tells the story of ancient Near Eastern peoples who migrated to the Americas: the Jaredites, the Nephites, and the Lamanites (the latter designated as ancestors of the American Indians). The account culminates with the visit of Jesus Christ, shortly after His resurrection, to the Nephites. Read metaphorically, the book depicts the success of those civilizations that follow the Commandments of the Lord and the collapse of those that become filled with pride and arrogance. In either case, *The Book of Mormon* was America's first indigenous holy scripture.

The Mormons invoked controversy wherever they settled. Their new scripture, Smith's 130 special revelations from the Lord—especially those concerning polygamy (an open secret, fueled by rumor, from the late 1830s until officially proclaimed in 1852), Mormon "bloc voting," and their alleged violation of the church-state separation—all played on Gentile fears. The culmination came on 29 January 1844, when Joseph Smith, Jr., announced that he was a candidate for the presidency of the United States.

Consequently, what the novelist William Dean Howells once termed "the foolish mob which helps to establish each new religion" proved a major factor in early Mormon history. Many church leaders, including Smith, were either tarred and feathered or thrown in jail on trumped-up charges. Their northern origins made them especially suspect in slaveholding Missouri, where proslavery settlers and politicians persecuted them mercilessly. As a Mormon hymn writer put it: "Missouri/Like a whirlwind in its fury,/And without a judge or jury,/Drove the Saints and spilled their blood."

When the Saints established the Mississippi town of Nauvoo, Illinois—a well-run prototype for the later Mormon communities in the Great Basin—local outrage could no longer be contained. On 27 June 1844, an angry mob stormed the jail at Carthage, Illinois, to martyr both Joseph Smith, Jr., and his brother Hyrum.

Virtually all observers expected the Saints to collapse with the death of the prophet. Indeed, several schisms weakened them considerably. Sidney Rigdon led a fragment to Pittsburgh, Pennsylvania; James J. Strang headed a larger remnant that thrived in a communal setting on Beaver Island in Lake Michigan, until his assassination; and Joseph Smith III, the prophet's son by his first wife, Emma Hale Smith, rejected polygamy to lead a group that became the Reorganized Church of Jesus Christ of Latter Day Saints, with headquarters in Independence, Missouri. That the entire body of Saints did not similarly fracture may be credited to the skills of the newly appointed prophet, Brigham Young, and his decision to move to the West.

The historian Jan Shipps has argued that the great trek from Missouri and Illinois to Utah formed the central event in Mormon history. The journey to the Great Basin carried the Saints not simply to the promised land of Deseret but also "backward" into a primordial sacred time. From this journey, Shipps has suggested, the Mormons emerged as a distinctly new religious faith, as different from Christianity as Christianity was from Judaism.

Both Mormon social practices and theology proved unique. The Saints rejected the Christian trinity and downplayed the concept of original sin. Their communalism, polygamy, and authoritarian church polity formed a sharp contrast to the romantic individualism that dominated contemporary American Protestantism. Believing that God "was once as we are now," the Mormons taught that most devout male Saints would eventually hold similar dominion over future worlds of their own. Their maxim phrased it thus: "As God is at present Man may become." Essentially universalists, the Saints maintained that all of humanity would achieve salvation but that Mormon believers would reach a higher degree of glory. The King James translation of Scripture, *The Book of Mormon* (written in the King James idiom), and Smith's subsequent revelations were accorded equal divine status. The head of the church was assigned the mantle of contemporary prophet.

The evolving Mormon folk religion transcended even the official pronouncements from church leaders. The Saints celebrated special holidays: Joseph Smith's birthday, Brigham Young's birthday, the birthday of the church; the day of arrival in the Salt Lake Valley (still observed in Utah on 24 July as Pioneer Day). They wove heroic legends of the "Great Trek" west and the suffering of the later emigrants, some of whom pushed handcarts over twelve hundred miles to their new home. They commemorated the sego lily, whose roots the early pioneers ate to avoid starvation, and seagulls, which arrived to devour a plague of crickets that threatened to consume the Saints' first wheat crop. They danced and sang with vigor. When their hymns spoke of "Israel" or the "Camp of Israel," they claimed these concepts for themselves, and thus the term *Gentiles* took on new meaning in the Mountain West. Like the ancient Hebrews, the Saints forged a separate concept of "peoplehood" that persists up to the present day.

The federal government, however, viewed the rise of a semi-independent kingdom in the Great Basin with considerable suspicion. In the mid-1850s, Congress accused Brigham Young of complicity in the harassment of Utah's federal officials. Spurred on by exaggerated coverage by the eastern press, President James Buchanan ordered federal troops to Utah in 1857 to bring the Saints into line.

The Saints viewed the arrival of the federal army as reminiscent of their persecution in Missouri and Illinois. The Mormon leaders seriously considered relocating to Central America or elsewhere. Eventually cooler heads prevailed, and the "Mormon War" ended without direct confrontation. But the tension caused by the war did lead to bloodshed. In August 1857, a wagon train of Missouri and Arkansas settlers crossed southern Utah, where they were attacked by a band of Mormons and their Indian allies. This raid, in which 130 people died, ranks as one of the worst examples of religious violence in American history. The Mountain Meadows Massacre, as it is known, assumed a symbolic role in defining Mormon-Gentile relations.

Politics and religion were equally intertwined in the story of religious expansion into the Pacific Northwest. In 1833, four Flathead and Nez Percé Indians journeyed to St. Louis to inquire about Christian missionaries. This seemingly inconsequential request would help to determine the course of the history of the Northwest. It opened the door for missionaries and migrants and thus became the basis for America's claim to the Oregon Country.

The native appeal for "white religion" probably implied a desire for increased knowledge of a general, all-defusing cultural power. In 1833 and 1837, other groups of Salishan and Sahaptian natives traveled the same path to St. Louis. The retelling of the story created one of the most famous legends of nineteenth-century western religious history. Catholic journals broadcast the Indian journey as a call for "Black Robes" who said "Great Prayers" (the Mass). Protestants declared that the Indians had requested the "white man's book of heaven." Within a few years, both Catholic and Protestant missionaries had begun the arduous trek to the Columbia River Plateau and the Northwest Coast.

In June 1840, the Jesuit Pierre Jean De Smet made the journey from St. Louis to the Flatheads and Pend d'Oreilles. The next year he returned with two more Jesuits, Nicholas Point and Gregory Mengarini, thus inaugurating what a later Jesuit termed "the grandest missionary work of the nineteenth century in its religious, social, economical and political aspect."

De Smet and his fellow Jesuits hoped to encourage the Indians to abandon their nomadic life and adopt a settled agrarian existence. In September 1841, De Smet began St. Mary's Mission in the Bitter Root Valley of Montana. The next year he helped create the Coeur d'Alene Mission of the Sacred Heart on the St. Joe River. The St. Ignatius mission to the Flatheads, St. Paul's to the San Poils, and St. Michael's to the Spokans soon followed.

Generally speaking, the Jesuits looked to their own history, especially their "holy experiment" in the Central Highlands of South America, as a model for this endeavor. During the seventeenth and eighteenth centuries, the Jesuits had established a string of over thirty settlements (called *reducciones,* from the Spanish *reducir,*

217 • THE ANTEBELLUM FRONTIER WEST

"to bring together") in the region that is now largely Paraguay. Centered around a market square and a plaza, these communities consisted of several thousand Indians managed by only a handful of clerics. The Jesuits taught the Natives European forms of agriculture, music, architecture, and religion during an experiment that lasted over a century.

Although De Smet's dream of establishing "a new Paraguay," never occurred, these Northwest missions did serve many functions similar to those of their earlier counterparts. St. Ignatius provided a hospital, sawmill, flour mill, and printing press. All missions boasted schools that taught theology, English, and other skills. Rumor had it that every Jesuit mission contained at least one resident genius. Father Anthony Ravalli certainly qualified. During his career at St. Mary's he served as doctor, architect, sculptor, linguist, and expert manager. De Smet himself also proved a skilled negotiator. His peacekeeping efforts on the northern plains saved hundreds of lives, and many regional native leaders held him in esteem.

De Smet also drew on the romantic appeal of the American West to encourage numerous European novices and priests to follow his footsteps. Over the course of the century, perhaps two hundred Jesuits crossed the ocean to serve missions in the northern Rockies and Plateau regions. In spite of this effort, however, the string of Jesuit missions never fulfilled their founders' hopes. The harsh climate of the region proved unsuitable for extensive agriculture, and the Indians preferred their traditional hunting, fishing, and gathering cycle to a settled mission life. (To follow the tribe, for example, Sacred Heart Mission moved three times in thirty-six years.)

Some of these Jesuit missions remain modest tourist attractions today, such as St. Ignatius in Montana or the Cataldo Mission (Sacred Heart) in Idaho. As an entity, however, these missions are not well-known outside the region, and they pale when compared with their internationally known California counterparts. The life of De Smet is respected, but it has never engendered the romance that surrounds California's mission founder, the Franciscan Junípero Serra.

The Methodists were the first Protestant denomination to respond to the Indian journey to St. Louis. In 1834, Rev. Jason Lee, his nephew Rev. Daniel Lee, and three lay associates traveled to the Northwest Coast, settling in the Willamette Valley. Within a few years the Presbyterians sent out Revs. Elkanah Walker and Cushing Eells and their wives, Dr. Marcus and Narcissa Whitman, and Rev. Henry and Eliza Spalding. Narcissa and Eliza were the first European-American women to cross the Rockies into the Columbia River Plateau. Unlike Jason Lee, these missionaries were drawn to the Plateau tribes: Walker and Eells to the Spokans at Tshimakain; the Spaldings to the Nez Percés at Lapwai; and the Whitmans to the Walla Wallas and Cayuses at Waiilatpu. Like the Jesuits, the Whitmans built a gristmill, sawmill, blacksmith shop, and school; their mission also served as an "emigrant house" for Oregon Trail travelers.

In 1842, when the American Board of Commissioners for Foreign Missions determined to close these missions to the Plateau tribes, an equally determined Whitman traveled east in a dangerous mid-winter trek to argue their case. Like the Nez Percé-Flathead trip to St. Louis, Whitman's dramatic journey to the East has also ballooned into legend. Those who argue that Whitman "saved Oregon" through his travels neglect the fact that by the 1840s, Midwesterners with "Oregon fever" were already beginning the migration that led to the resolution of the Oregon boundary issue. The Whitmans' contribution to the American cause may have come later. When Congress learned of the November 1847 native uprising against the Waiilatpu Mission and of the deaths of Marcus, Narcissa, and others, it responded by creating a government for the Oregon Territory, the first official American government established west of the Rockies.

As Protestant and Catholic missionaries competed among the tribes living in the Northwest Coast, Plateau, and northern Rockies, they carried out in microcosm the most persistent American religious theme of the century: Protestant-Catholic hostility. This theme echoed and reechoed throughout the West, where it affected both native and immigrant. The Protestant and Catholic "ladders" developed in the Northwest Coast and the Plateau reflected this antagonism. Borrowing from the Salishan concept of a *sahale* stick ("wood from above"), the French-Canadian father Francois Norbert Blanchet created a large (six-feet-by-two-feet) paper chart with a time line portraying the life of Christ and basic Christian principles. One version of the "Catholic ladder" depicted Martin Luther as branching off on a road that led to hell. By contrast, Spalding's "Protestant ladder" for the Nez Percés peopled the road to hell with worldly popes and immoral priests.
. . .

Many European immigrants to the Pacific Northwest, like the natives, responded to the missionaries with indifference. By the late twentieth century, this area was widely acknowledged as "the least churched region" of the nation. The nineteenth-century boasts "the Sabbath shall never cross the Missouri" and "no Sunday west of St. Louis" proved prescient. They pointed to the fact that the eastern religious institutions would have difficulty establishing themselves in the wide-open society of the trans-Mississippi West.

Nowhere was the secular image of the new West more pronounced than in California. In 1849, the cry of "Gold, Gold, from the American River" drew thousands around the Horn, across Panama, or over the trail to San Francisco. The chief goal of forty-niners was seldom that of the spirit. "The Americans," complained a visiting Catholic priest, "think only of dollars, talk only of dollars, seek nothing but dollars."

Nevertheless, a group of clerical forty-niners did their best to stem the tide. By one estimate, four denominations had established about fifty small churches throughout the early "Mother Lode" country. A Unitarian pulpit orator, Thomas Starr King, tried to replicate Boston's values in San Francisco during the 1850s and early 1860s while the Congregationalist Timothy Dwight Hunt attempted to "make California the Massachusetts of the Pacific."

Such was not to be. The historian Kevin Starr has noted that the tumultuous nature of California life could never be confined within traditional religious norms, be they New England parish, Virginia plantation, or Mexican village. California manifested a religious "openness" from its earliest days.

California life also muted all the traditional religious antagonisms. The fact that the territory's first American governor, Peter H. Burnett, was a Catholic convert played absolutely no role in his political career. As a Catholic archbishop noted in 1864, his church "did not face the prejudice which is encountered elsewhere." A generation later, California's small Seventh-Day Adventist community led a successful fight to repeal the state's Sunday regulations. In the cities, the African Methodist Episcopal and African Methodist Episcopal Zion churches provided strong voices for racial equality. John Muir's "religion of nature," a transcendental appreciation for the magnificence of Creation (with little or no role for a redeemer), also drew a number of followers. Worship services by Asian faiths generally went unmolested. In religion, as in so many other areas, California became "the great exception."

Politics and religion were equally intertwined in the American Southwest. In Texas, the nineteenth century was a postmission era. The Franciscan missions, especially those among the Caddo, established in the early 1700s in part to counteract French movement in the lower Mississippi Valley, were defunct, and in the 1840s only a handful of priests still served the Texas Catholic community. After the independence movement established freedom of religion, Jean Marie Odin, the first bishop of Galveston, oversaw the rejuvenation of Texas Catholicism. In addition to the Mexicans, his diocese consisted largely of European immigrants. For example, a band of German Catholics settled the hill country during the mid- 1840s, and the Polish Franciscan Leopold Moczygemba led a group of Silesian Poles to Panna Maria in 1856. By the 1850s, however, American immigration had thrust the Baptists, Methodists, and Disciples of Christ into dominance. These evangelical groups have played a major role in Texas religious history to the present day.

The political-religious connection was even more sensitive in the lands taken from Mexico in 1848. All of the Hispanos of the American Southwest were titular Catholics, but everywhere the faithful had long suffered from want of clerical attention. In southern Texas, Arizona, California, and especially New Mexico, the Hispanic settlers had responded to the dearth of priests by creating their own version of folk Catholicism.

This included an intense respect for local patron saints, many of whom were credited with frequent miracles, and a strong Mariolatry, represented by devotion to the Virgin of Guadalupe. The Hispanic communities of the borderlands celebrated a steady round of religious holidays: 17 January, the feast of San Antonio, a day for the blessing of the animals; 24 June, San Juan's Day, which became associated with the first fruits and vegetables of the season; the feast of Corpus Christi, celebrated in the seventh week after Easter; the solemn 1 November, All Saints' Day, and 2 November, All Souls' Day. December was the climax month of celebration, with *Los Pastores,* a Spanish medieval miracle play, plus a reenactment of the nine days that Mary and Joseph wandered in search of shelter in Bethlehem before the birth of Jesus. The historian Arnoldo De Leon has argued that the faith of the Rio Grande borderlands expressed "an attitude consonant more with life experience than theology."

Folk Catholicism permeated the territory of New Mexico. The healing skills of *curanderas,* the lay brotherhood of Penitentes, and the folk carvings of *Santos, bultos,* and *retablos* reflected a deeply held cultural faith. From the early nineteenth century forward, the little chapel at Chimayo, New Mexico, known as "The Lourdes of the Southwest," has drawn those seeking healing. This pervasive New Mexico folk Catholicism proved remarkably tolerant of the influx of Anglo Protestants.

The same basic toleration may be seen in the story of western Judaism. From the 1850s, Jews composed perhaps 10 percent of San Francisco's merchant community. Relying on a credit network that included family members and coreligionists, Jewish families provided vital economic services, both in rural areas, such as New Mexico, and urban centers, such as San Francisco, Portland, Los Angeles, Denver, and Seattle.

Contemporary visitors marveled at how well the western Jews had succeeded. In the Los Angeles 1876 centennial celebration, a young Jewish woman portrayed the "Spirit of Liberty" while a rabbi helped preside over the festivities. In San Francisco's first *Elite Directory* (1870-79), Jews composed over one-fifth of the city's "elite." The historians Harriet Rochlin and Fred Rochlin have counted over thirty nineteenth-century western Jewish mayors, plus countless sheriffs, police chiefs, and other elected officials. Although one can find traces of anti-Semitism, it played a much smaller role in western life than n the contemporary South or Northeast. The historian Eldon Ernst has concluded that California's failure to produce a "religious mainstream" allowed all faiths to flourish on roughly equal basis. The same could be said for many other subregions in the trans-Mississippi West. . . .

Temples in the Forest

ROBERT F. BERKHOFER, JR.

SOURCE: From *Salvation and the Savage* by Robert F. Berkhofer, Jr. Pp. 44-63, 68-69. Copyright © 1972 by The University of Kentucky Press. Reprinted with permission.

The propagation of the Gospel was the professed goal of all missionary societies, and the creation of self-sustaining native churches was the abiding hope of all missionaries. Although each denomination in theory furthered the same Church and preached the same Gospel, each considered its presentation the superior view and hoped its meetinghouse would be the abode of the Indian convert. To the people of the period, considerable differences existed between denominations and their work. Yet in observing their efforts in the Indian tribes, little variety is seen because of the uniform extrareligious assumptions. . . . For this reason, [what follows] will stress the similarity of the missionaries' religious approach rather than the specific theological doctrines and practices, believed so vital at the time, which separated Protestants.

Two means existed for the spread of the Gospel—oral and printed. The oral method was more widely used, particularly at the beginning of a mission. Missionaries were instructed to preach and talk at every opportunity, and they heeded their orders. When a Sioux requested from Stephen Riggs a piece of cloth to make a sacrifice to the great spirit, the missionary lectured the Indian on Christ's sacrifice and refused the favor. Another time this missionary occupied the place just vacated by the medicine man to tell a dying girl about Heaven. One missionary's wife resorted to an interesting stratagem to gain access to the pagan town upon the Cattaraugus Reservation of Senecas. She loaded a harmonium on a wagon and played at the edge of the town, knowing the Indians could not resist music of any kind. After many weeks of playing and singing, she gained their confidence sufficiently to meet her in their schoolhouse. After the usual instrumental and vocal music, she knelt to pray. Fear gripped her listeners. The frightened pagans rushed for the door and leaped from the windows in panic.

In a less dramatic manner the missionaries usually itinerated from house to house and grove to grove at the commencement of missions. Rarely was the opposition to preaching so great that the missionary was compelled to talk only to people at scattered huts or on the edge of crowds as happened among the Creeks during one period. Occasionally a missionary preached with amazing success upon entering a tribe, because the Indians were curious and knew nothing about missionaries. Samuel Parker met such enthusiasm among the Nez Percés in 1837. He explained to a few chiefs the significance of the Sabbath and asked them to construct a shaded place to preach. Lured by the novelty of the occasion, an audience of four or five hundred men, women, and children knelt before the blackcoat dressed in their best clothing. In a more usual circumstance, the missionary gradually assembled a small Sabbath audience after much visiting, without the secrecy of the Creek efforts or the extraordinary numbers of Nez Percé labors.

When the missionaries first arrived in a new field, they optimistically wrote their home boards describing in glowing terms how ripe the field was for a harvest of converts; they soon discovered Indians attended the Sabbath services as infrequently as they did school. When the Indians did attend the meetings, apathy at best and hostility at worst prevailed. At an Iowa missionary's meeting, the women continued their work in the tent without paying any attention to the preaching and made so much noise that no one else could hear the preacher. The women in typical Indian fashion, the missionary noted, "seem to view it as a council into which the principal men only are necessary." An Indian advised this missionary to offer the traditional feast if he wished their attendance, and one of his fellow laborers offered each attendant at Sabbath meeting a slice of bread with molasses. Although his board disapproved of his bribery, his audience increased. During cold weather a warm, snug meetinghouse lured more listeners than the cheering Word, but spring dispelled such a congregation. Even if the audience was attentive and assented to all said, it was mere Indian courtesy at most times.

Even after long contact with missionaries, Indian congregations were not regular. Among the Cherokees in 1855 a missionary noted attendance as variable after a half century's mission work. Attendance figures at the popular communion seasons varied from a high of 200 to a low of 145. With such extraordinary occasions deducted, the maximum figure equaled only 140 and the minimum figure totaled only fourteen one cold winter's day. As in the schools, the missionaries could not secure punctual attendance at a given time, and so Sabbath services were often repeated three or four times a day. Other missionaries discovered Sabbath attendance depended directly on the number of house visits made during the week. In some cases religious instruction could only be accomplished by visits to the Indian lodges.

Attendance at church as at school was a result of transformed values. Halfbreeds early attended church and were converted. The longer a tribe was in contact with whites and missionaries, the larger the congregation. This slow process embittered many a missionary to think as one missionary's wife complained: "But should an angel, or the Lord of glory himself come and preach to them, I see no reason to believe they would regard the message." In spite of disappointment, most missionaries doggedly remained in the field and hoped and prayed. At times their prayers seemed answered when a revival swept through a tribe. To aid the revival spirit, the Methodists and American Board missionaries held protracted meetings and camp meetings, especially among the southern Indians.

Even with an audience gathered, the missionaries found preaching the Word difficult in an alien language. At the mission's commencement, interpreters were employed. Frequently it was next to impossible to obtain such help, for these essential intermediaries were already hired by traders or demanded high wages. The missionaries considered most of these hirelings immoral or infidels and wondered whether such a "cracked vessel," should carry the precious Gospel tidings. Trans-Mississippi American Board and United Foreign Missionary Society missionaries at a joint meeting decided the Lord's Word could work its miracles even if interpreted by these people. Many other workers recognized the simple necessity of having interpreters regardless of their purity.

Because the missionaries believed a "simple" people must possess a "simple" language, they considered the Indian languages deficient in abstractions suitable for theology. From this conception flowed two complaints. Missionaries found the language barren of concepts to express God's relation to man in terms of king, government, and court, which were alien to Indian thinking. In addition many thought an interpreter must be converted in order to enrich his vocabulary through his own pious experience. The missionaries only realized their assumption unfounded after long study revealed an Indian language rich in abstraction sufficient for all religious purposes.

For the most effective preaching, the missionary had to learn the native language. He approached the task with confidence, for he assumed that the language was so simple that he would master it in a short time. After a year or so, he realized the language was far more complex than he at first thought and extraordinarily difficult to learn. After much study he sometimes concluded he would never fully learn the language. Cyrus Kingsbury admitted he had not mastered the Choctaw language after twenty years of residence in the tribe. In 1851 none of the Cherokee missionaries of the American Board preached in Cherokee, though the mission had been founded thirty-six years earlier. Some missionaries did compile dictionaries and even preached in the aboriginal languages, but these were few.

Even with the words at hand, the missionaries differed over what the Word should be. Some ministers and the Quakers believed it best merely to advance a system of morality—the "simple and intelligible moral precepts of Gospel, which have a reforming and purifying influence on the temper and conduct." Most Protestants preferred urging their religions' "most sublime and distinctive truths" on the natives from the very commencement of the mission. After adopting the latter view, most missionaries and their patrons argued to what extent subtle and complex doctrines should be propagated. All agreed that man's fall, his subsequent depravity, the redemption of man through Christ's atonement, and his future happiness or misery after death dependent upon his life on earth were doctrines of primary importance. But should predestination and the details of sacred history, for instance, be taught the natives? Should sectarianism be propagated?

Debate on these questions continued throughout the seventy-five years under study. Moravians felt only Christ's suffering and death affected heathen hearts and eschewed all discussion of God's majesty as tending to alienate the Indians and all talk of denominational differences as confusing to their hearers. Similarly the New York Missionary Society in 1799 instructed its missionaries to stress only the great doctrines of divine revelation. In the 1790s John Sergeant did not instruct his Stockbridge charges in the "high points, such as predestination, and the origin of evil," but preached "faith, repentance, and morality," while his neighboring colleague, Samuel Kirkland, discoursed to the Oneidas on all the intricate points of Calvinism. In 1821 the United Foreign Missionary Society directed its men to adapt their preaching to the capacity of their hearers by employing simple terms, short sentences, and plain language as well as dwelling only on the more prominent doctrines of the divine truth. On the other hand, the American Board desired its agents to preach the law of God in all its holy strictness as well as the fullness of the Saviour's mercy and love. Many of the board's missionaries lectured on subjects bound to confuse the Indian. A Nez Percé missionary presented a detailed chronological view of the Bible and prepared maps showing the Israelites' journey to Canaan. This missionary also orated at length on Protestant church history with its many denominational differences.

Regardless of the missionaries' position in this debate, they had to teach the Indians the conception of sin before they could save them. To this mighty task of value transformation, the missionaries bent their every effort. A sincere belief in the depravity of human nature divided the Christian Indian from his pagan brother just as it did among the whites. Only after an acceptance of human depravity was hope on Christ's atonement meaningful. In fact, only prior acceptance of man's fall made Christ's sacrifice sensible. So important was the concept of sin that the Bishop of Mann in his book, *The Knowledge and Practice of Christianity Made Easy to the Meanest Capacities; or, an Essay towards an Instruction for the Indians* made his dialogue, "Of the Corruption of Our Nature," second only to the explanation of God.

For this reason missionaries of all denominations endeavored to convince the Indians of their sinfulness. The first missionary sent out by the New York Missionary Society directors was charged to impress on the "rude minds" of the Cherokees "that all have sinned and come short of the glory of God—*that by the works of the law no flesh living can be justified—that sinners are justified, freely by God's grace, through the redemption that is in Christ Jesus*—and that his blood cleanseth from all sin." One of Kingsbury's first sermons to this tribe nearly two decades later endeavored to "explain and enforce the doctrine of total depravity." In his first sermon to the Nez Percés, Samuel Parker explained man's fall, the transgressor's deserts, and Christ's atonement. Later, Marcus Whitman pressed this tribe with "their lost ruined and condemned state in a particular manner, in order to remove the hope that worshiping will save them. It has stired [*sic*] up no little opposition of heart to the truth," he wrote, "but I trust it may result in striping [*sic*] them from a reliance which I think was given them [by Catholic missionaries], before we came into the country; that worshiping will aid them." Baptists and Methodists also emphasized this sinfulness. A Methodist missionary to Choctaws explained clearly his successful approach to Indian conversion: "Our plan of preaching to them was, to convince them of their guilt, misery, and helplessness by reason and experience: not appealing to the Scriptures as the law by which they were condemned, but to their own knowledge of right and wrong; and the misery felt from the consciousness that they have done wrong. The gospel profferring to them an immediate change of heart, was seized by them as Heavens best blessing of ruined man."

At the heart of the conversion experience was a deep emotional conviction of one's depravity. A vivid example of such an emotional foundation was Jason Lee's letter about Sampson, a scholar who was a backslider.

> While one after another of his former associates had humbled themselves under the mighty hand of God, and came out rejoicing in God their saviour, Sampson had remained unmoved, and seemed to stand aloof, as if he had neither part nor lot in this matter. One of the boys commenced praying for Sampson, and *such* a prayer— oh! Who could hear it without having his sympathies moved for the poor culprit, on the brink of ruin? The Lord seemed, in a moment, to roll a burden of soul upon all his children present for poor Sampson. Their faith seemed to seize, instinctively, upon the promises of God with a death-like grasp, and claim them in his behalf. I heard the deep groan—the impassioned sigh. I gazed around upon the sight with astonishment, and it seemed to me that I was left alone in the plains of unbelief. I knew indeed, the Lord had power to save; I hoped he would save; but I doubted whether he would save *now*. Not so with the children, not so with the brethren present. Feeling deepened. Intensity increased to agony. Each, as if a host in himself and bent on victory, offered supplications; and these commingling with many sighs and tears, borne on the wings of faith, came up before the eternal throne. I looked again, and behold, Sampson was in the midst of a group, who, in their agony, had gathered about him to wrestle in his behalf; and behold, he trembled like a leaf in

the wind. He sprung up on his feet, and with a faltering voice, a tremulous tongue, and quivering lips, which almost refused to give utterance to his words, he stammered out, "My friends, I have been a great sinner. I fraid I go to hell. Pray for me, my friends, I pray for myself." Down he went on his knees, and with strong cries and tears confessed his sins, and cried out in agony for mercy. The emotions within were too big for utterance, and he could only groan (I was about to say) unutterable groans . . . . The enemy seemed determined not to give up his victim. The conflict was severe, but the united prayer of faith prevailed. The struggle ceased, bless the Lord. "Praise the Lord" was heard in soft accents throughout the room. Soon Sampson arose, with a smile on countenance, and said, "My friends, I happy now, the Lord has blest my Soul."

Without such emotional conviction full acceptance of certain Christian practices was not possible. Unless the supposed convert accepted his sinfulness, he confused repentance with oral confession, failed to appreciate Christ's atonement, considered goodness to be mere external good behavior, and believed Heaven was the just reward for following mere external forms of religion. Yet for a missionary to determine whether the convert genuinely practiced religion or merely masqueraded under a set of practices and words, he had to judge the genuineness of the conversion experience. The Baptists and Methodists found their converts fully aware of their sinfulness. Isaac McCoy reported his converts' evidence of "their discovery of the depravity of their natures and of their entire inability to contribute in any degree to their own salvation is remarkable." Missionary after missionary of the American Board, on the other hand, complained in much the same words as a Chippewa missionary, that even the church members "have never manifested such pungent convictions of sin, as I have desired to see, though I have taken much pains to instruct them correctly with regard to the nature of sin." If the missionary believed the Indians lacked a strong sense of sin, then he judged their religion to be mere outward display.

In light of such experience, the missionaries who were pessimistic about the Indians' convictions questioned whether the proofs of conversion should be as strict for red as for white Christians. Acculturation probably had much to do with the evidences given, for the red convert was more familiar with white expectations and practices after increased contact. Two American Board missionaries averred that proofs of piety among the Tuscaroras and Cherokees were the same as among whites. A factor equally powerful in judging the conversion experience was the missionary's and denomination's strictness in questioning the conversion narrative and observing the fruits of the conversion.

The only objective test of true conversion was its effect on the convert's life. Redemption from depravity made a difference in the conduct and psychology of the newborn Christian observable both to his fellow Christians and unredeemed tribesmen. His Christian brethren theoretically expected "fear, disquiet, anxiety, disharmony in personal relations, anger, malice, jealousy, hatred, cruelty, selfishness, give place to faith, confidence, joy, sympathy, peace, love, gentleness, meekness, unselfishness, and a purpose to live a life of service." They further looked for profound changes in the "very self" which were not "wrought by the subject but upon him by a power greater than himself; . . . the subjects' whole world acquired new meaning; . . . the change included a new sense of freedom and power, an enlargement of self, and attainment of a higher level of life both in a spiritual sense (relation to God) and in relations to others."

But church membership depended not solely on conversion and pious experience but also on doctrinal knowledge. The extent to which even the most Christian Indian comprehended the doctrines of his church was open to inquiry. The New York Missionary Society dispatched a special agent to investigate just this question among the Tuscaroras in 1806. He discovered all the candidates for church membership gave "a pretty satisfactory account of their sense of & sorrow for sin: of their dependence on the mercy of God through Christ for pardon & acceptance. But their knowledge and views of the person of Christ, of the way of salvation, through him, and of the exercises of the soul in believing appeared to me considerably imperfect." They could not, for example, distinguish between God and Christ. But a Methodist bishop was surprised the Wyandots understood the doctrine of "trinity in unity" so well. The Brothertown Indians understood the subtleties of doctrine sufficiently to divide into parties in favor of election versus free salvation. Yet a Seneca Quaker saw no difference between the Presbyterians and the Friends other than that the former sang at their services. After several years of missionary activity two Weas thought Methodism and Presbyterianism exactly alike. Such ignorance resulted not only from the deliberate obscuring of denominational differences at times but also from the Indians' lack of comprehension. Though an extensive knowledge of Scriptural history and appreciation of complex doctrinal views were infrequently found in even the most acculturated tribes, the fundamental "Truths" were understood by many in the farthest outposts of missionary expansion after a few years of Gospel propagation. Failure to convert was not from lack of knowledge, a missionary pointed out, but from "Human depravity, fortified by degrading superstition." The missionaries did not know, as anthropologists do today, that basic values change very slowly.

The extent of doctrinal knowledge and pious experience necessary for admittance to church membership varied among denominations. Almost every denomination possessed a standard procedure of examination into these two subjects and observation of the candidates' "walk and conversation" before a convert gained formal church membership. Moravian requirements were strictest. A converted person seeking entrance into the church of this denomination first enrolled for instruction as a candidate for baptism after learning some of the basic doctrines. Upon passing an examination, he was baptized and he became a candidate for communion, during which period he received further instruction. Finally after another examination he was admitted to communion and therefore church membership. These requirements proved so arduous to Cherokees that the Moravian

Church in the tribe contained only eight members after twenty years of missionary effort. Membership in the Methodists and Baptists appeared easiest. A prospective Methodist member met with the leader of a society for a trial of six months or more, after which time he was recommended for membership, examined by a minister before the church members for correctness of faith and willingness to observe the church rules, and admitted to the denomination. Privileges of Baptist membership were accorded in a similar manner. After satisfying all the church members of his real piety, a person was baptized and received in full membership. Between these positions lay Congregationalist and Presbyterian practice. Usually a person was examined as to his belief in sin and the atonement of Christ before he was admitted as a candidate for baptism by these denominations. After suitable instruction in the Shorter Catechism or by other methods, he was again examined by the church members if Congregational or by the minister and church elders if Presbyterian, baptized, and admitted to communion, that is, church membership. For baptism in the Episcopalian Church, some basic doctrinal knowledge was necessary; after receiving that sacrament, the candidate was catechised until confirmed by the bishop and admitted to communion. The Quakers did not encourage Indians to form First Day Meetings until sufficiently under the exercise of the spirit, and membership was long in coming and difficult to determine.

Every missionary society warned its workers to maintain the purity of the church by cautious admittance of members. Fears were expressed constantly that incomplete conversion led to apostasy which hurt not only the specific denomination but the entire cause of Christ in the eyes of the heathen. For this reason various denominations accused each other of lax membership requirements by admitting persons without sufficient faith or knowledge. All Protestants attacked Catholicism as mere "baptized heathenism," and the Catholics reciprocated the epithet with venom. Both the American Board and Baptist missionaries complained that Methodists allowed all persons who merely signified their intentions to join a society. Presbyterian and Congregationalist missionaries thought the Baptists fostered unsound doctrine and "ignorant fanaticism" as much as the Methodists. Yet a strict American Board laborer found the Baptist missionaries and their native assistants among the Cherokee fully orthodox and knowledgeable. Requirements varied from missionary to missionary as from denomination to denomination, but no society allowed a person into the church without proof of conversion and doctrinal knowledge. Many of the bickering letters to society headquarters reveal more about interdenominational jealousy than actual facts.

In many ways the process leading to and the reaction after church membership resemble the "rites of passage," which ease a transformation of social relations. The instruction and examinations guided the new convert on the path to his new life. As such, these rites marked a change from heathen aboriginal life to Indian Christianity, or as the *Christian Professor's Assistant,* a Baptist handbook for Delaware Indians, noted, "to become a church member is to leave the ranks of Satan, and join the friends of Christ; it is to give to the public a pledge to live as a Christian and an heir of heaven ought to live." Membership was an institutional approval upon the new way of life pursued by the Indian after conversion and introduced him to several organizational arrangements which remodeled his old view of social relations.

As a result of conversion the church member was expected by the missionaries to practice a new standard of behavior. Fundamental to this new life was the decalogue. In the eyes of the missionaries some of the commandments needed special emphasis in relation to Indian life. Sabbath observance was strictly enjoined upon the red churchmen. A new concept of time was thus introduced to the Indians, for the missionaries had to instruct them in the concept of the week and invent various devices to help the Indians keep track of the passage of days until Sunday. Missionaries repeatedly lectured on the seventh commandment against adultery, because they felt the aborigines too promiscuous and too quick to part from their spouses. Under the sixth commandment the missionaries condemned the warfare which in many Indian societies was a fundamental part of the whole male role. Though the Indians did not violate the dicta against false gods and images, the missionaries harangued against attendance at "heathenish" dances and witchcraft as well as the use of medicine men.

Missionaries urged certain practices upon their charges as essential to continued church membership. More words probably were devoted to the evils of intemperance than to any other subject. Liquor was evil not only because drinking wasted time but also because intoxication led to quarrels and murder. Idleness was condemned, as was gossip. Native dances, ball games, and "frolics" violated the dicta against intemperance and idleness. All church members had to pay their debts promptly or face expulsion. Church members were expected to attend Sabbath services regularly and support the cause of Christ among the heathen. Minor bickering, grudges, and other examples of selfishness were supposed to be erased from the new life.

For failure to practice these virtues a church member was subject to the discipline of his church. The church's reason for judging the lives of its members was stated succinctly by the *Christian Professor's Assistant*, "Its purity, its reputation, its efficiency, and its existence, all depend on the conduct, public and private, of its members. It has, therefore, the right to investigate and judge of their belief and conduct, so far as these affect their religious or moral characters and standing." The backslider could only retain his membership by confessing his faults to the minister and other responsible church members when his errors were called to his attention. Upon his failure to appear for trial or examination or to confess his fault, he was suspended or excluded from communion.

The missionaries found it difficult to maintain the strict discipline they thought desirable. Violations of Christian practices were so frequent that one missionary admitted that if all the immoral members were excommunicated, his church would have ceased to exist. An American Board agent reported in 1828 that half of one Cherokee church's members had been suspended and twenty out of fifty in another church since their founding. Most exclusions resulted from adultery and intemperance. Maintenance of discipline proved difficult also because in most churches fellow tribesmen participated as members or officers of the church in judging the Indian sinner. Either because the backsliders were chiefs or relatives, or merely because of sympathy for each other's failings, a vote of exclusion was seldom given. Frequently when one person was disciplined, many of his relatives left the church in umbrage. Compromise with Indian custom and fallibility varied according to the missionary. Such compromise prompted interdenominational accusations of hurting Christ's cause by lax discipline. A Presbyterian missionary accused the Catholics of permitting intemperance. American Board missionaries complained that members under censure or even exclusion in their churches were received into Methodist and Baptist churches. Yet all denominations possessed institutional procedures for insuring a certain standard of conduct for its members in an attempt to preserve a difference between Christians and pagans. . . .

Thus as a result of missionary enterprise, the Indian Christians gained a different outlook on life, new social institutions, new male and female roles, and novel techniques for altering the lives of their fellow tribesmen. The spread of the true faith, according to the Protestant missionaries, could only come at the expense of traditional native life. Not only was the convert to abandon his old rites and priests for new ones and alter his attitudes toward the universe and his neighbors about him, but he was to change profoundly his secular ways as well. Religion in addition to being a philosophy of the unknown is a system for ranking basic values, and thus a new religion implies new behavior. With the added stress on civilization in the promulgation of the Gospel, true Indian conversion meant nothing less than a total transformation of native existence. While the missionaries may not have instituted the New Jerusalem in the forests for which they hoped, they did destroy the Gehenna, in their eyes, of integrated traditional tribal life.

Questions for Reflection and Discussion

1. The documents show the West to be a cauldron of hope and despair—conflict and consensus. Identify several examples of this reality.

2. Does Scott Miyakawa describe the western frontier as a place of religious conflict, consensus, or both?

3. Ferenc and Margaret Szasz present the West as a place of tolerance and inclusion. How do they account for this? Were there any exceptions to this in the antebellum frontier West?

4. Discuss the coming together of missionaries and Native American cultures on the frontier. Does Robert Berkhofer describe it as conflict or consensus?

5. Which of the four tensions in American religion was (were) present in the antebellum frontier West?

Additional Readings

Arrington, Leonard J. and Davis Bitton. *The Mormon Experience: A History of the Latter-Day Saints.* 2ⁿᵈ ed. Urbana: University of Illinois Press, 1979.

Bowden, Henry Warner. *American Indians and Christian Missions: Studies in Cultural Conflict.* Chicago: University of Chicago Press, 1981.

Drury, Clifford M. *Marcus and Narcissa Whitman and the Opening of Old Oregon.* Reprint ed. Seattle: Northwest Interpretive, 1986.

Guarneri, Carl and Davis Alvarez, eds. *Religion and Society in the American West: Historical Essays.* Lanham, MD: University Press of America, 1987.

Horsman, Reginald. *Race and Manifest Destiny: The Origins of American Racial Anglo-Saxonism.* Cambridge: Harvard University Press, 1981.

McLoughlin, William. *Cherokees and Missionaries, 1789-1839.* Norman: University of Oklahoma Press, 1995.

Moore, Arthur K. *The Frontier Mind.* New York: McGraw-Hill Book Company, 1963.

Pessen, Edward. *Jacksonian America: Society, Personality, and Politics.* Homewood, IL: Dorsey Press, 1969.

Prucha, Paul. "Two Roads to Conversion." *Pacific Northwest Quarterly* 79 (October 1988): 30-37.

Schoenberg, Wilfred P. *A History of the Catholic Church in the Pacific Northwest, 1743-1983.* Washington, D.C.: Pastoral Press, 1987.

Smith, Henry Nash. *Virgin Land: The American West as Symbol and Myth.* New York: Vintage Books, 1950.

Szasz, Ferenc, ed. *Religion in the West.* Manhattan: Kansas State University Press, 1984.

Terrell, John U. *The Arrow and the Cross: A History of the American Indians and the Missionaries.* Santa Barbara, CA: Capra, Press 1979.

Tewksbury, Donald G. *The Founding of American Colleges and Universities before the Civil War, with Particular Reference to the Religious Influences Bearing on the College Movement.* New York: Columbia University Press, 1932.

Chapter 7

Slavery and American Religion

Issue

How did slavery coexist with religion in antebellum America?

In America's religious experience few issues have been more critical for the integrity of the nation's religious community than slavery. Much conflict blemished the American landscape as contrary beliefs produced contrary behaviors. The antagonistic beliefs were often the expressions of divergent interpretations of the Bible. In his 1837 tract The Bible Against Slavery, *abolitionist Theodore Weld declared that "God spake the ten commandments from the midst of clouds and thunderings. Two of those commandments deal death to slavery. 'THOU SHALT NOT STEAL' or, 'thou shalt not take from another what belongs to him.'" He went on to argue that "the eighth commandment forbids the taking away, and the tenth adds, "Thou shalt not covet any thing that is thy neighbor's. . . . Who ever made human beings slaves without coveting them?"*

Weld and other critics of slavery did not go unanswered. Many of their respondents were equally religious in their determination to preserve this peculiar institution; and their defense was often taken from the same source, the Bible. In his 1852 letter included in The Pro-Slavery Argument, *James H. Hammond, a Christian owner of slaves from South Carolina, offered a different commentary on the tenth commandment in asking, ". . . what is the plain meaning, undoubted intent, and true spirit of this commandment? Does it not emphatically and explicitly forbid you to disturb your neighbor in the enjoyment of his property; and more especially of that which is here specifically mentioned as being lawfully, and by this commandment made sacredly his?"*

During the early decades of the nineteenth century a widespread network of interdenominational voluntary societies emerged "to disseminate Christian values, improve the character of the nation's citizens, and restructure the nation's leisure patterns." This network, which has come to be known as the Benevolent Empire, was to restore the wayward nation to righteousness. Though the cause of antislavery was not generally included within the scope of the network, certainly the spirit of the Empire intersected with the benevolence of the antislavery movement. Here again, however, a conflict was in the making: Who was the more benevolent, the abolitionist or the slaveowner? Southern theologian and educator, James H. Thornwell, had the answer in his 1861 address to a Presbyterian assembly. "We cannot forbear to say, however, that the general operation of the system [of slavery] is kindly and benevolent; it is a real and effective discipline, and without it, we are profoundly persuaded that the African race in the midst of us can never be elevated in scale of being."

When the antagonists held to different interpretations of a book and different understandings of a word, there was little room for consensus-building. Why was slavery a critical issue for American religion? Did this conflict leave any lasting marks on the face of American culture?

Documents

Slavery in antebellum America intersected with religion at many points. In the first document, a reporter in attendance at an organizational meeting of the American Colonization Society in 1817 summarizes Henry Clay's comments in which he stated that slaves in America could bless Africa by taking Christianity with them there. During the next thirty years several thousand blacks were colonized in Africa, but the number of slaves in America increased. While many of them found refuge in Christianity, many did not. In the second selection, John England, bishop of the Charleston Diocese of the Roman Catholic Church, provides a biblical defense of slavery. The third document is a list of resolutions produced at the Methodist antislavery convention held in Boston on January 18, 1843. The convening Methodist abolitionists agreed that slavery was "a sin under all circumstances." In the fourth selection, former Kentucky slave Henry Bibb explains in his 1849 autobiography why some slaves had difficulty being part of a religion that taught them to be obedient to their masters. And, indeed, some Southern Christian slaveowners like South Carolinian James H. Hammond claimed it was presumptuous for those who attacked slavery to claim divine support. His pro-slavery argument appears in the fifth document. Among the more scathing rebukes leveled toward churched people who defended slavery was that delivered by former slave Frederick Douglass in his 1852 address in Rochester, New York. Excerpts from his address appear in the sixth selection. The seventh document is part of an address (composed by James Henley Thornwell) adopted by the General Assembly of the Presbyterian Church in the Confederate States of America. It served to justify the action of the Southern churchmen in seceding from the parent Assembly and creating a new denomination. Slave songs were drawn from Bible stories, sermons, African musical styles, and the slaves' experiences. Enslaved Christians believed that the supernatural (sacred) interacted with the natural (secular), and that all in the world ultimately rested in the hands of God. The documents section concludes with selected slave songs.

1. A View of the Exertions Lately Made for the Purpose of Colonizing the Free People of Colour, 1817

SOURCE: *A View of the Exertions Lately Made for the Purpose of Colonizing the Free People of Colour. . . .* (Washington: Jonathan Elliott, 1817), 4-6.

Mr. Clay (on taking the chair) . . . understood the object of the present meeting to be to consider of the propriety and practicability of colonizing the free people of color in the United States, and of forming an association in relation to that object. That class of the mixt population of our country was, [he said], peculiarly situated. They neither enjoyed the immunities of freemen, nor were they subject to the incapacities of slaves, but partook in some degree of the qualities of both. From their condition, and the unconquerable prejudices resulting from their color, they never could amalgamate with free whites of this country. It was desirable, therefore, both as it respected them and the residue of the population of the country, to drain them off. Various schemes of colonization had been thought of, and a part of our own continent, it was thought by some, might furnish a suitable establishment for them. But for his part, Mr. C[lay] said, he had a decided preference for some part of the coast of Africa. There ample provision might be made for the colony itself, and it might be rendered instrumental to the introduction, into that extensive quarter of the globe, of the arts, civilization and christianity. There was a peculiar, a moral fitness in restoring them to the land of their fathers. And if, instead of the evils and sufferings which we have been the innocent cause of inflicting upon the inhabitants of Africa, we can transmit to her the blessings of our arts, our civilization and our religion, may we not hope that America will extinguish a great portion of that moral debt which she has contracted to that unfortunate continent? We should derive much encouragement in the prosecution of the object which had assembled us together by the success which had attended the colony of Sierra Leone. That establishment had commenced 20 or 25 years ago, under the patronage of private individuals in Gr. Britain. . . . We have their example before us; and can there be a nobler cause than that which, while it proposed to rid our own country of a useless and pernicious, if not a dangerous portion of its population, contemplates the spreading of the arts of civilized life, and the possible redemption from ignorance and barbarism of a benighted quarter of the globe!

It was proper and necessary distinctly to state, [Mr. Clay added], that he understood it constituted no part of the object of this meeting to touch or agitate, in the slightest degree, a delicate question connected with another portion of the coloured population of our country. It was not proposed to deliberate on, or consider at all, any question of emancipation, or that was connected with the abolition of slavery. It was upon that condition alone, he was sure, that many gentlemen from the south and the west, whom he saw present, had attended or could be expected to co-operate. It was upon that condition, only, that he himself had attended. He would only further add that he hoped, in their deliberations, they would be guided by that moderation, politeness and deference for the opinions of each other, which were essential to any useful result. But when he looked around and saw the respectable assemblage, and recollected the humane and benevolent purpose which had produced it, he felt it unnecessary to insist farther on this topic.

2. A Catholic Defense of Slavery, 1840
SOURCE: *Letters of the Late Bishop England to the Hon. John Forsyth, on the Subject of Domestic Slavery* (Baltimore, 1844), 34-39.

In the New Testament we find instances of pious and good men having slaves, and in no case do we find the Saviour imputing it to them as a crime, or requiring their servants' emancipation. In chap. viii, of St. Matthew, we read of a centurion, who addressing the Lord Jesus, said, v. 9, "For I also am a man under authority, having soldiers under me, and I say to this man, go, and he goeth: and to another, come, and he cometh: and to my servant, do this and he doth it." v. 10. "And Jesus hearing this wondered, and said to those that followed him: Amen, I say to you, I have not found so great faith in Israel." v. 13. ["] And Jesus said to the centurion, go, and as thou hast believed, so be it done to thee. And the servant was healed at the same hour." St. Luke, in ch. vii, relates also the testimony which the ancients of Israel gave of this stranger's virtue, and how he loved their nation, and built a synagogue for them.

In many of his parables, the Saviour describes the master and his servants in a variety of ways, without any condemnation or censure of slavery. In Luke xvii, he describes the usual mode of acting towards slaves as the very basis upon which he teaches one of the most useful lessons of Christian virtue, v. 7. "But which of you having a servant ploughing or feeding cattle will say to him, when he is come from the field, immediately, go sit down." 8. "And will not rather say to him, make ready my supper, and gird thyself, and serve me while I eat and drink, and afterwards, thou shalt eat and drink?" 9. "Doth he thank that servant because he did the things that were commanded him?" 10. "I think not. So you also, when you shall have done all the things that are commanded you, say: we are unprofitable servants, we have done that which we ought to do."

After the promulgation of the Christian religion by the apostles, the slave was not told by them that he was in a state of unchristian durance. I Cor. vii, 20. "Let every man abide in the same calling in which he was called." 21. "Art thou called being a bond-man? Care not for it; but if thou mayest be made free, use it rather,"

22. "For he that is called in the Lord, being a bond-man, is the free-man of the Lord. Likewise he that is called being free, is the bond-man of Christ." 23. "You are bought with a price, be not made the bond-slaves of men." 24. "Brethren, let every man, wherein he was called,   therein abide with God." Thus a man by becoming a Christian was not either made free nor told that he was free, but he was advised, if he could lawfully procure his freedom, to prefer it to slavery. The 23rd verse has exactly that meaning which we find expressed also in chap. vi, v. 20. "For you are bought with a great price, glorify and bear God in your body,["] which is addressed to the free as well as to the slave: all are the servants of God, and should not be drawn from his service by the devices of men, but should "walk worthy of the vocation in which they are called." Eph. iv, i. and the price by which their souls, (not their bodies) were redeemed, is also described by St. Peter I, c. i, 10.

"Knowing that you were not redeemed with corruptible gold or silver from your vain conversation of the tradition of your fathers" 19. "but with the precious blood of Christ, as of a lamb unspotted and undefiled." —That it was a spiritual redemption and a spiritual service, St. Paul again shows, Heb. ix, 14. "How much more shall the blood of Christ, who through the Holy Ghost, offered himself without spot to God, cleanse our conscience from dead works to serve the living God?" It is then a spiritual equality as was before remarked, in the words of St. Paul, I Cor. xii, 13. "For in one spirit we are baptized into one body, whether Jews or Gentiles, whether bond or free." And in the same chapter he expatiates to show that though all members of the one mystical body, their places, their duties, their gifts are various and different. And in his epistle to the Galatians, chap. iv. he exhibits the great truth which he desires to inculcate by an illustration taken from the institutions of slavery, and without a single expression of their censure.

Nor did the apostles consider the Christian master obliged to liberate his Christian servant. St. Paul in his epistle to Philemon acknowledges the right of the master to the services of his slave for whom however he asks, as a special favor, pardon for having deserted his owner. 10. "I beseech thee for my son Onesimus whom I have begotten in my chains." 11. Who was heretofore unprofitable to thee, but now profitable both to thee and to thee [sic]." 12. "Whom I have sent back to thee. And do thou receive him as my own bowels." Thus a runaway slave still belonged to his master, and though having become a Christian, so far from being thereby liberated from service, he was bound to return thereto and submit himself to his owner. . . .

Again it is manifest from the Epistle of St. Paul to Timothy that the title of the master continued good to his slave though both should be Christians, c. vii. "Whosoever are servants under the yoke, let them count their masters worthy of all honor, lest the name and doctrine of the Lord be blasphemed." 2. "But they who have believing masters, let them not despise them because they are brethren, but serve them the rather, because they are faithful and beloved, who are partakers of the benefit. These things exhort and teach." And in the subsequent part he declares the contrary teaching to be against the sound words of Jesus Christ, and to spring from ignorant pride. . . .

It will now fully establish what will be necessary to perfect the view which I desire to give, if I can show that masters who were Christians were not required to emancipate their slaves, but had pointed out the duties which they were bound as masters to perform, because this will show under the Christian dispensation the legal, moral and religious existence of slave and master.

The apostle, as we have previously seen, I Tim. vi, 2, wrote of slaves who had believing or Christian masters. The inspired penman did not address his instructions and exhortations to masters who were not of the household of the Faith. I Cor. v, 12. "For what have I to do, to judge them that are without?" 13. "For them that are without, God will judge; take away the evil one from amongst yourselves." Thus when he addresses masters; they are Christian masters. Ephes. vi, 9. "And you, masters, do the same things to them (servants) forbearing threatenings, knowing that the Lord both of them and you is in heaven: and there is no respect of persons with him,"—and again, Colos. iv, i, "Masters do to your servants that which is just and equal: knowing that you also have a master in heaven."

We have then in the teaching of the apostles nothing which contradicts the law of Moses, but we have much which corrects the cruelty of the Pagan practice. The exhibition which is presented to us is one of a cheering and of an elevated character. It is true that the state of slavery is continued under the legal sanction, but the slave is taught from the most powerful motives to be faithful, patient, obedient and contented, and the master is taught that though despotism may pass unpunished on earth it will be examined into at the bar of heaven: and though the slave owes him bodily service, yet that the soul of this drudge, having been purchased at the same price as his own, and sanctified by the same law of regeneration, he who is his slave according to the flesh, is his brother according to the spirit. —His humanity, his charity, his affection are enlisted and interested, and he feels that his own father is also, the father of his slave, hence though the servant must readily and cheerfully pay him homage and perform his behests on earth, yet, they may be on an equality in heaven. . . .

To the Christian slave was exhibited the humiliation of an incarnate God, the suffering of an unoffending victim, the invitation of this model of perfection to that meekness, that humility, that peaceful spirit, that charity and forgiveness of injuries which constitute the glorious beatitudes. He was shown the advantage of suffering, the reward of patience, and the narrow road along whose rugged ascents he was to bear the cross, walking in the footsteps of his Saviour. The curtains which divide both worlds were raised as he advanced, and he beheld Lazarus in the bosom of Abraham, whilst the rich man vainly cried to have this once miserable beggar allowed to dip the tip of his finger in water and touch it to his tongue, for he was tormented in that flame.

Thus, sir, did the legislator of Christianity, whilst he admitted the legality of slavery, render the master merciful, and the slave faithful, obedient and religious, looking for his freedom in that region, where alone true and lasting enjoyment can be found.

3. Slavery and Methodist Schism, 1843

SOURCE: Charles Elliot, *History of the Great Secession from the Methodist Episcopal Church in the Year 1845* . . . (Cincinnati, 1855), 970-71.

1. *Resolved,* That the holding or treating human beings as property, or claiming the right to hold or treat them as property, is a flagrant violation of the law of God: it is sin in itself, a sin in the abstract, and in the concrete: a sin under all circumstances, and in every person claiming such right; and no apology whatever can be admitted to justify the perpetration.

2. *Resolved,* That as the unanimity and harmony of feeling which should ever characterize the people of God, can not exist so long as slavery continues in the Church, we feel it our imperative duty to use all such means as become Christians, in seeking its immediate and entire abolition from the Church of which we are members.

3. *Resolved,* That the Methodist Episcopal Church, being a unit in its doctrine and Discipline, in its legislative and judicial departments, and almost one in its executive operations, is, as a body, responsible for the existence of slavery in its pale, but more especially the ministry, with whom the legislative, judicial, and executive duties rest, and who have the power to purge the Church of this shocking abomination.

4. *Resolved,* That slavery being a sin, and this sin in the Methodist Episcopal Church, and the Church a unit as above, nothing short of a speedy and entire separation of slavery from the Church can satisfy the consciences of honest and faithful abolitionists; and, therefore, reformation or division is the only alternative.

5. *Resolved,* That we all unitedly and solemnly pledge to God and each other, our zealous and unceasing efforts, while there is hope, to purge the Methodist Episcopal Church and the land from slavery.

Whereas, all slaveholding, that is, all claim of the right of property in human beings, is essentially a sin against God; and whereas, every slaveholder is, per consequence, a sinner; therefore.

6. *Resolved,* That we do not and will not fellowship a person claiming the above right, or holding slaves, as a Christian; nor ought he to be admitted to the pulpit or the communion.

7. *Resolved,* That while we do all we can in the several relations we sustain to the Church, to extirpate the great sin of slavery from her pale, we do not, by remaining members, either countenance or fellowship the slaveholder. . . .

11. *Resolved,* That the Methodist Episcopal Church being governed by a majority of the General conference, and as the north have a majority in the legislative, judicial, and executive branches of the Church, the sin of slavery in the Methodist Episcopal Church is emphatically a sin of the north, as it exists by their consent, and could be abolished from the Church by their votes at any time.

12. *Resolved,* That as our bishops and presiding elders have most authority as judicial and executive officers of the Methodist Episcopal Church, they can do more in the intervals of the General conference than any other portion of the Church, for

the overthrow of slavery in it, and therefore are more responsible in the premises, and are hereby earnestly requested to cooperate with us for its removal. . . .

14. *Resolved,* That the passage of the resolution at out late General conference, by which the colored members of our Church in such states as reject their testimony in courts of law, are denied the right of bearing testimony against white persons in Church trials, is an alarming and arbitrary exercise of arbitrary ecclesiastical power, subversive of the inalienable right of every member of the Church of Christ, contrary to the spirit of the Gospel, and inflicted a blot on the reputation of the Methodist Church that time can never efface.

15. *Resolved,* That the passage of the colored testimony resolution, at our late General conference, demands the interference of every member of the Church, and that it is the imperative duty of all who do not wish to be held responsible, for its continuance to protest against it in a decided and earnest memorial to the next General conference, and we hereby call on all the members of our Church to record their disapprobation of the above resolution, and require, in terms that can not be misunderstood, its immediate repeal. . . .

Whereas, the Discipline of the Methodist Episcopal Church, p. 176, provides, in substance, that no slaveholder shall be eligible to any official station in the Church, where the laws of the state in which he lives will admit of emancipation, and permit the liberated slave to enjoy freedom therein; and whereas, it appears that one of the bishops of said Church did, in the month of May, 1840, set apart and ordain to the holy office of elder in said Church, a man who was a slaveholder, and lived *at the time* in a state where the laws did allow of emancipation, and did permit the emancipated person to enjoy freedom therein; therefore,

17. *Resolved,* That this convention respectfully request the New England conference of the said Church, at its next session, to address the next General conference on this subject, and to instruct their delegates to that body to take such means as shall bring the matter fully before said General conference, for full examination and adjudication.

18. *Resolved,* That, whereas, in the sight of the most high God, it is not the color of the skin, but the state of the heart which is regarded, it is inconsistent with our Christian profession and character to despise or slight, or make any difference among men on account of their color, but especially in the house of God, and at the communion; and that all legislative enactments, based on this fact, are founded in injustice, contrary to every principle of humanity, and the government of God, who unequivocally declares that he is not a respecter of persons.

4. Slave Religion, 1849
SOURCE: Willie Lee Rose, *A Documentary History of Slavery in America* (New York: Oxford University Press, 1976), 458-59.

In 1833, I had some very serious religious impressions, and there was quite a number of slaves in that neighborhood, who felt very desirous to be taught to read the Bible. There was a Miss Davis, a poor white girl, who offered to teach a Sabbath

School for the slaves, notwithstanding public opinion and the law was opposed to it. Books were furnished and she commenced the school; but the news soon got to our owners that she was teaching us to read. This caused quite an excitement in the neighborhood. Patrols were appointed to go and break it up the next Sabbath. They were determined that we should not have a Sabbath School in operation. For slaves this was called an incendiary movement.

The Sabbath is not regarded by a large number of the slaves as a day of rest. They have no schools to go to; no moral nor religious instruction at all in many localities where there are hundreds of slaves. Hence they resort to some kind of amusement. Those who make no profession of religion, resort to the woods in large numbers on that day to gamble, fight, get drunk, and break the Sabbath. This is often encouraged by slaveholders. When they wish to have a little sport of that kind, they go among the slaves and give them whiskey, to see them dance, "pat juber," sing and play on the banjo. Then get them to wrestling, fighting, jumping, running foot races, and butting each other like sheep. This is urged on by giving them whiskey; making bets on them; laying chips on one slave's head, and daring another to tip it off with his hand; and if he tipped it off, it would be called an insult, and cause a fight. Before fighting, the parties choose their seconds to stand by them while fighting; a ring or a circle is formed to fight in, and no one is allowed to enter the ring while they are fighting, but their seconds and the white gentlemen. They are not allowed to fight a duel, nor to use weapons of any kind. The blows are made by kicking, knocking, and butting with their heads; they grab each other by their ears, and jam their heads together like sheep. If they are likely to hurt each other very bad, their masters would rap them with their walking canes, and make them stop. After fighting, they make friends, shake hands, and take a dram together, and there is no more of it.

But this is all principally for want of moral instruction. This is where they have no Sabbath Schools; no one to read the Bible to them; no one to preach the gospel who is competent to expound the Scriptures, except slaveholders. And the slaves, with but few exceptions, have no confidence at all in their preaching, because they preach a pro-slavery doctrine. They say, "Servants be obedient to your masters; —and he that knoweth his master's will and doeth it not, shall be beaten with many stripes; —" means that God will send them to hell, if they disobey their masters. This kind of preaching has driven thousands into infidelity. They view themselves as suffering unjustly under the lash, without friends, without protection of law or gospel, and the green eyed monster tyranny staring them in the face. They know that they are destined to die in that wretched condition, unless they are delivered by the arm of Omnipotence. And they cannot believe or trust in such a religion, as above named.

5. Letters on Slavery, 1852

SOURCE: James H. Hammond, *The Pro-Slavery Argument* (Charleston, S. C., 1852), 104-9.

If you were to ask me whether I am an advocate of Slavery in the abstract, I should probably answer, that I am not, according to my understanding of the question. I do not like to deal in abstractions. It seldom leads to any useful ends. There are few universal truths. I do not now remember any single moral truth universally acknowledged. We have no assurance that it is given to our finite understanding to comprehend abstract moral truth. Apart from revelation and the inspired writings, what idea should we have even of God, salvation and immortality? . . . I might say that I am no more in favor of Slavery in the abstract, than I am of poverty, disease, deformity, idiocy, or any other inequality in the condition of the human family; that I love perfection, and think I should enjoy a millennium such as God has promised. But what would it amount to? A pledge that I would join you to set about eradicating those apparently inevitable evils of our nature, in equalizing the condition of all mankind, consummating the perfection of our race, and introducing the millennium? By no means. To effect these things, belongs exclusively to a higher power. And it would be well for us to leave the Almighty to perfect his own works and fulfil his own covenants. . . . On Slavery in the abstract, then, it would not be amiss to have as little as possible to say. Let us contemplate it as it is. And thus contemplating it, the first question we have to ask ourselves is, whether it is contrary to the will of God, as revealed to us in his Holy Scriptures—the only certain means given to us to ascertain his will. If it is, then Slavery is a sin. And I admit at once that every man is bound to set his face against it, and to emancipate his slaves, should he hold any.

Let us open these Holy Scriptures. In the twentieth chapter of Exodus, seventeenth verse, I find the following words: "Thou shalt not covet they neighbor's house, thou shalt not covet they neighbor's wife, nor his man-servant, nor his maid-servant, nor his ox, nor his ass, nor anything that is thy neighbor's"—which is the tenth of those commandments that declare the essential principles of the great moral law delivered to Moses by God himself. Now, discarding all technical and verbal quibbling as wholly unworthy to be used in interpreting the Word of God, what is the plain meaning, undoubted intent, and true spirit of this commandment? Does it not emphatically and explicitly forbid you to disturb your neighbor in the enjoyment of his property; and more especially of that which is here specifically mentioned as being lawfully, and by this commandment made sacredly his? Prominent in the catalogue stands his "man-servant and his maid-servant who are thus distinctly *consecrated as his property*, and guaranteed to him for his exclusive benefit, in the most solemn manner. . . .

You cannot deny that there were among the Hebrews "bondmen forever." You cannot deny that God especially authorized his chosen people to purchase "bondmen forever" from the heathen, as recorded in the twenty-fifth chapter of Leviticus, and that they are there designated by the very Hebrew word used in the tenth commandment. Nor can you deny that a "BONDMAN FOREVER" is a "SLAVE;" yet you endeavor to hang an argument of immortal consequence upon the wretched subterfuge, that the precise word "slave" is not to be found in the *translation* of the Bible. As if the translators were canonical expounders of the Holy Scriptures, and *their words*, not *God's meanings*, must be regarded as his revelation.

It is vain to look to Christ or any of his Apostles to justify such blasphemous perversions of the word of God. Although Slavery in its most revolting form was everywhere visible around them, no visionary notions of piety or philanthropy ever tempted them to gainsay the LAW, even to mitigate the cruel severity of the existing system. On the contrary, regarding Slavery as an *established,* as well as *inevitable conditions of human society,* they never hinted at such a thing as its termination on earth, any more than that "the poor may cease out of the land," which God affirms to Moses shall never be: and they exhort "all servants under the yoke" to "count their masters as worthy of all honor:" "to obey them in all things according to the flesh; not with eyeservice as men-pleasers, but in singleness of heart, fearing God;" "not only the good and gentle, but also the froward:" "For what glory is it if when ye are buffeted for your faults ye shall take it patiently, but if when ye do well and suffer for it ye take it patiently, this is acceptable of God." St. Paul actually apprehended a runaway slave, and sent him to his master! Instead of deriving from the Gospel any sanction for the work you have undertaken, it would be difficult to imagine sentiments and conduct more strikingly in contrast, than those of the Apostles and the abolitionists. . . .

I think, I may safely conclude, and I firmly believe, that American Slavery is not only not a sin, but especially commanded by God through Moses, and approved by Christ through his apostles. And here I might close its defence; for what God ordains, and Christ sanctifies, should surely command the respect and toleration of man. But I fear there has grown up in our time a transcendental religion, which is throwing even transcendental philosophy into the shade—a religion too pure and elevated for the Bible; which seeks to erect among men a higher standard of morals than the Almighty has revealed, or our Savior preached; and which is probably destined to do more to impede the extension of God's kingdom on earth than all the infidels who have ever lived. Error is error. It is as dangerous to deviate to the right hand as the left. And when man, professing to be holy man, and who are by numbers regarded, declare those things to be sinful which our Creator has expressly authorized and instituted, they do more to destroy his authority among mankind than the most wicked can effect, by proclaiming that to be innocent which was forbidden. To this self-righteous and self-exalted class belong all the abolitionists whose writings I have read. With them it is no end of the argument to prove your propositions by the text of the Bible, interpreted according to its plain and palpable meaning, and as understood by all mankind for three thousand years before their time. They are more ingenious at construing and interpolating to accommodate it to their new-fangled and etherial [*sic*] code of morals, than ever were Voltaire and Hume in picking it to pieces, to free the world from what they considered a delusion. When the abolitionists proclaim "man-stealing" to be a sin, and show me that it is so written down by God, I admit them to be right, and shudder at the idea of such a crime. But when I show them that to hold "bondmen forever" is ordained by God, *they deny the Bible, and set up in its place a law of their own making.* I must then cease to reason with them on this branch of the question. Our religion differs as widely as our manners. The great judge in our day of final account must decide between us.

6. What to the Slave is the Fourth of July?, 1852

SOURCE: Text of speech based on pamphlet published by Lee, Mann and Company, 1852.

. . . Fellow citizens, I am not wanting in respect for the fathers of this republic. The signers of the Declaration of Independence were brave men. They were great men too—great enough to give fame to a great age. It does not often happen to a nation to raise, at one time, such a number of truly great men. The point from which I am compelled to view them is not, certainly, the most favorable; and yet I cannot contemplate their great deeds with less than admiration. They were statesmen, patriots and heroes, and for the good they did, and the principles they contended for, I will unite with you to honor their memory.

They loved their country better than their own private interests; and, though this is not the highest form of human excellence, all will concede that it is a rare virtue, and that when it is exhibited, it ought to command respect. He who will, intelligently, lay down his life for his country, is a man whom it is not in human nature to despise. Your fathers staked their lives, their fortunes, and their sacred honor, on the cause of their country. In their admiration of liberty, they lost sight of all other interests.

They were peace men; but they preferred revolution to peaceful submission to bondage. They were quiet men; but they did not shrink from agitating against oppression. They showed forbearance; but that they knew its limits. They believed in order; but not in the order of tyranny. With them, nothing was "*settled*" that was not right. With them, justice, liberty and humanity were "*final*"; not slavery and oppression. You may well cherish the memory of such men. They were great in their day and generation. Their solid manhood stands out the more as we contrast it with these degenerate times.

How circumspect, exact and proportionate were all their movements! How unlike the politicians of an hour! Their statesmanship looked beyond the passing moment, and stretched away in strength into the distant future. They seized upon eternal principles, and set a glorious example in their defence. Mark them!

Fully appreciating the hardship to be encountered, firmly believing in the right of their cause, honorably inviting the scrutiny of an on-looking world, reverently appealing to heaven to attest their sincerity, soundly comprehending the solemn responsibility they were about to assume, wisely measuring the terrible odds against them, your fathers, the fathers of this republic, did, most deliberately, under the inspiration of a glorious patriotism, and with a sublime faith in the great principles of justice and freedom, lay deep the corner-stone of the national superstructure, which has risen and still rises in grandeur around you.

Of this fundamental work, this day is the anniversary. Our eyes are met with demonstrations of joyous enthusiasm. Banners and pennants wave exultingly on the breeze. The din of business, too, is hushed. Even Mammon seems to have quitted his grasp on this day. The ear-piercing fife and the stirring drum unite their accents with the ascending peal of a thousand church bells. Prayers are made, hymns are sung, and sermons are preached in honor of this day; while the quick martial tramp of a great and multitudinous nation, echoed back by all the hills, valleys and mountains of a vast continent, bespeak the occasion one of thrilling and universal interest—a nation's jubilee.

Friends and citizens, I need not enter further into the causes which led to this anniversary. Many of you understand them better than I do. You could instruct me in regard to them. That is a branch of knowledge in which you feel, perhaps, a much deeper interest than your speaker. The causes which led to the separation of the colonies from the British crown have never lacked for a tongue. They have all been taught in your common schools, narrated at your firesides, unfolded from your pulpits, and thundered from your legislative halls, and are as familiar to you as household words. They form the staple of your national poetry and eloquence.

I remember, also, that, as a people, Americans are remarkably familiar with all facts which make in their own favor. This is esteemed by some as a national trait—perhaps a national weakness. It is a fact, that whatever makes for the wealth or for the reputation of Americans, and can be had *cheap*! will be found by Americans. I shall not be charged with slandering Americans, if I say I think the American side of any question may be safely left in American hands.

I leave, therefore, the great deeds of your fathers to other gentlemen whose claim to have been regularly descended will be less likely to be disputed than mine!
. . .

The Church Responsible

But the church of this country is not only indifferent to the wrongs of the slave, it actually takes sides with the oppressors, It has made itself the bulwark of American slavery, and the shield of American slavehunters. Many of its most eloquent Divines, who stand as the vary lights of the church, have shamelessly given the sanction of religion and the Bible to the whole slave system. They have taught that man may, properly, be a slave; that the relation of master and slave is ordained of God; that to send back an escaped bondman to his master is clearly the duty of all the followers of the Lord Jesus Christ; and this horrible blasphemy is palmed off upon the world for Christianity.

For my part, I would say welcome infidelity! welcome atheism! welcome anything! in preference to the gospel, *as preached by those Divines*! They convert the very name of religion into an engine of tyranny, and barbarous cruelty, and serve to confirm more infidels, in this age, than all the infidel writings of Thomas Paine, Voltaire, and Bolingbroke, put together, have done! These ministers make religion a cold and flinty-hearted thing, having neither principles of right action, nor bowels of compassion. They strip the love of God of its beauty, and leave the throne of religion a huge, horrible, repulsive form. It is a religion for oppressors, tyrants, man-stealers, and *thugs*. It is not that "*pure and undefiled religion*" which is from above, and which is "*first pure, then peaceable, easy to be entreated*, full of mercy and good fruits, *without partiality, and without hypocrisy.*" But a religion which favors the rich against the poor; which exalts the proud above the humble; which divides mankind into two classes, tyrants and slaves; which says to the man in chains, *stay there*; and to the oppressor, *oppress on*; it is a religion which may be professed and enjoyed by all the robbers and enslavers of mankind; it makes God a respecter of person, denies his fatherhood of the race, and tramples in the dust the great truth of the brotherhood of man. All this we affirm to be true of the popular church, and the popular worship of our land and nation—a religion, a church, and a worship which, on the authority of inspired wisdom, we pronounce to be an abomination in the sight of God. In the language of Isaiah, the American church might be well addressed, "Bring no more vain oblations: incense is an abomination unto me; the new moons and Sabbaths, the calling of assemblies, I cannot away with; it is iniquity, even the solemn meeting. Your new moons and your appointed feasts my soul hateth. They are a trouble to me; I am weary to bear them; and when ye spread forth your hands I will hide mine eyes from you. Yea! when ye make many prayers, I will not hear. YOUR HANDS ARE FULL OF BLOOD; cease to do evil, learn to do well; seek judgement; relieve the oppressed; judge for the fatherless; plead for the widow."

The American church is guilty, when viewed in connection with what it is doing to uphold slavery; but it is superlatively guilty when viewed in connection with its ability to abolish slavery.

The sin of which it is guilty is one of omission as well as of commission. Albert Barnes but uttered what the common sense of every man at all observant of the actual state of the case will receive as truth, when he declared that "There is no power out of the church that could sustain slavery an hour, if it were not sustained in it."

Let the religious press, the pulpit, the Sunday school, the conference meeting, the great ecclesiastical, missionary, Bible and tract associations of the land array their immense powers against slavery and slaveholding; and the whole system of crime and blood would be scattered to the winds; and that they do not do this involves them in the most awful responsibility of which the mind can conceive.

In prosecuting the anti-slavery enterprise, we have been asked to spare the church, to spare the ministry; but *how*, we ask, could such a thing be done? We are met on the threshold of our efforts for the redemption of the slave, by the church and ministry of the country, in battle arrayed against us; and we are compelled to fight or flee. From what quarter, I beg to know, has proceeded a fire so deadly upon our ranks, during the last two years, as from the Northern pulpit? As the champions of oppressors, the chosen men of American theology have appeared—men, honored for their so-called piety, and their real learning. The LORDS of Buffalo, the SPRINGS of New York, the LATHROPS of Auburn, the COXES and SPENCERS of Brooklyn, the GANNETS and SHARPS of Boston, the DEWEYS of Washington, and other great religious lights of the land, have, in utter denial of the authority of *Him*, by whom they professed to be called to the ministry, deliberately taught us, against the example of the Hebrews and against the remonstrance of the Apostles, they teach "*that we ought to obey man's law before the law of God.*"

My spirit wearies of such blasphemy; and how such men can be supported, as the "standing types and representatives of Jesus Christ," is a mystery which I leave others to penetrate. In speaking of the American church, however, let it be distinctly understood that I mean the *great mass* of the religious organizations of our land. There are exceptions, and I thank God that there are. Noble men may be found, scattered all over these Northern States, of whom Henry Ward Beecher of Brooklyn, Samuel J. May of Syracuse, and my esteemed friend on the platform, are shining examples; and let me say further, that upon these men lies the duty to inspire our ranks with high religious faith and zeal, and to cheer us on the great mission of the slave's redemption from his chains. . . .

7. Slavery and Southern Presbyterian Secession, 1861

SOURCE: *Minutes of the General Assembly of the Presbyterian Church in the Confederate States of America, Vol. I, A.D. 1861* (Augusta, GA, 1861), 55-59.

The antagonism of Northern and Southern sentiment on the subject of slavery lies at the root of all the difficulties which have resulted in the dismemberment of the Federal Union, and involved us in the horrors of an unnatural war. . . .

And here we may venture to lay before the Christian world our views as a Church, upon the subject of slavery. We beg a candid hearing.

In the first place, we would have it distinctly understood that, in our ecclesiastical capacity, we are neither the friends nor the foes of slavery, that is to say, we have no commission either to propagate or abolish it. The policy of its existence or non-existence is a question which exclusively belongs to the State. We have no right, as a Church, to enjoin it as a duty, or to condemn it as a sin. Our business is with the duties which spring from the relation; the duties of the masters on the one hand, and of their slaves on the other. These duties we are to proclaim and to enforce with spiritual sanctions. The social, civil, political problems connected with this great subject transcend our sphere, as God has not entrusted to His Church the organization of society, the construction of Governments, nor the allotment of individuals to their various stations. The Church has as much right to preach to the monarchies of Europe, and the despotism of Asia, the doctrines of republican equality, as to preach to the Governments of the South the extirpation of slavery. This position is impregnable, unless it can be shown that slavery is a sin. Upon every other hypothesis, it is so clearly a question for the State, that the proposition would never for a moment have been doubted, had there not been a foregone conclusion in relation to its moral character. Is slavery, then, a sin?

In answering this question, as a Church, let it be distinctly borne in mind that the only rule of judgment is the written word of God. The Church knows nothing of the intuitions of reason or the deductions of philosophy, except those reproduced in the Sacred Canon. She has a positive constitution in the Holy Scriptures, and has no right to utter a single syllable upon any subject, except as the Lord puts words in her mouth. She is founded, in other words, upon express *revelation*. Her creed is an authoritative testimony of God, and not a speculation, and what she proclaims, she must proclaim with the infallible certitude of faith, and not with the hesitating assent of an opinion. The question, then, is brought within a narrow compass: do the Scriptures directly or indirectly condemn slavery as a sin? If they do not, the dispute is ended, for the Church, without forfeiting her character, dares not go beyond them.

Now, we venture to assert that if men had drawn their conclusions upon this subject only from the bible, it would no more have entered into any human head to denounce slavery as a sin, than to denounce monarchy, aristocracy or poverty. The truth is, men have listened to what they falsely considered as primitive intuitions, or as necessary deductions from primitive cognitions, and then have gone to the Bible to confirm the crotchets of their vain philosophy. They have gone there determined to find a particular result, and the consequence is, that they leave with having made, instead of having interpreted, Scripture. Slavery is not a new thing. It has not only existed for ages in the world, but it has existed, under every dispensation of the covenant of grace, in the Church of God. Indeed, the first organization of the Church as a visible society, separate and distinct from the unbelieving world, was inaugurated in the family of a slaveholder. Among the very first persons to whom the seal of circumcision was affixed, were the slaves of the father of the faithful, some born in his house, and others bought with his money. Slavery again re-appears under the Law. God sanctions it in the first table of the Decalogue, and Moses treats it as an institution to be regulated, not abolished; legitimated and not condemned. We come down to the age of the New Testament, and we find it again in the Churches founded by the Apostles under the plenary inspiration of the Holy ghost. These facts are utterly amazing, if slavery is the enormous sin which its enemies represent it to be. It will not do to say that the Scriptures have treated it only in a general, incidental way, without any clear implication as to its moral character. Moses surely made it the subject of express and positive legislation, and the apostles are equally explicit in inculcating the duties which spring from both sides of the relation. They treat slaves as bound to obey and inculcate obedience as an office of religion—a thing wholly self-contradictory, if the authority exercised over them were unlawful and iniquitous.

But what puts this subject in a still clearer light, is the manner in which it is sought to extort from the Scriptures a contrary testimony. The notion of direct and explicit condemnation is given up. The attempt is to show that the genius and spirit of Christianity are opposed to it—that its great cardinal principles of virtue are utterly against it. Much stress is laid upon the Golden Rule and upon the general denunciations of tyranny and oppression. To all this we reply, that no principle is clearer than that a case positively excepted cannot be included under a general rule. Let us concede, for a moment, that the law of love, and the condemnation of tyranny and oppression, seem logically to involve, as a result, the condemnation of slavery; yet, if slavery is afterwards expressly mentioned and treated as a lawful relation, it obviously follows, unless Scripture is to be interpreted as inconsistent with itself, that slavery is, by necessary implication, excepted. The Jewish law forbade, as a general rule, the marriage of a man with his brother's wife.

The same law expressly enjoined the same marriage in a given case. The given case was, therefore, an exception, and not to be treated as a violation of the general rule. The law of love has always been the law of God. It was enunciated by Moses almost as clearly as it was enunciated by Jesus Christ. Yet, notwithstanding this law, Moses and the Apostles alike sanctioned the relation of slavery. The conclusion is inevitable, either that the law is not opposed to it, or that slavery is an excepted case. To say that the prohibition of tyranny and oppression include slavery, is to beg the whole question. Tyranny and oppression involve either the unjust usurpation or the unlawful exercise of power. It is the unlawfulness, either in its principle or measure, which constitutes the core of the sin. Slavery must, therefore, be proved to be unlawful, before it can be referred to any such category. The master may, indeed, abuse his power, but he oppresses not simply as a master, but as a wicked master.

But, apart from all this, the law of love is simply the inculcation of universal equity. It implies nothing as to the existence of various ranks and gradations in society. The interpretation which makes it repudiate slavery would make it equally repudiate all social, civil, and political inequalities. Its meaning is, not that we should conform ourselves to the arbitrary expectations of others, but that we should render unto them precisely the same measure which, if we were in their circumstance, it would be reasonable and just in us to demand at their hands. It condemns slavery, therefore, only upon the supposition that slavery is a sinful relation—that is, he who extracts the prohibition of slavery from the Golden Rule, begs the very point in dispute.

We cannot prosecute the argument in detail, but we have said enough, we think, to vindicate the position of the southern Church. We have assumed no new attitude. We stand exactly where the Church of God has always stood—from Abraham to Moses, from Moses to Christ, from Christ to the Reformers, and from the Reformers to ourselves. We stand upon the foundation of the Prophets and Apostles, Jesus Christ Himself being the Chief corner stone. Shall we be excluded from the fellowship of our brethren in other lands, because we dare not depart from the charter of our faith? Shall we be branded with the stigma of reproach, because we cannot consent to corrupt the word of God to suit the intuitions of an infidel philosophy? Shall our names be cast out as evil, and the finger of scorn pointed at us, because we utterly refuse to break our communion with Abraham, Isaac and Jacob, with Moses, David and Isaiah, with Apostles, Prophets and Martyrs, with all the noble army of confessors who have gone to glory from slave-holding countries and from a slave-holding Church, without ever having dreamed that they were living in mortal sin, by conniving at slavery in the midst of them? If so, we shall take consolation in the cheering consciousness that the Master has accepted us. We may be denounced, despised and cast out of the synagogues of our brethren. But while they are wrangling about the distinctions of men according to the flesh, we shall go forward in our Divine work, and confidently anticipate that, in the great day, as the consequence of our humble labors, we shall meet millions of glorified spirits, who have come up from the bondage of earth to a nobler freedom than human philosophy ever dreamed of. Others, if they please, may spend their time in declaiming on the tyranny of earthly masters; it will be our aim to resist the real tyrants which oppress the soul—Sin and Satan. These are the foes against whom we shall find it employment enough to wage a successful war. And to this holy war it is the purpose of our Church to devote itself with redoubled energy. We feel that the souls of our slaves are a solemn trust, and we shall strive to present them faultless and complete before the presence of God.

Indeed, as we contemplate their condition in the Southern States, and contrast it with that of their fathers before them, and that of their brethren in the present day in their native land, we cannot but accept it as a gracious Providence that they have been brought in such numbers to our shores, and redeemed from the bondage of barbarism and sin. Slavery to them has certainly been overruled for the greatest good. It has been a link in the wondrous chain of Providence, through which many sons and daughters have been made heirs of the heavenly inheritance. The Providential result is, of course, no justification, if the thing is intrinsically wrong; but it is certainly a matter of devout thanksgiving, and no obscure intimation of the will and purpose of God, and of the consequent duty of the Church. We cannot forbear to say, however, that the general operation of the system is kindly and benevolent; it is a real and effective discipline, and without it, we are profoundly persuaded that the African race in the midst of us can never be elevated in the scale of being. As long as that race, in its comparative degradation, co-exists, side by side, with the white, bondage is its normal condition.

As to the endless declamation about human rights, we have only to say that human rights are not a fixed, but a fluctuating quantity. Their sum is not the same in any two nations on the globe. The rights of Englishmen are one thing, the rights of Frenchmen another. There is a minimum without which a man cannot be responsible; there is a maximum which expresses the highest degree of civilization and of Christian culture. The education of the species consists in its ascent along this line. As you go up, the number of rights increases, but the number of individuals who possess them diminishes. As you come down the line, rights are diminished, but the individuals are multiplied. It is just the opposite of the predicamental scale of the logicians. There comprehension diminishes as you ascend and extension increases, and comprehension increases as you descend and extension diminishes. Now, when it is said that slavery is inconsistent with human rights, we crave to understand what point in this line is the slave conceived to occupy. There are, no doubt, many rights which belong to other men—to Englishmen[,] to Frenchmen, to his master, for example—which are denied to him. But is he fit to possess them? Has God qualified him to meet the responsibilities which their possession necessarily implies? His place in the scale is determined by his competency to fulfil its duties. There are other rights which he certainly possesses, without which he could neither be human nor accountable. Before slavery can be charged with doing him injustice, it must be shown that the minimum which falls to his lot at the bottom of the line is out of proportion to his capacity and culture—a thing which can never be done by abstract speculation. The truth is, the education of the human race for liberty and virtue, is a vast Providential scheme, and God assigns to every man, by a wise and holy decree, the precise place he is to occupy in the great moral school of humanity. The scholars are distributed into classes, according to their competency and progress. For God is in history.

To avoid the suspicion of a conscious weakness of our cause, when contemplated from the side of pure speculation, we may advert for a moment to those pretended intuitions which stamp the reprobation of humanity upon this ancient and hoary institution. We admit that there are primitive principles in morality which lie at the root of human consciousness. But the question is, how are we to distinguish them? The subjective feeling of certainty is not adequate criterion, as that is equally felt in reference to crotchets and hereditary prejudices. The very point is to know when this certainty indicates a primitive cognition, and when it does not. There must, therefore, be some eternal test, and whatever cannot abide that test has no authority as a primary truth. That test is an inward necessity of thought, which, in all minds at the proper stage of maturity, is absolutely universal. Whatever is universal is natural. We are willing that slavery should be tried by this standard. We are willing to abide by the testimony of the race, and if man, as man, has every where condemned it—if all human laws have prohibited it as crime—if it stands in the same category with malice, murder and theft, then we are willing, in the name of humanity, to renounce it, and to renounce it forever. But what if the overwhelming majority of mankind have approved it? What if philosophers and statesmen have justified it, and the laws of all nations acknowledged it; what then becomes of these luminous intuitions? They are *ignis fatuus*, mistaken for a star.

8. Slave Songs and Spirituals, 1867
SOURCE: "Negro Spirituals." *Atlantic Monthly* 19, no 116 (June 1867), 685-94.

Hold Your Light.
> Hold your light, Brudder Robert,—
> Hold your light,
> Hold your light on Canaan's shore.
> What make ole Satan for follow me so?
> Satan ain't got notin' for do wid me.
> Hold your light,
> Hold your light,
> Hold your light on Canaan's shore."

Bound to Go.
> Jordan River, I'm bound to go,
> Bound to go, bound to go,—
> Jordan River, I'm bound to go,
> And bid 'em fare ye well.

My Brudder Robert, I'm bound to go,
Bound to go, &c.

My Sister Lucy, I'm bound to go,
Bound to go, &c.

Room in There.

O, my mudder is gone! my mudder is gone!
My mudder is gone into heaven, my Lord!
I can't stay behind!
Dere's room in dar, room in dar,
Room in dar, in de heaven, my Lord!
I can't stay behind,

Can't stay behind, my dear,
I can't stay behind!

O, my fader is gone! &c.

O, de angels are gone! &c.
O, I'se been on de road! I'se been on de road!
I'se been on de road into heaven, my Lord!
I can't stay behind!
O, room in dar, room in dar,
Room in dar, in de heaven, my Lord!
I can't stay behind!

Hail Mary.

One more valiant soldier here,
One more valiant soldier here,
One more valiant soldier here,
To help me bear de cross.
O hail, Mary, hail!
Hail, Mary, hail!
Hail, Mary, hail!
To help me bear de cross.

My Army Cross Over.

> My army cross over,
> My army cross over.
> O, Pharaoh's army drownded!
> My army cross over.
>
> We'll cross de mighty river,
> My army cross over;
> We'll cross de river Jordan,
> My army cross over;
> We'll cross de danger water,
> My army cross over;
> We'll cross de mighty Myo,
> My army cross over. (*Thrice.*)
> O, Pharaoh's army drownded!
> My army cross over."

Ride In, Kind Saviour

> Ride in, kind Saviour!
> No man can hinder me.
> O, Jesus is a mighty man!
> No man, &c.
> We're marching through Virginny fields.
> No man, &c.
> O, Satan is a busy man,
> No man, &c.
> And he has his sword and shield,
> No man, &c.
> O, old Secesh done come and gone!
> No man can hinder me.

I Want To Go Home.

> Dere's no rain to wet you,
> O, yes, I want to go home.
> Dere's no sun to burn you,
> O, yes, I want to go home;
> O, push along, believers,
> O, yes, &c.

Dere's no hard trials,

O, yes, &c.

Dere's no whips-a-crackin',

O, yes, &c.

My brudder on de wayside,

O, yes, &c.

O, push along, my brudder,

O, yes, &c.

Where dere's no stormy weather,

O, yes, &c.

Dere's no tribulation,

O, yes, &c.

The Coming Day.

I want to go to Canaan,

I want to go to Canaan,

I want to go to Canaan,

To meet 'em at de comin' day.

O, remember, let me go to Canaan.

(*Thrice.*)

To meet 'em, &c.

O brudder, let me go to Canaan,

(*Thrice.*)

To meet 'em, &c.

My brudder, you—of!—remember

(*Thrice.*)

To meet 'em at de comin' day.

Essays

The pro-slavery and anti-slavery arguments of religious Americans during the middle decades of the nineteenth century are well known. Less attention has been given, however, to the religious lives of the slaves. Albert J. Raboteau of Princeton University distinguishes between the visible, institutional religion of slaves who attended independent black churches, and the invisible, noninstitutional religion, which was informal, spontaneous, and secretive. In the first essay, Raboteau describes the "invisible institution" of slave religion, which often provided an important network of slave communication. At the heart of the antebellum reform movement was the anti-slavery crusade. Evangelical church

*leaders were at the center of the crusade, as noted by Bertram Wyatt-Brown of
the National Center for the Humanities, in the second essay. He describes the
activities of Lewis Tappan and other abolitionists who faced numerous challenges in their efforts to eradicate slavery from America.*

Religious Life in the Slave Community
ALBERT J. RABOTEAU

SOURCE: From *Slave Religion: The "Invisible Institution" in the Antebellum South* by Albert
J. Raboteau, copyright © 1978 by Oxford University Press, Inc. Used by permission of
Oxford University Press, Inc.

By the eve of the Civil War, Christianity had pervaded the slave community. The
vast majority of slaves were American-born, and the cultural and linguistic barriers
which had impeded the evangelization of earlier generations of African-born slaves
were generally no longer a problem. The widespread opposition of the planters to
the catechizing of slaves had been largely dissipated by the efforts of the churches
and missionaries of the South. Not all slaves were Christian, nor were all those who
accepted Christianity members of a church, but the doctrines, symbols, and vision
of life preached by Christianity were familiar to most. During the closing decades
of the antebellum period the so-called invisible institution of slave Christianity
came to maturity. The religious life of slaves in the late antebellum period is well
documented by sources from the slaves themselves.

At first glance it seems strange to refer to the religion of the slaves as an invisible institution, for independent black churches with slave members did exist in
the South before emancipation. In racially mixed churches it was not uncommon for slaves to outnumber masters in attendance at Sunday services. But the
religious experience of the slaves was by no means fully contained in the visible
structures of the institutional church. From the abundant testimony of fugitive
and freed slaves it is clear that the slave community had an extensive religious life
of its own, hidden from the eyes of the master. In the secrecy of the quarters or
the seclusion of the brush arbors ("hush harbors") the slaves made Christianity
truly their own.

The religion of the slaves was both institutional and noninstitutional, visible
and invisible, formally organized and spontaneously adapted. Regular Sunday
worship in the local church was paralleled by illicit, or at least informal, prayer
meetings on weeknights in the slave cabins. Preachers licensed by the church and
hired by the master were supplemented by slave preachers licensed only by the
spirit. Texts from the Bible which most slaves could not read were explicated by
verses from the spirituals. Slaves forbidden by masters to attend church or, in some
cases, even to pray risked floggings to attend secret gatherings to worship God.

His own experience of the "invisible institution" was recalled by former slave
Wash Wilson:

When de niggers go round singin' 'Steal Away to Jesus,' dat mean dere gwine be a 'ligious meetin' dat night. De masters . . . didn't like dem 'ligious meetin's, so us natcherly slips off at night, down in de bottoms or somewhere. Sometimes us sing and pray all night.

Into that all-night singing and praying the slaves poured the sufferings and needs of their days. Like "Steal Away" and the rest of the spirituals, Christianity was fitted by the slave community to its own particular experience. At the same time the symbols, myths, and values of Judeo-Christian tradition helped form the slave community's image of itself.

"Steal Away"

Slaves frequently were moved to hold their own religious meetings out of disgust for the vitiated Gospel preached by their masters' preachers. Sermons urging slaves to be obedient and docile were repeated ad nauseam. The type of sermon to which he and other slaves were constantly subjected was paraphrased by Frank Roberson:

You slaves will go to heaven if you are good, but don't ever think that you will be close to your mistress and master. No! No! there will be a wall between you; but there will be holes in it that will permit you to look out and see your mistress when she passes by. If you want to sit behind this wall, you must do the language of the text 'Obey your masters.'

Another former slave, Charlie Van Dyke, bitterly complained: "Church was what they called it but all that preacher talked about was for us slaves to obey our masters and not to lie and steal. Nothing about Jesus, was ever said and the overseer stood there to see the preacher talked as he wanted him to talk." Consequently, even a black preacher "would get up and repeat everything that the white preacher had said, because he was afraid to say anything different."

For more authentic Christian preaching the slaves had to turn elsewhere. Lucretia Alexander explained what slaves did when they grew tired of the white folks' preacher:

The preacher came and . . . He'd just say, 'Serve your masters. Don't steal your master's turkey. Don't steal your master's chickens. Don't steal your master's hawgs. Don't steal your master's meat. Do whatsomever your master tells you to do.' Same old thing all the time. My father would have church in dwelling houses and they had to whisper. . . . Sometimes they would have church at his house. That would be when they would want a real meetin' with some real preachin'. . . . They used to sing their songs in a whisper and pray in a whisper. That was a prayer-meeting from house to house once or twice—once or twice a week.

Slaves faced severe punishment if caught attending secret prayer meetings. Moses Grandy reported that his brother-in-law Isaac, a slave preacher, "was flogged, and his back pickled" for preaching at a clandestine service in the woods. His listeners were flogged and "forced to tell who else was there." Grandy claimed that slaves were often flogged "if they are found singing or praying at home." Gus Clark reported: "My Boss didn' 'low us to go to church, er to pray er sing. Iffen he ketched us prayin' er singin' he whupped us . . . . He didn' care fer nothin' 'cept farmin.'" According to another ex-slave, "the white folks would come in when the colored people would have prayer meeting, and whip every one of them. Most of them thought that when colored people were praying it was against them. For they would catch them praying for God to lift things out of their way and the white folks would *lift them.*" Henry Bibb was threatened with five hundred lashes on the naked back for attending a prayer meeting conducted by slaves on a neighboring plantation, because he had no permission to do so. The master who threatened Bibb with this punishment was, incidentally, a deacon of the local Baptist church. Charlotte Martin asserted that "her oldest brother was whipped to death for taking part in one of the religious ceremonies." Despite the danger, slaves continued to hold their own religious gatherings because, as Grandy stated, "they like their own meetings better." There the slaves could pray and sing as they desired. They were willing to risk threats of floggings at the hands of their earthly masters in order to worship their "Divine Master" as they saw fit.

Slaves devised several techniques to avoid detection of their meetings. One practice was to meet in secluded places—woods, gullies, ravines, and thickets (aptly called "hush harbors"). Kalvin Woods remembered preaching to other slaves and singing and praying while huddled behind quilts and rags, which had been thoroughly wetted "to keep the sound of their voices from penetrating the air" and then hung up "in the form of a little room," or tabernacle. On one Louisiana plantation, when "the slaves would steal away into the woods at night and hold services," they "would form a circle on their knees around the speaker who would also be on his knees. He would bend forward and speak into or over a vessel of water to drown the sound. If anyone became animated and cried out, the others would quickly stop the noise by placing their hands over the offender's mouth." When slaves got "happy an' shout[ed]" in their cabins, "couldn't nobody hyar 'em," according to George Young, "'caze dey didn't make no fuss on de dirt flo,'" but just in case, "one stan' in de do' an' watch." The most common device for preserving secrecy was an iron pot or kettle turned upside down to catch the sound. The pot was usually placed in the middle of the cabin floor or at the doorstep, then slightly propped up to hold the sound of the praying and singing from escaping. A variation was to pray or sing softly with heads together around" the "kettle to deaden the sound." Clara Young recalled, "When dark come, de men folks would hang up a wash pot, bottom upwards, in de little brush church house us had, so's it would catch de noise and de overseer wouldn't hear us singin' and shoutin'." According to one account, slaves used the overturned pot to cover the sound of more worldly amusements too: "They would have dances sometimes and turn a pot upside down right in front of the door. They said that would keep the sound from going outside."

Whether the pots were strictly functional or also served some symbolic purpose is not clear. The symbolic element is suggested by Patsy Hyde, former slave in Tennessee, who claimed that slaves "would tek dere ole iron cookin' pots en turn dem upside down on de groun' neah dere cabins ter keep dere white folks fun herein' w'at dey waz sayin'. Dey claimed dat hit showed dat Gawd waz wid dem." The origin of this custom also remains unclear. When asked about the custom, one ex-slave replied, "I don't know where they learned to do that. I kinda think the lord put them things in their minds to do for themselves, just like he helps us Christians in other ways. Don't you think so?" One theory has been advanced which explains the slaves' use of the pot as a remnant of African custom. Sidney Mintz has offered an interesting suggestion: "One is entitled to wonder whether a wash-tub that 'catches' sound, rather than producing it, may not represent some kind of religious symbolic inversion on the part of a religious group particularly since the suppression of drumming by the masters was a common feature of Afro-American history." He explains further: this is perhaps "a case in which some original symbolic or instrumental commitment has outlived its original circumstantial significance. Rather than disappearing however, that commitment is somehow transmitted and preserved." Whatever the origin of this folk custom, the widespread belief among slaves was that the pots worked. The need for secrecy even dictated that children keep quiet about what went on in the slave quarters. "My master used to ask us children," recalled one former slave, "'Do your folks pray at night?' We said 'No' cause our folks had told us what to say. But the Lord have mercy, there was plenty of that going on. They'd pray, 'Lord, deliver us from under bondage.'"

Looking back at these secret and risky religious gatherings, an ex-slave declared, "Meetings back there meant more than they do now. Then everybody's heart was in tune, and when they called on God they made heaven ring. It was more than just Sunday meeting and then no godliness for a week. They would steal off to the fields and in the thickets and there . . . they called on God out of heavy hearts." Truly communal, these meetings, as Hannah Lowery noted, needed no preacher because "everyone was so anxious to have a word to say that a preacher did not have a chance. All of them would sing and pray." A description of a secret prayer meeting was recorded by Peter Randolph, who was a slave in Prince George County, Virginia, until he was freed in 1847:

> Not being allowed to hold meetings on the plantation, the slaves assemble in the swamp, out of reach of the patrols. They have an understanding among themselves as to the time and place of getting together. This is often done by the first one arriving breaking boughs from the trees, and bending them in the direction of the selected spot. Arrangements are then made for conducting the exercises. They first ask each other how they feel, the state of their minds, etc. The male members then

select a certain space, in separate groups, for the division of the meeting. Preaching
. . . by the brethren, then praying and singing all around, until they generally feel
quite happy. The speaker usually commences by calling himself unworthy, and
talks very slowly, until feeling the spirit, he grows excited, and in a short time, there
fall to the ground twenty or thirty men and women under its influence. . . .

Randolph went on to elucidate the importance of these gatherings for the life of
the slave community:

The slave forgets all his sufferings, except to remind others of the trials during the
past week, exclaiming: 'Thank God, I shall not live here always!' Then they pass
from one to another, shaking hands, and bidding each other farewell . . . . As they
separate, they sing a parting hymn of praise.

Prayer, preaching, song, communal support, and especially "feeling the spirit" re-
freshed the slaves and consoled them in their times of distress. By imagining their
lives in the context of a different future they gained hope in the present.

The contrast between present pain and future relief formed the matter of slave
prayer and song. From his memory of slavery, Anderson Edwards cited a song
which starkly combined suffering and hope.

We prayed a lot to be free and the Lord done heered us. We didn't have no song
books and the Lord done give us our songs and when we sing them at night it jus'
whispering so nobody hear us. One went like this:

> My knee bones am aching,
> My body's rackin' with pain,
> I 'lieve I'm a chile of God,
> And this ain't my home,
> 'Cause Heaven's my aim.

Slaves sought consolation in the future, but they also found it in the present. Exhausted from a day of work that stretched from "day clean" to after sundown, the
slaves sometimes found tangible relief in prayer, as Richard Caruthers attested: "Us
niggers used to have a prayin' ground down in the hollow and sometime we come
out of the field . . . scorchin' and burnin' up with nothin' to eat, and we wants to
ask the good Lawd to have mercy . . . . We takes a pine torch . . . and goes down in
the hollow to pray. Some gits so joyous they starts to holler loud and we has to stop
up they mouth. I see niggers git so full of the Lawd and so happy they draps
unconscious."

Freedom was frequently the object of prayer. According to Laura Ambromson,
"Some believed they'd git freedom and others didn't. They had places they met and

prayed for freedom." Others were certain it would come. "I've heard them pray for freedom," declared another former slave. "I thought it was foolishness then, but the old time folks always felt they was to be free. It must have been something 'vealed unto 'em." Mingo White remembered: "Somehow or yuther us had a instinct dat we was goin' to be free," and "when de day's wuk was done de slaves would be foun' . . . in dere cabins prayin' for de Lawd to free dem lack he did chillun of Is'ael." Andrew Moss revealed that his mother would retreat to her private praying ground, "a ole twisted thick-rooted muscadine bush," where she prayed for the deliverance of the slaves. George Womble, former slave from Georgia, recalled that "slaves would go to the woods at night where they sang and prayed" and some used to say, "I know that some day we'll be free and if we die before that time our children will live to see it." The father of Jacob Stroyer, before his family went to bed, would pray that "the time which he predicted would come, that is, the time of freedom when . . . the children would be [their] own masters and mistresses." Forbidden to pray for liberation, slaves stole away at night and prayed inside "cane thickets . . . for deliverance."

Secrecy was characteristic of only part of the slave community's religious life. Many slaveholders granted their slaves permission to attend church, and some openly encouraged religious meetings among the slaves. Baptisms, marriages, and funerals were allowed to slaves on some plantations with whites observing and occasionally participating. Annual revival meetings were social occasions for blacks as well as for whites. Masters were known to enjoy the singing, praying, and preaching of their slaves. Nevertheless, at the core of the slaves' religion was a private place, represented by the cabin room, the overturned pot, the prayin' ground, and the "hush harbor." This place the slave kept his own. For no matter how religious the master might be, the slave knew that the master's religion did not countenance prayers for his slaves' freedom in this world. . . .

Antislavery and the Evangelical Movement
BERTRAM WYATT-BROWN

SOURCE: From *Lewis Tappan and the Evangelical War against Slavery* by Bertram Wyatt-Brown. Pp. 310-22. Copyright © 1969 by Press of Case Western Reserve University. Reprinted with permission of the author.

Throughout the 1840's, Lewis Tappan and William Lloyd Garrison shared the leadership of the antislavery crusade. Garrison retained his control of the radical elements, exercising an influence that was perhaps disproportionate to his effective power and the size of his following, but Tappan served as the coordinator of the activities of a great number of abolitionists. His influence cannot be measured by popular vote, since he made no serious attempt to gain political or church office, nor can it be assessed by his management of the "new organization" or the A.M.A., important though that was. Instead, his correspondence and other association with hundreds of clergymen, reformers, and pious laymen both here and abroad gave him a wide network of channels of advice and persuasion, actively maintained from 1840 to 1860. He owed his pre-eminence in religious antislavery circles not primarily to his speaking abilities (though he was a good orator) but to his persistence. With the exception of Garrison, J. Miller McKim, John Greenleaf Whittier, and perhaps a few other delegates to the Philadelphia Convention of 1833, no other abolitionist could boast a longer or more dedicated life of reform. None had a more consistent policy spanning the antebellum and war years. No layman in the evangelical movement used his influence on clerical policies to better purpose.

Attrition among the ecclesiastical reformers also helped to single him out. Some died or retired, but many renounced their orthodox faith. Elizur Wright, for instance, published an attack in 1846 on the doctrine of future punishment in a weekly paper he had started in Boston. In spite of Lewis Tappan's rejoinder, Wright also denied the Hopkinsian principles of a "hell-spurred religion." Gerrit Smith, the eccentric Stephen Pearl Andrews, the Welds, Joshua R. Giddings, James Birney, George W. Julian, and Julia Ward Howe were among those outside the Garrisonian camp who also adopted some form of a religion of humanity. According to Julian, an antislavery Congressman from Indiana, "They were theologically reconstructed through their unselfish devotion to humanity and the recreancy of the churches to which they had been attached. They were less orthodox, but more Christian." Giddings, who was raised in the same faith as the Tappans, could shiver nostalgically when he recalled his childhood faith, for he considered himself as having been emancipated from a fear-ridden cult. By 1856, he was predicting that slavery and other kinds of oppression and barbarism would be wrecked upon "the sterile coast of political and religious conservatism" and that a new world, free from corruption and outmoded superstitions, would emerge. For him, humanitarianism and Calvinism were irreconcilable, as they had been for the Garrisonians since 1837. In general, the ideas of what was sometimes called Free Religion were not formally institutionalized, partly in reaction to the formalism of the orthodox churches, but their popularity among intellectuals, in New England especially, was bound to affect the abolitionist leaders. Ironically, Lewis Tappan, leader of the traditional wing of the antislavery movement, had helped to engender the new spirit, for his own agitation for immediate and unconditional emancipation had been one of the causes of the weakening of the church system to which he was so faithful.

William Jay was particularly alarmed by the development of religious deviancy, writing his old friend Lewis Tappan, "Very many abolitionists are running headlong into infidelity & jacobinism; & thus absolutely exclude from all co-operation with them the sober-minded men. . . ." He was not complaining only about the Garrisonians. Though few abolitionists went so far as to deny the validity of institutional Christianity itself, the rebellion against Calvinism was reaching its climax.

Tappan's loyalty to church antislavery in a sense increased his own power with the rank-and-file abolitionists in the forties, although it cut him off from some former associates. A new generation of clerical abolitionists appeared in the 1850's— Henry Ward Beecher, George B. Cheever, and others—whose fame outdistanced his own as the spokesmen of ecclesiastical antislavery. The new group was rather distinct from the old abolitionists who had attended the Philadelphia Convention of 1833. Perhaps the character of a second generation of reformers or revolutionaries is always somewhat different from that of the first. In the antislavery movement, this later set did not have to face the degree of scorn and rough handling that had been the lot of Tappan and his associates. Perhaps because violence had impinged less directly upon them, they were generally less hesitant to advocate it—for righteous purposes to be sure. But to Beecher antislavery was less a commitment burned into the soul than a badge memorializing that conviction. Tappan and his friends had convinced the truehearted Yankee evangelical that antislavery was his birthright and the proper means of expressing his sectional identity. The new generation of church-minded reformers to carry forward the banner of antislavery acted mostly from force of habit and therefore felt the need of reassurance and recommitment, sometimes in calls to arms. Just as evangelicalism for Lewis Tappan was an emotional allegiance to but not an intellectual acceptance of the faith of his mother, so antislavery was becoming by the 1850's an expression of something imperfectly remembered but nostalgically moving. Antislavery was gradually being modified to fit the growing complacency of the reformers themselves. Antislavery success, though still modest, was breeding its own failure; abolitionists of the Cheever and Beecher stripe (and also the former Liberty men like Leavitt and Stanton) could be reasonably well satisfied with the Free Soil and Republican movements as the embodiments of the antislavery tradition. At the same time they were beginning to look upon Garrisonian disunion with a disapproval that time had somewhat tempered. The radical rhetoric had lost some of its novelty and thus some of its impact; they could even listen to the speeches and conversations of Garrison, dean of antislavery, with that respect and indulgence that is usually accorded chieftains past their prime and retired statesmen.

Lewis Tappan prepared the way for these new leaders; he tried to keep them true to the old doctrines of racial equality and immediate emancipation. But the lines of argument that he took in the 1840's to bring the evangelical movement to what seemed to him the right ground were developed by others in the following decade. Beecher, Cheever, and their kind did not urge a renewed effort to bring Negroes into white churches in fellowship; they did not add new ideas to those that Lewis Tappan helped to promulgate; principally, they repeated the antisouthern abolitionist arguments, with increasing effect, following along the paths that Lewis had laid out.

As early as 1834, the American Anti-Slavery Society had tried to convert the other benevolent societies to its position. Initial rebuffs, however, kept the Society from pursuing that aim with much vigor thereafter, and it concentrated upon building a hard core of antislavery followers. Once the evangelicals separated from Garrison, however, the attack against the so-called "benevolent empire" was renewed in earnest. Most conservative and powerful among these agencies was the American Board of Commissioners for Foreign Missions (the A.B.C.F.M.). In 1842, Lewis Tappan was writing colleagues that the Board ought to be investigated and exposed. What aroused his attention was the fact that its missionaries to the Cherokee and Choctaw tribes condoned slaveholding as well as polygamy. The Board defended the policy on the grounds that it was hard enough to win converts to Christianity without interfering in established customs. Antislavery sentiment grew, however, and the Board took a strongly antislavery position at its meeting in Brooklyn in 1845, though it left the missionaries in the field with discretionary powers. Tappan was pleased with this change, even if it was not up to the abolitionist mark. "We think," he wrote Sturge optimistically, "that when the 'American Board' gets right we shall have but little difficulty in persuading the people that Slavery is altogether disgraceful to church & state."

Three years passed without further developments in the Board's policies, and Tappan grew impatient. "Nothing will bring the A.B.C.F.M. to right action so soon as outspoken remonstrance, withholding of funds, and commendation of the A.M. Assoc.," he wrote a clerical supporter. Abolitionist agitation, which included the jabs of the Garrisonians, was constant against the Board throughout the 1850's. No less concerned than Tappan, William Jay published articles announcing that the pro-slavery agency winked at "atrocities unknown to the despotisms of Europe." It was wrong, the abolitionists declared, to misrepresent Christianity in this way by not preaching the sinfulness of enslaving fellow creatures. A clergyman at an antislavery gathering in Chicago in 1851 urged his audience thereafter to give its money to the American Missionary Association. The propaganda began to have its effect, as evangelicals transferred their allegiance in growing numbers to the A.M.A. Under these pressures, the Board endorsed some modestly liberal suggestions of its secretary Selah Treat in 1854 and denounced the Cherokee nation for not allowing Negro children the chance for education. Such a display was not enough to satisfy Tappan, but what irked him especially was that so slight a thaw encouraged the northern religious press, including the *Independent,* which represented Beecherite antislavery, to hail the Board for its courage and humanity. He protested vigorously and with telling effect.

The following year the A.B.C.F.M. elected General John Hartwell Cocke as one of its vice-presidents. Tappan was outraged. The general held over a thousand slaves, he reported, in gross exaggeration. Undoubtedly, Lewis was really trying to embarrass his brother John, who he knew had engineered the appointment for his friend. Appearing as a card in the New York *Tribune,* Tappan's attack on the Christian slaveholder aroused considerable agitation. Conservatives maintained that Lewis had gone too far. The publicity may have been a factor in the more liberal line adopted at the next A.B.C.F.M. convention, when a resolution inimical to slavery passed, much to Tappan's satisfaction.

The Board's responses to pressure from proslavery and antislavery forces were characteristically nerveless, and its ultimate decision was to abandon the Indian missions altogether. By 1861 all missionary stations in the Indian territories were closed, and the Board contented itself with maintaining a sulky neutrality on these moral issues. Tappan had won no commanding victory by the time war began, but he had awakened the conscience of many northern clergymen and laymen and gained their support for his own A.M.A.

The other benevolent societies were hardly less conservative than the A.B.C.F.M. The American Bible Society, for instance, had long been the target of the Tappan brothers, ever since the Tappans' 1834 campaign to supply Bibles for distribution to slaves. In 1851, William Jay examined the Society's records and discovered that the fund allocated for southern Negro efforts varied from $1,222.69 in 1848, when Joshua Leavitt had conducted a drive for that purpose, to an absurd $5.50 in 1851. Tappan and Jay wrote resolutions for the American and Foreign Anti-slavery Society conventions, published articles, and made other kinds of entreaties of the usual pattern, but the Bible Society, though embarrassed, refused to be coerced, insisting that its auxiliaries had full autonomy to treat the slave issue as they chose.

Other organizations also received the attention of the two antislavery partners. While Jay, for his part, protested the absence of antislavery materials in the American Tract Society catalogue, Tappan, for his, exposed the expurgations of unfriendly comments on slavery from the Sunday School Union publications. The publicity worried Francis Packard, secretary of the latter group, but no substantial change of policy resulted. Taking over from Judge Jay, who was seriously ill, Tappan spoke for over an hour before the Life Directors of the Tract Society in 1858, but his proposal that the Society publish a mild admonition to slaveholders on the treatment of slaves was soundly defeated.

Although primarily concerned with the conversion of the Congregational-Presbyterian denominations and the benevolent associations they led, Tappan did not spare any evangelicals who deviated from abolitionist principles. Generally, he could count on the support of British Dissenting churchmen. Though they sometimes failed to speak out against slavery when traveling in America, they usually aligned themselves with his branch of the cause when they were on safer soil. "We are strengthened by the sympathy and example of the abolitionists of Great Britain," he once wrote.

American Protestants rejoiced at the founding of the Scottish Free Kirk, led by Dr. Thomas Chalmers, in 1843. Not only was the Free Kirk a blow to the prestige of the Established Church of Scotland, but it constituted a powerful addition to the Calvinistic forces in both countries. Chalmers, however, solicited "bloodstained" money from Southern Presbyterians on a tour in 1844. In vain Tappan urged the Free Kirk representatives to avoid that sort of compromise. When Chalmers vigorously assailed his abolitionist critics, Tappan wrote Sturge that he was afraid that the churchman's defense "is to put down what we have been attempting for 10 years to build up. . . . It is administering an opiate to Northern proslavery ministers who have been placed in an awkward position by Anti-Slavery arguments & entreaties." Since Scotland was perhaps more thoroughly attuned to antislavery principles than other parts of the Kingdom, Chalmers' policy was a serious defeat for American abolitionists. Tappan urged his British friends "to bring public sentiment to bear" on the Free Kirk through the regular means of agitation. Meanwhile, the American and Foreign Anti-Slavery Society issued a strong "Remonstrance," which circulated widely as a pamphlet and in the religious press of both countries. Not surprisingly, Garrison also turned his guns on the Scottish sect and sent Frederick Douglass and James Buffum to join George Thompson on the rostrum against it in Great Britain. Later, he went over himself. The Garrisonians were as convinced as Tappan "that there is no power out of the Church that could maintain Slavery, if the Church attacked it in earnest." For all their contempt for each other's "bigotry" and "infidelity," both antislavery groups attached more importance to the reformation of the churches than to any other aspect of the cause.

So virulent was the abolitionists' reaction to the Chalmers' American tour that the Evangelical Alliance, formed to unite all evangelical elements in the United States and England against the threat of popery and other "heresies," was seriously weakened, though it continued to exist. Chalmers, the American Old School Presbyterian Robert Baird, who had once helped Arthur with his Mississippi Valley missionary campaign, and its other leaders could blame the rise of antislavery for their failure. Writing to John Scoble, then secretary of the British and Foreign Anti-Slavery Society, Tappan boasted that the Alliance stood "but little better here than the Colonization Society," which by this time had fallen on very evil days.

Tappan was always vigilant in insuring that his English friends did not accept every American clerical visitor at face value. Some years later, a member of the Alliance, Dr. Chickering of Maine, took a clear antislavery position while in England. When Tappan learned of it, he publicized the incident thoroughly, pointing out that moderate clergymen like Chickering seldom spoke out at home. "It is no libel on our great body of Northern clergy to say that, in regard to the wrongs of the colored people . . . their highest merit consists in [not] afflicting new injuries on their wounded brother." While a few Yankee pastors—"Cotton Parsons," they were called—such as Nehemiah ("Southside") Adams of Boston, defended slavery on humanitarian and Biblical grounds as if they had been southerners themselves, most Protestant ministers were sluggishly indifferent and timid. Tappan's unremitting efforts had the limited effect of pressing some of the national benevolent institutions into a defensive position, creating a new moral spirit in regard to slavery, particularly among the churchmen of the North, and frightening Southerners into an awareness of their growing isolation.

In the early 1850's, the evangelical movement, which had lain in the doldrums in the 1840's, regained impetus. After the split between the New and Old School Presbyterians in 1837, new leaders appeared to take the place of Lyman Beecher, Nathaniel Taylor, Finney, and the other figures of the first crusade. Though these men were still active, a new breed arose to preach much the same message, though adapting it to the task of evangelizing the cities. Included in this new group were such men as Albert Barnes, Edward N. Kirk, and Horace Bushnell.

In New York City, the younger generation was more powerful than it had been in the heyday of Arthur Tappan and Finney. George Barrell Cheever, Joseph P. Thompson, Richard S. Storrs, and Henry Ward Beecher held churches fully independent of the discipline of Old School Presbyterians like Gardiner Spring. They were liberal in theology, alive to reform issues, and less sectarian in approach than the Old School Presbyterians. While these four were all preachers of rare ability, Beecher outshone the rest. Like his father, Lyman, he was more politician than theologian, dressing his religion in the accepted styles of the middle-class churchgoer of the day. His power came not from doctrinal orthodoxy but from an easy manner and flamboyant flights of oratory. "Popularity," a contemporary remarked, "has clothed him with pomposity and egotism," leading him to a strenuous over-use "of the mighty 'I'! and 'Myself'!" Yet, even Lewis and Sarah Tappan were impressed enough to join his Brooklyn parish in 1856, "after long hesitation."

Brooklyn had grown from a little town across the river to a city of over two hundred thousand by 1855, third largest in the nation. It was known as a hotel and bedroom city, where "all the world comes to stay over night, to rise up early in the morning, to quarry its breakfast from a mountain of hash, and go on its way grumbling." Beecher's Plymouth Church, located strategically in the center of city life, became the spiritual capital of middle-class America. Henry C. Bowen, Tappan's son-in-law, not only had personally hired Beecher from Indianapolis but also had loaned the money (at some profit to himself) for the huge auditorium structure on prime Brooklyn Heights property. Arthur and Lewis Tappan had sent the senior Beecher west and been disappointed by his performance there; Bowen had brought his son East and also regretted the decision, though many years later. Tappan never fully trusted Beecher, but he welcomed his rising fame, admired his ability to raise thirteen thousand dollars for the pew rentals (Tappan had abandoned the free-church idea), enjoyed his company when they met in Lucy Maria's parlor, and served with him on several antislavery rostrums. Beecher strengthened the cause of antislavery Christianity, whenever popular Yankee opinion indicated that it was safe to do so.

Tappan liked George Barrell Cheever better, but his church was in New York and Tappan refused to cross the river by ferry on Sunday. More than once, Cheever had stirred up his congregation by preaching on the sinfulness of slaveholding without the equivocations that marked Beecher's statements (though Cheever's outbursts were not sustained long enough to have much permanent effect). Tappan urged Cheever to greater efforts for the cause. "I pray you," he wrote him in 1856, "to sound the gospel trumpet, on the walls of Zion [?], in thunder tones," since the voluntary associations "are doing more to undermine & bring into contempt the religion of Christ than the efforts of all the Infidels, sceptics & non-professors in the land." Although he sometimes backslid, Cheever complied this time by denouncing the American Tract Society, the A.B.C.F.M., and the others for their policy of silence. "In reference to this iniquity [of slavery]," he declared, "they hate him that speaketh at the gate, and they abhor him that speaketh uprightly."

The new evangelists were free of some of the quixoticism of their predecessors, but their methods of reaching the people by press and pulpit were identical. Cheever re-established and edited the New York *Evangelist*, and in 1848 Henry Bowen started the *Independent*, which dominated the religious press of the North with a circulation of thirty thousand by the end of 1856. According to Theodore Tilton, one of its youngest and ablest editors, its original purpose was twofold: to promote "the Congregational as against the Presbyterian Church polity" and "the freedom of the slave against the tyranny of his master." Though forceful in pursuing the former goal, it did not show the spirit Tappan would have liked to see on the latter. The trouble, he said, was that the journal, "though called an anti-slavery, is not an abolition paper."

Tappan did not blame the proprietors, for Henry Bowen, Seth Hunt, and Thomas McNamee were all loyal alumni of Arthur Tappan's school at 122 Pearl, and the publisher was Seth W. Benedict, who had long been one of the brothers' printers. Besides, the *Independent* was not always neutral about slavery. In 1850, an editorial on the Fugitive Slave Act went so far as to urge Christians to disobey it. When Samuel Chittenden, another merchant-member of this latter-day Association of Gentlemen, resigned in protest and pro-slavery merchants denounced the paper and its managers, Bowen and McNamee inserted a card in the New York *Herald* declaring that "our goods, not our principles, are on the market." Tappan was proud of their stand and their paper, on that occasion at least. For its neutrality at other times he blamed the editors—Richard S. Storrs, Leonard Bacon, and especially Joseph P. Thompson, pastor of the Broadway Tabernacle. Antislavery though these men were, they were closer to the Free Soil position than to abolitionism.

In 1854, Thompson denounced the A.M.A., claiming that it duplicated the work of the A.B.C.F.M. and was schismatic and radical. Calling the accusation "wholly unjustifiable," Tappan launched a vigorous barrage of explanations and exhortations. Soon the controversy spilled into all the major Congregational newspapers on both sides of the Atlantic. The *Independent* also criticized the Reform Book and Tract Society, which Tappan and the Rev. James Vincent of Cincinnati founded in 1852 to fill the gap left by the Tract Society. On that subject, however, Tappan was silent, perhaps because he had to admit privately that Vincent was indeed rather hotheaded.

On only one occasion did Tappan chastise Bowen himself, noting that the *Independent* too often boasted about its influence among the leading men of the age. "Refuting the charge of being abolitionist! Placing stress on the fact that distinguished men, instead of God and Truth, are on the side of the paper! . . . I feel ashamed. . . ." He was uneasy about the materialism and irreligious behavior of these evangelicals as well as their circumspect, casual attitude toward reform. "My heart has ached at the supineness, man-worship, and expediency-policy of the ministry," he wrote Richard Storrs, another editor and clergyman.

In spite of these failures to win over the *Independent* and the leading clergy of New York City and Brooklyn to his abolitionist position, Tappan hoped that many Christians were at last awakened to the issue. Time and unceasing agitation would eventually bring them to right ground. The most optimistic sign was the development of an antislavery Congregational church. In 1852, Lewis attended the Maine Religious Convention, where speakers called for the organization of abolitionist Christians. There had been many such conferences before, but this conclave, coupled with similar gatherings in Ohio, led to another and larger affair at Albany the following October. Joshua Leavitt, Seth Gates (the old antislavery Congressman from western New York), Henry Bowen, George Cheever, Richard Storrs, Joel Hawes, Henry Ward and Lyman Beecher, Absolom Peters of the American Home Missionary Society, and Lewis Tappan were among the leading delegates. The chief business at hand, aside from dealing with slavery in the churches, was to strengthen Congregationalism outside New England. Bitter complaints were heard about the treatment of Congregational and New School Presbyterian missionaries in the West. Old School Presbyterians, still distrustful of Finney, Lyman Beecher, and Taylor, quizzed their missionaries unmercifully, threatened them with heresy trials, and sometimes actually brought them before ecclesiastical tribunals. Denouncing the Plan of Union, which forbade Congregational expansion, one delegate declared that Presbyterians "have often come from the West to our New England, and ranged over our fat pastures, and borne away the fleece from our flocks; they have milked our Congregational cows, but they have made nothing but Presbyterian butter and cheese."

Shortly after this debate, Henry Bowen rose to announce that his silk house would offer ten thousand dollars toward a drive for forty thousand in matching funds to support western missions. The proposal had as electrifying an effect as Arthur Tappan's offer to support the Mississippi Valley campaign of 1830. No longer was the barbarism of the frontier the issue, but the aim was basically the same—the extension of New England religion into the West. "Silks, feathers and piety" had combined once more to leave Presbyterian conservatism behind in a great effort to evangelize the New England way. By the terminal date of the drive, the fund was oversubscribed.

Unlike Arthur Tappan's original crusade, this one included antislavery as a chief goal. The convention endorsed the proposition that slavery was an individual as well as a social sin. Unless this line was adopted, Jonathan Blanchard of Illinois predicted that the western churches "would wheel off." The proslavery Home Missionary Society, which operated fifty missions in the South, was in danger of losing its Congregational support unless it adopted the same position on individual responsibility. When Peters, the Society's secretary, sought to prevent that loss, Leonard Bacon, formerly a colonizationist and a critic of the Tappans' measures, made it clear that he would not be disturbed if the A.M.A. replaced the older group entirely. When such men as Leonard Bacon could speak favorably of antislavery measures and organizations, there had indeed been a rather serious shift in Yankee opinion about the antislavery cause. Tappan had every reason to suspect that many of the delegates to the convention were adopting liberal positions simply to be abreast of the times or for reasons of political convenience. If he entertained such doubts, he kept them to himself and did not apparently take much part in these proceedings on the floor. He was pleased, however, with the debate about the Home Missionary Society. Later, he said, "It was no part of the design of the Convention to *dictate* to the Home Missionary Society [but] to inform . . . the public respecting the views" of Congregationalists on the slave issue. But the A.H.M.S. did not surrender to the demands.

Even though the *Independent* continued to be indifferent to the issues raised by the A.M.A., Congregationalists gradually left the A.H.M.S. Its treasury became depleted, and the rival group gained ground. Throughout the 1850's, the warfare between the Presbyterians and the Congregational missionaries continued. One A.M.A. agent reported, "Sectarian Presbyterians are very much afraid of Anti-Slavery preaching, & unite with. . . the lager beer, & whiskey drinkers [to drive] *political* preachers from their schoolhouse." Gradually, the A.M.A. lost its ecumenicism and took on something of the character of an institutional element of the Congregational church.

Tappan considered Congregational expansion a fulfillment of a quarter-century dream—the creation of a denomination dedicated to Christian reform. The old benevolent societies had not lived up to his expectations, but he was gratified that the church of his fathers was proving to be an effective alternative for the encouragement of antislavery beliefs among Yankee Christians. Yet he realized that even the Congregational church was too often timid and its spokesmen too preoccupied with pew sales and too little concerned with principles. In some ways, Lewis was not very far from Garrison's "come-outer" position. Even before the Albany meeting, he had written a Cincinnati convention of antislavery Christians, "We ought not to continue in Church relations where we cannot have freedom of speech and action in regard to . . . Slavery." Tappan continued to work alone with his Bible and mission classes for Negro children; he seldom had much support from his antislavery pastors. Despite the shortcomings that Tappan recognized in the churches, he wished not to disband "the divinely appointed institutions and instrumentalities of Christianity" but to save them from "disgrace" and to put them into a right relationship with God and man. Those who, like Giddings and Garrison, followed the path toward a secular humanitarianism despaired that the American church would ever accept the racial challenge. Lewis Tappan, on the other hand, believed that his son-in-law Henry Bowen, Beecher, Cheever, and other members of the new generation of reform-minded, practical men of affairs might succeed in making the Congregational church the vehicle of millennial reform that Lewis and Arthur had for so long tried to create.

Questions for Reflection and Discussion

1. How do the documents in this chapter reveal gaps between beliefs and behaviors, and between inclusion and exclusion in religion's struggle over the issue of slavery?

2. Describe the distinction Albert Raboteau makes between the visible, institutional religion of slaves and their invisible, noninstitutional religion.

3. Discuss the methods used by evangelical church leaders in their efforts to eliminate slavery, as noted by Bertram Wyatt-Brown.

4. How did American religion deal with the conflict produced by slavery? Was consensus possible?

Additional Readings

Barnes, Gilbert H. *The Anti-Slavery Impulse, 1830-1844.* New York: Harper and Row, 1933.

Carwardine, Richard. *Evangelicals and Politics in Antebellum America.* New Haven: Yale University Press, 1993.

Cole, Charles C. *The Social Ideas of the Northwestern Evangelists, 1826-1860.* New York: Columbia University Press, 1954.

Davis, Cyprian. *The History of Black Catholics in the United States.* New York: Crossroad, 1990.

Foster, Charles I. *An Errand of Mercy: The Evangelical Front, 1790-1837.* Chapel Hill: University of North Carolina, 1960.

Goen. C. C. *Broken Churches, Broken Nation: Denominational Schisms and the Coming of the Civil War.* Macon, GA: Mercer University Press, 1985.

Griffin, Clifford S. "Religious Benevolence as Social Control, 1815-1860." In *Ante-Bellum Reform,* ed. David Brion Davis, pp. 81-96. New York: Harper and Row, 1967.

Howe, Daniel Walker. "Religion and Politics in the Antebellum North." In *Religion and American Politics,* ed. Mark A. Noll, pp. 121-145. New York: Oxford University Press, 1990.

Johnson, Curtis D. *Redeeming America: Evangelicals and the Road to the Civil War.* Chicago: Ivan R. Dee, 1993.

Lesick, Lawrence. *The Lane Rebels: Evangelicalism and Abolitionism in Antebellum America.* Lanham, MD: Scarecrow Press, 1980.

McInerney, Daniel J. "'A Faith for Freedom': The Gospel of Abolition." *Journal of the Early Republic* 11 (Fall 1991): 371-393.

McKivigan, John, and Mitchell Snay, eds. *Religion and the Antebellum Debate over Slavery.* Athens: University of Georgia Press, 1998.

Smith, Timothy L. *Revivalism and Social Reform: American Protestantism on the Eve of the Civil War.* Nashville: Abingdon Press, 1957.

Swift, David E. *Black Prophets of Justice: Activist Clergy Before the Civil War.* Baton Rouge: Louisiana State University Press, 1989.

Yee, Shirley. *Black Women Abolitionists: A Study in Activism, 1828-1860.* Knoxville: University of Tennessee Press, 1992.

Chapter 8

Religion and America's Civil War

Issue

How did religion impact the Civil War?

It was as though God were "dressed in gray" in 1861 when Episcopalian bishop Leonidas Polk of Louisiana set aside his churchly duties and entered the Confederate army as a major-general. Writing to a fellow bishop to explain his action, Polk contended: "I believe most solemnly that it is for constitutional liberty, which seems to have fled to us [Southerners, especially churchmen] for refuge, for our hearth-stones, and our altars that we strike. I hope I shall be supported in the work and have grace to do my duty."

About the same time, though hundreds of miles to the north, another Episcopalian bishop, Thomas Clark of Newport, Rhode Island, addressed a farewell service for state militia as they left for war. For Clark it was as though God were "dressed in blue" when he stated: "Your country has called for your service and you are ready. It is a holy and righteous cause in which you enlist. . . . God is with us; . . . the Lord of hosts is on our side." He concluded his comments with prayer, asking for divine protection for the soldiers "now going forth to aid in saving our land from the ravages of sedition, conspiracy, and rebellion."

And so it was—though built on a consensus of religious tradition and symbolism, the religious community nevertheless in conflict over how to put into practice beliefs held in common. For decades prior to the war, through years following its conclusion, both the North and South believed they were in the right and had God's approval. As President Abraham Lincoln stated in his Second Inaugural Address in 1865, "Both [sides] read the same Bible, and pray to the same God."

The religious impact on the Civil War was aptly summarized years ago by religious historian William Warren Sweet when he stated: "There are good arguments to support the claim that the split in the churches was not only the first break between the sections, but the chief cause of the final break." Religious rhetoric claimed divine support for the direction each side took before, during, and for decades after the war. From politician to soldier to chaplain, a "divine logic" convinced many Americans that God would "make their paths straight." How might the conviction held by both sides that "God is on our side" have affected the plotting of military strategy by political and military leaders? Could it be argued that the religious rhetoric claiming divine support actually lengthened the war? How did the "divine logic" affect the sides' interpretation of the military outcome of the war?

Documents

Many voices from both sides expressed a wide range of thoughts grounded in religion during the several decades of the Civil War era. The documents reprinted here represent some of these compelling thoughts. In the first selection, Abraham Lincoln, a profoundly religious man though not a formal churchman, expresses his moral uneasiness in 1855 over the devastation of "bleeding Kansas" in the aftermath of the adoption of the Kansas-Nebraska Law the year before. The second and third documents are Southern voices heard during the war. In the second, a convention of confederate ministers assembled at Richmond, Virginia, in April 1863 launched a verbal barrage against the North in which they describe the internecine struggle as a "holy war." A year and a half later, as told in the third document, President Jefferson Davis invoked God's aid on behalf of the South with his Proclamation of October 26, 1864, calling for a Day of Prayer.

Six weeks before his death, and less than five weeks before the end of the war, President Lincoln delivered his Second Inaugural Address, which is the fourth selection that follows. In the third paragraph of the speech he states his interpretation of God's purposes in the war. Near the conclusion of the war, and on the anniversary of the fall of Fort Sumter, the Union government invited Henry Ward Beecher, one of America's most influential preachers of the nineteenth century, to deliver an address at Charleston, South Carolina. In the fifth document, he identifies seven "benefits" of the war that accrued to the South, some of which soon turned into obstacles on the path to national reconstruction. The final selection is an 1867 account by Baptist chaplain Reverend John J. D. Renfroe of the 1863-1864 religious revivals in the 19th Alabama Regiment.

1. Abraham Lincoln's Letter to Joshua F. Speed, 1855

SOURCE: J. G. Nicolay and John Hay, eds., *Complete Works of Abraham Lincoln* (New York: Lamb Publishing Co., 1905), II, 281-87.

SPRINGFIELD AUGUST 24, 1855.

Dear Speed: You know what a poor correspondent I am. Ever since I received your very agreeable letter of the 22d of May I have been intending to write you an answer to it. You suggest that in political action, now, you and I would differ. I suppose we would; not quite as much, however, as you may think. You know I dislike slavery, and you fully admit the abstract wrong of it. So far there is no cause of difference. But you say that sooner than yield your legal right to the slave, especially at the bidding of those who are not themselves interested, you would see the Union dissolved. I am not aware that any one is bidding you yield that right; very certainly I am not. I leave that matter entirely to yourself. I also acknowledge your rights in my obligations under the Constitution in regard to your slaves. I confess I hate to see the poor creatures hunted down and caught and carried back to their stripes and unrequited toil; but I bite my lips and keep quiet. In 1841 you and I had together a tedious low-water trip on a steamboat from Louisville to St. Louis. You may remember, as I well do, that from Louisville to the mouth of the Ohio there were on board ten or a dozen slaves shackled together with irons. That sight was a continued torment to me, and I see something like it every time I touch the Ohio or any other slave border. . . .

. . . You say that if Kansas fairly votes herself a free State, as a Christian you will rejoice at it. All decent slaveholders talk that way, and I do not doubt their candor. But they never vote that way. Although in a private letter or conversation you will express your preference that Kansas shall be free, you would vote for no man for Congress who would say the same thing publicly. No such man could be elected from any district in a slave State. You think Stringfellow and company ought to be hung; and yet at the next presidential election you will vote for the exact type and representative of Stringfellow. The slave-breeders and slave-traders are a small, odious, and detested class among you; and yet in politics they dictate the course of all of you, and are as completely your masters as you are the master of your own negroes. You inquire where I now stand. That is a disputed point. I think I am a Whig; but others say there are no Whigs, and that I am an Abolitionist. When I was at Washington, I voted for the Wilmot proviso as good as forty times; and I never heard of any one attempting to unwhig me for that. I now do no more than oppose the expansion of slavery. I am not a Know-nothing; that is certain. How could I be? How can any one who abhors the oppression of negroes be in favor of degrading classes of white people? Our progress in degeneracy appears to me to be pretty rapid. As a nation we began by declaring that "all men are created equal." We now practically read it "all men are created equal, except negroes." When the Know-nothings get control, it will read "all men are created equal, except negroes and foreigners and Catholics." When it comes to this, I shall prefer emigrating to some country where they make no pretense of loving liberty, —to Russia, for instance, where despotism can be taken pure, and without the base alloy of hypocrisy.

2. An Address to Christians Throughout the World, 1863

SOURCE: Speech delivered to convention of Confederate ministers at Richmond, Virginia, in April 1863.

The Christians of the South, we claim, are pious, intelligent and liberal. Their pastoral and missionary works have points of peculiar interest. There are hundreds of thousands here, both white and colored, who are not strangers to the blood that bought them. We rejoice that the great Head of the Church has not despised us. We desire, as much as in us lieth, to live peaceably with all men, and though reviled, to revile not again.

Much harm has been done to the religious enterprises of the Church by the war; we will not tire you by enumerating particulars. We thank God for the patient faith and fortitude of our people during these days of trial.

Our soldiers were before the war our fellow citizens, and many of them are of the household of faith, who have carried to the camp so much of the leaven of Christianity, that amid all the demoralizing influence of army life, the good work of salvation has gone forward there.

Our President, some of our most influential statesmen, our commanding General, and an unusual proportion of the principal Generals, as well as scores of other officers, are prominent and we believe consistent members of the Church. Thousands of our soldiers are men of prayer. We regard our success in the war as due to divine mercy, and our government and people have recognized the hand of God in the normal and humble celebration of his goodness. We have no fear in regard to the future. If the war continues for years, we believe God's grace sufficient for us.

In conclusion, we ask for ourselves, our churches, our country, the devout prayers of all God's people—"the will of the Lord be done."

Christian brethren, think on these things and let your answer to our address be the voice of an enlightened Christian sentiment going forth from you against war, against persecution for conscience' sake, against the ravaging of the Church of God by fanatical invasion. But if we speak to you in vain, nevertheless we have not spoken in vain in the sight of God: for we have proclaimed the truth—we have testified in behalf of Christian civilization—we have invoked charity—we have filed our solemn protest against a cruel and useless war. And our children shall read it and honor our spirit, though in much feebleness we may have borne our testimony.

"Charity beareth all things, believeth all things, hopeth all things, endureth all things." We desire to "follow after charity"; and "as many as walk according to this rule, peace be on them and mercy, and upon the Israel of God."

3. President Davis Seeks God's Aid and Mercy, October 1864

SOURCE: Reprinted in Michael Perman, ed., *Major Problems in the Civil War and Reconstruction* (Lexington, MA: D. C. Heath and Company, 1991), 210-11.

A Proclamation

It is meet that the people of the Confederate States should, from time to time, assemble to acknowledge their dependence on Almighty God, to render devout thanks to his holy name, to bend in prayer at his footstool, and to accept, with fervent submission, the chastening of his all-wise and all-merciful providence.

Let us, then, in temples and in the field, unite our voices in recognizing, with adoring gratitude, the manifestations of his protecting care in the many signal victories with which our arms have been crowned; in the fruitfulness with which our land has been blessed, and in the unimpaired energy and fortitude with which he has inspired our hearts and strengthened our arms in resistance to the iniquitous designs of our enemies.

And let us not forget that, while graciously vouchsafing to us his protection, our sins have merited and received grievous chastisement; that many of our best and bravest have fallen in battle; that many others are still held in foreign prisons; that large districts of our country have been devastated with savage ferocity, the peaceful homes destroyed, and helpless women and children driven away in destitution; and that with fiendish malignity the passions of a servile race have been excited by our foes into the commission of atrocities from which death is a welcome escape.

Now, therefore, I, Jefferson Davis, President of the Confederate States of America, do issue this my proclamation, setting apart Wednesday, the 16th day of November next, as a day to be specially devoted to the worship of Almighty God; and I do invite and invoke all the people of these Confederate States to assemble on the day aforesaid, in their respective places of public worship, there to unite in prayer to our Heavenly Father that he bestow his favor upon us; that he extend over us the protection of his almighty arm; that he sanctify his chastisement to our improvement, so that we may turn away from evil paths and walk righteously in his sight and that he may restore peace to our beloved country, healing its bleeding wounds, and securing to us the continued enjoyment of our own right to self-government and independence, and that he will graciously hearken to us while we ascribe to him the power and glory of our independence.

Given under my hand and the seal of the Confederate States at Richmond, this 26th day of October, in the year of our Lord 1864.

Jefferson Davis.

By the President:
J.P. Benjamin, *Secretary of State.*

4. Abraham Lincoln's Second Inaugural Address, 1865

SOURCE: J. G. Nicolay and John Hay, eds., *Complete Works of Abraham Lincoln* (New York: Lamb Publishing Co., 1905), XI, 45-47.

Fellow Countrymen:

At this second appearing to take the oath of the presidential office, there is less occasion for an extended address than there was at the first. Then a statement, somewhat in detail, of a course to be pursued, seemed fitting and proper. Now, at the expiration of four years, during which public declarations have been constantly called forth on every point and phase of the great contest which still absorbs the attention, and engrosses the energies of the nation, little that is new could be presented. The progress of our arms, upon which all else chiefly depends, is as well known to the public as to myself; and it is, I trust, reasonably satisfactory and encouraging to all. With high hope for the future, no predication in regard to it is ventured.

On the occasion corresponding to this four years ago, all thoughts were anxiously directed to an impending civil-war. All dreaded it—all sought to avert it. While the inaugural address was being delivered from this place, devoted altogether to *saving* the Union without war, insurgent agents were in the city seeking to *destroy* it without war—seeking to dissolve the Union, and divide effects, by negotiation. Both parties deprecated war; but one of them would *make* war rather than let the nation survive; and the other would *accept* war rather than let it perish. And the war came.

One-eighth of the whole population were colored slaves, not distributed generally over the Union, but localized in the Southern part of it. These slaves constituted a peculiar and powerful interest. All knew that this interest was, somehow, the cause of the war. To strengthen, perpetuate, and extend this interest was the object for which the insurgents would rend the Union, even by war; while the government claimed no right to do more than to restrict the territorial enlargement of it. Neither party expected for the war, the magnitude, or the duration, which it has already attained. Neither anticipated that the *cause* of the conflict might cease with, or even before, the conflict itself should cease. Each looked for an easier triumph, and a result less fundamental and astounding. Both read the same Bible, and pray to the same God; and each invokes His aid against the other. It may seem strange that any men should dare to ask a just God's assistance in wringing their bread from the sweat of other men's faces; but let us judge not that we be not judged. The prayers of both could not be answered; that of neither has been answered fully. The Almighty has His own purposes. "Woe unto the world because of offences! for it must needs be that offences come; but woe to that man by whom the offence cometh!" If we shall suppose that American Slavery is one of those offences which, in the providence of God, must needs come, but which, having continued through His appointed time, He now wills to remove, and that He gives to both North and South, this terrible war, as the woe due to those by whom the offence came, shall we discern therein any departure from those divine attributes which the believers in a Living God always ascribe to Him, Fondly do we hope—fervently do we pray—that this mighty scourge of war may speedily pass away. Yet, if God will that it continue, until all the wealth piled by the bond-men's two hundred and fifty years of unrequited toil shall be sunk, and until every drop of blood drawn with the lash, shall be paid by another drawn with the sword, as was said three thousand years ago, so still it must be said "the judgements of the Lord, are true and righteous altogether."

With malice toward none; with charity for all; with firmness in the right, as God gives us to see the right, let us strive on to finish the work we are in; to bind up the nation's wounds; to care for him who shall have borne the battle, and for his widow, and his orphan—to do all which may achieve and cherish a just, and a lasting peace, among ourselves, and with all nations.

5. Address at the Raising of the Flag over Fort Sumter, 1865

SOURCE: *Patriotic Addresses in America and England, from 1850-1855* (New York: Ford, Howard, and Hulbert, 1891), 676-97.

. . . I now pass to the considerations of benefits that accrue to the South in distinc-tion from the rest of the nation. At present the South reaps only suffering, but good seed lies buried under the furrows of war, that peace will bring to harvest.

1.   Deadly doctrines have been purged away in blood. The subtle poison of secession was a perpetual threat of revolution. The sword has ended that danger. That which reason has affirmed as a philo-sophy, the people have settled as a fact. Theory pronounces, "There can be no permanent government where each integral particle has liberty to fly, off." Who would venture upon a voyage on a ship, each plank and timber of which might withdraw at its pleasure? But the people have reasoned by the logic of the sword and of the ballot, and they have declared that States are inseparable parts of national government. They are not sovereign. State *rights* remain; but *sovereignty* is a right higher than all others; and that has been made into a common stock for the benefit of all. All further agitation is ended. This element must be cast out of our political problems. Henceforth that poison will not rankle in the blood.

2.   Another thing has been learned: the rights and duties of minorities. The people of the whole nation are of more authority than the people of any section. These United States are supreme over Northern, Eastern, Western, and Southern States. It ought not to have required the awful chastisement of this war to teach that a minority must submit the control of the nation's government to a majority. The army and the navy have been good political schoolmasters. The lesson is learned. Not for many generations will it require further illustration.

3.   No other lesson will be more fruitful of peace than the dispersion of those conceits of vanity, which, on either side, have clouded the recognition of the manly courage of all Americans. If it be a sign of manhood to be able to fight, then Americans are men. The North certainly are in no doubt whatever of the soldierly qualities of Southern men. Southern soldiers have learned that all latitudes breed

courage on this continent. Courage is a passport to respect. The people of all the regions of this nation are likely hereafter to cherish generous admiration of each other's prowess. The war has bred respect, and respect will breed affection, and affection peace and unity.

4.   No other event of the war can fill an intelligent Southern man of candid nature with more surprise than the revelation of the capacity, moral and military, of the black race. It is a revelation, indeed. No people were ever less understood by those most familiar with them. They were said to be lazy, lying, impudent, and cowardly wretches, driven by the whip alone to the tasks needful to their own support, and the functions of civilization. They were said to be dangerous, blood-thirsty, liable to insurrection; but four years of tumultuous distress and war have rolled across the area inhabited by them, and I have yet to hear of one authentic instance of the misconduct of a colored man. They have been patient and gentle and docile in the land, while the men of the South were away in the army, they have been full of faith and hope and piety; and when summoned to freedom they have emerged with all the signs and tokens that freedom will be to them what it was to be—the swaddling band that shall bring them to manhood. And after the Government, honoring them as men, summoned them to the field, when once they were disciplined and had learned the art of war, they proved themselves to be not second to their white brethren in arms. And when the roll of men that have shed their blood is called in the other land, many and many dusky face will rise, dark no more, when the light of eternal glory shall shine upon it from the throne of God.

5.   The industry of the Southern States is regenerated and now rests upon a basis that never fails to bring prosperity. Just now industry is collapsed; but it is not dead. It sleepeth. It is vital yet. It will spring like mown grass from the roots, that need but showers and heat and time to bring them forth. Though in many districts not a generation will see wanton wastes of self-invoked war repaired, and many portions may lapse again to wilderness; yet, in our life-time we shall see States, as a whole, raised to a prosperity, vital, wholesome and immovable.

6.   The destruction of class interests, working with a religion which tends towards true democracy in proportion as it is pure and free, will create a new era of prosperity for the common laboring people of the South. Upon them has come the labor, the toil, and the loss of this war. They have fought for a class that sought their degradation, while they were made to believe that it was for their own homes and altars. Their leaders meant a supremacy which would not long have left them political liberty, save in name. But their leaders are swept away. The sword has been hungry for the ruling classes. It has sought them out with remorseless zeal. New men are to rise up; new ideas are to bud and blossom; and there will be men with different ambition and altered policy.

7.   Meanwhile, the South, no longer a land of plantations, but of farms; no longer tilled by slaves, but by freemen, will find no hindrance to the spread of education. Schools will multiply. Books and papers will spread. Churches will bless every hamlet. There is a good day coming for the South. Through darkness and

tears, and blood she has sought it. It has been an unconscious *Via Dolorosa*. But, in the end, it will be worth all it has cost. Her institutions before were deadly. She nourished death in her bosom. The greater her secular prosperity, the more sure was her ruin. Every year of delay but made the change more terrible. Now, by an earthquake, the evil is shaken down. Her own historians, in a better day, shall write that from the day the sword cut off the cancer she began to find her health.

What, then, shall hinder the rebuilding of this republic? The evil spirit is cast out: why should not this nation cease to wander among tombs, cutting itself? Why should it not come, clothed in its right mind, to "sit at the feet of Jesus?" Is it feared that the Government will oppress the conquered States? What possible motive has the Government to narrow the base of that pyramid on which its own permanence stands? . . .

From this pulpit of broken stone we speak forth our earnest greeting to all our land.

We offer to the President of these United States our solemn congratulations that God has sustained his life and health under the unparalleled burdens and sufferings of four bloody years, and permitted him to behold this auspicious consummation of that national unity for which he has waited with so much patience and fortitude, and for which he has labored with such disinterested wisdom.

To the members of the Government associated with him in the administration of perilous affairs in critical times: to the Senators and Representatives of the United States who have eagerly fashioned the instruments by which the popular will might express and enforce itself, we tender our grateful thanks.

To the officers and men of the army and navy, who have so faithfully, skillfully, and gloriously upheld their country's authority, by suffering, labor, and sublime courage, we offer here a tribute beyond the compass of words.

Upon those true and faithful citizens, men and women, who have borne up with unflinching hope in the darkest hour, and covered the land with the labors of love and charity, we invoke the divinest blessing of Him whom they have so truly imitated.

But chiefly to Thee, God of our fathers, we render thanksgiving and praise for that wondrous providence that has brought forth, from such a harvest of war, the seed of so much liberty and peace.

We invoke peace upon the North. Peace be to the West. Peace be upon the South!

In the name of God, we lift up our banner, and dedicate it to Peace, Union, and Liberty, now and forevermore. Amen.

6. A Confederate Chaplain Recounts His Experience of the Revivals (1863-1864), January 1867

SOURCE: Reprinted in Michael Perman, ed., *Major Problems in the Civil War and Reconstruction* (Lexington, MA: D. C. Heath and Company, 1991), excerpted from pp. 211-15.

Dear Brother Jones: In attempting to give you some account of the religious character of Wilcox's old brigade, in the army of Northern Virginia, I find that I am entirely dependent upon my memory. I loaned my "notes" of events to a brother, who now informs me that he cannot lay his hand on them, having mislaid them.

The Tenth Alabama was the regiment of which I was chaplain. The brigade was composed of the Eighth, Ninth, Tenth, Eleventh and Fourteenth Alabama Regiments. I reckon this brigade comprised as noble a body of men as ever served in any army. I reached my post of duty while the army was in winter-quarters at Fredericksburg, in the early part of the year 1863. There were then three other chaplains in that brigade, but they were all then absent but one. Very little preaching had been done in the brigade up to that time. Many Christian soldiers and other good-disposed men told me that I could do no good in preaching to soldiers, but all seemed glad to welcome me among them. I was acquainted with a large number of the regiment before the war. The first Sabbath after I got there I preached twice, and from that time until I left them, I had a large attendance upon worship, and as good order in my congregations as I ever had at home. About that time the Rev. Mr. Bell, of Greenville, Alabama, visited the Eighth, which had no chaplain. He and I preached daily for two weeks. He baptized a Mr. Lee, of Marion, Alabama, the first profession that I saw in the army; though there were many men in the brigade who were Christians before they went to the army, and who maintained their religion. The chaplains of the brigade soon returned. We built arbors, and preached regularly to large and attentive congregations—on through the spring this continued—only interrupted by the battle of Chancellorsville. Then came the campaign to Gettysburg. I preached thirteen sermons on that campaign, but not more than half of them to our own brigade. I preached several sermons in line of battle. After we returned to the south side of the Potomac, at Bunker's Hill, we had several sermons in the brigade. Two of the chaplains (Mr. Rains, of the Fourteenth, and Mr. Whitten, of the Ninth) remained at Gettysburg with the wounded. Up to this time I saw but few signs of the good work—I saw no evidences of revival—I heard of no conversions in our brigade. Then we fell back to Orange Court House. There we at once established arbors—one in the Fourteenth, one in the Tenth, and began to preach. Rev. Mr. Johnson, chaplain of the Eleventh, and Mr. Cumbie, Lieutenant in the Fourteenth, did the preaching at the Fourteenth's preaching place. Their labors were blessed, and many were converted. At the preaching place of the Tenth I did the preaching for the most part. This lasted for about six weeks, in which time I was visited and aided by Rev. A. E. Dickinson, of Richmond, who preached for me a week; then by Rev. J.B.F. Mays, of Alabama, who preached nearly a week for me. God greatly blessed our efforts. I have stood at that place at night and on Sabbaths and preached, as it seemed to me, to a solid acre of men. I think I have seen as many as five or six hundred men, in one way and another, manifest at one time a desire to be prayed for. I have never seen such a time before or since. There were as many evidences of genuine penitence as I ever noticed at home—yes, more. Almost every day there would be a dozen conversions, and there were in the six weeks in the brigade, not less than five hundred who professed conversion. Not all of our brigade, for there was a battalion of artillery camped near us, and other brigades, who attended our preaching, many of whom professed religion. We estimated the conversions then at five hundred and fifty. I baptized about one hundred, Brother Cumbie about fifty, and most of the others joined the Methodist. This work, as you know, prevailed nearly all through the army. But it was partially interrupted by the fall campaign, when we drove Meade back to Bull Run. But the army returned from the campaign to Orange, went into winter-quarters and spent the winter there. Part of this winter I was at home on furlough. But prayer-meetings, Bible-classes and preaching were successfully kept up through the winter. And the revival also, in a less degree, continued. The Young Men's Christian Association was largely attended, many went to exhorting, and a great many prayed in public. Some of whom were greatly gifted. A most interesting feature was the large number who would retire after the evening "roll-call" in groups, to pray. Walk out from camp at that hour in any direction and you would find them, two, three, half-dozen and a dozen, in a place, all bowed in the dark, earnestly praying for themselves and the conversion of their comrades; they nearly always took some unconverted ones with them.

Through the awful campaign of 1864 there were very limited opportunities to preach to this brigade. It was almost constantly under fire or on the march. From the Wilderness to Petersburg and around Petersburg, this was the case. Though I preached to them as often as I could, yet most of my preaching was to other commands. I have several times preached when shot and shell were flying over our heads, and also several times I had minnie-balls to strike my congregation while preaching. We often had prayer-meetings in the trenches, where God did greatly bless and comfort our hearts. In the winter-quarters at Petersburg there was much faithful preaching, and regular prayer-meeting kept up in this brigade. . . .

Brother Jones, I am aware that this letter is a very poor and indifferent account of the religious standing of my old brigade. Maybe, however, that you can get something out of it. I baptized about two hundred while I was in the army, two years, but nearly half of them were men of other brigades than my own, and converted under the ministry of other men. The Lord bless you in your good work,

Yours fraternally,

J.J.D. Renfroe

Essays

The three essays reprinted here examine the reciprocal relationship between religion and the American Civil War. The first, by Mitchell Snay of Denison University, shows how at some times the symbiotic relationship between religious and political discourse in the antebellum South consisted of the adapting of ideas and rhetoric from religion to politics, while at other times the interplay between Southern religion and politics resulted in their convergence and mutual reinforcement. The second essay is by James H. Moorhead of North Carolina State University, who demonstrates the interaction of the churches' millennial perspective with the issues of nationalism, slavery, dissent, and postwar crisis of faith. Finally, Drew Gilpin Faust of the University of Pennsylvania discusses the spiritual life of the Confederate soldier and the religious revivals in the Army of Northern Virginia.

Religion, the Origins of Southern Nationalism, and the Coming of the Civil War
MITCHELL SNAY

SOURCE: From *Gospel in Disunion: Religion and Separatism in the Antebellum South* by Mitchell Snay. Copyright © Cambridge University Press 1993. Reprinted with the permission of Cambridge University Press.

The men who helped inaugurate Jefferson Davis as the first president of the Confederacy in February 1861 personified the different ways Southerners came to secession. First and foremost were the politicians. Those who assembled in Montgomery represented the various political paths that converged on the road to disunion. William L. Yancey, who had introduced Davis to a welcoming throng the night before, was a radical fire-eater as was the South Carolinian Robert Barnwell Rhett, who escorted the new Confederate president up the steps of the capitol. Davis himself, though not as radial as Yancey or Rhett, was a staunch defender of Southern rights. Two Georgians represented a more moderate and halting approach to disunion. Howell Cobb, who administered the oath of office to Davis, was a late convert to Southern nationalism. A supporter of the Union party in the early 1850s, Cobb had but recently joined the Georgia secessionists. Alexander Stephens, the first and only vice-president of the Confederacy, was a former Whig who only a few months before had opposed separate state secession.

The Rev. Basil Manly represented another course that led down the road to disunion. His presence and prayer at the inauguration of Jefferson Davis symbolically recognized the role that religion played in preparing Southerners for separate nationhood. Beginning in the early 1830s, religious discourse and institutions strengthened the sectionalization of Southern culture and politics. Religion invested the sectional controversy over slavery with moral and religious significance, reinforced important elements in Southern political culture, and fostered a sense of separate sectional identity among Southerners.

The inauguration of Jefferson Davis crowned the antebellum drive toward Southern nationalism. By placing the clergy at the birth of the Confederacy, it points to the larger historical issues raised in this book: the role of Southern religion in the origins of Southern nationalism and the coming of the Civil War. At first glance, the essentially political nature of the antebellum sectional controversy discourages such an inquiry. Explanations about why the war happened have traditionally focused on politics. The major sectional incidents of the prewar period were political and constitutional in nature. Secession itself was a political event, triggered by a string of events that eventually led to the disintegration of the second American party system. Yet despite this political tenor, several themes in Civil War historiography may now be profitably addressed on the basis of what we have learned about religion and sectionalism in the antebellum South. By summarizing the most important ways in which religion contributed to the growth of Southern distinctiveness and placing these themes in their historiographical context, this conclusion offers a modest contribution to explaining the coming of the Civil War.

I

The relationship between religious and political discourse was one way in which religion shaped the development of antebellum Southern separatism. Often, as with the biblical defense of slavery, this interaction worked simply as a borrowing of language and ideas from religion to politics. At other times, such as the denominational schisms, religious and political discourse converged and became mutually reinforcing. In two particular cases, this confluence of religious and political discourse strengthened preexisting elements in Southern political culture that were crucial in leading the South down the road to disunion.

The coming of the Civil War was in a fundamental sense a constitutional crisis. As historian Arthur Bestor suggested, the Constitution played a configurative role in the sectional controversy, providing the "narrow channel" through which all aspects of the slavery debate flowed. During the 1840s, the simultaneous appearance of the Methodist and Baptist schisms with the annexation of Texas and the Wilmot Proviso reinforced the constitutionalism in Southern political discourse. While politicians insisted that Congress had no right to legislate against slaveholders in the territories, Southern churchmen claimed that the exclusionary actions of Northern dominated church bodies were unconstitutional. During the secession crisis, clergymen again contributed to Southern constitutionalism by defending states' rights in their religious vindications of secession. Religion then reinforced the Southern habit of thinking about the sectional controversy over slavery in constitutional terms, which gave it a configuration capable of disrupting the Union.

The concept of honor was another central element in Southern political culture that has been used recently to explain secession. With its emphasis on a personal sense of worth and visible signs of respect from others, the code of honor gave Northern attacks on slavery and slaveholders a peculiarly intense emotional charge that demanded immediate vindication from Southerners. The well-known caning of Massachusetts Senator Charles Sumner by the South Carolinian Preston Brooks in 1856 is perhaps the clearest illustration of how honor inflamed sectional passions. Although they are often seen as separate and distinct ethical systems, religion reinforced the importance of honor, especially during the sectional politics of the 1840s. The controversies over the annexation of Texas and the Wilmot Proviso were seen by Southerners as attacks on their honor and equality. Barring slaveholders from the new territories was particularly insulting, for it implied moral inferiority. Similarly, Southern Baptists and Methodists claimed that by banning slaveholders, national denominations were depriving Southern Christians of their honor and equality. By employing the rhetoric of honor, religion fortified a distinctive element in Southern society and politics.

II

The variety of political persuasions represented at the inauguration of Jefferson Davis hints at the diversity and division that characterized the Old South. Historians have become increasingly aware of the extent to which the antebellum South was a dynamic and diverse society in which "change was omnipresent, varieties abounded, visions multiplied." Coupled with the recognition that the question of internal unity was paramount in the minds of Southern secessionists, this recent emphasis on Southern diversity poses perhaps the most pressing problem in interpreting secession. If there was not *a* single monolithic South committed to disunion, what made secession possible and successful? What centripetal forces helped achieve a working unity in 1861? Historians have suggested compelling answers to these questions: the obvious racial fears of slave rebellion, the widespread commitment to white supremacy, and the belief that containing slavery would ultimately doom the institution.

I suggest that religion served as one of these unifying forces. It helped forge a moral consensus around slavery, a consensus capable of encompassing differing political views and uniting a diverse and disharmonious South behind the banner of disunion. Religion contributed to this moral consensus primarily through the "spiritualization" of the sectional controversy over slavery. In several ways explored in this study, Southern clergymen invested the sectional conflict with religious meaning. They sanctified slavery through a scriptural justification of human bondage, a slaveholding ethic to guide the conduct of Christian masters, and efforts to bring the Gospel to the slaves. By translating secession into an evangelical language meaningful to Southern Christians, the ritual of the fast day sermon transformed the crisis of the Union into a larger struggle between the forces of orthodoxy and infidelity. The ways in which the spiritualization of the sectional controversy created a moral consensus around slavery provides additional insight into our understanding of the coming of the Civil War.

The sanctification of slavery was perhaps the most important element in this moral consensus. The biblical justification of human bondage, pervasive in the religious and secular discourse of the antebellum South, served as one of the common denominators on which Southerners of differing political perspectives could agree. It could legitimately unite radical secessionists and Unionists on a shared platform. A meeting for the religious instruction of slaves held in Charleston in 1845 reveals the consensual potential of religious proslavery. At this meeting, former opponents during the nullification controversy submerged their political differences for this common cause. The radical nullifier and Southern nationalist Robert Barnwell Rhett was joined by former Unionists Daniel Huger and Joel R. Poinsett. Indeed, the scriptural defense of slavery might well have functioned as a sectional counterpoint to the free soil ideology of the Republican party, which could unite radical abolitionists with moderate Northerners who opposed the extension of slavery but believed in the racial inferiority of blacks.

As the keystone of the religious contribution to a Southern moral consensus, the sanctification of slavery affirms the centrality of slavery in explaining the coming of the Civil War. Throughout the antebellum era, slavery remained at the center of Southern clerical thought on the sectional controversy. It was precisely their belief that slavery involved moral and religious issues that justified their entrance into the arena of sectional politics in 1835. The denominational schisms were in essence a division between Northern and Southern churchmen over the morality of slavery. Slavery was also at the base of the religious logic of secession, which rested on the assumptions that human bondage was sanctioned by God and that abolitionism was infidelity. The manner in which Southern clergymen invested sectional politics with religious significance lends support to those secessionists and later historians who placed slavery at the heart of their explanations of why the Union dissolved.

Besides the sanctification of slavery, religion worked in another way to create a moral consensus. By validating a hierarchical and organic vision of society and a particularistic and egalitarian approach to social relations, religious proslavery could incorporate the world views of both planters and yeomen. Two recent studies of South Carolina suggest the unifying power of evangelical religion. In her investigation of the formation of the planter class in upcountry South Carolina, Rachel Klein has shown how the hierarchical vision of religion provided the basis for a proslavery Christianity that was accepted by both wealthy planters and yeomen evangelical communities. This point is reinforced by Stephanie McCurry in her study of the South Carolina lowcountry: "[R]eligion and politics shared a discourse that effectively broached the divide between high and low culture and articulated the southern rights position in terms that appealed to both the yeoman majority and the planter elite." These works then demonstrate how religion could draw together in ideological wholeness the social visions of different and often conflicting classes.

The moral consensus that the Southern clergy helped to create emphasizes the crucial role of ideology in the coming of the Civil War. Historians during the past few decades have paid a great deal of attention to sectional ideologies, those world views or belief systems that allowed both Northerners and Southerners to see the other as a mortal peril to their existence. Whereas Northerners came to believe that the extension of slavery threatened a social order based on free soil, free labor, and free men, Southern slaveholders saw their peculiar institution menaced by a hostile and aggressive North bent on stopping the spread of slavery. As soon as these ideologies entered and came to dominate American politics during the 1840s, historian Eric Foner has argued, the Civil War was inevitable. They injected basic values and moral judgments into a party system the very existence of which was predicated on compromise. Once this happened, the two major national parties lost their ability to reconcile domestic conflict and to serve as bonds of national unity. By creating and sustaining a moral dimension to sectional politics, religion played a key role in infusing sectional ideologies into the political process. Indeed, the spiritualization of the sectional controversy helped bring about secession by enhancing the notion of an "irrepressible conflict," the idea that the North and South were different civilizations with incompatible labor systems, institutions, and values. Most often associated with a speech given in 1858 by William H. Seward, the Republican Senator from New York, this idea had widespread support in both sections immediately before the Civil War.

Despite its contribution to the formation of Southern nationalism and the eventual dissolution of the Union, the moral consensus about slavery was severely strained during the Civil War. For one thing, the hierarchical religious vision that bonded planter and yeoman in a common world view was obviously not strong enough to prevent the open class conflict so evident in the Confederate South. In addition, the Civil War exposed more fully the latent threats to slavery hidden in the Christian doctrine of slavery. As previously discussed, the slaveholding ethic established rigorous moral standards for masters that could easily become an invitation to judge and perhaps condemn the practice of slavery. Confederate clergymen increasingly discussed what they saw as the disparity between the ideals of Christian slaveholders and the actual practice of slavery itself, dissolving one of the ideological bonds that held the Confederate South together.

III

Religion played an important role in the shaping of antebellum Southern separatism. It reinforced important elements in Southern political culture, invested sectional politics with a charged religious significance, and contributed to a moral consensus that made secession possible. It helped convince Southerners that slavery and Southern civilization were best protected in a separate Southern nation. In tandem with a variety of other social, political, economic, and ideological factors, religion helped lead the South toward secession and the Civil War.

Yankee Protestants and the Civil War: From Confusion to Crusade
JAMES H. MOORHEAD
SOURCE: From *American Apocalypse: Yankee Protestants and the Civil War* by James H. Moorhead. Copyright © 1978 by Yale University Press. Reprinted with permission.

By the winter of 1860-61 the plight of the nation had become fully apparent. The Democrats were hopelessly divided into Northern and Southern wings, and the Republican party had elected its first president on a purely sectional basis. Although Lincoln tempered his opposition to the extension of slavery by a promise to respect the institution where it already exists, the South regarded such assurances as illusory. On 20 December South Carolina seceded, and by late February six more states had withdrawn from the Union to form the Confederate States of America. The federal government was paralyzed by the crisis. Alternately lecturing the South on the illegality of secession and wringing his hands because he had no authority to stop it, President James Buchanan successfully alienated almost every sector of public opinion. Senator John Crittenden of Kentucky suggested the restoration of the Missouri Compromise, and others proposed a constitutional convention. These were futile gestures, for the departed states had already made an irrevocable choice, and the incoming administration was uninterested in any compromise that might repudiate the platform on which it had come to power. When Lincoln assumed office on 4 March 1861, he pledged his government to enforce the laws "in all the States." Beyond this aim, he would attempt no coercion. "There will be no invasion," said the president. It was, however, not clear how the first item could be achieved without resort to the second.

The cautious policy of the central government under two presidents reflected the lack of a national consensus that would sustain military action against the Confederacy. Many citizens, especially those in large metropolitan business firms with Southern investments, advocated sectional conciliation, and that policy received venerable support from the Websterian notion of a sacred Union worthy of any compromise. On the other hand, a majority within the free states had voted for a presidential candidate opposed to the extension of slavery, and they were not willing to throw away their victory. Confident that secession had been the work of a small conspiracy, they believed that a show of Yankee determination would bring the Southern majority to its senses and that the Confederacy would collapse without the firing of a shot. The few who did contemplate a permanent dismemberment of the Union wondered if the result might not prove a disguised blessing, freeing the North from the taint of slavery. A divided public, in short, could agree on only one point: the inadvisability of armed intervention in the South. The restrictions imposed by popular opinion and the need to secure the loyalty of the border states effectively limited the president's options to tactical maneuvers. Lincoln strove to ensure that if war did some, its terms might promote Northern unanimity. Whether by artifice or bungling, he accomplished this goal. Northern unity and a holy crusade emerged out of the mouth of a cannon in Charleston harbor.

Initial Responses to Secession

During the presidential interregnum, the threat of national dismemberment prompted numerous clerical pleas for reason and forbearance. "The Union," explained Henry A. Boardman to his Philadelphia congregation, "is too sacred a trust to be sacrificed except upon the most imperative grounds. It has cost too much blood and treasure: it is freighted with too much happiness for this great nation: it is too closely linked with the cause of human liberty, and with the salvation of the world. To destroy it at the bidding of passion; to destroy it until every practicable means for preserving it has been tried and exhausted, would be a crime of appalling turpitude against patriotism, against religion, and against humanity."

To avoid that disaster, would-be conciliators offered various remedies to mollify the South. A circular letter signed by various clergy in the New York-Philadelphia area decried the inflammatory rhetoric that supposedly characterized many pulpits, North and South, and urged Southern Christians to join in an open-minded and conciliatory regard for the feelings of those in all sections of the country. A widely disseminated sermon by Old School Presbyterian Henry J. Van Dyke of Brooklyn branded abolitionism as "the great mischief maker between the North and the South, . . . the great stumbling block in the way of a peaceful settlement of our difficulties." Although he professed loyalty to the principal of free speech, Van Dyke proposed rigorous' slander laws to brindle the "utterance of libelous words" from antislavery zealots. Such would be a minor sacrifice compared to the imminent dissolution "amid confused noise, and garments rolled in blood" of the "brightest prospect the world ever beheld." Others suggested that the North might demonstrate good faith by altering the laws that the South deemed a violation of its constitutional rights. Several free states had adopted so-called personal liberty laws that forbade state officials from enforcing the Fugitive Slave Act. The *Presbyterian* observed: "If our present government is to be perpetuated, nullification, in all its forms, must be abandoned on all sides. The few Northern states which have adopted personal liberty bills, thereby, to all intents and purposes, setting at naught the provision of the Constitution guarantying protection to the South, should recede from this legislation. They must revert to the Constitution as it is, or not complain if the South, in equal disregard of the Constitution, should take measures to protect itself." If this measure should prove insufficient, a few were prepared to move to the ultimate compromise: a constitutional convention that would ensure the perpetuity of slavery where it already existed. No sacrifice could be too great, in the words of a New Hampshire clergyman, for a Union that was "the palladium of your political safety and prosperity."

The advocates of compromise believed that disunionists, whether of the Garrisonian or Confederate variety, were a small, self-serving band who could be isolated by a prudent majority. In an article published in the *Methodist Quarterly Review* shortly before the November election, Reverend J. Townley Crane offered the conservative analysis: "In our national legislature there is a little faction of agitators, who aim at the dismemberment of the Union. They are not numerous, or influential, nor do they represent any important division of the nation." As secession began this reassuring argument was reiterated to suggest that the movement was a minority effort destined to failure unless the North foolishly provoked Southern feeling. The best counsel for the present, asserted the *Presbyterian*, was to avoid any action that might lead to confrontation: "If South Carolina in its ill-judged enterprise is determined to set up a government for itself, and if, through her example, several other States should also prove recreant, it is a question whether they should not be foreborne with without conceding the right of secession, while they try their impracticable experiment, and wait for the inevitable disastrous results of it, rather than precipitate a war, which might involve the Border states that we might readily retain. Such forbearance, in the long run, would promote and strengthen our future union."

From our vantage point the deep-seated sectional animosities may appear to have predetermined an irrepressible conflict before which the optimism of the *Presbyterian* and kindred spokesmen looks naive; but in the winter of 1860, a people desperate for hope could see an inviting plausibility to this logic. Pockets of nationalist sentiment had been disclosed in most of the seceded states; and until Lincoln requested volunteers after the bombardment at Fort Sumter, only seven states in the Deep South had left the Union. Had the Confederacy not been ultimately strengthened by the addition of the Upper South, primarily Virginia, it would have remained a weak, truncated political unit with a doubtful future. After a trip through the South in these months, the aging Methodist preacher Heman Bangs surveyed the uncertainties of the moment and summed up the conservative credo: avoid "rash judgment" and await the decision of God in future events.

This call fell upon a Protestant community impatient with further accommodation. Numerous churchmen believed that a Union purchased at the price of another compromise with slave interest would forfeit the respect of true patriots. Few used stronger language than Lester Williams, Jr., of Holden, Massachusetts. Commenting upon President Buchanan's January 4 Fast Day, Williams noted acerbically:

> For the continuance of this Union we are exhorted to pray. Can we do it? Can we in conscience? Let us see. Once the Union of the State meant something. It meant fraternity, mutual regard, forbearance, sympathy, brotherly help. . . . What is the Union worth to-day? Every good thing pertaining to it is sacrificed to *one* thing in one half of the country. Trade, Friendship, Comity, Religion, Honor, Civilization, all yield to the clamors of slavery, and are brushed away before it. It is the Dagon god of the South to which everything else must fall down. The wrathful cry is, "Slavery shall have new and stronger guarantees, or the Union shall be dissolved." The Union if it exists, must be made to bear slavery on its shoulders, and so become a bond of iniquity. Shall we be called upon to pray for *such* a Union? I don't believe God can regard with complacency such a prayer. It is too repulsive to all Christian faith to think it. I could as soon pray that Satan might be prospered and his kingdom come.

The sacred trust as defined by the tradition of Webster was now perceived in many quarters an instrument of evil.

In these polemics the essence of American nationalism was defined as adherence to righteous principles requiring every iniquity to be purged from the land. At a Thanksgiving service in Ellenville, New York, the Reverend Edward Bentley told the Methodist and Dutch Reformed congregations that perpetual "agitation is the inevitable consequence" of the national faith. "This is a Christian nation. It has avowed the Lord to be its God. It has deliberately made God's revealed will its standard of morality, and this agitation is but the utterance of a Christian desire that its conduct should conform to its standard.'Stop this agitation!' As well command, the national pulse to stop its beating, or the national conscience to sheathe its stings." Bentley was certain that this "throbbing" of the "national heart" would not cease "till this crowning curse and sin is wiped from out national fame."

To persons of Bentley's opinion, the United States represented commitment to a universal ideal. True loyalty to the Republic meant devotion to the mission of spreading freedom and religion throughout the world, and unless the Union promoted these high aims, it ceased to be a legitimate object of reverence. "God is rebuking our idolatry of the Union," Joseph P. Thompson told his audience in the Broadway Tabernacle in New York City. "I value the Union of these States as a means of peace and prosperity to them all. I value the Union and Constitution, as ordained for freedom and justice, and capable of bringing out the highest development of self-government under recognized law." American nationality, however, had become sadly debased; what God intended as a vehicle of his grace was worshiped in its own right. "But some, instead of valuing the Union as the means to the great ends of order, freedom, and peace, have glorified it as in itself an END, and have vaunted the Constitution above the 'higher law' of God. When the advocates of Slavery have demanded some palpable wrong under the threat of breaking up the Union, these worshipers of the Union, as such, have conceded the wrong to save the Union. . . . We have assumed that the Union was the perfection of human government, and necessary to the advancement of religion in the world. God is rebuking our pride and idolatry. He is teaching us that no human agency is indispensable to his plans, and that He can overthrow our Constitution with a breath." Thompson, one of the editors of the *Independent*, had for years maddened abolitionist zealots by his cautious antislavery position. His harsh rhetoric indicated the rapidly failing appeal of further political accommodation.

Mere disapproval of slavery did not alone make Northern moderates adamant against further compromise. Although ever larger numbers of Protestants had come to detest the institution as a barbaric anachronism, they were willing to tolerate it, within present limits, in the confidence that it would collapse from internal weakness. Horace Bushnell suggested that the economic unprofitability of slavery would gradually float the system away, and others agreed that if shut up to its present domains, the peculiar institution would be set, in Lincoln's evocative phrase, in the course of ultimate extinction. Northern churchmen were aroused from these optimistic slumbers by the conviction that the South had adopted a concerted rule-or-ruin policy. Unwilling to accept the existing confines of slavery, the Southern leadership demanded that it have unlimited access to all portions of the nation and the unqualified sanction of the federal government. The correspondence of the Northern perception of a slave power conspiracy with the actuality of Southern intention is dubious; and, or course, the latter's counterbias that a sinister cabal of abolitionist forces directed Northern policy departs even further from reality. These beliefs cannot be dismissed as totally mythic constructions, however. Repeated accusations of malevolence heightened sectional estrangement, drove some to extreme positions, and thus gave the dire warnings a measure of self-fulfillment. The issue for most Northern Protestants had ceased to be whether slavery as a local institution should be grudgingly endured. The struggle now concerned the very core of American nationality: whether the South should be allowed to foist its iniquity upon the entire nation. The answer seemed clear.

D. D. Whedon, the editor of the *Methodist Quarterly Review*, epitomized the shift in mood. In earlier years a conciliator willing to mute his antislavery convictions, he now believed that the nation had been summoned to an irrevocable moral Rubicon. In the April 1861 issue of the *Review*, he tried to set the problem in historical perspective. When the Constitution was adopted, freedom was held to be the normal condition of man, "slavery the dark and terrible exception." Initially all Americans, including Southerners, had accepted this doctrine; but at length the South had sought to make slavery a permanent national institution to which all other interests must submit. Disregarding the threat for decades, the North had finally roused itself from its torpor to save the nation from total humiliation at the hands of the slavocracy.

> But one more national victory of the proslavery Democracy [the Democratic party], and the decision of the Lemmon case would have opened the door to the remanding of slavery to the free states. But one turn still farther of the judicial screw, and emancipation even in our Northern states would have been decided to be subversive of the rights of property and contrary to the Constitution, and the plot would have been completed. Slavery would have been pronounced national; abolitionists and anti-slavery men would have been lynched and hung as freely in New England as in Carolina, and Senator Toombs [of Georgia] might have built his slave-pen under the shadow of Bunker Hill. To such a denouement were we firmly and rapidly marching. From it we were saved, not by the advocates of compromise and pseudo-conservatism, but by fearless hearts and unshrinking choices; by men in Church and State who breasted the brunt of battle and won the victory that culminated in the election of Abraham Lincoln.

The issue had been fairly joined, and no further conciliation could be honorable. Either the North would yield no further ground to the South, or it would submit to "complete subjugation" by the slave power. The latter alternative might indeed preserve the political unity of the nation but it would do so "at the expense of all that renders the Union dear."

A more remarkable conversion occurred in an even less likely quarter. Throughout his long career Charles Hodge, the doyen of Old School Presbyterianism, had vehemently opposed abolitionism and had urged ecclesiastical silence on such secular matters. Yet in the January 1861 issue of the *Princeton Review*, he indicated that his patience, too, had worn thin. Having dominated the national government during most of the Republic's history, Southerners now decided that they could not bear the loss of one election and that they could not "live in any political community which they do not control." This attitude, he concluded, was "unrighteous and unreasonable," a constitutional "impossibility." Hodge insisted that he still abhorred abolition and favored just compromise, but he believed that the South had drawn a line that could not be honorably crossed. Southern intransigence had transformed an essentially political question into a moral imperative. "There are occasions," he suggested, "when political questions rise into the sphere of morals and religion; when the rule for political action is to be sought not in the considerations of state policy, but the law of God." The present crisis was such an occasion. As he prepared his article for the printer, Hodge wrote to his brother that he had become thoroughly disgusted with the "poltroonery of Northern men" who "go down on their knees" before the South. The time had come to take "just ground, and take it firmly."

This attitude indicated a negative program more than a positive one. The opponents of further compromise knew fairly well what they did not want: personal liberty laws should not be rescinded, the Crittenden proposal should be rejected, and the Constitution should not be altered. Left undetermined was what policy the government should pursue in regard to the seceded states: whether they should be permitted to depart in peace, or whether coercion should be employed to retain them.

This painful question was blunted by the continued faith in America's providential mission. When Protestants examined world events, they saw everywhere evidence that the Kingdom of God was hastening among men. Cavour and Garibaldi led the Italian risorgimento that would usher in a democratic era in that land, the papal states teetered on the verge of collapse, and heathen powers relaxed barriers to the missionary. "The redemption of the world draw nigh," observed the *Christian Watchman and Reflector*, "and if our faith and labors go hand in hand, it may be given to our generation to see the knowledge of the Lord covering the earth as the waters cover the sea." With all omens pointing to the progress of Christian civilization, it was inconceivable that the United States should be left behind. Heman Humphrey, one of Congregationalism's most venerable pastors, queried: "Would He have brought us hither and given us so much work in prospect for bringing in the millennium, if He had intended to pluck us up, just as we are entered upon the work?"

Viewed from this perspective, disunion appeared to be the dying gasp of an exhausted despotism. After the election of Lincoln, Gilbert Haven predicted that the South's intransigence would soon be overcome and that its people would soon breathe "the summer morning air of freedom." "The day is nigh at hand. It has already dawned. It shall speedily arise." And then with the benediction to the Apocalypse, Haven concluded: "Surely I come quickly. Amen! Even so, come, Lord Jesus!" In similar language the *Independent* predicted that Southern resistance presaged the early collapse of the slave power. "Slavery rocks and reels with the premonitory symptoms of its overthrow. If we hold fast our faith in God, we shall see 'greater things than these'—the Son of Man taking to Himself the power over the nations." A few weeks later in opposing the Crittenden compromise, the paper suggested: "This is the last hope of the slave power. After the fourth of March the cry of compromise will be heard no more; the necessity for compromise will be felt no more, the Government will go forward in the exercise of all its Constitutional functions, the slave power will know its place; and, by degrees, business and public affairs will return to their accustomed channels."

As it became clear that the affairs of state would not return to "accustomed channels," many clergy began to suggest that dismemberment of the Union might bring unexpected benefits. D. D. Whedon remarked: "Even disunion has its compensations. It will make us what we have never yet been, fully and consistently a FREE nation. Countless will be the blessings of a full emancipation from the dread evils not only of slavery domination but of union with slaveholders. That disunion will hasten the downfall of slavery and perhaps a reconstruction on a free basis." Cut loose from the burden of a union with the South, suggested Zachary Eddy of Northampton, Massachusetts, the remainder of the nation might more fully "develop all the forces of a high, Christian civilization." According to the Reverend Sefferenas Ottman of Branchport, New York, there existed the additional consolation that the system of human bondage would die soon whether the Union persisted or not. "In the Union or out of it, Slavery must die. God has written upon it its inevitable doom; and universal civilization has pronounced against it."

A clean break with decades of Union sentiment was not easy, but the step was being taken. In January, for example, the *Independent* urged the nation to bear any "extremity" for the maintenance of the Union; by February the paper concluded that coercion would be unwise.

> God, who controls the destiny of nations, is opening a new chapter in the history of the world's wickedness. He has permitted the apostasy of Southern Christianity and the incendiary sophistry of Southern politics to work out their results. He has permitted that revolutionary frenzy to sweep over so many states. *Quis vult perdere, dementat.* It is for us to accept the fact. Those states must be permitted to work out their own destruction under that retributive Providence which is ordering their dreadful destiny. . . . Let the boundaries between them and the United States be defined by negotiation and peaceful agreement, if possible; and then let their destiny and ours be developed.

Even those advocating coercion suggested a minimum response. The *Christian Watchman and Reflector* favored reinforcement of arsenals in Southern territory, blockades of the region's ports, and a suspension of the postal service, but the paper explicitly insisted that such was "the only force we advocate." The editor hoped to maintain the laws, without a full-scale invasion of the South, until the "disaffected States" could be legally dismissed from the Union.

By April 1861 it was clear that the churches were inching into the future cautiously and uncertainly. Although many continued to exalt the Union as the zenith of value, a majority of clergy insisted that American nationality was essentially commitment to an ideal that could admit no further compromise. Most, of course, hoped that the harsh choice between liberty and Union would not be forced upon them. The South—pacified according to some, treated firmly according to others—would perhaps come scurrying back to the fold; and if that happy end did not result, a few concluded that disunion was not the unbearable option that a generation of Americans had thought. In spite of millennial rhetoric about a coming conflict, Protestants were not yet prepared to fight that battle with the weapons of the flesh.

The Holy Crusade

After December 1860 federal property within the territory of seceded states presented a dilemma to both the United States and to the fledgling Confederacy. The problem was focused by the existence of Fort Sumter in the harbor of Charleston, South Carolina. By early April it was apparent that the garrison could not hold out much longer without resupply. A decision not to provision Sumter would signal a tacit recognition of disunion, and Lincoln therefore informed the governor of South Carolina on 6 April that fresh supplies would shortly be sent. The Southern government saw in this action the threat of an indefinite federal presence astride one of its leading ports—a situation that President Jefferson Davis believed could not be endured if the Confederacy's independence were to be credible. Accordingly he decided on 12 April to demand the surrender of Sumter and, when this ultimatum was rejected, to seize the arsenal by force. After a few hours of token resistance, Major Robert Anderson surrendered the garrison. Several days later Lincoln issued a proclamation calling for 75,000 volunteers to suppress the rebellion. Throughout the North the fall of Sumter was received as evidence that peaceful secession was impossible.

The loyal states—their clergy not least among them—responded to the president's call with an éclat of patriotic devotion submerging the doubts and divisions of the previous weeks. A year later Unitarian Edmund Willson of Salem, Massachusetts, assessed the remarkable transformation in sentiment. "One week before all was uncertainty; there was apathy, doubt, gloom. The uncrystallized atoms floated loose and uncohesive. . . .[But in the wake of Sumter] the problem which no man could work out was solved. Deeplying affinities were found beneath all our repulsions; surface seams were healed; and we were one people"—one people, he might have added, firmly committed to restore the Union by force of arms.

Conservatives recently dallying with conciliation turned upon the South with the anger of friends betrayed. "When the first indications of this conflict made their appearance," explained Dr. Gardiner Spring of New York's Brick Presbyterian Church, "all my prepossessions, as is well known, were with the Southern states. If their leading statesmen had conducted themselves like Christians and as friends of peace—for myself, I would have been the advocate of some amicable arrangement rather than have been forced to the arbitrament of the sword. But when I hear so few kind words, and these suppressed by violence or fear; when crafty politicians eager for fame, and panting for place and power, blind and enslave the minds of the people; when I learn that this secession was preconcerted and determined in years gone by, and was only biding its time, . . . when I see these things my convictions are strong that we have reached the limit beyond which forbearance may not be extended." It was, in fact, Spring who introduced in the May session of the Old School General Assembly a motion that firmly allied the denomination with the federal cause. Passed after considerable debate about their propriety, the so-called Spring resolutions marked a significant departure from the Old School's often reaffirmed policy of not pronouncing upon secular issues.

Enraged conservatives now believed that previous talk of a diabolical slave power conspiracy had proven all too accurate. The Baptist *Christian Review* had previously sidestepped political issues for the sake of sectional amity, but now the journal pictured a fiendish South greedy for every inch of Northern territory, and it called for the military obliteration of the Confederacy. Bishop Thomas A. Morris, a Southerner by birth and a sectional peacemaker by conviction, insisted in an open letter to border state Methodists that treason foreclosed all alternatives to an unsparing "destruction of its authors." As Henry Boardman explained, it was no longer possible to maintain any sympathy for those by whom "this rebellion was concocted many years ago." A "cumulative series of proofs" had unmasked the utter duplicity of the Southern leadership. More than any other factor, said Boardman, this revelation of Southern character "has brought the prudent and conservative classes of society into full sympathy with this war for the defense of the Union. . . . And now, that the treachery is laid open, and they see that all the while, the one cherished object of these men was to *destroy* the Union, they have the double mixture of personal wrong and public duty to inflame their zeal on behalf of the cause of their country."

The assault against the flag worked a different alchemy upon those who had rebuked the idolatry of the Union. Some of these people suggested that peaceful secession be allowed as a means of purging the nation of slavery. It will never be known whether they seriously wished this outcome or were instead expressing passionately a hypothetical possibility preferable to further compromise with the South. In any case, the outbreak of violent revolution cut short these speculations, and the proponents of the higher law enlisted with enthusiasm in the war for the Union. The *Independent* epitomized the new war spirit:

> The question of the hour is a new question. What is now to be decided is not the Nebraska question, nor the Lecompton question, nor the question of the fugitive slave law. The question is not whether the Union shall be divided. . . . Had the seceding states proposed a peaceable division of the Union, by any method consistent with the forms and spirit of the Constitution, the question now to be decided would not have arisen. . . . All other questions are now merged in one: Have we a Government? Is the Union of these states a solid reality, or only an airy vision? Can citizens of the United States make war upon the United States not be

guilty of treason? Shall the Government and Union of these states be defended against the enemies that have planned all this treason, and are now marching upon the capital? This is the question of the hour. Let all questions heretofore debated be foreborne.

In short, the problem of slavery had been supplanted by the issue of constitutional legitimacy, and staple sermon texts shifted to Romans 13: "Let every soul be subject to the higher powers. For there is no power but of God: the powers that be are ordained of God."

Protestants were convinced that failure to uphold the Union would set in motion centrifugal tendencies that would not halt until the nation and its cherished freedom were in ruins. The *Christian Watchman and Reflector* predicted that a United States which allowed revolution would recapitulate the history of Europe "with bitter local jealousies and antipathies, and large standing armies, and frequent wars and crushing debts." The Reverend William Dwight of Portland, Maine, pushed the warning a step further: broken into a half-dozen or so confederacies, the former nation would lapse into the colonial orbit of England or France. At stake, said A. L. Stone of Park Street Church in Boston, was the principle of law. If successfully challenged by the rebellion, legitimate authority would disappear, forcing Americans "back from friendships and brotherhoods and all alliances, to the instincts of the forest brute." Foreswearing momentarily his antislavery convictions, Stone urged citizens to "strike for Law and Union, for country and God's great ordinance of Government."

It would not be accurate to infer that the claims of transcendent morality had been completely displaced in the clamor to maintain the Union. Rather, the preservationist rhetoric had itself been infused with a new moral significance. Formerly an argument in behalf of concession to the South, such language now summoned the nation to battle against an iniquitous slave power. The holy Union that Northerners defended was no longer the compromise-tainted object of earlier years; it was democratic civilization in collision with an alien way of life. Thus the Vermont Baptist Association declared in October 1861: "We witness the culmination of a strife which has long been progressing between the principles of freedom incorporated into the framework of our government and lying at the foundation of our national existence on the one hand, and the system of American slavery on the other." In its Independence Day issue the *Christian Advocate and Journal* saw the conflict as the reflection of the universal struggle between aristocracy and democracy. After alluding to the economic and political differences between the two sections, the paper suggested that these were only surface difficulties: "But beneath all these is the predisposing cause. . . . The sentiment of the South is aristocratic, that of the North democratic. Its community is a rural aristocracy, resting like that of ancient Sparta, upon a helotry. Here lies the heart of our trouble." At a superficial glance the war might be called merely a struggle to vindicate legitimate government, but on the deeper level it was a great people's war for Christian democracy.

As the editor of the *Advocate* expressed the matter succinctly, "Directly we are contending for government, but indirectly for freedom."

The significance of such an ideological conflict could not be restricted to one nation alone, and Protestants asserted vigorously that in fighting the battle for liberty in America they were waging a war of universal significance. The *Independent* suggested that the war should not be categorized "with ordinary instances of international hostility." Unlike petty dynastic squabbles or commercial imbroglios, this struggle reached beyond local interests and constituted "a crisis in the world's history." By resolving a fundamental issue, the war would prove one of the "hinges on which the destiny of nations and of ages" turns. That question was starkly simple: was democracy a viable form of government? "Free institutions," said Francis Wayland in a pamphlet for the American Tract Society, "have been established in this country under every advantage, and have achieved a material, social, and intellectual progress wholly without a parallel. If they cannot be maintained here, in the midst of a Protestant population, with a Bible in every house, and education as free as air, and in the enjoyment of 'perfect liberty in religious concernments,' then it may be reasonably believed that they can be sustained nowhere. Crushed and degraded humanity must sink down in despair, and centuries must elapse before this experiment can be made again under so favorable auspices."

In the vanguard of the worldwide struggle for liberty, Americans bore a responsibility unlike that of any other people. They were in the deepest sense the representatives of humanity, and their government was the property of all. After a trip to the Levant in the spring of 1861, Daniel C. Eddy of Boston's Harvard Street Baptist Church was impressed anew by the unique position of the United States. "That flag belongs to the world; it is the ensign of the oppressed of all lands. The soil we tread! it is not yours or mine. It does not belong to the cotton lords of the South, nor to the merchant princes of the North. It belongs to constitutional government and human happiness." The Union had to be preserved because it freighted the hopes of all people. Although narrow chauvinism contributed, as it does in all wars, to the burst of military ardor that followed the start of hostilities, the patriotic spirit of 1861 was nourished also by the conviction that the cause was mankind. America's sacred trust was holy because it was held for all humanity and not for America alone. As Albert Barnes, New School Presbyterianism's best-known spokesman, said: "Of all the civil and political trusts ever committed to any generation of men, that Constitution is the most precious, for it guards higher interests and secures richer blessings to the world than any other."

By any standard of judgment, the metamorphosis of feeling in April 1861 was remarkable. The unthinkable war had become the irrepressible conflict in which the clergy eagerly volunteered their oratorical services. Conservatives who had urged conciliation set their faces against further compromise, and those who had talked glibly of sundering the nation suddenly bowed in reverence before the ark of the Union. As a symbol of political and religious meaning for all Protestants, the Union had been rehabilitated and suffused with new moral vitality. Virtually without exception, the clergy united with Zachary Eddy, whose conversion from an apostle of peaceful disunion to a drum major in the war effort was complete. "If the crusaders, seized by a common enthusiasm, exclaimed, 'IT IS THE WILL OF GOD! IT IS THE WILL OF GOD!'—much more may we make this our rallying cry and inscribe it on our banners." The late 1850s witnessed an upsurge in the expectation of a titanic conflict; in 1861 that apocalyptic struggle started to assume tangible definition.

Christian Soldiers: The Meaning of Revivalism in the Confederate Army

DREW GILPIN FAUST

SOURCE: From Drew Gilpin Faust, "Christian Soldiers: The Meaning of Revivalism in the Confederate Army," *Journal of Southern History,* 53 (February 1987):63-90. Copyright 1987 by the Southern Historical Association. Reprinted with permission of the Managing Editor.

From the fall of 1862 until the last days of the Civil War, religious revivalism swept through Confederate forces with an intensity that led one southerner to declare the armies had been "nearly converted into churches." A remarkable phenomenon in the eyes of contemporary observers, these mass conversions have been largely ignored by modern scholars. The attention recent historians have devoted to other manifestations of nineteenth-century Evangelicalism makes this neglect of Civil War religion seem all the more curious, for scholarly findings about the relationship between revivalism and the processes of social and cultural transformation suggest that an exploration of army Evangelicalism should yield important insights into the meaning of the South's experience in an era of profound dislocation and change.

The centrality of religion within antebellum southern culture gave sacred language and perception a prominent place in the region's response to war. The South had not only embraced evangelical Protestantism with a uniformity and enthusiasm unmatched in the rest of the nation but had also used religion as a crucial weapon in the sectional propaganda battle. Defining itself as more godly than the North, the South turned to the Scriptures to justify its peculiar institution and its social order more generally. With its declaration of nationhood and the subsequent outbreak of war, the Confederacy identified its independence and success as God's will. Their cause, southerners insisted until the very last days of the conflict, was God's cause; the South's war of defense against invasion was unquestionably a just war.

The prominence of such sentiments in public discourse—in the Confederate Constitution itself, in Jefferson Davis's proclamations of fast days, in generals' announcements of military victory, not to mention in church sermons and denominational publications—established religion as the fundamental idiom of national and personal identity; southerners' responses to the unanticipated horrors of the first modern, total war were almost necessarily articulated within a religious framework and in religious language. But if religion was central to the Confederacy as a whole, it was perhaps of greatest importance to the common southern soldier, whose life was most dramatically altered—if not actually ended—by war's demands. The widespread army revivals directly reflected the stresses of the soldier's life and death situation: the strains of life in the ranks of a mass army; the pressures of daily confrontation with death—and with a rate of mortality unmatched in any American war before or since.

Although the southern religious press reported scattered conversions of soldiers from the time fighting broke out, Confederates did not begin to identify what one Evangelical called a "genuine and mighty work of grace" until the fall of 1862. At first confined to the Army of Northern Virginia, and always strongest there, significant religious awakenings spread to the Army of Tennessee and to the Trans-Mississippi forces in 1863 and 1864. One observer later calculated that as many as 150,000 soldiers were "born again" during the war, but even if far fewer actually converted, thousands more participated in the revival without themselves undergoing the dramatic personal experience of grace.

For large numbers of men the struggle against the Yankees on the field had its parallel in the battle against Satan in the camp. Soldiers' diaries and letters make clear how widely the phenomenon extended. As one participant expressed it, "'We sometimes feel more as if we were in a camp-meeting than in the army expecting to meet an enemy'." A less sympathetic observer found he could not even write a peaceful letter to his wife. "It seems to me that whereever [sic] I go I can never get rid of the 'P-salm'- singers—they are in full blast with a Prayer meeting a few rods off. . . ." To many of those neither directly involved nor firmly opposed, the pattern of Evangelicalism and conversion became simply a part of army routine. One captain wrote indifferently yet revealingly in his diary in mid-1863, "Today is Sunday. Nothing unusual. . . .-preaching in the afternoon and evening. Many joined the church." . . .

Curiously, the evangelical fervor of the Confederate troops was not paralleled by enthusiasm at home, and, as self-righteous southerners loved to charge, "nothing like this occurred in the Yankee army." Despite the widespread perception of the conflict as a holy war, southern civilians, even church members, were not experiencing God's grace in substantial numbers. The coldness of established congregations throughout the war years troubled southern clergy, who attributed their failures to the preoccupation of their flocks with the secular realities of politics and economic survival. But surely the Confederacy's soldier-converts were even more concerned with the actualities of war. For them, perhaps, the ever-present threat of death gave battle a transcendent, rather than primarily worldly, significance, or possibly the enthusiasm within the army reflected Evangelicals' concerted efforts with the troops.

The comparison with soldiers' experiences in the northern army is more problematic, for revivals did occur with some frequency among Yankee troops. Most nineteenth-century observers, as well as twentieth-century scholars, have remarked, however, upon significant differences in the scale and in the intensity of army religion North and South. Abraham Lincoln himself worried that "rebel soldiers are praying with a great deal more earnestness . . . than our own troops. . . ." A number of explanations for this contrast seem plausible. The greater homogeneity of religious outlook within the overwhelmingly evangelical and Protestant southern army was certainly significant. The more profound stresses on southern soldiers, who because of shortages of manpower and material served for longer periods of time, with fewer furloughs, and with greater physical deprivation, undoubtedly played a role as well, for it was as the war increased in duration and intensity that revivalism began to spread.

Men donning the Confederate uniform did not at first demonstrate unusual piety. At the outset the devoted found themselves very much on the defensive, for religious leaders felt obliged to combat a widespread view that godliness would undermine military effectiveness. There "is nothing in the demands of a just and defensive warfare at variance with the spirit and duties of Christianity," an oft-reprinted tract urged. "Piety will not make you effeminate of cowardly." Godly southerners at first feared that the influences might work in just the opposite direction: that battle would prove an impediment to piety. "War is the hotbed of iniquity of every kind," wrote the Reverend Charles Colcock Jones. The army had in all ages been "the greatest school of vice." History showed that men removed from the restraining, "softening" moral influences of womanhood and hearth easily succumbed to the temptations of camp life. One tract drawing soldiers' attention to the grave yawning open before them pointedly summarized the dilemma. "Men, by associating in large masses, as in camps and cities, improve their talents, but impair their virtues." The South, happily free of significant urban centers, must not now abandon her comforting moral advantage.

The initial experience of camp life seemed to bear out these dire expectations. "I think the majority of the men of our Regt. are becoming very wild & contracting many bad habits," a private wrote home from Virginia in November 1861. The Sabbath brought "no preaching, no service" to counteract Satan's growing influence. "The religious destitution of the Army," a soldier confided to his diary, "is awful. . . ." By far the largest portion of the troops appeared to one tract agent as entirely godless. Of the three hundred men in three companies that he visited in the summer of 1861, only seven were "professors of religion." The army presented a moral picture that was "dark indeed." . . .

The mobilization of the southern clergy to confront the wartime challenge paralleled the mobilization of Confederate military resources. Identifying both the hazards and the opportunities that war offered the church ministers worked to devise a strategy for conquering army camps, and not incidentally, for making religion—and its preachers—a central force in the creation of the new nation. With the successes of the church among the troops, a chaplain declared to a gathering of his colleagues, "the foundation for a wide religious power over the country is now lain. . . . We, then here and now, stand at the fountain head of the nation's destiny. We lay our hands upon its throbbing heart. Never again shall we come so near having the destiny of a great nation in our own hands." . . .

In the fall of 1862 these religious labors began to bear fruit, as circumstances came to the aid of the southern churches. The timing of evangelical successes during the war offers important clues to the meaning of the conversion experience. By late 1862 many initial illusions had begun to disappear; after more than a year of "hard service," as one chaplain explained, "the romance of the soldier's life wore off, a more sober and serious mood seemed to prevail in the camps." Conscription had begun the previous spring, and by fall soldiers without the romantic zeal and optimism of the original volunteers had joined the ranks. Perhaps most significantly, however, revivals first broke out among troops retreating from Maryland after the Confederate loss at Antietam, which represented not only the first major southern defeat in the eastern theater but the bloodiest single battle day of American history as well. The experiences of slaughter and military failure surely had their impact in encouraging the "serious reflection and solemn resolve" that preceded evangelical commitment. There was great "eloquence" in the "din" and "carnage" of the field. "We are so much exposed," one soldier observed, as he explained why he had quit "light trashy novels" for the Bible, "we are likely to be called off at any moment."

During the rest of the war the most dramatic outbursts of religious enthusiasm followed fierce and bloody battles—especially losses. The "great revival along the Rapidan" in the late summer and fall of 1863 swept through troops encamped for the first time since their retreat from Gettysburg. The pattern was clear to contemporary observers. As one army correspondent explained in 1863 to the *Confederate Baptist*, "There have been always among us, some pious men, but until that time nothing like a general revival or even seriousness. The regiment had just returned from the disastrous Pennsylvania expedition, and a few days before had the closest and most desperate encounter with the enemy that they had ever had. The minds of the men were fresh from scenes of danger and bloodshed and were forced thereby to contemplate eternity, and in many cases, to feel the necessity of preparation." In the West, Vicksburg and Chattanooga had a similar effect. Individual experiences of grace were closely connected to the wider search for God's favor implicit in the divine gift of military victory. As one recently converted soldier wrote in a letter home, he hoped the revival in his camp would bring "a great blessing nationally as well as Spiritually."

Religion thrived, however, not just on growing personal and national insecurity, not just on individual and collective fear of the Yankees, but on anxieties related to social realities within the Confederate army itself. Chaplains, missionaries, and colporteurs had begun to make clear that rather than hinder military effectiveness, they could do a great deal to enhance it. Officers previously indifferent, if not openly hostile, to religion in the camps came to encourage piety and to provide spaces and occasions for the evangelization of their troops. "It is an interesting fact," observed Baptist preacher J.J.D. Renfroe in November 1863, "that most of our officers have undergone some change on the subject of chaplains. . . . when they first started out it made no difference with them what sort of man they had for chaplain, or whether they had any at all; but now you will not talk with an officer ten minutes about it until you will discover that he does not want a chaplain simply to 'hold service,' but he wants a man who will promote the religious good of his regiment. I have had irreligious officers to tell me that a good chaplain is worth more for the government of troops than any officer in a regiment." Colonel David Lang communicated his satisfaction that his chaplain's efforts in the fall of 1863 were "making good soldiers of some very trifling material."

Despite the notable and inspiring exceptions of Robert E. Lee, Stonewall Jackson, and other pious commanders, army evangelism had its greatest impact among the common soldiers. Missionaries, chaplains, and even Jackson himself complained repeatedly of the religious indifference of the officers. The rhetoric of the Confederate revival, the themes of its sermons and its tracts, suggest one obvious explanation of why so many southern leaders encouraged piety among their troops while they remained largely aloof. "Irreligious colonels," the *Religious Herald* explained, "seek the cooperation of a good chaplain in their desire to render their regiment as efficient as possible." Religion promised significant assistance in the thorny problem of governing the frequently intractable Confederate troops.

From the outset the Confederate army experienced great difficulties with discipline, for the southern soldier was most often a rural youth who had every expectation of becoming—if he was not already—an independent landholding farmer. Despite the uneven distribution of wealth and particularly of slaveownership in the prewar South, the common man ordinarily had no direct experience with political or social oppression, for he lived in a democratic political and social order where decentralization minimized perceptions of sharp stratification between planters and plain folk. The prevalent ideology of republicanism had encouraged rich and poor whites alike to cherish their "independence" and autonomy, emphasizing a sharp contrast between their status and that of enslaved blacks. But the army was to demand a hierarchy and a discipline that the prewar situation had not, even if practice such as election of officers might seem to symbolize the soldier's willing contractual surrender of control over his own life. Previously masterless men were compelled in the army to accept subordination for the first time, and many recruits complained bitterly about this change in expectations and circumstances. As one young soldier wrote home in the summer 1861, "we are not lowd to go to the Shops without a permit and we are not lowd to miss a drill without a furlo sickness or permit, we are under tite rules you dont know how tite they are I wish I coul see you and then I could tell you what I thought of campt life it is very tite rules and confinen."

Religion promised considerable assistance in easing this difficult transition. Élie Halévy, E. P. Thompson, and others have described the role of Methodism in the transformation of English workers into an industrial proletariat, and more recently Anthony F. C. Wallace has explored the influence of evangelical Protestantism upon laborers in nineteenth-century Pennsylvania textile mills. In the South of the 1860s the role of religion was somewhat different, for young rural Confederates were going to war, not to the factories. But the requirements of industrialized work and industrialized warfare are alike in important ways—in their demand for new levels of discipline, regularity, and subordination. Daniel T. Rodgers has described a process of "labor commitment—. . . by which new industrial employees adjusted deeply set rural loyalties and work habits to the disrupting demands of factory labor." In their identity shift from farmers to soldiers, young southerners needed to make analogous changes in internal values and expectations. A soldier "must be trained," insisted the *Religious Herald,* "and willing to submit to thorough training. . . .There is a *moral* requirement as important as the material one—an inward man as indispensable as the outward one. . . ." Religious conversion and commitment could serve as the vehicle accelerating and facilitating this necessary personal transformation. Both southern military and religious leaders recognized that Evangelicalism could contribute to internalizing discipline and enhancing the efficiency of the Confederate soldier; the church could help to mold disorganized recruits into an effective fighting force. "A spirit of subordination and a faithful discharge of duty," the *Biblical Recorder* summarized, "are [as] essential to the good soldier" as they are to the good Christian.

The term "efficiency" appeared again and again in evangelical rhetoric. The Christian soldier would be an efficient soldier because he would not be afraid to die; he would be obedient and well disciplined because he would understand the divine origin of earthly duty. One army chaplain offered a striking illustration of the *"military power of religion.* In a brigade of five regiments, where there has recently been a glorious revival, two of the regiments, which had not shared in the revival, broke, while the three which had been thus blessed stood firm. . . ." A missionary of the Army of Tennessee made an even more dramatic claim. "Preaching," he asserted, had "corrected" one of "the greatest evils of our army, in a military point of view . . .—that of straggling." The servant of God, he explained, learned that he must execute all earthly as well as all spiritual obligations "conscientiously," and that meant keeping up with your regiment even if you were ill or had no shoes. A colonel of the South Carolina Volunteers emphasized the point when he congratulated a colporteur on the usefulness of his tracts, which he found "of incalculable service in encouraging the soldier to a continuation of his hard duties, and making him feel contented with his lot." The Reverend R. N. Sledd no doubt won similar approval from Confederate military leaders when he insisted to a congregation of common soldiers about to depart for war that "it is . . . not only wise, but necessary to your efficiency, that for the time you surrender your will to that of your officers, . . . This lesson of submission to control is a difficult one for many to learn; but until you have completely mastered it, . . . you are not prepared to behave yourself the most valiantly and the most efficiently in the field of conflict." Significantly, religious leaders stressed the profitable management of time as well as the adoption of regular personal habits, and often chose the bourgeois language of commerce and the marketplace to emphasize the productive uses of religion. A correspondent to the *Religious Herald* suggested in 1863 that chaplains on the field make themselves easily identifiable by wearing badges emblazoned with the epigraph, "Godliness is profitable unto all." Another article reported an imaginary dialogue between an officer and a recently converted private who assured his superior, "'I used to neglect your business; now I perform it diligently.'" . . .

In writing of World War I, Eric J. Leed has argued that there occurred a "militarized proletarianization" of European soldiers. Certainly no such dramatic transformation took place in the Confederate South, for this first modern war fell far short of the 1914 conflict in its demands for hierarchy, routine, and control. Nevertheless, Leed's observation, combined with the rhetoric of Confederate army religion, cannot help but draw attention to the new work patterns warfare imposed and to the loss of autonomy and independence it implied for the average southerner. As one Virginia private tellingly observed, "A soldier in the ranks is like a piece of machinery—he moves and acts as commanded." Even though his salary was often not even paid, the Confederate soldier was in most cases undergoing his first experience as a wage laborer subordinate to the direction of his employer. When at the end of the war the *Nation* called for the North to "turn the slothful, shiftless Southern world upside down," little would editor E. L Godkin have guessed that the leaders of the Confederate army and churches had already been acting as his unwitting allies. For four years they had struggled—albeit with uncertain success—to teach the southern soldier the very same values of training, regularity, and industry that Godkin hoped northern victory might now impose.

Yet such a view of the role of Confederate religion—as manipulative and hegemonic—is partial and one-dimensional. Recent scholarly work has justly insisted that monolithic emphasis on the aspects of social control within evangelicalism must not distort its larger meaning or impugn the authenticity of revivalists' piety and sacred commitment by casting them simply as conspirators seeking to enhance their own social power. Most advocates of the order and discipline central to the revivalistic impulse sincerely believed that their goals were above all to fulfill God's design and only secondarily to serve the needs of men. The perceptions of the common Confederate soldiers who were the targets of army revivalists' efforts is less clear. Certainly the impact of the evangelical message among the troops was profound, as the large number of conversions attests. And many of these converts readily accepted the notion of a regenerate life as one of discipline and self-control, for soldiers frequently wrote home that revivals had made it impossible to find a cardplayer or a profane swearer in the regiment. It seems likely, however, that the cynicism of some reductionist twentieth-century social control historians may have been shared by at least some nineteenth-century soldiers. The suspicion and hostility toward evangelical hegemony expressed by the plain folk who participated in the anti-mission movement in the prewar South had not, in all probability, entirely disappeared, even though there is scant surviving evidence of its existence in the Confederate army. The revivals could not in any case have completely succeeded in transforming southern soldiers into a tightly disciplined fighting force, for complaints about insubordination continued throughout the war and even increased as the desertion rate rose dramatically in 1864 and 1865.

Common soldiers may well have ignored much of the rhetoric of control in tracts and sermons to appropriate from the evangelical message truths that they found more meaningful. The notion of a disciplined and deferential Christian soldier undoubtedly had a greater appeal to religious and military leaders than to the common fighting man instructed that it was his "business . . . to die." Yet Evangelicalism met important needs for the soldiers themselves as well as for their military masters. Like religion among black slaves or working-class Methodists, army evangelism did what E. P. Thompson has described as a "double service," appealing in different ways both to the powerful and to the powerless. In the Old South the Christianity preached by masters to their bondsmen was quite different from that embraced by the slaves.

Similarly, common Confederate soldiers used religion in their own ways, focusing on the promise of salvation from death as well as upon the reality of an evangelical community that recreated some of the ideals of a lost prewar world. The experience of conversion served as the basis for a shared equality of believers and an Arminian notion of ultimate self-determination that in profound ways replicated the antebellum republican order that military hierarchy and command had obliterated. There was, as the *Religious Herald* observed in 1863, a sense of real "homogeneity and fellow-feeling" within the brotherhood of believers. The comradeship of the regenerate encouraged as well the group solidarity that modern military analysts have identified as critical to the maintenance of morale. Converts formed Christian Associations within their brigades and regiments to assume communal responsibility for evangelical discipline, and, in the words of the constitution of one such organization, "to throw as many strengthening influences around the weak . . . as it is possible to do. . . ." The associations ran Bible and reading classes, established camp libraries of tracts and religious newspapers, but, perhaps most significantly, confronted the fear of death—and of dying abandoned and alone—that haunted so many soldiers. The believers of the Seventh Virginia Infantry covenanted, for example, to "care specially for each other in all bodily or mental suffering, to show each other respect in case of death. . . ." In practice this usually meant that association members would try to identify comrades disabled on the field of battle in order to provide them either with medical care or with Christian burial.

On a more individual level, evangelical religion provided psychological reassurance to southern soldiers struggling with the daily threat of personal annihilation. In its Christian promise of salvation and eternal life, conversion offered a special sort of consolation to the embattled Confederate. In striking ways accounts of camp conversions parallel descriptions of what in World Wars I and II was first known as "shell shock," then as "combat exhaustion" or "combat stress." Shaking, loss of speech, paralysis of limbs, uncontrolled weeping, and severe emotional outbursts often appeared among twentieth-century soldiers when they reached safety after military action. Similar behavior characterized many Confederate converts who found Christ in the emotion-filled revival meetings held in the intervals between Civil War battles. The fiercest encounters brought the largest harvests of souls, just as the most desperate fighting of World Wars I and II yielded the highest incidence of combat stress. These similarities in nineteenth- and twentieth-century soldiers' responses suggest that analogous psychological processes might well have been involved.

Twentieth-century scholars have often commented on the seeming failure of the Civil War soldier to grapple with the emotional significance of his experience.

"Much in the Civil War was to be forgotten," Marcus Cunliffe has observed. "Involvement in it was intense yet oddly superficial." Unlike World War I, which yielded its Wilfred Owen, its Siegfried Sassoon, its Ernest Hemingway, the Civil War remained in a real sense unwritten, its horrors, if not unnoticed, at least denied. Yet in their own way and in their own particular idiom, Confederate soldiers were just as expressive as their World War I counterparts. Southerners were very articulate, for example, about their *inability* to portray what they had witnessed. After his first battle in 1861 one infantryman wrote home, "I have not power to describe the scene. It beggars all description." Kate Cumming, working as a nurse in a military hospital, commented even more tellingly on the inability of all those around her to communicate their experiences: "Nothing that I had ever heard or read had given me the faintest idea of the horrors witnessed here. I do not think that words are in our vocabulary expressive enough to present to the mind the realities of that sad scene."

The language of post-Freudian self-scrutiny used by World War I participants was not available to Civil War soldiers. But their silences are eloquent. Their speechlessness was part of a process of numbing, of the denial that is a widespread human response to stress. "We hurry," one soldier wrote, "through the dreadful task apparently unconscious of its demoralizing influences and destructive effects." The war, another confirmed, "is calculated to harden the softest heart." The majority came to act as "unconcerned as if it were hogs dying around them." A correspondent writing to the *Religious Herald* in 1862 understood well, however, "the true fountain" of this apparent indifference. Soldiers' unconcern, he explained, was "the result of an effort to *banish*, not to *master*, the fear of death. . . . the expedient of the ostrich [who acts] . . . as though refusing to look on a peril were to escape from it."

Modern-day analysts of combat stress point out, however, that such denial has its limits, that numbness and indifference can only be retained for so long. Eventually extreme stress results in the appearance of symptoms in virtually everyone. Often denial begins to be interrupted by what psychiatrists call "intrusions," nightmares or irrepressible and unwelcome daytime visions of stress-producing events. One Confederate soldiers who had previously told his wife that he found the battle of Shiloh indescribable wrote again several weeks later, "I've had great and exciting times at night with my dreams since the battle; some of them are tragedies and frighten me more than ever the fight did when I was awake. . . ." Another soldier was obviously more profoundly affected, for, as a friend described him, he began reliving battles in his everyday life. "He became more and more alarmed, and, at last, became so powerfully excited—to use his own words—he felt as if some one was after him with a bayonet, and soon found himself almost in a run, as he moved backwards and forwards in his beat." . . .

The broader significance of army religion may thus be the way in which it points to the importance of the experience of war itself in establishing a framework for the social and political conflicts of a New South. In the Confederate army, as in the South of the postwar years, the protean nature of the evangelical message permitted its adherents to appropriate it to satisfy very different purposes and needs.

Revivalism served at once as an idiom of social strife and a context for social unity in an age of unsettling transition; it became a vehicle both for expression and resolution of conflict about fundamental transformations in the southern social order.

The identity crisis of the Confederate soldier adjusting to distressing new patterns of life and labor was but a microcosm of the wartime crisis of a South in the throes of change. Military service inaugurated for many southerners a new era characterized by a loss of autonomy and self-determination that even peace would not restore. In the postwar years a southerner was far more likely to be a tenant and far less likely to be economically self-sufficient than he had been in the antebellum period. He might even follow his experience of military wage labor with that of factory employment, as the cotton mill campaign drew thousands of white southerners into industry.

But perhaps the most profound transformation for many Confederate soldiers was deeply personal. In the past decade we have been made sharply aware of the lingering effects of another lost war upon its veterans' years after their return to civilian life. Irrational outbursts of violence and debilitating depression are but two characteristic symptoms of what psychiatrists have come to see as a definable "post-Vietnam" syndrome. Southerners deeply scarred by their experiences of horror in the world's first total war may have been affected in similar ways. Perhaps part of the explanation for the widespread violence of the postwar South should be psychological; Klan activity, whitecapping, and lynching may have been a legacy of soldiers' wartime stresses as well as a political response to new and displeasing social realities.

In the clues that it offers to the profound impact of battle and to the social origins of a new South, revivalism is central to the Confederate experience. The Civil War challenged both the South and her fighting men to be "born again."

Questions for Reflection and Discussion

1. According to the documents, what role did religion play in the Civil War?

2. Describe the case Mitchell Snay makes in his argument that religion was a key ingredient in the forming of Southern nationalism.

3. How does James Moorhead demonstrate that Yankee Protestants were significant in the North's Civil War cause?

4. What role does Drew Gilpin Faust ascribe to Southern Christian soldiers for revivalism in the Confederate army?

5. How did a national consensus of religious tradition and symbolism degenerate into a conflict between the people of the nation?

Additional Readings

Armstrong, Warren. *For Courageous Fighting and Confident Dying: Union Chaplains in the Civil War.* Lawrence: University Press of Kansas, 1998.

Blied, Benjamin J. *Catholics and the Civil War.* Milwaukee: Privately Printed, 1945.

Carwardine, Richard. *Evangelicals and Politics in Antebellum America.* New Haven: Yale University Press, 1993.

Chesbrough, David B., ed. *"God Ordained This War": Sermons on the Sectional Crisis, 1830-1865.* Columbia: University of South Carolina Press, 1991.

Dunham, Chester F. *The Attitude of the Northern Clergy toward the South, 1860-1865.* Toledo, Ohio: Gray Co., 1942.

Evans, Eli. *Judah P. Benjamin: The Jewish Confederate.* New York: Free Press, 1988.

Goen, C. C. *Broken Churches, Broken Nation: Denominational Schisms and the Coming of the Civil War.* Macon, Ga.: Mercer University Press, 1985.

Guelzo, Allen C. *Abraham Lincoln: Redeemer President.* Grand Rapids, MI: Wm. B. Eerdmans Publishing Co., 1999.

Howe, Daniel Walker. "Religion and Politics in the Antebellum North." *Religion and American Politics,* ed. Mark A. Noll, pp. 121-145. New York: Oxford University Press, 1990.

Johnson, Curtis D. *Redeeming America: Evangelicals and the Road to the Civil War.* Chicago: Ivan R. Dee, 1993.

Korn, Bertram W. *American Jewry and the Civil War.* Cleveland: Meridian Books, 1961.

Miller, Randall, Harry Stout, and C. R. Wilson, eds. *Religion and the American Civil War.* New York: Oxford University Press, 1998.

Noll, Mark A. "The Puzzling Faith of Abraham Lincoln." *Christian History* 11 (1991): 10-20.

Shattuck, Gardiner H., Jr. "Revivals in the Camp." *Christian History* 11 (1991): 28-38.

Silver, James W. *Confederate Morale and Church Propaganda,* Tuscaloosa, Ala.: Confederate Publishing Co., 1957.

Smith, Timothy L. *Revivalism and Social Reform: American Protestantism on the Eve of the Civil War.* Nashville: Abingdon Press, 1957.

Wolf, William J. *The Almost Chosen People: A Study of the Religion of Abraham Lincoln.* Garden City, N.Y.: Doubleday & Co., 1959.

Chapter 9

"And God said, Let us make man in our image, after our likeness: and let them have dominion over the fish of the sea, and over the fowl of the air, and over the cattle, and over all the earth, and over every creeping thing that creepeth upon the earth.

"So God created man in his own image, in the image of God created he him; male and female created he them."

—Genesis 1:26-27

Religion & Science in Confrontation

Issue

How did religion in America respond to the "new" voice of science?

"Darwin threw down a challenge to the old rigidities, and his doctrine of evolution made everything a matter of degree, obliterating the absoluteness of white-and-black, right and wrong. . . . It seemed that everything, instead of being so or not so, as in the logic books, was only more so or less so. And in this mush of compromise all the old splendid certainties dissolved."

—Bertrand Russell, 1949

The truth of Bertrand Russell's analysis in 1949 was fully apparent a half century earlier. The "new" voice acquired by science in the last half of the nineteenth century prompted a range of responses from defenders and critics alike. While Princeton theologian Charles Hodge was referring to Darwinism as atheism, Brooklyn minister Henry Ward Beecher was defending his acceptance of Darwinism with the remark that evolution "lifted [divine Design] to a higher plane, and made it more sublime than it ever was contemplated to be under the old reasonings." A consequence of these different responses was a new level of conflict among both divines and laity.

Additionally, Darwinism accelerated the secularization of American society and thought that had appeared early in the nineteenth century. Formal, organized religion was losing control of more areas of American life. The new ideas of science were overturning a traditional understanding about the nature of the universe. "Whereas before, stability had been considered the ideal state of things, now change was taken as typical of nature and hence equated with the good." As for any problem this caused for religion, educator John Dewey stated in 1909: "Intellectual progress usually occurs through sheer abandonment of ques-

tions. . . . We do not solve them; we get over them." What did Dewey's comment mean for religion? How would the confrontation between religion and science impact American society? What evidence is there that the tension between religion and science produced both conflict and consensus?

DOCUMENTS

The documents below represent some of the variety of religious responses to the ideas of evolutionary naturalism. In the first document, Charles Hodge, a foremost Presbyterian theologian of the nineteenth century, pronounces natural selection to be a contradiction to the traditionally held belief in an omnipotent, omniscient Creator. James Woodrow, the uncle of President Woodrow Wilson and professor of natural sciences, argues in the second selection that the content of the Bible and science are so different that it is futile to identify consistencies. The accommodation of evolutionary principles to traditional biblical teaching was accelerated through the influence of Brooklyn minister Henry Ward Beecher. In the third document, he discusses the bearing of evolution on the fundamental doctrines of orthodox Christianity. In the fourth selection, Catholic scholar Father John Zahm not only argued that science and scripture could never really conflict, but also that evolution supported dogma "by requiring man to presuppose the existence of an intelligent and purposeful God." In the final selection, scholar-diplomat Andrew Dickson White, who elsewhere had argued that "the old theory of direct creation is gone forever," describes here the final effort of theology to withstand the onslaught of Darwinism at the end of the century.

1. What is Darwinism?, 1874

SOURCE: Charles Hodge, *What is Darwinism?* (New York: Scribner, Armstrong and Company, 1874), *passim.*

This is a question which needs an answer. Great confusion and diversity of opinion prevail as to the real views of the man whose writings have agitated the whole world, scientific and religious. If a man says he is a Darwinian, many understand him to avow himself virtually an atheist; while another understands him as saying that he adopts some harmless form of the doctrine of evolution. This is a great evil. It is obviously useless to discuss any theory until we are agreed as to what that theory is. The question, therefore, What is Darwinism? must take precedence of all discussion of its merits.

The great fact of experience is that the universe exists. The great problem which has ever pressed upon the human mind is to account for its existence. What was its origin? To what causes are the changes we witness around us to be referred? As we are a part of the universe, these questions concern ourselves. What are the origin, nature, and destiny of man?. . . Mr. Darwin undertakes to answer these questions. He proposes a solution of the problem which thus deeply concerns every living man. Darwinism is, therefore, a theory of the universe, at least so far as the living organisms are concerned. . . .

The Scriptural solution of the problem of the universe is stated in words equally simple and sublime: "In the beginning God created the heavens and the earth." We have here, first, the idea of God. The word God has in the Bible a definite meaning. It does not stand for an abstraction, for mere force, for law or ordered sequence. God is a spirit, and as we are spirits, we know from consciousness that God is, (1) A Substance; (2) That He is a person; and, therefore, a self-conscious, intelligent, voluntary agent. He can say I; we can address Him as thou; we can speak of Him as He or Him. This idea of God pervades the Scriptures. It lies at the foundation of natural religion. It is involved in our religious consciousness. It enters essentially into our sense of moral obligation. It is inscribed ineffaceably, in letters more or less legible, on the heart of every human being. The man who is trying to be an atheist is trying to free himself from the laws of his being. He might as well try to free himself from liability to hunger or thirst.

The God of the Bible, then, is a Spirit, infinite, eternal, and unchangeable in his being, wisdom, power, holiness, goodness, and truth. As every theory must begin with some postulate, this is the grand postulate with which the Bible begins. This is the first point.

The second point concerns the origin of the universe. It is not eternal either as to matter of form. It is not independent of God. It is not an evolution of his being, or his existence form. He is extramundane as well as antemundane. The universe owes its existence to his will.

Thirdly, as to the nature of the universe; it is not a mere phenomenon. It is an entity, having real objective existence, or actuality. This implies that matter is a substance endowed with certain properties, in virtue of which it is capable of acting and of being acted upon. These properties being uniform and constant, are physical laws to which, as their proximate causes, all the phenomena of nature are to be referred.

Fourthly, although God is extramundane, He is nevertheless everywhere present. That presence is not only a presence of essence, but also of knowledge and power. He upholds all things. He controls all physical causes, working through them, with them, and without them, as He sees fit. As we, in our limited spheres, can use physical causes to accomplish our purposes, so God everywhere and always cooperates with them to accomplish his infinitely wise and merciful designs.

Fifthly, man a part of the universe, is, according to the Scriptures, as concerns his body, of the earth. So far, he belongs to the animal kingdom. As to his soul, he is a child of God, who is declared to be the Father of the spirit of all men. God is a spirit, and we are spirits. We are, therefore, of the same nature with God. We are God-like; so that in knowing ourselves we know God. No man conscious of his manhood can be ignorant of his relationship to God as his Father.

The truth of the theory of the universe rests, in the first place, so far as it has been correctly stated, on the infallible authority of the word of God. In the second place, it is a satisfactory solution of the problem to be solved: (1) It accounts for the origin of the universe. (2) It accounts for all the universe contains, and gives a satisfactory explanation of the marvelous contrivances which abound in living organisms, of the adaptations of these organisms to conditions external to themselves, and for those provisions for the future, which on any other assumption are utterly inexplicable. (3) It is in conflict with no truth of reason and with no fact of experience. (4) The Scriptural doctrine accounts for the spiritual nature of man, and meets all his spiritual necessities. It gives him an object of adoration, love, and confidence. It reveals the Being on whom his indestructible sense of responsibility terminates. The truth of this doctrine, therefore, rests not only on the authority of the Scriptures, but on the very constitution of our nature. The Bible has little charity for those who reject it. It pronounces them to be either derationalized or demoralized, or both. . . .

We have not forgotten Mr. Darwin. It seemed desirable, in order to understand his theory, to see its relation to other theories of the universe and its phenomena, with which it is more or less connected. His work on the "Origin of Species" does not purport to be philosophical.... Darwin does not speculate on the origin of the universe, on the nature of matter, or of force. He is simply a naturalist, a careful and laborious observer; skillful in his descriptions, and singularly candid in dealing with the difficulties in the way of his peculiar doctrine. He set before himself a single problem, namely, How are the fauna and flora of our earth to be accounted for? In the solution of this problem, he assumes: (1) The existence of matter, although he says little on the subject. Its existence however, as a real entity, is everywhere taken for granted. (2) He assumes the efficiency of physical causes, showing no disposition to resolve them into mind-force, or into the efficiency of the First Cause. (3) He assumes also the existence of life in the form of one or more primordial germs. He does not adopt the theory of spontaneous generation. What life is he does not attempt to explain. . . . (4) To account for the existence of matter and life, Mr. Darwin admits a Creator. This is done explicitly and repeatedly. Nothing, however, is said of the nature of the Creator and of his relation to the world, further than is implied in the meaning of the word. (5) From the primordial germ or germs (Mr. Darwin seems to have settled down to the assumption of only one primordial germ), all living organisms, vegetable and animal, including man, on our globe, through all the stages of its history, have descended. (6) As growth, organization, and reproduction are the functions of physical life, as soon as the primordial germ began to live, it began to grow, to fashion organs, however simple, for its nourishment and increase, and for the reproduction, in some way, of living forms like itself. How all living things on earth, including the endless variety of plants, and all the diversity of animals—insects, fishes, birds, the ichthyosaurus, the mastodon, the mammoth, and man—have descended from the primordial animalcule, he thinks, may be accounted for by the operation of the following natural laws:

First, the law of Heredity, or that by which like begets like. The offspring are like the parent.

Second, the law of Variation, that is, while the offspring are, in all essential characteristics, like their immediate progenitor, they nevertheless vary more or less within narrow limits, from their parent and from each other. Some of these variations are indifferent, some improvements, that is, they are such as enable the plant or animal to exercise its functions to greater advantage.

Third, the law of Over Production. All plants and animals tend to increase in a geometrical ratio; and therefore tend to overrun enormously the means of support. . . . Hence of necessity arises a struggle for life. Only a few of the myriads born can possibly live.

Fourth, here comes in the law of Natural Selection, or the Survival of the Fittest. That is, if any individual of a given species of plant or animal happens to have a slight deviation from the normal type, favorable to its success in the struggle for life, it will survive. This variation, by the law of heredity, will be transmitted to its offspring, and by them again to theirs. Soon these favored ones gain the ascendancy, and the less favored perish; and the modification becomes established in the modification becomes established in the species. After a time another and another of such favorable variations occur, with like results. Thus very gradually, great changes of structure are introduced, and not only species, but genera, families, and orders in the vegetable and animal world, are produced. Mr. Darwin says he can set no limit to the changes of structure, habits, instincts, and millions or milliards of centuries may bring into existence. He says, "we cannot comprehend what the figures 60,000,000 really imply, and during this, or perhaps a longer roll of years, the land and waters have everywhere teemed with living creatures, all exposed to the struggle for life, and undergoing change.". . .Years in this connection have no meaning. We might as well try to give the distance of the fixed stars in inches. As astronomers are obliged to take the diameter of the earth's orbit as the unit of space, so Darwinians are obliged to take a geological cycle as their unit of duration. . . .

We have not reached the heart of Mr. Darwin's theory. The main idea of his system lies in the word "natural." He uses that word in two senses: first, as antithetical to the word artificial. Men can produce very marked varieties as to structure and habits of animals. This is exemplified in the production of the different breeds of horses, cattle, sheep, and dogs; and specifically, as Mr. Darwin seems to think, in the case of pigeons. . . . If, then he argues, man, in a comparatively short time, has by artificial selection produced all these varieties, what might be accomplished on the boundless scale of nature, during the measureless ages of the geologic periods?

Secondly, he uses the word natural as antithetical to supernatural. Natural selection is a selection made by natural laws, working without intention and design. It is, therefore, opposed not only to artificial selection, which is made by the wisdom and skill of man to accomplish a given purpose, but also to supernatural selection, which means either a selection originally intended by a power higher than nature; or which is carried out by such power. In using the expression Natural Selection,

Mr. Darwin intends to exclude design, or final causes. All the changes in structure, instinct, or intelligence, in the plants or animals, including man, descended from the primordial germ, or animalcule, have been brought about by unintelligent physical causes. On this point he leaves us in no doubt. It is affirmed that natural selection is the operation of natural laws, analogous to the action of gravitation and of chemical affinities. It is denied that it is a process originally designed, or guided by intelligence, such as the activity which foresees an end and consciously selects and controls the means of its accomplishment. Artificial selection, then, is an intelligent process; natural selection is not. . . .

The conclusion of the whole matter is, that the denial of design in nature is virtually the denial of God. Mr. Darwin's theory is virtually atheistical; his theory, not he himself. He believes in a Creator. But when that Creator, millions on millions of ages ago, did something—called matter and a living germ into existence—and then abandoned the universe to itself to be controlled by chance and necessity, without any purpose on his part as to the result, or any intervention or guidance, then He is virtually consigned, so far as we are concerned, to nonexistence. . . . This is the vital point. The denial of final causes is the formative idea of Darwin's theory, and therefore no teleologist can be a Darwinian. . . .

We have thus arrived at the answer to our question, What is Darwinism? It is Atheism.

2. Evolution, 1884

SOURCE: Joseph L. Blau, ed., *American Philosophic Addresses, 1700-1900* (New York: Columbia University Press, 1946), excerpted from pp. 488-513.

. . . When thinking of the origin of anything, we may inquire, Did it come into existence just as it is? Or did it pass through a series of changes from a previous state in order to reach its present condition? For example, if we think of a tree, we can conceive of it as having come immediately into existence just as we see it; or, we may conceive of it as having begun its existence as a minute cell in connexion with a similar tree, and as having reached its present condition by passing through a series of changes, continually approaching and at length reaching the form before us. Or thinking of the earth, we can conceive of it as having begun to exist in the simplest possible state, and as having reached its present condition by passing through a long series of stages, each derived from its predecessor. To the second of these modes, we apply the term "Evolution." It is evidently equivalent to "derivation"; or, in the case of organic beings, to "descent."

This definition or description of Evolution does not include any reference to the power by which the origination is effected; it refers to the mode, and to the mode alone. So far as the definition is concerned, the immediate existence might be attributed to God or to chance; the derived existence to inherent uncreated law, or to an almighty personal Creator, acting according to laws of his own framing. It is important to consider this distinction carefully, for it is wholly inconsistent with much that is said and believed by both advocates and opponents of Evolution. It is not unusual to represent Creation and Evolution as mutually exclusive, as contradictory: Creation meaning the immediate calling out of non-existence by divine power; Evolution, derivation from previous forms or states by inherent, self-originated or eternal laws, independent of all connexion with divine personal power. Hence, if this is correct, those who believe in Creation are theists; those who believe in Evolution are atheists. But there is no propriety in thus mingling in the definition two things which are so completely different. . . .

The definition now given, which seems to me the only one which can be given within the limits of natural science, necessarily excludes the possibility of the questions whether the doctrine is theistic or atheistic, whether it is religious or irreligious, moral or immoral. It would be as plainly absurd to ask these questions as to inquire whether the doctrine is white or black, square or round, light or heavy. In this respect it is like every other hypothesis or theory in science. These are qualities which do not belong to such subjects. The only question that can rationally be put is, Is the doctrine true or false? If this statement is correct—and it is almost if not quite self-evident—it should at once end all disputes not only between Evolution and religion, but between natural science and religion universally. To prove that the universe, the earth, and the organic beings upon the earth, had once been in a different condition from the present, and had gradually reached the state which we now see, could not disprove or tend to disprove the existence of God or the possession by him of a single attribute ever thought to belong to him. How can our belief in this doctrine tend to weaken or destroy our belief that he is infinite, that he is eternal, that he is unchangeable, in his being, or his wisdom, or his power, or his holiness, or his justice, or his goodness, or his truth? Or how can our rejection of the doctrine either strengthen or weaken our belief in him? Or how can either our acceptance or rejection of Evolution affect our love to God, or our recognition of our obligation to obey and serve him—carefully to keep all his commandments and ordinances?

True, when we go outside the sphere of natural science, and inquire whence this universe, questions involving theism forthwith arise. Whether it came into existence immediately or mediately is not material; but what or who brought it into existence? Did it spring from the fortuitous concurrence of eternally-existing atoms? Are the matter and the forces which act upon it in certain definite ways eternal; and is the universe, as we behold it, the result of their blind unconscious operation? Or, on the other hand, was the universe in all its orderly complexity brought into existence by the will of an eternal, personal, spiritual God, one who is omniscient, omnipresent, omnipotent? These questions of course involve the very foundations of religion and morality; but they lie wholly outside of natural science; and are, I repeat, not in the least affected by the decision of that other question, Did the universe come into its present condition immediately or mediately; instantly, in a moment, or gradually, through a long series of intermediate stages? They are not affected by, nor do they affect, the truth or falsehood of Evolution. . . .

Believing, as I do, that the Scriptures are almost certainly silent on the subject, I find it hard to see how any one can hesitate to prefer the hypothesis of mediate creation to the hypothesis of immediate creation. . . .

I cannot take time to discuss at length objections which have been urged against this hypothesis, but may say that they do not seem to me of great weight. It is sometimes said that, if applied to man, it degrades him to regard him as in any respect the descendant of the beast. We have not been consulted on the subject, and possibly our desire for noble origin may not be able to control the matter; but, however that may be, it is hard to see how dirt is nobler than the highest organisation which God had up to that time created on the earth. And further, however it may have been with Adam, we are perfectly certain that each one of us has passed through a state lower than that of the fish, then successively through states not unlike those of the tadpole, the reptile, and the quadruped. Hence, whatever nobility may have been conferred on Adam by being made of dust has been lost to us by our passing through these low animal stages.

It has been objected that it removes God to such a distance from us that it tends to atheism. But the doctrine of descent certainly applies to the succession of men from Adam up to the present. Are we any farther from God than were the earlier generations of the antediluvians? Have we fewer proofs of his existence and power than they had? It must be plain that, if mankind shall continue to exist on the earth so long, millions of years hence the proofs of God's almighty creative power will be as clear as they are today.

It has been also objected that this doctrine excludes the idea of design in nature. But if the development of an oak from an acorn in accordance with laws which God has ordained and executes, does not exclude the ideas of design, I utterly fail to see how the development of our complex world, teeming with co-adaptations of the most striking character, can possibly exclude that idea.

I have now presented briefly, but as fully as possible in an address of this kind, my views as to the method which should be adopted in considering the relations between the Scriptures and natural science, showing that all that should be expected is that it shall be made to appear by interpretations which may be true that they do not contradict each other; that the contents and aims of the Scriptures and of natural science are so different that it is unreasonable to look for agreement or harmony; that terms are not and ought not to be used in the Bible in a scientific sense, and that they are used perfectly truthfully when they convey the sense intended; that on these principles all alleged contradictions of natural science by the Bible disappear; that a proper definition of Evolution excludes all reference to the origin of the forces and laws by which it works, and therefore that it does not and cannot affect belief in God or in religion; that, according to not unreasonable interpretations of the Bible, it does not contradict anything there taught so far as regards the earth, the lower animals, and probably man as to his body; that there are many good grounds for believing that Evolution is true in these respects; and lastly, that the reasons urged against it are of little or no weight.

I would say in conclusion, that while the doctrine of Evolution in itself, as before stated, is not and cannot be either Christian or anti-Christian, religious or irreligious, theistic or atheistic, yet viewing the history of our earth and inhabitants, and of the whole universe, as it is unfolded by its help, and then going outside of it and recognising that it is God's PLAN OF CREATION, instead of being tempted to put away thoughts of him, as I contemplate this wondrous series of events, caused and controlled by the power and wisdom of the Lord God Almighty, I am led with profounder reverence and admiration to give glory and honor to him that sits on the throne, who liveth for ever and ever; and with fuller heart and a truer appreciation of what it is to create, to join in saying, Thou art worthy, O Lord, to receive glory and honor and power; for thou hast created all things, and for thy pleasure they are and were created.

3. Evolution and Religion, 1886

SOURCE: Henry Ward Beecher, *Evolution and Religion* (New York: Ford, Howard, and Hulbert, 1886), excerpted from pp. 112-17.

The law of cause and effect is fundamental to the every existence of science, and, I had almost said, to the very operation of the human mind. So, then, we gain nothing by excluding divine intelligence, and to include it smooths the way to investigation, and is agreeable to the nature of the human mind. It is easier to conceive of the personal divine being with intelligence, will and power, than it is to conceive of a world of such vast and varied substance as this, performing all the functions of intelligence and will and power. That would be giving to miscellaneous matter the attributes which we denied to a personal God.

The doctrine of Evolution, at first sight, seems to destroy the theory of intelligent design in creation, and in its earlier states left those who investigated it very doubtful whether there was anything in creation but matter, or whether there was a knowable God.

So sprang up the Agnostic school, which includes in it some of the noblest spirits of our day. "God may exist, but we do not know it." That is what the Bible says from the beginning to end; that is what philosophy is now beginning to explain. We cannot understand the divine nature, so exalted above everything that has yet been developed in human consciousness, except it dawns upon us when we are ourselves unfolding and rising to such a higher operation of our minds as does not belong to the great mass of the human race. God is to be seen only by those faculties that verge upon the divine nature, and to them only when they are in a state of exaltation. Moral intuitions are not absolute revelations, but they are as sure of higher truths as the physical senses are of material truths.

But the question of design in creation, which has been a stable argument for the proof of the existence of God and his attributes, seems to have been shaken from its former basis. It is being restored in a larger and grander way, which only places the fact upon a wider space, and makes the outcome more wonderful. Special creation, and the adaptation in consequence of it, of structure to uses in animals, and in the vegetable kingdom to their surroundings, has always been an element of God's work regarded as most remarkable. How things fit to their places; how regular all the subordinations and developments that are going on; how fit they are to succeed one another! Now the old theory conceived God as creating things for special uses, When the idea of the lily dawned on him, he smiled and said: "I will make it"; and he made it to be just as beautiful as it is. And when the rose was to be added, like an artist God thought just how it should be all the way through. That is the old view that some plants were made to do without water and could live in parched sands; and that some could live only in the tropics; and thus God adapted all his creation to the climate and the soil and the circumstances, and it was a beautiful thing to see how things did fit, by the divine wisdom, the place where they were found.

Then comes Evolution and teaches that God created through the mediation of natural laws; that creation, in whole or detail, was a process of slow growth, and not an instantaneous process, that plants and animals alike were affected by their surrounding circumstances favorably or unfavorably; and that, in the long run, those which were best adapted to their environment survived, and those perished which could not adapt themselves to the conditions of soil, climate, moisture, cold or heat which in the immeasurable periods of creation befell them. The adaptation then of plants to their condition did not arise from the direct command of the Great Gardener; but from the fact that, among these infinite gradations of plants, only those survived and propagated themselves which were able to bear the climate and soil in which they found themselves; all others dwindled and perished. Of course there would be a fine adjustment of the plant to its condition; it came to this by a long preparation of ancestral influences. . . .

Through long periods all things intended to vary more or less from their original forms, and adapted themselves to their necessary conditions; and what could not do this perished; for the theory of Evolution is as much a theory of destruction and degradation as of development and building up. As the carpenter has numberless shavings, and a vast amount of wastage of every log which he would shape to some use, so creation has been an enormous waste, such as seems like squandering, on the scale of human life, but not to Him that dwells in Eternity. In bringing the world to its present conditions, vast amounts of things have lived for a time and were unable to hold on, and let go and perished. We behold the onflowing, through immeasurable ages of creation, of this peculiar tendency to vary, and in some cases to improve. The improvement is transmitted; and in the battle of life, one thing conflicting with another, the strong or the best adapted crowd out the weak, and these continue to transmit their qualities until something better yet shall supplant them. . . .

If single acts would evince design, how much more a vast universe, that by inherent laws gradually builded itself, and then created its own plants and animals, a universe so adjusted that it left by the way the poorest things, and steadily wrought toward more complex, ingenious, and beautiful results! Who designed this mighty machine, created matter, gave to it its laws, and impressed upon it that tendency which has brought forth the almost infinite results on the globe, and wrought them into a perfect system? Design by wholesale is grander than design by retail.

You are familiar with the famous illustration of Dr. Paley, where a man finds a watch, and infers irresistibly that that watch was made by some skillful, thoughtful watchmaker. Suppose that a man, having found a watch, should say to himself, "Somebody thought this out, somebody created this; it was evidently constructed and adapted exactly to the end in view the keeping of time." Suppose, then, that some one should take him to Waltham, and introduce him into that vast watch factory, where watches are created in hundreds of thousands by machinery; and suppose the question should be put to him, "What do you think, then, about the man who created this machinery, which of itself goes on cutting out wheels, and springs, and pinions, and everything that belongs to making a watch? If it be an argument of design that there is a man existing who could create a manufactory turning out millions of watches, and machinery too, so that the human hand has little to do but to adjust the parts already created by machines?" If it be evidence of design in creation that God adapted one single flower to its place and functions, is it not greater evidence if there is a system of such adaptations going on from eternity to eternity? Is not the Creator of the system a more sublime designer than the creator of any single act?

Or, let me put down before you an oriental rug, which we all know has been woven by women squatting upon the ground, each one putting in the color that was wanted to form the figure, carrying out the whole with oriental harmony of color. Looking upon that, you could not help saying, "Well, that is a beautiful design, and these are skillful women that made it, there can be no question about that." But now behold the power loom where not simply a rug with long, drudging work by hand is being created, but where the machine is creating carpets in endless lengths, with birds, and insects, and flowers, and scrolls, and every elements of beauty. It is all being done without a hand touching it. Once start the engine, and put the perforated papers above the loom, and that machine turns out a carpet that puts to shame the beauty of these oriental rugs. Now the question is this: It is evidence of design in these women that they turn out such work, and is it not evidence of a higher design in the man who turned out that machine—that loom—which could carry on this work a thousandfold more magnificently than human fingers did?

It may be safely said, then, that Evolution, instead of obliterating the evidence of divine Design, has lifted it to a higher plane, and made it more sublime than it ever was contemplated to be under the old reasonings.

4. A Catholic Reconciles Evolution and Church Dogma, 1896
SOURCE: John Augustine Zahm, *Evolution and Dogma* (Chicago: D. H. McBride & Co., 1890), excerpted from pp. xiv-xix, 378-434.

Can a Catholic, can a Christian of any denomination, consistently with the faith he holds dear, be an evolutionist; or is there something in the theory that is so antagonistic to faith and Scripture as to render its acceptance tantamount to the denial of the fundamental tenets of religious belief? The question . . . has been answered both affirmatively and negatively. But, as is evident, the response cannot be both yea and nay. It must be one or the other, and the query now is, which answer is to be given, the negative or the affirmative?

Whatever may be the outcome of the controversy, whatever may be the results of future research and discovery, there is absolutely no room for apprehension respecting the claims and authority of Scripture and Catholic Dogma. Science will never be able to contradict aught that God has revealed; for it is not possible that the Divine works and the Divine words should ever be in any relation to each other but one of the most perfect harmony. Doubts and difficulties may obtain for a time; the forces of error may for a while appear triumphant; the testimonies of the Lord may be tried to the uttermost; but in the long run it will always be found, as has so often been the case in the past, that the Bible and faith, like truth, will come forth unharmed and intact from any ordeal, however severe, to which they may be subjected. For error is impotent against truth; the pride of man's intellect is of no avail against the wisdom of the Almighty. . . . The fictions of opinions are ephemeral, but the testimonies of the Lord are everlasting. . . .

I am not unaware of the fact that Evolution has had suspicion directed against it, and odium cast upon it, because of materialistic implications and its long anti-Christian associations. I know it has been banned and tabooed because it has received the cordial *imprimatur* of the advocates of Agnosticism, and the special commendation of the defenders of Atheism; that it has long been identified with false systems of philosophy, and made to render yeoman service in countless onslaughts against religion and the Church, against morality and free-will, against God and His providential government of the universe. But this does not prove that Evolution is ill-founded or that it is destitute of all elements of truth. Far from it. It is because Evolution contains so large an element of truth, because it explains countless facts and phenomena which are explicable on no other theory, that it has met with such universal favor, and that it has proved such a powerful agency in the dissemination of error and in giving verisimilitude to the most damnable of doctrines. Such being the case, ours is the duty to withdraw the truth from its enforced and unnatural alliance, and to show that there is a sense in which Evolution can be understood—in which it must be understood, if it repose on a rational basis—in which, far from contributing to the propagation of false views of nature and God, it is calculated to render invaluable aid in the cause of both science and religion. From being an agency for the promulgation of Monism, Materialism and Pantheism, it should be converted into a power which makes for righteousness and the exaltation of holy faith and undying truth. . . .

The evolutionary idea is not . . . the late development it is sometimes imagined to be. On the contrary, it is an idea that had its origin in the speculations of the earliest philosophers, and an idea which has been slowly developed by the studies and observations of twenty-five centuries of earnest seekers after truth.

In reading over the history of Greek philosophy, we are often surprised to see how the sages of old Hellas anticipated many of the views which are nowadays so frequently considered as the result of nineteenth century research. . . . No one can read of the achievements of Aristotle, or recall his marvelous anticipations of modern discoveries, without feeling that it was he who supplied the germs of what subsequently became such large and beautiful growths. As one of the greatest, if not the greatest, of the world's intellects, he accomplished . . . far more than is usually attributed to him, especially in all that concerns the now famous theory of Evolution. . . . In the Stagirite's doctrine, too, we find the germs of those views on creation which were developed later on with such wonderful fullness, and in such marvelous perfection, by those great Doctors of the church, Gregory of Nyssa, Augustine and Thomas Aquinas. According to Aristotle it was necessary, that is, in compliance with natural law, that germs, and not animals, should have been first produced; and that from these germs all forms of life, from polyps to man, should be evolved by the operation of natural causes. How like St Augustine's teaching, that God in the beginning created all things potentially . . . and that these were afterwards developed through the action of secondary causes . . . during the course of untold ages. . . .

No; it is a mistake to suppose that the theory of Evolution, whether cosmic or organic, is something new and the product solely of modern research. It is something old, as old as speculative thought, and stripped of all explanations and subsidiary adjuncts, it is now essentially what it was in the days of Aristotle, St. Augustine, and the Angel of the Schools. Modern research has developed and illustrated the theory, has given it a more definite shape and rendered it more probable, if indeed it has not demonstrated its truth, but the central idea remains practically the same. . . .

Darwinism . . . is not Evolution; neither is Lamarckism nor Neo-Lamarckism. The theories which go by these names, as well as sundry others, are but tentative explanations of the methods by which Evolution has acted, and of the processes which have obtained in the growth and development of the organic world. They may be true or false, although all of them undoubtedly contain at least an element of truth, but whether true or false, the great central conception of Evolution remains unaffected. . . . What shall ultimately be the fate of the arguments now so confidently advanced in favor of Evolution by its friends, and against it by its enemies, only the future can decide. The grounds of defense and attack will, no doubt, witness many and important changes. Future research and discovery will reveal the weakness of arguments that are now considered unassailable, and expose the fallacies of others which, as at present viewed, are thoroughly logical. But new reasons in favor of Evolution will be forthcoming in proportion as the older ones shall be modified or shown to be untenable. And, as the evolutionary idea shall be more studied and developed, the objections which are now urged against it will, I doubt not, disappear or lose much of their cogency. . . .

In proportion as Evolution shall be placed on a solider foundation, and the objections which are now urged against it shall disappear, so also will it be evinced, that far from being an enemy of religion, it is, on the contrary, its strongest and most natural ally. Even those who have no sympathy with the traditional forms of belief, who are, in principle, if not personally, opposed to the Church and her dogmas, perceive that there is no necessary antagonism between Evolution and faith, between the conclusions of science and the declarations of revelation. Indeed, so avowed an opponent of Church and Dogma as Huxley informs us that: "The doctrine of Evolution does not even come into contact with Theism, considered as a philosophical doctrine. That with which it does collide, and with which it is absolutely inconsistent, is the conception of creation which theological speculators have based upon the history narrated in the opening book of Genesis."

In other words, Evolution is not opposed to revelation, but to certain interpretations of what some have imagined to be revealed truths. It is not opposed to the dogmas of the Church, but to the opinions of certain individual exponents of Dogma, who would have us believe that their views of the Inspired Record are the veritable expressions of Divine truth.

To say that Evolution is agnostic or atheistic in tendency, if not in fact, is to betray a lamentable ignorance of what it actually teaches, and to display a singular incapacity for comprehending the relation of a scientific induction to a philosophical— or, more truthfully, an anti-philosophical— system. . . .Rather should it be affirmed that Evolution, in so far as it is true, makes for religion and Dogma; because it must needs be that a true theory of the origin and development of things must, when properly understood and applied, both strengthen and illustrate the teachings of faith. "When from the dawn of life," says Prof. Fiske, who is an ardent evolutionist, "we see all things working together towards the Evolution of the highest spiritual attributes of man, we know, however the words may stumble in which we try to say it, that God is in the deepest sense a moral being." Elsewhere the same writer truly observes: "The doctrine of Evolution destroys the conception of the world as a machine. It makes God our constant refuge and support, and nature His true revelation." And again he declares: "Though science must destroy mythology, it can never destroy religion; and to the astronomer of the future, as well as to the Psalmist of old, the heavens will declare the glory of God."

Evolution does, indeed, to employ the words of Carlyle, destroy the conception of "an absentee God, sitting idle, ever since the first Sabbath, at the outside of His universe and seeing it go." But it compels us to recognize that "this fair universe, were it in the meanest province thereof, is, in very deed, the star-domed city of God; that through every star, through every grass-blade, and most, through every living soul, the glory of a present God still beams. . . ."

But the derivation of man from the ape, we are told, degrades man. Not at all. It would be truer to say that such derivation ennobles the ape. Sentiment aside, it is quite unimportant to the Christian "whether he is to trace back his pedigree directly or indirectly to the dust." St. Francis of Assisi, as we learn from his life, "called the birds his brothers." Whether he was correct, either theologically or zoologically, he was plainly free from that fear of being mistaken for an ape which haunts so many in these modern times. Perfectly sure that he, himself, was a spiritual being, he thought it at least possible that birds might be spiritual beings, likewise incarnate like himself in mortal flesh; and saw no degradation to the dignity of human nature in claiming kindred lovingly with creatures so beautiful, so wonderful, who, as he fancied, "praised God in the forest, even as angels did in heaven."

Many, it may here be observed, look on the theory of Evolution with suspicion, because they fail to understand its true significance. They seem to think that it is an attempt to account for the origin of things when, in reality, it deals only with their historical development. . . . Evolution, then postulates creation as an intellectual necessity, for if there had not been a creation there would have been nothing to evolve, and Evolution would, therefore, have been an impossibility. And for the same reason, Evolution postulates and must postulate, a Creator, the sovereign Lord of all things, the Cause of causes. . . . But Evolution postulates still more. . . . To suppose that simple brute matter could, by its own motion or by any power inherent in matter as such, have been the sole efficient cause of the Evolution of organic from inorganic matter, of the higher from the lower forms of life, of the rational from the irrational creature, is to suppose that a thing can give what it does not possess, that the greater is contained in the less, the superior in the inferior, the whole in a part.

No mere mechanical theory, therefore, however ingenious, is competent to explain the simplest fact of development. No only is such a theory unable to account for the origin of a speck of protoplasm, or the germination of a seed, but it is equally incompetent to assign a reason for the formation of the smallest crystal or the simplest chemical compound. Hence, to be philosophically valid, Evolution must postulate a Creator not only for the material which is evolved, but it must also postulate a Creator . . . for the power or agency which makes any development possible. God, then, not only created matter in the beginning, but He gave it the power of evolving into all forms it has since assumed or ever shall assume.

But this is not all. In order to have an intelligible theory of Evolution, a theory that can meet the exacting demands of a sound philosophy as well as of a true theology, still another postulate is necessary. We must hold not only that there was an actual creation of matter in the beginning, that there was potential creation which rendered matter capable of Evolution, in accordance with the laws impressed by God on matter, but we must also believe that creative action and influence still persist, that they always have persisted from the dawn of creation, that they, and they alone, have been efficient in all the countless stages of evolutionary progress from atoms to monads, from monads to man.

This ever-present action of the Deity, this immanence of His in the work of His hands, this continuing in existence and developing of the creatures He has made, is what St. Thomas calls the "Divine administration," and what is ordinarily known as Providence. It connotes the active and constant cooperation of the Creator with the creature, and implies that if the multitudinous forms of terrestrial life have been evolved from the potentiality of matter, they have been so evolved because matter was in the first instance proximately disposed for Evolution by God Himself, and has even remained so disposed. . . . Evolution, therefore, is neither a "philosophy of mud," nor "a gospel of dirt," as it has been denominated. So far, indeed, is this from being the case that, when properly understood, it is found to be a strong and useful ally of Catholic Dogma. For if Evolution be true, the existence of God and an original creation follow as necessary inferences.

5. The Final Effort of Theology, 1896

SOURCE: Andrew Dickson White, *A History of the Warfare of Science with Theology in Christendom* (New York, 1896).

Darwin's *Origin of Species* had come into the theological world like a plough into an ant-hill. Everywhere those thus rudely awakened from their old comfort and repose had swarmed forth angry and confused. Reviews, sermons, books light and heavy, came flying at the new thinker from all sides.

The keynote was struck at once in the *Quarterly Review* by Wilberforce, Bishop of Oxford. He declared that Darwin was guilty of "a tendency to limit God's glory in creation"; that "the principle of natural selection is absolutely incompatible with the word of God"; that it "contradicts the revealed relations of creation to its Creator"; that it is "inconsistent with the fulness of his glory"; that it is "a dishonouring view of Nature"; and that there is "a simpler explanation of the presence of these strange forms among the works of God": that explanation being—"the fall of Adam." Nor did the bishop's efforts end here; at the meeting of the British Association for the Advancement of Science he again disported himself in the tide of popular applause. Referring to the ideas of Darwin, who was absent on account of illness, he congratulated himself in a public speech that he was not descended from a monkey. The reply came from Huxley, who said in substance: "If I had to choose I would prefer to be a descendant of a humble monkey rather than of a man who employs his knowledge and eloquence in misrepresenting those who are wearing out their lives in the search for truth."

This shot reverberated through England, and indeed through other countries.

The utterances of this most brilliant prelate of the Anglican Church received a sort of antiphonal response from the leaders of the English Catholics. In an address before the "Academia," which had been organized to combat "science falsely so called," Cardinal Manning declared his abhorrence of the new view of Nature, and described it as "a brutal philosophy—to wit, there is no God, and the ape is our Adam."

These attacks from such eminent sources set the clerical fashion for several years. One distinguished clerical reviewer, in spite of Darwin's thirty years of quiet labour, and in spite of the powerful summing up of his book, prefaced a diatribe by saying that Darwin "might have been more modest had he given some slight reason for dissenting from the views generally entertained." Another distinguished clergyman, vice-president of a Protestant institute to combat "dangerous" science, declared Darwinism "an attempt to dethrone God." Another critic spoke of persons accepting the Darwinian views as "under the frenzied inspiration of the inhaler of mephitic gas," and of Darwin's argument as a "a jungle of fanciful assumption."

Another spoke of Darwin's views as suggesting that "God is dead," and declared that Darwin's work "does open violence to everything which the Creator himself has told us in the Scriptures of the methods and results of his work." Still another theological authority asserted: "If the Darwinian theory is true, Genesis is a lie, the whole framework of the book of life falls to pieces, and the revelation of God to man, as we Christians know it, is a delusion and a snare." Another, who had shown excellent qualities as an observing naturalist, declared the Darwinian view "a huge imposture from the beginning."

Echoes came from America. One review, the organ of the most widespread of American religious sects, declared that Darwin was "attempting to befog and to pettifog the whole question"; another denounced Darwin's views as "infidelity"; another, representing the American branch of the Anglican Church, poured contempt over Darwin as "sophistical and illogical," and then plunged into an exceedingly dangerous line of argument in the following words: "If this hypothesis be true, then is the Bible an unbearable fiction; . . . then have Christians for nearly two thousand years been duped by a monstrous lie. . . .Darwin requires us to disbelieve the authoritative word of the Creator." A leading journal representing the same church took pains to show the evolution theory to be as contrary to the explicit declarations of the New Testament as to those of the Old, and said: "If we have all, men and monkeys, oysters and eagles, developed from an original germ, then is St. Paul's grand deliverance—'All flesh is not the same flesh; there is one kind of flesh of men, another of beasts, another of fishes, and another of birds'—untrue."

Another echo came from Australia, where Dr. Perry, Lord Bishop of Melbourne, in a most bitter book on *Science and the Bible*, declared that the obvious object of Chambers, Darwin, and Huxley, is "to produce in their readers a disbelief of the Bible."

Nor was the older branch of the Church to be left behind in this chorus. Bavma, in the *Catholic World*, declared, "Mr. Darwin is, we have reason to believe, the mouthpiece or chief trumpeter of that infidel clique whose well-known object is to do away with all idea of a God."

Worthy of especial note as showing the determination of the theological side at that period was the foundation of sacro-scientific organizations to combat the new ideas. First to be noted is the "Academia," planned by Cardinal Wiseman. In a circular letter the cardinal, usually so moderate and just, sounded an alarm and summed up by saying, "Now it is for the Church, which alone possesses divine certainty and divine discernment, to place itself at once in the front of a movement which threatens even the fragmentary remains of Christian belief in England." The necessary permission was obtained from Rome, the Academia was founded, and the "divine discernment" of the Church was seen in the utterances which came from it, such as those of Cardinal Manning, which every thoughtful Catholic would now desire to recall, and in the diatribes of Dr. Laing, which only aroused laughter on all sides. A similar effort was seen in Protestant quarters; the "Victoria Institute" was created, and perhaps the most noted utterance which ever came from it was the declaration of its vice-president, the Rev. Walter Mitchell, that "Darwinism endeavours to dethrone God."

In France the attack was even more violent. Fabre d'Envieu brought out the heavy artillery of theology, and in a long series of elaborate propositions demonstrated that any other doctrine than that of the fixity and persistence of species is absolutely contrary to Scripture. The Abbé Désorges, a former Professor of Theology, stigmatized Darwin as a "pedant," and evolution as "gloomy"; Monseigneur Ségur, referring to Darwin and his followers, went into hysterics and shrieked: "These infamous doctrines have for their only support the most abject passions. Their father is pride, their mother is impurity, their offspring revolutions. They come from hell and return thither, taking with them the gross creatures who blush not to proclaim and accept them."

In Germany the attack, if less declamatory, was no less severe. Catholic theologians vied with Protestants in bitterness. Prof. Michelis declared Darwin's theory "a caricature of creation." Dr. Hagermann asserted that it "turned the Creator out of doors." Dr. Schund insisted that "every idea of the Holy Scriptures, from the first to the last page, stands in diametrical opposition to the Darwinian theory"; and, "if Darwin be right in his view of the development of man out of a brutal condition, then the Bible teaching in regard to man is utterly annihilated." Rougemont in Switzerland called for a crusade against the obnoxious doctrine. Luthardt, Professor of Theology at Leipsic, declared: "The idea of creation belongs to religion and not to natural science; the whole superstructure of personal religion is built upon the doctrine of creation"; and he showed the evolution theory to be in direct contradiction to Holy Writ.

But in 1863 came an event which brought serious confusion to the theological camp: Sir Charles Lyell, the most eminent of living geologists, a man of deeply Christian feeling and of exceedingly cautious temper, who had opposed the evolution theory of Lamarck and declared his adherence to the idea of successive creations, then published his work on the *Antiquity of Man*, and in this and other utterances showed himself a complete though unwilling convert to the fundamental ideas of Darwin. The blow was serious in many ways, and especially so in two— first, as withdrawing all foundation in fact from the scriptural chronology, and secondly, as discrediting the creation theory. The blow was not unexpected; in various review articles against the Darwinian theory there had been appeals to Lyell, at times almost piteous, "not to flinch from the truths he had formerly proclaimed." But Lyell, like the honest man he was, yielded unreservedly to the mass of new proofs arrayed on the side of evolution against that of creation.

At the same time came Huxley's *Man's Place in Nature*, giving new and most cogent arguments in favour of evolution by natural selection.

In 1871 was published Darwin's *Descent of Man*. Its doctrine had been anticipated by critics of his previous books, but it made, none the less, a great stir; again the opposing army trooped forth, though evidently with much less heart than before. A few were very violent. The *Dublin University Magazine*, after the traditional Hibernian fashion, charged Mr. Darwin with seeking "to displace God by the unerring action of vagary," and with being "resolved to hunt God out of the world." But most notable from the side of the older Church was the elaborate answer to Darwin's book by the eminent French Catholic physician, Dr. Constantin James. In his work, *On Darwinism, or the Man-Ape*, published at Paris in 1877, Dr. James not only refuted Darwin scientifically but poured contempt on his book, calling it "a fairy tale," and insisted that a work "so fantastic and so burlesque" was, doubtless, only a huge joke, like Erasmus's *Praise of Folly*, or Montesquieu's *Persian Letters*. The princes of the Church were delighted. The Cardinal Archbishop of Paris assured the author that the book had become his "spiritual reading," and begged him to send a copy to the Pope himself. His Holiness, Pope Pius IX, acknowledged the gift in a remarkable letter. He thanked his dear son, the writer, for the book in which he "refutes so well the aberrations of Darwinism." "A system," His Holiness adds, "which is repugnant at once to history, to the tradition of all peoples, to exact science, to observed facts, and even to Reason herself, would seem to need no refutation, did not alienation from God and the leaning toward materialism, due to depravity, eagerly seek to support in all this tissue of fables. . . ." Wherefore the Pope thanked Dr. James for his book, "so opportune and so perfectly appropriate to the exigencies of our time," and bestowed on him the apostolic benediction. Nor was this brief all. With it there came a second, creating the author an officer of the Papal Order of St. Sylvester. The cardinal archbishop assured the delighted physician that such a double honour of brief and brevet was perhaps unprecedented, and suggested only that in a new edition of his book he should "insist a little more on the relation existing between the narratives of Genesis and the discoveries of modern science, in such fashion as to convince the most incredulous of their perfect agreement." The prelate urged also a more dignified title. The proofs of this new edition were accordingly all submitted to His Eminence, and in 1882 it appeared as *Moses and Darwin: the Man of Genesis compared with the Man-Ape, or Religious Education opposed to Atheistic*. No wonder the cardinal embraced the author, thanking him in the name of science and religion. "We have at last," he declared, "a handbook which we can safely put into the hands of youth."

Scarcely less vigorous were the champions of English Protestant orthodoxy. In an address at Liverpool, Mr. Gladstone remarked: "Upon the grounds of what is termed evolution God is relieved of the labour of creation; in the name of unchangeable laws he is discharged from governing the world"; and, when Herbert Spencer called his attention to the fact that Newton with the doctrine of gravitation and with the science of physical astronomy is open to the same charge, Mr. Gladstone retreated in the *Contemporary Review* under one of his characteristic clouds of words. The Rev. Dr. Coles, in the *British and Foreign Evangelical Review*, declared that the God of evolution is not the Christian's God. Burgon, Dean of Chichester, in a sermon preached before the University of Oxford, pathetically warned the students that "those who refuse to accept the history of the creation of our first parents according to its obvious literal intention, and are for substituting the modern dream of evolution in its place, cause the entire scheme of man's salvation to collapse." Dr. Pusey also came into the fray with most earnest appeals against the new doctrine, and the Rev. Gavin Carlyle was perfervid on the same side. The Society for Promoting Christian Knowledge published a book by the Rev. Mr. Birks, in which the evolution doctrine was declared to be "flatly opposed to the fundamental doctrine of creation." Even the *London Times* admitted a review stigmatizing Darwin's *Descent of Man* as an "utterly unsupported hypothesis," full of "unsubstantiated premises, cursory investigations, and disintegrating speculations," and Darwin himself as "reckless and unscientific." . . .

ESSAYS

In the first essay, Paul A. Carter of Northern Illinois University discusses the religious unrest produced by Charles Darwin and others who introduced new ideas of science. "If God didn't die in the late nineteenth century," Carter writes, "He received many mortal wounds." He describes some of the roots of hostility that produced extensive cultural hostility among Protestants, Catholics, and Jews during the final decades of the nineteenth century. The second essay, by James Turner of the University of Notre Dame, discusses how religion's traditional doctrine of the existence of a transcendent God was challenged by Darwin and other scientists. "After Darwin's Origin of Species appeared in 1859, God rapidly became redundant in the whole business [of scientific practice]," Turner maintains.

The Ape in the Tree of Knowledge
PAUL A. CARTER

SOURCE: From *The Spiritual Crisis of the Gilded Age* by Paul A. Carter, 1971, Northern Illinois University Press. Copyright © 1971 by Northern Illinois University Press. Used by permission of the publisher.

I

The self-love of mankind has "been three times severely wounded by the researches of science," said Freud. It suffered the first blow when men learned that their small planetary home was not the center of the universe; the second, when the presumed gulf between themselves and the rest of the animal kingdom was bridged by the theory of evolution; the third, when sleuths like Freud himself showed them that the ego was not master even in its own house. With a certain professional bias, perhaps, the Viennese doctor declared the third of these shocks to have been probably the most severe; but he would have been the first to acknowledge that Nicolaus Copernicus and Charles Darwin had also taken their historic toll.

The new astronomy of the seventeenth century prompted Blaise Pascal to exclaim: "The eternal silence of these infinite spaces frightens me," and the new biology of the nineteenth century, writes one leading cultural historian, "seemingly made final the separation between man and his soul." Small wonder, then, that some who heard this dismal news fell back upon the most traditional means available for the defense of human dignity. "When you read what some writers say about man and his bestial origin your shoulders unconsciously droop. . . . Your self-respect has received a blow," wrote Dyson Hague, Professor of Liturgics in Wycliffe College, Toronto, around 1909. "When you read Genesis, your shoulders straighten, your chest emerges. You feel proud to be that thing that is called man."

With any trauma, according to Freud, goes repression; the victim is naturally inclined to forget how deep these cultural shocks were. The humiliation implicit in civilized man's discovery that he is just another of the animals may have been dispelled for many by the comfortable words of Dr. Benjamin Spock, whose well-thumbed baby book has within the past decade begun to rival the Bible in sales; certainly it has been read by many a woman of childbearing age with more attention than she had free to devote to Scripture. "Each child as he develops is retracing the whole history of mankind, physically and spiritually [sic]. . . . A baby starts off in the womb as a single tiny cell just the way the first living thing appeared in the ocean. Weeks later . . . he has gills like a fish," et cetera. To the twentieth-century American mother, as she anxiously watches her one-year-old "celebrating that period millions of years ago when man's ancestors got up off all-fours," the theory of evolution is not exactly news; in fact, if she has time to reflect, she is likely aware that the good doctor's version of the doctrine that ontogeny recapitulates phylogeny is somewhat inaccurate and out of date.

Nevertheless, viewers of the National Geographic Society's 1966 television documentary on man's lowly origins may have squirmed a bit as the homely likeness of Zinjanthropus swung into focus before the camera. Desmond Morris's book *The Naked Ape* made the best-seller lists in 1968 partly because its subject matter, man, still seemed a bit scandalous under that title; and at some showings of Stanley Kubrick's remarkable motion picture *2001* the physically and morally ugly ape-men depicted in its opening "dawn of man" sequence drew an audience response of nervous laughter. Freud's "wound," however forgotten it may sometimes seem at the conscious level, is an historical reality. As for its implications for religion, a graduating high school senior in Grafton, Ohio, in 1964 said to his teacher: "I suppose that if you really think about it, you can't believe in God and evolution at the same time. We just don't like to think about it."

In the 1920's the edges of the wound were more raw. "'Close your eyes and think of some muddy gutter or frog pond full of stagnant water with a scorching sun glittering down on the green slime'," one Fundamentalist leader cried, quoting from a pamphlet he had found in the hands of a twelve-year-old boy. "'. . . Those cesspools, geologists tell us, were the cradle of life on earth'." Outraged at this "sample of the stuff some of our children are getting," he urged the church to do something about it—which indeed it did. In the same spirit Alfred W. McCann in his prosecutor's brief *God—or Gorilla?*, published in 1922 and illustrated with vivid photographs of unattractive anthropoids, denounced Darwinism as "this new 'chemic creed,' that out of the lowest clod man has developed in common with the toad and the cockroach." Such a creed was a denial of civilization, of conscience, of manhood itself: "For what law, except the law of fear, shall this soulless THING have respect?"

Forty or fifty years earlier some Americans had found little difficulty in reconciling respect—sometimes exaggerated respect—for conventional morality with the belief that man had sprung from more lawless breeds. Kinship with toad and cockroach could be taken not only as a reminder of how humble man's poor relations were but also as an assurance of how far above their social level he had climbed, in the spirit caricatured by Gilbert and Sullivan in the haughty Pooh-Bah, who was proud to claim that he could trace his family tree back to a "protoplasmal primordial atomic globule." "People who get up in the world are sometimes ashamed of their parentage," conceded the American Unitarian Minot J. Savage, but "since my line runs back millions of years, and ends in God, I see no good cause for being ashamed of the long and wondrous way by which it has come." He was not half as anxious to find out that he did not come from an ape, Savage declared, as he was to know that he was not traveling toward one.

Father John Augustine Zahm, professor of physics at Notre Dame University, pointed to the precedent of Saint Francis of Assisi, who had called creatures even humbler than the primates his brothers; "whether he was correct, either theologically or zoologically, he was plainly free from that fear of being mistaken for an ape which haunts so many in these modern times." The fears of theologians lest Darwinism shatter their souls were likened by one British writer to the panic of a man who clings to a precipice all night and then, his strength failing, lets go—only to learn that his feet have been hanging within a few inches of the ground all the while. In other words Darwinian evolution, rationally considered, was not really a crippling wound to the human ego at all, but only a bad scare.

II

But to some evolutionist Victorians in England and America such an answer smacked less of science than of Christian science. At the very least, the blow struck at man's self-esteem had been experienced as if it were real. "The fears that were felt when the doctrine of evolution was first offered to the world were not unnatural," wrote Theodore T. Munger in 1886. When a new doctrine with revolutionary implications for the nature and destiny of man is put forth, this Protestant liberal acknowledged, "there is an intuitive wisdom or instinct of self-preservation in man that prompts him to turn on it with resentment and denial." Freud of course would have called this the ego's refusal to believe and accept the awful truth. But since evolution, rightly understood, was (in John Fiske's words) "God's way of doing things," and therefore was an exalting, not a humbling, doctrine, it followed that "if we shrink from linking our nobler faculties with preceding orders, it is because we have as yet no proper conception of the close and interior relation of God to all his works," preached Munger. "Let us be thankful for existence, however it came about, and let us not deem ourselves too good to be included in the one creation of the one God."

And yet, even though man ought not to regard himself as "too good" to be only a part of God's whole world, the acceptance of evolution on terms such as these betrayed a subtle man-centeredness nevertheless. While some of the religious liberals did not shrink from linking their nobler faculties with preceding orders, it was often at the price of sentimentalizing those more distant animate cousins into a spurious resemblance to man. "Have Animals Souls?" asked James Freeman Clarke in the *Atlantic Monthly* for October, 1874. He testified that he himself owned a horse that he believed could distinguish Sunday from the other days of the week, and that had shown "a very distinct feeling of the supernatural." The other animals are "made 'a little lower' than man," Clarke concluded, "and if we are souls so surely are they." Still, even with souls, they were lower than man, and in the theological tradition of Genesis 1:28 they had to be kept firmly in their place. We can "adore the directing Power and delight in His method" while we study the developing animal forms in the evolutionary series, Theodore Munger wrote in *The Appeal to Life*, "but the feeling of reverence only possesses us as we discern that creative process issuing in man as a moral being."

High religion had once known reverence elsewhere. "Hast thou entered into the springs of the sea? or hast thou walked in the search of the depth?" the Voice out of the Whirlwind asked Job; and, viewing with awe the mighty works of Yahweh, the Psalmist cried "What is man, that thou art mindful of him?" Or, as a reflective conservationist in the last half of the twentieth century like Joseph Wood Krutch might have said, Who is man, to be so little mindful of his environment? Must modern man save his sense of awe for himself as made in God's image, sharing a little of it perhaps with a few of the lesser species that are safely housebroken? Or might he share with Blake in the *mysterium tremendum,* as he contemplates the

> Tyger, Tyger burning bright
>
> In the forest of the night,

and then shudderingly asks

> Did He who made the Lamb make thee?

If the creative process is only worthy of reverence when it issues in man as a moral being, may one then experience no sense of wonder at solar flares, or the weird behavior of Helium II, or the craters of the moon?

Measured by standards such as these, Theodore Munger's cosmos turns out after all to be a remarkably impoverished one, precluding any religious dimension to the vast remainder of the universe which is left over after we have discovered man and morality in one cozy corner of it. Comfortable in its narrow confines, a defender of that rather dowdy faith would have been able to concede Freud's point but deny its significance. The human ego turns out once more to be remarkably adaptable; in the words of the modern humorist James Thurber "The noblest study of mankind is Man—says Man."

Some of the Gilded-Age liberals went even further, arguing that Darwinism had left man more at home in the universe, not less. Only ten years after *The Origin of Species* Alexander Winchell, a professor of geology, zoology, and botany at the University of Michigan and director of that state's geological survey, published his *Sketches of Creation*. Ambitiously subtitled "A popular view of some of the grand conclusions of the sciences in reference to the history of matter and of life, together with a statement of the intimations of science respecting the primordial condition and the ultimate destiny of the solar system"—the work assumed throughout that this vast panorama of natural wonders confirmed its author's faith that "science prosecuted to its conclusions leads to God." Far more cautiously, but with equal religious serenity, the great American botanist Asa Gray found his way back to theism. Darwinism itself prosecuted to its conclusions might not lead inevitably to God. "Darwinian evolution . . . is neither theistical nor nontheistical," Gray asserted, but the alternative to a belief in a Divinely based order in nature was a belief in chaos, a belief which for both the religionist and the materialist in the Gilded Age would have been difficult to accept; and Gray's own option was for God.

Arguments like these by scientists were quickly seized upon by liberal clergymen. The first tendency of Darwin's hypothesis had indeed been "toward infidelity and skepticism," wrote a theological professor in 1889 in the *Cumberland Presbyterian Review*. But with greater familiarity, placed alongside the researches of Newton, Copernicus, Laplace, and Lyell, "it has ceased to be atheistic, and is likely to become itself one of the arguments of natural theologians." Washington Gladden, the kindly minister of the Social Gospel, found in the doctrine of evolution "a most impressive demonstration of the presence of God in the world." And in any event, Gladden wrote to Lyman Abbott, if we can't lick them we will have to join them: "Our theology must adjust itself to evolutionary conceptions; we can not now think in any other terms."

III

Other inquirers, seeking out the fuller meaning of the logic and grammar of science, were disinclined to let these ministers of reconciliation get away with it. "Those scientific men who have sought to make out that science was not hostile to theology have not been so clear-sighted as their opponents," declared the cantankerous Charles Sanders Peirce in 1878. The same could have been said of many of their allies among the clergy. When Theodore Munger, for example, argued that "evolution not only perfects our conception of the unity of God, but . . . strengthens the argument from design," he ignored an evolutionary mechanism (random variation of individuals) and method (the struggle for existence) which logically seemed not to strengthen the design-argument but to shatter it.

"Certain theories"—for example, "that matter has within itself the potentiality of all terrestrial life, and goes on in its development alone, and by its own energy"—would be grounds for the fears some had voiced about evolution, Munger admitted, but only if such theories "were to be accepted as settled." He clearly implied that they were not. "But that *is* 'evolution'!" one reader of this defensive essay exclaimed. The uncompromising materialism which Munger claimed was only one theory among many "is the definition of evolution given by the most conspicuous scientific men on that side of the question," including Thomas Henry Huxley, whose definitive *Britannica* article on the subject could hardly have been classed as (in Munger's words) "'an outcast in the world of thought'"!

Those who rejected the whole proposition, asserting that if evolution were true then theism was false, had at least the virtue of consistency. Furthermore, as Edward Lurie has pointed out, judging solely on the character of the evidence available in 1859 when *The Origin of Species* first appeared it was respectably possible to disagree with Darwin. Edward Youmans of the *Popular Science Monthly* had to defend himself and his magazine from attacks for his "strong bias . . . as an evolutionist" not only by clergymen but also by the prestigious *Scribner's Monthly*, which editorially declared in 1872 that "the doctrine of Evolution, with its offspring, Darwinism, is nothing more than a provisional hypothesis, based upon *a priori* reasonings, and not on any valid induction of facts." Youmans gave a good account of himself in reply, reviewing the scientific evidence for evolution and then advising the editor of *Scribner's* to "stick to his fiction and his verse-making." Such arguments continued, however, to the joy and solace of distressed churchmen.

They were particularly comforted by Louis Agassiz, who brought his meticulous Swiss mind and the prestige of Harvard to bear against Darwinism to his dying day, and by such lay partisans as the proprietors of the New York *Tribune* when they inserted an advertisement in the *Nation* proclaiming "'the Darwinian theory utterly demolished' (or words to that effect) 'by AGASSIZ HIMSELF!'" The year before Darwin's *Origin of Species* appeared, Louis Agassiz had published two massive volumes of *Contributions to the Natural History of the United States of America*, in which he argued that the relationships of life-forms man finds were a witness not to the random selection of a blind mechanical process but to the deliberate intent of the Hand that had made them; God the Creator was also a professor of taxonomy, grouping species and genera together into larger units of classification in order that men might learn clues of His overall plan for the universe. "If we can prove premeditation prior to the act of creation, we have done, once and forever, with the desolate theory which refers us to the laws of matter as accounting for all the wonders of the universe, and leaves us with no God," Agassiz wrote in the opening pages of this work. Reviewing it for the *Atlantic Monthly*, Oliver Wendell Holmes, Sr., was "thankful that so profound a student of nature as Mr. Agassiz has tracked the warm foot-prints of divinity throughout all the vestiges of creation."

Having taken this stand, the formidable Swiss scientist never budged. "Darwin's theory, like all other attempts to explain the origin of life, is thus far merely conjectural," Agassiz concluded in his last, posthumously published article, and Darwin had "not even made the best conjecture possible in the present state of our knowledge." The Harvard biologist based his case strictly on the evidence from embryology, paleontology, and comparative anatomy, kept God out of the argument until the closing paragraphs, and brought in a convincing verdict of "Not Proven." Quite understandably an obituary to a leading Methodist weekly summed up Louis Agassiz's lifework as "a demonstration of the baselessness of all atheistical philosophy."

Two years after the death of Agassiz a contributor to *Scribner's Monthly* returned to the attack: "The truth is more in danger in our day from the prejudice that accepts without question the new, than from that which unreasonably holds to the old," J. B. Drury declared. Like Agassiz, this opponent of the new theory addressed himself primarily to the scientific issues, although Drury also argued that Darwinism left "no room for providence, prayer, or redemption." But what seems to have bothered him even more was that the doctrine of evolution pointed toward some rather horrible consequences for human society, along with its merely biological humiliations.

> Darwinism in deriving man from the brute, making him an improved ape rather than a fallen spirit, at one blow robs morality of its sanctions. . . . Might, and cunning, and whatever tends to advance self-interest, will more and more tell in the struggle for existence, and be the goal of human progress. The Christian virtues of self-denial, thoughtfulness for others, care for the infirm, the destitute, and the aged . . . must, under such evolution, be eliminated.

The Reform rabbi Isaac Mayer Wise, striking his own balance between science, philosophy, and religion in a book entitled *The Cosmic God* (1876), called Darwinism "Homo-Brutalism," and condemned it as a doctrine of might makes right. Some of Darwinism's defenders, including T. H. Huxley and Darwin himself, were worried about the possibility of this same conclusion being drawn and they therefore argued that man—naked ape or not—was somehow *ethically* different from other species. But their logic was inconsistent, argued the American Catholic writer John S. Vaughan in 1890. If conscience itself should turn out to be no more than a product of trial-and-error (of evolution, that is to say, by Darwin's definition), so that "virtue" meant only whatever traits or practices had proved "most serviceable" for "groups of human animals" struggling to survive, and "vice" merely "that which is disadvantageous to the race," then why should man not engage in morally repugnant but racially enhancing practices such as eugenic infanticide? And from an evolutionary standpoint why had such policies once adopted, as in Sparta and ancient Rome, not spread throughout mankind by "natural selection" and become universally accepted practice? (We may add that in the cruel twentieth century certain "Aryan" post-Darwinists did ask "Indeed, why not?")

Alas, the mere unpleasantness of an idea is no guarantee of its untruth. As late as 1889 so notable an American cleric as Cardinal Gibbons could call Darwinism "an unproven and disproven theory that will soon be forgotten to give place to some other phantom of a futile brain," and Isaac Wise continued into the Nineties to hold fast to his earlier belief that "the gorilla theory is a dream without a foundation in science." But sadly for those who would refute evolution on such grounds a rising generation of younger Darwinists had been busy replacing that theoretical phantom with solid flesh.

John Wesley Powell's spectacular boat trip down the canyon of the Colorado in 1869 and the quiet eloquence of his *Geology of the Uinta Mountains* both dramatized convincingly the uniformitarian geology of Sir Charles Lyell. A vast Western land required a vast time scale for its making, vast enough to meet the requirements for evolution, rather than the cramped six thousand years called for by Archbishop Ussher's Biblical chronology. Man himself had been on this stage long before 4004 B.C.; "The great antiquity of mankind upon the earth," said the anthropologist Lewis Henry Morgan in the preface to his pioneering and widely influential study of *Ancient Society* (1877), "has been conclusively established." Judging from the Eohippus fossil sequence which the Yale paleontologist O.C. Marsh convincingly assembled (to Thomas Huxley's delight), man's perennial companion the horse had been around even longer. And in the great Cretaceous beds of the Rocky Mountain West a host of bone hunters were disclosing to a startled Victorian world the splendor of the dinosaur. On the strength of these and other discoveries one of those hunters, Marsh, told the American Association for the Advancement of Science: "To doubt evolution today is to doubt science, and science is only another name for truth."

IV

By that time the battle lines had shifted. With the publication in 1871 of Darwin's *The Descent of Man,* the argument begun over *The Origin of Species* moved from the evolution of life in general to that of man in particular. Conceding to science the geological time scale and the evolution of life, some of the defenders of Genesis 1, 2, and 3 drew the line at Adam and Eve.

Reviewing the evidence, pro and con, from stratigraphy, paleontology, geography, physiology, morphology, and embryology, the Rev. A. F. Hewitt, a founder of the Paulist order, concluded in 1887: "The hypothesis of evolution must stop short of man." This was an echo of what soon became—and, technically, still remains— the official position of the Roman Catholic Church on evolution. In post-*Kulturkampf* Germany the scientist-politician Rudolph Virchow, physical anthropologist, physician, and distinguished lecturer at the University of Berlin, drew the line against the new doctrines at the same point. Opening an international scientific congress in Moscow in 1892, Professor Virchow told his professional colleagues: "There exists a definite barrier separating man from the animal, which has not yet been effaced." Most other scientists hopefully focused their attention on the word "yet," but Virchow was more pessimistic or, in terms of Freud's argument, optimistic. He concluded that all the studies undertaken with the purpose of discovering biological continuity between the other animals and man had been a failure: "There exists no *proanthropos,* no man-monkey, and the 'connecting link' remains a phantom."

Twenty and thirty years later American Fundamentalists girding themselves for the Scopes Trial would still be clinging to Virchow's words. But it was an increasingly untenable position. In 1857 Virchow had pronounced Neanderthal Man not to be an ancient human fossil at all, but a relatively modern man whose bones had been shaped not by evolution but by rickets, arthritis, and heavy blows on the skull. *One* Neanderthal Man might have been such a fluke, but could the same be said of the dozens or hundreds of fragments that later came to light, not only in Europe but in the Near and Far East? Even though Virchow had been only thirty-six years old at the time of that first discovery, his expert opinion on that first Neanderthal skull has been judged "a masterpiece of senile resistance to new ideas."

As the nineteenth century rushed on toward its end, the mounting scientific consensus in favor of evolution, including that of man, became an embarrassment for men like Cardinal Gibbons, who was having trouble enough as it was reconciling his own Church with the American cultural ethos, and like Phillips Brooks, who bravely preached that "the Church . . . will have nothing to do with the false awe of the *Credo quia impossible.*" For such men, to reject the evidence of all the patient investigators in the field solely because it conflicted with dogma was out of the question. "The truths of Heaven and the truths of earth are in perfect sympathy; every revelation of the Bible is clearer the more it is to be found in the speaking conscience, or in the utterance of history, or in the vocal rocks," Brooks insisted. In fact, far from contradicting the Darwinian hypothesis, declared the Southern Presbyterian chemist and theologian James Woodrow, if rightly interpreted "the Bible, implicitly yet distinctly, teaches the doctrine of Evolution."

Even before Lyell's time the theologians had begun to make this adjustment, allowing that the Hebrew word ordinarily translated "day" might in fact allude to periods millions of years long, punctuated not by "the evening and the morning" as in Genesis 1 but by intervals of mountain-building. Now, in Darwin's era, biology as well as astronomy and geology came under the tent. In the pages of *Popular Science Monthly* for January, 1874, George Henslow argued that the very grammar of the Divine commands (as in verse 21, "Let the waters bring forth") was consistent with an evolutionary origin for marine life: "The use of the imperative mood can only signify an agent other than the speaker," an agent corresponding to "natural law, which, after all, is but a synonym for the will of God." Theodore T. Munger reasoned, "When there is such an accumulation of knowledge and of evidence against the apparent meaning" of a passage in the Bible "that the mind cannot tolerate the inconsistency, it must search the text to see if it will bear a meaning . . . consistent with ascertained facts."

But was this not twisting the words of Scripture in the manner of Humpty Dumpty, to make them mean whatever the apologist wanted them to mean? "Let the waters bring forth abundantly" might be stretched into consistency with man's fragmentary factual knowledge about the rise of life in the ocean, but what of the astronomical havoc wrought by having the sun and moon wait in the wings until the fourth day (Gen. 1: 16-19)? One pious Prussian professor, who believed in the literal truth of the Bible but who also believed that a day really meant a day, told his class that the chronology of creation was unfortunate; God ought logically to have begun with those cosmic time pieces, since without them "the first three days, vaguely composed of morning and night," saw no real order and discipline in the world!

Sometimes this puzzling passage has been made to read that God "caused the sun and moon to appear," i.e., break through the clouds; but pretty quickly one is torturing the text as with Shakespeare's plays, in order to make them yield Baconian cryptograms. For the more literal-minded of the harmonizers of science with Scripture, "the accommodation was often grotesque, resulting in a strained 'reconciliation' of Biblical passages to make the facts of evolution fit them," George Daniels has written, and "most modern readers will be inclined to think that if the Bible is as wondrously plastic" as such interpreters assumed, "there is little meaning in the claim that it is 'inspired truth.'" We are reminded further that in scientific investigation, or any other kind, a hypothesis becomes suspect the moment it stops explaining things and starts explaining things away.

And it was all so futile, for the same spirit of inquisitive investigation which was pushing back the mysteries of geologic time, of life, and of man, had been turned also to the study of the Bible. The book of Genesis itself was seen as the product of historical evolution, composed and collated over a span of centuries. In that case, what did it matter how much one stretched and shuffled the "days of creation" to make them fit the researches of Lyell and Darwin if those days turned out to have been not part of the original story at all, but interpolations by a later Hebrew editor into a more primitive narrative in order to make it square with a Babylonian calendar chronology? The new mode of Biblical criticism made it even more painfully evident that some critics of Darwin were not so much arguing a theory as making excuses. . . .

The Intellectual Crisis of Belief
JAMES TURNER

SOURCE: Turner, James C. *Without God, Without Creed: The Origins of Unbelief in America.* Pp. 171-173, 179-187. © 1985 by The Johns Hopkins University Press. Reprinted with permission of The Johns Hopkins University Press.

It was 1867 when Jonathan Harrison, in Illinois, complained that "even atheism" would be "a forward movement." Such a movement of thought was even then gathering momentum, culminating two centuries of struggle between those who sought to secure belief by fixing it in comprehensible reality and those who denied that God fit those familiar terms. However, *atheism,* implying a positive denial of God's existence, did not precisely define this emerging outlook. Two years later Thomas Huxley, in London, would coin a fitter word, *agnosticism.* Huxley put a name on what had grown common enough to need a name: a permanent suspension of belief in God. This settled inability to accept the reality of God, rather than positive atheism, became the distinctively modern unbelief.

Within twenty years after the Civil War, agnosticism emerged as a self-sustaining phenomenon. Disbelief in God was, for the first time, plausible enough to grow beyond a rare eccentricity and to stake out a sizable permanent niche in American culture. Two hundred years spent adapting belief to the cultural environment had paid off, in a way: unbelief now also fitted tolerably well into it—well enough to find sufficient intellectual and psychological nourishment to survive and reproduce itself. An agnostic subculture had taken root—not a geographic community, but a community of ideas, assumptions, and values. This shared world view gave agnostics a coherent understanding of reality without benefit of God. That their world view *was* shared reinforced their agnosticism, for they knew that many others, and no insignificant men, agreed with their doubts. That it was a *sub*culture—that agnosticism was broadly continuous with the fundamental assumptions of the larger culture—made their unbelief convincing. For agnosticism did not represent a sharp break from Victorian culture, but rather one plausible outgrowth of it.

This particular offshoot grew from a mass of ideas and attitudes so tangled and matted as to be at points almost impenetrable. These intertwined roots can, for analytic purposes, be cut apart into three sections—three "mental and moral states," in Harrison's words, that engendered unbelief. They are (1) intellectual uncertainties about belief that produced the conviction that knowledge of God lay beyond human powers, if such a Being existed; (2) moral problems with belief that led to the rejection as immoral of belief in God and the erection of a nontheistic morality; and (3) the transfer of reverence from God to other ideals.

These three categories should not be taken as chronological stages in the development of agnosticism or even as actually distinct in the thinking of agnostics. They are only the historian's tools, instruments for dissecting a knotted growth of opinion, a subculture of unbelief otherwise too complex and intertwined to allow coherent discussion.

Indeed, these elements must be considered together, for no one of them could have sufficed to sustain unbelief. To be sure, in individual cases, one or another often tipped the balance toward agnosticism—and in that sense "caused" a person's unbelief. But the fibers of belief twined so thoroughly through the common life that ripping it out did not come easily; the emergence of unbelief appears to have been a very near thing. Just when modern unbelief was appearing, modern belief was also gaining coherence and vigor. Church membership was rising, more sophisticated theologies taking shape to meet the challenge of doubt. In these circumstances, agnosticism might have proved as evanescent as the few atheist voices of the Enlightenment, might never have found a voice at all. It was the concurrent force of different doubts that gave birth to agnosticism, the multiplicity of its springs that gave it endurance.

Of these sources, the intellectual problems of belief provide the clearest entryway into agnosticism. True, people seldom defined explicitly the basic rationale for their faith (if indeed only one existed and if indeed they were fully aware of it). So one cannot be sure which intellectual prop bore most of the weight of belief. But the arguments for God common in the mid-nineteenth century fell into three categories. First, but scarcely persuasive to anyone inclined to doubt, was the testimony of Scripture. Reeling under the higher criticism, revelation now required rehabilitation itself; the Bible might unfold a God already believed in but could hardly convince the mildest of sceptics that He existed.

The two other styles of argument carried much more conviction. One was the quasi-scientific, empirical demonstration of God's existence embodied in the argument from design. The other looked beyond the sensible world, into man's heart, and found there primal religious impulses or immediate intuitions of the divine, deeper than reason, that testified to the reality of God. These two approaches might appear oddly yoked, but most early Victorians thought them complementary: a devastatingly persuasive pair that made unbelief preposterous beyond words. Though not the only rationales for belief, "scientific" natural theology and various forms of intuitionism so dominated discussion that they almost inevitably leapt to mind whenever the plausibility of belief came into question. . . .

Science and Knowledge of God

Before 1859, believers could rest secure in the conviction that the evidence for God was as certain as science itself. God remained central to thinking about important scientific questions. To be sure, scientists routinely distinguished their methods and their subject matter from those of theology. Nevertheless, such problems as the beginning of life and the origin of species required invoking some sort of creative force—which scientists and everyone else in fact thought of as God—or else they became incomprehensible. The adaptation of animals and plants to their environments provided both a central doctrine of natural history and obvious evidence of God's hand. Although scientists commonly thought of knowledge of God's nature as, technically, beyond science, they still believed that science pointed to Him; and, indeed, scientific explanations depended ultimately on the hypothesis of a First Cause.

Yet, by the end of the 1860s, science had little use for God. This was really no sudden transformation (though its last stages raised considerable noise around Charles Darwin). Rather, the excision of God from science culminated a long trend, the eventual outcome of which had been forecast long before by those disregarded prophets who warned that theologians had no business mixing God and science. And, in fact, ever since the seventeenth century, God—while remaining essential to the overall scientific enterprise—had become peripheral to progressively larger areas of scientific practice. After Darwin's *Origin of Species* appeared in 1859, God rapidly became redundant in the whole business.

Darwin's work played the largest part in the eviction of God. The Darwinian hypothesis of natural selection explained two of the three great instances of divine activity in biology—the origin of species and the adaptation of animals and plants to their environments—without reference to God. The theory of natural selection was hardly impregnable, but it broke the magic spell. Darwin showed that, in the one large area of science where God still retained an active explanatory function, He was not needed after all. A purely naturalistic account of the central phenomena of natural history could be laid out in a scientifically credible way.

Ten years later, Thomas Huxley proposed a solution to the great remaining mystery of biology, the origin of life. The basic unit of life, he claimed, was protoplasm. Having formed by purely chemical processes from inorganic material, protoplasm then aggregated into more complex forms, wiggling up the evolutionary tree until it appeared in frock-coat and spats. There was nothing very original or consequential in Huxley's speculations, but they created a tremendous stir at the time. John Morley, editor of the *Fortnightly Review,* where Huxley's musings first appeared in print, recalled fifty years after that no other article "in any periodical for a generation back," with possibly one exception, "excited so profound a sensation." The *New York World,* a penny daily, trumpeted "New Theory of Life" and reprinted the full text. Huxley's Ur-life formed the center of a scientific and popular controversy that raged into the 1880s. Lester Ward erected an elaborate description of the evolution of life on this gelatinous foundation As with Darwinism, the effect turned not on the final validity of the hypothesis—Huxley's was flabbier than its protagonist—but on its credibility. Darwin and Huxley might both be wrong, but they were plausible. They had proved that the big problems could be explained without God, and they had thus shown God to be unnecessary in biology. And if God was superfluous in the science of life, then He could call no part of science home.

Even His primal creative function—His role as First Cause—dissipated into mist. Most scientists, qua scientists, simply stopped talking about such metaphysical questions. Many of the amateurs of science, taking their cue from Herbert Spencer, solemnly if vaguely invoked Force as the primal creative power inherent in the universe, discarding "a divine Creator, a guiding intelligence, and a controlling purpose" in favor of "a force that is physical, persistent, ultimate, unintelligent, unconscious, unknowable." This "modern theory of forces" stemmed from the law of the conservation of energy, enunciated in the 1840s—a concept that had a fascination for some nonscientists almost equal to its scientific importance. Those who invoked Force as a creative power believed themselves to be speaking science. That they were, for the most part, speaking hokum only underlines again the enormous appeal of scientific explanations.

What really mattered was not that an agnostic had ready at hand a scientific explanation for the origin of life, the formation of the solar system, or any other specific problem; rather, it was that he had the impression that science could provide one—if not right away, then eventually. Awareness of the details of any particular theory was not key; awareness that such theories existed was. The scientific endeavor to understand reality—in both its professional and its vernacular versions—appeared to be dispensing with God.

Even the fundamental concept of scientific law had altered in a way that left God out. In its origins, the idea of natural laws presumed a Lawgiver. The very word *law* reveals this assumption of a personal governor. Although, by the early nineteenth century, scientists thought of laws as empirically discovered regularities, rather than in more explicitly theological terms, they still believed that law manifested God, for these universal and invariable causes reflected a regular order that could only have come from the hand of a divine Orderer. And this Orderer had to *will* the law-described behavior of the universe—execute His laws, as it were— for dead matter could not move of itself.

In the Darwinian universe, however, all the varieties of life developed as unintended consequences of chance variations. Evolutionists might speak of a "law" of natural selection, but this term only disguised a roulette wheel that earlier would have ranked as a natural law in no one's book, not even a French materialist's. Asa Gray of Harvard, though Darwin' s friend and defender, could scarcely digest so bizarre a notion. He went on insisting on "faith in an order" as "the basis of science" and assuring his readers that this inevitably led to "faith in an Ordainer, which is the basis of religion." Gray remained loyal not only to Christianity but to the Enlightenment; Darwin repudiated both. For the existence of order in nature, in the traditional sense, was precisely what Darwin put in question.

Natural selection reflected and speeded an expulsion of all metaphysical assumptions from the concept of natural law. One scientific popularizer warned his audience not to read too much into scientific talk of law; "for law is not an agent, but a conception, an intellectual summation in respect of the order of things." Indeed, a law might represent nothing more than a very high degree of statistical probability. No one could say that a God had not determined these regularities. But the regularities themselves—and that was all science could know—no longer implied a God.

"Principles of order, so pervasive, so permanent, so inflexible, lose their personal character, become a nature of things, and wholly separate the mind of man from God," warned the Reverend John Bascom of Williams College. What worried Bascom delighted the agnostic Robert Ingersoll. The fact that "the universe is governed by law," trumpeted Ingersoll, is not proof of God's existence but "the death-knell of superstition." Although many scientists clung to the faith that their work pointed to God, God no longer formed a necessary part of the scientific understanding of reality.

God's absence from scientific work constituted no logically valid argument against His existence, but it did mean one less reason to believe in Him. And precisely because both scientists and theologians had long assumed His necessity in science, His sudden departure could not but shake confidence. "Physical science, at the present day, investigates phenomena simply as they are in themselves. This, if not positively atheistic, must be of dangerous tendency. Whatever deliberately omits God from the universe is closely allied to that which denies him.'" This naturalizing of scientific explanations did not of itself sever the sturdy and reassuring connection between science and belief, because leaving God out of statements about physical reality did not prohibit scientific statements about metaphysical reality. But the weakening of the link was undeniable.

Nor was this the end of the problem. To the strongest ties that bound science and belief, Darwin applied an ax. No demonstration showed more forcefully how science led to nature's God than the argument from design. No proof of God compelled more nearly universal assent than the argument from design. No theology exuded more confidence than the argument from design. And no theology ever collapsed so rapidly. Darwin punctured it, and its plausibility fizzed away like air from a leaky balloon.

Just before Darwin, two species of design arguments flourished, a dominant utilitarian one and a less popular idealist version, both of which by separate paths led the scientific inquirer inexorably to God. The utilitarian species, stemming from Ray and Paley, hinged on two points. First, the complexity of living organisms evidenced design, and design implied a Designer. Second, the design of organisms fitted them to prosper in their specific environments, and this precise adaptation showed the benevolent concern of the Designer for His creatures. The idealist species of design focused not on complexity and adaptation but on the fundamental structures that pervaded nature: for example, the basic anatomy shared by all vertebrates. Not usefulness but uniformity mattered. Indeed, the very uselessness of male nipples showed a symmetry, a harmony, a fundamental plan carried through without regard to function. Thus, nature revealed intelligent planning; it embodied the thoughts of God.

Darwin not only disabled the dominant species, he laid waste the whole genus. Darwin showed how, through purely natural selection, organisms developed from the very simple to the extremely complex. And far from proving divine benevolence, adaptation to environment was nothing more than the mechanism and product of natural selection. Those scattered organisms that chanced to develop variations better fitting them to their environments survived and reproduced. The multitude of organisms that varied unfavorably or not at all survived less often and accordingly reproduced less often. Ultimately, the old form died out altogether, and a new variety, eventually a new species, emerged, better adapted to the environment—but only at the cost of millions of ill-adapted organisms dying of starvation, predation, and disease. Darwinian natural selection thus explained not only the appearance of benevolent design in complex organisms adapted to specific environments but also the uniformities ramifying through nature. These were not the enfleshed thoughts of God but the branching out of an evolutionary tree, through eons of trial and error, from a common ancestor.

If this were design, its sloppiness and inefficiency suggested gross incompetence; and if this were benevolence, the designer exercised it with a paradoxical delight in suffering. Darwin had shown that this cast-iron proof of God had a gaping hole in the bottom, that the scientific evidence of design had a wholly naturalistic explanation. Moreover, the wastefulness and suffering entailed in evolution made it harder to believe that God could be responsible for the process: the humanized God of the nineteenth century, the God who was expected to act like a perfect and all-powerful human being, could not plausibly have set in motion Darwinian evolution. Perhaps more shocking, Darwin implied that man was an accident, the human presence on earth a mere chance. Was this *design?*

It was, of course, still possible to believe in God. Darwin himself did when he published the *Origin of Species.* After all, natural selection did not explain why there should be order in the universe or why there should be a universe at all.

Admittedly, even order appeared less certain after Darwin made chance the mainspring of biology. And Darwin had blasted the natural theologies in which confidence had been vested: those that had tried to mimic science and carefully grounded themselves in detailed physical evidence. But he did not torpedo every possibility of natural theology. Moreover, the *Origin* itself was far from conclusive. The fossil evidence for evolution was closer to nonexistent than overwhelming. Darwin had no solid clue as to the mechanism that produced variations. And it shortly became clear that natural selection required more eons than Lord Kelvin and contemporary physics allowed. Indeed, many gentlemen of the cloth went blithely along spinning their design arguments as if Darwin had drowned on the voyage of the *Beagle*.

Yet these problems did not deflate Darwinism, far less revive the quasi-scientific proofs of God. Darwin had plausibly accounted for the appearance of design in purely naturalistic terms. The sheer audacity of this stroke shook confidence in natural theology and impressed people with the independent explanatory power of science. Less ready now to assume that the lack of a naturalistic explanation required invoking the hand of God—particularly since science had dispensed with God in its own work—people grew readier to trust that science would eventually unravel present mysteries. The gaps in Darwin's theory suggested limited knowledge rather than divine activity. It was natural theology, not natural selection, that found itself becalmed .

More specifically, Darwin's effect on design arguments could not be countered by pointing out his failure to prove his hypothesis. Simply by offering a plausible alternative explanation, Darwin had destroyed the proof value of design. God was no longer the only persuasive way to account for appearances of design. No wonder that an unbeliever in 1871 declared Darwinism "the most complete revolution which modern science has effected." One could still believe that evolution manifested God—as many scientists did—but to do so became an act of faith. One Christian apologist tried to slide around Darwin by pointing out that "evolution, if rightly understood, has no theological or anti-theological influence whatever." But that was just the point. After Darwin, there was no longer a scientifically persuasive argument for God.

Nor, more troubling still, could there be. Recovery from this blow was not possible. For Darwin's overthrowing of the design argument in particular, and the omission of God from science in general, manifested a basic change in the epistemology of science: a narrowing of the range of valid scientific knowledge so as to exclude all inferences about supposed nonphysical realities. The older idea of science, prevalent through the early decades of the century, envisioned a spacious and rather laxly policed territory of scientific knowledge. Science meant something like "orderly and methodically digested and arranged" knowledge of nature. No fortified frontiers prevented science from exploring metaphysical as well as physical questions about the natural world. To Francis Wayland, president of Brown University, for example, science included all "the knowledge of the laws of nature and of the modes in which they may be applied to increase the happiness of man."

No notion prevailed that this knowledge excluded conclusions unverifiable by direct physical consequences. So long as "laws" or "facts" (of which God was one) rested ultimately on observation of nature, they qualified as scientific knowledge. That science was still commonly called natural philosophy before 1850 signified more than a semantic accident. Natural philosophy shared the metaphysical concerns of all philosophy.

So broadly constructed a version of science flourished because standards of evidence and proof were similarly generous. Science typically concerned itself with physical data perceptible to the senses, but no barrier shut out other modes of knowing scientifically. Psychology, for instance, got most of its facts from introspection yet fell at least on the borders of science. As late as 1874, the erudite Presbyterian conservative Charles Hodge of Princeton did not conceive of science as limited to observable physical evidence. Most scientific work did not wander so freely; the point is that science did permit some fairly elastic conceptions of "fact."

Yet a good deal of tightening up took place in the decades before 1850. Research, even in natural history, exhibited greater precision. More and more scientists in other fields began to speak the exact language of mathematics. The Cambridge geologist Adam Sedgwick defined science in 1833 as "the consideration of all subjects, whether of a pure or mixed nature, capable of being reduced to measurement and calculation." Probably Sedgwick did not really intend to outlaw every phenomenon that defied counting or weighing. But his drift was revealing—and carried an implication that ought to have set natural theologians and Sedgwick himself back on their heels. For the creation could be measured, but the Creator could not. A process of self-limitation was already in train by which natural philosophy would shed its transcendental concerns and become "science" in the modern sense.

Sedgwick's student Charles Darwin did more than anyone else to bring this process to fruition (and earned in the process his teacher's undying enmity). Except for an enigmatic allusion on the last page, the Creator appeared nowhere in the *Origin of Species*. Darwin was, at least in 1859, not an agnostic; he certainly had no wish to deny God. But, as a scientist, he shrank from questions unanswerable in terms of observable, regular physical consequences and refused to treat as knowledge beliefs about the non-physical.

Darwin soon found a great deal of scientific company. In effect, science by fiat redefined its meaning of "natural" so as to preclude the traditional necessity of a supernatural on which nature depended. It did this de facto, not by denying the supernatural, but by refusing to consider as within the bounds of scientific knowledge anything but the physical. This was at root why scientific laws had to be reconceived as merely observed regularities rather than manifestations of divine will. By no means every well-read person understood what had happened, but one furious Presbyterian certainly did. Scientists, wrote Charles Hodge, perversely refuse to recognize that "there are other kinds of truth than the testimony of the senses." Instead, they limit themselves to "the external world": "A scientific fact is a fact perceived by the senses." The Johns Hopkins physiologist Henry Newell Martin fully agreed with this last statement; his "business was to study the phenomena exhibited by living things, and leave the noumena, if there were such, to amuse metaphysicians." Martin could afford to be snide. He had won. As far as science went, knowledge had shrunk to physical knowledge.

Nor should this contraction have surprised anyone, had the earlier warnings of the critics of natural theology been heeded. Since the seventeenth century, science had striven not just to describe nature but to control or at least predict its course. The prodigious American physicist Joseph Henry defined as essential to a "scientific truth" its enabling "us to explain, to predict, and in some cases to control the phenomena of nature." But what could be accurately predicted was inherently limited to what could be carefully and precisely observed; that is, to physical reality. Thus, this predictive drive demanded ever more rigorous verification by physical evidence of scientific hypotheses. Hypotheses projected beyond human experience of the natural world—even if formed by it—are worthless, George John Romanes insisted, because we have no way of testing them. The very purpose of modern science forced it gradually but inexorably to narrow its focus to physical reality alone. Darwin made this obvious at last—and owed much of his notoriety to the fact.

Darwin, then, not only torpedoed the argument from design but made clear that the whole enterprise of natural theology had foundered in very deep waters. The very idea of a scientific natural theology involved now a contradiction in terms. For science qua science, by definition, could now offer no foundation for belief in God.

Science hardly banned belief; indeed, most American scientists remained Christians. But they looked less and less to science for support of their faith, as science repudiated any claims to pronounce on such subjects. Increasingly, Christian scientists and clerical apologists concerned themselves not with proving God but with showing that science did not disprove Him. The botanist Asa Gray, a devout Presbyterian and ardent Darwinian, reconciled the two beliefs by severing them, arguing that science as such had no more bearing on religious truth than religion had on science. Only by such utter heresy to the tradition of natural theology could Gray preserve both his science and his Christianity. Gray's friend Chauncey Wright took this hint and elaborated it into a philosophical theory of the neutrality of science.

Where science had once pointed beyond nature to God, it now pointed only to nature, behind which lay, if anything, the Unknowable. One might choose to call nature or force or the Unknowable by the name of God. But science offered no justification. Only the "illegitimate pretensions of natural theology" asserted that there could be scientific knowledge of God. Thus, the enormous prestige and influence of scientific support for belief were cut away.

The loss of scientific knowledge of God would not necessarily have proved devastating, save for one fact. Religious leaders had, since Newton, insisted on linking science and God. In the half century before Darwin, the certainty of knowledge of God through science had been drummed into Christians more insistently than ever before. Natural theologians—ministers and scientists alike—had hoped thereby to capitalize on the rising stock of science, on the ever-growing confidence in its approach to knowledge.

Now those who thought science could find God were trapped by their own self-assurance. To be sure, many believers had never taken the bait, and they escaped the debacle. But the rest suffered a blow to the head. Assertions of absolutely certain knowledge turned into a desperate scramble for reassurance. Natural theology had invested huge sums of confidence in scientific knowledge. If it now turned out that science could give no knowledge of God, the question had to be asked whether knowledge of God was possible at all. . . .

Questions for Reflection and Discussion

1. Identify the principal points of conflict and consensus between science and religion described in the documents.

2. According to Paul Carter, what variety of religious responses were made to the new ideas of science?

3. Summarize James Turner's contention that with Darwin's writings "God rapidly became redundant in the whole business [of scientific practice]."

4. Describe the influence of the "new science" on the secularization of American culture during the final third of the nineteenth century.

Additional Readings

Boller, Paul F., Jr. *American Thought in Transition: The Impact of Evolutionary Naturalism, 1865-1900.* Chicago: University of Chicago Press, 1969.

Desmond, Adrian and James Moore. *Darwin: The Life of a Tormented Evolutionist.* New York: Warner Books, 1991.

Gillespie, Neal. *Charles Darwin and the Problem of Creation.* Chicago: University of Chicago Press, 1979.

Greene, John C. *Darwin and the Modern World View.* Baton Rouge: Louisiana State University Press, 1961.

_____. *The Death of Adam: Evolution and Its Impact on Western Thought.* Ames: Iowa State University Press, 1959.

Hofstadter, Richard. *Social Darwinism in the United States.* Revised edition. Boston:Beacon Press, 1955.

Lindberg, David C. and Ronald L. Numbers. "Beyond War and Peace: A Reappraisal of the Encounter Between Christianity and Science," *Church History* 55 (September 1986):338-54.

Livingstone, David N. *Darwin's Forgotten Defenders: The Encounter Between Evangelical Theology and Evolutionary Thought*. Grand Rapids:Eerdmans and Scottish Academic Press, 1987.

Mayr, Ernst. *One Long Argument: Charles Darwin and the Genesis of Modern Evolutionary Thought*. Cambridge: Harvard University Press, 1991.

Numbers, Ronald L. *Darwinism Comes to America*. Cambridge: Harvard University Press, 1998.

Persons, Stow, ed. *Evolutionary Thought in America*. New Haven: Yale University Press, 1950.

Russett, Cynthia Eagle. *Darwin in America: The Intellectual Response, 1865-1912*. San Francisco: W.H. Freeman and Company, 1976.

Webb, George E. *The Evolution Controversy in America*. Lexington: The University Press of Kentucky, 1994.

White, Edward A. *Science and Religion in American Thought: The Impact of Naturalism*. Stanford, Calif.: Stanford University Press, 1952.

Wilson, R. Jackson, ed. *Darwinism and the American Intellectual: An Anthology*. 2nd Edition. Chicago: The Dorsey Press, 1989.

Chapter 10

The late nineteenth-century influences of industrialization, immigration, and urbanization changed the face of America in incalculable ways. The giant corporate enterprise at the heart of the economic revolution produced a new class of wealth in the nation. A steady influx of new arrivals from abroad sparked the advent of a host of social challenges. The site of the economic revolution and the destination of millions of immigrants was the city, where crowded and unhealthy living conditions caused conflict and new debate over restricting their future numbers.

Religion in Industrializing America

Issue

How did the factory and the city influence American religion?

One historian describes the economic revolution as "probably the greatest secularizing force in the late 1800's." He notes that with the many changes brought on by the three influences noted above, Catholicism and Judaism took their places beside Protestantism as significant religions of Americans. All three religious categories, furthermore, went through a process of secularization, with Protestantism being altered the most.

Why did this happen? The new challenges of urban life produced new challenges for the churches. Many Protestant clergy and laity were troubled by the rising tide of crime and immorality that threatened to engulf the cities. And in the cities resided many of the churchless. "The American Protestant Church, as a whole," bemoaned one clergy in the 1880s, "has failed to win to itself the working class of the towns." Painfully admitting the negligence of the church, some Protestant clergymen called upon their churches to meet their responsibility in solving the problems of the world. What emerged from this call was a secularized gospel—a gospel that "provided the foundation for social and political reforms designed to eliminate poverty, disease, filth, and immorality."

Not all churched Americans agreed with the revamped gospel. Some conservative Protestant preachers holding to traditional theology contended that "un-

til Christ returned none of the basic problems of the world could be solved"—
and among these problems were social problems caused by immorality and poverty. Conflict and division arose over the social gospel, not only among Protestants,
but also among Catholics and Jews, as conservatives fought progressives for control of the church and the soul of the nation. Excluded from most of this turmoil
were black churchgoers, whose preoccupation with the effects of Jim Crowism
made the social gospel controversy less relevant to them.

Walter Rauschenbusch, one of the most articulate advocates for the social
gospel, wrote in his first book, Christianity and the Social Crisis (1907): "The
ministry must apply the teaching function of the pulpit to the pressing questions
of public morality." How did the social gospelers view the new urban world?
Why did conflict emerge from the social gospel movement? In what ways was
the social gospel a secularized gospel? How does the social gospel reflect a tension
between the secular and the sacred?

Documents

The first document, a tribute to temperance leader Frances Willard, illustrates
the social reform emphasis of the social gospel, in this case the effort to eliminate
alcohol from America. The second selection is taken from James Cardinal
Gibbons's communique to the Vatican in which he argues that the Knights of
Labor, two-thirds of whose members were Roman Catholic, should not be condemned as a secret society in the United States, as had been done in the Cana-
dian Province of Quebec in 1884. The third document includes excerpts from
Pope Leo XIII's encyclical in which he stated that it was the church's role to
provide spiritual and social leadership in a changing society. Though he was
probably not speaking directly to American Catholics, by the end of the century
his views were becoming the foundation of labor policy for Catholics in the
United States. In the fourth selection, the Rev. Charles M. Sheldon of the Central Congregational Church of Topeka, Kansas, asks the readers of his famous
work In His Steps, "What would Jesus do?" about the needs of the town if he
were attending Rev. Maxwell's First Church of Raymond. In the fifth document, the Rev. Reverdy C. Ransom of the A.M.E. Church calls upon member
churches to help make black America a more meaningful part of industrializ-
ing America. In the final selection, seminary professor Walter Rauschenbusch
challenged young men and women to a new apostolate in support of the social
gospel movement.

1. Frances Willard and the Women's Christian Temperance Union, 1883

SOURCE: Mary Lathbury, "Frances Willard of Illinois," in *Women and Temperance or The Work and Workers of the Women's Christian Temperance Union* (1883). (Chicago: Women's Temperance Publication Association, 1886), 28-32.

In October, 1874, a voice that had been thrilling [Frances Willard] strangely wherever she heard a sound of it, came to her with a personal appeal. It was from the Women's Christian Temperance Union, and the invitation to work with them was gladly accepted. She saw, with the clear intuition which is peculiar to her, that the little "root out of dry ground" was His promise of that which was to cover the land with a banyan-like growth. Said she, later: "I was reared on a western prairie, and often have helped kindle the great fires for which the West used to be famous. A match and a wisp of dry grass were all we needed, and behold the magnificent spectacle of a prairie on fire, sweeping across the landscape, swift as a thousand untrained steeds, and no more to be captured than a hurricane! Just so it is with the Crusade. . . . When God lets loose an idea upon this planet, we vainly set limits to its progress; and I believe that Gospel Temperance shall yet transform that inmost circle, the human heart, and in its widening sweep the circle of home, and then society, and then, pushing its argument to the extreme conclusion, it shall permeate the widest circle of them all, and that is, government."

So closely identified had she become with the womanhood of our country, that the question came very distinctly to her as a representative woman, "Who knoweth if thou be come into the kingdom for such a time as this?" The old feeling of being born to a work, a "destiny," had passed over from her own personality to the sex with which she is identified, as it is now passing over to the race, the "woman question" becoming the "human question."

There is much to be written from this point which cannot be brought within the limits of this sketch. It would be an unnecessary re-writing of the history of the Women's Temperance Movement. This seed of the kingdom, after its wonderful planting in Ohio during the winter and spring of 1873-4, was beginning to bear fruit through the Middle and Western States. In August of that year, at Chautauqua, the "birthplace of grand ideas," the Women's Christian Temperance Union was born. A convention was called for November of the same year, at Cleveland, Ohio, and the National W.C.T.U. was then organized, with Miss Willard as Corresponding Secretary. It was at this Convention that she offered the resolution which, springing from the inspirations and the aspirations of the hour, has proved to be, in its spirit, a glory and a defence: "Realizing that our cause is combated by mighty and relentless forces, we will go forward in the strength of Him who is the Prince of Peace, meeting argument with argument, misjudgment with patience, and all our difficulties and dangers with prayer." Her work grew with the growth of the Union, and that growth was largely due to the tireless pen and voice and brain of its Corresponding Secretary.

While holding this office there occurred two episodes—apparent digressions—which did not, however, sever her connection with the Temperance work. In 1876-7, on invitation from Mr. Moody, she assisted him in the Gospel work in Boston for several months. Her hope in undertaking this enterprise was that the Temperance work might be united with the Gospel work, and brought with it to the front. The meetings for women, filling Berkeley and Park Street churches, and her words before the thousands gathered in the great Tabernacle, are memorable.

Says one who lives "in the Spirit" as few women do, "I have never been so conscious of the presence of the Divine power, the unction of the Holy One, in the ministry of the Word, as under the preaching of Miss Willard."

In this connection we are tempted to quote from a published statement recently made by Miss Willard:

"The deepest thought and desire of my life would have been met, if my dear old Mother Church had permitted me to be a minister. The wandering life of an evangelist or a reformer comes nearest to, but cannot fill, the ideal which I early cherished, but did not expect ever publicly to confess. While I heartily sympathize with the progressive movement which will ere long make ecclesiastically true our Master's words, 'There is neither male nor female in Christ Jesus'; while I steadfastly believe that there is no place too good for a woman to occupy, and nothing too sacred for her to do, I am not willing to go on record as a misanthropic complainer against the church which I prefer above my chief joy."

2. Cardinal Gibbons Defends the Knights of Labor, 1887

SOURCE: Henry J. Browne, *The Catholic Church and the Knights of Labor* (Washington, D. C.: The Catholic University of America Press, 1949), 365-78.

To His Eminence Cardinal Simeoni, Prefect of the Sacred Congregation of the Propaganda:

Your Eminence:

In submitting to the Holy See the conclusions which after several months of attentive observation and reflection, seem to me to sum up the truth concerning the association of the Knights of Labor, I feel profoundly convinced of the vast importance of the consequences attaching to this question, which forms but a link in the great chain of the social problems of our day, and especially of our country. . . .

1. In the first place, in the constitution, laws and official declarations of the Knights of Labor, there can clearly be found assertions and rules [though there may be found . . . things—*peuvent bien se trouver des assertions ou des régles*] which we would not approve; but we have not found in them those elements so clearly pointed out by the Holy See, which places them among condemned associations. . . .

2. That there exists among us, as in the other countries of the world, grave and threatening social evils, public injustices, which call for strong resistance and

legal remedy, is a fact which no one dares to deny, and the truth of which has been already acknowledged by the Congress and the President of the United States. Without entering into the sad details of these wrongs,—which does not seem necessary here,—it may suffice to mention only that monopolies on the part of both individuals and of corporations, have already called forth not only the complaints of our working classes but also the opposition of our public men and legislators; that the efforts of these monopolists, not always without success, to control legislation to their own profit, cause serious apprehension among the disinterested friends of liberty; that the heartless avarice which, through greed of gain, pitilessly grinds not only the men, but particularly the women and children in various employments, make it clear to all who love humanity and justice that it is not only the right of the laboring classes to protect themselves, but the duty of the whole people to aid them in finding a remedy against the dangers with which both civilization and the social order are menaced by avarice, oppression and corruption. It would be vain to deny either the existence of the evils, the right of legitimate resistance, or the necessity of a remedy. At most doubt might be raised about the legitimacy of the form of resistance and the remedy employed by the Knights of Labor. This then ought to be the next point of our examination.

3.   It can hardly be doubted that for the attainment of any public end, association—the organization of all interested persons—is the most efficacious means, a means altogether natural and just. This is so evident, and besides so conformable to the genius of our country, of our essentially popular social conditions, that it is unnecessary to insist upon it. It is almost the only means to invite public attention, to give force to the most legitimate resistance, to add weight to the most just demands. . . .

3. Leo XIII's "Rerum Novarum", 1891

SOURCE: John A. Ryan and Joseph Husslein, ed., *The Church and Labor* (New York, 1920), 57-59, 74-75, 77-78, 93-94.

That the spirit of revolutionary change, which has long been disturbing the nations of the world, should have passed beyond the sphere of politics and made its influence felt in the cognate sphere of practical economics is not surprising. The elements of the conflict now raging are unmistakable: in the vast expansion of industrial pursuits and the marvellous discoveries of science; in the changed relations between masters and workmen; in the enormous fortunes of some few individuals, and the utter poverty of the masses; in the increased self-reliance and closer mutual combination of the working classes; as also, finally, in the prevailing moral degeneracy. The momentous gravity of the state of things now obtaining fills every mind with painful apprehension; wise men are discussing it; practical men are proposing schemes; popular meetings, legislatures, and rulers of nations are all busied with it—and actually there is no question which has taken a deeper hold on the public mind. . . .

The Church Alone Can Solve the Social Problem

We approach the subject with confidence, and in the exercise of the rights which belong to Us. For no practical solution of this question will ever be found without the assistance of Religion and of the Church. It is We who are the chief guardian of Religion, and the chief dispenser of what belongs to the Church, and we must not by silence neglect the duty which lies upon Us. Doubtless this most serious question demands the attention and the efforts of others besides Ourselves—of the rulers of States, of employers of labor, of the wealthy, and of the working population themselves for whom We plead. But We affirm without hesitation that all the striving of men will be vain if they leave out the Church. . . .

The Christian Interdependence of Capital and Labor

The great mistake that is made in the matter now under consideration, is to possess oneself of the idea that class is naturally hostile to class; that rich and poor are intended by nature to live at war with one another. So irrational and so false is this view, that the exact contrary is the truth. Just as the symmetry of the human body is the result of the disposition of the members of the body, so in a State it is ordained by nature that these two classes should exist in harmony and agreement, and should, as it were, fit into one another, so as to maintain the equilibrium of the body politic. Each requires the other; capital cannot do without labor, nor labor without capital. Mutual agreement results in pleasantness and good order; perpetual conflict necessarily produces confusion and outrage. Now, in preventing such strife necessary as this, and in making it impossible, the efficacy of Christianity is marvelous and manifold. First of all, there is nothing more powerful than Religion (of which the Church is the interpreter and guardian) in drawing rich and poor together, by reminding each class of its duties to the other, and especially of the duties of justice. Thus Religion teaches the laboring man and the workman to carry out honestly and well all equitable agreements freely made, never to injure capital, nor to outrage the person of an employer; never to employ violence in representing his own cause, nor to engage in riot and disorder; and to have nothing to do with men of evil principles, who work upon the people with artful promises, and raise foolish hopes which usually end in disaster and in repentance when too late. Religion teaches the rich man and the employer that their work-people are not their slaves; that they must respect in every man his dignity as a man and as a Christian; that labor is nothing to be ashamed of, if we listen to right reason and to Christian philosophy, but is an honorable employment, enabling a man to sustain his life in an upright and creditable way; and that it is shameful and inhuman to treat men like chattels to make money by, or to look upon them merely as so much muscle or physical power. Thus, again, Religion teaches that, as among the workmen's concerns are Religion herself, and things spiritual and mental, the employer is bound to see that he has time for the duties of piety; that he be not exposed to corrupting influences and dangerous occasions; and that he be not led away to neglect his home and family or to squander his wages. Then, again, the employer must never tax his work-people beyond their strength, nor employ them in work unsuited to their sex or age. His great and principal obligation is to give to every one that which is just. . . .

As far as regards the Church, its assistance will never be wanting, be the time or the occasion what it may; and it will intervene with greater effect in proportion as its liberty of action is the more unfettered; let this be carefully noted by those whose office it is to provide for the public welfare. Every minister of holy Religion must throw into the conflict all the energy of his mind, and all the strength of his endurance; with your authority, Venerable Brethren, and by your example, they must never cease to urge upon all men of every class, upon the high as well as the lowly, the Gospel doctrines of Christian life; by every means in their power they must strive for the good of the people; and above all they must earnestly cherish in themselves, and try to arouse in others, Charity, the mistress and queen of virtues. For the happy results we all long for must be chiefly brought about by the plenteous outpouring of Charity; of that true Christian Charity which is the fulfilling of the whole Gospel law, which is always ready to sacrifice itself for others' sake, and which is man's surest antidote against worldly pride and immoderate love of self; that Charity whose office is described and whose God-like features are drawn by the Apostle St. Paul in these words: *Charity is patient, is kind, . . . seeketh not her own, . . . suffereth all things, . . . endureth all things.*

On each of you, Venerable Brethren, and on your Clergy and people, as an earnest of God's mercy and a mark of our affection, We lovingly in the Lord bestow the Apostolic Benediction.

Given at St. Peter's in Rome, the fifteenth day of May, 1891, the fourteenth year of our Pontificate.

LEO XIII., Pope.

4. In His Steps, 1896

SOURCE: Charles M. Sheldon, *In His Steps* (Chicago: John C. Winston Co. 1957), *passim*.

The sermon was interesting. It was full of striking sentences. They would have commanded attention printed. Spoken with the passion of a dramatic utterance that has the good taste never to offend with a suspicion of ranting or declamation, they were very effective. If the Rev. Henry Maxwell that morning felt satisfied with the conditions of his pastorate, the First Church also had a similar feeling as it congratulated itself on the presence in the pulpit of this scholarly, refined, somewhat striking face and figure, preaching with such animation and freedom from all vulgar, noisy, or disagreeable mannerism.

Suddenly into the midst of this perfect accord and concord between preacher and audience, there came a very remarkable interruption. It would be difficult to indicate the extent of the shock which this interruption measured. It was so unexpected, so entirely contrary to any thought of any person present that offered no room for argument, or, for the time being, of resistance.

The sermon had come to a close. Mr. Maxwell had just turned the half of the big Bible over upon his manuscript and was about to sit down, as the quartette prepared to rise to sing the closing selection,

"All for Jesus, All for Jesus,
All my being's ransomed powers."

when the entire congregation was startled by the sound of a man's voice. It came from the rear of the church, from one of the seats under the gallery. The next moment the figure of a man came out of the shadow there and walked down the middle aisle.

Before the startled congregation barely realized what was going on, the man had reached the open space in front of the pulpit and had turned about, facing the people.

"I have been wondering since I came in here"—they were the words he used under the gallery, and he repeated them—if it would be just the thing to say a word at the close of this service. I'm not drunk and I'm not crazy, and I'm perfectly harmless; but if I die, as there is every likelihood I shall in a few days, I want the satisfaction of thinking that I said my say in a place like this, and before this sort of a crowd."

Mr. Maxwell had not taken his seat, and he now remained standing, leaning on his pulpit, looking down at the stranger. It was the man who had come to his house the Friday before—the same dusty, worn, shabby-looking young man. He held his faded hat in his two hands. It seemed to be a favorite gesture. He had not been shaved, and his hair was rough and tangled. It was doubtful if anyone like this had ever confronted the First Church within the sanctuary. It was tolerably familiar with this sort of humanity out on the street around the railroad shops, wandering up and down the avenue; but it had never dreamed of such an incident as this so near.

There was nothing offensive in the man's manner or tone. He was not excited, and he spoke in a low but distinct voice. Mr. Maxwell was conscious, even as he stood there smitten into dumb astonishment at the event, that somehow the man's action reminded him of a person he had once seen walking and talking in his sleep.

No one in the house made any motion to stop the stranger or in any way interrupt him. Perhaps the first shock of his sudden appearance deepened into genuine perplexity concerning what was best to do. However that may be, he went on as if he had no thought of interruption, and no thought of the unusual element which he had introduced into the decorum of the First Church service. And all the while he was speaking the minister leaned over the pulpit, his face growing more white and sad every moment. But he made no movement to stop him, and the people sat smitten into breathless silence. One other face, that of Rachel Winslow, from the choir, stared white and intent down at the shabby figure with the faded hat. Her face was striking at any time. Under the pressure of the present unheard-of incident, it was as personally distinct as if it had been framed in fire.

"I'm not an ordinary tramp, though I don't know of any teaching of Jesus that makes one kind of a tramp less worth saving than another. Do you?" He put the question as naturally as if the whole congregation had been a small Bible class. He paused just a moment, and coughed painfully. Then he went on. "I lost my job ten months ago. I am a printer by trade. The new linotype machines are beautiful specimens of inventions, but I know six men who have killed themselves inside of the year just on account of those machines. Of course, I don't blame the newspapers for getting the machines. Meanwhile, what can a man do? I know I never learned but the one trade, and that's all I can do. I've tramped all over the country trying to find something. There are a good many others like me. I'm not complaining, am I? Just stating facts. But I was wondering, as I sat there under the gallery, if what you call following Jesus is the same thing as what he taught. What did he mean when he said, 'Follow me?' The minister said,"—here the man turned about and looked up at the pulpit— "that it was necessary for the disciple of Jesus to follow his steps, and he said the steps were obedience, faith, love, and imitation. But I did not hear him tell you just what he meant that to mean, especially the last step. What do you Christians mean by following the steps of Jesus? I've tramped through this city for three days trying to find a job, and in all that time I've not had a word of sympathy or comfort except from your minister here, who said he was sorry for me and hoped I would find a job somewhere. I suppose it is because you get so imposed on the professional tramp that you have lost your interest in the other sort. I'm not blaming anybody, am I? Just stating facts. Of course, I understand you can't go out of your way to hunt jobs for people like me. I'm not asking you to, but what I feel puzzled about is, what is meant by following Jesus? What do you mean when you sing, 'I'll go with him, with him all the way'? Do you mean that you are suffering and denying yourselves and trying to save lost, suffering humanity just as I understand Jesus did? What do you mean by it? I see the ragged edge of things a good deal. I understand there are more than five hundred men in this city in my case. Most of them have families. My wife died four months ago. I'm glad she is out of trouble. My little girl is staying with a printer's family until I find a job. Somehow I get puzzled when I see so many Christians living in luxury and singing, 'Jesus, I my cross have taken, all to leave and follow thee,' and remember how my wife died in a tenement in New York City gasping for air, and asking God to take the little girl, too. Of course I don't expect you people can prevent everyone from dying of starvation, lack of proper nourishment, and tenement air, but what does following Jesus mean? I understand that Christian people own a good many of the tenements. A member of a church was the owner of the one where my wife died, and I have wondered if following Jesus all the way was true in his case. I heard some people singing at a church prayer meeting the other night,

'All for Jesus, all for Jesus;

All my being's ransomed powers:

All my thoughts and all my doings,

All my days and all my hours;'

and I kept wondering as I sat on the steps outside just what they meant by it. It seems to me there's an awful lot of trouble in the world that somehow wouldn't exist if all the people who sing such songs went and lived them out. I suppose I don't understand. But what would Jesus do? Is that what you mean by following his steps? . . .

"There is no other test that I know of. We shall all have to decide what Jesus would do after going to that source of knowledge." "What if others say of us when we do certain things, that Jesus would not do so?" asked the superintendent of railroads. "We cannot prevent that. But we must be absolutely honest with ourselves. The standard of Christian action cannot vary in most of our acts." "And yet what one church member thinks Jesus would do, another refuses to accept as his possible course of action. What is to render our conduct uniformly Christlike? Will it be possible to reach the same conclusions always in all cases?" asked President Marsh. Mr. Maxwell was silent some time. Then he answered: "No; I don't know that we can expect that. But when it comes to a genuine, honest, enlightened following of Jesus' steps, I cannot believe there will be any confusion either in our own minds or in the judgment of others. We must be free from fanaticism on one hand and too much caution on the other. If Jesus' example is the example for the world, it certainly must be feasible to follow it. But we need to remember this great fact. After we asked the Spirit to tell us what Jesus would do and have received an answer to it, we are to act regardless of the results to ourselves. Is that understood? . . ."

5. The Race Problem in a Christian State, 1906

SOURCE: From *The Spirit of Freedom and Justice* by Reverdy C. Ransom. Pp. 128-32. Copyright © 1926 by AMEC Sunday School Union/Legacy Publishing. Reprinted with permission.

There should be no Race problem in the Christian State.

When Christianity received its Pentecostal baptism and seal from heaven it is recorded that, "there were dwelling at Jerusalem Jews, devout men, out of every nation under heaven. Parthians, and Medes, and Elamites, and the dwellers in Mesopotamia, and in Judea, and Cappadocia, in Pontus and Asia. Phrygia, and Pamphylia in Egypt, and in parts of Lybia about Cyrene; and strangers of Rome; Jews and Proselytes, Cretes and Arabians."

St. Paul, standing in the Areopagus, declared to the Athenians that, "God hath made of one blood all nations of men for to dwell on all the face of the earth."

Jesus Christ founded Christianity in the midst of the most bitter and intense antagonisms of race and class. Yet be ignored them all, dealing alike with Jew, Samaritan, Syro-Phoenician, Greek and Roman. It is true that the Jewish religion and the entire social and political structure of Hebrew civilization rested upon the idea of race. "First the blade, then the ear, after that the full corn in the ear," is as true in human society as it is in nature. God, through the Jew, was educating the world, and laying a moral and spiritual foundation. That foundation was the establishment of the *one God idea*. Upon this foundation Jesus Christ builded the superstructure of "the Fatherhood of God," and its corollary, "the Brotherhood of man."

The crowning object at which Jesus Christ aimed was, to "break down the middle wall of partition," between man and man, and to take away all the Old Testament laws and ordinances that prevented Jew and Gentile from approaching God on an equal plane. And this He did, "that He might reconcile both unto God in one body by the cross, having slain the enmity thereby, so making peace."

What is a Christian State?

A Christian State is one founded upon the teachings of Jesus; being thus founded, its constitution and laws and all the complex social relations of its people's life will partake of the character and spirit of His teachings. This is the ideal which the Christian State has set before it, toward which it must ever strive. It cannot hesitate or turn back, without turning its back upon Him. From the time that St. Paul answered the Macedonians' cry by introducing Christianity into Europe down to the present hour, the states calling themselves Christian have had to deal with the race problem, and they have done it with the rack, the torch, the Spanish Inquisition, the Kishnev Massacre, political disability, social exclusion and by all other means passion and prejudice could devise. America has this right to call itself a Christian nation, that it is the first nation that was born with the Bible in its hands. It has had to face problems new to the civilization of Europe, and to walk in untried paths. The Negro Question has been with this nation from the time that the foundations of the government were laid. James G. Blaine in his "Twenty Years in Congress" says: "The compromises on the Slavery Question, inserted in the Constitution, were among the essential conditions upon which the federal government was organized. If the African slave trade had not been permitted to continue for twenty years; if it had not been conceded that three-fifths of the slaves should be counted in the apportionment of representatives in Congress, if it had not been agreed that fugitives from service should be returned to their owners, the Thirteen States would not have been able in 1787 "to form a more perfect union."

In dealing with this question, the history of our past is well known. The Race Problem in this country is not only still with us an unsolved problem, but it constitutes perhaps the most serious problem in our country today. In Church and State, from the beginning, we have tried to settle it by compromise, but all compromises have ended in failure. It is only when we have faced it courageously and sought to settle it right that we have triumphed, as in the case of Lincoln's immortal "Proclamation of Emancipation." American Christianity will un-christ itself if it refuses to strive on, until this Race Problem is not only settled, but settled right; and until this is done, however much men may temporize and seek to compromise, and cry "peace! peace!" there will be no peace until this is done.

Facing the Industrial Question

Those who brought the Negro to this country had no thought of him as a human being above the mere level of brute strength and animalism. The thought of admitting him even into the outer courts of opportunity for progress, much less according him the rights of a man, had never for a moment been entertained. He was to be forever tied to the soil, enjoy no rights nor privileges, exercise no will save the will of his master. Negro slavery was for generations, the corner-stone of Southern civilization. Whatever progress or prosperity the South enjoyed for two hundred years was based upon it. All the power of her pulpits, the learning of her schools, the ability of her statesmen were employed to justify, to uphold, to maintain and to defend it. It was, in fact, constitutional and it was declared to be also in accordance with the will of heaven, which had decreed that the Negro should be a servant forever. The North partly from climatic reasons and partly from differences of its political, intellectual and moral inheritance and training, was unfriendly to slavery; more than this, there were high-souled men and women who were sufficiently acquainted with the will of God and the teachings of Jesus Christ, to know that a Christian nation founded in liberty could not long survive upon the foundation of human slavery. At last God's hour came; He spoke from heaven; men's eyes were opened, their hearts were a flame of fire, they matched to the field of battle and fought until the ground ran red with blood; both North and South gave their beauty, their chivalry, their wealth, their brain and brawn. When the thick blackness piled up by the smoke from the cannon's roar was lifted, the world beheld the fetters of four million slaves piled up like a monument to heaven. After these days passed, men felt that the Negro would be permitted to tread the pathway of industrial opportunity with perfect freedom, according to his capability and desires, but not so. The attitude of this nation today both North and South, seems to be, that the Negro should live only upon the fringes of the industrial world, that his place should be that of a menial. This idea has become so fixed, that it is thought to be a presumption amounting to impertinence, for qualified Negro men and women to seek to enter the doors of the great banking, manufacturing, mercantile and business avenues open to all others with perfect freedom. Following upon this idea, a propaganda has arisen, which has found willing assent in the North, to the extent that it is shared by clergymen, newspapers, magazines and most of the great organs of public opinion, as well as the wealthy, who willingly contribute millions in its behalf. No one can successfully prove what is claimed, that industrial education will solve the Negro Problem. How can industrial education solve the Negro Problem? The South has assented to this proposition in which northern sentiment seems to have acquiesced; but what the South undoubtedly means by this solution, is that a great peasant class, composed of ten million Negroes shall be built up and established in this land; that they shall be trained to more intelligently till the soil, ply the trades and render domestic service. This Republic, conceived in liberty, cannot stand upon its foundation by establishing here a peasant class.

Rev. Thomas Dixon, Jr. has recently complained in the public prints that Dr. Booker T. Washington's great school at Tuskegee was not turning out servants, but men, who would go out into the world to be themselves leaders of men, as contractors, master mechanics and employers or directors of labor, and because of this, he says that Tuskegee will be a failure; that it cannot survive. Here in Massachusetts and throughout all the North and West, yea even in the Southland, colored boys and girls are studying the same books and drinking from the same fountains of aspirations as are the whites. They read the same books, papers and magazines; they cherish the same ideals and ambitions. Can one think of a greater crime, almost against the very life of human spirit, than this, that these youths should go thus out into life only to find that their ability, coupled with high character, counted for very little when they sought to enter the doors of industrial opportunity?

We admit that the Negro has been a servant, and only a servant, so long has been in a place of inferiority for so many generations, that it is difficult, no doubt, to conceive of him entering a path which character and fitness would permit any other person to tread with perfect freedom. The Negro does work, and has done nothing but work since he landed upon these shores centuries ago. He should become a more skilled, and a more intelligent worker, it is true; but he should be permitted to work not only as a servant, but as a man, with all the opportunities open to him that are open to others no better qualified than he. White men may not feel it thus and some Negroes may not see it, but the great and menacing danger that surrounds the Negro and the nation at this hour, is the circumscribed limitations which this nation has put around the opportunities of the Negroes of this land, to occupy themselves freely, in any sphere, according to their ambitions, capability and desire. The government does deal justly with the Negro so far as permitting him to be employed in its various branches which may be entered through Civil Service examination, but even here, when it comes to promotion for merit, the boundary line beyond which be may not go is fixed. This nation is not rich enough in trained minds, skilled hands and cultured brains to put a discount upon the ability and aspiration of any class of its citizens, nor will it act in the spirit of Christ toward the black toilers of this land, until Negroes are as freely permitted to run locomotive engines as they are elevators; to work in a national bank, as they are a coal bank; to sell dry goods over the counters of the store as they are to wash them in the laundry; to work in a cotton mill, as they are in a cotton field; and to follow the pig-iron from the furnace, all the way to the iron and steel mills, through all the various forms of utility into which it is capable of being manufactured; this and nothing less than this, is the justice which a Christian nation should be willing to give. Willing because such giving would not impoverish, but would greatly enrich it in all lines and branches by the reenforcement of these millions of eager hands, whose fingers have been twitching in hopeful anticipation for the day when they might seize these opportunities from which they have been so long debarred. It would add to the nation's strength by making so many more millions of her citizens prosperous; by permitting them to contribute to the upbuilding of the nation along all the lines of its defense, production, development and growth. . . .

6. Christianity and The Social Crisis, 1907

SOURCE: From *Christianity and the Social Crisis* by Walter Rauschenbusch. pp. 414-17, 420-21. Copyright © 1907 by Macmillan Publishing Co.

The first apostolate of Christianity was born from a deep fellow-feeling for social misery and from the consciousness of a great historical opportunity. Jesus saw the peasantry of Galilee following him about with their poverty and their diseases, like shepherdless sheep that have been scattered and harried by beasts of prey, and his heart had compassion on them. He felt that the harvest was ripe, but there were few to reap it. Past history had come to its culmination, but there were few who understood the situation and were prepared to cope with it. He bade his disciples to pray for laborers for the harvest, and then made them answer their own prayers by sending them out two by two to proclaim the kingdom of God. That was the beginning of the world-wide mission of Christianity.

The situation is repeated on a vaster scale to-day. If Jesus stood today amid our modern life, with that outlook on the condition of all humanity which observation and travel and the press would spread before him, and with the same heart of divine humanity beating in him, he would create a new apostolate to meet the new needs in a new harvest-time of history.

To any one who knows the sluggishness of humanity to good, the impregnable entrenchments of vested wrongs and the long reaches of time needed from one milestone of progress to the next, the task of setting up a Christian social order in this modern world of ours seems like a fair and futile dream. Yet in fact it is not one tithe as hopeless as when Jesus set out to do it. When he told his disciples, "Ye are the salt of the earth; ye are the light of the world," he expressed the consciousness of a great historic mission to the whole of humanity. Yet it was a Nazarene carpenter speaking to a group of Galilaean peasants and fishermen. Under the circumstances at that time it was an utterance of the most daring faith,—faith in himself, faith in them, faith in what he was putting into them, faith in faith. Jesus failed and was crucified, first his body by his enemies, and then his spirit by his friends; but that failure was so amazing a success that to-day it takes an effort on our part to realize that it required any faith on his part to inaugurate the kingdom of God and to send out his apostolate.

To-day, as Jesus looks out upon humanity, his spirit must leap to see the souls responsive to his call. They are sown broadcast through humanity, legions of them. The harvest-field is no longer deserted. All about us we hear the clang of the whetstone and the rush of the blades through the grain and the shout of the reapers. With all our faults and our slothfulness we modern men in many ways are more on a level with the real mind of Jesus than any generation that has gone before. If that first apostolate was able to remove mountains by the power of faith, such an apostolate as Christ could now summon might change the face of the earth.

The apostolate of a new age must do the work of the sower. When the sower goes forth to sow his seed he goes with the certainty of partial failure and the knowledge that a long time of patience and of hazard will intervene before he can hope to see the result of his work and his venture. In sowing the truth a man may never see or trace the results. The more ideal his conceptions are, and the farther they move ahead of his time, the larger will be the percentage of apparent failure. But he can afford to wait. The powers of life are on his side. He is like a man who has scattered his seed and then goes off to sleep by night and work by day, and all the while the seed, by the inscrutable chemistry of life, lays hold of the ingredients of its environment and builds them up to its own growth. The mustard-seed becomes a tree. The leaven assimilates the meal by biological processes. The new life penetrates the old humanity and transforms it. Robert Owens was a sower. His cooperative communities failed. He was able to help only a small fraction of the workingmen of his day. But his moral enthusiasm and his ideas fertilized the finest and most self-sacrificing minds among the working classes. They cherished his ultimate hopes in private and worked for realizable ends in public. The Chartist movement was filled with his spirit. The most influential leaders of English unionism in its great period after the middle of the nineteenth century were Owenites. The Rochdale Pioneers were under his influence, and the great cooperative movement in England, an economic force of the first importance, grew in some measure out of the seed which Owen had scattered. Other men may own the present. The future belongs to the sower—provided he scatters seed and does not mistake the chaff for it which once was so essential to the seed and now is dead and useless. . . .

In asking for faith in the possibility of a new social order, we ask for no Utopian delusion. We know well that there is no perfection for man in this life: there is only growth toward perfection. In personal religion we look with seasoned suspicion at any one who claims to be holy and perfect, yet we always tell men to become holy and to seek perfection. We make it a duty to seek what is unattainable. We have the same paradox in the perfectibility of society. We shall never have a perfect social life, yet we must seek it with faith. We shall never abolish suffering. There will always be death and the empty chair and heart. There will always be the agony of love unreturned. Women will long for children and never press baby lips to their breast. Men will long for fame and miss it. Imperfect moral insight will work hurt in the best conceivable social order. The strong will always have the impulse to exert their strength, and no system can be devised which can keep them from crowding and jostling the weaker. Increased social refinement will bring increased sensitiveness to pain. An American may suffer as much distress through a social slight as a Russian peasant under the knout. At the best there is always but an approximation to a perfect social order. The kingdom of God is always but coming.

But every approximation to it is worth while. Every stop toward personal purity and peace, though it only makes the consciousness of imperfection more poignant, carries its own exceeding great reward, and everlasting pilgrimage toward the kingdom of God is better than contented stability in the tents of wickedness. . . .

Essays

In the first essay, Susan Curtis of Purdue University describes how the problems caused by late nineteenth-century industrialization, immigration, and urbanization produced a social gospel movement among American Protestants—a gospel that would meet the needs of both the individual and society. Jay P. Dolan of the University of Notre Dame demonstrates in the second essay that the same influences of the factories and cities that produced the Protestant social gospel movement were also moving American Catholicism toward a social gospel. Conflict among both Protestants and Catholics surrounded the social gospel, however, as a consensus of support among churchgoers was building gradually but steadily. In the final essay, Timothy E. Fulop of King College (TN) contends that during the final decades of the nineteenth century when black Americans were pursuing the American dream in the age of industrialization, some black Americans emerging from the dark shadow of slavery could only hope for a future golden day fulfilled in the millennial reign of God on earth. The exclusion of most black Americans from the mainstream of the social gospel dynamic was apparent.

American Protestantism at a Crossroads

SUSAN CURTIS

SOURCE: From *A Consuming Faith: The Social Gospel and Modern American Culture* by Susan Curtis. Pp. 1-3, 3-4, 4-11, 12-15. Copyright © 2001 by University of Missouri Press. Reprinted with permission of the author.

When Walter Rauschenbusch wrote *Christianizing the Social Order* in 1912, he believed that the social gospel had become the dominant expression of Protestantism in America. He had returned to the United States in 1908 after a year-long stay in Europe to discover that his book *Christianity and the Social Crisis* had won popular approval beyond his "boldest hopes." He marveled at the "social awakening of our nation" that made people receptive to his ideas. Rauschenbusch applauded Americans' "enthusiastic turning toward real democracy" and the increasing intensity of "religious energy" that accompanied it. He discovered a vast array of programs and projects that heartened him. The Federal Council of Churches, the Social Creed of the Churches, an expanding YMCA, the blossoming of institutional churches across the country, the social interests of the Religious Education Association, the Men and Religion Forward Movement, and the Presbyterians' Labor Temple in New York City—all were evidence to him of a dramatic reordering of Protestant America. To his astonishment and delight, long-time defenders and advocates of the social gospel were not the only ones to sing its praises. "Perhaps the most convincing proof of the spread of the social interest in the ministry," he declared, "is the fact that the old men and the timid men are falling in line." By

1912, Rauschenbusch believed that his social message had become the legitimate expression of mainstream Protestantism in America.

From his vantage point as one of the vanguard of the social gospel movement, Walter Rauschenbusch considered the organizations and achievements that he praised in 1912 as evidence of the triumph of a new kind of Protestantism. The social gospel, as this new Protestantism was known, bolstered the age-old demand for individual regeneration with a powerful social message. It was a gospel that did not let the saved languish in smug self-satisfaction while the ills of society kept others from salvation. According to the social gospel, every Christian had a dual obligation: to himself and to society. As a result, the social gospel provided the foundation for social and political reforms designed to eliminate poverty, disease, filth, and immorality. And its advocates evangelized the unchurched. For example, social gospelers launched a campaign to attract the working class by supporting their class interests for fairer working conditions, by easing the discomfort of their lives with material and medical assistance, and by living among them, sharing their burdens and speaking to them as brothers and sisters with a message of hope. Social gospelers wrote hymns and compiled hymnals that reflected their Christocentric theology and their interest in the kingdom of God on earth. They rewrote Sunday school literature to instruct young people to balance individual piety with social responsibility. The social gospel asked Protestants to address the physical, emotional, and material, as well as spiritual, needs of men and women whether they belonged to a church or not.

The social gospel usually is described as the religious expression of progressivism in the early twentieth century. Like the progressive political culture of which it was a part, the social gospel was perceived by participants and observers alike as a departure from the Protestant emphasis in nineteenth-century Victorian America on individualism. Men and women born in the 1830s and 1840s—such as Elizabeth Stuart Phelps Ward, Josiah Strong, Washington Gladden, and Lyman Abbott—increasingly voiced their dissatisfaction with Protestant belief and practice in the 1860s and 1870s. Initially, their ideas met with disfavor, but beginning in the 1880s a rising generation identified more readily with their critique of individualism. By the 1890s Protestants had established a number of organizations devoted to social reform.

In 1908, when the Federal Council of Churches met in Philadelphia, delegates unanimously adopted the Social Creed of the Churches, which signaled the commitment of a significant portion of Protestant America to an agenda of social justice and social reform. By the time this creed was adopted, the "social question" absorbed the attention of many Protestants. Josiah Strong had announced the dawning of "a new era"; Rauschenbusch had alerted thousands to a serious "social crisis"; Washington Gladden had defined "social salvation" and George Herron, the "new redemption." It would have been difficult to avoid confronting the social gospel. Even conservatives, who later joined with fundamentalists in the 1920s, undertook various programs of reform and responded to the needs of society as well as to the souls of individual communicants. Inspired by the hope of ushering in the kingdom of God on earth, men like John Roach Straton attacked political corruption, prostitution, child labor, women's labor, and bad working conditions in the 1910s.

The social gospel is also explained as a response by late-nineteenth-century American Protestants to problems caused by industrialization, massive immigration, and chaotic urban development. The Labor Temple in New York City, the University Settlement House in Chicago, Walter Rauschenbusch in Hell's Kitchen in the 1880s, and Washington Gladden's political crusades on behalf of workers and reform in Columbus, Ohio, are among the treasured memories of the social gospel movement. Protestants in the late nineteenth century turned away from the accepted religious wisdom of their elders by formulating a theology and practice that redefined the categories of belief and that presented a serious challenge to industrial capitalist society. They exchanged the terror of the anxious bench for a commitment to altruism that would ensure their own and their brothers' salvation. In place of unbridled competition, individual responsibility for success, and government policies of laissez faire, social gospelers proposed cooperation, social responsibility for justice, and an interventionist welfare state. . . .

In addition to the well-known accomplishments of the social gospel movement, this major shift in Protestantism also resulted in different church services. Across the nation, Americans witnessed the emergence of "institutional" churches that remained open seven days a week and provided meals, employment, medical services, clothes, child care, and social activities that bound neighbors together in the quest for justice and nurture. Instead of limiting their service to people formally associated with the church or denomination, Protestants who supported the social gospel sought to serve all those in need. By the early twentieth century the majority of Protestants went beyond providing material and spiritual succor to support more fundamental assaults on the system that created inequality. The Social Creed of the Churches, for example, affirmed laborers' rights to organize unions and to bargain collectively with employers. Some congregations lent assistance to striking workers who tried to wrest a better life from a grudging industrial order, and at least one social gospeler arbitrated labor disputes in his community to the satisfaction and with the gratitude of unionists. . . .

Social gospelers also produced an extensive literature that helped to popularize the commitment to social justice. Novelists like Elizabeth Stuart Phelps Ward and Charles Sheldon created imaginary communities beset by social ills that flourished once they adopted the social gospel. *In His Steps* by Charles Sheldon became a best-seller in the 1890s and appeared in at least a dozen different languages and countries. The Religious Education Association oversaw the publication of new Sunday school texts that reflected the new social interests of Protestants and acquainted young people with the ideas of the social gospel in stories, object lessons, and community service projects. Most ministers in the movement wrote books aimed at the general educated reader concerned with social ills and reform, but many also tried to reach a working-class audience composed of men and women who had fallen away from the church. Their essays, collections of sermons, and blueprints for reform appeared in monographs, literary journals, and inexpensive religious magazines. William Bliss prepared an encyclopedia of social reform in 1897 that pulled together much of the pathbreaking work by men and women in the social gospel movement, and it remains an invaluable source for the ideas and accomplishments of twentieth-century Christian reformers. These writers shared a desire to improve the physical conditions of life for an urban underclass impoverished by industrial development, and they revolutionized the way middle-class adherents to the movement thought about religion.

These social gospel programs and literature reflected an important transformation of Protestant theology. While formal, academic statements of theology did not appear until later in the twentieth century, social gospelers redefined salvation, the nature of God, and religious commitment and in so doing, made an important departure from the Protestantism of the Second Great Awakening in the early 1800s. Eschewing the lonely struggle with sin for a sense of individual assurance, social gospelers insisted that salvation was a social matter—that Christians were responsible for their brothers' and sisters' redemption as much as their own. The social view of salvation required a united Christian attack on the poverty, vice, and filth that prevented many Americans from staying on the road to redemption. If the conditions that encouraged depravity were removed, these reformers argued, believers would be less likely to stray.

Given this commitment to changing the social environment, it is not surprising that social gospelers redefined the meaning of God as well. Instead of the angry Jehovah of the eighteenth century or even the judgmental God of the "burned-over district," the God of the social gospel was "immanent," "indwelling," and indulgent. A kind parent, God befriended man and surrendered to his moral creatures the agency to usher in his kingdom.

The idea of social salvation granted by an immanent God gave rise to a third important shift in Protestant thinking— away from a concern with the afterlife and toward a concern with this life. Social gospelers proposed active involvement in the affairs of the world, an agenda of reform, and a vital commitment to the kingdom of God on earth. Instead of viewing religion exclusively as a private matter to be addressed by each individual, Rauschenbusch and his colleagues believed in paving the way for individual assurance by removing the social barriers to righteousness. Rather than dwelling on future promises of celestial bliss, they occupied themselves with the evils of poverty, depravity, and injustice in this world.

Social gospelers hold a respected place in American history as Christian reformers in urban, industrial America; and many Americans, then and later, have drawn strength from the example they set. But much more can be learned from these Protestant men and women than how to translate Christian commitment into social action. The social gospel appeared at a critical moment in American history—a moment that marked the unraveling of the Victorian culture of the nineteenth century. Consequently, social gospelers were among those who experienced anxiety when the matrix of beliefs and values that had given life meaning in the nineteenth century began to make less and less sense. Struggling to find religious and personal meaning themselves, they gradually developed a social interpretation of religion that contributed to the formation of the new culture that emerged in the twentieth century. An examination of the social gospel can reveal the intersection of faith and culture and demonstrate how social and cultural facts of life impinged on religion. Such an inquiry also demonstrates the way in which an emergent pattern of religious belief conditioned the standards applied to work, family life, politics, individual personality, and social relationships.

Because of its origin in an era of cultural transformation, the social gospel can help explain how a modern, secular, consumption-oriented culture took root and flourished in Protestant Victorian soil. But gaining this understanding requires a fresh approach to the movement and its message. We must grant to the men and women of the social gospel their sincerity and earnestness in seeking religious and cultural certainty. But we must frame the phenomenon in cultural terms rather than narrowly religious ones. We must look at the relation of reverence and faith to their experience as members of families, as citizens, as workers, and as men and women of letters.

As children in the middle third of the nineteenth century, future social gospelers approached maturity with expectations implanted by their elders. They assumed that the key to their success and salvation lay inside themselves and that failure would be the result of inadequate effort or restraint. They looked forward to starting families and living among neighbors whose domestic harmony and order reflected their own. They never imagined that their Protestant world view, liberal political culture, and Victorian respectability would be significantly challenged.

Yet the Gilded Age called their lives and faith into question. An increasingly industrialized, bureaucratized, urban economy thwarted the efforts of many an ambitious individual to strive and succeed on his own. The demands of the market along with greater educational opportunities for women brought more women into the workplace as laborers and professionals, thus eroding the domestic ideal. Thousands of Catholic and Jewish immigrants from southern and eastern Europe began to undermine the Protestant majority and its outlook, and with the rise of urban political machines, they transformed American politics. While these external forces undermined the culture of Victorian Protestantism, the advent of biblical criticism, Darwin's theory of evolution, and Freudian psychology brought religious certainty under direct attack. Men and women raised to believe in individualism, self-restraint, domesticity, liberalism, and moral free agency found themselves in the late nineteenth century in a world that did not sustain their beliefs. They sought and eventually began to articulate a creed that would reassure them both culturally and spiritually.

American Protestants in the late nineteenth century responded to this changed world in a variety of ways, many of which became parts of the social gospel program. Some rejected trends in the economy as destructive of self-esteem and just rewards for labor. They opposed industrial capitalism because they believed it denied justice, fair distribution of rewards, and human dignity. These critics supported labor unions, socialism, or government intervention and regulation. Others looked nervously askance at an increasingly militant and foreign-born working class and escalating class warfare. Their Christian faith in brotherhood, charity, and harmony clashed with the hateful spirit of both labor activists and exploitative employers. Instead, they sought peace and generosity and social harmony. These Christian men and women wanted to ameliorate the conditions that evoked such fierce anger, which in turn elicited harsh repression.

Many American Protestants worried. They sensed that their beliefs were being drowned out by the plethora of voices, cultures, and creeds of an ever more diverse American society. They feared that Protestant beliefs would be swallowed by the creeds of Catholic and Jewish immigrants. They worried that family life, necessary to sustain and reproduce their values, would be destroyed by people whose circumstances demanded, by middle-class standards, unwholesome domestic arrangements. They predicted the demise of democratic institutions if the new immigrants were not tutored in American political practices. They wanted to combat their fears by reaching a new audience—not the already converted but the men and women thronging to America's shores. They groped toward a bigger and more inclusive way of conceiving a Protestant America.

Most people who embraced the social gospel questioned the beliefs or practices of their parents. They sensed that the lessons of their youth would not stand up to the demands being placed on them by a rapidly changing society. Personal experiences conditioned their reaction to their society and culture, and their formulation of the social gospel in its own way answered deeply felt needs to succeed, to help others, to restore social (Christian) harmony, to earn their birthright as good citizens, and to help see that justice was done. Protestants who embraced the social gospel did so because they saw it as a way of presenting new ideas, addressing their fears, and achieving their vision of a godly society.

Ministers of the social gospel at the turn of the century set themselves against their parents' professions of religion. They questioned the focus on individual salvation, not because they believed the individual soul was somehow unimportant, but because they believed it was not the only concern. They worried that too much attention to the afterlife would draw attention away from very real problems on earth that would delay the coming of the kingdom of God. They rejected the explanation of antebellum religion and postbellum liberal political economy, that people who failed did so on their own. Social gospelers were deeply aware of the limits of the individual's power, especially among the lower classes. They wanted religion to engage, even transform, politics and business. Though liberal Protestants before the Civil War had begun to blur the distinctions between heaven and earth, and antebellum Protestant reformers had begun to address a wide range of social problems, social gospelers shifted the emphasis and believed that they were breaking with the beliefs and practices of the past. Rauschenbusch remembered the years before 1900 as "a time of loneliness" for social Christians. Their elders chided Rauschenbusch and his peers for "wrecking" their careers by taking theological stands outside mainstream Protestantism. He recalled the "happy surprise" every time he met "a new man who had seen the light." Indeed, while some parents of social gospelers had fought against slavery, intemperance, ignorance, and poverty, they emphasized individual responsibility and individual solutions. Slaveholders were individual sinners, as were drinkers. The children of these earlier reformers, those who became a part of the social gospel movement, sponsored reform campaigns in municipalities and state legislatures that assumed individual responsibility but looked more often to collective solutions, to a socialized humanity. Social gospelers fought for higher standards of public sanitation, health, education, and working conditions; and they sought to abolish child labor, to protect women at work, and to improve the treatment of immigrant laborers. They placed the burden of responsibility on institutions rather than on the individual, and they proposed social, governmental solutions to problems that their parents had treated as individual failings.

Social gospelers' calls for social salvation, commitment to the kingdom of God on earth, new criteria for evaluating personal worth, cooperation, and involvement in the affairs of the world eventually gained wide acceptance. Certainly not every Protestant was a social gospeler, but in *Christianizing the Social Order* Rauschenbusch noted that the "contrast with the early days . . . makes the present situation in the churches . . . amazing." By 1912, many American Protestants accepted a creed of which the generation of the 1880s would have been skeptical.

The generation of Protestants who followed the original pathbreakers found that it was respectable to advocate a social gospel. In places like Grinnell College in the 1890s, they could take courses in applied Christianity. In leading theological seminaries they studied Christian sociology and wrote theses on various dimensions of the "social crisis." They had at their disposal a growing body of scholarship on Christians' responsibility for economic, social, and political reform. Religious literature for children reflected the interest in social salvation. It did not require the same act of courage for younger men and women to declare their support for the social gospel that it had for the first spokesmen. While this represented "progress" of an important source for the movement, it also changed the movement's character. The focus of the second generation would be different—that of broadcasting the movement.

Some social gospelers in the early twentieth century experimented with new ways of attracting adherents. Their aim was to win the adherence of people outside of Protestantism. Some tried innovations in worship services and in church life. Others dabbled in the new mass media—moving pictures and, later, radio. Some believed that advertising would augment the number of supporters for social Christianity. By the onset of the First World War, the social gospel had been transformed. A movement that had originated in the social problems produced by capitalist industrial production took on the coloration of a movement of a piece with an emergent consumer society.

America's involvement in the Great War in Europe illuminated both the achievements and the much-expanded ambition of the social gospel movement. While social gospelers were morally offended by war, many nonetheless saw a chance to influence society in the postwar Western world. They never wavered in their denunciation of the war's destruction and violence, but they believed that the war was a turning point in Western civilization. It was an opportunity to Christianize society, culture, religion, work, politics, and international relations in the United States and Europe. Social gospelers fused their aims with the nation's, and many became proud defenders of the American mission to make the world safe for democracy.

By the 1920s, the commitment of social gospelers to politics and reform as well as to publicity had been validated by their own involvement in the success of the state and corporate organization during the Great War. The shift must be described with some precision. Social gospelers still urged individuals to save their brothers and sisters as well as themselves. They still spoke of the need to redeem society. Increasingly, however, they articulated their beliefs and aspirations in terms drawn from secular society, terms, indeed, of secular society. They proposed to achieve social harmony and social justice by advocating social sensitivity to others, self-realization, and material abundance for all. The qualities of congeniality, inoffensiveness, and team spirit, evident in such secular settings as the college campus and the corporate white-collar world, promised, in the social gospel's terms, success, morality, and spiritual fulfillment. Participating in the modern workplace and marketplace provided material comfort, promised psychological security, involved the individual in something larger than himself, and thereby could invest religious meaning in secular acts. Affirmation through others, transcendence of the individualistic code, and faith in material comfort conferred a sense of well-being, gave people direction and attainable goals, and connected them to a larger social experience, all of which eased nagging fears of personal failure and eternal damnation. When social gospelers insisted that man could achieve salvation on earth, consumer goods and fellow-feeling came to be regarded among the tangible evidence of that salvation. . . .

The social gospel, then, is fruitfully studied in a broader cultural frame as cultural history. From its beginning in the late nineteenth century, the social gospel was a matter of men and women in search of cultural truth as well as spiritual fulfillment. For that reason, it was a "consuming faith," a term used in this study to refer both to the social gospeler' profound commitment to justice and reform and to their eventual adoption of secular and commercial language and methods for achieving their goals. Protestants were articulating the social gospel at the same time that they were experiencing a changing economy, the undermining of Victorian domesticity, the challenge of democratic citizenship in the face of widespread corruption, and eventually the horrifying and galvanizing years of the World War I. They lived in the years that marked an important transition from Victorianism to modern culture, and their religion bore the marks of that dramatic reordering. In order to appreciate these social gospelers as the authors of a new kind of Protestantism, we must also understand them as men and women, children and parents, workers and citizens.

Thus the experiences that shaped the beliefs and outlook of social gospelers—work, family, social and political changes, the war—take on a heightened significance in this study. It was the tedium of work in the 1870s and 1880s, for example, that first frustrated their quest for successful individual achievement. Many suffered because of their early disappointments as middle-class and professional workers and began to ask what work should yield in the modern world. Work, it seemed, ought to be more than physical effort or production: it should be, they thought, a source of personal worth and meaning. They came to seek social justice and individual validation in the experience of work. Such an understanding of work pointed to a more general revision of cultural and religious conceptions of both individual and social salvation. By examining the generational experiences of social gospelers as children and later as heads of families, one gains insights into their conception of the fatherhood of God and the brotherhood of Jesus. These understandings, in turn, led them to embrace new child-rearing practices, and it led them especially to value their social and professional peers. All of this was intertwined with the shift in family life and personal behavior from Victorianism to modern ways. As citizens of a nation marked by labor strife and by political ineffectiveness and corruption, these Protestants sought a place for religion in public life, and they looked for leaders who would respond to the social crisis in terms more vital than liberal self-interest. They were among the vanguard calling for political and social reform that culminated in Progressivism in the early twentieth century. All of these factors—work, family, and political culture—were responsible for creating the need for and the appeal of the social gospel. And the war reinforced the resulting changes. Most came out of the war years surer of the social gospel than they had been before the first American troops were sent to Europe.

These developments associated with the social gospel were parallel, even interactive, with similar shifts in the larger culture, as Victorianism gave way to a modern secular culture embracing self-realization, materialism, and consumerism. The approach proposed here is thus a bifocal one, recognizing that one must attend simultaneously to religious and general cultural developments if one is to grasp the qualities of either in this period of transformation. In arguing that the social gospel is a key part of the cultural mix that gave birth to modern American culture I attempt also to shed light on the complex legacy of the United States in the twentieth century. Much of the admirable strength of twentieth-century American culture—its commitments to activism in behalf of freedom, egalitarianism, social justice, and social unity—can be traced to the influence of the social gospel. But it can also be argued that the same social and moral movement furthered less welcome qualities of twentieth-century American culture—a vacuous mass culture; extreme fears of cultural, intellectual, and political decline in the international arena; political apathy; and pervasive materialism. Those who see the erosion of rugged individualism, the rise of a therapeutic ethos, and the embrace of commercialism as key sources of the United States' current problems might indict the social gospel movement as one of the factors responsible for cultural decline in the late twentieth century. Men and women from the social gospel tradition—Walter Rauschenbusch and Mary McDowell, for example—rank among the most committed and heroic citizens of the United States, yet, ironically, their message and values have undergirded the mass culture that many recent critics have denounced.

Finally, the social gospel movement provides some valuable lessons for latter-day reformers. Commitment to justice, equality, and abundance for all has not subsided. Indeed, through much of the past three decades reformers have struggled to remove the barriers to fulfillment that have been erected against minorities like African Americans and against women. The focus has been on personal liberation—the freedom to realize one's full potential. Like their counterparts in the social gospel movement, late-twentieth-century reformers hope to free themselves and others from economic exploitation, social ostracism, poverty, disease, crime, and discrimination. While they recognize that there is a power structure that limits opportunities, they tend to assume that continued economic growth and expansion, as well as a heightened consciousness, will lead to a more equitable, more democratic society.

When social gospelers in the early twentieth century followed the same tack, they gradually adopted the values and criteria for success of the dominant culture. By using the language and ideas of secular culture, they robbed their message of some of its sting; and as time passed, their followers found less disagreement between their religious values and secular formulas for success and fulfillment.

The lesson to be learned here is that by the 1920s, some social gospelers had lost sight of important questions. They no longer asked whether power was distributed equitably or exercised responsibly for the good of the whole society. They did not demand a structure of power in an industrial capitalist society that could achieve individual autonomy and the common good. The men and women who dominated the movement in the 1920s were satisfied with an ideology of self-realization, a diminution of private anxieties, and an improved standard of living for many Americans. They did not challenge power relationships that sustained social, economic, and political inequities. Those who had posed such challenges were either dead by 1920 or had been marginalized and denounced within the movement.

In 1912 when Walter Rauschenbusch wrote glowing reports about the triumph of the social gospel, Protestantism in America had reached a crossroads. The movement had produced admirable reformers, a pervasive consciousness of the need for social justice, and programs that would serve as prototypes for later governmental reforms. Nevertheless, the distinctly Protestant character of the movement had been muted by an increasing commitment to worldly affairs, and the influence of secular culture had left an unmistakable impression on both the style and message of the social gospel. In 1912 all of American society seemed to be poised on the brink of transformation. The midwestern writer Floyd Dell called 1912 "really an extraordinary year in America." For proof he offered the election of Woodrow Wilson, the heated woman-suffragist activity, Edna St. Vincent Millay's poem "Renascence," plans for the Post-Impressionist show, and the opening of Chicago's Little Theatre. All were "evidence," he insisted, "of a New Spirit suddenly come to birth in America." American culture and American Protestant faith were in the midst of change. In both Greenwich Village's Bohemia, where Dell now lived and wrote, and in the social gospel movement, the future of this new culture was un-clear. Malcolm Cowley, who lived through the period, suggested in *Exile's Return* the ironic proposition that the cultural radicals in fact furthered the development of a consumer-oriented, even a therapeutic, culture in America. . . .

Toward a Social Gospel

JAY P. DOLAN

SOURCE: From *The American Catholic Experience* by Jay P. Dolan, copyright © 1985 by Jay P. Dolan. Used by permission of Doubleday, a division of Random House, Inc.

In 1876 the nation celebrated its one hundredth birthday with a Centennial Exposition in Philadelphia. Spread across 236 acres of parkland were 180 build-ings housing such technological wonders as the telephone, the typewriter, and the self-binding reaper. A nineteenth-century world's fair, the Exposition celebrated technological progress by highlighting "the glorious triumphs of skill and inven-tion." A major attraction was the giant Corliss stream engine, which provided power for the exhibits in Machinery Hall. People strained their necks to get a good look at the twenty-five-hundred-horsepower engine that rose thirty-nine feet above the building floor. William Dean Howells, a noted essayist, called it a "giant," "an athlete of steel and iron"; in its presence, he wrote, "one thinks only of the glorious triumphs of skill and invention. . . . it is in these things of iron and steel that the national genius most freely speaks." Howells's paean to the machine age captured the meaning of the transformation that the United States was undergoing. For Howells and scores of other Americans the machine symbolized the industrial ep-och that the nation was passing through. . . .

Industrial Revolution had a profound impact on the lives of Americans. As the economy expanded, progress seemed natural, but the cycle of boom and bust dem-onstrated how fickle and fragile the economy really was. New titans of industry emerged, and names like Rockefeller and Carnegie were permanently etched into American history; alongside such great wealth was a sea of poverty that increased with each economic depression. In 1890 it was estimated that of the 12.5 million families in the United States, 11 million had an average income of less than $380 a year; and 1890 was a year of prosperity. In the cities, housing became a serious problem as more and more people crowded into already congested neighborhoods. Rows of four- and five-story tenements lined city streets, and families were packed into them like sardines in a can. To make ends meet, women and children went to work for meager wages in less than desirable conditions. Workers began to protest such low wages, and soon strikes and labor violence became commonplace. To many people, the nation seemed out of joint and too high a price was being paid for the dream of prosperity and success. Each age brought forth its reformers. At mid-century some looked to the school as the key to stability and social harmony; others championed the cause of temperance as a cure to social problems. Later on, labor saw the hope of the future in organizing; others advocated better housing legislation or political reform as the hoped-for salvation. Americans wanted decent housing, less poverty, and a better life. The urge for such basic human desires launched a moral crusade, and by the turn of the century reform had become part of the American way of life. The nation entered the twentieth century riding a crest of reform enthusiasm; labeled progressivism, this reform movement captured the idealism of many people who dedicated their energies and talents to building a better world for all.

No segment of American society was left untouched by the spirit of reform, least of all the churches. Some Protestants championed such traditional reform measures as temperance, the Sunday school, and moral conversion. Others were more socially oriented and wanted to reform society itself, the economic system which, they believed, was the major cause of poverty and the unequal distribution of wealth. By the 1890s this trend became known as the social gospel. Applying the principle of the gospel to all aspects of human life—the public and social realms as well as the private and individual spheres—the social-gospel movement transformed American Protestantism. The impact of the industrial age and the spirit of reform also affected American Catholicism.

In analyzing the Catholic response to the industrial age it is clear that a definite change of attitude took place in the 1880s. In order to understand the significance of this shift it is necessary to look at the previous period, 1820-80, when industrialization and urbanization first made their impact on the United States.

As thousands and eventually millions of Catholic immigrants from Ireland and Germany settled in the United States, Catholicism became a working-class church. Made up mainly of lower-class immigrants, the church was centered in the cities and towns of the Northeast, the economic core of the nation, where industrialization had its most visible impact. Given their heavy concentration in the working class, Catholics were especially vulnerable to the fickleness of the economy and the hard times of depression. They lived close to the edge economically; the slightest turn for the worse would have serious consequences in any Catholic community. The 1830s was a case in point. Transfiguration parish was situated in New York City's Sixth Ward; an Irish parish made up mostly of working-class people, it enjoyed the people's financial support during the early 1830s. When economic depression hit in 1837, however, the climate quickly changed. People who had loaned money to the church now besieged the trustees for return of their funds; others, out of work for months and "in the utmost distress," had to sell their furniture to pay the rent; other parishioners were running out of food and sent messages "from their bed of sickness begging a small portion of their money to procure necessary food and care." The finances of the parish deteriorated so badly that the church was scheduled to be sold at a public auction. When the economy collapsed again in the 1850s, Irish and German immigrants were hit hard once more. Some chose to return to the old country, rather than live in poverty in a strange city; the city's Alms House attracted large numbers of the poor, and the Irish led the way, constituting two thirds of its residents in 1858. Nor was New York unique. In such large cities as Boston and Philadelphia and in small towns like Troy, New York, and Newburyport, Massachusetts, similar patterns prevailed. Given their heavy concentration in the lower rungs of the occupational ladder, Catholics were especially vulnerable to the problems and distress that accompanied the emergence of the new industrial economy. Confronted with this reality, the church, through its laity and clergy, mounted a crusade of charity. . . .

The most visible and impressive aspect of the Catholic response to the social problems of the age was the founding of hospitals and orphanages. The people most responsible for this were women religious. Recruited by bishops and priests as teachers and missionaries, women religious soon involved themselves in a variety of ministries in the local church. Care of the sick and of orphans was an area that attracted their attention from the very beginning. When the Sisters of Mercy came to Chicago, in the 1840s, they founded not only schools but also a hospital and two orphan asylums. Mercy Hospital opened its doors in 1851 and to this day remains a symbol of Catholic charity. The Sisters of Charity arrived in Milwaukee at about the same time and repeated a similar pattern by founding orphan asylums and a hospital. Mother Joseph of the Sisters of Providence became a legend through her work in establishing fifteen hospitals in various cities throughout the Northwest. The dedicated service of women religious during the epidemics that periodically ravaged the nation won them public acclaim. In New York the Sisters of Charity were singled out for their work in the 1832 and 1849 cholera epidemics; when cholera struck again in 1866, hitting hardest in the immigrant neighborhoods, their services as nurses were once more requested. In San Francisco the Sisters of Mercy gained similar acclaim when cholera struck that city. By 1880, 119 Catholic hospitals were in operation, along with 267 orphan asylums. That was remarkable progress in a half century and underscored the commitment of the church to the care of the sick and the orphaned. Such a commitment had been a long-standing tradition within Roman Catholicism, and it met an obvious need in an immigrant community caught up in the industrial age.

The most obvious reason for the Catholic crusade of charity was the need of the people. Poverty, sickness, and death were frequent visitors to workingclass neighborhoods. Such misfortune and distress were hardly new to the United States, but in densely crowded nineteenth-century city neighborhoods their victims were very numerous, and this dramatically underscored the need for assistance. Moreover, poverty was no longer being accepted as a normal ingredient in the human community. The early-nineteenth century was a time when Americans were beginning to view poverty as a social problem, a disorder in society; with this change in attitude came a heightened sense of moral concern, which persuaded many people to work to alleviate human suffering. Numerous hospitals and public institutions to aid the orphans, the insane, the poor, and the delinquent were built during the pre-Civil War period. Through these institutions, Americans sought to correct disorders of society and in so doing bring order and harmony to the republic. The proliferation of charitable institutions and the general moral concern for the plight of the poor, noble as it was, posed a problem for Catholics. The reason was obvious. The institutions and the social workers were Protestant in spirit and ethos, and this caused grave concern among Catholics. Nor was the concern illusionary.

In many cities, Catholic clergy were refused admittance to public hospitals and asylums. Boston, long a citadel of anti-Catholic feeling, was a case in point. Catholic clergy were not welcome in the city's hospitals and orphanages. Even though they fought such discrimination in the courts, it was not until 1879 that priests were legally allowed to visit Catholics in such public institutions. In some cities such as Chicago and Milwaukee, where such institutionalized discrimination was absent, the needs of the community, rather than the fear of proselytization, was a major reason for establishing hospitals and asylums.

The Catholic crusade for charity prior to 1880 was quite traditional. Aimed at the poor, the sick, and the homeless, its emphasis was on bettering the lot of the individual, with the guiding principle always being the salvation of souls. This was the highest law, and ". . . as for the rest, though you should be stripped of all your worldly possessions, all this is nothing if you arrive at length at the happy term of salvation." Social disorders, those "social evils which afflict mankind are the result of Adam's sin," wrote one priest, and "all reform, properly understood, begins with a return to religion and the Church." Such thinking did not allow for social change and reform. According to Catholic thinking at this time, society was a static, stratified social system, and each level of this divinely designed order had its own responsibilities. John Hughes, the archbishop of New York, expressed this typically Catholic viewpoint to a Baltimore audience:

> To every class and condition [the church] assigned its own peculiar range of Christian obligations: to sovereigns and legislators, those of justice and mercy in the enactment and execution of laws. To the rich, moderation in enjoyment and liberality toward the poor. To the poor, patience under their trials and affection toward their wealthier brethren. Toward all, the common obligation of loving one another, not in word, but in deed.

Since God had permitted poverty, the church had to protect the poor; as representatives of Christ, Catholics were reminded that "to extend a generous and charitable hand to a fellow creature in distress is one of the most exalting and noble acts of man." This was the motivating impulse behind the crusade for charity, and traditional though it was, Catholics distinguished themselves, laymen and women religious especially, in bringing comfort and solace to the poor, the sick, and the homeless.

Such conservative social thought put Catholics out of step with any attempts at social reform during the pre-1880 period. The Protestant character of American reform movements made such a stance appear quite reasonable, given the hostile feelings between Catholics and Protestants at that time. Nevertheless, there was one reform cause to which Catholics gave their wholehearted support: temperance. Crusading for temperance was as Catholic as going to Sunday Mass. If there was poverty in society, it was because of intemperance. This was a popular American response to the social problems brought on by a flawed economy, and it fit right in with the Catholic mentality. The national president of the St. Vincent de Paul Society, Henry J. Anderson, put it very clearly: "Where there is health, temperance and industry, there cannot be poverty." It was as simple as that, and "Intemperance," Anderson went on to say, "is the great evil we have to overcome; it is a source of misery for at least three-quarters of the families we are called upon to visit and relieve." Church councils urged support for the temperance movement; parish communities sponsored local temperance societies; all revival preachers had temperance sermons in their repertoires, and they administered the total-abstinence pledge to thousands of people. A national society, the Catholic Total Abstinence Union of America, was formed in 1872; its annual conventions were national rallies for temperance. . . .

While many Americans were beating the drum of temperance, the economy was beginning to come apart. The most visible sign of this was the 1873 depression. One of the nation's worst depressions, it left one fifth of the nation's workers completely unemployed by 1877; another two fifths were able to find work for six or seven months a year, and only one fifth were working full-time. Wages were cut and working hours got longer. People lost their homes, ninety thousand in New York City alone; shantytowns sprung up, and parades of the unemployed dramatized the plight of the poor as people shouted, "Bread for the needy, clothing for the naked, and houses for the homeless." Then, in 1877, took place "the most violent and most significant labor upheaval in the nineteenth century—the Railway Strike of 1877." To protest continuous wage cuts, workers with the Baltimore and Ohio Railroad went on strike in July; with tornado force the strike spread to New York, Pennsylvania, and west across the country. A nationwide protest against the injustices of the railroad industry and the miseries endured during the depression, the strike involved thousands of workers; it also involved hundreds of militiamen and federal troops. When the strike ended, in early August, less than three weeks after it began, the toll was heavy: $10,000,000 in property damage, hundreds of people dead, countless numbers injured. The violence of the strike shocked the nation, but its true significance was that " . . . it gave working men a class consciousness on a national scale."

In the next quarter century, labor strikes became a way of life. In 1886 alone, 1,572 strikes took place, involving 610,000 workers; Homestead, Pennsylvania, was the site of a famous strike against the Carnegie Steel Corporation; the mining region of Coeur d'Alene, Idaho, was the scene of labor violence; Pullman, Illinois, where railroad cars were manufactured, was the scene of another violent strike, during the summer of 1894. The strikes at Homestead, Coeur d'Alene, Pullman, and hundreds of other, less notorious, places awakened the consciences of many Americans and made them more aware of and more sensitive to the social distress brought on by a flawed industrial capitalism. In Congress, churches, parlors, and saloons, people debated the social consequences of the unequal distribution of wealth. The relations between labor and capital were getting worse, not better. Many Americans questioned the prevailing economic doctrine of laissez-faire, which allowed the economy to proceed naturally, with no governmental regulation or modification; for many, such a theory was not only seriously defective, but also terribly insensitive to human needs. Poverty and unemployment were the result of this misguided economic doctrine and not the result of personal sin or laziness. This was the cry of the reformers, and increasingly people accepted their reasoning and voted for a reform of the economic and social system.

It was in this atmosphere of increased labor activity and a mounting call for reform that Catholics began to evaluate their response to the new social order brought on by industrialization. For the majority, the answer seemed very clear: more charity; for others, the times demanded something more.

After 1880 the Catholic crusade for charity intensified. At the parish level, the St. Vincent de Paul Society continued to be the mainstay of the charity apostolate; by 1902 the number of parish branches of the society had increased to 428. Though this was a significant increase since the 1880s, it was evident that most parishes still did not support the St. Vincent de Paul Society. It was clearly an English-speaking organization, with heavy concentration in Irish parishes. Among Eastern-European-immigrant parishes, it was the mutual benefit organization and not the St. Vincent de Paul Society that sought to provide relief in times of economic distress. In conjunction with St. Vincent de Paul Society, some parishes opened up employment bureaus; others provided day care for children of working mothers. . . .

A new dimension to the charity crusade after 1880 was the increased involvement of laywomen. With the emergence of a sizable middle class among Catholics of Irish and German descent, more women began to become involved in activities outside the home. The ideal and recommended type of involvement was charitable work. This was spelled out quite emphatically by a group of women who were forming a federation of women's societies in Louisiana; they resolved to "take up the work peculiar to women only, viz.: work of mercy and charity, on the lines of the St. Vincent de Paul Society, social work among the women such as establishing of girl's homes, protection of traveling girls and women, saving the wayward and fallen girls. . . ." Such a commitment led Catholic laywomen to organize citywide charitable organizations, and by the 1890s they were focusing their attention on the needs of the new immigrants. "They did for the new immigrants," wrote the historian of Catholic charities, "what the Vincent de Paul Society did for the older immigrants." Their most notable endeavor was their involvement in the social settlement movement. The late-nineteenth century witnessed the emergence of settlement houses in the United States, the most famous being Jane Addams's Hull House in Chicago. To meet the needs of the new immigrants and to counteract the work of Addams and other Protestant humanitarians, Catholic women began to organize settlement houses in cities across the nation. In opening these homes, laywomen chose to live among the poor and provide education classes for children and adults, health-care programs, cooking classes, English-language classes, and recreation. In this way they sought to improve the "moral, physical, educational and social welfare of the people in the neighborhood." In cities such as Chicago and New York, settlement houses were established in Italian and Polish neighborhoods; in Los Angeles they served the Mexican population. By 1915, twenty-seven such settlements were in operation across the country.

The crusade for charity that swept through the church in the late-nineteenth and early-twentieth centuries was rooted in traditional Catholic social doctrine. Conservative as regards social reform, its focus was individual, personal reform; in other words, it emphasized the corporal works of mercy. This differed very little from the earlier phase of the charity crusade; it meant more hospitals and more asylums; it added settlement houses and industrial schools to its list of charitable institutions and involved more women than previously. But many Catholics came to the conclusion during the 1880s that the times demanded more than charity and mercy; justice was also necessary, though clearly a minority in the Catholic community, those who called for social justice did make an impact on the clergy and lay people, so that by the time of World War I, American Catholicism had acquired a social-gospel tradition.

The catalyst for this change was the labor movement. Before the Civil War, workers began to organize and push for better wages and a ten-hour workday. The 1860s and 1870s witnessed increased labor activity in the organization of trade unions. Since Catholics were predominantly a working-class people, they were naturally attracted to the labor movement. The Irish were especially involved. In Lynn, Massachusetts, Irish factory workers joined the shoemakers' union, the Knights of St. Crispin, in the late 1860s; in San Francisco they rallied behind their countryman Denis Kearney and the Working Men's Party in the late 1870s; a similar pattern developed in other manufacturing towns and cities. But it was their involvement with the Knights of Labor in the 1880s that best illustrated the commitment of the Irish to the cause of labor and the problem this posed for clergy and bishops. . . .

Bishops and priests were suspicious of labor organizations from their very inception. Secrecy was a characteristic feature of labor organizations at the time, and this made them suspect in the eyes of the Catholic clergy; labor violence was also commonplace, and this, too, made the clergy wary of supporting labor. With the Knights of Labor, suspicion turned into open opposition. Though some clergymen were sympathetic to the Knights, the vast majority were not. Some priests even went so far as to deny the sacraments to people who belonged to the Knights; others refused them burial. Such strong opposition definitely slowed the growth of the union among Catholics and led one Knight to declare that "the greatest curse to our order seems to me to be the Priest." Powderly sought to defuse the opposition by having any hint of religious oath-swearing removed from the order's initiation ritual in 1881, but secrecy remained a feature of the union and so clerical opposition stood firm. . . .

The change taking place among the Irish was notable in other segments of the Catholic community as well. By the mid-1880s, the Catholic press, including both newspapers and journals of opinion, was much more sympathetic to the cause of labor and social problems than it had been a decade earlier. It was also more critical of laissez-faire economics and the injustices it caused in society. Clearly the 1880s was a heady time for all Americans. The depression of the 1870s and the great strike of 1877 ushered in a climate of crisis and an urge for reform. Labor was riding a wave of popularity, and criticism of capitalism and laissez-faire economics had become more commonplace. Catholic lay men and women, the Irish especially, were heavily committed to this call for reform. Nevertheless, some Catholic bishops still remained opposed to labor and social reform. One strong opponent was Peter Kenrick, archbishop of St. Louis. He showed his opposition by reprimanding Father Cornelius O'Leary for his support of the Knights of Labor in De Soto, Missouri, and transferring him out of town to another parish. Archbishop Corrigan of New York was strongly opposed to the work of Edward McGlynn on behalf of the Land League and Henry George; after repeated attempts to curb the work of McGlynn, he suspended him in 1886 from his priestly ministry. This created a public uproar in New York. Such actions tended to confirm the suspicion of many Americans that the Catholic hierarchy was opposed to labor and social reform. Fortunately the majority of bishops were not so reactionary. They began to follow the lead of the people by supporting labor unions and economic reform. The most dramatic and symbolic incident in this regard was the intervention in Rome of James Cardinal Gibbons on behalf of the Knights of Labor.

At the request of Archbishop Taschereau of Quebec, the Vatican had issued a ruling in 1884 that forbade Catholics to belong to the Knights of Labor. Most American bishops interpreted this as applying to Canada only and were reluctant to prohibit Catholics from joining the Knights of Labor, but Taschereau forced their hand by asking Rome to make the condemnation universal. At this juncture, Gibbons, who had previously counseled "a masterly inactivity and a vigilant eye" in the whole affair, decided to act. When in Rome in February 1887 to receive the red hat, the symbol of his recent elevation to the College of Cardinals, Gibbons presented Vatican officials with a lengthy statement defending the rights of workers to organize and urging that the Knights of Labor not be condemned. Written by Bishops John Ireland and John Keane and signed by Gibbons, the statement marked a major turning point in the church's position on labor and social reform.

The document recognized the "social evils, public injustices . . . heartless avarice" that plagued the nation, and the need, indeed the right, of workers to organize. It was foolish to think, stated Gibbons, that the "struggle of the great masses of the people against the mail-clad power which . . . often refuses them the simple rights of humanity and justice" and their desire for "organizing which is their only hope of success" can be deterred. Prudence forces the church to accept this fact of life. Then, in a manner quite typical of Gibbons and his episcopal collaborators, the document in a very shrewd political move went on to point out the consequences of a condemnation. As in Europe, the working class would become estranged from the church, souls would surely be lost, public opinion would turn against Catholics in the United States, the revenues of the church "would suffer immensely" (the effect of which would be felt in Rome), and the Holy See would be looked upon "as a harsh and unjust power." To prove his point, Gibbons cited the public outcry against the suspension of McGlynn; such deplorable consequences resulted "from the condemnation of only one priest, because he was considered to be the friend of the people, . . . what will not be the consequences to be feared from a condemnation which would fall directly upon the people themselves in the exercise of what they consider their legitimate right?"

A year and a half later, the Vatican finally rendered a decision. It lifted the ban on the Knights of Labor and stated that the organization could be tolerated on the condition that the Knights revise their constitution in order to omit any references "which seem to savor of socialism and communism." Hardly a resounding endorsement of labor, it was an approval of the Knights, nevertheless. More important, the American public perceived Gibbons's defense of the Knights and Rome's favorable decision as a victory for labor. Thenceforth, the leadership of the Catholic Church in the United States would officially be on the side of labor. This was a dramatic turnabout. For the first time, the bishops stood behind the people in their commitment to the cause of labor. This marked the first step in the formation of a Catholic social-gospel tradition. . . .

. . . Catholic journalists were also more critical of the abuses of industrial capitalism and laissez-faire economics. The commitment of the Catholic laity to the labor movement, together with Gibbons's strong defense of the Knights of Labor, were among the major reasons for this change in thinking. Another major influence was the publication in 1891 of the papal encyclical *Rerum Novarum*.

Compared to his predecessor, Pius IX, Pope Leo XIII was a progressive church leader. *Rerum Novarum* was an excellent example of such progressivism. Drawing upon a European tradition of social Catholicism, *Rerum Novarum* sought to analyze the conditions of labor in the modern world and offer a program of reform based on the concept of social justice. The Pope condemned socialism, the perceived archenemy of the church and the main target of the encyclical, but he also spoke out against the excesses of capitalism and individualism. In addition, he upheld the right to private property, the right of workers to organize, and the need for the intervention of the state to protect the rights of the people. Such an endorsement of the labor movement and the concept of social justice by the Papacy would ultimately have "a truly epoch-making effect in driving home the idea that Catholics must have a social conscience and above all that they must actively concern themselves with the conditions of workers." . . .

Catholics had come a long way since the days of John Hughes. The concept of justice was now central to their program of reform; in addition to a deeply engrained tradition of personal religion, a new dimension of public religion, or what can be called a social gospel, became part of the Catholic tradition. Catholics were now known not just for what they opposed—socialism—but also for what they advocated: social reform. Three major events stood out in this transition. The first was Gibbons's defense of the Knights of Labor; another was Pope Leo XIII's encyclical *Rerum Novarum;* and the final one was, of course, The Bishops' Program of Social Reconstruction. These were the high points of a transformation that took place over the course of some thirty years and more. During this period, the labor movement had come of age; a progressive reform movement had captured the imagination of Americans; Catholic workers joined unions in large numbers and rose to leadership positions; labor priests began to emerge, and charity workers sought to prevent poverty and social distress as well as lessen their harsh effects. Viewed from this long-range perspective, the bishops' statement was not "a miracle" at all; it represented the culmination of three decades of increased Catholic involvement on behalf of reform. Modest to be sure, but real nonetheless. Beginning with the people and the labor movement, expanding with the increased participation of the clergy, it finally reached the hierarchy in the wake of World War I. The absence of much episcopal support for reform prior to the postwar period should not obscure the reality of an impulse for reform at other levels in the Catholic community. Both people and priests provided the initial thrust for reform, and only after this gained headway during the progressive period did the hierarchy unite to support such reform.

Unfortunately the Bishops' Program came at a very inopportune time. The nation was heading into a decade when, in Ryan's words, ". . . social thinking and social action were chilled and stifled in an atmosphere of pseudo prosperity and thinly disguised materialism." During the 1920s the vitality of the progressive movement died out; the bishops, like most Americans, lost interest in plans for social reconstruction. Conservatism, rather than progressivism, characterized the spirit of the times, and social reform became a victim of the age. Nevertheless, American Catholicism had taken an important step forward in the development of a social-gospel tradition. Further development of this impulse would have to wait until another time.

"The Future Golden Day of the Race": Millennialism and Black Americans in the Nadir, 1877–1901
TIMOTHY E. FULOP

SOURCE: Copyright 1997 From *African-American Religion* by Timothy E. Fulop and Albert J. Raboteau. Reproduced by permission of Taylor & Francis, Inc./Routledge, Inc., http://www.routledge-ny.com

At the turn of the century, Edward W. Blyden, resident of Liberia and Presbyterian missionary from America, read to some African natives the description from the New York *Independent* of the burning of a black in Georgia:

> Sam Hose was burned on Sunday afternoon in the presence of thousands of people. Before the fire had been kindled the mob amused themselves by cutting off the ears, fingers, toes, etc. to carry away as mementos. After the burning and before the body was cool, it was cut to pieces, the heart and liver being especially cut up and sold. Small pieces of bone brought 25 cents, and "a bit of liver, crisply cooked, sold for 10 cents." So eager were the crowd to obtain souvenirs that a rush for the stake was made, and those near the body were forced against and had to fight for their escape.

The story was so shocking, Blyden recounted, that the African audience did not know whether to respond with indignation or incredulity:

> Their imagination had never pictured any tragedy so frightful or revolting. Nothing in their experience or their traditions could afford any parallel to such hideous barbarities practiced as they were by people supposed to be Christian and highly civilized.

The last twenty-five years of the nineteenth century have appropriately gone down in African-American history as "the Nadir." Disenfranchisement and Jim Crow laws clouded out any rays of hope that Reconstruction had bestowed in the American South. Darwinism and phrenology passed on new "scientific" theories of black inferiority, and the old racial stereotypes of blacks as beasts abounded in American society. The civil, political, and educational rights of black Americans were greatly curtailed, and lynching reached all-time highs in the 1890s. Conditions were not much better in Africa as European nations carved the continent into colonies and spread Western civilization, according to one critic, in "the proportion of hundreds of gallons of gin to a Bible or missionary." The Nadir was accompanied by a cacophony of black voices seeking to make sense of the history and destiny of African Americans. One strand of these voices proclaimed in song, sermon, and theological treatise that the millennial reign of God was coming to earth.

The study of millennialism in American religion has been a rich and popular field of study, yet as Leonard Sweet stated in a historiographical survey of American millennialism, "the manner in which millennial ideology fired faith and forged it to works in the black experience, and not just among insurrectionists like Nat Turner, has not been explored." From the images of a future Canaan held by slaves to the dream of the Promised Land in the sermons of Martin Luther King, Jr., millennialism in African-American religion remains largely unexamined. This article sheds further light on how African Americans in the Nadir period understood their destiny by exploring the neglected subject of black millennialism.

Millennialism is the belief rooted in Christian tradition and thought that history will be fulfilled in a golden age. The term itself comes from Rev 20:1-7, which predicts a thousand-year reign of Christ with the resurrected martyrs while Satan is bound and confined to the abyss. Though the millennium is explicitly mentioned only in this New Testament passage, older Hebrew Bible images and metaphors of a time of felicity on earth have played an important role in millennial movements.

Of particular importance in African-American thought is the biblical story of the Exodus and the image of Canaan. Thomas Wentworth Higginson in an 1867 article on Negro spirituals claimed that the books of Moses and the Revelation of St. John composed the Bible of American blacks, and "all that lay between, even the narrations of the life of Jesus, they hardly cared to read or to hear." It will become evident that the identification with ancient Israel and the hope for entering the Promised Land played an important role in black millennialism.

Toward a Typology of Black Millennial Thought

Several scholars claim that American slaves were primarily millennialists of the quietest sort who waited for Christ to intervene in history, release them from slavery, and usher them into Canaan as God had done for the ancient Israelites in delivering them from bondage in Egypt, though there were those, like Nat Turner, who were of a revolutionist sort and claimed a role for themselves in the apocalyptical drama. In contrast, black millennialism in the Nadir period exhibits great variety. Before proceeding, however, to an examination of the varieties of black millennial thought, it is useful to categorize black millennial thought in the Nadir period according to three types: cultural millennialism, millennial Ethiopianism, and progressive millennialism.

Cultural millennialism denotes the type of black millennial thinking most closely akin to the ideology of the United States as the redeemer nation of the world. The emphasis is on the working out of the millennium through the forces of Western civilization, education, Anglo-Saxon culture, American democracy, and republicanism.

Millennial Ethiopianism, as will become apparent in this article, is the most distinctively African-American millennial tradition, though there are elements unique to the black experience in each of these millennial types. In contrast to white millennial theories that emphasize America, Anglo-Saxon culture, and the radical break with the Old World, millennial Ethiopianism posits a pan-African millennium, a future golden age continuous with a glorious African past accompanied by God's judgment of white society and Western civilization.

Progressive millennialism is a more traditional type of millennial thought that emphasizes the role of the church, evangelism, missions, and reform in giving birth to the millennium on earth. This type is not without notes of pan-Africanism and strong social criticism concerning race relations, but, unlike millennial Ethiopianism, it reveals an optimism that the millennium will be marked by racial equality and harmony. Progressive millennialism is optimistic about the power of Christianity to transform and perfect American society, but it is not naive and takes a more religiously prophetic stance toward the United States than does cultural millennialism.

Descriptions of the Millennium

Different varieties of black millennial thought can be delineated by addressing questions of what the millennium will look like, where its location will be, how it will come about, and when it will occur. Attention to these issues makes it possible to distinguish between cultural millennialisrn, millennial Ethiopianism, and progressive millennialism.

Since the millennium is only mentioned formally in one opaque passage of scripture open to many different interpretations, a description of the millennium reveals much about the particular group that espouses this vision. The millennium proclaimed by African Americans during the Nadir period shared many of the spiritual priorities of white nineteenth-century American millennialism. J.W.E. Bowen, president of Gammon Theological Seminary, preached an enthusiastic sermon titled "What Shall the Harvest Be?"

> A belief in the future golden day of the race when men shall see, not through a glass darkly, but face to face, gives buoyancy and courage to the efforts of Christians in bringing all men to the knowledge of the truth as it is in Christ. The golden age is not in the past as the heathens ignorantly taught, but it is before us somewhere in the dim tracery of the future, and possibly we have come to the edge of this new heaven. I do not believe that that age will find its characteristics so much in the material acquisitions as in the spiritual triumphs of the soul and in a proper knowledge of our relation to God.

George W. Clinton, African Methodist Episcopal Zion Church bishop and editor of the *Star of Zion*, claimed that the tense of one well-known hymn "Jesus *shall* reign," would need to be changed to "Jesus *doth* reign where'er the sun. . . ." The unification of all Christians was anticipated by the African Methodist Episcopal (A.M.E.) Church bishop Daniel Alexander Payne:

> The name Christian—that and that alone—will be able to stand before enlightened, progressive humanity, the glory of the millennium and the consuming fires of the judgment-day, to which we all are hastening, and for which we all ought to live.

Black millennial visions also included social and political concerns common to reform-minded nineteenth-century evangelicals. Lucius H. Holsey, self-taught bishop of the Colored Methodist Episcopal Church, proclaimed a millennium without wars, "corrupting institutions," "massive conclaves of sin and infidelity," saloons, drunkenness, the opium traffic, "slavery in every form," "heathen priests and their superstitious systems," kingdoms and empires, and "every opposing foe and antagonizing power." Concerns of contemporary populists and Progressives are detected in an *A.M.E. Church Review* article by a layman, R. Henri Herbert of Trenton:

> The Government of the Future! A government whose primary object will be to make two blades of grass grow where but one did before; a government in which Taxation shall go hand in hand with Representation; a government in which every man shall be protected in the full enjoyment of his equal legal, political and religious liberty; a government in which education shall be as universal as the star-decked canopy of Heaven; a government in which there shall be no Pagan, no Mahomedan, no Catholic, no Protestant, no Negro, no Caucasian, no distinction of race or creed, but which will ever remember that "of one blood were created all the nations of the Earth;" a government in which there shall be neither wars nor

rumors of wars but over which shall everlastingly rest the sweet benison of Peace; a government so vast in its territory, so wonderful in its wealth, so stupendous in its resources, so God-like in its beneficence that the human mind can but poorly compass its grandeur—A GOVERNMENT THAT SHALL EMBRACE THE WHOLE EARTH, *THE REPUBLIC OF THE WORLD!* . . . Then shall have come the time of which sages have written and poets sung and which the great Jehovah Himself hath prophesied. Then upon earth shall be—THE MILLENNIUM!

Contemporary descriptions of the millennium by white Americans like Samuel Harris's *The Kingdom of Christ on Earth* lack a racial component, but in black depictions of the millennium, resolution of the "race problem" is primary. The millennium, according to James T. Holly, would "dissipate the darkness that has so long brooded over the sons of Ham." Holsey looked for an era of racial reconciliation inspired by "the fatherhood of God and the brotherhood of men." The fullest vision of racial harmony and equality is offered by the South Carolina politician and A.M.E. bishop R. H. Cain:

> Happy for the great country, happy for the negro and the nation when the great principles upon which our government is founded, when the genius of liberty as understood by the fathers, shall permeate this whole land, mold the opinions of statesmen, fix the decrees of judges, settle the decisions of Supreme Courts and executed by every law officer of this broad land; then there will need be no more discussion as to what of the negro problem. . . . There will be one homogeneous nation governed by intellectual, moral worth and controlled by Christian influences. Then there will be no East, no West, no North, no South, no Black, no White, no Saxon, no Negro, but a great, happy and peaceful nation.

Unlike white millennial thought, which was nearly unanimous about the focus of the millennium being on the United States, black millennial thought proposed a variety of locations for the millennium. A large segment of black millennial thought did locate the millennium in America, which was congruent with the dominant ideology of America as a redeemer nation and a "city upon a hill." Herbert is in this tradition for he reminds his readers that the Old World with its aristocracy, militarism, and despotism is in decay and that the future republic of the world has its foundation in the American republic. Many black Americans looked for the millennium to be located in America because they believed that America would also be as exceptional in race relations as it was thought to be in its republicanism, availability of "virgin land," growth of missions, expansion of evangelical religion, and technological accomplishments. . . .

In a discussion of how African Americans envisioned the millennium would come and when, it is helpful to be aware of the distinction between premillennialism and postmillennialism. Premillennialism locates the second coming of Christ before the millennium and is usually associated with apocalyptic tones of judgment and divine intervention. Postmillennialism argues that Christ will return after the millennium and is usually associated with a more evolutionary and optimistic view of the establishment of the kingdom of God in the world through spiritual and material triumphs.

James Holly's millennialism provides an example of premillennialism. He stated that "Christ shall come with His saints and give to our weary and sin cursed earth its long-lasted Sabbath by inaugurating a reign of a thousand years." There is a radical disjunction between the present and the millennium, as Holly believed that the "Christian" nations embody the spirit of the Antichrist and would aid the coming of the millennium only by destroying themselves at Armageddon. Steward is also a premillennialist in terms of judgment and a radical disjunction between the present and the future, though he is unsure whether Jesus will personally inaugurate the millennium: "The culminating stages of the Redeemer's glory will be marked by the coming of Jesus as King on earth, whether in a visible, personal form, or in effectual power only, it is not to our purpose to inquire."

The traditional, but tenuous, correlation between premillennialism and inaction or quietism is not found in the millennialism of Holly or Steward. Though Christ will inaugurate the millennium, Holly and Steward criticized the present social and racial situation through their theories and reserved an active role for blacks in spreading the millennium.

The driving force behind the coming of the millennium for postmillennialists is also God, though not in such a manner that the present and future is marked by a radical disjunction. Some postmillennialists, those I identify as cultural millennialists, found the millennium arising out of the forces of Western civilizations. Gaines, for example, saw God working through Anglo-Saxon civilization:

> Providence, in wisdom, has decreed that the lot of the negro should be cast with the white people of America. Condemn as we may the means through which we were brought here, recount as we may the suffering through which, as a race, we passed in the years of slavery, yet the fact remains that today our condition is far in advance of that of the negroes who have never left their native Africa. We are planted in the midst of the highest civilization mankind has ever known, and are rapidly advancing in knowledge, property and moral enlightenment. We might, with all reason, thank God even for slavery, if this were the only means through which we could arrive at our present progress and developments.

Herbert claimed that the millennium was arising from the spread of republicanism, justice, education, and civilization.

Most black millennialists who may be described as postmillennialists were not so naive and optimistic as to identify the kingdom of God with Western civilization. Their optimism lay, rather, in their belief that Christianity could be a leaven in history, transforming and redeeming it until the millennium emerged. I refer to this kind of millennialism as progressive. Bishop Clinton spoke for churchmen in emphasizing the role of the church as a leaven "for purifying, preserving and seasoning the world till 'Righteousness abound, As the great deep profound, And fill the earth with purity.'"

In addition to his statement that the millennium inspires Christians to evangelize, J.W.E. Bowen called black Americans to take the future into their own hands and acquire "Christian character"; actions that he optimistically believed would "assert and prophesy the incoming of the gray dawn of the millennium which shall ultimately usher in the blazing midday." The millennium, argued Holsey, will come about by the "hybridization" of Jesus' love, presence, and power in the world:

> Shiloh's empire still abides, and its magnetic embodiment in the person of the living Christ, marches on in stately tread, transversing the breadth of centuries, measuring the decades, and wrapping the string of days and the fibre of hours around his hand, and buckling the aged cycles and the countless trend of years to his belt.... But the Kingdom of Shiloh is progressive. It is educative and consequently slow in its progress. It is slow to the ideas and conceptions of men, but not slow to God . . . . The perfection of character is the ultimate end for which time is given, and the process and progress toward perfection cannot cease until the effort is coronated with the brightest gems of nature. The Kingdom of Shiloh cannot stand still, because its very life is in its thrift and activity.

Many black ministers in the "New South" were optimistic about the transforming powers of Christianity on race relations, according to Edward L. Wheeler, because of their belief in the "fatherhood of God and the brotherhood of man." This optimism is visible in the belief that the kingdom of God would triumph in the world.

The premillennial, or more appropriately millennial Ethiopian, beliefs of both Holly and Steward are accompanied by an apocalyptic urgency that sees the millennium as very near at hand. Holly argued for an imminent millennium both from the appearance of the spirit of the Antichrist in the "Christian nations" and the manipulation of "sacred chronology." He suggested that the "millennial Sabbath" would begin six thousand years after creation, which he claims was in 4124 BC and, thus, puts the end at 1876. Interestingly, Holly then added forty years of tribulation, a biblical number of "Trial and humiliation" (roughly the years of the Nadir period under study!), which points to 1916, though the millennium might come sooner because God "has promised to cut short those evil days for the sake of the elect." Steward was more tentative than Holly about calculating the end times by biblical prophecy and suggested several different tabulations. In addition, Steward argued for an imminent millennium based on the signs of the times (social and political unrest, increase in knowledge and travel, apostasy, and the emergence of the Antichrist).

James H. Moorhead has argued that postmillennialism, by placing the second coming after the achievements of evangelical Christianity in the world, "represented a compromise between an apocalyptic and an evolutionary view of time, between a history characterized by dramatic upheavals and supernatural events and one governed by natural laws of organic development." Apocalyptic elements can also be detected in the coming of the millennium in many of the millennial schemes under study that may loosely come under the rubric of postmillennialism. Though Holsey emphasized that the coming of the millennium is slow, it is also throbbing with an apocalyptic nearness:

> Everywhere Shiloh's empire touches the deep chores of human nature and human hearts, stirring, revolutionizing and unifying its forces and agencies, exhibiting those far-reaching plenitudes of power and throbbing energies and plenipotent activities that make up its irresistible character. Everyday the empire of Shiloh is making its onslaughts and encroachments upon the ramparts of sin and hell.

Likewise, Bowen preached that "the times are ominous; ominous I believe not for evil, but for good," and argued that the millennium would arise in the new century:

> I repeat, my hope is fixed, and standing upon the top of this present Mt. Nebo, and letting my eyes sweep through the dark past up along the shores of the river we have crossed, and now into the wilderness with our churches, school houses, trade schools, and various christian and civilizing agencies, with faith in God, I am certain that I see, though the thick darkness that envelopes us, the gray rays of a new morn, and I hear the tramp of a new civilization and the music of its avant courier joyfully shouting: "There's a good time coming boys, a good time coming."

Though there may be some overlap between cultural millennialism, millennial Ethiopianism, and progressive millennialism due to the elusive and elastic nature of millennial symbols as well as shared concerns and traditions, I contend that these three types portray distinct major themes. Likewise, I believe that the different types can be assigned to the great variety of millennial thought presented, while recognizing a degree of overlap between the types.

Cultural millennialism, with its strong identification with Western culture and American society, and its optimism that the forces of western civilization were working out into a millennial golden age is exemplified by the articles of Cain, Herbert, and Gaines. In a way, the racial amalgamation of Ruffin, Minton, and Downing represents an extreme form of cultural millennialism, yet falls short of complete identification with Anglo-Saxon culture because of notes of social criticism and black exceptionalism. Capitalism and economic growth are another such force of progress, according to Booker T. Washington and William Matthews. The latter, a wealthy lawyer and businessman in Washington, D.C., wrote an article in the *A.M.E. Church Review* titled "Money as a Factor in Human Progress" in which he argued that money is an indispensable "soldier" in the spread of Christian civilization:

> Those most deeply interested in the redemption of Africa frankly admit that their great hope is in the spirit of commercial enterprise; not in it alone to be sure, but that commerce will be the John the Baptist opening up a way and that the Christian missionary with an open Bible following in the furrows made by the invincible and remorseless plough of commerce, will drop his seed of truth, which will spring up into a magnificent harvest.

The religious nature of cultural millennialism is similar to what Robert Bellah has called civil religion. Though God is given recognition as working through the forces of culture, the prominent place of the deity in traditional Christian theology is either replaced or shared by a profound trust in American cultural principles and institutions. It may be more appropriate to consider this a rhetorical millennialism than a developed theological and biblical millennialism, though it is difficult to make a clear distinction. There is a certain elastic vagueness to millennial symbols that extends their powerful influence in culture, resulting in a millennial theory that may be diffuse, diluted, and secular.

The emphasis on pan-Africanism, the criticism or rejection of white society and culture, and the elevation of the African past characteristic of millennial Ethiopianism are found in the millennial language and thought of Perry, Brent, Cole, Bruce, Holly, and Steward. An extreme form is the millennialism of the latter three who espouse the total rejection of white society in terms of apocalyptic judgment. In general, millennial Ethiopianism stresses the supernatural intervention of God, a broader understanding of history in which Western civilization is seen as a stage and not the fulfillment of history, the importance of biblical prophecy centering on Ps 68:31, the moral leadership and prophetic insight of black peoples, and the judgment of American cultural forces.

Progressive millennialism is a more traditionally theological millennialism most akin to the prevailing white postmillennialism of the middle of the nineteenth century. Unlike millennial Ethiopianism, progressive millennialism as seen in the thought of Bowen, Clinton, Payne, and Holsey stresses the power of Christianity through the church's involvement in evangelism, missions, and reform in transforming American society and bringing about the millennium on earth. This type, however, does not share the more secular and uncritical optimism of cultural millennialism.

A discussion of millennial types is not complete without looking at a-millennialism among African-Americans. This theory interprets Revelation 20 symbolically as either the age of the church or the realm beyond this world. In the only biblical commentary on Revelation written by an African-American during this period, A.M.E. Zion bishop J. W. Hood argued that if there is to be a millennium and partial resurrection of the saints, it will occur in heaven. There will be no establishment of the millennium on earth, for the second coming of Christ will be at the end of time, and the "new heaven and new earth" will be beyond time. The only establishment of the kingdom of God, according to Hood, is within the heart, when Christ rather than Satan dwells in the hearts of men and women. In a collection of black Baptist sermons published to assure white missionaries that their work in the South had not been in vain, S.W. Anderson addressed the subject of eschatology in a-millennial fashion and argued that the only golden "world to come" would be in heaven. The Presbyterian minister Francis J. Grimke castigated this-worldly and otherworldy millennial talk of "golden streets, and pearly gates, and white robes, and a land flowing with milk and honey" because he believed that it distracted black Americans from the more pressing need for "character" and "Christian manhood and womanhood."

An a-millennial position tends to look toward the world with neither extreme optimism nor extreme pessimism. In an *A.M.E. Church Review* article from 1900, Du Bois looked to the dawning century with caution and modesty:

> The progress of the nation toward a settlement of the Negro is patent—the movement with all its retrogression is a spiral not a circle, and as long as there is motion there is hope. At the same time we must indulge in no fantastic dreams, simply because in the past this nation has turned back from its errors against the Negro and tardily sought the higher way is no earnest for the future. Error that ends in progress is none the less error.

Progress is neither inevitable nor impossible, but dependent on the hard work of Christian men and women rather than a millennial vision.

Conclusion

It is generally accepted by scholars today that millennialism should be described, as Hillel Schwartz states, "less often as the products of disease, more often as an arsenal of world-sustaining forces." Timothy L. Smith argues that black Americans in the nineteenth century grasped the radical and liberating nature of Christianity:

> Africans were pressed up against the wall by American slavery's vast assault upon their humanity. This tragic circumstance compelled them to discover in the religion of their white oppressors a faith whose depths few of the latter ever suspected, enabling the Black Christians to reconcile suffering and hope, guilt and forgiveness, tyranny and spiritual freedom, self-hate and divine acceptance. In that faith some of them found the strength to throw off their bonds, and many others the dignity, when once emancipated, to stand up free.

In like manner, many black Christians found great strength in the Christian millennial tradition because of its divinely inspired criticism and rebellion against the present social order. Regardless of form or type, millennialism sets a future perfect state over against the present and sows the seeds of social and religious criticism. Inherent in black millennialism is criticism against the unjust and unequal treatment of African Americans as well as criticism against white Christianity, which did little if anything to solve the "race problem."

Black millennialism of the Nadir period reveals several important things about the experience of African Americans. Blacks of this period were deeply religious and influenced by biblical symbols and passages. Jean Quandt has argued that postmillennialism during this period became secularized into a theory of human and natural progress. Although this can be seen in cultural millennialism, the greater part of black millennialism retained a strong emphasis on divine and spiritual activity, perhaps related to the fact that black Americans did not have many secular powers and institutions at their disposal. This religious emphasis, however, did not translate into a quietism or withdrawal from social criticism. Some of the strongest criticism of white Christianity and American society can be found in black millennialism.

It becomes clear in a study of black millennialism that a very important ingredient of the African-American Christian faith was the belief that history is divinely ordained, controlled by God, and moving toward its fulfillment. The belief in the millennium and the special destiny of the black race was part of a theodicy African Americans sought in order to make sense of their past in slavery, reaffirm meaning in their lives, and strengthen their trust in God. In the midst of the deteriorating conditions of the Nadir, black Americans may have differed in how they understood their destiny in different types of millennialism, but they were united in the strong belief that God was in control of history and their future.

Questions for Reflection and Discussion

1. Create a definition of *social gospel* based on your reading of the documents.

2. Summarize Susan Curtis's argument that the adoption of the social gospel represented a crossroads experience for American Protestantism.

3. According to Jay Dolan, what factors contributed to American Catholicism's adoption of a social gospel?

4. As white churches in America struggled over the implications of the social gospel, African Americans pursued a millennial golden age. Describe Timothy Fulop's account of this pursuit.

5. How and why did the social gospel produce both conflict and consensus during the industrial age?

Additional Readings

Abell, Aaron. *The Urban Impact on American Protestantism*, 1865-1900. Cambridge: Harvard University Press, 1943.

Browne, Henry J. *The Catholic Church and the Knights of Labor*. Washington, D.C.: Catholic University of America Press, 1949.

Crunden, Robert. *Ministers of Reform: The Progressives' Achievement in American Civilization*. New York: Basic Books, 1982.

Dorn, Jacob. *Washington Gladden: Prophet of the Social Gospel*. Columbus: Ohio State University, 1968.

Dorsett, Lyle. *Billy Sunday and the Redemption of Urban America*. Grand Rapids, MI: Wm. B. Eerdmans, 1991.

Gladden, Washington. *Social Salvation*. Boston: Houghton Mifflin, 1902.

Glazer, Nathan. *American Judaism*. Chicago: University of Chicago Press, 1957.

Handy, Robert R., ed. *The Social Gospel in America*. New York: Oxford University Press, 1966.

Higginbotham, Evelyn Brooks. *Righteous Discontent: The Women's Movement in the Black Baptist Church, 1880-1920*. Cambridge: Harvard University Press, 1993.

Hopkins, Charles H. *The Rise of the Social Gospel in American Protestantism, 1865-1915*. New Haven: Yale University Press, 1940.

Magnuson, Norris. *Salvation in the Slums: Evangelical Social Work, 1865-1920*. Lanham, MD: Scarecrow Press, 1977.

May, Henry F. *Protestant Churches and Industrial America*. New York: Harper and Row, 1949.

Rauschenbusch, Walter. *A Theology for the Social Gospel*. New York: Macmillan, 1917.

Szasz, Ferenc. "The Progressive Clergy and the Kingdom of God." *Mid-America: An Historical Review* 55 (January 1973):12-15.

White, Ronald, Jr. *Liberty and Justice for All: Racial Reform and the Social Gospel*. San Francisco: Harper and Row, 1990.

White, Ronald, Jr., and C. Howard Hopkins. *The Social Gospel: Religion and Reform in Changing America*. Philadelphia: Temple University Press, 1976.

Chapter 11

Manifest destiny as an American idea is probably as old as the "sea to sea" charters of the earliest colonies. The Puritans' sense of divine mission soon added a spiritual dimension to the quest for land acquisition. This spiritual dimension grew in 1776 when religious supporters of the American Revolution saw war as a means of establishing a Christian, democratic lighthouse in a world of political darkness.

Religion and American Empire Building

Issue

How did religion influence the emergence of America as a world power?

During the decades before the Civil War, evangelicals' dreams of an extensive Christian republic brought renewed support for the American destiny that was clearly manifested. Though the turmoil of the Civil War and the postbellum development of the giant industrial machine interrupted national expansion for several decades, by the final decade of the century the drive for empire-building was renewed, as many Americans looked beyond the seas, especially to the Caribbean and the Far East.

It was understandable, then, for the California Christian Advocate *to respond to the outbreak of the Spanish-American War in 1898 by declaring, "The war is the Kingdom of God coming!" Not to be outdone, the* Pacific Advocate *stated dogmatically, "The cross will follow the flag. . . . The clock of the ages is striking." Political and military figures responded favorably, too, to the new opportunity offered by Caribbean conquest. Here, sacred and secular were knit together, as patriotism, imperialism, and religion united more closely than perhaps at any other time in the nation's history.*

For Protestants the way was clear: "He (God) sends us, as He sent His well-loved Son, to serve the world, and thus to save the world," announced James W. Bashford, Methodist minister and president of Ohio Wesleyan University. For American Catholics, however, the "splendid little war" created special difficul-

ties. Just at the time when Catholics were seeking the approval of the pope to "Americanize" the American Catholic Church, the United States declared war on one of the oldest and most steadfast Catholic powers in the world. Then, too, Catholics were continuing to walk carefully in the Protestant-dominated nation that was still questioning whether they could be trusted to become "good Americans." After considerable soul-searching and hand-wringing, most Catholics resolved this critical issue by offering their support to United States military and political leaders. By the end of the short-lived war in Cuba, in most areas of America there was little noticeable difference between Catholic and Protestant support for American imperialism.

At a time when many voices in America were calling for the nation to fulfill its expansionist destiny, a smaller number of Americans were not. Among them were notables such as William James, William Graham Sumner, Mark Twain, and Andrew Carnegie. Joining them was William Jennings Bryan, who contended that America's behavior of imperialist "criminal aggression" contradicted its belief in liberty and morality. How did religionists argue the cause of empire-building? Why was American expansionism a critical issue for citizens who espoused religious convictions?

Documents

The remote vastness of Alaska was a new frontier for missions in the last quarter of the nineteenth century. In the first document, Presbyterian missionary John Brady writes to fellow missionary Sheldon Jackson about the potential for missions activities among the Native Americans of that region. In the second document, Protestant missionary to China S. Wells Williams makes clear that Christianity is China's means to salvation, as it had been for over forty years. Social gospeler Josiah Strong combined Anglo-Saxonism, social Darwinism, and the social gospel in his argument that Anglo-Saxons were destined to transmit their superior civilization to inferior races abroad. Excerpts from his influential book Our Country appear in the third selection. The fourth document consists of two views of "the Philippine Question." The first, by Catholic Archbishop John Ireland of Minneapolis, calls for Protestants to keep their hands off the Philippines. The second, by Arthur J. Brown, Secretary of the Presbyterian Board of Foreign Missions, argues that the old religious establishment of Catholicism should allow for Protestant input. In the fifth selection, participants in the Boxer Rebellion let Christian missionaries and converts know they are not welcome in China. In the final selection, United States Senator Albert J. Beveridge, a pronounced nationalist who was suspicious of foreign countries, joins profit and providence into a single argument on behalf of American expansion.

1. Reaching Alaska's Natives, 1878

SOURCE: Sheldon Jackson, *Alaska, and Missions on the North Pacific Coast* (New York: Dodd, Mead, & Co., 1880), 204-5, 206-7, 208.

Sitka, Alaska, May, 1878

Rev. Sheldon Jackson, D.D.

Dear Doctor: We arrived here the night of April the 11th. Our first meeting occurred on Sunday in the castle. The day was charming, for the clouds had vanished, the sun was warm, and the scenery was all that could be asked. Far out beyond the harbor, protected by innumerable green islets, lay the vast Pacific, in a sort of rolling calmness. At another point rose the funnel-topped Edgecumbe, crested with snow. Back of the town, and as far down the coast as the eye can reach, we have all the variety of grand mountain scenery. When these days come all nature seems to be still with solemnity, and one appears to be near the presence-chamber of the Almighty. Alaska scenery has a peculiar effect upon my emotions.

The castle has been stripped of everything, and is in a dilapidated condition. As we began to sing some of the Moody and Sankey hymns, the Indians began to steal in and squat themselves on the floor along the wall. Most of them had their faces painted black; some were black and red, and a few had the whole face black with the exception of the right eye, which was surrounded with a coat of red. All but a few of the chiefs were in their bare feet, and wrapped in blankets of various colors.

Sitka Jack is the chief who seems to have the most influence among them, and he is their orator. He and Annahootz, the war chief, were clad in some old suits of the naval officers who have been here. They think a great deal of the buttons, shoulder-pieces and the like. Several wore soldiers' caps. The rest were bareheaded.

The natives along the coast from Cape Fox to Mount St. Elias, speak the same tongue. Mr. Cohen, a Jew who keeps a store here, kindly volunteered to hunt up the old Russian interpreter. This man is about sixty years old. He is a half-breed. The Russian American Fur Company took him, when a boy, and educated him for a priest to the natives; but for some reason he was never ordained to that office. He has always been employed as interpreter. He speaks both languages well, and can read and write the Russian. Mr. George Kastrometinoff turned my English into Russian, and the interpreter turned that into good Indian. The people listened very attentively to all that I had to say. Jack, becoming impatient to speak, broke into a gesticulating speech, telling how bad they were heretofore, fighting and killing one another. Now they were glad that they were going to have a school and a church, and people to teach them. . . .

I explained to them why we wished them to go to school, and the advantages which they would have if they would learn English. I centred everything upon the

Bible, and tried to impress upon their minds its value to all men, because it is God speaking to us when we read it. . . .

I hired some Indians, and we all worked hard to put the upper floor of the soldiers' barracks in trim for our school and church services. Mr. Whitford, who bought nearly everything which the soldiers left, sold us twenty benches, a stove, cord of wood, two brooms, and a box of chalk. The Russian priest loaned us a blackboard with half-inch cracks between the boards. These things, together with two tables, make up the list of our furniture. The school opened on Wednesday, April 17th, with fifty present, and after asking God's blessing upon this beginning of a work, which will surely prove to be one of the most interesting in the history of missions. . . .

If our churches had known the facts concerning this people, and the wonderful coast upon which they live, missionaries would have been sent out years ago. The money spent in teaching and Christianizing these people will not be thrown away. "Blessed are they which do hunger and thirst after righteousness: for they shall be filled." This promise will surely be fulfilled to these people, for they are hungering and thirsting for more light. It would be a great wrong for the Church to neglect these people longer.

I hope that before the leaves fall we shall be able to organize the Presbytery of Alaska. This will be a great thing for this Territory, which has been so wilfully misrepresented to the public. Such a body can be the source of information concerning the people and the country and its resources which will be trusted by the reading public.

2. A Missionary Declares China's Salvation, 1883

SOURCE: S. Wells Williams, *The Middle Kingdom: A Survey of the Geography, Government, Literature, Social Life, Arts, and History of the Chinese Empire and Its Inhabitants*, rev. ed. (New York: Charles Scribner's Sons, 1882), I, xiii-xv, II, 333-36, 364-65.

My experiences in the forty-three years of my life in China were coeval with the changes which gradually culminated in the opening of the country. Among the most important of these may be mentioned the cessation of the East India Company in 1834, the war with England in 1841-42, the removal of the monopoly of the hong merchants [privileged Chinese merchants responsible to imperial officials for foreign trade], the opening of five ports to trade, the untoward attack on the city of Canton which grew out of the lorcha Arrow [In 1856, the Chinese searched this vessel and the British used the incident to recommence military operations against Canton; lorcha is the three-masted sailing ship], the operations in the vicinity of Peking, the establishment of foreign legations in that city, and finally, in 1873, the peaceful settlement of the *kotow* [*kowtow*, a royal court ritual of prostration], which rendered possible the approach of foreign ministers to the Emperor's presence. Those who trace the hand of God in history will gather from such rapid and great changes in this [Chinese] Empire the foreshadowing of the fulfilment of his purposes; for while these political events were in progress the

Bible was circulating, and the preaching and educational labors of missionaries were silently and with little opposition accomplishing their leavening work among the people. . . .

. . . I am assured of a great future for the sons of Han; but the progress of pure Christianity will be the only adequate means to save the conflicting elements involved in such a growth from destroying each other. Whatever is in store for them, it is certain that the country has passed its period of passivity. . . .

The time is speedily passing away when the people of the Flowery Land can fairly be classed among uncivilized nations. The stimulus which in this labor of my earlier and later years has been ever present to my mind is the hope that the cause of missions may be promoted. In the success of this cause lies the salvation of China as a people, both in its moral and political aspects. This success bids fair to keep pace with the needs of the people. They will become fitted for taking up the work themselves and joining in the multiform operations of foreign civilizations. Soon railroads, telegraphs, and manufactures will be introduced, and these must be followed by whatsoever may conduce to enlightening the millions of the people of China in every department of religious, political, and domestic life. . . .

In 1834 Dr. [Peter] Parker joined the mission at Canton, and opened a hospital, in October, 1835, for the gratuitous relief of such diseases among the Chinese as his time and means would allow, devoting his attention chiefly to ophthalmic cases and surgical operations. . . .

When Dr. Parker's scheme was made known to Howqua, the hong merchant, he readily fell in with it and let his building for the purpose, and after the first year gave it rent free till its destruction in 1856. It was opened for the admission of patients November 4, 1835. The peculiar circumstances under which this enterprise was started imposed some caution on its superintendent, and the hong merchants themselves seem to have had a lurking suspicion that so purely a benevolent object, involving so much expense of time, labor, and money, must have some latent object which it behooved them to watch. A linguist's clerk was often in attendance, partly for this purpose, for three or four years, and made himself very useful. The patients, who numbered about a hundred daily, were often restless, and hindered their own relief by not patiently awaiting their turn; but the habits of order in which they are trained made even such a company amenable to rules. The surgical operations attracted much notice, and successful cures were spoken of abroad and served to advertise and recommend the institution to the higher ranks of native society. . . .

The reports of this hospital in Sin-tau-lan Street gave the requisite information as to its operations, and means were taken to place the whole system upon a surer footing by forming a society in China. Suggestions for this object were circulated in October, 1836, signed by Messrs. [T. R.] Colledge, Parker, and [E. C.] Bridgman, in which the motives for such a step and the good effects likely to result from it were thus explained:

. . . In the vast conflict which is to revolutionize the intellectual and moral world, we may not underrate the value of any weapon. As a means, then, to waken the dormant mind of China, may we not place a high value upon medical truth, and seek its introduction with good hope of its becoming the handmaid of religious truth? If an inquiry after truth upon any subject is elicited, is there not a great point gained? And that inquiry after medical truth may be provoked, there is good reason to expect; for, exclusive as China is in all her systems, she cannot exclude disease nor shut her people up from the desire of relief. Does not, then, the finger of Providence point clearly to one way that we should take with the people of China, directing us to seek the introduction of the remedies for sin itself by the same door through which we convey those which are designed to mitigate or remove its evils? Although medical truths cannot restore the sick and afflicted to the favor of God, yet perchance the spirit of inquiry about it once awakened will not sleep till it inquires about the source of truth; and he who comes with the blessings of health may prove an angel of mercy to point to the Lamb of God. At any rate, this seems the only open door; let us enter it. A faith that worketh not may wait for other doors. None can deny that *this* is a way of charity that worketh no ill, and our duty to walk in it seems plain and imperative. . . .

The influence and labors of female missionaries in China is, from the constitution of society in that country, likely to be the only, or principal means of reaching their sex for a long time to come, and it is desirable, therefore, that they should engage in the work by learning the language and making the acquaintance of the families around them. No nation can be elevated, or Christian institutions placed upon a permanent basis, until females are taught their rightful place as the companions of men, and can teach their children the duties they owe to their God, themselves, and their country. Female schools are the necessary complement of boys', and a heathen wife soon carries a man back to idolatry if he is only intellectually convinced of the truths of Christianity. . . .

3. Our Country, 1885
SOURCE: Josiah Strong, *Our Country*, rev. ed. (New York: Baker and Taylor Co., 1891), 200-18, *passim*.

The Anglo-Saxon and the World's Future
Every race which has deeply impressed itself on the human family has been representative of some great idea—one or more—which has given direction to the nation's life and form to its civilization. Among the Egyptians this seminal idea was life, among the Persians its was light, among the Hebrews it was purity, among the Greeks it was beauty, among the Romans it was law. The Anglo-Saxon is the representative of two great ideas, which are closely related. One of them is that of

civil liberty. Nearly all of the civil liberty of the world is enjoyed by Anglo-Saxons: the English, the British colonists, and the people of the United States. To some, like the Swiss, it is permitted by the sufferance of their neighbors; others, like the French, have experimented with it; but, in modern times, the peoples whose love of liberty has won it, and whose genius for self-government has preserved it, have been Anglo-Saxons. The noblest races have always been lovers of liberty. The love ran strong in early German blood, and has profoundly influenced the institutions of all the branches of the great German family; but it was left for the Anglo-Saxon branch fully to recognize the right of the individual to himself, and formally to declare it the foundation stone of government.

The other great idea of which the Anglo-Saxon is the exponent is that of a pure *spiritual* Christianity. It was no accident that the great reformation of the sixteenth century originated among a Teutonic, rather than a Latin people. It as the fire of liberty burning in the Saxon heart that flamed up against the absolutism of the Pope. Speaking roughly, the peoples of Europe which are Celtic are Roman Catholic, and those which are Teutonic are Protestant; and where the Teutonic race was purest, there Protestantism spread with the greatest rapidity. But, with beautiful expectations, Protestantism on the continent has degenerated into mere formalism. By confirmation at a certain age, the state churches are filled with members who generally know nothing of a personal spiritual experience. In obedience to a military order, a regiment of German soldiers files into church and partakes of the sacrament, just as it would shoulder arms to obey any other word of command. It is said that, in Berlin and Leipsic, only a little over one percent of the Protestant population are found in church. Protestantism on the continent seems to be about as poor in spiritual life and power as Romanism. That means that most of the spiritual Christianity in the world is found among Anglo-Saxons and their converts; for this is the great missionary race. If we take all of the German missionary societies together, we find that, in the number of workers and amount of contributions, they do not equal the smallest of the three great English missionary societies. The year that the Congregationalists in the United States gave one dollar and thirty-seven cents per caput to foreign missions, the members of the great German State Church gave only three quarters of a cent per caput to the same cause. Evidently it is chiefly to the English and American peoples that we must look for the evangelization of the world.

It is not necessary to argue to those for whom I write that the two great needs of mankind, that all men may be lifted up into the light of the highest Christian civilization, are, first a pure, spiritual Christianity, and second, civil liberty. Without controversy, these are the forces which, in the past, have contributed most to the elevation of the human race, and they must continue to be, in the future, the most efficient ministers to its progress. It follows, then, that the Anglo-Saxon, as the great representative of these two ideas, the depository of these two greatest blessings, sustains peculiar relations to the world's future, is divinely commissioned to be, in a peculiar sense, his brother's keeper. Add to this the fact of his rapidly increasing strength in modern times, and we have well nigh a demonstration of his destiny. . . .

And it is possible that, by the close of the next century, the Anglo-Saxons will outnumber all the other civilized races of the world. Does it not look as if God were not only preparing in our Anglo-Saxon civilization the die with which to stamp the peoples of the earth, but as if he were also massing behind that die the mighty power with which to press it? My confidence that this race is eventually to give its civilization to mankind is not based on mere numbers—China forbid! I look forward to what the world has never yet seen united in the some race; viz., the greatest numbers, *and* the highest civilization.

There can be no reasonable doubt that North America is to the great home of the Anglo-Saxon, the principal of his power, the center of his life and influence. . .

America is to have the great preponderance of numbers and of wealth, and by the logic of events will follow the scepter of controlling influence. This will be but the consummation of a movement as old as a civilizations—result to which men have looked forward for centuries. . . . .

Mr. Darwin is not only disposed to see, in the superior vigor of our people, an illustration of his favorite theory of natural selection, but even intimates that the world's history thus far has been simply preparatory for our future, and tributary to it. He says: "There is apparently much truth in the belief that the wonderful progress of the United States, as well as the character of the people, are the results of natural selection; for the more energetic, restless, and courageous men from all parts of Europe have emigrated during the last ten or twelve generations to that great country, and have there succeeded best. Looking at the distant future, I do not think that the Rev. Mr. Zincke takes an exaggerated view when he says: 'All other series of events—as that which resulted in the Empire of Rome—only appear to have purpose and value when viewed in connection with, or rather as subsidiary to, the great stream of Anglo-Saxon emigration to the West!'"

There is abundant reason to believe that the Anglo-Saxon race is to be, is, indeed, already becoming, more effective here than in the mother country. The marked superiority of this race is due in large measure, to its highly mixed origin. . . .

It seems to me that God, with infinite wisdom and skill, is training the Anglo-Saxon race for an hour sure to come in the world's future. Heretofore there has always been in the history of the world a comparatively unoccupied land westward, into which the crowded countries of the East have poured their surplus populations. But the widening waves of migration, which millenniums ago rolled east and west from the valley of the Euphrates, meet today on our Pacific coast. There are no more new worlds. The unoccupied arable lands of the earth are limited, and will soon be taken. The time is coming when the pressure of population on the means of subsistence will be felt here as it is now felt in Europe and Asia. Then will the world enter upon a new stage of its history—*the final competition of races, for which the Anglo-Saxon is being schooled.* Long before the thousand millions are here, the mighty *centrifugal* tendency, inherited in this stock and strengthened in the United States, will assert itself. Then this race of unequaled energy, with all the majesty of numbers and the might of wealth behind it—the representative, let us hope, of the largest liberty, the purest Christianity, the highest civilization—having developed peculiarly aggressive traits calculated to impress its institutions upon mankind, will spread itself over the earth. If I read not amiss, this powerful race will move down upon Mexico, down upon Central and South America, out upon the islands of the sea, over upon Africa and beyond. And can any one doubt that the result of this competition of races will be the "survival of the fittest?" "Any people," says Dr. Bushnell, "that is physiologically advanced in culture, though it be only in a degree beyond another which is mingled with it on strictly equal terms, is sure to live down and finally live out its inferiority. Nothing can save the inferior race but a ready and pliant assimilation. Whether the feebler and more abject races are going to be regenerated and raised up, is already very much of a question. What if it should be God's plan to people the world with better and finer material?"

"Certain it is, whatever expectations we may indulge, that there is a tremendous overbearing surge of power in the Christian nations, which, if the others are not speedily raised to some vastly higher capacity, will inevitably submerge and bury them forever. These great populations of Christendom—what are they doing, but throwing out their colonies on every side, and populating themselves, if I may so speak, into the possession of all countries and climes?" To this result no war of extermination is needful; the contest is not one of arms, but of vitality and of civilization. "At the present day," says Mr. Darwin, "civilized nations are everywhere supplanting barbarous nations, excepting where the climate opposes a deadly barrier; and they succeed mainly, though not exclusively, through their arts, which are the products of the intellect." Thus the Finns were supplanted by the Aryan races in Europe and Asia, the Tartars by the Russians, and thus the aborigines of North America, Australia, and New Zealand are now disappearing before the all-conquering Anglo-Saxons. It seems as if these inferior tribes were only precursors of a superior race, voices in the wilderness crying: "Prepare ye the way of the Lord!"

Some of the stronger races, doubtless, may be able to preserve their integrity; but, in order to compete with the Anglo-Saxons, they will probably be forces to adopt his methods and instruments, his civilization and his religion. Significant movements are now in progress among them. While the Christian religion was never more vital, or its hold upon the Anglo-Saxon mind stronger, there is taking place among the nations a widespread intellectual revolt against traditional beliefs. "In every corner of the world," says Mr. Froude, "there is the same phenomenon of the decay of established religions. . . . Among the Mohammedans, Jews, Buddhists, Brahmins, traditionary creeds are losing their hold. An intellectual revolution is sweeping over the world, breaking down established opinions, dissolving foundations on which historical faiths have been built up." The contact of Christian with heathen nations is awakening the latter to new life. Old superstitions are loosening their grasp. The dead crust of fossil faiths is being shattered by the movements of life underneath. In Catholic countries, Catholicism is losing its influence over educated minds, and in some cases the masses have already lost all faith in it. Thus, while on this continent God is training the Anglo-Saxon race for its mission, a complemental work has been in progress in the great world beyond. God has two hands. Not only is he preparing in our civilization the die with which to stamp the nations, but, by what Southey called the "timing of Providence," he is preparing mankind to receive the impress.

Is there room for reasonable doubt that this race, unless devitalized by alcohol and tobacco, is destined to dispossess many weaker races, assimilate others, and mold the remainder, until, in a very true and important sense, it has Anglo-Saxonized mankind? Already "the English language, saturated with Christian ideas, gathering up into itself the best thought of all the ages, is the great agent of Christian civilization throughout the world; at this moment affecting the destinies and molding the character of half the human race." Jacob Grimm, the German philologist, said of this language: "It seems chosen, like its people, to rule in future times in a still greater degree in all the corners of the earth." He predicted, indeed, that the language of Shakespeare would eventually become the language of mankind. Is not Tennyson's noble prophecy to find its fulfillment in Anglo-Saxondom's extending its dominion and influence—

> "Till the war-drum throb no
> longer, and the battle-flags are
> furl'd, In the Parliament of man,
> the Federation of the world."

In my mind, there is no doubt that the Anglo-Saxon is to exercise the commanding influence in the world's future; but the exact nature of that influence is, as yet, undetermined. How far his civilization will be materialistic and atheistic, and how long it will take thoroughly to Christianize and sweeten it, how rapidly he will hasten the coming of the kingdom wherein dwelleth righteousness, or how many ages he may retard it, is still uncertain; but *is now being swiftly determined.* Let us weld together in a chain the various links of our logic which we have endeavored to forge. Is it manifest that the Anglo-Saxon holds in his hands the destinies of mankind for ages to come? Is it evident that the United States is to be the home of this race, the principal seat of his power, the great center of his influence? Is it true that the great West is to dominate the nation's future? Has it been shown that this generation is to determine the character, and hence the destiny of the West? Then may God open the eyes of this generation! When Napoleon drew up his troops before the Mamelukes, under the shadow of the Pyramids, pointing to the latter, he said to his soldiers: "Remember that from yonder heights forty centuries look down on you." Men of this generation, from the pyramid top of opportunity on which God has set us, *we look down on forty centuries!* We stretch our hand into the future with power to mold the destinies of unborn millions.

> "We are living, we are dwelling,
> In a grand and awful time,
> In an age on ages telling—
> To be living is sublime!"

Notwithstanding the great perils which threaten it, I cannot think our civilization will perish; but I believe it is fully in the hands of the Christians of the United States, during the next ten or fifteen years, to hasten or retard the coming of Christ's kingdom in the world by hundreds, and perhaps thousands, of years. We of this generation and nation occupy the Gibraltar of the ages which commands the world's future.

4. A Catholic and Protestant Debate Over the Philippines, 1899 and 1903

SOURCE: *Outlook,* no. 17 (Aug. 26, 1899), 933-34; A. J. Brown, *The New Era in the Philippines* (New York: Fleming H. Revell Co., 1903), 152-54.

1.

You ask me what I think of cooperation between Catholics and Protestants towards religious reconstruction in our new American possessions. I will speak frankly, and give expression to my convictions as a Catholic and as an American. As a Catholic, I cannot approve of any efforts of Protestants to affect the religious duties of the inhabitants of the islands. Catholics are there in complete control; they have a thorough church organization; the inhabitants are Catholics; some of them may not live up to the teachings of their faith, but they have no idea of abandoning that faith for another. It represents all they have ever known of a higher life. Protestantism will never take the place in their hearts of that faith. To take from them their faith is to throw them into absolute religious indifference. If the inhabitants of those islands were all Protestants, would Protestants ask Catholics to unite with them in the work of Protestant disintegration? Now, as an American I will no less object to efforts to implant Protestantism in those islands. Why? Because I want to see American rule made possible in those islands. Do your Protestant missionaries realize that they are doing the greatest harm to America by making her flag unpopular? Spain has already begun to say to her former subjects: "You have objected to our rule. Very well, what have you in place? You have given up to strangers not only your civil government; they are also taking away your religion." A great mistake was made, in my opinion, by one of our military officers in Porto Rico; he put himself forth as an official leader in establishing the Protestant Church. Now, as an American ruler he had no right, and he was not asked, to prevent the establishment there of a Protestant church; nor was he asked to take part in Catholic worship; but the fact that he was foremost in founding a Protestant church was enough to make the simple Porto Ricans take the new chapel to represent the established church of the United States. It was enough to make them think that America was officially opposed to the Catholic religion. If I were America's enemy today, I would say to American Protestants, Hurry on your missionaries to Cuba, Porto Rico, and the Philippines, and have them tell the inhabitants of those islands that their historic faith is wrong and that they ought to become Protestants. This would be the speediest and most effective way to make the inhabitants of those islands discontented and opposed to America.

2.

Archbishop Ireland and his sympathizers in the United States, the Roman Catholic bishops and priests in the Philippines, and a considerable number of Americans both at home and abroad, never tire of reminding us that the Filipinos had a form of the Christian religion before the Americans came, and that it is neither expedient nor just to attempt to change it.

I reply that the Filipinos had a form of civil government before the Americans came and also, a form of public education, forms which were as adequate to their needs as was their form of religion. Indeed, all competent testimony is to the effect that the dissatisfaction of the people with their civil governors and their schools was less than their dissatisfaction with their priests. Nevertheless, Americans have deemed it their duty to forcibly overthrow the entire governmental and educational systems, and to replace them with our own radically different ones. The wishes of the people were not considered. The Taft Commission reports: "Many witnesses were examined as to the form of government best adapted to these Islands and satisfactory to the people. All the evidence taken, no matter what the bias of the witness, showed that the masses of the people are ignorant, credulous and childlike, and that under any government the electoral franchise must be much limited, because the large majority will not for a long time be capable of intelligently exercising it."

So Americans have proceeded on the supposition that as the people did not know what was good for them, that good must be imposed by the strong arm of military power and civil law, confident that in time the Filipinos will see that it is for their welfare. Any argument that could be framed for the inadequacy of the former civil and educational systems would, *mutatis mutandis,* apply with equal force to the Roman Catholic *régime.* Indeed, if disinterested writers are to be trusted, the rottenness of the ecclesiastical administration was the source of nearly all the evils from which the Filipinos were suffering.

Protestant missionary methods are not a tenth part as drastic and revolutionary as the American civil and educational methods. Protestants ask no assistance from soldiers or policemen. They do not wish the Filipinos to be taxed to support their work, as they are taxed to maintain the public schools to which the Roman Catholic Church so strongly objects. The Protestant Churches of the United States rely wholly upon moral suasion and the intrinsic power of the truths which they inculcate. They send to the Philippines as missionaries men and women who represent the purest and highest types of American Christian character and culture. They propose to pay all costs out of voluntary contributions. Now we insist that our justification for this effort is as clear as the justification of the Department of Public Instruction, for example, in superseding the educational control of the Roman Catholics, and that our methods are far less apt to alarm and anger the Roman hierarchy and its followers.

5. Boxer Opposition to Christian Missionaries and Converts, 1900

SOURCE: Ssu-yu Teng and John K. Fairbank, *China's Response to the West* (Cambridge: Harvard University Press, 1954), 190.

Attention: all people in markets and villages of all provinces in China—now, owing to the fact that Catholics and Protestants have vilified our gods and sages, have deceived our emperors and ministers above, and oppressed the Chinese people below, both our gods and our people are angry at them, yet we have to keep silent. This forces us to practice the I-ho magic boxing so as to protect our country, expel the foreign bandits and kill Christian converts, in order to save our people from miserable suffering. After this notice is issued to instruct you villagers, no matter which village you are living in, if there are Christian converts, you ought to get rid of them quickly. The churches which belong to them should be unreservedly burned down. Everyone who intends to spare someone, or to disobey our order by concealing Christian converts, will be punished according to the regulation when we come to his place, and he will be burned to death to prevent his impeding our program. We especially do not want to punish anyone by death without warning him first. We cannot bear to see you suffer innocently. Don't disobey this special notice!

6. The March of the Flag, 1903

SOURCE: Thomas B. Reed, ed., *Modern Eloquence* (Philadelphia: John D. Morris and Co., 1903), II, 224-43, *passim*.

It is a noble land that God has given us; a land that can feed and clothe the world; a land whose coast lines would inclose half the countries of Europe; a land set like a sentinel between the two imperial oceans of the globe; a greater England and a nobler destiny. It is a mighty people that He has planted on this soil; a people sprung from the most masterful blood of history; a people perpetually revitalized by the virile working folk of all the earth; a people imperial by virtue of their power, by right of their institutions, by authority of their heaven-directed purposes, the propagandists and not the misers of liberty. It is a glorious history our God has bestowed upon His chosen people; a history whose keynote was struck by the Liberty Bell; a history heroic with faith in our mission and our future; a history of statesmen, who flung the boundaries of the Republic out into unexplored lands and savage wildernesses; a history of soldiers, who carried the flag across blazing deserts and through the ranks of hostile mountains, even to the gates of sunset; a history of a multiplying people, who overran a continent in half a century; a history divinely logical, in the process of whose tremendous reasoning we find ourselves today.

Therefore, in this campaign the question is larger than a party question. It is an American question. It is a world question. Shall the American people continue their restless march toward the commercial supremacy of the world? Shall free institutions broaden their blessed reign as the children of liberty wax in strength until the empire of our principles is established over the hearts of all mankind? Have we no mission to perform—no duty to discharge to our fellow man? Has the Almighty endowed us with gifts beyond our deserts, and marked us as the people of His peculiar favor, merely to rot in our own selfishness, as men and nations must who take cowardice for their companion and self for their deity as China has, as India has, as Egypt has? Shall we be as the man who had one talent and hid it, or as he who had ten talents and used them until they grew to riches? And shall we reap the reward that waits on the discharge of our high duty as the sovereign power on earth; shall we occupy new markets for what our farmers raise, new markets for what our factories make, new markets for what our merchants sell, aye, and please God, new markets for what our ships will carry? Shall we avail ourselves to new sources of supply of what we do not raise or make, so that what are luxuries today shall be necessities tomorrow? Shall we conduct the mightiest commerce of history with the best money known to man or shall we use the pauper money of Mexico, China, and the Chicago platform? Shall we be worthy of our mighty past of progress, brushing aside, as we have always done, the spider webs of technicality, and march ever onward upon the highway of development, to the doing of real deeds, the achievement of real things, and the winning of real victories?

In a sentence, shall the American people endorse at the polls the American administration of William McKinley, which, under the guidance of Divine Providence, has started the Republic on its noblest career of prosperity, duty and glory, or shall the American people rebuke that administration, reverse the wheels of history, halt the career of the flag. . . ?

William McKinley is continuing the policy that Jefferson began, Monroe continued, Seward advanced, Grant promoted, Harrison championed. Hawaii is ours; Puerto Rico is to be ours; at the prayer of its people Cuba will finally be ours; in the islands of the East, even to the gates of Asia, coaling stations are to be ours, at the very least the flag of a liberal government is to float over the Philippines, and it will be the stars and stripes of glory. And the burning question of this campaign is whether the American people will accept the gifts of events, whether they will rise, as lifts their soaring destiny; whether they will proceed along the lines of national development surveyed by the statesmen of our past, or whether, for the first time, the American people doubt their mission, question their fate, prove apostate to the spirit of their race, and halt the ceaseless march of free institutions?

The opposition tells us that we ought not to govern a people without their consent. I answer, the rule of liberty that all just government derives its authority from the consent of the governed, applies only to those who are capable of self-government. We govern the Indians without their consent; we govern our Territories without their consent; we govern our children without their consent. I answer, would not the natives of the Philippines prefer the just, humane, civilizing government of this Republic to the savage, bloody rule of pillage and extortion from which we have rescued them? Do not the blazing fires of joy and the ringing bells of gladness in Puerto Rico prove the welcome of our flag? And regardless of this formula of words made only for enlightened, self-governing peoples, do we owe no duty to the world? Shall we turn these peoples back to the reeking hands from which we have taken them? Shall we save them from those nations, to give them to a self rule of tragedy? It would be like giving a razor to a babe telling it to shave itself. It would be like giving a typewriter to an Esquimau and telling him to publish one of the great dailies of the world. . . .

Today, we are making more than we can use. Therefore, we must find new markets for our produce, new occupation for our capital, new work for our labor. And so, while we did not need the territory taken during the past century at the time it was acquired, we do need what we have taken in 1898, and we need it now. Think of the thousands of Americans who will pour into Hawaii and Puerto Rico when the Republic's laws cover those islands with justice and safety. Think of the tens of thousands of Americans who will invade the Philippines when a liberal government shall establish order and equity there. Think of the hundreds of thousands of Americans who will build a soap and water, common school civilization of energy and industry in Cuba, when a government of law replaces the double reign of anarchy and tyranny. . . .

The resources of the Philippines have hardly been touched by the finger tips of modern methods. And they produce what we cannot, and they consume what we produce—the very predestination of reciprocity. And William McKinley intends that their trade shall be ours. It means an opportunity for the rich man to do something with his money, besides hoarding it or lending it. It means occupation for every workingman in the country at wages which the development of new resources, the launching of new enterprises, the monopoly of new markets always brings. . . .

Why mumble the meaningless phrases of a tale that is told when the golden future is before us, the world calls us, its wealth awaits us and God's command is on us? . . .

Fellow-Americans, we are God's chosen people. Yonder at Bunker Hill and Yorktown His providence was above us. At New Orleans and on ensanguined seas His hand sustained us. Abraham Lincoln was His minister, and His altar of freedom the boys in blue set up on a hundred battlefields. His power directed Dewey in the east, and He delivered the Spanish fleet into our hands on Liberty's natal day as He delivered the elder Armada into the hands of our English sires two centuries ago. His great purposes are revealed in the progress of the flag, which surpasses the intentions of Congresses and Cabinets, and leads us, like a holier pillar of cloud by day and pillar of fire by night, into situations unforeseen by finite wisdom and duties unexpected by the unprophetic heart of selfishness. The American people cannot use a dishonest medium of exchange; it is ours to set the world its example of right and honor. We cannot fly from our world duties; it is ours to execute the purposes of a fate that has driven us to be greater than our small intentions. We cannot retreat from any soil where Providence has unfurled our banner; it is ours to save that soil for liberty and civilization. For liberty and civilization and God's promises fulfilled, the flag must henceforth be the symbol and the sign of all mankind.

Essays

In the first essay, Robert T. Handy, Professor Emeritus of Union Theological Seminary, describes the Protestant quest for a Christian America, and ultimately for a world won to Christ, during the final years of the nineteenth century and early years of the twentieth century. In the vanguard of the movement were both home missions and foreign missions societies that embraced the spread of American culture and democracy abroad. William R. Hutchison of Harvard University provides in the second essay a close examination of the role of Christian missions which, in the blending of secular and sacred themes, produced a form of "the Christ-and-culture tension." He points to this tension as a critical issue for America to the present time. In the third essay, Jane Hunter of Lewis and Clark College in Portland, Oregon, looks at the role of women missionaries in China and reveals the tension that existed between the mission enterprise and American cultural, political, and economic interests. Both the sacred and secular dynamics of American religion were at work in China as the missionaries performed their duties.

The Christian Conquest of the World, 1890-1920
ROBERT T. HANDY

SOURCE: From *A Christian America: Protestant Hopes and Historical Realities*, second edition by Robert T. Handy, copyright © 1984 by Oxford University Press, Inc. Used by permission of Oxford University Press, Inc.

American Protestantism approached and entered the twentieth century in a mood of great confidence. To be sure, the years from 1890 to 1920 were troubled by several periods of economic difficulty, by growing awareness of acute social problems and by participation in two wars, but the assurance of the churches that this was to be the "Christian century" was not seriously shaken. The churches themselves entered the period in a vigorous and growing condition; membership was continuing to increase proportionately faster than a rapidly expanding population. In the 1895 edition of his massive work, *Christianity in the United* States, Daniel Dorchester, a Methodist pastor, enthusiastically summarized the advances of evangelical Christianity during the nineteenth century. He said:

> Christ, reigning over a territory hitherto unrivaled in extent; great benevolences, awakened and sustained by a deeper religious devotion; rapidly multiplying home, city, and foreign mission stations, the outcome of intelligent consecration; magnificent departments of Christian labor, many of them heretofore unknown, and none

of them ever before so numerous, so vast, or so restlessly active; the great heart of the Church pulsating with an unequaled velocity; the fires of evangelism burning with unwonted brightness on multiplied altars; and a religious literature such as has characterized no other age, eminently practical, intensely fervid and richly evangelical, emanating from her presses; all conspire to show that more than ever before God has a living Church within the churches, towering amid them all in its mightiness—the strength, the support, the central life of all; and that an increasing number of true believers are " walking with him in white," a grand constellation of light and purity—a bright Milky Way from earth to heaven.

Dorchester sought to dramatize the strength of "evangelical" churches in a series of colorful charts, one of which showed that of all the church organizations in the country, 151,172 were "evangelical," 10,231 were Roman Catholic, while "all others" accounted for 3894. Evangelicals believed they would continue to dominate the religious scene.

Protestant confidence was sustained, not only by such optimistic observations, but also by the pervasive assumption that America was still a Christian nation. No less an authority than the Supreme Court in one of its famous cases gathered evidence to show how religious the nation was. Noting that the state constitutions provided "organic utterances" which speak for the voice of the entire people that the Christian religion was part of the common law, the court went on to say:

If we pass beyond these matters to a view of American life as expressed by its laws, its business, its customs and its society, we find everywhere a clear recognition of the same truth. Among other matters note the following: The form of oath universally prevailing, concluding with an appeal to the Almighty; the custom of opening sessions of all deliberative bodies and most conventions with prayers; the prefatory words of all wills, "In the name of God, amen"; the laws respecting the observance of the Sabbath; with the general cessation of all secular business, and the closing of courts, Legislatures, and other similar public assemblies on that day; the churches and church organizations which abound in every city, town, and hamlet; the multitude of charitable organizations existing everywhere under Christian auspices; the gigantic missionary associations, with general support, and aiming to establish Christian missions in every quarter of the globe. These, and many other matters which might be noticed, add a volume of unofficial declarations to the mass of organic utterances that this is a Christian nation.

The future seemed secure for the continued advance of the churches in such a nation.

The self-assurance of Protestants was based not only on religious belief but was also rooted in the relative stability and order of the life-style of nineteenth-century middle-class white Americans. Henry Seidel Canby once declared that "confidence is a habit which must be acquired young and from an environment that is constant and rhythmically continuous." The pace of life had been steadily quickening, especially in the cities, as the generation which was to lead the main line Protestant forces so confidently into the new century was growing up. But many evangelical leaders were products of the open country or small towns; as late as 1900 about two-thirds of the population of some seventy-five million was considered rural. More significantly, whether raised in country or city, most Protestants were schooled in an atmosphere in which the universe was felt to be friendly. The order and regularity of the natural order were pictured as a reflection of God's law. In such a universe, the eye of faith could see all things working together for good to them that loved God.

Evangelicals were certain that the universe was friendly both to the progress of Christianity and to the moral and spiritual advances in civilization for which the churches stood. In his Ely Lectures at Union Theological Seminary in New York in 1890, Lewis French Stearns, liberal theologian at the Congregational seminary at Bangor, Maine, employed the familiar argument that much of civilization's progress was due to Christian influences. He claimed that such things as the recognition of the rights of individuals and groups, the establishment of democratic government, the abolition of slavery, and the growth of charity were primarily the result of the Christian leaven. "In a word," he declared, "our many-sided modern civilization, with its immense superiority over that of the heathen and ancient times, is the effect of Christianity." Evangelical spokesmen were also sure that such a civilization would go on advancing, for divine influences were at work within it. Protestant confidence was sustained by the conviction that both natural and cultural environments were favorable to evangelical goals and hopes, for the power of God was working in both. Small wonder their optimism was so great! Regular services of worship, in which "God's great book" was constantly cited, provided them keys for understanding the plan of the ages as it was being worked out in nature and history to a glorious climax. Thus the buoyant faith that the great certainties remained untouched and were progressing to victory despite the vicissitudes of time were bolstered week by week. Evangelical confidence was deep-rooted in spiritual soil; that there were indeed those who could not or did not share in the brimming sense of self-assurance should not obscure for us how general and powerful that sense was.

Protestants believed that they were in the very vanguard of true progress, and that Christianity as they understood it "is the highest and purest form of religion in the world, and contains the highest and purest conception of man and society." Those words of a Baptist leader, Samuel Zane Batten, were axiomatic among his fellow evangelicals. Another Baptist, William Newton Clarke, the first prominent systematic theologian of evangelical liberalism, expressed the thought in a slightly different way: "Something has made Christianity the boldest of the religions that lay claim to universality; and that something is an inward sense of its own divine excellence, surpassing all other faiths." He admitted that there might be some truth and goodness in other religions, but "the sense of pursuing the unparalleled good is characteristic of Christianity, wherever Christianity is at its best."

It would unnecessarily belabor the obvious to show in detail how the sense of Christian confidence about the future of civilization and the church's place in it was operative in the life of the denominations. William E. Dodge, a noted lay leader and a conspicuous figure in the calling of the famous Ecumenical Missionary Conference in New York in 1900, expressed the prevailing view in saying: "We are going into a century more full of hope, and promise, and opportunity than any period in the world's history." Though of course in these years there were certain changes in mood as economic, social, and military crises came and went, in general a pervasive sense of confidence prevailed among Protestants and in the culture of which they were a part. Progress in science and technology, in democratic reforms, and in the expansion of industry and philanthropy was interpreted by religious leaders largely as a product of the advance of Christian civilization and as a sign of the coming of the kingdom.

Protestant Hope for World Civilization

From its earliest days, Christianity in America had a world vision, a dream of a world won to Christ. In the missionary thrust of the eighteenth and nineteenth centuries it sought to turn the dream into reality. As the nineteenth century drew to a close, the belief that Christian civilization would soon dominate the world primarily through the agency of Anglo-Saxon achievement seemed very near to fulfillment for great numbers of American Protestants. In 1890 Lewis French Stearns proclaimed:

> Today Christianity is the power which is moulding the destinies of the world. The Christian nations are in the ascendant. Just in proportion to the purity of Christianity as it exists in the various nations of Christendom is the influence they are exerting upon the world's destiny. The future of the world seems to be in the hands of the three great Protestant powers—England, Germany, and the United States. The old promise is being fulfilled; the followers of the true God are inheriting the world.

The forthcoming Christian conquest would be a peaceful one, as they saw it—a victory by the sheer weight of numbers and enthusiasm, of commitment and confidence. Stearns continued:

> Looking at the matter in the large, we can have no question that Christianity has been from the first certain of its universal conquest. No other religion can vie with it. There is no likelihood that any religion will ever appear to enter into rivalry with it . . . The facts are manifest. The unbeliever sees them as fully as the Christian. Deny them he cannot. To explain them in any other way than upon the assumption that Christianity is divine, is, to say the least, a difficult matter, with regard to which unbelievers are at cross-purposes among themselves.

Josiah Strong had been influential in spreading such views through his writings and his leadership in the Evangelical Alliance. His expectancies increased toward the end of the century. "We have seen that the world is evidently about to enter on a new era, that in this new era mankind is to come more and more under Anglo-Saxon influence," he declared in 1893, "and that Anglo-Saxon civilization is more favorable than any other to the spread of those principles whose universal triumph is necessary to that perfection of the race to which it is destined; the entire realization of which will be the kingdom of heaven fully come on earth." He believed that the perils to which he had called attention so dramatically a few years before would be overcome: "We have seen that the Anglo-Saxon is accumulating irresistible power with which to press the die of his civilization upon the world."

Similar attitudes were often expressed by foreign mission leaders, by those who had served the missionary cause in distant lands. For example, Sidney L. Gulick, missionary of the American Board of Commissioners for Foreign Missions, declared in 1897: "Christianity is the religion of the dominant nations of the earth. Nor is it rash to prophesy that in due time it will be the only religion in the world." He was convinced that the non-Christian religions would become Christian — such was the divine plan.

> By the intellectual, moral, commercial and political blessings—in a word, by the civilization which God has given and is still giving to those nations which have adopted Christianity—he has indicated His approval; it is evident that He intends that these Christian nations shall have the predominant and moulding influence in the world at this state of its development. The real reason why Christian nations are predominant is because they, more than others, have discovered and loved and lived the truth, the eternal principles on which God created this world.

Gulick was not hesitant to put this in general political terms, though he expected the conquest to be moral and peaceful:

> It is Protestant Germany and especially Puritan England that have grown in influence and power. No peoples have been so controlled by the religion of Jesus Christ as the Anglo-American. No peoples have absorbed it so fully into their national life, and have so embodied it in their language and literature and government. No peoples, as a natural consequence, have so succeeded in establishing prosperous, self-governing colonies and nations. . . . God means that the type of religion and civilisation attained by the Anglo-Saxon race shall have, for the present at least, the predominating influence in moulding the civilisation of the world. And everything points to the growing predominance of the Christian religion and Christian civilisation.

Such comments as Gulick's—there were many like it—point to the lack of a self-critical sense among the Protestant leaders of the time. But to them it seemed evident that Christianity would win the pagan world and that the future of the "Christian" nations was especially secure. . . .

Christians who did accept imperialism presented their cause in such a way as to appeal as widely as possible to a broad constituency. "American imperialism, in its essence," one spokesman declared, "is American valor, American manhood, American sense of justice and right, American conscience, American character at its best, listening to the voice of God, and His command nobly assuming this republic's rightful place in the grand forward movement for the civilizing and Christianizing of all continents and all races." Josiah Strong hastened to show that even the role of armies was shifting in the new era:

> But as the world is gradually being civilized and civilization is gradually being Christianized, armies are finding new occupations. As *The Outlook* says: "The army among Anglo-Saxon peoples is no longer a mere instrument of destruction. It is a great reconstructive organization. It is promoting law, order, civilization, and is fighting famine and pestilence in India. It is lightening taxes, building railroads, laying the foundations of justice and liberty, in Egypt."

Lyman Abbott, the editor of the influential journal cited by Strong, was a defender of Christian imperialism who proclaimed that "it is the function of the Anglo-Saxon race to confer these gifts of civilization, through law, commerce, and education, on the uncivilized people of the world." He met a criticism posed by anti-imperialists with these words:

> It is said that we have no right to go to a land occupied by a barbaric people and interfere with their life. It is said that if they prefer barbarism they have a right to remain barbarians. I deny the right of a barbaric people to retain possession of any quarter of the globe. What I have already said I reaffirm: barbarism has no rights which civilization is bound to respect. Barbarians have rights which civilized people, are bound to respect, but they have no right to their barbarism.

In the debates about the war, imperialism, and expansionism, the various Protestant parties may have disagreed about many details, but they rarely disagreed about the importance of missionary expansion everywhere in the world.

In the denominational presses and at religious assemblies confident expectation that Christianity was on the way to world conquest was frequently expressed. The Quadrennial Address of the Bishops of the United Brethren Church in 1901 was characteristic:

> In a political sense Christendom is today the world. If we take the map of the globe and mark off the possessions and spheres of influence of the Christian powers, there will be little or nothing left to the independent control of non-Christian

governments. The islands of the sea are all appropriated; the Western Continent is wholly under Christian rule; the partition of Africa among the Christian nations of Europe is well-nigh complete; Asia is slowly coming under the control of Christian nations.

England and America were considered to be in the very forefront of Christianity's world conquest. A representative of the British Wesleyan Conference, Thomas Allen, brought greetings from English Methodism to the General Conference of the Methodist Episcopal Church in 1900. "I believe in the election of nations to work out definite purposes of the divine mind," he said. "And England's mission seems to be to serve the purposes of colonization and Christianity. . . . We are a ruling race, and no doubt we have got the defects as well as the excellencies of our qualities." Then he linked Christians on both sides of the Atlantic in a common enterprise: "We are allied in blood, our principles of self-government are the same, our interests are identical in various parts of the world; and there are strong reasons why we should be friends, and why we should cooperate for the advancement of civilization and for the triumph of Christianity throughout the earth." The next morning an enthusiastic delegate moved that inasmuch as the "cooperation of America and Great Britain makes for peace on earth, Christian civilization, and the holding of the open door for the propagation of the Gospel," the British colors should fly beside the American flag. The motion was tabled—after all, it was only at that very conference that it had been decided permanently to display the *American* flag on the platform—but the sentiment was widely shared. A Southern Baptist paper, the *Christian Index* of Atlanta, had the year before rejoiced in the new *rapprochement* of England and America, exclaiming: "Oh, let the stars and stripes, intertwined with the flag of old England, wave o'er the continents and islands of earth, and through the instrumentality of the Anglo-Saxon race, the kingdoms of this world shall become the kingdoms of our Lord and His Christ!" Protestant spokesmen often expressed the hope that American evangelicals, in cooperation with those of other lands, especially England, would lead the way in the Christian conquest of the world.

New Thrusts in World Missions

The expectation of peaceful world conquest by Christian civilization, an expectation that seemed to come dramatically nearer with the exciting events around the turn of the century, gave a new intensity to the already pronounced missionary concerns of evangelical Protestantism. "Missionary fervor reached a high water mark during the imperial years after 1890 and the first two decades of the twentieth century," declared Paul H. Varg in his study of American Protestant missions in China. The missionary advances of those years caught the interest of almost all groups of Protestants, for it was widely believed that this was the way the world was being made Christian and was being prepared for the coming of the kingdom of God. Foreign missions provided the means for pressing toward world Christian civilization. Though various theological tensions were felt within and between the communions, a unifying partnership was found in facing the challenge of missions. The Protestant Episcopal Church, for example, had its share of internal tensions, but the Pastoral Letter for 1901 sought to gather all the faithful for a great missionary crusade: "And lastly, beloved in the Lord, we bid you carry away from our great synod as the watchword of our battle for the time to come—missions, missions, missions." Home missions were included, but the greater excitement centered on foreign missions.

The backbone of the Protestant missionary thrust was the denominational missionary society, assisted by a member of nondenominational and interdenominational agencies. In the last third of the nineteenth century, the missionary force was rapidly increasing. By 1900 there were over fifty mission boards in the United States and eight closely associated agencies in Canada which were directly involved in sending missionaries abroad. There were nearly fifty auxiliary societies. The total North American missionary staff overseas was about five thousand.

A powerful movement that added great numbers and resources to Protestant missions and exerted effective unifying tendencies emerged in the late nineteenth century. The story of the Student Volunteer Movement for Foreign Missions with its various related movements and the impact they made on the whole Protestant missionary enterprise under the leadership of Robert P. Wilder, John R. Mott, Robert E. Speer, Sherwood Eddy, and others has been told many times. At an international student conference at Mt. Hermon, Massachusetts, in 1886 under the leadership of the famous revivalist, Dwight L. Moody, a group of some two hundred and fifty college men found their attention arrested by an enthusiastic minority of missionary-minded students. A Baptist missionary who had come uninvited, Dr. William Ashmore, was asked to speak. He took as his theme, "The work of missions is not a wrecking expedition, but a war of conquest." Robert Wilder, born of missionary parents in India, had just graduated from Princeton and had much to do with the major outcome of the conference—the commitment to overseas service of one hundred of those present. With an associate, Wilder toured American colleges the year following that famous summer conference. More than two thousand volunteers for foreign missions were enrolled, of whom about five hundred were women. In 1888 the Student Volunteer Movement was formally organized, and John R. Mott, Cornell graduate and Methodist layman, took the chairmanship, which he held for some three decades. . . .

The crusading missionary spirit continued to flow unchecked until much of it was redirected and absorbed by World War I. When he thought back on those years, Walter M. Horton, theologian at the Oberlin Graduate School of Theology, recalled that:

> The generation that fought the First World War was led to Christian commitment by a triumvirate of great lay leaders, continuators of the tradition of lay evangelism which formerly centered at Northfield in Dwight L. Moody. No one who went to student conferences or Church mass meetings in those days could be in any doubt

as to who the real leaders of American Christendom were. Their names were Mott, Speer, Eddy—the inevitable three to call upon when a Christian movement was to be launched or a national convention held.

The crusade for a Christian civilization in America which they and so many others like them sponsored was set in a world context; not only at home but abroad was the expectation of the victory of Christianization and civilization high among Protestants.

Nationalism and Religion

Looking back from the last third of the twentieth century to its first two decades, we can see how the Protestant denominations rather easily idealized the culture and democracy of America. There was a considerable transfer of religious feelings to the civilization and the nation. "This was still a period of fervent devotion, but the object of devotion had been subtly changed under the appearance of enlargement to include a particular system of social, political, and economic life," Sidney E. Mead has observed. "Consequently under the system of official separation of church and state the denominations eventually found themselves as completely identified with nationalism and their country's political economic systems as had ever been known in Christendom." The world setting of American Protestantism did not seriously work against this, for the flow was largely one way. In Varg's judgment, "missionary activity, although an exercise in both an intellectual and a practical philanthropy, was nonetheless subject to the usual egotistical elements and caught in the vortex of nationalistic crosscurrents. In the end American nationalism threatened to triumph over the religious."

Nationalism did not succeed overtly in triumphing over the religious, though its influence was pervasive. For the Protestant leaders and their followers in that period were for the most part religiously sincere and devout men, earnestly seeking to follow God's will as they understood it. Beaver's observation catches the right balance: "Nationalism provided a powerful incentive to the development of the missionary movement, but, nevertheless, it was secondary to the spiritual and theological motivation." The missionary forces, home and foreign, were more involved than they knew in a form of religious nationalism from which they thought the separation of church and state had delivered them. Their religious devotion could and did unwittingly bolster a nationalist spirit. Greatly impressed by the achievements of Western, especially American, civilization, they attributed its remarkable progress primarily to the working of Christianity within it. Though they strove as Christians to keep the priority on spiritual religion and to be aware of the differences between faith and culture, it was not difficult in the spirit of those times to lose the distinction and to see Christian civilization as a main outcome of faith, if not its chief outcome. . . .

By the early years of the new century, then, the long search for a Christian America seemed to many Protestants to be nearing fulfillment in the spread of democratic civilization. All of the American presidents of this period were spokesmen for the advance of Christian civilization. Referring to the foreign policies of McKinley, Roosevelt, and Taft and their associates, Washington Gladden could say: "I cannot doubt that because of these benign interventions of our national government the people of many of the eastern lands must be more ready than they have ever been to listen to the message of the gospel of Christ." For many in the nation and in the churches, Christianity and American civilization seemed so intimately related that religious duties patriotic feeling appeared to be but the two sides of the same coin of Christendom. Religion and nationalism lived in intimate association, long after the fact of the separation of church and state.

Threats to be Faced and Overcome

The confidence and enthusiasm of Protestant leaders did not mean that they were unaware of serious problems and dangers in American life. There was uneasy recognition that forces were at work in society which were threatening Protestant values. The range of such concerns was wide, and it affected different groups in the Protestant world with varying intensities. The perplexing realities of social and economic problems, the transforming effects of immigration which cascaded to unprecedented heights in the early years of the present century, the numerical growth of Roman Catholicism and Mormonism, the changing patterns of family life and the increase in the divorce rate—such matters worried the Protestant forces. At many types of church gatherings a familiar rhythm was followed: the identification of problem areas, the acceptance of responsibility to do something about them, and the arousing of enthusiasm to get the job done. The analyses of the problem differed, the proposed solutions varied widely, but in arousing enthusiasm Protestant leaders of many types sounded much alike. It was believed that good intentions and an abundance of zeal would with God's help be adequate to handle the difficult problems. . . .

The Great Crusade

The Protestant hope for world conquest for Christ and civilization was to be realized primarily by voluntary means, by the spirit, commitment, and sacrifice of those who believed it would soon be realized, with God's help. But when civilization was threatened, then the Protestant forces could include war in their crusading pattern—it happened in 1898, and on a much larger scale it happened in 1917-18. Though there had been much sentiment for peace and a desire to remain neutral, when America finally entered the war in April 1917, the churches generally supported the military effort, and with serious determination.

Lyman Abbott spoke for the majority of American Christians in calling the war a "twentieth century crusade." On the title page of his book by that title, he stated its thesis: "A crusade to make this world a home in which God's children can live in peace and safety is more Christian than a crusade to recover from pagans the tomb in which the body of Christ was buried." He interpreted the war as a struggle of civilization against barbarism. "In strictness of speech there is no war in Europe. There is an international *posse comitatus*, representing more than twenty civilized nations, summoned to preserve the peace and protect peaceable the nations of Europe from the worst, most highly organized and most efficient band of brigands the world has ever known." Along with many others, he idealized American anticipation in the war as an illustration of its Christian character:

> A nation is made Christian, not by maintaining an established church, nor by building cathedrals, nor by writing a confession of its faith into its constitution. It is made Christian by the spirit of love, service, and sacrifice. When did a nation ever show so much of this spirit of love, service and sacrifice as the American Nation does today? . . .

. . . much that the Protestant churches did from 1890 to 1920 was largely a continuation of the familiar patterns of the nineteenth-century search for a Christian America by voluntary means—the missionary enterprise, the temperance drive, and the crusades of 1898 and 1918 have provided illustrations. In these movements, the main line evangelical denominations felt themselves to be allies in the great cause of Christianizing American civilization. Though the churches prided themselves on their own denominational particularities, they recognized other evangelical bodies as partners in the crusade for a Christian America and a Christian world. . . .

God's Mission and America's
WILLIAM R. HUTCHISON

SOURCE: From *Errand to the World: American Protestant Thought and Foreign Missions* by William R. Hutchison. Reprinted with permission of the University of Chicago Press.

Don't apologize. All Americans are missionaries.

—Arnold Rose

The foreign mission enterprise in its heyday (about 1890 to 1930) was a massive affair, involving tens of thousands of Americans abroad and millions at home. Even in the early nineteenth century, as a movement of huge aspiration but more modest dimensions, it exceeded most other reform or benevolent organizations in size and resources. It sent abroad, through most of its history, not only the largest contingents of Americans—dwarfing all other categories except that of short-term travelers—but also the most highly educated. Missionaries on the whole belonged to the tiny cohort of the college-trained; and male missionaries generally had been educated beyond college. If deficient from a modern point of view in sensitivity to foreign cultures, they were measurably superior in that regard to most contemporaries at home or abroad.

The missionaries' considerable influence among other peoples and in America, while hard to quantify, has usually been acknowledged both by those who feel kindly disposed toward them and by others who wish fervently that these religious couriers had stayed home. People of varying persuasions may wince at John K. Fairbank's listing of ten Chinese Communist programs originated by the missionaries, but few could take factual exception to it. Nor would they be likely to dispute the conclusion, now common in the scholarly literature, that the missionaries were the chief interpreters of remote cultures for the people at home, and as such played a central role in the shaping of American public attitudes. The large number of missionary offspring that observers noted among the foreign-culture experts of the Second World War era (roughly 50 percent came from such a background) suggested that the enterprise had had many forms of continuing impact, and perhaps vouched for a certain quality in the original personnel.

One could, however, make more modest claims for the movement and still find it remarkable that missionaries and their sponsors have on the whole remained shadowy figures in narrations of religious and general history. The reason for neglect is plain enough: these overseas Americans and their best-known objectives have seemed more than a little embarrassing, and especially so to those who might have struck some balance between appreciation and criticism; that is, to those engaged in the study of religion.

The problem has been that the missionaries' stated purposes, while expressive of service and sacrifice, bespoke a supercilious and often demeaning attitude toward religions that the recipient peoples considered integral to their own cultures. The missionaries who embodied such complexities have seemed too admirable to be treated as villains, yet too obtrusive and self-righteous to be embraced as heroes. The most common reaction, therefore, has been simple avoidance.

Distortion, in the form both of hagiography and of negative stereotyping, was available to fill some of the vacuum. Whether the missionaries, when recognized in these ways, suffered more at the hands of detractors or of admirers would be hard to say; both types of biographer created abstract and unreal figures. Stereotyping led to more avoidance and disdain, and the more we disdained the less we learned; thus the cycle of neglect and bad history become well established.

From the outset, of course, there were noteworthy exceptions—historians who viewed missionaries as typical Americans working abroad and who dealt with the movement as they would any other. Then, in the Vietnam era, amid an increasing sense on all sides that we must learn what our overseas compatriots of the past had done and thought, the cycle was broken. Like the study of Puritanism in the 1930s, or of Protestant revivalism in the 1950s and of Indian missions in the 1960s, the study of foreign mission history began in the 1970s to take its place as a worthwhile subject for ordinary scholarly inquiry and classroom discussion. In this latest instance of revision, as in the Puritan and other cases, it was "secular" scholars, more than those associated with seminaries or religion departments, who called for a new look at a neglected subject.

Though developments even then were scarcely epochal, one could adopt a modest biblical phrasing to say that in the 1970s many ran to and fro, and knowledge of foreign missions was increased. But it increased unevenly, rapidly with respect to some vital foreign areas (such as China), scarcely at all in relation to others (Iran, Korea). And despite a highly developed scholarship on related matters of American ideology—dealing, for example, with Americans' sense of themselves as a chosen people and a redeemer nation—the ideological assumptions behind foreign missions were as yet touched only incidentally and sporadically. Several years earlier, Pierce Beaver of the University of Chicago had agreed to discuss missionary ideas and motivation in a volume of "reinterpretations" in American religious history; but he had remarked wryly that the task was really not feasible since "first interpretation" had not occurred. Even an adequate narrative of American participation, he argued, had not yet appeared. By the 1980s, despite noticeably increased interest and effort, Beaver's observation still held.

In some respects the goal of adequate generalization and chronicling came to seem farther away than ever. Historians of missions for some time had known that in reconstructing the story they would have to look beyond official pronouncements and publicity, and beyond the sanitized reports in mission-board archives, into the actual day-to-day experience of workers in the field. But by the 1980s they also realized that women, both at home and abroad, had constituted a clear if relatively silent majority in the movement; and that women's experience must be heeded far more than it had been. They saw that they must consider the ventures and ideas of American Catholics, blacks, pentecostals, and other distinctive groups outside the Protestant mainline even though foreign mission activity in most such cases had been minimal, and theorizing nonexistent before the Second World War. Finally, scholars grasped that beyond all this they would need to view the enterprise through the eyes and sensibilities of those whom the missionaries had set out to convert. If adequate accounts could be achieved of what mainline Protestants had done, and of what their mostly male theorists had said and written, that would be only a beginning.

Yet beginnings must be attempted. If one does presume at this point to offer a general analysis, he or she must be content either to write a preliminary institutional survey, or else to trace a limited theme or relationship. As a student of American thought with little background in "missiology" or even in institutional Church history I found it more natural and engrossing to adopt the second of these approaches, and to do so with an emphasis on the ideas that informed the movement. I have chosen, therefore, to explore the changing relations between missionary ideology (here meaning simply "body of ideas") and several pertinent and well-known themes in American thought. I have responded to the need for choice and limitation by looking intently at the missionary (or mission theorist) as American.

To adopt such a line of inquiry could mean that one is actually reducing American missionary operatives *to* their American identity, and contending that they were little more than spokespersons for nation and societal values. I do not mean to fall into that common simplification. Confusing as it may be, missionaries and mission theorists claimed a number of identities, and with something like equal conviction. They always, by explicit career choice and almost by definition, insisted that their Christian identity transcended any other. They were aware, moreover, to a greater degree than most of us would have suspected, that Western forms, language, and cultural trappings could complicate or nullify what they considered was their essential witness. But none of this prevented them from acknowledging and glorying in their identities as Westerners and as Americans.

Which is to say that in the missionary context as in its other manifestations the "Christ and culture" dilemma was almost never put to rest by a simple choice. For most missionaries, as for most Christians, such a choice would have seemed unnecessary; but in any case it was just not possible. Customarily, for example, they assumed both a deeply affirming and a sharply critical stance toward their own culture. They were not alienated from it, but neither were they about to identify it, straight out, with Christ or Christianity: preachers and Christian workers did not, just because they became overseas missionaries, cease to feel strongly about debaucheries and structural evils in American society. Since the missionaries, once they had fashioned a satisfactory working relation between their own religious and cultural identities, had to make this formula effective within a quite different milieu, the difficulties in balancing its various elements were especially complex. The missionary's problem was, one might say, the Christ-and-culture problem squared.

Solutions—in particular, the formulas for relating Christian outreach to its Western cultural embodiment and vocabulary—were correspondingly varied, indeed multitudinous; and they of course changed over time as well as in response to the challenges presented by particular overseas situations. One can best chart a path through these mission ideologies, can begin to organize the varied prescriptions without doing violence to them, by calling attention at the outset to the ways in which mission theories affirmed Western and American culture; and then to the ways in which they either disavowed elements of both, or attempted for practical reasons to divorce the Christian message and outreach from the cultural trappings.

The movement in its culturally affirmative mode drew, first of all, upon many of the biblical ideas and metaphors that historians have discerned in American literary expression and the rhetoric of secular expansionism. Convictions about the Adamic or Christlike innocence of the Americans, a national destiny made manifest in biblical prophecy, and America's redemptive role within the divine plan were as evident, especially in the founding years of the missionary movement, as was the biblical injunction to "go into all the world and preach the gospel." The latter, the so-called Great Commission, authorized foreign missions; biblical typologies, read as expressing God's dear intent for the New World societies, explain why the Americans bore special obligations toward foreign missions.

Among the several explanations of America's unique responsibility that were offered by biblical models, the most directly appropriate was the one that had been phrased in the latter part of the seventeenth century as a Puritan "errand into the wilderness." While the imagery of a city on a hill suggested the influence of an exemplary society, that of an errand into the wilderness suggested a heightened activism—the actual transporting of a message and witness to unknown, possibly fearsome and uncivilized places.

Among Puritans and other early Americans who drew on this set of ideas, "wilderness" meant the environment into which the Church flees for protection and nurture, but also the Church's resting-place on the way to triumphs for Christ in a wider world. Insofar as the errand had looked to the saving or improving of others, it had involved a fitful concern about the Indians, and a somewhat steadier sense of obligation toward England and Protestant Europe: colonial spokesmen, during the Cromwellian era and recurrently thereafter, looked to Europe as they elaborated John Winthrop's famous warning that "the eyes of all people are upon us." The more sanguine expected the societies on the North American strand to provide examples, but also active instigation and personnel, for a British and European renovation that must occur before the Church could fulfill her destiny throughout the world.

Such aspirations, limited though they were, ended in defeat. Or so Puritan leaders lamented during their seasons of discouragement. The historian Perry Miller suggested in an influential essay of the 1950s that the Stuart restoration of 1660 persuaded many that, though God was surely noting the successes of his American couriers, Englishmen were not. Miller concluded poignantly that the colonists, with all Europe ignoring and slighting them, found themselves "left alone with America."

Yet the ideal, far from being permanently defeated or suppressed, was revived repeatedly, often in grander forms. The epoch of the American and French revolutions constituted another great cycle of hope and despair; an ecstatic conviction, as the French Revolution began, that wicked old Europe was at least listening and taking note; then a new round of disappointment, lasting from the Thermidorean reaction through the Napoleonic era; and after 1815 a resigned determination on the part of Americans to tend their own garden and come to terms with the American environment. Again the world had not heard, or not heard well; and our frustration, we have thought, helped engender the various forms of cultural nationalism and hemispheric thinking that marked the period from 1820 to the Civil War. Somewhat later, the American retreat from internationalism after the First World War and the Versailles Conference provided merely the most acute latter-day instance of a dialectical process evident throughout American history.

As that term "dialectical" suggests, even the periods that have seemed clearly isolationist or clearly internationalist have shown contrary tendencies that complicate the historian's simpler generalizations. A parochial nationalism after 1815 could be transmuted almost overnight, by a Latin American or Central European revolution, into something recalling older commitments to an American errand. "Young America" in the mid-nineteenth century not only could feel kinship for Young Germany or Young Hungary (as Americans lined the parade routes for the Hungarian insurgent Kossuth); it could also take pride in having provided an example and a set of instructions. The dream of renovating old Europe and the world never fully receded.

The American foreign mission enterprise of the early nineteenth century is best understood not as a majority expression—whether it was that, even at its apogee a hundred years later, can be questioned—but as one of these countercyclical gestures of openness to the world in a period better known for cultural nationalism and relative isolationism. As the movement grew, dispatching some two thousand missionaries over a sixty-year period, it could be said to represent a substantial bloc of Americans who after the disappointments of the Napoleonic era had resolved to do what the preachers of the "Jeremiads" had always instructed them to do at such junctures: to pick themselves up and try again; to repent their own sinfulness as well as indict that of the wicked uncaring world; to reaffirm their covenant with God. In this new version of the errand they would seek to establish "that true Church which is to be as a garden in the wilderness of the world beyond the seas."

Even more than earlier embodiments of the errand ideal, the foreign mission effort placed a premium on activism and motion, doing and going. To set an example, to send forth beams from the American hilltop, was seen as essential but not sufficient. Americans as Christ's special messengers were a people sent as well as chosen. Later, when the movement had grown to huge proportions and great public notice, those who could not go were admonished that the foreign missionaries were couriers on their behalf, that this was the mission of an entire, favored people. In moments of special enthusiasm or compulsiveness, for example during the campus recruitments for the Student Volunteer Movement at the end of the century, Christians were made to feel they must justify, to God if to no one else, a decision not to run the errand themselves. Those with compelling reasons for staying home were in effect expected to pay for a substitute by tithing or otherwise supporting the effort in a sacrificial way.

The missionaries, on their part, were obliged to report back to the home churches. This was not merely to inspire or shame those who stayed behind, or to assure them the job was being done; it was also because the missionaries were considered important to the renovation of their own churches and society. In that respect this nineteenth-century errand retained much of the Puritans' sense of going into the wilderness to nurture and preserve Christ's church. One of the most common arguments for missions (also one of the most problematic as a contribution to the way Americans conceive their relations to others) was that missions must be pursued for the health and fulfillment of the churches at home. Christianity itself would expire, mission publicists warned, if it denied its true nature and ceased to expand all over the world.

Once more, as in the Puritan formulation of the American errand, spokesmen referred constantly to the manner in which God's providence had opened the way for the couriers. In that earlier instance God had provided Protestant winds that defeated Romish armadas or that propelled settlers off-course to New England; he had sent plagues to reduce the numbers of "savages" and make it evident that the white men were to occupy their lands; above all, God had wondrously kept the New World hidden from human knowledge until the Protestant movement had gained leverage against Antichrist and could assure settlement under the auspices of true religion. In the analogous thinking of nineteenth-century mission spokesmen, God had given his signs in the new winds of Western technology and power, in the timely debilitation of rival religions, and in the opening of treaty ports through which religion could flow along with commerce. The potential converts, in both epochs, were said to be pleading with Christ's servants to bring them the Gospel. Whenever the work seemed to be faltering, in the later instance as in the earlier one, the tendency was to conclude, not that God's intent or the natives' wishes had been misinterpreted, but rather that Christians had been failing in their clear obligations.

To propose that the analogies between the Puritan migration and the missionary enterprise are exact, or the continuities complete, would be mistaken and is by no means necessary. What does seem reasonable is to interpret this major nineteenth-century movement, in its American expressions, as rooted both in a Christian, a-nationalistic zeal for expansion and active evangelization, and equally in a fervent belief, less obviously Christian but just as religious, that Americans were under special obligation to save and renovate the world.

In theory, the first of these motivations could have operated without aid from the second. American promoters of foreign missions, conscious of an active and continuing collaboration with British and other European colleagues, could plausibly have contended that Christian world obligations were essentially unrelated to national ideology. In fact, however, they seldom advanced such an argument; they were much less concerned to disentangle Christian missions and the American mission than later apologists have been on their behalf. The religious rationale did have to be primary; and as far as possible the Gospel was to be offered in universal rather than parochial terms. But, given those caveats, spokesmen were comfortable with formulations that pictured a universal, nonparochial faith being carried to the world by certain clearly chosen emissaries by the Protestant West, by the Anglo-Americans, and above all by God's New Israel.

Cultural affirmation in these very fundamental forms deserves to be called a dominant motif in this nineteenth-century version of the American errand. Indeed the affirmations, responding to the youthful enthusiasm of the Americans in nearly all their endeavors, tended to be extreme or at least ebullient. While sharing the Puritans' confidence in the renovating possibilities of Reformed Christianity, the nineteenth century envoys far exceeded the Puritans in their certitude that they represented a society in which the possibilities were being realized. Yet the elements of tension between Christ and culture, between religion the missionaries sought to represent and the civilization or society of which they were a part, qualified this affirmation, greatly complicated the missionaries' task and their seemingly straightforward agenda, and accounted for much of the controversy within and surrounding the movement. Three forms of this tension stand out.

One form, already mentioned, was an intense disapproval of certain features of the sending culture. The missionary coming out of a revivalist tradition was most likely to deplore the sins, back home, that were associated with individual morality, while the "Social Gospel" missionary common in the later stages of the movement deplored collective sins. Because neither was prone to hang out this dirty linen when preaching to benighted heathen, one might be tempted to suppose that such reservations were unimportant. But they were enormously important, and in very practical ways. The missionaries and mission boards frequently clashed with the commercial, the military, and even the diplomatic representatives of their own and other Western countries—with the rumrunners, landgrabbers, slavetraders, and other less flagrantly evil compatriots. The missionary interests, if restrained about discussing these hostilities before foreign audiences, made them part of the rhetoric when exhorting the folks at home. In the latter setting they complained loudly about the ways in which imperfections in the Western societies, of whatever description, were undercutting their best efforts.

Another form of the Christ-and-culture tension, rarely encountered yet providing prophetic counterpoint when it did occur, extended these selective reservations into much broader indictments of the home culture. From the sixteenth-century Spanish priest Bartolomé de Las Casas, railing against a society that had institutionalized Indian slavery: through Roger Williams, proclaiming the superior virtue of the native Americans; the premillennialists and social radicals of the late nineteenth and early twentieth centuries; one could always hear a few voices within the churches and the missionary enterprise raising sharp questions about the purported overall superiority of Western or American civilization.

Far more common than either of these forms of outright hostility was a third form of tension between Christ and culture that related less to missionary ideals than to missionary practice. Mission theorists debated incessantly about the extent to which Western and American culture, however one might evaluate them, were what the missionary was commissioned to transmit; whether the cultural baggage the missionary carried did not in fact get in the way of his or her proper business. . . .

A persistent minority, throughout the history of the missionary movement, questioned the right to impose one's own cultural forms, however God-given and glorious; and doubted the complementary "right" to suppress or seek to displace another culture, however crude or benighted. When an abstract right of cultural displacement was conceded (as it usually was, especially in the early decades), the question nonetheless arose whether it was politic to act on that right; whether the urging of particular cultural forms aided or impeded the reception of the religious message. Finally, if one did espouse aggressive civilizing aims, serious questions remained about the sequence: must one educate and civilize before evangelization can be effective? Or should one concentrate upon evangelization, confident that civilization will follow? Or should the two processes be simultaneous?

Here again, as in the matter of cultural self-criticism, we could question whether tortured, seemingly abstract issues of "evangelization or civilization" carried much meaning for working missionaries, or even for mission executives with their tidy public pronouncements. Certainly the executives and theorists . . . spent more time and ink on these controverted issues than on the straightforward advocacy and cheerleading for which they were best known. From the beginning, mission boards, executives, and all but the most superficial advocates dealt constantly with the "cultural" questions: whether or not to teach in English; whether to send out "farmers and mechanicks" or only preachers; how to relate to governments and other secular entities.

As for missionaries in the field (it is well to remember, incidentally, that many theorists had themselves been missionaries in the field), they not only cared about such issues; they confronted them as matters of daily experience, as truly agonizing questions affecting their own sense of duty and purpose. The dispiriting gap between the generally tiny harvests of converts and the plethora of successful civilizing ventures (a gap that was not emphasized in reports to the home churches, yet was well understood by both missionaries and executives) made the issue of "civilizing or evangelizing" a personal and often painful one for devoted workers who had been recruited to evangelize the world. Even for the many missionaries, perhaps a majority, who went about their teaching or healing with little sense of personal strain, the questions that others were debating as grand theory impinged in a thousand disconcerting ways. Whether the captive audiences of proud Moslems or Buddhists in a hospital ward were to be preached to and prayed over, or just healed, was the sort of symbolic and practical issue that could determine the nature, and sometimes the fate, of any missionary endeavor.

Both for individual missionaries and for the movement at large, moreover, the build-in difficulties were intensified by outside criticism that, intentionally or not, presented them with a classic "no-win situation." If, recognizing the dangers and counterproductive effects of imposing their cultural forms, they resolved to preach "Christ only," they would be criticized for ignoring the need for material and social amelioration. If they came to see, intuitively or otherwise, that the attempt to undermine someone's religion is the ultimate cultural aggression; and if, as happened repeatedly, they therefore turned from proselytizing to social amelioration coupled with personal witness; they were then criticized as relatively unsanctified promoters of Western technology and ideology. If, finally, they tried to ignore criticism and go about their business for Christ, they were rewarded with a reputation for insular thinking.

All three missionary responses were common, and all are highly important to an understanding of the changing contours of the movement. The third stance—Bunyan's brave "I'll care not what men say"—was probably the most usual reaction. As such it goes far to explain what was most mundanely productive. But it also helps account for a fortress mentality more intense and pervasive than that of most other religious movements.

None of this means that the dilemmas of missions and of missionary rationales were manufactured by captious critics. The quandaries were real enough, and indeed intrinsic not just to this enterprise but, it would seem, to any venture in which one culture attempts to apply its ideals and technologies to the supposed benefit of another.

By the same token, the dilemmas are still with us. This is not to say that the historian's criticism is out of order; the missionaries and their sponsors were guilty of miscalculations and lapses of logic that are such not merely in privileged hindsight by the light of their own knowledge and their own Bible. Yet the fact that a later, purportedly more enlightened age makes similar errors in a more dangerous world means that any wholesale condescension toward the religious and cultural ambassadors of an earlier century would be clearly be inappropriate. . . .

Women Missionaries and Cultural Conquest

JANE HUNTER

SOURCE: From *The Gospel of Gentility: American Women Missionaries in Turn-of-the-Century China* by Jane Hunter. Copyright © 1984 by Yale University Press. Reprinted with permission.

To American women, more than to any others on earth, is committed the exalted privilege of extending over the world those blessed influences, which are to renovate degraded man, and "to clothe all climes with beauty."

—Catharine Beecher, *A Treatis on Domestic Economy* (1842)

Catharine Beecher's practical guide of the nineteenth-century housewife included this tribute to the glorious possibilities of the woman's sphere. Woman's chores might seem menial and inconsequential, but she should make no mistake: well executed in the proper spirit, they contained enormous power. Through her improving influence on her husband and children, she might reform American society. By introducing her special qualities into the public arena, through schoolteaching or church work, she might reform all peoples. Diffused beyond her home, woman's nurture and refinement carried the miraculous potential to conquer and redeem the entire world.

Even as Beecher wrote, the female voluntary societies of the Christian benevolent empire were working to fulfill her mandate. Women's "cent" and "mite" societies gathered housewives' extra pennies to add women's subsidies to the support of the foreign missionary movement. Female supporters thrilled to the courage and heroism of young missionary women who accompanied their husbands to the jungles of Asia and Africa, and who suffered and perished nobly there. After the Civil War, American women founded agencies of their own to send unmarried female missionaries to the heathen in foreign lands. By 1890, the married women of the general missionary boards and the single women of the women's boards together composed 60 percent of the mission force.

Simultaneous with the feminization of the mission force, the movement became important to a nation newly intrigued by the possibilities of international expansion. Empire seemed to offer an appealing resolution to the dissonance between growing industrial capacity and the limits of the American frontier. It promised new markets for American goods, new challenges for the American spirit, new moral wilderness for American civilization. The Spanish-American War inspired a burst of fresh support for the flagging foreign mission movement. Even after passions for territorial expansion had cooled, the mission movement would continue to tap a rich vein of American nationalism.

Throughout the nineteenth century, women's contributions to the American missionary impulse were unique both in style and substance. In accordance with their stations within American families, women relied particularly on "blessed influence" rather than on direct authority to win compliance from other peoples. Their approach was intimate and personal rather than directive. They associated their Christian mission with their domestic responsibility to instill moral character ("to renovate degraded man") and to breed refinement (to "clothe all climes with beauty"). As in their homes, women's moral and material responsibilities were closely connected. Their special concern with the details of domestic life made them both the most dedicated and the most successful emissaries of an entire civilization. As one of the celebrants of the missionary enterprise put it, "Every home they set up, every school they establish, is an object lesson in the art of living." . . .

The Protestant women who volunteered for missionary service represented an important sector of the native-born population. Women of an appropriate background might gravitate toward mission service for any number of reasons, ranging from a divine call to a family death, from marriage to a male missionary to accommodation to spinsterhood. Like other American women of the late Victorian period, missionary volunteers participated in a national, feminine culture reinforced by church institutions, publishers of women's periodicals, and producers of domestic bric-a-brac. Missionary service represented a courageous decision but not an extraordinary one, and those who made it shared many values and attitudes with schoolteachers and ministers' wives at home. . . .

As China became more receptive to the lessons of the West, the American missionary force in China increased rapidly; it more than doubled between 1890 and 1905, and by 1919 had more than doubled again, to thirty-three hundred workers. This rapid growth in the American force reflected a resurgent interest in missions accompanying late-nineteenth-century American expansion, and a particular enthusiasm for the development of the "New China" rising from the ashes of the Boxer debacle. By the early twentieth century, American missionaries seeking a hearing from the Chinese had replaced their reliance on military force with a reliance on the broad appeals of their culture. American national leaders supported this shift in strategy, and with missionaries, sought cultural rather than political empire in China. . . .

The treaty accompanying the end of the Opium War granted missionaries and Chinese converts the right to practice Christianity in five coastal cities. But missionaries were largely unsuccessful in converting the heathen of the treaty ports. Their struggles to acquire land within the walls of such cities as Foochow excited antipathies, and popular association of them with the sailors and merchants of the opium trade did not enhance their stature. One Canton native described the Westerner as one who "loved to beat people and to rob and murder" and often "could be seen reeling drunk." Missionaries succeeded in winning their first convert in Foochow only after a decade of proselytizing in the crowded streets. By the end of 1860, four years later, the fifty missionaries from several denominations could still count only sixty-six converts.

The Treaty of Tientsin (1858) extended rights to proselytize to the countryside, and there missionaries discovered more fruitful territory. Using Chinese workers, hired and trained as they went, missionaries poured more energy into opening outstations, shifting their focus from the major ports. By 1880, for example, the Congregational missionaries at Foochow had opened ninety-six new outstations in the countryside with Chinese help, and claimed three thousand new adherents. Outstations were the scenes of some of the greatest victories; perhaps not surprisingly, they were also the scenes of some of the greatest victories; perhaps not surprisingly, they were also the scenes of frequent antiforeign disturbances. The less sophisticated peoples of the interior were both more susceptible to the heterodox appeals of Christian ritual and more suspicious of its magical powers.

When missionaries were threatened, they unambivalently called for protection. "Missionary incidents" of the 1860s, 1870s, and 1880s, in which outraged Chinese attacked foreign intruders, involved far more French Catholics and British than American, but property disputes and popular outbreaks occasionally sent American missionaries to their legation demanding that their rights be defended or avenged. At the time of the Boxer uprising in 1900, of course, voices from the field were particularly loud. They demanded full American participation in any allied European military solution and vigorously protested the early withdrawal of American troops. The retaliatory raids of American board missionaries William Ament and Gardner Tewksbury received immediate coverage, first by *The New York Sun* and then by Mark Twain, in his famous essay, "To the Person Sitting in Darkness." . . .

. . . Church and state found . . . common ground during the early decades of the twentieth century. Wary political leaders and missionary supporters of the social gospel converged in a campaign for American influence rather than empire in China. The attendance at a 1900 Conference on Missions in New York suggested what would be a new compromise coalition of American leaders supporting informal empire in China. In addition to noted imperialists Admiral George Dewey and Alfred Mahan, many opponents of empire also attended. Former President Benjamin Harrison, the honorary president of the conference, had refused to endorse McKinley that year because of his expansionist policies. And Grover Cleveland, also in attendance, like most Democrats opposed territorial aggrandizement. Supporters of American empire considered Christian religion a necessary accompaniment to American expansionism, and in some cases the very justification for it. (In fact, the patriotic and militarist enthusiasms of the Spanish-American War were responsible for a needed outpouring of contributions to the mission cause.) But when the costs of imperialism because apparent, American leaders withdrew their support for political expansion and used mission organizations as a partial strategy to retain the exhilaration of empire without paying its bills or taking on its corrupting responsibilities. . . .

Missionaries remained ambivalent about commercial efforts to introduce the products of the West into China. Women favored the importation of some goods, such as oil and sewing machines, but like women reformers at home, they fought a vigorous battle against efforts to disseminate Western vices. The introduction of such products as alcohol and cigarettes discredited the moral claims of the West, as had opium imports before, but it also threatened to draw souls already benighted by heathendom further from the missionary grasp. Missionary women felt that China itself was at contest in their competition with Western vice industries. Sarah

Goodrich, an early representative of the China chapter of the Women's Christian Temperance Union, launched a concerted attack on the British American Tobacco Company and its goal to put "a cigarette in the mouth of every man, woman and child in China." Imported liquor never became a major problem in China except with the foreign community, but Goodrich's participation in the WCTU suggests that at some level and for some women, the missionary battles of China were the same as those of women reformers in the United States. . . .

Missionary men as well as women sometimes spoke as self-appointed advocates for China. But women were more likely than men to express sympathy for China's powerlessness at the hands of the West. The reaction of American women in China to the Boxer uprising presents an opportunity to contrast male and female attitudes. . . .

. . . Luella Miner remarked that for all the Boxer atrocities there had been no incidents of Chinese rape, and Emma Martin wrote, "It is just outrageous the way the allied powers especially the soldiers have behaved in China. If our indemnities have to come out of the poor people I don't feel as if I want any." Sarah Conger, whose husband was the American minister to Peking, wrote a letter of sympathy for the Chinese position shortly after her release: "Poor China! Why cannot foreigners let her alone with her own? China has been wronged, and in her desperation she has striven as best she could to stop the inroads, and to blot out those already made. My sympathy is with China. A very unpopular thing to say but it is an honest conviction, honestly uttered." . . . Sarah Conger reacted differently from her husband, who favored decisive reprisals. The previous year Edwin Conger had proposed that the United States seize the province of Chihli, which included the capital Peking, as a base in China.

Women like Sarah Conger and Emma Martin responded to intrusions on Chinese sovereignty with sensibilities that they seldom used to defend their own autonomy as women. Lida Ashmore, for instance, who acquiesced in her husband's domination of her daily life, criticized him sharply for a constriction of Chinese rights. When he suggested that a Chinese missionary society consult with foreign representatives, Lida Ashmore wrote, "they did not like it. You could see how they would resent asking a foreigner if they could go into a field to work, where no work is done, when they are Chinese and this is China." Lucy Mead, with other American women not yet eligible for the vote in the United States, wrote possessively of China, "Why can't we decide what kind of government we want, no matter what our neighbor advises?" Like many other missionary women, Lucy Mead did not comment on public affairs in the United States, nor did she protest the lack of a voice in determining public policy. Yet Japanese threats to Chinese prerogative inspired her instinctive, proprietary ire. Of course, American missionary women never surrendered their own interests to China's, but at some level they identified the two. In defending China, they defended their own right to feel responsible, competent, empowered.

American women were also defending a female kind of authority when they defended China. According to the tenets of domestic ideology, authority was best applied directly, it should be done according to rules of decorum. Luella Miner wrote that she was particularly offended by a medial imprinted as a memento for the survivors of the siege: "I do not at all approve of the design on one side, Europe, America and Japan trampling on the Dragon. . . . I object to this first because it isn't true to fact, as the dragon came out on the top side, and second because it isn't polite." . . .

Like the anti-imperialist Mugwumps, missionary women lacked a political base and tended to oppose the exercise of military, imperial, or commercial power in which they could have no part. Instead they mounted a moral crusade based on premises of social elitism which played up to their perceptions of themselves as guardians and founts of civilization. This women's crusade, for once in the early twentieth century, corresponded with the interests and policies of the American government in China. The American decision to preserve an open door and to work to maintain Chinese sovereignty enhanced the importance of missionary influence to American purposes and also encouraged a shared posture of national righteousness. . . .

The Protestant missionary effort was unsuccessful in achieving the wide-scale conversions in China hoped for by the American churches. In contrast to Africa, where entire tribes fell under Christian sway, Chinese conditions were not conducive to mass conversion. Official hostility and a strong state orthodoxy, combined with the thriving heterodox Taoist and Buddhist folk traditions, left little room for a demanding and exclusive Christian God. The precariousness of the Chinese economy, however, presented opportunities to missionaries which Christian ideology alone could not have done. The Taiping uprising and the colonial wars of the mid-nineteenth century added political unrest to the ongoing problems of population expansion, and the once stable Manchu court began to lose control. Family and clan organizations helped provide relief to those left helpless by the century's devastations, but many destitute remained for missionaries to approach with the possibilities they offered for employment, for schooling, and many Chinese thought, for legal intercession. As one woman put it, "the unspeakable conditions of physical suffering constitute both our call and our opportunity to minister."

Women in China, as in most societies, suffered disproportionately in hard times. Considered economic liabilities, they were less valued at time of birth and more subject to abandonment or sale in times of famine. At marriage, women were cut off from friends and family and transferred as property to husbands and families they knew little of. Though a woman's family, particularly her brothers, retained some responsibility for her well-being, only the most visible and well-substantiated abuse could free her from a disastrous match. Missionaries gained their early converts from a disadvantaged class; the significant numbers of women converts could be explained in part by the disadvantages of their sex.

Tales of abandoned children, daughters rescued from sale or death, and women saved from cruel mothers-in-law and brutal husbands filled missionary letters and propaganda. In the retelling, they assumed the proportions of melodrama. Jessie Ankeny wrote of a woman who overtook her in the road and "told me about her daughter who was about to commit suicide because of the cruelty of the mother-in law 'Ah let me give her to you and you can do with her as you like—let her study of be your *slave*'!" Emma Martin, too, wrote of a woman attempting suicide to escape a "wretch" of a husband; she had been adopted by a Bible woman "till she can find new courage to live." Ella Glover provided care for a sick woman whose mother-in-law, according to mission story, had instructed her "never mind, let her die." Although the numbers and the circumstances of needy women were exploited and perhaps exaggerated, they were not fabricated. Women missionaries working in China used their abilities to offer economic and institutional support to the needy as perhaps their most powerful means of recruiting loyal converts and Christian workers. . . .

When missionary women encouraged Chinese women's independence, they incurred responsibilities to provide them with support and protection. Missions offered a variety of occupations to uprooted Chinese women, including training as teachers and nurses for young women, training as Bible women to assist in the preaching of the gospel for older women, and assorted menial jobs as cooks, seam-stresses, and amahs for women of all ages. These occupations were frequently tem-porary and did not guarantee security, but they did offer short-term relief. Christian women, as well as many Christian men, found that their religion cut them off from old sources of support. The gradually narrowing restriction of support to the mission community inevitably increased the personal dependence of Chinese Chris-tians on foreign missionaries. . . .

The women's missionary enterprise . . . never departed far in theory from the domestic ideology which sanctioned it. Woman's extended responsibility for nur-ture allowed her to teach school and care for the sick, but the home remained her central province and sentiment her central strategy of conversion. Missionary women carried on a personal evangelism which aimed to gain access to women's houses and their hearts. Anna Kauffman explained her belief that the "greatest sphere for any woman is the sphere of the home," which influenced her plan to bring her "deepest and best vision of home and womanhood" to the homes that most needed it. "I have found no greater opportunity than to place my life in the rising homes of China," she wrote. Gaining access to those "rising homes" presented missionar-ies with major challenges. The missionary women of Peking, Luella Miner wrote in 1893, had had no success at all in securing admission to family courtyards. Nellie Russell of T'ungchow, however, with her more winning style, had succeeded in gaining access to over thirty homes "and is making the work boom."

Even for those who taught Chinese girls in schools, entry to the Chinese home remained symbolically important. Miss R. J. Miller, who ran a Presbyterian girls' school in T'ungchow, frequently went on three-week trips through the country-side visiting the homes of her schoolgirls. Her reason for these trips, she explained, was that "it brings these girls nearer to me." Entry to the home represented an important physical analogue for the entry to the heart which was the ultimate missionary goal.

Justifying their service on the basis of the uniqueness of their gifts, missionary women emphasized the power of Christian love to stimulate individual conversion. Of course, the evangelical tradition which spawned the mission movement had always placed a strong emphasis on the power of love and a faith founded on feeling. Whether the large female church memberships of the nineteenth century encouraged this emotional strategy or were recruited by it is unclear. But, as Ann Douglas has argued, as the century progressed, Protestant religion and female culture became sentimentalized in tandem. Distinctions between the evangelism of men and women were reinforced by the ordination requirements of the majority of the Protestant churches. Male preachers assembled congregations to hear the Word, while women were more likely to "look love." . . .

Ideally, the missionary encounter consisted of an effusion of encouragement and love on the part of the missionary, manifested in soulful eye contact and frequently a held hand, to be met with an outpouring of guilt and remorse, leading to conversion, on the part of the potential convert. The intensity of the individual attention was the key. When YWCA evangelist Ruth Paxson came to China in 1918, she emphasized that souls could be conquered only one at a time. Missionaries customarily targeted particularly promising souls in advance. Congregationalist Sarah Goodrich hoped to "get hold of the heart of young Mrs. Wei," and added, "I covet her womanhood for Christ," When a Baptist woman's "special one" had become a believer, she selected another, a friend wrote. Anna Hartwell wanted every Christian to be a "soul-winner" and seemed to advocate totting up souls as if they were scalps, when she described a dying Chinese woman as "one of the trophies our Tommie [Jane Thompson] will lay at the Savior's feet." . . .

The Christian conversion involved . . . a surrender of will itself. With such high stakes missionaries ardently entered the fray. Luella Huelster described one conversion battle:

> Gwei Lan's whole body was in a tremor. Her teacher, sitting beside her, took her hands and held them firmly in her own as she prayed that the soul-struggle, so evidently going on, might cease. She hastily penned an informal little pledge and placed it in Gwei Lan's hands; but she, reading it, smiled and shook her head in negation; she was not ready to sign it. But the Father coveted her, and less than ten minutes had passed before the little pledge, which no other eyes were to see, was quietly signed and slipped into the teacher's hand, and Gwei Lan was on her feet.

Gwei Lan's surrender was a victory not only for the Lord but also for his insistent aide, who in His name had presumed an awesome intimacy. . . .

Missionaries did not find the Chinese easy to influence, and that perhaps helps to explain their particular preoccupation with this problem. Chinese propriety demanded polite toleration of a stranger's viewpoint. Missionaries railed with frustration at the impenetrable "face" which thwarted their efforts to get in "vital touch." They complained about problems ranging from the lack of student responsiveness in class to the formalism of the Chinese religious tradition, but their dissatisfactions stemmed from a fundamental difference in the etiquette of emotion. . . .

Although missionaries admired Confucian ethics, they agreed that Chinese religion lacked feeling and "hasn't the life." They considered Chinese obeisance to Taoist and Buddhist deities to be empty ritual. "Keeping up appearances before the images seems to be the sole end of religion, if one can judge from outward show," Elsie Clark wrote. Monona Cheney judged that she "had more comprehension of things spiritual at five years old" than most Chinese did at seventy-five, so "narrow and materialist" were their backgrounds. Even when Chinese did accept Christianity, missionaries worried that they did so in the wrong spirit. There is much evidence for Elsie Clark's impression that many times converts simply added Christian sacraments to Taoist and Buddhist practices. "Christian religion is made a fetish to many of these people. Prayer and the Holy Spirit are to them tools to be used, forces to have on one's side, magic to be evoked," Clark wrote. With probably less basis, Clara Foster saw Christian belief in China as a rational decision within a Confucian tradition and thought that such belief lacked "the sorrow for sin and the joy of knowing Christ as their Savior which are experienced in the homeland." She went on, "They are ready to talk glibly of all being great sinners and only by accepting Christ's righteousness can we be saved, but somehow it is difficult for them to make it a personal matter."

Helping Chinese to make it "a personal matter" was at the heart of the missionary's self-appointed task in China. Professional, religious, and feminine traditions would have directed women toward personal work in any case, but the stubbornness of Chinese cultural resistance seemed to intensify missionary efforts. Their instructions in character became also lessons in culture. Alice Reed lamented that the Chinese lack entirely "what we call pep," and Agnes Scott, who had taught music at Fukien Christian College, felt that music offered an important emotional outlet to students and gave the school "college spirit." In 1894 Luella Miner delighted that "our Chinese associates are learning better every year how to be informal and 'folksy,'" but Frederica Mead in 1915 still lamented that "our girls have lots to learn in being at ease in entertaining and loosing themselves in the fun of it." When missionaries stressed the personal nature of their work, they were in part stressing the fundamental changes they were seeking. Their lessons in Christian "character" frequently also fostered Western personality.

Missionaries' highest triumphs came when they could participate in a moment of personal transformation. Usually the moment involved a debate within an individual between "right" and "face." Florence Manly remembered some private talks with a Christian "in which my view of what he ought to do meant losing face and was at first intolerable to him, but I held firm and he finally gave in." When the potential convert had been recalcitrant, the victory was most gratifying. Lucy Mead described the resistance of one girl in her school to the conversion efforts of a YWCA evangelist:

> She came to the first meeting and sat thru it with a straight back, arms folded, and scorn on her face, even all thru the prayer. The next meeting was about the same

attitude, an occasional expression in the following meetings betrayed a struggle in her soul, still she would not admit it, the girls still worked and all prayed. As she started to the last meeting she said with pride and scorn "She can't touch me, I'm not going to be affected by anything she says."

When by the end of the service she had confessed her sins and surrendered her pride, her missionary sponsors were euphoric. Clearly, delight in conquering such a proud resister exceeded the delight in a less challenging conquest, though both alike totted up a soul for God. . . .

The Western infatuation with Asian people has been compared to a masculine desire for possession. [The novelist] Pearl Buck portrayed her father as emotionally impotent in his relations with his family, as a man who could only find enthusiasm among the Chinese he felt superior to. "I think he felt about souls very much as some people feel about eggs," Buck wrote. "He wanted them brown." Only through racial domination, Buck implied, could her father feel sexually and emotionally competent. Edward Said, too, has employed the metaphor of male sexual possession to explain the protective condescension and benign violation which French Orientalists expressed toward the supine East. Han Su-yin's account of the Belgian railroad man who befriended her as a Eurasian schoolgirl in Peking presented the metaphor most dramatically:

> Like so many Europeans in China, Joseph Hers began to "love" China, a fierce, dominating, anxious, all-conquering possessiveness, characteristic of the warped, twisted, and altogether vicious relationships miscalled "love" between the dominating and the suppressed; the powerful and the weak; the spoiler and the cheated. Like many other foreigners he expressed this "love" in sexual imagery; to all of them, China was the WOMAN, the all-enveloping, soft, weak women, who actually welcomed rape, welcomed being invaded. "Don't worry, China is feminine, she has always ended by absorbing all her conquerors," was their favourite explanation, and Hers said this too when I spoke about the Japanese. A great part of this love for China was their attraction to Chinese women; none of them, I think, realized how much this was resented by the Chinese. . . .

Missionary women's love for China shared some of the condescension and arrogance which Han saw in Joseph Hers; yet the sexual basis of the metaphor must, at least temporarily, ally missionary women with Asia itself. Both felt, without fully knowing, the threat which Western masculine authority posed to their autonomy. Both felt without articulating it their need for unconstricted life. Before arriving in China, missionary women expressed their ambition in a conventional vocabulary of self-sacrifice and Christian service rather than in the big terms with which they celebrated their later triumphs. Those who discovered the richness of experience in

China had been seeking more modest rewards. Docile and sometimes frail, missionary women anticipated a more useful life doing the Lord's work in China, but they could not imagine the way in which colonial inequalities would cancel out American sexual imbalances and help them to liberation.

Once in China, however, the balance tipped too far. The politics of fulfillment has rarely been democratic, and the richness of life afforded one group inevitably occurs at cost to another. Missionaries did offer economic opportunities and educational advantages to Chinese men and women, but these advantages often came at the expense of Chinese independence and pride. Women differed from men in the intimacy of their missionary contacts and the nature of their evangelical techniques, but they frequently shared with men a sense of the limitless reaches of their authority. An article published in 1911, the year of the Chinese revolution, explained the exhaustive responsibility of women missionaries: "What the Chinese learn to do, we must first do for them. The most startling thing to be realized back of that statement is the fact that what the Chinese *live*, we must first live for them." Although there were many distinctions between men and women in turn-of-the-century America, conservative Protestant women could share with men an appreciation for personal freedom and vocational competence and also an enthusiasm for the possibilities of power.

Questions for Reflection and Discussion

1. Summarize the variety of religious opinions about America's empire-building a century ago.

2. Describe the convergence of American secular and sacred interests abroad as described by Robert Handy.

3. What evidence does William Hutchison provide that American missionaries made a significant contribution to the blending of secular and sacred interests abroad?

4. How does Jane Hunter's discussion of women missionaries in China illustrate one or more of the four dimensions of religious tension?

5. Why did Americans divide over the issue of empire-building?

6. How did the tension between secular and sacred interests abroad produce a form of "the Christ-and-culture tension"?

Additional Readings

Beisner, Robert L. *Twelve Against Empire: The Anti-Imperialists, 1898-1900*. New York: McGraw-Hill Books Co., 1968.

Breslin, Thomas A. *China, American Catholicism, and the Missionary.* University Park: Pennsylvania State University Press, 1980.

Carpenter, Joel and Wilbert R. Shenk, eds. *Earthen Vessels: American Evangelicals and Foreign Missions, 1880-1980.* Grand Rapids: Eerdmans Publishing Co., 1990.

Cherry, Conrad, ed. *God's New Israel: Religious Interpretations of American Destiny.* Revised and Updated Edition. Chapel Hill: University of North Carolina Press, 1998.

Cowen, Paul A. *China and Christianity: The Missionary Movement and the Growth of Chinese Antiforeignism, 1860-1870.* Cambridge: Harvard University Press, 1963.

Fairbank, John K., ed., *The Missionary Enterprise in China and America.* Cambridge: Harvard University Press, 1963.

Flynt, Wayne, and Gerald W. Berkeley. *Taking Christianity to China.* Tuscaloosa: University of Alabama Press, 1997.

Horsman, Reginald. *Race and Manifest Destiny: The Origins of American Racial Anglo-Saxonism.* Cambridge: Harvard University Press, 1981.

MacKenzie, Kenneth M. *The Robe and the Sword: The Methodist Church and the Rise of American Imperialism.* Washington, D.C.: Public Affairs Press, 1961.

May, Ernest. *Imperial Democracy: The Emergence of America as a Great Power.* Chicago: Imprint Publications, 1991.

Pratt, Julius W. *Expansionists of 1898: The Acquisition of Hawaii and the Spanish Islands.* Baltimore: The Johns Hopkins University Press, 1936.

Stephanson, Anders. *Manifest Destiny: American Expansion and the Empire of Right.* New York: Hill and Wang, 1995.

Tuveson, Ernest L. *Redeemer Nation: The Idea of America's Millennial Role.* Chicago: University of Chicago Press, 1968.

Weinberg, Albert K. *Manifest Destiny: A Study of Nationalist Expansionism in American History.* Gloucester, Mass.: Peter Smith, 1958.

Chapter 12

Fundamentalism vs. Modernism

Issue

What were the factors that divided Protestants at the beginning of the 20th century?

In his monumental work A Religious History of the American People *(1972), Sydney E. Ahlstrom states that "No aspect of American church history is more in need of summary and yet so difficult to summarize as the movements of dissent and reaction that occurred between the Civil War and World War I." Recognizing that the reasons for the difficulty are obscure, he observes that "After 1865 the problems of Reconstruction, urbanization, immigration, natural science, and modern culture destroyed the great evangelical consensus [of the pre-Civil War period], leaving a situation wherein dissenters were merely angry and frustrated." All of this eventually led to a showdown when "conservatives and liberals simply lost contact with each other, both culturally and religiously."*

What were fundamentalism and modernism, and why was the pre-Civil War evangelical consensus replaced by conflicts between these two warring factions in the early decades of the twentieth century? In his Fundamentalism and American Culture: The Shaping of Twentieth-Century Evangelicalism, 1870-1925 *(1980), George M. Marsden defines fundamentalism as "a loose, diverse and changing federation of co-belligerents united by their fierce opposition to modernist attempts to bring Christianity into line with modern thought." In the midst of the fundamentalist-modernist controversy in 1924, liberal theologian Shailer Mathews defined modernism (also known on some fronts as liberalism) as "the use of the methods of modern science to find, state and use the permanent and central values of inherited orthodoxy in meeting the needs of a modern world." Hence, modernists utilized "the results of scientific research as data with which to think religiously."*

Taken together, Ahlstrom, Marsden, and Mathews suggest that the same social and economic forces of secularism that forged the social gospel in the late nineteenth century were at work then and early into the next century to create sharp theological divisions in American Protestantism. In the wake of World War I, when optimism was high for a unified nation, denominational rivalries and conflicts erupted into the fundamentalist-modernist controversy. Fundamentalists coalesced as a distinct movement, and the differences that had developed over several decades produced a battle both within the churches and the culture as a whole. As a critical issue, the controversy left lasting marks on America's religious landscape.

Early in the conflict conservative theologian J. Gresham Machen drew his line in the sand, declaring, "A separation between the two parties [fundamentalists and modernists] in the Church is the crying need of the hour." What were the principal worldview differences between conservative fundamentalists and liberal modernists? How did these differences translate into denominational and theological warfare? Why was this a critical issue for American religion?

Documents

The Fundamentals *were published in twelve paperback volumes from 1910 to 1915 as a response to modernist teaching during the previous decades. In the first document, Jean Frederic Bettex, a professor of science and apologetics in Stuttgart, Germany, provides his opinion of modern criticism in his article "The Bible and Modern Criticism." In the second selection, an editorial in the conservative Baptist publication* The Watchman *responds to a rival Baptist publication's claim in 1921 that fundamentalism was dead. The next year the popular liberal Baptist preacher Harry Emerson Fosdick launched a liberal counteroffensive in his sermon titled "Shall the Fundamentalists Win?" Excerpts from the sermon appear in the third document. In the fourth selection, conservative professor of New Testament at Princeton Seminary, J. Gresham Machen, presents his view of liberalism (modernism). The liberal* Christian Century *editorializes in the final document that the fundamentalist-modernist controversy is essentially a clash between a traditional view and a modern view of the world.*

1. The Bible and Modern Criticism, 1910–1915

SOURCE: From *The Fundamentals: the Famous Sourcebook of Foundational Biblical Truths* by R. A. Torrey. Pp. 29-31, 32-33. Copyright © 1958, 1990 by Biola University and Kregel Classics. Reprinted with permission.

How does the Bible prove itself to be a divinely inspired, heaven-given book, a communication from a Father to His children, and thus a revelation?

First, by the fact that, as does no other sacred book in the world, it condemns man and all his works. It does not praise either his wisdom, his reason, his art, or any progress that he has made; but it represents him as being in the sight of God, a miserable sinner, incapable of doing anything good, and deserving only death and endless perdition. Truly, a book which is able thus to speak, and in consequence causes millions of men, troubled in conscience, to prostrate themselves in the dust, crying, "God be merciful to me a sinner," must contain more than mere ordinary truth.

Secondly, the Bible exalts itself far above all merely human books by its announcement of the great incomprehensible mystery that, "God so loved the world that He gave His only begotten Son; that whosoever believeth in Him should not perish, but have everlasting life" (John 3:16). Where is there a god among all the heathen nations, be he Osiris, Brahma, Baal, Jupiter or Odin, that would have promised those people that, by taking upon himself the sin of the world and suffering its punishment, he would thus become a savior and redeemer to them?

Thirdly, the Bible sets the seal of its divine origin upon itself by means of the prophecies. Very appropriately does God inquire, through the prophet Isaiah, "Who, as I, shall call, and shall declare it, and set it in order for Me since I established the ancient people? and the things that are coming and shall come to pass, let them declare" (Ch. 44:7). Or says again, "I am God, declaring the end from the beginning, and from ancient times, things not yet done, saying, My counsel shall stand, and I will do all My pleasure; calling a ravenous bird from the east, and the man of My counsel from a far country. Yea, I have spoken, I will also bring it to pass; I have purposed, I will also do it" (Ch. 46:10, 11). Or, addressing Pharaoh, "Where are thy wise men, and let them tell thee, and let them know what the Lord of Hosts hath purposed upon Egypt" (Ch. 19:12). Again we say, where is there a god, or gods, a founder of religion, such as Confucius, Buddha, or Mohammed, who could, with such certainty, have predicted the future of even his own people? Or where is there a statesman who in these times can foretell what will be the condition of things in Europe one hundred or even ten years from now? Nevertheless the prophecies of Moses and his threatened judgments upon the Israelites have been literally fulfilled. Literally also have been fulfilled (although who at the time would have believed it?) the prophecies respecting the destruction of those great ancient cities, Babylon, Nineveh, and Memphis. Moreover, in a literal way has been fulfilled what the prophets David and Isaiah foresaw concerning the last sufferings of Christ—His death on the cross, His drinking of vinegar, and the casting of lots for His garments. There are also other prophecies which will still be most literally fulfilled, such as the promises made to Israel, the final judgment, and the end of the world. "For," as Habakkuk says, "the vision is yet for an appointed time, and will not lie. Though it tarry, wait for it; it will surely come" (Ch. 2:3).

Fourthly, the Bible has demonstrated its peculiar power by its influence with the martyrs. Think of the hundreds of thousands who, at different times and among different peoples, have sacrificed their all, their wives, their children, all their possessions, and finally life itself, on account of this book. Think of how they have, on the rack and at the stake, confessed the truth of the Bible, and born testimony to its power.

Lastly, the Bible shows itself every day to be a divinely given book by its beneficent influence among all kinds of people. It converts to a better life the ignorant and the learned, the beggar on the street and the king upon his throne, yonder poor woman dwelling in an attic, the greatest poet and the profoundest thinker, civilized persons and uncultured savages. Despite all the scoffing and derision of its enemies, it has been translated into hundreds of languages, and has been preached by thousands of missionaries to millions of people. It makes the proud humble and the dissolute virtuous; it consoles the unfortunate, and teaches man how to live patiently and die triumphantly. No other book or collection of books accomplishes for man the exceeding great benefits accomplished by this book of truth.

Modern Criticism and Its Rationalistic Method

In these times there has appeared a criticism which, constantly growing bolder in its attacks upon this sacred book, now decrees, with all self-assurance and confidence, that it is simply a human production. Besides other faults found with it, it is declared to be full of errors, many of its books to be spurious, written by unknown men at later dates than those assigned, etc., etc. The fundamental principle upon which this verdict is based is, as Renan expressed it, reason is capable of judging all things, but is itself judged by nothing. However, a purely rational revelation would certainly be a contradiction of terms; besides, it would be wholly superfluous. But when reason undertakes to speak of things entirely supernatural, invisible and eternal, it talks as a blind man does about colors, discoursing of things concerning which it neither knows nor can know anything; and thus it makes itself ridiculous. It has not ascended up to heaven, neither has it descended into the deep; and, therefore, a purely rational religion is no religion at all. . . .

What Are the Fruits of This Criticism?

In the classroom it ensnares, in lecture halls it makes great pretences, for mere popular lectures it is still serviceable; but when the thunders of God's power break in upon the soul, when despair at the loss of all one has loved takes possession of the mind, when remembrance of a miserable lost life or of past misdeeds is felt and realized, when one is on a sickbed and death approaches, and the soul, appreciating that it is now on the brink of eternity, calls for a Savior—just at this time when its help is most needed, this modern religion utterly fails.

But suppose all the teachings of this criticism were true, what would it avail us? It would put us in a sad condition indeed. For then, sitting beside ruined temples and broken-down altars, with no joy as respects the hereafter, no hope of everlasting life, no God to help us, no forgiveness of sins, feeling miserable, all desolate in our hearts and chaotic in our minds, we should be utterly unable either to know or believe anything more. Can such a view of Christianity be true? No! If this modern criticism were true, then away with all so-called Christianity, which only deceives us with idle tales! Away with a religion which has nothing to offer us but the commonplace teachings of morality! Away with faith! Away with hope! Let us eat and drink, for tomorrow we die!

Conclusion

Let us then, by repudiating this modern criticism, show our condemnation of it. What does it offer us? Nothing. What does it take away? Everything. Do we have any use for it? No! It neither helps us in life nor comforts us in death; it will not judge us in the world to come. For our Biblical faith we do not need either the encomiums of men, nor the approbation of a few poor sinners. We will not attempt to improve the Scriptures and adapt them to our liking, but we will believe them. We will not criticize them, but we will ourselves be directed by them. We will not exercise authority over them, but we will obey them. We will trust him who is the way, the truth, and the life. His Word shall make us free.

"Lord, to whom shall we go? Thou hast the words of eternal life. And we believe and are sure that Thou art that Christ, the Son of the living God" (John 6:68, 69). "And he answered, Behold, I come quickly: hold that fast which thou hast; that no man take thy crown" (Rev. 3:11).

2. Fundamentalism Is Very Much Alive, 1921

SOURCE: *Watchman-Examiner* 9 (July 28, 1921), 941.

Agitation, perturbation, mortification, mystification reign supreme among the enemies of fundamentalism. The fundamentalists at Des Moines did not prove themselves to have horns and hoofs and fangs and claws as had been freely predicted and confidently expected. Their dignity, their fraternity, their moderation, their enthusiasm for the work of the Convention were a sore disappointment to many. Their confession of faith was so simple, so comprehensive, so scriptural that no one has dared to pick a flaw in it.

With a twist of mind almost serpentine *The Baptist* declares that fundamentalism is dead, because forsooth the fundamentalists at Des Moines refused to dance to the music of the extravaganza composed for them by the enemies of our historic and holy faith. Because the fundamentalists proved themselves loyal Baptists, without *plus* or *minus*, therefore "fundamentalism is dead!"

Now, be it known unto all men everywhere that Baptist fundamentalism is a spontaneous movement within our beloved denomination, which seeks to reaffirm and re-emphasize the age-long principles for which our fathers suffered and died. It seeks to unite our denomination rather than to divide it. The name of the movement is a mere incident and is relatively unimportant. The movement itself will never die because always there will be men brave enough to contend earnestly for the faith delivered once for all to the saints. And it is this condition—sharp, vigorous, insistent—that is so distasteful to men without convictions.

Fundamentalists will not abandon the implements of work for the weapons of war. While fighting rationalism to the bitter end, whether it be found in our schools, our pulpits, our papers, or our denominational organizations, genuine fundamentalists will give themselves unceasingly to the work of the Lord in their local churches, their associations and their conventions.

We are proud of being in the Baptist fellowship of love and labor. No one desires or proposes any addition to or subtraction from that honored name. But as all of us know, because a man is known as a Baptist is no guarantee that he is a Baptist, provided that name connotes the faith of our fathers. Therefore the tragic airs that some assume when pleading that we shall be known as "just Baptists" is almost ridiculous. The Baptists who are standing for the fundamentals care not a fig by what name they are designated, but it seems necessary to designate them because of the battle that they are waging. In our issue of July 1, 1920, just after the Buffalo Convention, we said in discussing the Conference on Fundamentals:

The program was of high order, the subjects discussed being of the first importance to our Christian and denominational life. The Conference exerted a large influence upon the Convention. It brought together hundreds of able ministers who have hitherto been willing to leave the management of denominational affairs in the hands of others. They have now waked up to the fact that they have no right voluntarily to absent themselves from the Convention and then to criticise the decisions of the Convention. The Convention belongs to us all, and more fully this time than ever before all shades of opinion were represented.

We here and now move that a new word be adopted to describe the men among us who insist that the landmarks shall not be removed. "Conservatives" is too closely allied with reactionary forces in all walks of life." "Premillennialists" is too closely allied with a single doctrine and not sufficiently inclusive. "Land-markers" has a historical disadvantage and connotes a particular group of radical conservatives. We suggest that those who still cling to the great fundamentals and who mean to do battle royal for the fundamentals shall be called "Fundamentalists." By that name, the editor of THE WATCHMAN-EXAMINER is willing to be called. It will be understood therefore when he uses the word it will be in compliment and not in disparagement.

Since that time aggressive conservatives—conservatives who feel that it is their duty to contend for the faith—have by common consent, been called "fundamentalists." Thus far we are not ashamed of the name. It is not the name, however, but the cause represented by the name, in which we are interested. If the editor of *The Baptist* feels that fundamentalism is dead, he is probably the only man in the United States cherishing that delusion.

3. Shall the Fundamentalists Win?, 1922

SOURCE: *The Christian Work,* CII (June 10, 1922), 716-19.

. . . all of us must have heard about the people who call themselves the Fundamentalists. Their apparent intention is to drive out of the evangelical churches men and women of liberal opinions. I speak of them the more freely because there are no two denominations more affected by them than the Baptists and the Presbyterians. We should not identify the Fundamentalists with conservatives. All Fundamentalists are conservatives, but not all conservatives are Fundamentalists. The best conservatives can often give lessons to the liberals in true liberality of spirit, but the Fundamentalist program is essentially illiberal and intolerant. The Fundamentalists see, and they see truly, that in this last generation there have been strange new movements in Christian thought.

The New Knowledge

A great mass of new knowledge has come into man's possession: new knowledge about the physical universe, its origin, its forces, its laws; new knowledge about human history and in particular about the ways in which the ancient peoples used to think in matters of religion and the methods by which they phrased and explained their spiritual experiences; and new knowledge, also, about other religions and the strangely similar ways in men's faiths and religious practices have developed everywhere.

Now, there are multitudes of reverent Christians who have been unable to keep this new knowledge in one compartment of their minds and the Christian faith in another. They have been sure that all truth comes from the one God and is his revelation. Not, therefore, from irreverence or caprice or destructive zeal, but for the sake of intellectual and spiritual integrity, that they might really love the Lord their God not only with all their heart and soul and strength, but with all their mind, they have been trying to see this new knowledge in terms of the Christian faith and to see the Christian faith in terms of this new knowledge. Doubtless they have made many mistakes. Doubtless there have been among them reckless radicals gifted with intellectual ingenuity but lacking spiritual depth. Yet the enterprise itself seems to them indispensable to the Christian Church. The new knowledge and the old faith cannot be left antagonistic or even disparate, as though a man on Saturday could use one set of regulative ideas for his life and on Sunday could change gear to another altogether. We must be able to think our modern life clear through in Christian terms and to do that we also must be able to think our Christian life clear through in modern terms.

New Knowledge in Former Times

There is nothing new about the situation. It has happened again and again in history, as, for example, when the stationary earth suddenly began to move and the universe that had been center in this planet was centered in the sun around which the planets whirled. Whenever such a situation has arisen, there has been only one way out: the new knowledge and the old faith had to be blended in a new combination. Now, the people in this generation who are trying to do this are the liberals, and the Fundamentalists are out on a campaign to shut against them the doors of the Christian fellowship. Shall they be allowed to succeed? . . .

What Has Intolerance to Offer?

Here in the Christian churches are these two groups of people and the question which the Fundamentalists raise is this: Shall one of them throw the other out? Has intolerance any contribution to make to this situation? Will it persuade anybody of anything? Is not the Christian church large enough to hold within her hospitable fellowship people who differ on points like this and agree to differ until the fuller truth be manifested? The Fundamentalists say not. They say that the liberals must go. Well, if the Fundamentalists should succeed, then out of the Christian church would go some of the best Christian life and consecration of this generation—multitudes of men and women, devout and reverent Christians, who need the church and whom the church needs. . . .

Here in the Christian church today are these two groups, and the question which the Fundamentalists have raised is this: Shall one of them drive the other out? Do we think the cause of Jesus Christ will be furthered by that? If he should walk through the ranks of this congregation this morning, can we imagine him claiming as his own those who hold one idea of inspiration and sending from him into outer darkness those who hold another? You cannot fit the Lord Christ into that Fundamentalist mold. The church would better judge his judgment. For in the middle west the Fundamentalists have had their way in some communities and a Christian minister tells us the consequence. He says that all the educated people are looking for their religion outside the churches. . . .

. . . it is true that just now the Fundamentalists are giving us one of the worst exhibitions of bitter intolerance that the churches of this country have ever seen. As one watches them and listens to them, he remembers the remark of General Armstrong of Hampton Institute: "Cantankerousness is worse than heterodoxy."

Opinions May Be Mistaken; Love Never Is

There are many opinions in the field of modern controversy concerning which I am not sure whether they are right or wrong, but there is one thing I am sure of: courtesy and kindliness and tolerance and humility and fairness and right. Opinions may be mistaken; love never is. . . .

4. Christianity and Liberalism, 1923

SOURCE: From J. Gresham Machen, *Christianity and Liberalism,* © 1923 J. Gresham Machen, published by Wm. B. Eerdmans Publishing Co., Grand Rapids, Michigan. Reprinted by permission; all rights reserved.

What is the relation between Christianity and modern culture; may Christianity be maintained in a scientific age?

It is this problem which modern liberalism attempts to solve. Admitting that scientific objections may arise against the particularities of the Christian religion— against the Christian doctrines of the person of Christ, and of redemption through His death and resurrection—the liberal theologian seeks to rescue certain of the general principles of religion, of which these particularities are thought to be mere temporary symbols, and these general principles he regards as constituting "the essence of Christianity."

It may well be questioned, however, whether this method of defence will really prove to be efficacious; for after the apologist has abandoned his outer defences to the enemy and withdrawn into some inner citadel, he will probably discover that the enemy pursues him even there. Modern materialism, especially in the realm of psychology, is not content with occupying the lower quarters of the Christian city, but pushes its way into all the higher reaches of life; it is just as much opposed to the philosophical idealism of the liberal preacher as to the Biblical doctrines that the liberal preacher has abandoned in the interests of peace. Mere concessiveness, therefore, will never succeed in avoiding the intellectual conflict. In the intellectual battle of the present day there can be no "peace without victory"; one side or the other must win.

As a matter of fact, however, it may appear that the figure which has just been used is altogether misleading; it may appear that what the liberal theologian has retained after abandoning to the enemy one Christian doctrine after another is not Christianity at all, but a religion which is so entirely different from Christianity as to belong in a distinct category. It may appear further that the fears of the modern man as to Christianity were entirely ungrounded, and that in abandoning the embattled walls of the city of God he has fled in needless panic into the open plains of a vague natural religion only to fall an easy victim to the enemy who ever lies in ambush there.

Two lines of criticism, then, are possible with respect to the liberal attempt at reconciling science and Christianity. Modern liberalism may be criticized (1) on the ground that it is un-Christian and (2) on the ground that it is unscientific. We shall concern ourselves here chiefly with the former line of criticism; we shall be interested in showing that despite the liberal use of traditional phraseology modern liberalism not only is a different religion from Christianity but belongs in a totally different class of religions. But in showing that the liberal attempt at rescuing Christianity is false we are not showing that there is no way of rescuing Christianity at all; on the contrary, it may appear incidentally, even in the present little book, that it is not the Christianity of the New Testament which is in conflict with science, but the supposed Christianity of the modern liberal Church, and that the real city of God, and that city alone, has defences which are capable of warding off the assaults of modern unbelief. However, our immediate concern is with the other side of the problem; our principal concern just now is to show that the liberal attempt at reconciling Christianity with modern science has really relinquished everything distinctive of Christianity, so that what remains is in essentials only that same indefinite type of religious aspiration which was in the world before Christianity came upon the scene. In trying to remove from Christianity everything that could possibly be objected to in the name of science, in trying to bribe off the enemy by those concessions which the enemy most desires, the apologist has really abandoned what he started out to defend. Here as in many other departments of life it appears that the things that are sometimes thought to be hardest to defend are also the things that are most worth defending.

In maintaining that liberalism in the modern Church represents a return to an un-Christian and sub-Christian form of the religious life, we are particularly anxious not to be misunderstood. "Un-Christian" in such a connection is sometimes taken as a term of opprobrium. We do not mean it at all as such. Socrates was not a Christian, neither was Goethe; yet we share to the full the respect with which their names are regarded. They tower immeasurably above the common run of men; if he that is least in the Kingdom of Heaven is greater than they, he is certainly greater not by any inherent superiority, but by virtue of an undeserved privilege which ought to make him humble rather than contemptuous.

Such considerations, however, should not be allowed to obscure the vital importance of the question at issue. If a condition could be conceived in which all the preaching of the Church should be controlled by the liberalism which in many quarters has already become preponderant, then, we believe, Christianity would at last have perished from the earth and the gospel would have sounded forth for the last time. If so, it follows that the inquiry with which we are now concerned is immeasurably the most important of all those with which the Church has to deal. Vastly more important than all questions with regard to methods of preaching is the root question as to what it is that shall be preached. . . .

. . . The condition of mankind is such that one may well ask what it is that made the men of past generations so great and the men of the present generation so small. In the midst of all the material achievements of modern life, one may well ask the question whether in gaining the whole world we have not lost our own soul. Are we forever condemned to live the sordid life of utilitarianism? Or is there some lost secret which if rediscovered will restore to mankind something of the glories of the past?

Such a secret the writer of this little book would discover in the Christian religion. But the Christian religion which is meant is certainly not the religion of the modern liberal Church, but a message of divine grace, almost forgotten now, as it was in the middle ages, but destined to burst forth once more in God's good time, in a new Reformation, and bring light and freedom to mankind. What that message is can be made clear, as is the case with all definition, only by way of exclusion, by way of contrast. In setting forth the current liberalism, now almost dominant in the Church, over against Christianity, we are animated, therefore, by no merely negative or polemic purpose; on the contrary, by showing what Christianity is not we hope to be able to show what Christianity is, in order that men may be led to turn from the weak and beggarly elements and have recourse again to the grace of God.

5. Fundamentalism and Modernism: Two Religions, 1924

SOURCE: Copyright 1924 Christian Century Foundation. Reprinted with permission from Jan. 2, 1924, issue of *Christian Century*.

How deep-going is the fundamentalist-modernist controversy? Is it an issue worth serious attention? Does it matter vitally which way it all comes out? Is not the course of neutrality and even unconcern the better course for strong, level-headed leaders to adopt, leaving "partisan" alignment to those of more impetuous temperament? Is not the whole controversy, after all, scarcely more than a tempest in a teapot? Or are the fundamentalists right in claiming that the issue is a grave one, going to the roots of religious conviction and involving the basic purposes and almost the genius of Christianity itself?

A candid reply to such inquiries must be one of agreement with the fundamentalist claim. It is to be doubted that the average churchman whose sympathies are in the main with modernism has any adequate appreciation of the sharpness and depth of the issue, and it would seem that the time has come to say to the rank and file of church folk and of the religiously disposed outside the churches that the differences between fundamentalism and modernism are not mere surface differences, which can be amiably waved aside or disregarded, but that they are foundation differences, structural differences, amounting in their radical dissimilarity almost to the differences between two distinct religions. The fact that the modernist and the fundamentalist groups both call themselves Christians, both derive their theological standards from the historic tradition of the Christian church, and are both sheltered under the roofs of the same established ecclesiastical institutions, should not blind any one to the profound disparity which characterizes not only their respective intellectual processes, but their objective goals and even their spiritual experiences. Two world-views, two moral ideals, two sets of personal attitudes have clashed, and it is a case of ostrich-like intelligence blindly to deny and evade the searching and serious character of the issue. Christianity according to fundamentalism, is one religion. Christianity according to modernism, is another religion. Which is the true Christian religion, is the question that is to be settled in all probability by our generation for future generations.

By drawing the antitheses thus sharply it is not meant to say that there are no points of contact between these two religions, that there are no convictions and ideals and experiences held in common between them. Even between religions historically alien to each other there are substantial common possessions, as our modern missionaries with true insight not only discern but declare. Neither does the antithesis imply that the body of common spiritual possession between the religion of fundamentalism and the religion of modernism is no more substantial than that which obtains in the case, let us say, of Confucianism and Christianity. It implies only that the differences which characterize fundamentalism and modernism are so broad and deep and significant that, if each group holds its respective views consistently and acts upon them with conscientious rigor, they find an alienating gulf fixed between them.

This view of the gravity of the issue is not customarily expressed by voices representing the liberal wing. But the voice of fundamentalism is in stern and aggressive agreement with what we have just said. This difference in attitude involves considerations which deserve to be examined, as they will be, at another time. But without accepting the fundamentalist conclusion that division in the churches is inevitable, it would seem that the moment is long since due for believers in the modernist conception of Christianity to recognize and reverently to deal with the fact that there exists in present-day Christianity two structurally distinct religions, irreconcilable not alone on the side of apologetics but of churchly function and ideal and of missionary propagation.

Brave—or should we say *brave?*—attempts have been made by many ministers of liberal intellectual outlook to carry on their church life without either themselves bringing in or allowing others to introduce into their pulpits or parishes any teaching tending to enlighten their people with respect to the issues which from year to year for nearly a generation have been growing more and more acute. They have assumed that the differences were superficial, "merely intellectual" or theological, and that the course not only of professional security but of essential Christianity lay in steering their ministry away from the controversies that have been disquieting the souls of multitudes.

Looking at the outcome of certain long-time pastorates of this sort which have come under our observation—pastorates characterized by this middle-of-the-road neutrality and evasion—one's heart is touched with pity. The minister himself, at the beginning equipped with a thoroughly modern faith but shrinking from the hazard and labor of uttering it, now finds his leadership hedged about with inhibitions which he cannot break through, and in this crucial hour to which all of us have come finds in his care a flock utterly without understanding, which would be equally responsive to the appeal of reactionism and legalism on one side or liberalism on the other. Both shepherd and flock are deserving of pity in that case. For the day of neutrality has all but passed. This "protected" parish is now compelled to face the issue for which other parishes have had years of preparation. Christianity is hardly likely to last much longer half fundamentalist and half modernist. It is not merely the aggressiveness of fundamentalism that is forcing a choice, it is the inherent nature of the issue itself.

Two worlds have crashed, the world of tradition and the world of modernism. One is scholastic, static, authoritarian, individualistic; the other is vital, dynamic, free, social. There is a clash here as profound and as grim as that between Christianity and Confucianism. Amiable words cannot hide the differences. "Blest be the tie" may be sung until doomsday but it cannot bind these two worlds together. The God of the fundamentalist is one God; the God of the modernist is another. The Christ of the fundamentalist is one Christ; the Christ of modernism is another. The Bible of fundamentalism is one Bible; the Bible of modernism is another. The church, the kingdom, the salvation, the consummation of all things—these are one thing to fundamentalists and another thing to modernists. Which God is the Christian God, which Christ is the Christian Christ, which

Bible is the Christian Bible, which church, which kingdom, which salvation, which consummation are the Christian church, the Christian kingdom, the Christian salvation, the Christian consummation? The future will tell. But that the issue is clear and that the inherent incompatibility of the two worlds has passed the stage of mutual tolerance is a fact concerning which there hardly seems room for any one to doubt.

Essays

In the first essay, George M. Marsden of the University of Notre Dame discusses the rise of theological liberalism as a response to a troubled culture that was rapidly becoming secularized. In the second essay, Willard B. Gatewood, Jr., of the University of Georgia notes that the cultural forces that produced the controversy between fundamentalists and modernists also produced the showdown at Dayton, Tennessee, over the teaching of evolution in the state's public schools. In the final essay, Ferenc M. Szasz of the University of New Mexico describes how intense divisions developed within denominations between conservatives and liberals in spite of post-World War I hope and optimism for an armistice.

Tremors of Controversy
GEORGE M. MARSDEN
SOURCE: From *Fundamentalism and American Culture: The Shaping of Twentieth-Century Evangelicalism, 1870-1925* by George M. Marsden, copyright © 1980 by Oxford University Press, Inc. Used by permission of Oxford University Press, Inc.

In almost every major American denomination, sometime between the late 1870s and World War I, serious disagreements broke out between conservatives and liberals. In these struggles the traditionalists were not necessarily fundamentalists in any strict sense. They were first of all denominational conservatives who had their own distinct traditions and characters. Some, like the traditionalists among the Disciples of Christ, were regarded as a part of the fundamentalist movement largely because their aims were parallel and in certain of their attacks they had common opponents. What made others more fundamentalist was their combination of militant antimodernism with participation in a larger movement that, despite its mix of separable elements, possessed some degree of conscious unity. The active cooperation of denominational traditionalists with the theologically innovative dispensationalists and holiness advocates in the battle against modernism was particularly important in shaping a distinct fundamentalism. These traditionalists were found mostly among Baptists and Presbyterians. B. B. Warfield is a striking example. Warfield apparently despised the newer holiness teachings and certainly disdained dispensationalism. His own position was Old School Presbyterian traditionalism. Yet he cooperated with the larger fundamentalist movement, even with dispensationalist and holiness teachers, and in fact made an important contribution to fundamentalism, as did the Old School Presbyterian tradition generally.

The issues debated so intensely in the denominations usually centered on the authority of Scripture, its scientific accuracy, or the supernatural elements in Christ's person and work. There were also parallel and closely related disputes over denominations' distinctive doctrines or traditions—strict Calvinism among Presbyterians, immersion among Baptists and Disciples of Christ. Almost every major denomination struggled with some such issue, although some denominations avoided at least temporarily any dramatic disruption.

In the South the debates were in most cases short-lived, because dissent was simply not tolerated. As early as the first half of the nineteenth century, advanced theological views had usually been associated with advanced social views and abolition. Southern theology already had a strong conservative bent. The War Between the States simply intensified Southern determination to resist change. Hence there was a strong anti-modernist impulse in Southern religion well before modernism became a distinct movement in America. This theological conservatism, often combined with the warm revivalist evangelicalism inherited from the early nineteenth century, created in Southern religion many characteristics that resembled later fundamentalism. Until the 1920s, however, Southern revivalist conservatism and Northern fundamentalism developed more or less independently, although in parallel ways. The principal direct connection between the two movements was that several important fundamentalist leaders came from the South. When in the twentieth century fundamentalism became a distinct entity, Southerners with a long history of revivalist conservatism eventually flocked to the movement.

An early sign that sparks of liberalism would quickly be snuffed out in the Southern atmosphere came in 1878 when Alexander Winchell was forced by the Southern Methodist denomination out of his position at Vanderbilt for holding questionable views on Genesis. In the following year Crawford H. Toy's resignation from the Southern Baptist Seminary at Louisville had similar causes. The Toy case was followed some years later by that of his friend, William H. Whitsitt, who had the indiscretion to publicize historical research showing that baptism by immersion had not continued as an unbroken tradition since apostolic times. The Landmark Baptists, an especially rigid traditionalist group, speaking through the vitriolic *Western Recorder* of Tennessee, led the fight that forced Whitsitt's resignation as president of the Southern Baptist Seminary.

Among Southern Presbyterians serious scholarly discussion of the issues was similarly brought to a quick end with the dismissal of James Woodrow, uncle of Woodrow Wilson, from Columbia Theological Seminary for his claim that evolution was compatible with the teachings of Scripture. In the South, but not in the North, evolution was already a chief symbol of heresy. Southern thought had been shaped by Puritan, Scottish philosophical, and Baconian influences, which together encouraged an enormous reverence for Scripture as a source of hard fact, as opposed to speculative hypotheses such as those of Darwin.

In the North, by contrast, the cultural forces for change which fanned the new religious ideals were so strong that stamping out the spark in one place could not prevent a general conflagration. Many of the major Northern denominations suffered through painful heresy trials. Even conservative victories turned out to be largely illusory. Liberalism continued to grow almost as though the trials had never taken place. Among the Congregationalists, from the time of the flurry over future punishment in 1877 through the 1880s, conservatives were temporarily successful in their efforts to restrain liberalism. At Andover Seminary, where the move toward the New Theology centered, they even managed to have Professor Egbert C. Smyth removed from the faculty for a time. Yet by the 1890s the issues were settled in favor of the progressives and conservativism was defunct as an ecclesiastical force. Among Northern Methodists, the emphasis on the experiential religion of the heart and its practical moral consequences was congenial to a rapid development of liberal theology during the last fifteen years of the nineteenth century. Conservatives made some counter-efforts in the early twentieth century and charged Boston University theologians Hinkley G. Mitchell and Borden P. Bowne, two leading advocates of a personalistic theology, with holding lax views of Scripture. Bowne was acquitted, but Mitchell was dismissed from his post. In 1908, however, in connection with appeals of the Mitchell case, the General Conference effectively ended such trials of professors. The Protestant Episcopal Church had a similar isolated case in 1906 when the Reverend Algernon Sidney Crapsey was convicted for denying the Virgin Birth. In general, however, the Episcopal tradition of toleration for diversity prevailed.

The Northern Baptist and Northern Presbyterian controversies had the most to do with the development of interdenominational fundamentalism. The Baptists, who had much greater local autonomy, developed much greater diversity, with all the major parties—denominational traditionalists, dispensational premillennialists, and avowed liberals—well represented within the same denomination. In America, the Baptists had long been a coalition of diverse elements. On the one hand they had a confessional Calvinist tradition; yet at the same time they had a strong emphasis on doctrinal freedom. Calvinism was strong in the seventeenth-century Puritan origins of the American movement and also in the important eighteenth-century separation of New England Baptists from Congregationalism after the Great Awakening. Baptists, however, had an individualistic view of the church as a voluntary association of individuals who had experienced conversion. The Calvinist confessionalism was qualified by opposition to ecclesiastical centralization and vigorous affirmation of the individual right to theological freedom. Moreover, the emphasis on conversion in the pietist camp and especially in nineteenth-century frontier revivalism reinforced Arminian doctrines which emphasized human freedom of choice and were, as much as Calvinism, a venerable part of the diverse Baptist heritage.

In this relatively open atmosphere Biblical criticism and liberal theological tendencies appeared early among Baptists in the Northern United States and soon flourished as in no other evangelical denomination, except perhaps the Congregational-ist. By the 1870s three positions on Scripture were already perceptible. Some scholars, under German influences, rejected the infallibility of Scripture in favor of subjec-tive experiential verification of the truth of Christianity; most still assumed that the Bible was infallible in doctrine and without error in detail; others stood in a middle position. During the next decades militant conservatives won two isolated victories, removing Ezra P. Gould from Newton Theological Seminary in 1882 and Nathaniel Schmidt from Colgate in 1896. Nevertheless, they could not begin to hold back the liberal enthusiasm which swept over all of the Northern Baptist seminaries regardless of the degree of their earlier orthodox opposition. By 1900 liberals were well represented everywhere and by World War I strict conservatives had almost disappeared from the older seminaries. Moreover, under the leadership of President William Rainey Harper, the (Baptist) Divinity School at the Univer-sity of Chicago became after the 1890s the leading American center for aggressive theological liberalism, including on its faculty such outstanding "modernists" as Shailer Mathews, George Burman Foster, Gerald Birney Smith, and Shirley Jack-son Case. At Colgate Theological Seminary William Newton Clarke, whose views on the kingdom we have already encountered, was another outstanding voice for Baptist liberalism. Perhaps most important was the combination of pragmatic lib-eral theology with the new "Social Gospel" in the work of Walter Rauschenbusch at Rochester Theological Seminary. Rauschenbusch developed the liberal idea of the kingdom into an optimistic social theology that explicitly opposed the indi-vidualistic and otherworldly emphases often associated with revivalist evangelicalism.

Most striking in these Baptist developments is the degree of tolerance and room for open discussion that most representatives of both liberal and conservative views showed toward each other. During the decades spanning the turn of the century the "Baptist Congress" provided a forum in which both sides vigorously repre-sented their views. During the same period most Baptist seminaries still included both conservatives and liberals. Even in the midst of the ongoing debates, the various traditional segments of Northern Baptists strengthened their ties by the formation in 1907 of the Northern Baptist Convention. Yet the new Convention included explosive new elements that could easily trigger a chain reaction. In 1897 one astute observer predicted that "old and new will wage a war of extermination, and neither will live to gain the satisfaction of having destroyed the other." The explosion was delayed, however, and ten years later a similar analyst did not find the outlook so clear. "Two parties are in process of formation in the denomi-nation. . . ," said Professor H. C. Vedder. "At times there are symptoms that their opposition may break out into an open warfare; at times a peaceful issue seems not only hopeful, but certain."

In part this hope must simply have reflected the enthusiastic optimism and activism of the evangelicalism of the age. These years were, as Gaius Glann Atkins in retrospect described them, "the Age of Crusades." They were filled with "a su-perabundance of zeal, a sufficiency of good causes, unusual moral idealism, exces-sive confidence in mass movements and leaders with rare gifts of popular appeal."

Although they had deep-seated ideological differences, most American Protestants were not first of all ideological in orientation. So, in spite of the ongoing debates, they were uniting on the home front, as the formation of the Federal Council of Churches in 1908 best attests. Looking abroad, the fires of revival could be seen around the world and certainly the rank and file of American Protestants saw no conflict between revivalism and the essence of Christianity. Considering the advance of missions, the nineteenth seemed Protestantism's greatest century and many a judicious observer supposed that the new century might be greater still. The clouds of emerging controversy, however real and ominous, were in most of America hardly noticed in the midst of the bright halos of surrounding light of evangelical idealism. "On the whole," recalled Atkins, "the ten or fifteen years before the war were, controversially, a kind of Truce of God."

There was another reason why this was a time of peace even within a group with as much diversity as the Baptists. Although the issues were well aired and strenuously debated in the seminaries and among the denomination's leadership, they were not well known on a popular level. Albert H. Newman, probably the leading Baptist historian of the time, in 1905 provided an unusually clear analysis of the current status of the theological debates. Newman identified three major parties among Baptists in America. At one extreme were the liberals with their dazzlingly impressive academic strength. On the other extreme were the premillennialists, whom Newman characterized as "intensely anti-rationalistic," uncompromising concerning Scripture, tending to equate higher criticism with the Devil, and working through independent agencies and Bible institutes. In the middle was a moderate conservative party, "still in the vast majority" and controlling most of the working forces of the denomination. Despite these major divisions, the debates inspired no large-scale public interest. "Even in New England and the Middle States," Newman estimated, "not one Baptist member in ten is conscious of any important change in theology or departure from the old Baptist orthodoxy." For the Western and Southeastern states his estimate was not one in twenty; for the Southwest, not one in a hundred. Newman, who himself apparently considered such ignorance compatible with invincibility, concluded that the denomination "never possessed so many advantages and never encountered so few obstacles to progress." "'Things are getting better,'" he said, "and not worse."

The moderate character of the dominant conservative party, standing between the two aggressive new movements on the extremes, was one reason for optimism. Although some Baptist conservatives insisted on the inerrancy of Scripture in detail, this position was far from being a test of Baptist orthodoxy. The leading conservative Baptist theologian of the time, Augustus H. Strong, president of Rochester Theological Seminary, had a concept of truth that reflected the influence of some of the same philosophical trends that were shaping theological liberalism. While holding a high view of Biblical authority, Strong's starting point was that truth was not doctrinal or propositional, but rather "the truth is a personal Being, and that Christ himself is the Truth." Strong attributed the intellectual difficulties in the church to a view of truth that was too abstract and literal. People mistakenly supposed that the perfection attributed to the deity could be attributed equally to statements about Christ made by the church, the ministry, the Bible, or a creed. "A large part of the unbelief of the present day," he said, "has been caused by the unwarranted identification of these symbols and manifestations with Christ himself. Neither the church nor ministry, Bible or creed, is perfect. To discover imperfection in them is to prove that they are not in themselves divine."

Strong rejected very explicitly the idea of Scripture as inerrant and in his influential *Systematic Theology* eventually dropped language that might even suggest such a conclusion. Statements similar to Strong's could readily be found elsewhere among Baptist conservatives. Robert Stuart MacArthur, pastor of Calvary Baptist Church in New York City (which became a fundamentalist center under his successor, John Roach Straton), in 1899 strongly defended traditional Christianity while maintaining that "A true doctrine of inspiration may admit mistakes, or at least the possibility of mistakes, in history and biographical statements, while it denies error in matters of faith and morals . . . . " Even Curtis Lee Laws, editor of the conservative *Watchman-Examiner* (and in 1920 inventor of the word "fundamentalist" to describe this Baptist party), did not insist on inerrancy, emphasizing the "experimental" verification of the Bible's truth rather than its value as scientific statement. Like the dispensationalists and (as will be seen shortly) the Princeton theologians, Laws viewed the objective character of Biblical truth as analogous to the laws of physics. Like the Princetonians, he viewed Biblical truth as known by common sense. "The infallibility of the Bible is the infallibility of common sense, and of the experimental triumph within us." Yet, as this last phrase suggests, the truth of Scripture known by common sense was the truth of its "living power." "It is our authority," he said, "because it does for us what our souls need." In Laws's view this was by no means subjectivism. But one's common sense knowledge of the objective truth of Scripture came by way of intuitive confirmation, not as scientific demonstration. This view separated Laws from the more characteristic fundamentalist insistence on inerrancy. An intuitive sense of the "living power" of Scripture was not dependent on the Bible's accuracy in scientific detail.

Such emphasis on the personal, the dynamic, and the experiential gave conservative Baptists something in common with their liberal brethren who carried these principles to more controversial conclusions. The real problem for conservatives such as Strong, MacArthur, and Laws was the liberal drift away from supernaturalism in Christianity. In 1897 Strong argued against those who loudly proclaimed "Back to Christ," but who meant "Christ as a merely ethical teacher—a teacher who made no claim to supernatural knowledge and power." Said Strong:

> It is not such a Christ as this to whom the penitent has looked for forgiveness and the sorrowing for comfort. It is not for such a Christ as this that the martyrs have laid down their lives.

By 1907 Strong, unlike some of his Baptist contemporaries, was genuinely alarmed. "We seem upon the verge of a second Unitarian defection," he observed, "that will break up churches and compel secession, in a worse manner than did that of Channing and Ware a century ago."

Despite the relatively good feelings that prevailed among Baptists in the decades before the Great War, there had been scattered forebodings of things to come. In 1907 a large element in southern Illinois left the Illinois Baptist Convention to join the Southern Baptist Association, in protest over the liberalism at the University of Chicago. In 1909 a dispensationalist-inspired secession from the leading Baptist church in Grand Rapids provided the nucleus for a secessionist Baptist association which formed in Michigan during the next decade. In 1913 moderate conservatives founded Northern Baptist Seminary in Chicago to counter the influence of the Divinity School at the University. The same year the Baptist Congress came to an end, partly because the debates between extreme liberals and extreme conservatives had become too acrimonious. Yet among Baptists in general there was little to presage what was to come. A spirit of harmony, cooperation, and activism seemed to prevail.

Introduction
WILLARD B. GATEWOOD, JR.

SOURCE: From *Controversy in the Twenties: Fundamentalism, Modernism, and Evolution* by Willard B. Gatewood, Jr. Pp. 3-7, 19-23, 23-26, 43-46. Copyright © 1969 by Vanderbilt University Press. Reprinted with permission of the author.

In many respects, World War I was the signal for a series of tremors that reverberated in American society throughout the postwar decade. Many agreed with Richard Le Gallienne's observation in 1924 that society was going "through a process of reconstruction, and the process, as it has always been, is disquieting." More graphic was Willa Cather's simple pronouncement that "the world broke in two in 1922 or there-abouts." The novelist obviously referred to the cumulative impact of a half-century of social, economic, and intellectual changes, as well as the host of new forces unleashed by the war, which collectively created a new America where traditional formulas for the good life seemed strangely inappropriate. Revolutionary developments in science, technology, and psychology substantially altered man's view of himself and his universe as well as his ways of making a living. The easy access of radios, movies, and automobiles in the postwar era had an immeasurable effect upon American culture and contributed significantly to changes in morals, manners, and mobility. Urbanization gathered such new momentum that during the 1920s, for the first time in the nation's history, more people lived in the city than in the country. This shift in population reflected the dramatic growth of industrialism that characterized the period and gained for it the epithet "second industrial revolution." As old ways changed, so did old certainties. A rash of social and cultural innovations threatened traditional concepts and values. Gone was that "ineffable certainty which made God and his plan as real as the lamp-post."

The impact of the "new era" was nowhere more evident than in American religious life. The postwar climate witnessed significant changes in both the institutional and theological positions of the Protestant churches. The decline in church attendance, missionary efforts, and the Social Gospel during the 1920s coincided with an increasing interest in humanism, scientism, and behaviorism. "The agony of a spiritual quest in a world that regarded spiritual matters with indifference," wrote one student of postwar American literature, "was one of the most profound emotional experiences of the 1920's." Many churchmen disturbed by the plight of Protestantism demanded a religious revival. They agreed with Bishop Francis J. McConnell of the Methodist Church who in 1924 declared: "we were told that an upward moral movement was sweeping us in spite of ourselves. The events of the last eight years have pretty well knocked this notion to splinters." Some Americans actually thought they detected the beginning of a "New Reformation." Unable to decide whether religion was in the midst of a reformation or a decline, the distinguished theologian William Pierson Merrill was nonetheless certain that "Protestantism is at the crossroads!" Perceptive foreign observers generally agreed with his assessment. In their view, America's "man-made, not time-made, commonwealth" was in the midst of an awesome "social and moral crisis." In a sense Americans were in the throes of their first major confrontation with the twentieth century.

So direct was the confrontation that Americans could scarcely have failed to recognize that the old order was rapidly disintegrating. Some welcomed the opportunity to overhaul senile institutions and to chart new courses; others were profoundly and genuinely disturbed by what appeared to them to be sheer chaos. All the changes, so it seemed especially to the latter, conspired to dehumanize man, to obliterate areas of certainty in human affairs, and to clear the right-of-way for the triumph of secularism. Such anxiety often induced popular spasms of disorientation characterized by indiscriminate, almost blind, assaults upon all phenomena associated with the new order. One critic, agonized by the irreverence of postwar America, declared:

> This is an age of new things. So many new discoveries—so many new inventions—so many combinations that the people are all at sea. In this age we have new thought, new voices, new books, new theology, new psychology, new philosophy, new religion, and everything that hell can suggest and the devil concoct.

Groups and individuals in search of normalcy and the return of certitude often employed the tactic of excluding both ideas and practices which they held responsible for the breakdown of traditional codes and the destruction of eternal verities. Such ideas and practices were considered "subversive," a term used widely in the 1920s in a variety of contexts. Both New York's Lusk Laws of 1921 and the Tennessee anti-evolution law of 1925 were essentially designed to prevent subversion and to protect the American Way. To a large extent, the Sacco-Vanzetti case and the "Monkey Trial" at Dayton were products of the same exclusionist mood.

The head-on collision between those determined to recapture the past and those desirous of coming to terms with the new conditions filled the air with controversy. Since many were convinced that the battle to preserve American values would be decided on the religious front, it was not surprising that few of these clashes generated more furor than the so-called war in the churches. Throughout most of the decade, theological conservatives or "fundamentalists" waged a militant offensive against religious modernism. The martial language and biblical symbolism employed in their warfare seemed calculated to conjure up the image of an epic struggle between rival contenders for the faith. The martial quality of their combat reached a climax in the controversy over evolution—the most dramatic aspect of a many-sided struggle. A Louisiana clergyman, opposed to all types of modernists, provided some insight into the complexity and pervasiveness of the "enemy" against which many fundamentalists were actually fighting. "I would say," he declared, "that a modernist in government is an anarchist and Bolshevik; in science he is an evolutionist; in business he is a Communist; in art a futurist; in music his name is jazz; and in religion an atheist and infidel." The sustained intensity of the modernist-fundamentalist encounters prompted Professor Richard Hofstadter to describe the 1920s as "the focal decade in the Kulturkampf of American Protestantism."

Contemporary accounts of the conflict generally described it in terms of the polarization of Protestantism. Certainly, as it intensified, those who occupied a theological ground between modernism and fundamentalism tended to move to one extreme or the other. Professor Robert T. Handy has noted that in the heat of the battle, when Protestantism seemed bifurcated between modernism and fundamentalism, extremists had their opportunity. Contemporary observers who attempted to explain the origins of the disturbance almost invariably stressed the role of World War I. Some suggested that the shock of war and the "nervous overstrain" that it produced drove people to extremes, "making liberals more liberal and reactionaries more reactionary." Others saw the war as creating a fighting spirit that outlived the war. And still others held the war primarily responsible for the spread of a "great fear, with a craving for something solid and a return to normalcy." More specifically, the war stimulated discussions of church unity and a demand by liberal churchmen for "deliverance from sectarianism." A church "open free without test or barrier of belief" was essential, declared one modernist, if the church was to "stand the test of our logical and searching years." The relaxation of creedal requirements implicit in such proposals was anathema to the defenders of orthodoxy who generally interpreted the church unity movement as a deceptive tactic by modernists to substitute a commitment to social service for any "declaration of fundamentals." To thwart this "journey into apostasy," the fundamentalists felt compelled to organize an all-out offensive against modernism. . . .

Obviously another reason why evolution evoked such hostile reaction among fundamentalists was its apparent attack upon their view of revelation. Theirs was a transcendent deity who entered the world in the form of miracles and special acts of revelation such as those recorded in the verbally inspired scriptures. To question any biblical account of these extraordinary events, as indeed higher critics and modernists did, was the first step toward a total denial of the basic premises of Christianity. T. T. Martin, secretary of the Anti-Evolution League, summarized much of the fundamentalist objection to the evolutionary hypothesis when he declared:

> Every honest man knows that accepting evolution means giving up the inspiration of Genesis; and if the inspiration of Genesis is given up, the testimony of Jesus to the inspiration of the scriptures goes with it; and if his testimony to the scriptures is given up, his deity goes with it, and with that goes his being a real Redeemer and we are left without a Savior and in the darkness of our sins.

Since such fundamentalist crusaders as Martin made virtually no distinction between organic evolution, Darwinism, and evolutionary philosophy, they found little difficulty in linking evolution with atheism, secularistic trends, "godless education," sexual immorality, disintegration of the family, German militarism, and Communism. In their vocabulary, evolution became a catchall, scare word meaning modern evils in general. One zealot even insisted upon spelling it "devilution."

Even those shocked by the renewal of the nineteenth-century debate over evolution recognized that it was only one ingredient in a many-sided conflict. Watson Davis, the science editor of *Current History*, noted that "evolution and the science of biology seem to have been picked by the fundamentalists as symbols of modernism." "The Darwinian doctrine," W. J. Cash observed, "was indeed no more than the focal point of an attack for a program, explicit or implicit, that went far beyond evolution laws." In fact the disturbance over evolution in the 1920s symbolized a direct confrontation between widely dissimilar mentalities which had previously operated virtually independent of each other at different levels in American culture. But by 1920, advances in education and mass communication largely precluded the continuation of such independence and, according to Richard Hofstadter, "threw the old mentality into direct and unavoidable conflict with the new." A variety of other scientific or psychological theories might well have served as the focus of the conflict; yet the choice of evolution was in many ways a natural one because it was more familiar and less abstract than some of the more recent theories. Perhaps another reason for the fundamentalists' choice was related to the nature of modernism itself. The variety and fluidity of modernist theology tended to make it an elusive enemy. But Darwinian evolution, which was a basic part of the modernist structure, particularly the concept of an immanent deity, provided fundamentalists with a concrete target. To discredit evolution was to destroy the underpinnings of modernism.

By 1921 the fundamentalist crusade, especially as evidenced by the strategy of the World's Christian Fundamentals Association, had aimed its heaviest artillery at

Darwinian evolution. The strategic shift in the campaign first became evident late in 1920 when the association invited William Jennings Bryan to lead a "laymen's movement" against modernism and evolution. At the time Bryan was not prepared to accept the offer. "It was not until the spring of 1921," according to Professor Lawrence Levine, "that Bryan's toleration of the evolution theory, which had been wearing thin gradually, finally came to an end." The folk hero of rural America ultimately decided that he was as unwilling to be crucified on the cross of evolution as on the cross of gold. Convinced that his defense of the old-time religion against evolution was the "greatest" of all his reform efforts, Bryan emerged as one of the most significant spokesmen for militant fundamentalism. Evolution, he claimed, was "the only thing that has seriously menaced religion since the birth of Christ, and it menaces . . . civilization as well as religion." It was responsible for "the destruction of faith" and the modern sin of "mind worship." "But the mind is a mental machine," Bryan insisted, "and needs a heart to direct it. If the heart goes wrong, the mind goes with it." He pursued these themes in numerous speeches, books, pamphlets, and syndicated columns. His personal crusade against evolution was not only a significant part in the fundamentalist effort to achieve restrictive legislation in the various states but also figured prominently in disturbances which rocked the Presbyterian General Assembly and the University of Wisconsin.

The campaign to obliterate modernism by striking at what was considered its chief handmaiden, evolution, was in large part the work of interdenominational fundamentalist groups. Numerous organizations such as the Anti-Evolution League and the Bible Crusaders of America later joined the crusade launched by the World's Christian Fundamentals Association. Collectively these organizations dedicated themselves to the mobilization of public opinion in defense of the orthodox faith and against the "creeping humanism" represented by modernists and evolutionists. William Bell Riley, John Roach Straton, and other fundamentalist leaders stormed the country on forensic tours. Such cities as New York, Philadelphia, and San Francisco, no less than obscure hamlets throughout the nation, were the scenes of their highly publicized debates with evolutionists. At the same time free-lance evangelists contributed to the air of controversy with their flamboyant rhetoric which pinpointed Darwinism as the principal cause for the sorry predicament of modern America. The evolution sermons of Billy Sunday, Mordecai F. Ham, J. Frank Norris, and a host of lesser lights brought into question the fidelity of both denominational and public schools to the historic faith. Testimonials of students whose faith had been wrecked by the teaching of evolution in schools and colleges became standard fare in many tent-revival services.

The antievolution crusaders indicted Darwin's theory on both theological and scientific grounds. Evolutionists, they maintained, substituted a belief in man's ascent from primitive conditions to a fuller life for the Christian concept of the fall of man. This substitution, which contradicted the biblical account of man's origins, invalidated the whole basis of the doctrine of sin and erased all hope of salvation. Lacking a sense of sin, man reverted to the brute morality of his monkey ancestors. Those who espoused the "God-or-gorilla" approach left no room for reservation or equivocation regarding evolution and branded the theistic evolutionist as "the very worst sort of infidel" because his sin included deceit as well as unbelief. But not only was evolution theologically unacceptable, it was also scientifically unacceptable. Fundamentalists insisted that the theory was a "mere guess" first propounded by the pagan Greeks of antiquity. Since evolution was "unproved and unprovable" it should not be taught as science. In 1923 William Jennings Bryan assured the West Virginia legislature that of all the sciences, chemistry most conclusively contradicted evolution because "it proves that degeneration and not progress, disintegration and not construction, is the rule of mankind." Leander S. Keyser, a professor in the Hamma Divinity School and probably the most prominent Lutheran identified with the fundamentalist cause, argued that "the upright posture" of man was itself a denial of biological evolution. The fact that man alone among the animals "naturally stands and walks uprightly" was proof of "the doctrine of special creation in the divine image." "Note," Keyser concluded, "that man can cast his vision toward the transcendent God in no other way than by looking up from the earth." To support their claims that the evolutionary theory was a "biological absurdity" the fundamentalists marshaled an impressive array of evidence from nineteenth-century scientists who denied the validity of Darwin's hypothesis. They also seized upon any divergence in interpretation regarding evolution within contemporary scientific circles as evidence of its falsity. . . .

Both the free-lance evangelists and spokesmen for national antievolution organizations took advantage of the prejudices and anxieties of the postwar era. The wartime hysteria against all things German made it easier for them to characterize Darwinism as the basic cause of Germany's guilt in bringing about World War I. Oddly enough, Vernon Kellogg, a well-known scientist who served with the American Relief Association in Europe during the war, provided support for such an interpretation in his little volume *Headquarters Nights,* which recorded his conversations with high-ranking German officials. Kellogg concluded that Neo-Darwinism explained Germany's adherence to the "creed of the *Allmacht* of natural selection based on violent and fatal competitive struggle." Germany, so the fundamentalist argument ran, had replaced the standards of Christ with those of the evolution-oriented philosophy of Nietzsche. German universities, gripped by evolutionary heresies, had divested Christianity of its supernatural qualities and moral precepts by embracing higher criticism, rationalism, and modernism. The obvious implication was that America's continued deviation from the orthodox faith would lead to the same catastrophic fate that engulfed Germany.

But the antievolution crusaders not only capitalized on the anti-German sentiment, they also found the mood engendered by the Red Scare useful in the promotion of their cause. In fact, the same highly emotional vocabulary that characterized the Red Scare pervaded the fundamentalist campaign against evolution. They began with the assumption that a belief in evolution, no matter how one attempted to reconcile it with the Protestant faith, led inescapably to atheism. Modernists were, by their reasoning, nothing more than atheists who clothed their infidelity in high-sounding phrases borrowed from Christian theology. Since the Red Scare had pointed up atheism as an important attribute of Communist belief, fundamentalists identified modernism with Communism and evolutionists with Bolsheviks. Albert S. Johnson, a well-known Presbyterian clergyman, assured his congregation that evolution led "to sensuality, carnality, Bolshevism, and the Red Flag." Mordecai F. Ham charged that the teaching of evolution at the University of Oklahoma was financed by "Red money" from Soviet Russia and that the legal war against Tennessee's evolution law was "the work of the anti-Christ Communists." Convinced that evolutionists encouraged all forms of immorality by dispensing with the fall of man and by rationalizing sin out of existence, Amzi C. Dixon concluded: "If Darwin was right and the evolutionists . . . are right, Germany was right and Lenine and Trotsky are right."

A belief in evolution, then, involved more than religious loyalty; it was a threat to American democracy. To accept the biological theory was to risk being accused of un-Americanism. James M. Gray of the Moody Bible Institute insisted that modernism in general and evolution in particular were "bringing into general practice the red doctrine of the Third International of Moscow, and if allowed to grow it can result in only one thing, and that is the overthrow of our government." John Roach Straton was even more explicit in equating the orthodox faith with patriotism:

> The very foundations of the American Republic were laid down upon the open Bible. The most significant fact, at last, in the history of our country is the fact that the Plymouth fathers, before they ever left the Mayflower and set foot upon these wild shores, opened the Bible in the cabin of the ship and drew up the first charter for their colony in the light of its teachings. The foundation stones in this country's greatness were not laid by men who doubted the Bible, who desecrated the Lord's Day, and who neglected the church. . . . No, the greatness of our country was founded by men and women who held to the old faith, who lived lives of usefulness and service, who walked in the light of God's law, whose sorrows were comforted by the truths of His word, and whose hopes of Heaven were the mainstay and anchorage of their souls.

By relating evolution and modernism to un-Americanism, the fundamentalist crusaders won support from civic and patriotic groups whose primary concern was not ordinarily the protection of religion. Some observers, in fact, suggested that the fundamentalist movement received encouragement from economic conservatives interested in it primarily as an aid in maintaining the politico-economic status quo. "It may well appear to large financial interests," noted Kirsopp Lake of Harvard in 1925, "that industrial stability can be safeguarded by Fundamentalists who can be trusted to teach 'antirevolutionary' doctrines in politics and economics as well as theology." Gerald Johnson claimed that southern cotton manufacturers had long recognized the advantages to be reaped from the work of the fundamentalist evangelist who discouraged strikes by "exhausting the honest workman's capacity for emotion."

Since the fear of conspiracy flourishes in times of anxiety, it is not surprising that the conspiratorial theme appeared so often during the evolution controversy. The defenders of evolution viewed their opposition as a combination of semiliterate elements whose mentality and methods smacked of the Ku Klux Klan. Nowhere was the idea of a fundamentalist conspiracy against education and culture elaborated in greater detail than in the works of Upton Sinclair during the 1920s. Implicit in much of the fundamentalist rhetoric was the idea that a small coterie of intellectuals in colleges and seminaries, constituting a so-called educational soviet, was involved in a clandestine plot to undermine the Christian faith of their students. As evidence that such a conspiracy existed, fundamentalists cited textbooks, personal affidavits of college students, questionnaires, and passages excerpted from scholarly journals. Professional evangelists invariably struck a responsive chord when they lashed out at the small group of arrogant intellectuals who monopolized the control of education financed by Christian taxpayers. In a facetious definition of evolution, Baxter F. McLendon traced man's ancestry from the amoeba to the gorilla, then concluded: "and the gorilla, thank God, begat pin-whiskered professors who draw their breath and salary and use big jaw-breaking words, and talk about the Bible being allegoric, figurative, probable, inferential, and hypothetical." Others such as Billy Sunday, who specialized in attacking the manhood of liberal intellectuals in general, characterized evolutionist professors as "sissies" too cowardly to admit that their aim was to destroy "the faith of our boys and girls." At times the conspiratorial theme assumed overtones of sectionalism, anti-Semitism, and antiforeignism. In the South, for example, antievolutionists blamed "outsiders," notably "Yankee infidels," for undermining the religious beliefs of college students. Fundamentalist zealots were not satisfied merely with exposing the conspiracy; they insisted that all the conspirators be driven from the classrooms and pulpits of institutions whose existence depended upon the support of evangelical Christians. In short, those who deviated from the fundamentalist credo should establish their own schools and churches.

Fundamentalists generally defined their antievolution crusade as an effort to save the children—the future generations of America—from the soul-destroying influence of the Darwinian heresy. In fact, theirs was an attempt to insulate all the family pieties from the "subtle poison" of evolutionary teachings. Billy Sunday described, in his own inimitable way, the theological and moral diet of American school children as a mixture of "this evolution hokum, this gland bunk, this protoplasm chop suey, this ice water religion, this mental-disease crime stuff, this mortal-thought-instead-of-sin blah." A devout mother characterized evolutionist teachers as "German throwbacks" who blighted the lives of her children by "destroying their faith, lowering their ideals, and paralyzing their constructive ability." Teachers who exposed the young to Darwin's "slime theory," according to a lady evangelist in Texas, committed a sin greater than murder, because a murderer only destroyed the physical life of his victim while such teachers "crushed the soul."

The fundamentalists' battle against evolution represented, among other things, their reaction to the new ideal of education which was rapidly gaining ascendancy by the 1920s. The new ideal was "not that the child shall acquire the wisdom of his elders, but that he shall revise and surpass it." Such a concept was manifestly unacceptable to those who equated wisdom and righteousness with "the unchanging Word of God." For their children to attempt revisions was to insure moral deterioration rather than improvement. But the fundamentalists faced a difficult dilemma in saving the future generations: the success they desired for their children required an ever-increasing amount of formal education which would almost certainly expose these "impressionable minds" to all the intellectual trends symbolized by evolution. Their problem was to provide their children with the educational requirements of success without alienating them from parental ways and pieties. . . .

Fundamentalism, then, may well have become "a lost cause," but it had raised issues, often in a crude, unsophisticated manner, on which others would call modernism to account. True to Nixon's prediction in 1925, no sooner had modernists claimed victory over the fundamentalists than they encountered challenges from diverse nonfundamentalist sources whose intellectual prowess and mode of criticism clearly placed modernism on the defensive once again. Perhaps the most immediate threat was the blossoming of a humanist movement in the late 1920s. Although the Humanist Manifesto, signed by John Dewey, Harry Elmer Barnes, and thirty other notables, was not issued until 1933, humanism was a lively topic of discussion during the previous decade. In 1928, a nonfundamentalist critic, pursuing a favorite theme of fundamentalism, claimed that modernists were "finding their faith evaporating into the thin air of agnosticism." The humanist, opposed to supernaturalism and committed to human values, claimed that his position was merely the logical end of modernism, an argument persistently used by fundamentalist crusaders. If modernism had made God immanent, so the argument ran, humanism made him completely immanent. God became the world, man, and his dreams; religion became human experience. "Fundamentalism is skeptical of science," a humanist wrote in 1927; "Modernism merely flirts with science; but humanism says that while science may give us inadequate knowledge, it gives us all we have and we must make the most of it." By expressing similar views before the American Association for the Advancement of Science late in 1928, Harry Elmer Barnes of Smith College created a storm of controversy and was severely arraigned by scientists and modernist theologians. According to the proponents of theological orthodoxy, Barnes's forthright declaration of humanism without the paraphernalia of Christian theological terminology was less obnoxious than the deceitful discourses of scientists and modernist theologians. Humanists like Barnes rejected modernism as a "half way reform" and took upon themselves to complete what modernism had begun but had been unwilling to complete.

Obviously modernism was still under siege at the end of the 1920s. What Nixon had described in 1925 as "the flank attack of scientific Naturalism" and the "frontal attack of conservative religion" had in effect been reversed. In the face of assaults from so many directions, a majority of modernists began to adjust their positions without succumbing to humanism. Harry Emerson Fosdick, busily combating humanism as "a tentative makeshift," represented those who gradually shifted their stance in order to keep "the cosmic rootage for truth, goodness, and beauty." Fosdick's sermons offered a rather reliable chart of his changing position: his famous "Beyond Modernism" in 1935 was a theological descendant of his "Beyond Reason" in 1928. As one church historian has indicated, the majority of modernist theologians, though still dedicated to reason, an open mind, and the currents of modernity, attempted "to keep the God of Jesus Christ and to keep Jesus as the revelation of God." Even so, their theology continued to elicit criticism from diverse sources.

A recent study of American Protestantism concludes that "Fundamentalism drew a necessary line between historic Christianity and naturalism but it drew the line at the wrong place." With the gradual decline of the modernist-fundamentalist controversy, "the way was open for a more profound and more creative discussion of basic Christian truths." Such a reorientation of Protestant thought, heralded by the translation of treatises by Karl Barth and other Europeans late in the 1920s as well as the maturing of Reinhold Niebuhr's theology, was evident in the emergence of a theocentric neo-orthodoxy and the re-thinking of liberalism. Although neo-orthodoxy diverged sharply from the theological position of fundamentalism, it represented an indictment of modernism and embraced tenets that tended to "dull the cutting edge of the fundamentalists' argument." Despite the influence of such theologians as Niebuhr upon American Protestantism between 1930 and the opening of World War II, the older type of fundamentalism continued to flourish even if it rarely captured the headlines. By 1941 fundamentalism had undergone a considerable transformation in organization, education, scholarship, and sophistication. After World War II, in a socio-psychological climate similar in some respects to that of the 1920s, fundamentalists returned to militant revivalism. The new fundamentalism reached a wide audience through television and other media of mass communication. The popular response was spectacular. Again, evolution was the focus of an insignificant skirmish by combatants "trapped in the stereotypes of previous generations." In the 1950s and 1960s the agitation over Darwin in Arizona, California, and Texas prompted brief notice in the press; in Tennessee it resulted in the repeal of the "monkey law" of 1925. As Reinhold Niebuhr witnessed the re-emergence of virile fundamentalism after World War II, he undoubtedly had little reason to question the validity of his observation made a quarter of a century earlier:

> Frantic orthodoxy is never rooted in faith but in doubt. It is when we are not sure that we are doubly sure. Fundamentalism is, therefore, inevitable in an age which has destroyed so many certainties by which faith once expressed itself and upon which it relied.

But, as Niebuhr also observed in the mid-1920s, neither modernism nor any other theology which took "refuge in various kinds of pantheism" provided a satisfactory alternative. Only a "transcendentally oriented religion" which boldly faced "the moral implications of its faith" would suffice.

The Fundamentalist-Modernist Controversy, 1918-1930

FERENC M. SZASZ

SOURCE: From *The Divided Mind of Protestant America, 1880-1930* by Ferenc M. Szasz. Pp. 92, 95-101, 101-2, 103, 104-5, 106. Copyright © 1982 by University of Alabama Press. Reprinted with permission.

A wave of optimism swept across the nation after the signing of the 1918 armistice. The war, one commentator noted, had formed "an abyss of fire and death between the past and the future." Peace, said another, would usher in "a new age; not so much because the map of Europe will be changed but rather because the map of the human mind will be changed." "This," said Presbyterian minister J. Wilbur Chapman in January 1919, "is the day of the churches' glorious opportunity."

Failure of these grand hopes to come about is the key to understanding the Protestant reaction in the 1920s. The despair was almost as great as the hopes that had been raised. In addition to despair over Christianity's failure to capture the world in the 1920s, the churches were troubled by: the growing conservative conviction that liberalism was in the ascendancy in many denominations, a militant premillennialism that had entrenched itself in many Bible schools and was not yet viewed by other conservatives as appreciably different from their own position, new aggressive conservative leadership under William B. Riley, and the evolution issue as revived by William Jennings Bryan. Here were all the necessary ingredients for a major social upheaval. Disruption took the form of the Fundamentalist-Modernist controversy that racked the churches during the 1920s, with consequences that remain evident today. . . .

The Fundamentalist-Modernist conflict really began with the conservatives' action within the denominations. The stakes were high, for the ultimate question was which group and which theological position would control the churches. Religious affairs, especially when they are plagued by dispute, make interesting reading, and the nation's press was not long in publicizing the clash. An age that later would be labeled "post-Christian" was momentarily filled with heated discussions over the Westminster Confession, miracles, various creeds of belief, and the meaning of the biblical narratives. But the Bible is complex, and discussions over fine points were soon lost in the two issues around which most of the debate during the 1920s revolved: the imminent second coming of Christ and His Virgin Birth.

The Baptists were especially susceptible to controversy of this type because of the nature of their polity. The Northern Baptist Convention is simply a gathering of the individual Baptist churches to carry out their common interests. Consequently, it had not the power, as did the General Assembly of the Presbyterians, for example, to affirm any major position. In addition, Baptists have always been proud of the fact that they have never been bound by any creed. Their past contains confessions of faith, but these have never been seen as binding in the sense of a creedal commitment. The creedal question, however, threw the 1922 Indianapolis convention into turmoil. The previous year the Fundamentalists had adopted a statement of doctrine introduced by Frank M. Goodchild, but they had not introduced it at the convention. The journals predicted that a showdown on this issue might come at Indianapolis. The first two conservative preconvention meetings had been chiefly concerned with doctrine, but at Indianapolis they tried to put their beliefs into action. Jasper C. Massee of Tremont Temple in Boston emerged as floor leader of the Baptist Fundamentalist Fellowship, but the *Christian Century* hinted that someone else (perhaps Riley) was backing him. After interviewing some of the men involved, Robert Delnay felt that it was part of Riley's plan that the gentle Massee be the one to lead the initial fight. The Fundamentalists' goal in Indianapolis was to get the New Hampshire Convention of Faith adopted by the convention, and their position received publicity from Bryan's trip to the city to speak to them. The liberals halted this maneuver, however, when Cornelius Woelfkin introduced a counterresolution stating that the New Testament was sufficient for all Baptists. After a fierce debate, Woelfkin's resolution was finally passed. The liberals were greatly relieved, and the elected president, Mrs. W. A. Montgomery, noted that adopting an official confession of faith "would come perilously near to abandoning one of our fundamental principles." After the convention, Laws, Goodchild, and Massee went to the Moody Bible Institute to give addresses. In his speech there, Laws noted, "We have lost a battle, but we have not lost the war." In large part, however, the war had been lost. Had the Fundamentalists won control of the Baptist denomination, that victory would have had a major impact on main line Protestantism. Instead, they were soundly defeated, and within three years the moderate J. Whitcomb Brougher had inaugurated a widespread campaign to institute peace.

One reaction to this failure to secure a creedal commitment was the creation in 1923 of a separate conservative organization, the Baptist Bible Union (BBU) with Riley, T. T. Shields of Toronto, and J. Frank Norris of Fort Worth serving as its guiding lights. At Riley's insistence, Shields, whom the *Christian Century* labeled "the very incarnation of fanatical conviction," took over as president. Riley's *Beacon* and Shields's *Gospel Witness* became the voices of their position. The historian of the Baptist Bible Union has claimed that, as originally established, it was primarily separatist in intent and that only the objections of Riley kept it from publishing a separatist pamphlet and immediately taking that position. The goal of the BBU was to organize all the Baptists of North America into one unit—Norris leading the South, Riley, the North, and Shields, Canada—and thus destroy Modernism. They saw themselves as the only true heirs of the Baptist democratic tradition. "Modernists are not Baptists, even though they are called by that name," said William M. Pettingill. "The name belongs to Bible believers and to no others." Riley scoffed at the liberal use of the term "liberty of conscience," for he said that the liberties of the faith consisted in the liberty of believing what was written in the Bible and in Christ. "Every man has a right to independent thought," he said, "but he who thinks 'above that which is written,' apart from that which is revealed, is using his 'liberty for an occasion to the flesh,' and comes under the condemnation of the Scriptures."

Shields insisted that the BBU and the fundamentalists in the Northern Baptist Convention were one ideologically, but others were not so certain. Curtis L. Laws wrote a lengthy editorial in the *Watchman-Examiner* pointing out their differences. Laws was afraid that the new organization would destroy what the more moderate Fundamentalists were trying to do. This division of forces caused considerable harm to their efforts. Eventually the BBU moved to establish separate foreign missionaries and, on their own, took over Des Moines University. By 1929, they were close to becoming a new denomination, and in 1932, they formed the heart of the group that split off to form the General Association of Regular Baptist Churches.

Because many foreign missionaries were supported by the denominations, the Fundamentalist controversy soon became international. China seems to have been the major area of concern, but Africa was also involved. The problems of getting an accurate view of the situation in the foreign missions field were many. The standard approach was for each denomination to send a person to visit the missions and mission schools and then write a report on his discoveries. The mission question, along with that of the soundness of schools, troubled the Baptists for many years.

John R. Straton's interest in the Baptist missions arose when Bertha Henshaw, who had served in China for some years but was then working for the American Baptist Foreign Missionary Society (ABFUS), became suspicious of the theological views of some of the current missionaries. A member of Straton's Calvary Church, she allied herself with his Fundamentalist league. For a while, she was both working for the ABFMS and preparing articles for Straton's *Fundamentalist*, a position she found decidedly uncomfortable. "If I speak of things, I feel like a traitor," she wrote, "if I keep still, I feel like a coward."

In his magazine and his sermons, Straton suddenly began to demand an investigation of the foreign missionary situation. The Fundamentalist group that he led finally arranged a meeting with the Board of Managers of the ABFMS but they sustained an earlier ruling that Straton and his followers not be allowed access to the records. Straton claimed that they did not want to rummage through the files, but only to examine a few specific items. A stockholder should have access to a company's records, he declared. The board, however, decided that many of the letters had been written in confidence and that to allow any such examination would be a violation of trust. The agitation Straton caused had considerable effect, and when the Northern Baptist Convention met in Milwaukee in 1924, Jasper C. Massee led the floor fight to get a commission to investigate their foreign missions. A group was organized and given $25,000 for this purpose. Straton proposed that he and Riley do the investigating, but this was shouted down. The committee reported the next year that the sweeping criticism of the missionaries could not be verified and that the spreading of such rumors caused severe harm to their denominational efforts. They urged peace on the issue. The plan they adopted was the so-called "inclusive policy," which recognized the existence of two points of view within the denomination. This decision was not satisfactory to many of the Fundamentalists. Bertha Henshaw exchanged sad letters with Riley about the ineffectiveness of Massee's leadership, and Straton exchanged harsh letters with the moderate Frank M. Goodchild, who suffered a heart attack because of the strain of his activities. Straton and the others then began talking about a new foreign mission society, which eventually the more extreme Fundamentalists set up in the BBU. Eastern Baptist Seminary also was born in 1925 to counter Crozer, following the path of Northern, which had been established in 1913 to counter the influence of Chicago. For many, the only solution was to separate.

The last important fight in the Northern Baptist Convention came in 1926. Riley played an especially important role in that stormy gathering in Washington, D.C. The failure of the Fundamentalists to unseat the New York Park Avenue Church delegates the previous year at Seattle promised a fierce controversy, for the issue at stake was who should determine what constituted a true Baptist church. Harry Emerson Fosdick's Park Avenue Church administered baptism according to the joiner's wishes, but certain groups of Fundamentalists felt this was contrary to the traditional Baptist position. If the convention determined the practices of a local church, however, it would be taking upon itself the powers of a general assembly—which it had never done. By 1926, Jasper C. Massee had divested himself of the leadership of the Fundamentalist Fellowship, and Frank M. Goodchild and J. Whitcomb Brougher had replaced him as the moderate leaders. Brougher proposed a standing resolution that the Northern Baptist Convention recognize its constituency as consisting of those churches "in which the immersion of believers is recognized and practiced as the only Scriptural baptism; and the Convention hereby declares that only immersed members will be recognized as delegates to the Convention." Riley, however, felt that immersion and regeneration were irrevocably connected and proposed as an amendment that "the Northern Baptist Convention recognizes its constituency as consisting solely of those Baptist Churches in which the immersion of believers is recognized and practiced as a pre-requisite to membership."

The fight on the floor was fierce. Holding the Bible in the air, Straton declared the Baptists would be aiding those who were out to destroy it if they failed to pass Riley's motion. He also criticized John D. Rockefeller's role in the denomination. Riley's motion was finally defeated 1,084 to 2,020, and Brougher's was then adopted. This was the last great Baptist floor fight for twenty years, for it was obvious by 1926 that the denomination was tiring of controversy. Although clearly a conservative, J. Whitcomb Brougher had spent the previous six months traveling across the nation urging one hundred thousand Baptists to "play ball." As a gesture of reconciliation, he was elected president of the convention. Jasper C. Massee proposed a six months' "armistice" on the controversy, which was well received except by a few extremists. The 1927 convention was billed as the "harmony" meeting, but it did not receive much publicity because Charles Lindbergh's solo transatlantic flight occurred at the same time. The meetings in 1928 and 1929 were also quiet, and in 1930 William B. Riley and Harry Emerson Fosdick appeared on the same platform. The controversy among the Baptists seemed to be over.

The Northern Presbyterians experienced only slightly less internal dissension than the Baptists. One contemporary declared the fight within the ranks to be "that of the Protestant Reformation over again." The Baptists had no figure of national importance. William Jennings Bryan was the most widely known Presbyterian layman, however, and a good part of the denomination's troubles could be laid at his doorstep. Bryan had long been a frequent delegate to the Presbyterian General Assembly. He was there in 1919, and in 1920, although he was not scheduled to speak, in answer to demands from the crowd, he arose to deliver a few words. His major impact upon the Presbyterians, however, came in the 1923 convention when he ran for moderator of the General Assembly. Paolo Coletta's contention that Bryan was a shrewd politician is well borne out in his fight for moderator. Before he entered the race, he asked several prominent Presbyterians whose opinions he valued whether he should run. Not all of the replies were favorable, but he decided to have his name entered. The battle on the floor was long and heated, and although he led on the first two ballots, his opponent, Charles F. Wishart of Ohio, finally won on the third. Thus, the "most widely influential layman in the church," as the *Christian Century* called him, went down to defeat in what would be his last major bid for elected office. This fight created the most strain the General Assembly had seen for years..

Had Bryan been elected moderator in 1923 the Northern Presbyterians might well have split into two factions, for he had been a divisive force in the denomination for over two years on the question of evolution. The prospect of the head of a major Protestant denomination traversing the land denouncing evolution would have caused untold controversy. In addition, 1923 was to be a year of organizational revision, and Bryan had never been closely involved with the inner workings of the church. Eventually, the issue of evolution swallowed up most of the doctrinal issues that had caused the appearance of the Auburn confession and the General Assembly's periodic reaffirmation of the points of the Westminster Confession. Theology did not come under consideration again until 1927-28, when J. Gresham Machen and his followers split from the church over the issue of Calvinism.

The man at the center of both of these denominational controversies was Harry Emerson Fosdick. Fosdick was ordained to the Northern Baptist ministry in 1903, and he was a popular preacher from the beginning. One of his best books, *The Meaning of Prayer,* was published in 1915. He served as professor at Union Theological Seminary from 1915 to 1946 and as minister of the Riverside Church from 1926 to 1946. Before that, however, he served as a permanent Baptist "special minister" in New York City's Park Avenue Presbyterian Church. Thus, he was susceptible to attacks from both denominations.

A satisfactory definition of Protestant Modernism or liberalism (for the too terms were used interchangeably) has so far eluded historians. "I am not going to undertake to give you a single definition of Modernism," said the president of Columbia Theological Seminary in South Carolina in an article entirely devoted to the subject, because "the modernist has a manifold personality. Modernism has many phases." Sydney E. Ahlstrom, for example, in A *Religious History of the American People,* has a section entitled "The Varieties of Religious Liberalism." Understanding of the term thus has revolved around the people concerned, and because of his great reputation as a preacher, Harry Emerson Fosdick came to be seen as the chief exemplar of the new theology. The *New Republic* claimed that he had made himself into "the prophet of modernism."

When he visited the mission field in China in 1921, Fosdick found Fundamentalists engaged in an aggressive campaign against the liberals, even to the extent of trying to force their retirement. He saw similar troubles when he returned to the United States and was motivated to preach a sermon on May 22, 1922, called "The New Knowledge and the Christian Faith," which was also circulated under the title, "Shall the Fundamentalists Win?" Essentially pleading for tolerance, Fosdick also presented a good case for the liberal position on the major issues of the Virgin Birth, the second coming, and biblical interpretation.

The reaction to the distribution of this sermon was unprecedented. Conservatives in all denominations rushed to answer it. Presbyterian Clarence Macartney of Philadelphia published "Shall Unbelief Win?" Conservative *Bible Champion* editor William H. Bates replied with "Fundamentalism vs. Liberalism," Presbyterian Harry Bochne with "Can the Fundamentalists Lose?" Disciples minister Rupert C. Foster with "Shall the Fundamentalists Win?" and Baptist John R. Straton with "Shall the Funnymonkeyists Win?"

Fosdick's sermon became one of the most important pulpit statements of the decade. It caused a minor pamphlet war, and it thrust Fosdick onto center stage as the archetypal liberal. Conservative attacks on him knew no bounds. This view of Fosdick was unfortunate for all concerned, for, in spite of his prominence, he was not a representative figure for the new theology. As later studies have shown, his thinking was not typical. He was chiefly a preacher and a religious counselor, and the main burden of his message concerned the integrity of the human personality. Even more important, Fosdick was not aggressive, and, unlike many Fundamentalists, he never relished controversy. Eventually, the *Christian Century* urged the Fundamentalists to find another target, but the abuse he received did not cease until his death.

Because of the premillennial issue, the presence of Harry Emerson Fosdick and William Jennings Bryan, and (perhaps) more aggressive conservative leadership, the Northern Baptists and the Northern Presbyterians were the denominations most disturbed by the Fundamentalist-Modernist controversy. But the other main line groups were also affected. The theological issues raised moved from denomination to denomination with conservatives and liberals each bending them to their own specifications.

Disciples of Christ members were never prominent in any of the interdenominational Fundamentalist organizations, nor was the denomination much concerned with the premillennial issue, but the controversy had considerable impact upon them. They had been divided into conservative and liberal wings for years, and the polarization of the issues exacerbated these divisions. Disciples' periodicals were filled with articles agonizing over the question of whether or not their conservatives were really Fundamentalists. The liberal periodicals declared they were not. Fundamentalism, they argued, was based on a creed, whereas the Disciples based their beliefs solely on the Bible. At the end of the decade, however, the two distinct views were clearly evident in their churches.

Liberal denominations such as the Congregationalists and Unitarians watched the fray from one sideline. Congregationalists seemed little affected at the time, for they had long resolved the issues involved to their own satisfaction. In the 1920s, for example, the Tucson Congregationalists described themselves as "a liberal church." But aggressive conservatism made advances even there. Today, examples can be found of Fundamentalist Congregational churches (now called the United Church of Christ) in rural areas. Albert C. Dieffenbach, able editor of the Unitarian *Christian Register*, saw the rise of Modernism as a vindication of the Unitarian position. In issue after issue he urged the liberals to leave their churches and join his. He especially pressured Fosdick along these lines. Yet, surprisingly, few did so. Unitarians did not gain large numbers during the decade because most Modernists remained within their own denominations.

The Missouri Synod Lutherans cheered on the Fundamentalists from the conservative sidelines. They had no interest in premillennialism, but were sympathetic to conservative theology. The Missouri Synod leaned heavily on a literal interpretation of Scripture, and, of course, had little interest in materialistic evolution or the liberal view of Jesus. In the early 1970s, however, the synod split in two over issues almost identical to those raised in the 1920s: the historicity of Scripture, the use of higher criticism, and the rise of liberalism in their seminaries.

The Seventh-Day Adventists, Pentecostals, Holiness groups, Church of the Nazarene, Mormons, Salvation Army, and independent sects also sided with the Fundamentalists. They all shared a common conservative interpretation of Scripture. The Seventh-Day Adventist, moreover, attacked evolution with special vehemence. Some of them saw the struggle over the theory as the predicted battle with Anti-Christ. . . .

At first, the Fundamentalist organizations, such as the WCFA, disliked being lumped with such groups as the Pentecostals, Adventists, or Holiness churches. But eventually they realized they had more in common than they had first thought. Moreover, the popular mind rarely made fine distinctions, viewing all such groups as Fundamentalists.

In general, the Roman Catholics were bewildered by the controversy. They had effectively halted "Modernism" (the same name but a slightly different movement) in their churches by Pius X's 1907 encyclical, *Pascendi dominici gregis*. They were also little bothered by the evolution issue, for they made the distinction between the body (which might have come via materialistic evolution) and the soul (which came from God). One prelate even suggested that the controversy signaled the death knell of American Protestantism.

Although Methodists, both North and South, prided themselves on being free from Fundamentalist agitation, whether they were is open to doubt. The quasi-official three-volume *History of American Methodism* credited their lack of involvement to three causes: Methodist theology, which stressed the personal experience of each individual as the only test of faith, could not be easily polarized; their central governing body met every four years and it was not in session in 1925; and no strong Methodist Fundamentalist leaders emerged.

Historian William W. Sweet, who lived through the fracas, however, remembered it differently. He recalled that the Methodists were troubled. Their conservatives were centered in New Jersey, Philadelphia, and Baltimore, and in 1920 and 1924, they questioned the denomination's "course of study" program. They feared that reading liberal materials would cause young ministers to lose their faith. In 1925, they formed themselves into a Methodist League for Faith and Life, with a monthly periodical, *The Call to Colors.* The league's express purpose was "to reaffirm the vital and eternal truths of the Christian religion, such as the inspiration of the Scriptures, the deity of Jesus, his Virgin Birth, etc." In 1923 the WCFA annual convention met in Fort Worth to hold a sensational "trial" of three Methodist schools: Texas Women's College, Southwestern University, and Southern Methodist University. Six students confessed that they had been taught evolution in these schools. Leander W. Munhall, irascible editor of the *Eastern Methodist,* frequently denounced liberal denominational leaders. In spite of claims to the contrary, Methodist periodicals for this time show much concern over the issues raised, especially the proper interpretation of Scripture. . . .

Although the Episcopalians were bothered by neither evolution nor premillennialism and could hardly be classified as Fundamentalists, they were considerably affected by the theological issues raised by the controversy. For them the issue revolved around the interpretation of the historic church creeds: a "creedal traditionalism" versus a more liberal interpretation. Episcopalians had long been divided into conservative and liberal camps, and their denominational conflict formed over the necessity for belief in the Virgin Birth and bodily resurrection of Jesus. Liberals, such as Bishop William Lawrence of Massachusetts, argued that this might not be essential doctrine; conservatives, such as Bishop William T. Manning of New York, insisted that it was.

The quarrel was focused by Reverend Percy Stickney Grant's assertion that the church should allow for liberalism within its walls, a view for which his bishop, William Manning, rebuked him. Simultaneously, an obscure Texas rector named Heaton was cited for trial for his liberal views. In their Dallas meeting of 1923, the bishops of the church issued a pastoral letter affirming the Virgin Birth and bodily resurrection of Christ. Publication of this statement was expected to quiet the controversy, but it had the opposite effect. Dr. Leighton Parks attacked the pastoral letter and pleaded for intellectual integrity on the part of the clergy in their recitation of the Apostles' Creed. Parks challenged Manning to leave Heaton alone and bring both Lawrence and himself to trial as an object lesson. The faculty of the Episcopal Theological School at Cambridge sent out an official alumni bulletin suggesting more liberty by allowing recitation of the creeds to be permissive instead of obligatory. The 1924 Church Congress solemnly discussed the question of how the church should deal with Fundamentalism.

One of the most articulate defenders of the conservative position among the Episcopalians was New York's Bishop Manning. Much to his dismay, his defense of conservative Christianity caused him to be lumped with the antievolutionists, premillennialists, and biblical literalists. In a widely publicized sermon in 1923, he argued that Episcopal conservatism and Fundamentalism were completely different. Fundamentalism rested on sixteenth-century confessions of faith that did not affect Episcopalians, he declared. "The question with us in this Church," he said, "is not Fundamentalism or Modernism but belief in Jesus Christ, the Son of God."' In his 1924 message to the diocese, he tried to reaffirm what he saw as basic Christian principles. Although few Episcopalians could legitimately be termed Fundamentalists, many of them were decidedly conservative Christians in their interpretation of theology. The Fundamentalist-Modernist controversy helped reawaken these old grievances. . . .

Except for the issue of the second coming, the South congealed quickly on the points raised. While the Northern churches were smoothing over their science-religion difficulties, in 1926 the powerful Southern Baptist Convention unanimously passed a resolution rejecting evolution and supporting Genesis. Bryan placed his faith primarily in the southern colleges, and in 1925 Southern Methodist Bishop Warren A. Candler declared that "the churches of the South must save the cause of evangelical Christianity in the United States or it will be lost." The Fundamentalist controversy was instrumental in calling the South to a renewed consciousness of its distinctive religious position. The southern denominations are today one of the last remnants of Puritan America.

As the southern churches closed ranks, the incipient liberal trends of the previous decade came under fire. Even the moderate liberals such as Southern Baptist William L. Poteat, president of Wake Forest College, and Edgar Y. Mullins, president of the Southern Baptist Theological Seminary, Louisville, were denounced for their views on theistic evolution. Southern Baptist periodicals rejoiced that their churches were relatively free from northern heresy. Historian James J. Thompson, Jr., has concluded that virtually all Southern Baptists during the 1920s disbelieved in the theory of evolution. Not all of them, however, wished to see its teaching prohibited by law.

Southern Presbyterians equally rejoiced that their denomination was not much affected by Modernism. They were especially acerbic in their attacks on this point of view. In 1923, the president of their seminary in Columbia, South Carolina, declared Modernism "the greatest danger that menaces the world today." Their prestigious *Presbyterian of the South* (Richmond) cheered the legislature of Tennessee for decreeing that evolution would not be taught in that state. Although there were few liberals within the denomination proper, considerable division existed among their foreign missionaries.

The Southern Methodists also had few liberals within their denomination, but those often were harassed. Local pressure forced the resignation of Dr. John Rice from the School of Theology at Southern Methodist University in Dallas, and at the May 1922 General Conference, a special commission urged responsible officials to take all necessary steps to drive out heretical doctrines. When a visiting speaker presented the Wellhausen theory of the Pentateuch at a Lake

Junaluska conference in 1925, he was severely attacked by Bishop James Cannon.

Because most of the southern churches held some type of conservative position, the South proved an especially congenial home for the last wave of Fundamentalist organizations in the 1920s, the most important of which was the Bible Crusaders. Born from a conversation between John R. Straton and wealthy real estate broker George F. Washburn, the Crusaders hoped to unify all the Fundamentalist forces of the country. "If this movement only stops the invasion of modernists," Washburn was quoted as saying, "I would rather be known as the founder of it than President of the United States."

In spite of the hopes with which they began, however, the Crusaders were never able to gain momentum. Their threats to "make and unmake" southern governors, senators, and state officials on the textbook question came to nothing. Their only success occurred when, through the efforts of T. T. Martin in the house and I. R. Deal and L. B. Morony in the senate, they were able to push an antievolution bill through the Mississippi legislature. The Crusaders did not become the clearing house for a federation of Fundamentalists as had been hoped. Their magazine, *Crusader's Champion,* ceased publication in October 1926, after having existed about a year. In 1929, Washburn reported that the collapse of the Florida land speculation in which he was engaged had forced him to consolidate his enterprises, discontinue his Crusaders work, and resign from all but the most essential business activity, and even so, he was barely able to save his Florida estate.

The South's most controversial Fundamentalist leader, J. Frank Norris, also fell on hard times after 1925. Pastor of the First Baptist Church in Fort Worth since 1909, Norris stepped onto the national stage in the early 1920s. His continual attacks on Modernists, evolutionists (especially those on the faculty of Baylor University), Roman Catholics, city officials, and other Texas Baptists helped keep him in the public eye for many years.

Although the Texas Baptist Convention refused to seat his delegates in 1922 and 1923 and permanently removed his church from their organization in 1924, Norris continually insisted that 90 percent of the Southern Baptists were in his camp. Gradually, however, he separated himself from all local Baptist fellowship. Although his dreams of establishing a premillennial organization in every southern state never materialized, he did succeed in setting up his own Bible seminary. The graduates from this school helped keep his militant conservatism alive. . . .

. . . by the late 1920s, the Fundamentalist-Modernist controversy had diminished. The great crash of 1929 and the ensuing Depression administered what appeared to be the final blow. Yet during the 1920s, this social and religious movement proved of the utmost importance. It severely disrupted the Northern Baptists and Northern Presbyterians. It reaffirmed long-standing divisions within the Disciples, Episcopalians, and Northern and Southern Methodists. It caused the popular mind to consider Seventh-Day Adventists, Pentecostals, the Church of the Nazarene, and all other conservative groups as Fundamentalists, and it brought these groups to a realization of how many points they shared in common. It called the southern churches to a consciousness of their own distinctive conservative heritage. It confirmed the fact that the major divisions among the main line Protestant churches were really not denominational but based on whether one were liberal or conservative. . . .

Questions for Reflection and Discussion

1. How do the documents reveal conflicting worldviews of fundamentalism and modernism?

2. How does George Marsden account for the rise of theological liberalism and hence its emerging tension with fundamentalism?

3. According to Willard Gatewood, what were the connections between the controversy over evolution and the tension between fundamentalism and modernism?

4. To what social and religious factors does Ferenc Szasz attribute the fundamentalism-modernist controversy?

5. How does the fundamentalist-modernist controversy reflect the "nervous and uncertain" character of American society in the decade after World War I?

Additional Readings

Appleby, R. Scott. *Church and Age Unite: The Modernist Impulse in American Catholicism.* Notre Dame: University of Notre Dame Press, 1991.

Cauthen, Kenneth. *The Impact of American Religious Liberalism.* New York: Harper and Row, 1962.

Dollar, George. *A History of Fundamentalism in America.* Greenville, SC: Bob Jones University Press, 1973.

Furniss, Norman F. *The Fundamentalist Controversy, 1918-1931.* New Haven: Yale University Press, 1954.

Hart, D. G. *Defending the Faith: J. Gresham Machem and the Crisis of Conservative Protestantism in Modern America.* Baltimore: The John Hopkins University Press, 1994.

Hutchison, William R. *The Modernist Impulse in American Protestantism.* Cambridge: Harvard University Press, 1976.

Kraut, Benny. "A Wary Collaboration: Jews, Catholics, and the Protestant Goodwill Movement." In William R. Hutchison, ed., *Between the Times: The Travail of the Protestant Establishment in America, 1900-1960*, 193-230. Cambridge: Cambridge University Press, 1989.

Marty, Martin. *Modern American Religion: The Noise of Conflict, 1919-1941*. Chicago: University of Chicago Press, 1991.

_____. *The Modern Schism: Three Paths to the Secular*. New York: Harper and Row, 1969.

Russell, C. Allyn. *Voices of American Fundamentalism: Seven Biographical Studies*. Philadelphia: Westminster Press, 1976.

Sandeen, Ernest. *The Roots of Fundamentalism: British and American Millenarianism*. Chicago: University of Chicago Press, 1970.

Weber, Timothy. *Living in the Shadow of the Second Coming: American Premillennialism, 1875-1925: with a New Preface*. Chicago: University of Chicago Press, 1987.

Chapter 13

American Religious Ferment During the Depression Era

Issue

How did American religion respond to the secular challenges of the depression period?

"The man who builds a factory builds a temple. The man who works there, worships there," remarked President Calvin Coolidge in the midst of America's unprecedented prosperity during the 1920s. With the factory largely responsible for the rise in per capita GNP from $719 in the prosperous years of 1917-21 to $857 in 1929, and the growth of the national income from $63 billion in 1922 to $88 billion in 1929, Coolidge declared confidently that "the business of America is business." But with the plummeting of stock prices beginning in October of 1929, panic set in and the economy went into a tailspin that resulted in the drop of per capita GNP to $590 in 1933 and the rise of unemployment to 25 percent.

The economic trauma affected not only the pocketbooks of the American people, but also their minds and their souls. How did America respond religiously to the challenges of the decade-long depression? Unlike prior occasions of widespread economic hardship, this time no wave of revival spread among the people. Was this, mused the editors of Christian Century, *because for once people did not blame God for hard times? Maybe this time their troubles were due not to a collective offense against God, but to the failure of a humanly invented economic system. This response from the houses of worship in America reflected the ongoing secularization of American society.*

In the midst of the economic revolution of the late nineteenth century, America's turn toward secular values accelerated. Many in the nation relegated their religious beliefs to the back of their minds while they preoccupied themselves with the material world during the next quarter century. But as the fundamentalist-modernist controversy of the 1920s discussed in the previous chapter showed, religious beliefs were not abandoned—only increasingly secularized. This process redefined the boundaries of the religious establishment in the depression decade. How inclusive would the liberalized, ecumenical Federal Council of Churches be in the matter of race? And would secularized Jews be more inclusive toward women? The fundamentalists' contest against secularists in the 1920s ended in apparent failure, but not death. As fundamentalism became more exclusive in the 1930s, it gained a new vitality as a viable grassroots movement. All of this activity, however, failed to produce a new wave of revival among the hurting, confused people of America.

Documents

How inclusive American religion would be along inter-faith lines was a matter of considerable discussion during the depression era. During the 1920s some Protestants promoted a "goodwill movement" among the three major faiths, but the encyclical of Pope Pius XI in 1928 expressly forbade Catholic participation with Protestants in Christian congresses, such as the one at Lausanne the year before. The first document is an excerpt from the encyclical. The extent of the secularization of American culture is reflected in the Humanist Manifesto I, *signed in 1933 by fourteen Unitarian and Universalist ministers, a rabbi, eleven professors, and a number of independent writers and thinkers. It is the second document printed below. In the third selection, Esther Bengis wrote in her short work* I am a Rabbi's Wife *(1934) of her activity as the young, orthodox wife of Rabbi Bengis (never identifying him by his first name.) The final two documents note two widely varied religious responses to the travail of capitalism and the New Deal response to it. In the fourth reading, a* New York Times *article of August 3, 1936, reflects Father Charles Coughlin's continuing secular involvement as a Roman Catholic voice of exclusion in his attack on President Franklin Roosevelt and the New Deal, and Coughlin's move toward fascism. The next year Quaker pacifist (and socialist) Kirby Page insisted in* Must We Go to War? *that pacifism remained the best option for bringing about change in American capitalism. His comments appear in the final selection.*

1. The Promotion of True Religious Unity, 1928

SOURCE: Excerpted from Pope Pius XI's encyclical *Mortalium animos*, on "Fostering True Religious Unity" delivered in 1928.

The teaching authority of the Church, which by divine plan was established on earth that revealed truths might be preserved untouched forever, and quickly and safely come to the minds of men, is daily exercised by the Roman Pontiff and the bishops in communion with him.

Still it has the duty to proceed opportunely in defining points of faith with solemn rites and decrees, when there is a need to declare them to resist more effectively the errors and assaults of heretics or to impress upon the minds of the faithful clearer and more profound explanations of points of sacred doctrine.

However, in this extraordinary use of the teaching authority nothing is invented nor is anything new added to the sum of truths that are, at lease implicity [sic], contained in the deposit of divine revelation that was entrusted by God to the Church. Instead points of faith are defined that could by chance still seem obscure to some or truths are established as matters of faith that for the first time were called into question.

Therefore, Venerable Brethren, it is clear why the Apostolic See has never permitted its children to take part in these congresses. The unity of Christians cannot be otherwise obtained than by securing the return of the separated to the one true Church of Christ from which they once unhappily withdrew. To the one true Church of Christ, We say, that stands forth before all and that by the will of its Founder will remain forever the same as when He Himself established it for the salvation of all mankind.

The mystical Spouse of Christ has in the course of the centuries remained unspotted nor can it ever be contaminated. St. Cyprian says: "The Spouse of Christ cannot commit adultery; she is incorrupt and modest, she knows one house, she guards with chaste modesty the holiness of one room." This same holy martyr marveled, and with reason, how anyone could think that "the unity which proceeds from the stability of God and is bound together by the sacraments of heaven could be torn asunder in the church or separated by the wills of the discordant."

Since the Mystical Body of Christ, that is to say, the Church, is, like the physical body, a unity, a compact thing closely joined together, it would be false and foolish to say that Christ's Mystical Body could be composed of separated and scattered members. Whoever therefore is not united with it is not a member of it nor does he communicate with its Head Who is Christ.

No one is found in the one Church of Christ and no one perseveres in it unless he acknowledges and accepts obediently the supreme authority of St. Peter and his legitimate successors. Did not the very ancestors of those who are entangled in the errors of Photius and the Protestants obey the Roman bishop as the high shepherd of souls?

Children did, alas, abandon their father's house but the house did not therefore fall in ruins, supported as it was by the unceasing help of God. Let them return, then, to the common father of all. He has forgotten the unjust wrongs inflicted upon the Holy See and will receive them most lovingly. If, as they often say, they desire to be united with Us and with Ours, why do they not hasten to return to the Church, "the mother and mistress of all the followers of Christ ?"

Let them listen to Lactantius crying: "It is only the Catholic Church that retains the true worship. It is the fountain of truth, it is the household of the faith, it is the temple of God: if anyone does not enter it or if anyone departs from it, he is a stranger to the hope of life and salvation. Let no one deceive himself by continuous wranglings. Life and salvation are in the balance, which if not looked to carefully and diligently will be lost and destroyed."

Let these separated children return to the Apostolic See established in this city which the Princes of the Apostles, Peter and Paul, consecrated with their blood, to this See, "the root and matrix of the Catholic Church," not indeed with the idea or hope that "the Church of the living God, the pillar and ground of truth" will abandon the integrity of the faith and bear their errors, but to subject themselves to its teaching authority and rule.

Would that what has not been granted to many of Our predecessors would be granted to Us, to embrace with the heart of a father the children over whom We mourn, separated by an evil discord from Us. May God Our Saviour "Who will have all men to be saved and to come to the knowledge of the truth" hearken to our ardent prayer and vouchsafe to call back all wanderers to the unity of the Church!

2. Humanist Manifesto I, 1933

SOURCE: Paul Kurtz, *Humanist Manifestos I and II*, pp. 7-10, (Amherst, NY: Prometheus Books), Copyright 1973. Reprinted by permission of the publisher.

Preface

Humanism is a philosophical, religious, and moral point of view as old as human civilization itself. It has its roots in classical China, Greece, and Rome; it is expressed in the Renaissance and the Enlightenment, in the scientific revolution, and in the twentieth century.

Each age seeks to define what its distinctive values are, what it seeks to cherish and enhance. Each age has to contend with alienating and restrictive forces that seek to denigrate the individual, undermine humane values, and suppress social justice.

In the twentieth century, humanist awareness has developed at a rapid pace; yet it has to overcome powerful antihumanist forces that seek to destroy it.

In 1933 a group of thirty-four liberal humanists in the United States defined and enunciated the philosophical and religious principles that seemed to them fundamental. They drafted *Humanist Manifesto I*, which for its time was a radical document. It was concerned with expressing a general religious and philosophical outlook that rejected orthodox and dogmatic positions and provided meaning and direction, unity and purpose to human life. It was committed to reason, science, and democracy. . . .

* * * * *

The time has come for widespread recognition of the radical changes in religious beliefs throughout the modern world. The time is past for mere revision of traditional attitudes. Science and economic change have disrupted the old beliefs. Religions the world over are under the necessity of coming to terms with new conditions created by a vastly increased knowledge and experience. In every field of human activity, the vital movement is now in the direction of a candid and explicit humanism. In order that religious humanism may be better understood we, the undersigned, desire to make certain affirmations which we believe the facts of our contemporary life demonstrate.

There is great danger of a final, and we believe fatal, identification of the word *religion* with doctrines and methods which have lost their significance and which are powerless to solve the problem of human living in the Twentieth Century. Religions have always been means for realizing the highest values of life. Their end has been accomplished through the interpretation of the total environing situation (theology or world view), the sense of values resulting therefrom (goal or ideal), and the technique (cult) established for realizing the satisfactory life. A change in any of these factors results in alteration of the outward forms of religion. This fact explains the changefulness of religions through the centuries. But through all changes religion itself remains constant in its quest for abiding values, an inseparable feature of human life.

Today's man's larger understanding of the universe, his scientific achievements, and his deeper appreciation of brotherhood, have created a situation which requires a new statement of the means and purposes of religion. Such a vital, fearless, and frank religion capable of furnishing adequate social goals and personal satisfactions may appear to many people as a complete break with the past. While this age does owe a vast debt to traditional religions, it is none the less obvious that any religion that can hope to be a synthesizing and dynamic force for today must be shaped for the needs of this age. To establish such a religion is a major necessity of the present. It is a responsibility which rests upon this generation. We therefore affirm the following:

First: Religious humanists regard the universe as self-existing and not created.

Second: Humanism believes that man is a part of nature and that he has emerged as the result of a continuous process.

Third: Holding an organic view of life, humanists find that the traditional dualism of mind and body must be rejected.

Fourth: Humanism recognizes that man's religious culture and civilization, as clearly depicted by anthropology and history, are the product of a gradual development due to his interaction with his natural environment and with his social heritage. The individual born into a particular culture is largely molded to that culture.

Fifth: Humanism asserts that the nature of the universe depicted by modern science makes unacceptable any supernatural or cosmic guarantees of human values. Obviously humanism does not deny the possibility of realities as yet undiscovered, but it does insist that the way to determine the existence and value of any and all realities is by means of intelligent inquiry and by the assessment of their relation to human needs. Religion must formulate its hopes and plans in the light of the scientific spirit and method.

Sixth: We are convinced that the time has passed for theism, deism, modernism, and the several varieties of "new thought."

Seventh: Religion consists of those actions, purposes, and experiences which are humanly significant. Nothing human is alien to the religious. It includes labor, art, science, philosophy, love, friendship, recreation—all that is in its degree expressive of intelligently satisfying human living. The distinction between the sacred and the secular can no longer be maintained.

Eighth: Religious humanism considers the complete realization of human personality to be the end of man's life and seeks its development and fulfillment in the here and now. This is the explanation of the humanist's social passion.

Ninth: In place of the old attitudes involved in worship and prayer the humanist finds his religious emotions expressed in a heightened sense of personal life and in a cooperative effort to promote social well-being.

Tenth: It follows that there will be no uniquely religious emotions and attitudes of the kind hitherto associated with belief in the supernatural.

Eleventh: Man will learn to face the crises of life in terms of his knowledge of their naturalness and probability. Reasonable and manly attitudes will be fostered by education and supported by custom. We assume that humanism will take the path of social and mental hygiene and discourage sentimental and unreal hopes and wishful thinking.

Twelfth: Believing that religion must work increasingly for joy in living, religious humanists aim to foster the creative in man and to encourage achievements that add to the satisfactions of life.

Thirteenth: Religious humanism maintains that all associations and institutions exist for the fulfillment of human life. The intelligent evaluation, transformation, control, and direction of such associations and institutions with a view to the enhancement of human life is the purpose and program of humanism. Certainly religious institutions, their ritualistic forms, ecclesiastical methods, and communal activities must be reconstituted as rapidly as experience allows, in order to function effectively in the modern world.

Fourteenth: The humanists are firmly convinced that existing acquisitive and profit-motivated society has shown itself to be inadequate and that a radical change in methods, controls, and motives must be instituted. A socialized and cooperative economic order must be established to the end that the equitable distribution of the means of life be possible. The goal of humanism is a free and universal society in which people voluntarily and intelligently cooperate for the common good. Humanists demand a shared life in a shared world.

Fifteenth and last: We assert that humanism will: (a) affirm life rather than deny it; (b) seek to elicit the possibilities of life, not flee from it; and (c) endeavor to establish the conditions of a satisfactory life for all, not merely for the few. By this positive *morale* and intention humanism will be guided, and from this perspective and alignment the techniques and efforts of humanism will flow.

So stands the theses of religious humanism. Though we consider the religious forms and ideas of our fathers no longer adequate, the quest for the good life is still the central task for mankind. Man is at last becoming aware that he alone is responsible for the realization of the world of his dreams, that he has within himself the power for its achievement. He must set intelligence and will to the task.

[concluded with names of 34 signers]

3. I am a Rabbi's Wife, 1934

SOURCE: Esther Bengis, *I am a Rabbi's Wife* (Moodus, CT: Esther Bengis, 1934), 80-84.

The work of women is of great importance in the community. In many communities the labors and achievements of "women of valor" surpass the efforts of the men. Often, this becomes so apparent that the masculine leaders will hesitate to undertake any community or congregational project of any magnitude, unless they feel certain of the moral backing and support of the women.

My husband would ask the congregational Board of Directors to appoint two women of the Ladies' Auxiliary as members of the Board. Usually the Auxiliary president and another of her officers would serve. This proved most helpful. By attending Board meetings, these ladies would keep in close touch with congregational needs, and be prepared to present these needs at their own Board or general meetings.

To the congregation, the Ladies Auxiliary is all that the name implies. Often it is even more. I have known Auxiliaries to cover Hebrew School deficits, raise funds to pay the mortgage interest, contribute a good portion of the general congregational budget, maintain the synagogue office and secretary and render a host of similar valuable services.

During the depression period, especially, the women proved most heroic. They often succeeded where the men failed. Jobs that the men despaired of they gladly undertook, and as a rule they succeeded. Whether it was a bazaar, the raffling of an automobile, the publishing of a congregational year book, or running a kitchen for a week in one of the leading stores downtown—they undertook these tasks courageously, worked faithfully, and secured results.

One Auxiliary president stands out preeminently in my mind. She had served most faithfully and capably for nearly a score of years. Hers was a long record of usefulness and of achievement.

I have often wondered why it is that women who have servants and do no hard work at home will, on the eve of an Auxiliary affair, come to the synagogue and cheerfully cook, wash dishes, scrub and do other such tasks they would not dream of doing at home. I can ascribe it to one thing only, an earnest and spirited desire to be of service. This readiness to serve is a tribute to their loyalty.

As a rule, the work of the women is earnest and sincere. Feuds and squabbles among the leaders of women's organizations are inevitable, but less frequent than among the men.

In the furtherance of congregational and community projects Rabbi Bengis realized and appreciated the value of the women. He was always prepared to give them full credit and recognition for their labors, as well as encouragement in all their undertakings. His relations with the Auxiliary, its officers and workers were most cordial and pleasant. He attended their meetings, helped in their plans and cheered them in their endeavors.

It is a most happy memory that the Ladies' Auxiliary in one of my husband's early positions was responsible for the gift of an automobile to us. Many other gifts which adorned our home, including floor lamps, articles of silver and even our radio came from the Auxiliary.

Besides the congregational Auxiliary, there is the Hadassah which is really the Zionist Auxiliary, doing splendid work in sanitation, hospitalization and child welfare in Palestine. The leaders of these organizations, unless they were tactful and clever, would sometimes come into conflict, since one stressed local synagogue work and the other emphasized the national, or Palestine need. The rabbi, who urged the support of both, would now and then be called in as mediator and arbitrator of these disputes. Of late, a better understanding of both needs is being cultivated and developed with beneficial results. Thus in our last position it was nothing new for both organizations to enter into a partnership on a rummage sale proposition or jointly sponsor a picnic. Of course, there will always be the rabid and fanatic extremists who will not listen to reason, but fortunately they are few in number and their influence is not felt.

There is still another organization worthy of note: namely, the Council of Jewish Women. While giving itself mainly to civic and philanthropic work, it has other worth-while achievements to its credit. I have known small communities in which the Council of Jewish Women maintained a synagogue or a Hebrew School. The Council does one other commendable work, and that is, the aiding of Jewish college students. Its Student Loan Fund and scholarships have proved a blessing to many a Jewish student. I knew a number of young men and women who owed their college education to the Council.

The Council also fosters and aids Jewish boys and girls who have talent for drama and art.

There are other women's organizations, such as Auxiliaries to the Hebrew School, Relief Societies, etc., each doing a definite and specific piece of work. There is scarcely a Jewish woman in the community who is not affiliated with one or more of these organizations. Many women are members of all.

4. Coughlin Attacks Roosevelt as Red, 1936

SOURCE: From "Coughlin Attacks Roosevelt as Red," *The New York Times,* Aug. 3, 1936. Copyright © 1936 by United Press International. Reprinted with permission.

New Deal Is Surrounded by Atheists and Communists, He Says at Providence.

LANDON IS 'THIS FELLOW'
Name 'Forgotten' by Priest, Who Praises Hoover's 'Honesty' but Deplores 'Ignorance.'

PROVIDENCE, Aug. 2 (AP),—Father Coughlin declared here this afternoon that under the New Deal "the forgotten man has been remembered" in time to pay the government's bills. He spoke at an outdoor rally, which he said was attended by 25,000 persons.

"With the New Deal the forgotten man has been remembered, because every gallon of gas you buy, every pound of butter, every loaf of bread, all your groceries and drugs, have posted on them a mortgage to the United States in favor of international bankers," he said.

He asserted that "one day out of every three you work is taken out of your payroll for hidden taxes."

He argued that the New Deal was "surrounded by its atheists" and "surrounded by its red and pink Communists and by 'frankfurters of destruction.'"

"Look and behold, and see if you want to follow that kind of New Deal that is digging us into a ditch from which we shall never return," he said.

Herbert Hoover was "supremely honest, but supremely ignorant," he asserted, adding that "Hoover with his rugged individualism was more dangerous than Stalin with his communism," and the "worst menace America has ever known."

Revolution "Surely" Coming

"If Herbert Hoover had been re-elected there would have been more bullet holes in the White House than you could count with an adding machine," he said.

"But Roosevelt only stemmed the revolution. It is coming as surely as God is in heaven unless the money changers are driven from the temple. And the National Union is going to drive the servants of the money changers out of the temple and those who keep them there—the politicians."

Father Coughlin said that when the President's father "made his will he would not entrust his money to Franklin Delano Roosevelt because he did not know how to handle his own money."

"And this is the same man we are entrusting with millions of dollars to spend," he added.

He lauded the Union party candidate for President, Representative Lemke, as "honest and sincere." Then he turned to the Union candidate for Vice President, Thomas C. O'Brien of Boston, who was on the platform. Clapping him on the back, he declared:

"We don't believe in the Roosevelt-Tugwell program of destroy and devastate."

Urging each one in the audience to obtain two new members in the National Union for Social Justice, he warned "and if they lose their jobs over it I want an affidavit of the fact and I'll publicize the name of the company that fired them."

"The old corpses of the Democratic and Republican parties are stinking in our nostrils," he asserted.

At another point he declared that "the Republican party is so dead it is a corpse buried beneath the waves of memory."

He referred to Governor Landon as "this fellow from out West—what's his name?"

"When he goes on the radio, everybody shuts it off," he added. "That's why I don't know his name."

5. Must We Go to War?, 1937

SOURCE: From *Must We Go to War?* by Kirby Page. Copyright © 1937 by Henry Holt and Company, LLC. Reprinted with permission.

Is pacific transformation of the property system in the United States probable? Will the effort to achieve this result incite vested interests to overthrow parliamentary government and establish a fascist dictatorship?

In laying foundations strong enough to sustain arguments in favor of peaceable methods of revolution it is not necessary to prove that success is inevitable or even highly probable. It is sufficient to demonstrate the *relative* advantages of this strategy in contrast to revolution through civil war. The fact that the odds are heavily against victory in the effort to transform capitalism through non-warlike means does not invalidate this procedure, since the barriers to triumph through violent seizure of power are far higher. To struggle only when the tides are running in one's favor means that a just society will never be created. Epoch-making social changes have usually been brought about in the face of titanic obstacles. Pacifists should therefore refuse to be discouraged by assertions that in no country has non-warlike revolution ever abolished capitalism. It is equally true that *in no highly industrialized and urbanized nation with conditions at all comparable to those existing in the United States has victory been achieved through violent means.* Indeed, the fact must be emphasized that even in Russia, success was made possible both in March and in November precisely because the revolutionists were not compelled to seize power through armed violence, as I pointed out in an earlier section. It is sheer nonsense to maintain that the Bolsheviks overthrew czarist tyranny. Lenin, Trotsky and a large proportion of other Bolshevik leaders were living in exile and did not return to Russia until after the collapse of czardom. Persons seeking pacific revolution in the United States have more valid reasons for hope than have their opponents who rely upon civil war.

Advocacy of pacific revolution is preferable to reliance upon armed seizure of power for three primary reasons: it is more likely to succeed in the United States; its processes are accompanied by less destruction of human values; and, on grounds of religion, its means are more consistent with the ends sought.

Revolution by any strategy is dependent upon winning the active support or friendly acquiescence of an outright majority of the population, and in the United States there is a far higher possibility of enlisting the required support in behalf of pacific processes than of gaining a sufficient number of adherents in the ranks of armed revolutionists. Lenin was emphatic in repeated assertions that the winning of a majority is a condition of successful revolution, and this is still the orthodox position of the Community Party. The notion that a small company of revolutionists through a *coup d'etat* can inaugurate a revolutionary regime is sheer sentimentalism.

To win a majority in this country means gaining the support of a substantial proportion of skilled workers, white-collar employees, professional men, women and farmers There are not enough genuine proletarians in the United States to seize power, even if the prevailing lethargy and impotence of a large section of this group could be overcome. It is easy to point out obstacles in the way of winning a majority of the population for any strategy of revolution, but surely the evidence is beyond dispute that the task of enlisting sufficient adherents in the ranks of armed revolutionists is far more formidable than the winning of a majority for pacific processes of revolution. . . .

The responsibilities of the churches in this connection are tremendous. Millions of individuals are powerfully affected by the message proclaimed from pulpit and class room of religious education. If even a substantial minority of ministers and other religious educators would throw themselves vigorously into the crusade for a cooperative commonwealth, their influence would prove to be of incalculable value. That this very thing is happening constitutes one of the hopeful signs of the times. It is probably true to say that the minds of religious leaders concerning economic questions have been changed more drastically during the past six years than in the preceding century. The 1934 questionnaire, which was responded to by nearly 21,000 clergymen and rabbis, showed that 18,324 of these ministers favor a cooperative commonwealth, as contrasted with 1,035 supporting rugged individualism. Moreover, 87 per cent of those replying were willing to have their answers made public. Approximately 6,000 expressed themselves as favoring socialism, and nearly 11,000 as supporting drastically reformed capitalism.

The speed with which the public mind is being changed with regard to economic questions stands out vividly when viewed from the perspective of history. The degree of regulation to which railways and other public utilities are now subjected was simply unthinkable a generation ago and would have then been regarded as rankest radicalism. The heresy of rate regulation was so obnoxious that even the *Nation* raved against it as "confiscation, or, if another phrase be more agreeable, the change of railroads from pieces of private property, owned and managed for the benefit of those who have invested their money in them, into eleemosynary or charitable corporations, managed for the benefit of a particular class of applicants for outdoor relief—the farmers." So far has public opinion moved that today no sane man objects to governmental regulations of railway rates. . . .

Essays

In the opening essay, Alan Brinkley of Columbia University describes the tension experienced by Father Charles Coughlin in his relationship with President Franklin Roosevelt and the New Deal. He also notes the tension between Coughlin and his own church, whose representatives were divided on how to respond to arguably the most visible religious spokesman of the decade. Norma Fain Pratt, professor emerita of Mt. San Antonio College, argues in the second essay that secular forces set in motion during the late nineteenth century formulated new patterns of inclusion and exclusion in the new culture of American Jewry by 1940. One manifestation of this was the extensive involvement of American Jewish women in religious and community affairs during the 1930s. In the final essay, Joel A. Carpenter of Calvin College contends that while fundamentalism emerged intellectually bankrupt and publicly disgraced after its bitter battles with secularized religion in the 1920s, it used its exclusion from the public forum during and immediately after the depression era to build new strength from within.

Searching for Power

ALAN BRINKLEY

SOURCE: From *Voices of Protest* by Alan Brinkley, copyright © 1982 by Alan Brinkley. Used by permission of Alfred A. Knopf, a division of Random House, Inc.

Coughlin undoubtedly realized that he owed much of his new popularity to his prominent identification with Franklin Roosevelt and the New Deal. Yet such was his thirst for power and acclaim that when, early in 1934, he finally recognized that he was not to play the major role in the Administration he had envisioned, he began to explore the possibilities of charting an independent course. His break with Franklin Roosevelt was not sudden; indeed, not until 1936 would it become complete. But the days of his rapturous and unwavering support of the New Deal came to an end in the spring of 1934.

No single factor or incident soured the relationship. Coughlin's excesses of 1933, had, perhaps, begun the process, eroding what little confidence members of the Administration may once have had in him and producing an attitude from the White House that Coughlin recognized as increasingly hostile. He was particularly upset by Roosevelt's refusal to endorse or even acknowledge his defense of the President's monetary policies at the New York Hippodrome in November. Coughlin had telephoned the White House shortly before the meeting to inform McIntyre that he was "going the limit" for the President and would appreciate some informal sign of approval. There was no response. "I was never stupid," he recalled years later of the last months of 1933. "I realized the President now considered me burdensome." Yet for a while he remained confident that the men around Roosevelt had misled the President, and that Coughlin could still "win him back over to my side."

At the same time, however, he was growing impatient with New Deal monetary policies. It was clear by 1934 that the President was not going to remonetize silver, as Coughlin was urging, and the confident public predications to the contrary were ringing more and more hollow. Yet Coughlin might have been willing to swallow even this disappointment, at least for a time, had it not been for the crude tactics of the Treasury Department, which began trying to discredit members of the "silver bloc" in the spring of 1934. Late in April, Treasury Secretary Henry Morgenthau (who had succeeded Woodin) authorized the release of a list of major speculators in silver. On it was the name of Amy Collins—personal secretary to Father Coughlin. She was, the report indicated, the holder of contracts for 500,000 ounces of silver, purchased for $20,000 on behalf of the Radio League of the Little Flower. No one believed her when she explained that she had made the investment on her own initiative, that Coughlin had known nothing about it.

There was, of course, nothing illegal or even necessarily unethical about investing in silver futures. Yet Coughlin's critics could now accuse him of advocating silver remonetization for the sake of personal profit. It was an embarrassing incident, one that provided the foundation for years of characterizations of Coughlin as a financial charlatan and a fraud, and one for which he never fully forgave Roosevelt. Publicly, he lashed out only at Morgenthau and some of the President's "assistants." Privately, however, he blamed Roosevelt himself. "We were supposed to be partners," he remarked acidly many years later. "He said he would rely on me. That I would be an important adviser. But he was a liar. He never took my advice. He just used me and when he was through with me he double-crossed me on that silver business." His pride wounded, Coughlin was developing a personal bitterness toward Franklin Roosevelt that would last for over three decades.

Disenchantment with the New Deal now crept into Coughlin's public statements, inaugurating a period of marked ambivalence toward the Administration that continued for more than two years. Never entirely certain that his popularity could survive an open break with the President, still hopeful that Roosevelt would turn to him again for advice, Coughlin alternated erratically and often confusingly between enthusiastic support and open hostility. But the trend was unmistakable. Slowly, tentatively, he was putting distance between himself and the White House.

Even before the appearance of the Morgenthau list, Coughlin had expressed reservations about the course of the New Deal. In January, in an open letter to a supporter in the House of Representatives, Coughlin urged the Congress to "take the initiative" away from the President and launch a recovery program of its own. Roosevelt's monopoly of power was, he warned, beginning to resemble a dictatorship; it was time for members of Congress to become "imbued with the idea of your personally rectifying our rotten financial system instead of becoming a group of acquiescing sycophants." On March 4, the anniversary of Roosevelt's inauguration, Coughlin reviewed the first year of the New Deal and could muster only enough enthusiasm to call it "more or less successful." He openly criticized the administration of the National Recovery Administration and charged that the Home Owners' Loan Act, an effort to prevent foreclosures on mortgages, "has not functioned at all." One year ago, he added, "we were an optimistic people"; now, "something like consternation is beginning to be felt as the clouds of suspicion are darkening our hope."

His drift away from the President accelerated in the months following his dispute with the Treasury Department. There were new criticisms of New Deal actions, but the most noticeable change was perhaps an even more ominous one: he ceased for a time to speak about the Administration much at all. While his sermons through much of 1933 had often been little more than admiring catalogues of Roosevelt initiatives, his 1934 discourses concentrated instead on Coughlin's own monetary programs, on his harsh denunciation of bankers, on his impatience with "modern capitalism," and on his vision of a reformed system that would eliminate the cruelest abuses of the present one. He did not have to speak about Roosevelt directly, for implicit in all this was Coughlin's rejection of some of the major premises of the Administration.

By the end of the year, he was once again talking openly about the New Deal, and he was now making his reservations explicit. "The Democratic party," he said threateningly in November, "is merely on trial. Two years hence it will leave the courtroom of public opinion vindicated and with a new lease on life, or will be condemned to political death if it fails to answer the simple question of why there is want in the midst of plenty." And later in the same sermon: "Our Government still upholds one of the worst evils of decadent capitalism, namely, that production must be only at a profit for the owners, for the capitalist, and not for the laborer." When he spoke now about specific New Deal programs, he was more likely to mention those he detested—the crop and livestock destruction of the AAA, the cartelization that had resulted from the NRA, the restrained monetary policies that failed to offer sufficient inflation—than those he had once publicly admired. And when he insisted on his loyalty to the President, he measured his words carefully. "More than ever," he said in one of the first broadcasts of his fall 1934 season, "I am in favor of *a* New Deal."

Both Coughlin's own supporters and the Administration itself, however, made it difficult for him to move quickly toward an open break. Every time he criticized the President even indirectly, he received anguished and occasionally angry responses from members of his audience imploring him to reconsider. Every time he thought the President had written him off for good, a tantalizing bit of flattery or conciliation would emerge from the White House. When Coughlin cautiously asked Marvin McIntyre for help in the fall of 1934 in securing an appointment as a navel chaplain for one of his friends, the President himself wrote the Navy Department to expedite the matter. Several weeks later, Roosevelt received Coughlin at the White House and listened patiently for over an hour as the priest explained a proposal for allotting federal jobs to college graduates. (The President agreed to "study" the plan, but took no action on it.) And when relations became particularly strained, the President would send a friendly emissary like Frank Murphy or Joseph P. Kennedy to intercede with Coughlin and persuade him to return to the fold. He nearly always did—briefly.

What made Coughlin's public statements seem particularly vacillating during this period were his painful efforts to repudiate many of the major initiatives of the New Deal without denouncing the President himself. It was an impossible task, but one Coughlin approached with alacrity. When he resumed his sermons in the fall of 1934 after his usual summer hiatus, he was once again outspoken in support of the President, yet once again ambivalent about some of the central policies of the New Deal. "It is not fair," he insisted, "for our citizens to suspect even momentarily the motives of our President. He is endeavoring to bring about a union of forces, a union of efforts." In the same sermon, however, he referred obliquely to the government as the "slave" of the "unbridled ambition" of "modern capitalism." It was a continual balancing act: at one moment, a denunciation of New Deal policies; at the next, an insistent reminder of Coughlin's continued loyalty to Roosevelt. The harsher the attack, it sometimes seemed, the more enthusiastic the ensuing praise.

Despite the occasional gestures of conciliation, Franklin Roosevelt had by mid-1934 already decided privately to break with Coughlin. Thus, at the same time that some members of the White House staff were treading carefully to avoid antagonizing Coughlin, others were working quietly to undermine and perhaps to destroy him. James Farley initiated a study of the Coughlin radio network, complete with research into the finances and political connections of station owners. If the situation deteriorated too far, he may have reasoned, the Administration could use its considerable power over the broadcasting industry to force Coughlin off the air. Another government investigation examined Coughlin's finances, attempting to assess the extent and source of his wealth. The Immigration and Naturalization Service, apparently at the request of Louis Howe, undertook a study of Coughlin's citizenship status to determine whether he was living in the country legally. (They concluded that he was.) And at the top of a memorandum explaining one such inquiry was a cryptic but significant handwritten note: "Mac—This will help in your talk with Father Burke. FDR." Cautiously but deliberately, the Administration was trying to put pressure on Coughlin through the one institution capable of stopping him entirely—the Catholic Church.

II

The story of Coughlin's relations with his own Church during the 1930s is a confused and murky one. A controversial figure from the moment his radio sermons began, he attracted both praise and criticism from American Catholic officials until the end of his public career. Yet, despite the often outraged attacks by eminent cardinals, despite occasional indications of displeasure from the Vatican, despite Franklin Roosevelt's cautious efforts to mobilize Catholic leaders against Coughlin, the Church appeared for nearly a decade to have virtually no control over its most famous and outspoken priest.

The reason was simple: Bishop Michael J. Gallagher of Detroit. No matter how harshly Catholics elsewhere denounced Coughlin, as long as he retained the support of his own bishop, the only official outside the Vatican with any statutory control over his activities, he could operate with impunity. And Gallagher continued not only to defend but to encourage his priest even as Coughlin's sermons became harsher and more inflammatory.

Coughlin's standing within the Church was important to him, both personally and politically. There is no reason to doubt his repeated claims that nothing, not even the loss of his political career, could make him abandon the priesthood. "A Catholic priest who is not a Catholic priest is a washout," he said in 1935. "I am a priest and I hope to die as one." Indeed, when in 1942 he finally did receive orders from his ecclesiastical superiors to cease his public activities, he unhappily but obediently complied. Equally important to him, perhaps, was that the priesthood— its mystique, its prestige, its image of integrity, respectability, and compassion— may have been his most valuable political asset. Time and again, Coughlin's supporters referred to his clerical status as evidence of his credibility and his self-lessness. Time and again, political figures who might otherwise have openly attacked him restrained themselves for fear of appearing irreverent. The approval of his own bishop, essential as it was, was not all Coughlin needed to be concerned about. It was important, too, that he retain a reasonable standing within the Church at large, that he keep the respect and admiration of leading Catholics throughout the nation. Yet, just as he seemed unable to maintain cordial relations with the President despite the importance of such relations to his popularity, so he was increasingly incapable of, and apparently increasingly uninterested in, mollifying his critics within the Church. For the controversy that he created among Catholic leaders as early as 1931 grew steadily each year thereafter.

Attacks came from many quarters: from Boston's William Cardinal O'Connell, who was opposed in principle to political activities among the clergy; from New York's William Cardinal Hayes, who resented Coughlin's 1932 appearance in Manhattan to defend that embarrassingly prominent Catholic Jimmy Walker; from clergy and laymen throughout the Church who were offended by Coughlin's harsh attacks upon Al Smith in the fall of 1933. For a time, however, Coughlin's defenders within the Church far outnumbered his detractors. Among liberals, he seemed at first to be the most eloquent and powerful spokesman for the newly revived spirit of Catholic social activism.

The Catholic social-justice movement, which had displayed great strength in the early years of the century, had shown signs of ebbing during the 1920s. The Depression infused it with new life; and the appearance in 1931 of an important papal encyclical inspired even greater interest in social reform. Pius XI's *Quadragesimo Anno (After Forty Years)*, like Leo XIII's influential *Rerum Novarum* of 1891, which it was intended to commemorate, called upon Catholics to re-examine the teachings of St. Thomas Aquinas and to oppose the unjust economic conditions that had created the present crisis. It is the "function of government," Pius urged, "to adjust ownership to meet the needs of the public good." Where government had a special obligation was in the case of excess wealth and power, for "a man's superfluous income is not left entirely to his own discretion."

Coughlin seized upon the encyclical almost at once as justification for his own public role, and he referred to it constantly, both in his sermons and in private communication. In March 1934, he sent copies both to Marvin McIntyre (whom he urged to "Take time off—if necessary go and sit on the toilet while you read the enclosed book") and to Franklin Roosevelt (to whom he wrote somewhat more respectfully that "I hope the contents of this book will help to guide you during these troublesome days"). But Coughlin was not alone in his enthusiasm. Liberal Catholics throughout the nation interpreted the encyclical as a mandate for involvement with social problems, and they quickly moved to the fore in many areas of the Church. Taking control of existing publications or establishing new ones, they made Catholic periodicals into forceful advocates of reform. *America*, long one of the most conservative of Catholic magazines, began in 1932 to support the concept of labor unions and call for expanded government control of the economy. "Suppression of the corporation or business by the state is not merely permissible," claimed a 1932 editorial, "but the state's duty." A year later, it spoke even more strongly: "Capitalism as we have known it in this country has ever been a stupid and malicious giant." *Commonweal,* too, was expressing reservations about capitalism and echoing Pius XI's cry for reform: "the system is vicious, both ethically and ontologically. . . . capitalism degrades men to mere economic factors of cost, to be bargained for at lowest possible market prices." Others—the radical *Catholic Worker* and the Catholic Trade Unionists' *Michigan Labor Leader*—were even more outspoken.

Catholic organizations, too, began to shed the apolitical demeanor they had adopted in the 1920s and work actively for social change. The National Catholic Welfare Conference, for example, was openly critical of Herbert Hoover in 1931 and consistently urged the government to become more responsive to the needs of the unemployed. A year later, the Catholic Alumni Federation called for a reconstruction of the capitalist order. The Catholic Central Verein likewise advocated major reforms.

Most important, perhaps, individual priests were becoming influential spokesmen for social justice. While none ever rivaled Coughlin in popularity or influence, several had significant impact. Father James R. Cox of Pittsburgh, for example, began in the early 1930s to broadcast political sermons over a local radio station, and he soon developed a large and impassioned following among his city's jobless. In January 1932, he addressed a shivering crowd of 60,000 in Pitt Stadium, denounced the government and the banks for their indifference and inaction, and then led a motley army of some 12,000 protesters to Washington, where he was received at the White House by an uncomfortable President Hoover.

By the middle of 1933, the diffuse reform efforts of liberal Catholics had begun to congeal, and the Church's social activists became among the loudest and most enthusiastic supporters of Franklin Roosevelt and the New Deal. Virtually every major Catholic publication and organization went on record in support of the new President. Church officials, from Cardinal Mundelein in Chicago and Cardinal O'Connell in Boston to obscure parish priests throughout the nation, praised the administration's efforts. "All Catholics who desire to give practical effect to the principles of social justice laid down by Pope Pius XI," wrote *Commonweal*, "will see that . . . Roosevelt's opportunity to lead . . . is likewise the Catholic opportunity to make the teachings of Christ apply to the benefit of all."

To some such Catholics, Father Coughlin appeared for a while not only a welcome and compatible ally but the Church's brightest hope. Although organizational pronouncements and Catholic publications could influence clergy and lay officials, only Coughlin, it seemed, had ready access to the Catholic masses. The man most aware of Coughlin's potential importance was Father John A. Ryan, a professor of theology at Catholic University in Washington. A leader of the National Catholic Welfare Conference, an outspoken admirer of Pius XI's teachings, and a harsh critic of traditional capitalism, he had long been one of the most prominent and influential of the Catholic liberals. It was his influence, perhaps more than anyone else's, that persuaded Church intellectuals to support Roosevelt. And he attempted simultaneously to convince his colleagues of the importance of Coughlin's work as well. Coughlin was "on the side of the angels," he claimed after the 1933 Al Smith imbroglio, and was performing an essential and difficult task:

> . . . he is stirring up the animals, and that has got to be done by some one. The masses are sluggish-minded and have not shown any faint signs of rebellion until recently. The recovery program opposed by the moneyed interests cannot be carried through on an intellectual plane alone. The masses must be enlisted to fight for it before you can put it over. Father Coughlin is arranging that kind of thing to a considerable extent, and in doing so is a useful citizen.

It was, however, conditional praise. Catholic intellectuals such as Ryan were willing to defend Coughlin, even to praise him, as long as his message remained compatible with their own. But they never considered him an intellectual equal. He was performing a useful service by bringing the messages of the encyclicals to the masses, but that did not make him a serious social theorist or a real leader among Catholic liberals. Thus, in 1934, when Coughlin began to repudiate Franklin Roosevelt, whom Ryan and most other Catholic liberals continued strongly to support, his standing among them started to erode.

Open criticism of Coughlin was slow to emerge, but by early 1935 the warm references to him by other Church activists, the indications that they considered him a welcome ally, had all but ceased. *Commonweal*, for example, commented less and less frequently on Coughlin's activities throughout 1934; and in the spring of 1935, it remarked that he was "following up the work begun through his radio addresses with extraordinary personal success, but with extremely dubious results." John Ryan, beginning along the road that would by 1936 take him to an ugly, open confrontation with Coughlin, issued intermittent rebuttals in 1935 to Coughlin's attacks upon the Roosevelt Administration.

Occasionally, evidence of lingering collegiality would surface briefly. Increasingly, however, its character suggested less admiration for Coughlin than a general defensiveness among Catholics against attacks from outsiders, a lingering sensitivity to the anti-Catholic prejudice that had afflicted the Church in the 1920s. When, for example, the interdenominational *Christian Century* published a savage attack upon Coughlin by David Carl Colony, an Episcopal minister, the magazine was flooded with letters from Catholics protesting what they saw as the religious bigotry of the polemic. A letter from John Ryan called the article "extremely interesting," but concluded that "it includes a considerable amount of exaggeration, some pretty faulty logic, and a small bit of anti-Catholic bias."

Yet even this limited camaraderie was becoming rare, partly because of Coughlin's own provocative belligerence. When he learned late in 1934 that Cardinal O'Connell of Boston had once again publicly criticized him, he replied with what even the most progressive of his Catholic colleagues considered unwarranted and unseemly harshness:

> For forty years William Cardinal O'Connell has been more notorious for his silence on social justice than for any contribution which he may have given either in practice or in doctrine toward the decentralization of wealth and toward the elimination of those glaring injustices which permitted the plutocrats of this nation to wax fat at the expense of the poor.

Besides, Coughlin somewhat gracelessly added, O'Connell "has no authority to speak for the Catholic Church in America." He had jurisdiction only inside his own diocese. The remark was not, perhaps, directed only at O'Connell. Coughlin seemed also to be writing off many of his other colleagues in the Church, reminding them that he did not need their support and was not subject to their authority.

What, then, of those who did have authority over Coughlin? The question arose with growing frequency as he turned more forcefully against Franklin Roosevelt. Neither the White House officials seeking leverage with Coughlin nor the members of the Church growing impatient with him could find a clear answer. Bishop Gallagher, certainly, could not be expected to curb his devoted priest. In the spring of 1935, he went out of his way to announce his full support for the Coughlin broadcasts: "I pronounce Father Coughlin sound in doctrine, able in his application and interpretation. Freely I give him my imprimatur on his written work and freely I give him my approval on the spoken word. May both be circulated without objection throughout the land."

Critics of Coughlin continued to hope that, if Gallagher would not discipline him, the Vatican might. But from Rome came only confused and conflicting signals. On the one hand, there were recurrent rumors that Coughlin was soon to be removed from Gallagher's jurisdiction, even reassigned to the Vatican itself. On the other, there were reports that he retained the confidence of the Pope himself (who was a longtime person friend of Bishop Gallagher). One journalist recounted a conversation that supposedly occurred in Washington in 1935 between an American Church official critical of Coughlin and a highly placed papal delegate. "But my dear sir," the delegate told the American, "what the Holy Father teaches, Father Coughlin preaches!" Occasionally, there were veiled criticisms of Coughlin's most inflammatory statements in the Vatican newspaper, *Osservatore Romano;* even more occasionally, Gallagher himself, perhaps on orders from Rome, would direct Coughlin to retract some particularly troublesome comment. But until the fall of 1936, when Papal Secretary of State Eugenio Cardinal Pacelli (later Pope Pius XII) visited the United States and reportedly ordered Coughlin to moderate his public statements, there was virtually nothing to suggest how the Vatican viewed the priest's political activities.

Under such circumstances, Coughlin was willing to weather the increasing hostility of other Catholic leaders in America. Although their criticisms did his public image no good, the alternative—moderating his positions to regain their approval—was unacceptable. As long as he retained the tacit approval of the Vatican and the open support of his own bishop, he reasoned, he could afford to ignore the attitudes of other members of his Church. About the long-range consequences of this growing gulf, he was, for the present, unconcerned.

Transitions in Judaism: The Jewish American Woman Through the 1930s

NORMA FAIN PRATT

SOURCE: Norma Fain Pratt. "Transitions in Judaism: The Jewish American Woman through the 1930s." *American Quarterly* 30(5): 681-702 (1978). © The American Studies Association. Reprinted by permission of The Johns Hopkins University Press.

"To be a Jew in the twentieth century is to be offered a gift," wrote Muriel Rukeyser, the New York-born Jewish poet. "If you refuse, wishing to be invisible, you choose death of the spirit. . . ." Most American Jewish women accepted this gift, even though the tenets of Judaism circumscribed the role of women in worship and community activity. Women had never been encouraged to examine the nature of their own religious beliefs, nor had the traditional assumptions about their inferiority and subservience to men been challenged. In the late nineteenth and early twentieth centuries, however, a minority of women began to redefine their place within Jewish life, and in the 1920s and 1930s patterns perceptibly changed for the majority. Women became participants in the synagogue, the schools, and the social institutions which expressed the new culture of American Jewry. Nevertheless they continued to face limitations and intolerance; by the 1940s, a new pattern had been established with its own forms of inclusion and exclusion.

In order to distinguish the ways in which women altered their role, it is important to consider the nature of American Judaism and its course of development. American Jews never centralized their religious institutions. What could be termed "organized" Judaism was congregational. Essentially, public rituals were practiced in local synagogues whose congregations selected a mode of worship and expressed their preference for certain Jewish theological interpretations. In popular parlance, the types of worship came to be categorized as Orthodox, Conservative, and Reform. National synagogue unions were formed at the turn of the present century.

In the seventeenth century, Sephardic Jews brought to British America from Spain and the Middle East a variation of the ritual and theology of medieval Judaism practiced by their co-religionists in Western and Eastern Europe. A few Sephardic women took an active part in business and in the high cultural life of American urban centers. German Jews arrived in considerable number just before the middle of the nineteenth century. Between 1840 and 1880 some 250,000 settled in the eastern and midwestern United States, mainly in the cities. Many had already been influenced by secular European culture and in America they created their own version of Reform Judaism. The Reform synagogues, now called temples, eliminated some of the ancient ritual, substituted English for Hebrew, altered the theological emphasis of the liturgical literature, and departed substantially from the traditional orthodox service.

Reform Jews initiated radical innovation in the position of women. The temples permitted the desegregation of the sexes; women and men now sat together in the family pews. Women were allowed to sing in the choir. Girls were confirmed. The Reform prayerbook eliminated the male benediction thanking God "that I am not a woman." Women were counted as part of the *minyan* (the ten-person quorum necessary to hold services). Through the temple "sisterhood" organizations women participated in the administration of charitable and other social services; they were granted the privileges of tending to temple upkeep and to the religious education of children . These changes did not come without opposition. One dissenter posed the argument familiar in the Judaeo-Christian tradition in his article "God's Curse on Womanhood," published in 1864 in the popular Philadelphia German-Jewish English-language periodical, *The Occident:*

> Now when Eve was created she was made equal to Adam in every respect, and by no means had he any power or authority over her whatever. . . . But after she had induced him to break the commandment of God, and he was cursed to labor and to toil for his living, and to support her, to supply all their wants through hard work, she was also cursed by losing her right to be equal to him. . . . Now this was the curse pronounced against her, that she should always remember and repent of what she had done. She shall always desire to be equal with him, as before she sinned, but he shall rule over her. . . .

By 1900, many middle-class Jewish American women of German descent had assumed responsibilities in the work of their Reform temples. A National Federation of Temple Sisterhoods was founded in 1913 with a membership of 5,000, representing 52 local groups. Sisterhoods met, both for recreation and for temple and community work. Contemporary feminist thought has variously interpreted such voluntarism as a cult of the leisured woman; as an aspect of middle-class conspicuous consumption; as an outlet for female energies which did not conflict with home duties and which in fact translated women's work in the home into social terms; as an expression of a feminist consciousness; or as a factor of labor division in a developing capitalist economy. While all these theories might be applied to the women of the Reform movement, as well as to the voluntary work of American women of other faiths, the leadership of the Federation understood their own purpose in specifically Jewish terms. "The increased power which has come to the modern American Jewess ought to be exercised in congregational life," stated the NFTS constitution. Another motif, the future of Judaism, pervaded their ideology. "Woman is the bearer, the guardian and the preserver of the nation," the feminist Bertha Pappenheim proclaimed. This is her "primary function—on which depends the welfare and continued existence of the people, Israel. . . ."But guardianship was not enough. By the 1890s German Jewish American women also defended the faith. The founding convention of the National Council of Jewish Women in 1893 stood aggressively against anti-Semitism. Along with religious understanding, philanthropy, and education, the purpose of the NCJW was "to secure the interest and aid of influential persons in arousing the general sentiment against religious persecutions whenever and by whomever shown, and in finding means to prevent such persecutions."

German Jewish women also defended the faith by taking measures to prevent assimilation. Although, like the men, they responded to the temptations of Americanization by adopting aspects of the dominant culture, they also wanted to retain their individuality as Jews. Zionism served this purpose. Hadassah, the women's division of the Zionist Organization of America, founded in 1912, planned to foster Judaism at home through the propagation of Zionist ideals. Books for young women explained that the chief problem for Jews in America was "finding a way back to the original Jewish National life and thereby defeating assimilation." The solution was "a return to the sources of Jewish culture, to the Bible and to the study of Hebrew and by contact with the living Jewry of the East." Ida Adlerblum, the head of Hadassah's Cultural Committee, boasted in 1930 (when the organization had the largest membership of any Zionist group in the United States) that "The future historian of the twentieth century will reckon Hadassah among the forces which operate in creating Judaism anew. . . . From a mere organization, Hadassah has become a spiritual historical movement knitted with the life of Palestine as well as with Jewish life in America."

The migration of Eastern European Jews began in 1880; by the early 1920s more than 2 1/2 million had immigrated. The place of Eastern European immigrant women in Judaism was far different from that of their American German-Jewish co-religionists. Some inequalities, explicit and implicit, still existed in the Reform community (for example, women could not join the rabbinate or hold administrative posts in their temples), but in the orthodox system segregation and subordination of women was the rule. . . .

For nearly 40 years after 1880, Jews who were no longer orthodox and yet could not accept Reform Judaism had no form of Judaism through which to express their changing mode of behavior. Conservative Judaism, a movement attracting mainly second- and third-generation American Jews of Eastern European background, was still in its formative stages. The majority of Conservative congregations were established during or soon after World War I, their synagogues located in the newer non-ghetto neighborhoods where the Jewish population was in the minority and where living conditions expressed middle class tastes. Marshall Sklare has described Conservatism as a mediation "between the demands of the Jewish tradition . . . and the norms of middle class worship." The new patterns altered the liturgy, showed tolerance toward personal deviation from traditional practices like *kashruth* or rest on the Sabbath, and created social clubs as part of the function of the synagogue. Following somewhat the practice of Reform Judaism, Conservatives adjusted the status of women. Men and women were seated together. Women's synagogue organizations participated in the upkeep of the synagogue and in the religious education of the children. Women, however, still were excluded from significant parts of the worship, for instance the rituals surrounding the handling and reading of the Torah. In the 1920s and 1930s Conservative women wrestled with a felt dichotomy between the new position in synagogue life and the traditional home. Some thought that things had gone too far. "At the risk of being declared a reactionary, a menace to women's freedom," wrote Rose Goldstein in the Conservative Women's League paper *Outlook,* "I maintain that the greatest part the Jewish woman can play in the future of a healthy American Judaism is through the conduct of her own household."

Beside the Orthodox, Conservative, and Reform modes, a secular form of Judaism developed in the late nineteenth century which offered women a different place in Jewish society. While secular Jews rejected most theological values, they retained *Yidishkayt,* a sense of Jewishness embracing a respect for the Yiddish language and traditions and for the contemporary common Jewish fate. One could observe secular Judaism without prayer and without joining a special group. The *veltlekhe* (secular) Jews did organize, since they not only accepted a Jewish identity in theory but put this into practice by creating a cultural life for themselves and their children. The study of Jewish history, appreciation of Yiddish and Hebrew literature, celebration of Jewish holidays, and support of a Yiddish theatre were characteristic expressions.

A vital part of the secular movement, which divided along sectarian lines, was radical political ideology in such forms as socialism, Zionist-socialism, and anarchism. Actually, the roots of secular Judaism were found in Eastern European Jewish radical and labor movements that provided doors through which working-class men and women entered the secular world. Some radical groups like the Marxist Jewish Labor Bund discouraged workers from following religious customs since religion was held to reflect the Jewish bourgeois power structure. Bund ideology transformed the special Jewish religious identity into a national one, urging Bundists to work for a socialist revolution in which Jews would obtain cultural autonomy.

Radical Jewish movements accepted equality between the sexes and this made political radicalism attractive to women. Because Jewish women had been excluded from those male sanctuaries, the orthodox synagogues, women intellectuals and workers joined radical organizations expecting to find equality within the movement. For these women, a nonreligious mode of life within a Jewish community became bound with socialism and equality. When an increasing number of Eastern European radicals emigrated to America after the unsuccessful Russian revolution of 1905, many of the politically conscious women began participating, soon after their arrival, in the feminist and suffrage movements. Esther Luria, a Bundist who in Europe had engaged in revolutionary activities, played a role in the suffrage and labor movements among Jewish immigrant women in New York. Far less known than Emma Goldman, Luria tried to provide Jewish women with role models through her writings and the example of her own life. Her biography had the romantic ring of that first generation of immigrant radical intellectuals. Born in Warsaw in 1877, Luria completed the Russian gymnasium and studied at the University of Bern in Switzerland, where she received the degree of doctor of humanistic studies. In Bern she joined the socialist movement, and she returned to Russia as an active member of the Bund. Arrested there several times, she was sent to Siberia in 1906. She escaped in 1912 and came to New York City. Luria made her debut in the Yiddish-language socialist literary and political monthly *Zukunft* (Future). She wrote more than sixty articles about Jewish and non-Jewish women who broke out of traditional molds, including "Famous Jewish Women in America and England," "Marx's Wife and Daughter," "The Russian Women and the Revolution," and the "Life and Works of Liebknecht and Luxemburg." Her contributions to the International Ladies Garment Workers' Union Yiddish weekly *Glaykhhayt* (Equality) advocated political activism for women in America. Without a family, impoverished, and in poor health Luria disappeared in the early 1920s and her fate is unknown.

Women in these Jewish circles had more equality with men than their sisters in the Orthodox, Conservative, and even Reform movements. In theory, at least, they were unencumbered by religious traditions, restrictions, and ancient prejudices. As a consequence, working-class women joined trade unions and occasionally were trade organizers; literary women wrote fiction or poetry and were employed on the staff of the Yiddish press and in the Yiddish theatre; women were active within political groups. Nevertheless there were inequalities. Ambivalent or negative attitudes toward the "emancipated" Jewish woman existed in subtle, perhaps unconscious form, and the contradiction between the ideal and the real would become more apparent by the 1920s. Such attitudes could be found in the literature of the time. The novel *Worshippers* (1906) by Henry Berman (who was sympathetic to socialism and thus to the rights of women) centers upon Katherine Bronski, the creatively frustrated and sexually unsatisfied wife of a Philadelphia pharmacist. Katherine leaves her husband to follow a stage career and to engage in an extramarital affair with a New York Yiddish socialist poet. According to Berman, Katherine's emancipation illustrates the fallacy of the socialist aspiration for sexual equality. Katherine's freedom is merely a mask for her egotism, her desire to dominate males, and her inability to understand political commitment. Berman assigns all the affirmative values to her lover, whose virtues include intelligence, idealism, compassion, and a sense of responsibility. In the end Katherine, a failure on the stage, deserts her lover to return to Philadelphia and the pharmacist. Berman's novel focused some of the traditionally negative attitudes upon the so-called emancipated woman: her intellectual inferiority, the superficiality of her political and artistic purpose, and her destructive sexual powers.

By the early 1920s Jews had ceased to be an immigrant nation in America. Increasing numbers left immigrant work to enter business and the professions. Jewish women and men moved out of the old ghetto-like neighborhoods into newer, more middle-class parts of town. Although occasional anti-Semitism created feelings of insecurity, social mores in the United States permitted Jews to retain their religion, sacred or secular, and still become American. In fact the American partiality for religious affiliation encouraged Jews to identify themselves in religious terms. Concurrently, most became convinced that an American style of life was appropriate for all citizens.

Far from merging into their surroundings, however, the Jews developed a particular culture during the years between the two world wars. A myriad network of institutions demonstrated this adherence to what Horace Kallen called "cultural pluralism": Jewish congregations (3,118 in 1927), theological seminaries, religious schools and secular Yiddish culture schools, local and national philanthropic agencies, and social and recreational groups. At least four organizations dealt with the problem of Jewish rights in America and abroad. The Jewish socialists and communists ran their own political sections, children's schools, camps, and cultural and social groups, and published books and periodical literature.

Within this structure the functions women performed expanded. The status of all American women had been enhanced by their enfranchisement in 1920. Jewish women had benefited both economically and educationally during the movement into the middle class and were now capable of shouldering the burdens and privileges of community life; many accepted civic duties. One slogan of a girl's youth organization in 1930 declared: "Every member of Junior Hadassah is an American, a Jew and a Zionist. She is not one time one, another time another; she is all three in one."

Changes in the practice of Judaism itself contributed to the new involvement of women. Orthodox Judaism, regulating all daily life (secular and sacred) by religious law, made heavy demands upon the male. The Reform movement of the nineteenth century and the new Conservative movement, by separating the sacred and secular, left only the actual religious service in the realm of the sacred. The male was no longer required to uphold the faith of his fathers by daily worship, religious study, and synagogue attendance. Jewish education, philanthropy, social services, and sociocultural expression had moved out from under Talmudic-rabbinic regulation. Under these circumstances, women became more participant in all areas of Jewish life while men became less so. . . .

The number of national women's organizations founded in the 1920s and 1930s testified to the vitality of Jewish women and to their interest in religion and community affairs, as well as to the strength of the separatist tradition. The list includes Junior Hadassah (1921); Conference Committee of National Jewish Women's

Organizations (1923); Women's Branch of the Union of Orthodox Jewish Congregations of America (1924); Women's Division of the Communist Workers' Order (1924); Women's Organization of the Pioneer Women of Palestine (1925); Women's American ORT (1927); Women's League for Palestine (1927); American Beth Jacob Committee (1928); Mizrachi Women's Organization of America (1930); and the Menorah League (1935).

Along with the older groups like the National Council of Jewish Women, the National Federation of Temple Sisterhoods, or the Women's League of the United Synagogues of America (1918), all these associations provided a complex Jewish "woman's world." She could choose to work at several levels—congregational or civic, national or international. The range of her activities might encompass personal study of history, politics, and religion; mundane social events; teaching children; social work in the community with the poor, with recent Eastern European immigrants or, in the 1930s, with refugees from Germany; programs to aid impoverished Eastern European girls or to settle Jews in Palestine; assistance to universities and Jewish libraries; or the publication of periodical literature. Not all commitments were alike: some women contributed money to their favorite cause, while others joined the rank and file or took active leadership roles. These positions were exacting and prestigious, and women like Henrietta Szold emerged as heroic role-model figures. Nor were all workers volunteers. Jewish social services were becoming professionalized; the Graduate School of Jewish Social Work was organized in 1925 and attracted young women in search of socially approved careers.

Trends in Jewish education generally reinforced women's interest in perpetuating their religious, social, and cultural life. By the 1920s, the example of American coeducational public schooling, the increased number of organized Jewish women, and changes in rituals like the introduction of a *bas mitzvah* or female confirmation ceremony in the Conservative synagogues all encouraged the inclusion of girls in Jewish educational programs. These were held after regular school hours or on Sunday. Hebrew or Yiddish and Jewish rituals, holidays, and history were the major subjects. The Conservative schools, however, emphasized the male *bar mitzvah* and offered girls a less intensive and hence less socially important program. By the 1930s one-third of the pupils enrolled in Jewish schools were girls. The Reform Sunday schools and the secular Yiddish schools had still higher female enrollments, mainly because their programs were not *bar mitzvah* oriented. . . .

Women teachers, who by 1935 made up about one-third of the teaching force, were in the forefront of developing not only new methods but a new philosophy for Jewish education. For example, Fannie R. Neumann, an articulate educational theoretician at the Brooklyn Jewish Center, hoped to create a method of rearing Jewish children which would offer them a "cultural synthesis." She envisioned a way to educate "a new type of Jew—steeped in Jewish culture, yet thoroughly at home in . . . [the] American milieu, disciplined yet free, adjusted to the machine age but saved from its serfdom by a critical eye and a sentient heart."

In the 1930s, girls seemed to respond more enthusiastically than boys to Jewish education. This was especially true in the secular Jewish schools, where preparation for the *bar* or *bas mitzvah* was not the final goal and where girls were taught the same curriculum as boys. In fact, Leibush Lehrer, a leading educator in the Yiddishist Sholom Aleichem Folkschule, was struck by the differences in male and female reactions to Jewish interests. Interviewing former students, Lehrer found young women to have a more tenacious identification with Yiddish. Many more women than men continued to read Yiddish fiction and poetry and to attend Yiddish theatre after they had ceased their formal education. Discussing the possible reasons for the differences, Lehrer suggested that the female students were more intellectually mature than the males during the ages from 8 to 14 when they were studying Yiddish culture. He attributed the male students' lack of interest to an overemphasis on sports in American culture. Not being involved in sports, the girls had time for languages and literatures. It was likely, too, although Lehrer did not state this, that Jewish girls were encouraged to study humanistic subjects as part of the feminine ideal of a "cultured lady," while the boys rejected these subjects for that very reason.

Although by the end of the 1930s women were thus taking a prominent part in public aspects of American Jewish life, the extent of their exclusion and segregation continued to be profound. In fact the changes tended to mask the remaining inequalities. The unresolved problems in the most "progressive" Jewish sectors illustrate the biases that operated throughout the community. Reform Judaism, for instance, had integrated women into the temple and into the religious service for almost a hundred years. Reform women were lawyers, judges, and doctors. Nevertheless, in 1922 when Martha Neumark, a student at the Reform seminary, Hebrew Union College, expressed her intention to seek ordination as a rabbi, her request was denied. The lay members of the Board of Governors who opposed her ordination argued that such a departure from tradition was too radical and might alienate the Conservative and Orthodox co-religionists. The calling of rabbi required strenuous full-time activities and complete devotion; the essential role of the Jewish woman was to cultivate a Jewish home life and family. The board could not encompass the thought of combining the two. Dr. Jacob Z. Lauterbach, one of the more articulate members, assured the rejected candidate that there was "no injustice done to woman by excluding her for this office. There are many avenues open to her if she chooses to do religious and educational work. . . ."

Jewish women in the 1920-1940 period lived within a pattern of seeming acceptance combined with implicit exclusion that remained characteristic of American Judaism until the 1970s, when Jewish feminists pressed for new changes. Obviously they were not unique. Women were socially and organizationally segregated for the most part in American Protestant and Catholic society as well. But American Judaism did not merely imitate American culture, although imitation was an aspect of Jewish historical development. The perspective which Jewish women faced in the 1920s was complex. For most Jewish women secularization was of recent origin. The traditions of orthodox Judaism explicitly, even legally, maintained separate worlds for women and men. The meeting of these worlds within a secular frame of reference had brought about a radical change. Comparing their own position with that of their grandmothers, most women believed themselves to be already living a revolution; few developed much insight into the contradictions of their situation.

It was difficult, too, for women to form a common ground upon which to base criticism of their role within Judaism. The myriad women's organizations reflected the structural decentralization of the faith. Identification as a Reform, Orthodox, Conservative, Yiddishist, or Socialist Jew obfuscated the sense of being a Jewish woman at odds with a set of common limitations. Furthermore, since the Jewish education of women was not grounded in theological literature, they did not feel qualified to muster arguments in their own defense.

Despite their many successful adjustments, Jews additionally did not feel secure in their newfound homeland in the 1920s and 1930s. The sense of existing as foreigners, as immigrants, was still a part of Jewish thinking. The threat of anti-Semitism combined with the apprehensions regarding assimilation had marked ramifications for women. Anti-Jewish sentiments were commonly expressed during the First World War, and immediately following the war restrictions were placed upon Jewish immigration to the United States. In the 1930s the rise of Nazism and echoes of fascism in the Coughlinites, Pelley's Silver Shirts, and others intensified Jewish anxiety. Anti-Semitism acted as a centripetal force exacting solidarity. In the face of external hostility, Jewish women were not able to begin their own crusade as women.

Concurrently, the perceived threat of assimilation kept Jewish women in their place. Since Biblical times Judaism had been inherited genetically through the mother. In America women had increasingly shouldered the responsibility of preserving a faith which men often found burdensome. The school and the social institutions became part of the domain of women—even if men controlled the upper reaches of power. Thus as newly installed defenders of the faith, it seemed contradictory for women also to be critics of that faith.

In the early 1970s Jewish feminists began to battle these contradictions. They questioned power relationships in Jewish institutions, religious inequality in Judaic practices, and anti-female bias expressed in some traditional Jewish literature. Concurrently, feminists sought Jewish precedent to legitimize the concept of equality of the sexes in Judaism. Like many religious reformers in the past, feminists have turned to a reinterpretation of the Bible. Rabbi Laura Geller, one of several women ordained in Reform Judaism, noted during a recent interview that Jewish feminists can look to another creation story than that of a masculine God creating in male terms. The first chapter of Genesis reads, "in the image of God created He them, male and female . . . . and he called their name 'adam' (human beings)." Thus all human beings are created in the image of God. "Just as God is the father, God is also the mother," said the Rabbi.

A Thriving Popular Movement

JOEL A. CARPENTER

SOURCE: From *Revive Us Again* by Joel Carpenter, copyright © 1997 by Joel Carpenter. Used by permission of Oxford University Press, Inc.

How was fundamentalism faring by the end of the 1920s? That question is more complicated than it first appears, but the common perception has been that it was, as one historian put it, "split and stricken." Many observers would go further and judge that fundamentalism was rapidly declining and would soon die out altogether. Indeed, the movement was in retreat. Without a doubt it had lost influence and respect. Yet fundamentalism remained a viable grassroots religious movement and it prospered as such in the 1930s, in spite of its defeats and disgrace. In order to see fundamentalism in this light, however, we need to know how and where to look for it.

A Dying Crusade?

The first part of that task is to see why fundarnentalism's survival and continuing vitality has not been duly acknowledged. The conclusion that fundamentalism was dying by 1930 has been based on a variety of perceptions, notably those formed by the movement's opponents, by fundamentalist leaders themselves, and, more recently, by historians. The major problem was in a sense a definitional one. If fundamentalism was viewed as the organized offensive against liberalism in the denominations and evolution in the schools, then it was a spent force. There was little doubt in the mind of the movement's secular and religious critics; they were certain that fundamentalism was finished. To religious liberals especially, its death seemed imminent. In the wake of the Scopes trial, the *Christian Century* described the fundamentalist movement as "an event now passed," a brief, dysfunctional mutation away from the main line of religious evolution. Theologian H. Richard Niebuhr's article on fundamentalism in the 1931 edition of the *Encyclopedia of the Social Sciences* assumed that the movement was finished, for Niebuhr referred to it exclusively in the past tense. While these diagnoses probably owed much to wishful thinking, secular critics with less at stake in the church fights, such as H. L. Mencken and Walter Lippmann, observed that the movement, if not dead, certainly was no longer a significant force in American thought and culture. Mencken relegated fundamentalists to the "mean streets" of America, "everywhere where learning is too heavy a burden for mortal minds to carry." Lippmann observed that fundamentalists' ideas no longer appealed to "the best brains and the good sense of the modern community."

Fundamentalists themselves often developed a martyr's mentality in the 1930s and spoke as though theirs was a lost cause. Northern Baptist separatist leader Oliver W. Van Osdel, for example, urged his colleagues not to seek the world's acceptance, but to emulate "the rejected Son of God in these days of declension and compromise." A rhetoric of martyrdom, fortified with biblical imagery of persecuted faithful remnants, prevailed in many fundamentalist circles. Such talk was an important device for counteracting the world's scorn and restoring a sense of mission, but it has added to the illusion of fundamentalism's dying.

Historians are also responsible for the myth of fundamentalism's demise. A number of leading American historians have argued that fundamentalism was a momentary reaction to the irresistible tide of America's passage into modern, cosmopolitan secularity. They suggested that the movement had been an obstacle to enlightened and rational public discourse. Consequently, many American history texts ignore fundamentalism and other kinds of evangelical Christianity after 1920. By eliminating fundamentalism from any sustained treatment in the narrative, American historians have betrayed a secular and progressivist bias that, as one critic pointed out, has led them to try to "write Americans beyond their religious backwardness as quickly as possible ."

Two recent historians of fundamentalism, Ernest R. Sandeen and George M. Marsden, have argued to the contrary that America's cultural breadth and multiplicity give dissenting movements the space and freedom to survive, and that fundamentalism found a lasting niche for itself in modern America. Their treatments have a rather elegiac tone, however, since they focus on fundamentalism's role as a defender of nineteenth-century religious ideas whose influence and credibility were failing. Sandeen summed up his story as "the decline if not the collapse" of premillennialism as a "valiant nineteenth-century minority view." Marsden likewise insisted that the fundamentalist impulse still carries much force today, but he saw that tendency primarily as a symptom of American evangelicals' loss of intellectual vigor and cultural influence. Following in this vein, Mark Noll's recent commentary on evangelicals and the life of the mind more generally treats fundamentalism as an intellectual disaster.

The dominant story line for fundamentalism's career, then, has been declension and dissolution. Fundamentalists' opponents gave them premature burials or banished them to the outer darkness of cultural marginality; fundamentalists gloried in their tribulations; liberal historians passed fundamentalists off as marginal and vestigial; and even the historians who rehabilitated fundamentalists as worthy of scholarly attention considered them to be the tattered remnant of a once-powerful tradition.

Each of these judgments about fundamentalism's state of health conveys some truth, but the movement's career during the 1930s and 1940s demands a different sort of treatment. *Movement,* indeed, is the operative term, for fundamentalism was not merely a collection of mental or religious proclivities, nor was it simply a defeated party in ecclesiastical politics, nor solely the guardian of spent ideas. It was a comprehensive religious movement with a whole panoply of aims and aspirations. Loss of the respect of intellectual elites does not necessarily mean loss of popular support, and it may actually enhance a group's appeal in some circles. The rhetoric of heroic alienation can also be misinterpreted, for popular movements often ascribe more marginal status to themselves than a realistic assessment would dictate. Indeed, the "outsider" pose was an important tool in shaping fundamentalists' sense of mission for their movement. While it certainly suffered from external defeats and a variety of internal fractures and strains, and contributed few if any fresh and powerful ideas, fundamentalism provided a believable faith and a strong, lively religious community for hundreds of thousands in the 1930s and 1940s. Indeed, the movement's success posed a double irony: while liberal Protestant spokesmen smugly predicted that such "belated forms" of religious life would "gradually be starved out," their own mainline Protestant denominations suffered a severe religious depression during the 1930s. At the same time, the fundamentalists—who talked melodramatically about being a tiny, despised minority—prospered."

It was an odd sort of prosperity, one must admit, for scarcely anyone, fundamentalists included, recognized it at the time. Fundamentalists had been conditioning others and themselves to associate their movement with antimodernist crusading in the nation's public forum. But by 1930 or so, the antievolution crusades and the pressure groups that mounted them had failed, and the once-formidable coalitions of conservatives who were determined to drive modernism from the churches had been split and scattered. So where was fundamentalism to be found? If the answer was, among the "come-outer" sects and fellowships—such as the Union of Regular Baptist Churches of Ontario and Quebec (founded 1927), the Independent Fundamental Churches of America (founded 1930), the General Association of Regular Baptist Churches (founded 1932), the Orthodox Presbyterian Church (founded 1936) or the Bible Presbyterian Church (founded 1937)—then the movement had diminished indeed.

Another common answer has been that fundamentalism revolved around the empires of its most prominent champions, such as William Bell Riley of First Baptist Church in Minneapolis, J. Frank Norris of First Baptist Church in Fort Worth, John Roach Straton of Calvary Baptist Church in New York, and Mark Matthews of Seattle's First Presbyterian Church. The fact that these regional "warlords" were fiercely independent, jealous guardians of their freedoms and scarcely able to get along on a personal level, much less continue any cooperative ventures, adds to the impression that fundamentalism was thoroughly fragmented by the 1930s and lacking in any basic cohesion.

Another common way of locating fundamentalism has been by identifying it with the ultra-right-wing fringe of the movement that continued to campaign against evolution and communism. The bizarre words and deeds of this "Old Christian Right" helped to confirm the movement's stereotype as rural, bigoted, and pathological in mindset. If fundamentalism is equated with any of these features, each of which reveals a facet of the movement's character, then it truly was performing its death dance by the 1930s.

The best that fundamentalists could say for themselves was, in the words of the North Carolina Baptist preacher Vance Havner, that "just because the great broadcast chains do not carry our message and because popular periodicals give us no space, it need not be deduced that we are bound for extinction." There were still many "old-fashioned Christians" around, Havner pointed out, who "have not bowed to the modern Baal." It was the age's "moderns" who were frantic self-wounders, not the fundamentalists. Echoing the apostle's words to the Philippian jailer, Havner quipped that fundamentalists would "say to this bewildered age, 'Do thyself no harm, we are all here.'"

But where was "here"? Simply put, fundamentalism in the 1930s and 1940s was not to be found primarily within the broken ranks of the antimodernist crusades, nor was it limited to the small and alienated groups of separatists or the "super-church" empires of some of its chieftains. Fundamentalism was a popular movement and, as such, its strength was not to be measured according to the degree of its organizational unity. Movements commonly have internal variation and tensions. This is not a sign of declension so much as of vitality, for movements, like patches of dandelions, grow and spread when they are agitated. Movements have horizontal, web-like, informal lines of leadership and organization, not vertical, pyramid-like ones. So if we are to see how fundamentalism was doing in the 1930s, we must explore its major network of operations, the grid of institutions bequeathed to it by the revivalistic and premillennial pastors, evangelists, missions leaders, and Bible teachers who had laid the foundations of the movement at the turn of the century. One of the most important developments in fundamentalists' career during the 1930s and 1940s was their growing dependence upon this web of agencies as the channel for their work, the mediator of their message, and the focus of their affiliation and identity. How was this fundamentalist enterprise faring during the 1930s? It was thriving and growing. Its network of institutions was expanding in order to accommodate the movement's demand for trained leaders, popular religious knowledge, and vehicles for evangelism.

Training Leaders

Without a doubt, the most important terminals in the fundamentalist network were its Bible institutes. These schools, which were tightly knit, familial, and religiously intense places, had been founded to train lay volunteers and full time religious workers such as evangelists, Sunday school superintendents, and foreign missionaries. By the early 1930s there were at least fifty of them, according to one report, that served fundamentalist constituencies. Some, like the Detroit Bible Institute, were little more than evening classes run out of a local church for training Sunday school teachers. But over time, as some of the institutions became well established, they developed into comprehensive centers of religious activity. The largest and most important of the fundamentalist Bible institutes by the early 1930s were the Bible Institute of Los Angeles (known as BIOLA), Gordon College of Theology and Missions in Boston, Moody Bible Institute in Chicago, National Bible Institute in New York City, Northwestern Bible and Missionary Training School in Minneapolis, Nyack Missionary Training Institute (in Nyack-on-the-Hudson, New York), the Philadelphia School of the Bible, and the Bible Institute of Pennsylvania (also in Philadelphia). Two other schools that were founded in the 1920s but were developing rapidly were Columbia Bible College in South Carolina and the Prairie Bible Institute in Three Hills, Alberta. For fundamentalist pastors and parishioners who were weary of the theological tensions they felt with their denominational neighbors and wary of the perspectives emanating from their denominational agencies, Bible schools often became denominational surrogates. These agencies provided educational and other religious services, a support structure for fellowship and inspiration, and opportunities to participate in such "Christian work as evangelism and foreign missions. . . .

Without a doubt, the Bible school was the dominant fundamentalist educational institution. Fundamentalists' tendency to reduce the church's mission to evangelism and their premillennial urgency to get the job done predisposed them to favor the pragmatic, trade-school approach of Bible school training for their leaders over the more extensive and cosmopolitan approach of college and seminary education. Furthermore, they had been dispossessed of the colleges and seminaries in their home denominations, since liberal theological views now prevailed in those institutions. Thus it was tempting to depend on the Bible institutes to train pastors, even though their founders had not intended them for that purpose. By the 1930s, several of the larger Bible institutes had added a "pastoral course" to their programs.

Fundamentalists also built some theological seminaries of their own. They felt keenly the "loss" of denominational theological schools to the control of their moderate and liberal opponents, and sought to replace them. These new seminaries were less central than the Bible schools to the general fundamentalist enterprise, but they were important incubators of the movement's next generation of leaders. . . .

Fundamentalists did have some purely post-baccalaureate theological seminaries. The three most important of these were independent, but served mostly Presbyterian constituencies in the 1930s and 1940s. The Evangelical Theological College (later Dallas Theological Seminary) was founded in 1926 in Dallas, Texas, by close colleagues of the late C. I. Scofield, the eminent dispensationalist Bible teacher. In its early years Dallas Seminary had many Presbyterians on its faculty and in its student body. It grew at a healthy rate throughout its first twenty-five years to nearly two hundred students in 1950, and became probably the most influential fundamentalist seminary. Another influential independent seminar of Presbyterian heritage was Westminister, founded in Philadelphia by J. Gresham Machen and three other dissident Princeton Seminary professors after Princeton's reorganization in 1929. While it developed informal ties to the Presbyterian Church of America after the latter's founding in 1936, Westminster attracted intellectually aspiring fundamentalists of many varieties in its early years. After Machen died in 1937 and a controversy over eschatology and Christian lifestyle split the separatist Presbyterians later that year, Westminster suffered. It enrolled seventy-two students in 1937 but in 1946 had only about half that many. Nevertheless, its faculty upheld high intellectual standards and produced some valuable scholarship.

The faction that left the Presbyterian Church in America to form the Bible Presbyterian Church also founded Faith Theological Seminary in Wilmington,

Delaware, in 1937. Faith Seminary had thirty-five students enrolled by 1940, and it continued to grow. Unlike Westminster, which became more exclusively Calvinist and distanced itself from the mainstream of fundamentalism, Faith built ties to other separatists by including independent Baptist and "Bible church" pastors on its board of trustees and adding J. Oliver Buswell, Jr., former president of Wheaton College, to its faculty.

Seminaries could not carry as much associational freight as Bible institutes, but they served fundamentalism in another fashion. They kept an intellectual spark alive in an otherwise activistic and often anti-intellectual movement. Seminaries provided institutional homes for fundamentalist thought leaders, a few of whom were able to rise above the movement's intellectual stagnation and, in spite of crushing institutional demands and paltry resources, produce some conservative scholarship of lasting merit. These schools also provided a nurturing environment for the coming generation of fundamentalist leaders, some of whom eventually headed up the postwar movement to reform fundamentalism, revive evangelical thought, and restore evangelical Christianity's cultural influence.

Acquiring a college diploma in an evangelical academic setting was not a major priority among fundamentalists in the 1930s and 1940s, but those who sought a Christian liberal arts education encountered problems. Liberal theological perspectives were as pervasive in the colleges of the old-line northern denominations as in the seminaries. These colleges were also following the universities' lead in divorcing theological thought from other forms of learning. Perhaps more disturbing for conservative pastors and parents was the waning of evangelical piety, moral constraints, and religious idealism on these campuses. The Bible institutes responded to this change by offering to fortify young people with a year of biblical and doctrinal studies and spiritual growth before setting out for more secular campuses. Thousands of families chose that route, and in the process they permanently changed the character of these Bible schools, many of which previously had limited admission to adults.

The older evangelical ideal of a liberal arts education still had influence within fundamentalism, however, and a number of institutions were available to serve the movement. In some cases, schools that were founded as Bible or missionary training institutes developed bachelor's degree programs and course offerings in the arts and sciences. That is what was happening at Gordon College in Boston and at Nyack, just north of New York City, during the 1930s. In some other instances, fundamentalists created new schools, such as Bob Jones College, founded by evangelist Bob Jones in Florida in 1926 but relocated in 1933 to Cleveland, Tennessee; William Jennings Bryan University, begun in 1930 in Dayton, Tennessee, as a memorial to the Great Commoner's last stand at the Scopes trial; youth evangelist Percy Crawford's The King's College, which first held classes in 1938 in Belmar, New Jersey; and Westmont College, begun in Los Angeles in 1940. Fundamentalists also attended liberal arts colleges operated by the holiness Wesleyans, such as Taylor University in downstate Indiana and Houghton College in upstate New York; and a few enrolled in conservative Calvinist church-related institutions such as Geneva College in Beaver Falls, Pennsylvania, and Grove City College in another western Pennsylvania town. All told, these conservative colleges prospered during the depression years. A survey of evangelical higher education in 1948 found that the total enrollment of seventy such schools in the United States doubled between 1929 and 1940.

There was only one college of thoroughly fundamentalist pedigree, however, that was neither just half-evolved from Bible school origins nor still waiting for the ink to dry on its charter. That was Wheaton College, in the town of Wheaton, thirty miles west of Chicago. Wheaton had started as a secondary academy under Wesleyan Methodist auspices in the late 1850s, but was reorganized in 1860 by its first president, the Congregationalist reformer and educator Jonathan Blanchard. Wheaton's history to about 1900 was unexceptional for a small midwestern college. But, probably because of its leaders' ties to Dwight L. Moody and his protégés. Wheaton had not become a theologically liberal or an academically and socially secularizing institution like most of its sister colleges. Indeed, the Wheaton of the 1930s and 1940s was something of a throwback to an earlier era, with a pervasively evangelical emphasis and atmosphere, an accent on Christian service, and a strong penchant for training young apologists to defend the faith J. Oliver Buswell, Jr., who was president of Wheaton from 1926 to 1940, was particularly proud of the school's champion debate teams.

Buswell labored to promote the school far and wide, sending its student musicians, debaters, and athletes on tours during vacations and advertising Wheaton as a "safe school" in all the leading fundamentalist magazines. The president worked hard on Wheaton's academic standing as well. During his administration the college won a high accreditation rating and for three years led all the nation's liberal arts colleges in growth of enrollment. By 1941 Wheaton's 1,100 students, up from about 400 in 1926, made it the largest liberal arts college in Illinois. The school was well on its way toward becoming a "Harvard of the Bible Belt," the foremost fundamentalist college in the nation and a producer of such future leaders as theologians Carl F. H. Henry and Edward John Carnell and evangelist Billy Graham. . . .

Proclaiming the Gospel
Fundamentalists were activists par excellence in a nation whose most distinctive religious trait has been activism. They pursued their evangelistic mandate by creating a variety of new ministries and sustaining many older ones. Virtually the only limit to what these ministries might do for the gospel's sake was the imagination of their founders. But of all the activities the fundamentalists pursued outside of their own congregations, perhaps the most important to them and the most indicative of their contrasting fortunes with the major Protestant denominations was their foreign missionary work. The missionary enterprise of the Protestant churches had entered the twentieth century with unbounded hope and zeal, but the liberal theological movement had introduced some second thoughts about aggressive evangelizing in other cultures, and this, coupled with inflation, a cooling of popular ardor for overseas crusades, and some explosive controversies over the allegedly liberal

character of denominational mission boards added up to a major downturn in missions commitment even before the economic depression set in. The Northern Baptist Convention provides an especially dramatic example of the missions declension in mainline Protestantism. Its overseas staff dwindled from 845 in 1930 to 508 in 1940. In the disastrous year of 1936, the denomination's budget for missions totaled $2.26 million, down 45 percent from 1920. That year no new missionaries went out, and many returned from overseas fields for lack of support.

Some blamed fundamentalism for this sorry state of affairs. Before the fundamentalist-modernist controversies, conservatives and liberals had worked together on denominational boards under a broadly evangelical consensus about the missionary's task. That consensus now was destroyed, the missions community was badly polarized, and conservative constituents had lost confidence in the denominational boards. It is a mistake, however, to infer that fundamentalists were driven to contend with the denominational boards out of sheer dogmatic zeal or desire for denominational control. They were intensely committed to foreign missions, and they were eager to get on with the task of world evangelization. Fundamentalists recoiled from the denominational boards when they found that they could not change the boards' policy of including theological liberals as well as conservatives and social gospel programs as well as evangelization. But fundamentalists' missions interest did not flag. They supported independent "faith" mission societies and founded new denominational agencies. During the mid-1930s fundamentalists contributed about one out of every seven North American Protestant missionaries (about 1,700 of the 12,000 total), and by the early 1950s fundamentalists' portion of the total (5,500 out of 18,500) had doubled. . . .

The faith missions in particular developed many connections with the Bible schools. Retiring missionaries often settled nearby to recruit, encourage, and screen potential candidates. Several schools had interlocking directorates with the mission boards. At one time or another in the 1920s and 1930s, the Philadelphia School of the Bible shared trustees and administrators with four different societies: Africa Inland Mission, China Inland Mission, the Inland South America Missionary Union, and the Central American Mission.

Bible conferences and magazines also promoted the missionary enterprise. Established conference centers might have week-long conferences exclusively focused on missions, while more general conferences would have at least one missionary speaker. Annual missionary conferences in the leading regional "cathedrals" of fundamentalism such as Park Street Church in Boston, the People's Church in Toronto, or the Church of the Open Door in Los Angeles, also publicized the enterprise and afforded recruiting opportunities. Fundamentalist magazines, such as the *Sunday School Times* and the *Moody Bible Institute Monthly,* featured regular missions pages and frequent missions articles and news.

Fundamentalists' primary institutions—their homes, Sunday schools, congregations and local leaders—all served the missions cause as well. Young people received missionary biographies for gifts from friends and relatives. Parents may have dedicated their children as babies—as in the Old Testament story of Hannah and her son, Samuel—to "full-time Christian service." Other exposure and encouragement abounded in the form of Sunday school missions stories and offerings, visiting missionary speakers, and encouraging pastors and pastors' wives. So fundamentalist young people grew up in a subculture that saw evangelism as the church's all-consuming priority and vocational religious careers as the highest calling. Missionaries were the noblest models of all for the life of heroic Christian service; they beckoned devoted, visionary, and adventuresome young people to join them on the front lines of spiritual warfare. The result, once most of the fundamentalist volunteers and supporting churches decided to bypass the older denominational mission boards, was the dramatic growth of a distinctly fundamentalist mission force.

Conclusion

This survey should dispel any doubts about the vitality of fundamentalism in the wake of its public defeats in the 1920s. The movement was thriving; it was developing a complex and widespread institutional network to sustain its activities. Indeed, perhaps the best way to think about the fundamentalist movement and its location in the American social, cultural, and religious landscapes is to remember these interconnections: the ties between people and institutions, the collective interests and concerns being expressed, the mutual involvement in religious projects. These different kinds of fundamentalist activity—education, "conferencing," publishing, radio broadcasting, and evangelization—each connected individuals and congregations to endeavors of a larger scope. Like overlaid map transparencies showing the highways, railroads, waterways, air routes, and communications lines that connect a modern society, each kind of collective undertaking gave fundamentalism another layer of infrastructure as a movement. Fundamentalists surged out of the older institutional structures partly out of protest and alienation, but also because they wished to do many things not possible within mainline Protestantism. Fundamentalists created a host of new agencies and retrofitted many older ones to do their work, and their work prospered.

The success of fundamentalism and other evangelical groups, which also grew very rapidly during the 1930s and 1940s, came at the very time that mainline Protestantism was experiencing decline. Yet there was not a general "religious depression" during the 1930s, as has been supposed, but a crisis mainly among the older or more prestigious denominations. The contrasts in religious fortunes between the two major parties of Anglo-American Protestantism in this period are striking. While fundamentalists' missions and ministries grew, Southern Baptists gained almost 1.5 million members between 1926 and 1940, and the Pentecostal denomination the Assemblies of God quadrupled during the same period to total some two hundred thousand members. At the same time, almost every mainline Protestant denomination declined in membership, baptisms, Sunday school enrollments, total receipts, and foreign missions.

Although the mainline Protestants still commanded immense wealth, membership, and cultural prestige, and the evangelicals of various stripes still occupied the margins of public life, a historic shift was beginning. Not only was mainline Protestantism being confronted with its final "disestablishment" in an irreversibly pluralistic nation, but by the 1930s it had reached its apogee as the dominant expression of Protestantism. The mainline was engaged in what would become a long decline, with only a brief respite after the Second World War. Conservative evangelicals, including the fundamentalists but also many others, were perhaps at their lowest point of visibility and respect during the 1930s, but they were thriving and picking up institutional momentum.

By 1950 hints of a changed religious order were beginning to appear. The new pattern in American Christianity has been not so much a challenge to mainline denominations' influence by ascendant conservative denominations as the declining importance of denominations. Like the holiness Wesleyans and pentecostals before them, fundamentalists contributed to the decline of the mainline denominations by promoting dissatisfaction with those bodies' work. Yet fundamentalists were much less prone than the holiness and pentecostal people to solidify their movement around new, break-away denominations. They adopted the parachurch pattern of associational life and, as we have seen, they thrived on it. Instead of compelling its followers to choose between fundamentalism and their home denominations, the movement allowed many to maintain membership in the older denominations while shifting their support to independent ministries. This pattern of forming special-purpose parachurch groups to accomplish religious purposes rather than working through denominational agencies is now increasingly the preference of Catholics and mainline Protestants and as well as conservative evangelicals.

The result, according to sociologist Robert Wuthnow, has been a renewed polarization of American religious life. In their heyday, the mainline denominations were broad enough to include varied viewpoints, mediate differences, and forge the consensus needed to do the church's work. But in the freewheeling world of special purpose religious groups that has grown up since the great Protestant divide in the 1920s, the mainline denominations' power to perform these functions has been seriously weakened, and liberals and conservatives have fewer compelling reasons to resolve their disputes. Ironically, fundamentalists' institution-building in the 1930s and 1940s has become not only the compensatory action of a defeated protest movement, but an important step in the weakening of the American denominational system.

But we are getting ahead of the story. During the 1930s and 1940s, many fundamentalist leaders did indeed feel defeated, and seemed to be trying to compensate for their losses and find their bearings. If the movement's identity was tied up in battling for the "fundamentals" of the faith, what was its purpose when the opponent no longer felt the need to honor the call to come out and fight? Some of the movement's leaders continued their combative posturing, while others focused more intently on evangelizing the neighbors and providing an institutional base for their dispossessed followers. Many felt the need to do both. President James M. Gray of Moody Bible Institute epitomized this complex mood fairly early on when he advised his graduating class of 1922 that they would need to work, like Nehemiah's band, with "a trowel in one hand and . . . a sword in the other."

Questions for Reflection and Discussion

1. As the forces of secularization intensified in the 1930s, what evidence is there that the tension between religious inclusion and exclusion increased, according to the documents?

2. According to Alan Brinkley, why and how did Charles Coughlin foster tension toward the Roosevelt administration?

3. Trace Norma Fain Pratt's argument that secularizing forces in the first quarter of the twentieth century produced new patterns of inclusion and exclusion in the new culture of American Jewry by 1940.

4. What evidence does Joel Carpenter provide in support of his argument that the same secularizing forces which made fundamentalism more exclusive in the 1920s helped it rebuild from within during the depression era?

5. Was America more inclusive or exclusive in the years before World War II?

Additional Readings

Abrams, Ray H. *Preachers Present Arms.* New York: Round Table Press, 1933.

Bengis, Esther. *I am a Rabbi's Wife.* Moodus, Conn.: Esther Bengis, 1934.

Bennett, David H. *Demagogues in the Depression: American Radicals and the Union Party, 1932-36.* New Brunswick, N.J.: Rutgers University Press, 1969.

Carter, Paul A. *The Decline and Revival of the Social Gospel: Social and Political Liberalism in American Protestant Churches, 1920-1940.* Ithaca: Cornell University Press, 1956.

Handy, Robert T. "The American Religious Depression, 1925-35," *Church History* 29 (March 1960): 1-29.

Marsden, George M. *The Soul of the American University: From Protestant Establishment to Established Nonbelief.* New York: Oxford University Press, 1994.

Meyer, Donald B. *The Protestant Search for Political Realism, 1919-1941.* Berkeley: University of California Press, 1960.

Miller, Robert M. *American Protestantism and Social Issues, 1919-1939.* Chapel Hill: University of North Carolina Press, 1958.

Reimers, David M. *White Protestantism and the Negro.* New York: Oxford University Press, 1965.

Ribuffo, Leo P. *The Old Christian Right: The Protestant Far Right from the Great Depression to the Cold War.* Philadelphia: Temple University Press, 1983.

Sklare, Marshall. *Conservative Judaism: An American Religious Movement.* New York: Shocken, 1972.

Sobran, Joseph. "Secular Humanism and the American Religion," In *Piety and Politics,* ed. Richard John Neuhaus and Michael Cromartie, pp. 395-410. Washington, DC: Ethics and Public Policy Center, 1987.

Weisenfeld, Judith. *African American Women and Christian Activism: New York's Black YWCA, 1905-1945.* Cambridge: Harvard University Press, 1998.

Wolters, Raymond. *Negroes and the Great Depression.* Westport, Conn.: Greenwood Press, 1970.

Chapter 14

For American religion the decades of the 1940s and 1950s was a time of consolidation and consensus with occasional eruptions of conflict. As noted by historian Martin Marty in Under God, Indivisible, 1941-1960 *(1996), during the war years there was* "the need for national unity and harmony." *With the development of the Cold War from 1945 to 1952,* "a need for common symbols and energies" *emerged. Mainline Protestantism coalesced in the spirit of ecumenism. In his*

American Religion from World War II to Vietnam

Issue

How would American religion respond to the pressures of the post-World War II period?

1948 book Can Protestantism Win America?, Christian Century *editor Charles Clayton Morrison spelled out his formula. What was needed was a new, reformed "ECUMENICAL CHURCH OF CHRIST." He argued that "Only such a church can win the America that now is or the America that is to be, to the Christian faith." But this church unity movement could only be "Protestant: in the sense that it rests upon the ecumenical basis of the sovereignty of Christ."*

With this spirit of ecumenism among Protestants, it was no mystery why occasional conflagrations broke out between the Protestant and Catholic faiths during this era. After all, Morrison could claim that his book merely responded to the series of articles recently published in the Christian Century *(an ecumenical, Protestant voice) by his colleague Harold E. Fey titled "Can Catholicism Win America?" Did the American profession of inclusion and belief in cultural pluralism extend to the ranks of American religion? George Seldes had already answered that question in his 1939 work* Catholic Crisis, *which forthrightly summed up the liberal case against the Catholic church.*

Furthermore, the spirit of Morrison-style ecumenism did not attract a large number of fundamentalist Protestants. Divisive features of the earlier funda-

mentalist-modernist controversy carried over into the post-World War II era and kept the two branches of Protestantism far apart. A hopeful sign of cooperation from some conservative Protestants did appear in the early 1950s when the spirit of revivalism reappeared among evangelicals, led by the youthful revivalist Billy Graham. As noted by Marty, Graham's preaching of an exclusive gospel during the unrest produced by the Korean War meant he could turn his spotlight on the persistent threat of atheistic communism from abroad while continuing to alert his audiences to the rise of immorality at home— audiences that were inclusive of Protestant, Catholic, and Jew, black and white, and male and female. Even some Morrison-style ecumenists conceded that Graham presented the masses with a "more readily digestible form" of the gospel than elsewhere available.

How did American religion deal with the pressures of the post-World War II period? For some who sought unity, unity could be found. For others who spurned unity, the differences that divided were expressions of conscience and duty. What new issues of gender and race arose after World War II? Was American religion more unified or divided in the early 1960s than two decades earlier?

Documents

In the first document, journalist-turned-theologian Carl F. H. Henry called upon fundamentalists to maintain their support of orthodox theology, but also to address social evils in the mid-twentieth century. Henry was in the forefront of the new evangelicalism. The persistent tension between church and state is presented in the second document, which is an excerpt from School District of Abington Township v. Schempp *(1963). In this decision the Supreme Court ruled that public school opening exercises which used Bible reading were in violation of the First Amendment's establishment clause. The third selection, by the Rev. John Courtney Murray, S.J., is his effort to deflect criticism of traditional interpretations of Roman Catholic teaching on state-church practices, and to present a more rational and dynamic theory of state-church relations. The critical issue of ordination of women is discussed in the fourth document by a spokesperson of the Presbyterian Church of the USA. In the fifth selection, non-Catholic professor of theology John C. Bennett discusses the prospect of electing a Catholic president in 1960. Important ecumenical changes for the Roman Catholic Church were sparked at the gathering of church leaders in Rome known as Vatican Council II (1962-63). In the sixth document, an anonymous insider at the opening session writes of the high drama over which Pope John XXIII presided.*

1. The Uneasy Conscience of Modern Fundamentalism, 1947

SOURCE: From Carl F. H. Henry, *The Uneasy Conscience of Modern Fundamentalism,* © 1947 Wm. B. Eerdmans Publishing Co., Grand Rapids, Michigan. Reprinted by permission; all rights reserved.

Some of my evangelical friends have expressed the opinion that nobody should "perform surgery" on Fundamentalism just now, thinking it wiser to wait until the religious scene is characterized by less tension.

I do not share this view that it is wiser to wait, for several reasons.

It is a sober realism, rather than undue alarm, that prompts the fear that, unless we experience a rebirth of apostolic passion, Fundamentalism in two generations will be reduced either to a tolerated cult status or, in the event of Roman Catholic domination in the United States, become once again a despised and oppressed sect. The only live alternative, it appears to me, is a rediscovery of the revelational classics and the redemptive power of God, which shall lift our jaded culture to a level that gives significance again to human life. It was the rediscovery of classic ancient philosophy that gave incentive to Renaissance humanism with its disastrous implications for Western culture. The hour is ripe now, if we seize it rightly, for a rediscovery of the Scriptures and of the meaning of the Incarnation for the human race.

Further, Fundamentalism is a constant object of surgery anyway. One can hardly move about the campuses of the large universities and secular college—let alone some religious schools—without awareness of the constant assault on our position. Numbers of clergymen who minister to university students repudiate the doctrine of substitutionary atonement as doing violence to man's moral sense. [To us who insist on the abnormality of man's religious affections, there is no infallibility of man's moral sense. The latter leads away from redemption's path those who walk in the confidence of man's inherent goodness. One of the things which modern man most needs to be saved from, is a moral sense which is outraged at a divine provision of redemption.] But it is not this doctrinal assault on the central affirmations of our faith that here distresses me; it must always be, preceding that future day when we shall no longer move by faith, that revelational and nonrevelational views shall stand in sharp conflict. What concerns me more is that we have needlessly invited criticism and even ridicule, by a tendency in some quarters to parade secondary and sometimes even obscure aspects of our position as necessary frontal phases of our view. To this extent we have failed to oppose the full genius of the Hebrew-Christian outlook to its modern competitors. With the collapse of Renaissance ideals, it is needful that we come to a clear distinction, as evangelicals, between those basic doctrines on which we unite in a supernaturalistic world and life view and the area of differences on which we are not in agreement while yet standing true to the essence of Biblical Christianity. But even beyond this, I voice my concern because we have not applied the genius of our position constructively to those problems which press most for solution in a social way.

Unless we do this, I am unsure that we shall get another world hearing for the Gospel. That we can continue for a generation or two, even as a vital missionary force, here and there snatching brands from the burning, I do not question. But if we would press redemptive Christianity as the obvious solution of world problems, we had better busy ourselves with explicating the solution. . . .

Moreover, I am well aware that some who have no sympathy for a supernaturalistic viewpoint, will likely distort and misrepresent the sentiments voiced in these pages. But I do not consider it needful on that account to hesitate. Those who read with competence will know that the "uneasy conscience" of which I write is not one troubled about the great Biblical verities, which I consider the only outlook capable of resolving our problems, but rather one distressed by the frequent failure to apply them effectively to crucial problems confronting the modern mind. It is an application of, not a revolt against, fundamentals of the faith, for which I plead.

That it may be somewhat optimistic to speak of a widespread uneasiness, I also recognize. Many of our Bible institutes, evangelical colleges, and even seminaries, seem blissfully unaware of the new demands upon us. My hope is that some, who were not troubled at the outset of these pages, will become concerned before they finish.

One last word is almost superfluous. It will be almost too evident that the formulation of a solution requires much more constructive treatment. At times, I have been content with a minimal statement, seeking to provoke a united effort, rather than to dogmatize. I address my words to fellow evangelicals in the hope that they shall not make every faltering word an occasion of calumny, but rather inviting them to stand firm in the recognition that, while we are pilgrims here, we are ambassadors also. . . .

2. *School District of Abington Township, Pennsylvania* v. *Schempp*, 1963

SOURCE: *School District of Abington Township, Pennsylvania* v. *Schempp* 374 U.S. 203; 10 L. Ed. 2d 844; 83 S. Ct. 1560 (1963).

MR. JUSTICE CLARK *delivered the opinion of the Court.*

Once again we are called upon to consider the scope of the provision of the First Amendment to the United States Constitution which declares that "Congress shall make no law respecting an establishment of religion, or prohibiting the free exercise thereof. . . ." These companion cases present the issues in the context of state action requiring that schools begin each day with readings from the Bible. While raising the basic questions under slightly different factual situations, the cases permit of joint treatment. In light of the history of the First Amendment and of our cases interpreting and applying its requirements, we hold that the practices at issue and the laws respecting them are unconstitutional under the Establishment Clause, as applied to the states through the Fourteenth Amendment. . . . [In] No. 142 [t]he Commonwealth of Pennsylvania by law, 24 Pa. Stat. Sec. 15–1516, as amended, . . . requires that "At least ten verses from the Holy Bible shall be read, without comment, at the opening of each public school on each school day. Any child shall be excused from such Bible reading, or attending such Bible reading, upon the written request of his parent or guardian." The Schempp family, husband and wife and two of their three children, brought suit to enjoin enforcement of the statute, contending that their rights under the Fourteenth Amendment to the Constitution of the United States are, have been, and will continue to be violated unless this statute be declared unconstitutional as violative of these provisions of the First Amendment. They sought to enjoin the appellant school district. . . from continuing to conduct such readings and recitation of the Lord's prayer in the public schools of the district. . . . . A three-judge statutory District Court for the Eastern District of Pennsylvania held that the statute is violative of the Establishment Clause of the First Amendment as applied to the States by the Due Process Clause of the Fourteenth Amendment and directed that appropriate injunctive relief issue. . . .

The appellees . . . are of the Unitarian faith . . . [and] they . . . regularly attend religious services. . . . The . . . children attend the Abington Senior High School, which is a public school operated by appellant district.

On each school day at the Abington Senior High School between 8:15 and 8:30 A.M., while the pupils are attending their home rooms or advisory sections, opening exercises are conducted pursuant to the statute. The exercises are broadcast into each room in the school building through an intercommunications system and are conducted under the supervision of a teacher by students attending the school's radio and television workshop. Selected students from this course gather each morning in the school's workshop studio for the exercises, which include readings by one of the students of 10 verses of the Holy Bible, broadcast to each room in the building. This is followed by the recitation of the Lord's Prayer, likewise ever the intercommunications system, but also by the students in the various classrooms, who are asked to stand and join in repeating the prayer in unison. The exercises are closed with the flag salute and such pertinent announcements as are of interest to the students. Participation in the opening exercises, as directed by the statute, is voluntary. The student reading the verses from the Bible may select the passages and read from any version he chooses, although the only copies furnished by the school are the King James version, copies of which were circulated to each teacher by the school district. During the period in which the exercises have been conducted the King James, the Douay and the Revised Standard versions of the Bible have been used, as well as the Jewish Holy Scriptures. There are no prefatory statements, no questions asked or solicited, no comments or explanations made and no interpretations given at or during the exercises. The students and parents are advised that the student may absent himself from the classroom or, should he elect to remain, not participate in the exercises.

It appears from the record that in schools not having an intercommunications system the Bible reading and the recitation of the Lord's Prayer were conducted by the homeroom teacher, who chose the text of the verses and read them herself or had students read them in rotation or by volunteers. . . .

At the first trial Edward Schempp and the children testified as to specific religious doctrines purveyed by a literal reading of the Bible "which were contrary to the religious beliefs which they held and to their familial teaching.". . . Edward Schempp testified at the second trial that he had considered having. . . [his children] excused from attendance at the exercises but decided against it for several reasons, including his belief that the children's relationships with their teachers and classmates would be adversely affected.

* * * * *

The trial court, in striking down the practices and the statute requiring them, made specific findings of fact that the children's attendance at Abington Senior High School is compulsory and that the practice of reading 10 verses from the Bible is also compelled by law. It also found that:

> The reading of the verses, even without comment, possesses a devotional and religious character and constitutes in effect a religious observance. The devotional and religious nature of the morning exercises is made all the more apparent by the fact that the Bible reading is followed immediately by a recital in unison by the pupils of the Lord's Prayer. . . . The exercises are held in the school buildings and perforce are conducted by and under the authority of the local school authorities and during school sessions. Since the statute requires the reading of the "Holy Bible," a Christian document, the practice . . . prefers the Christian religion. . . .

[The facts in] no. 119 [show that] [i]n 1905 the Board of School Commissioners of Baltimore City adopted a rule pursuant to . . . [state law which] . . . provided for the holding of opening exercises in the schools of the city, consisting primarily of the "reading, without comment, of a chapter in the Holy Bible and/or the use of the Lord's Prayer." The petitioners, Mrs. Madalyn Murray and her son, William J. Murray III, are both professed atheists. Following unsuccessful attempts to have the respondent school board rescind the rule, this suit was filed for mandamus to compel its rescission and cancellation. It was alleged that William was a student in a public school of the city and Mrs. Murray, his mother, was a taxpayer therein; . . . that at petitioners' insistence the rule was amended to permit children to be excused from the exercise on request of the parent and that William had been excused pursuant thereto. . . .

The respondents demurred and the trial court, recognizing that the demurrer admitted all facts well pleaded, sustained it without leave to amend. The Maryland Court of Appeals affirmed, the majority of four justices holding the exercise not in violation of the First and Fourteenth Amendments, with three justices dissenting. . . .

It is true that religion has been closely identified with our history and government. . . .The fact that the Founding Fathers believed devotedly that there was a

God and that the unalienable rights of man were rooted in Him is clearly evidenced in their writings, from the Mayflower Compact to the Constitution itself. This background is evidenced today in our public life through the continuance in our oaths of office from the Presidency to the Alderman of the final supplication, "So help me God." Likewise each House of the Congress provides through the Chaplain an opening prayer, and the sessions of this Court are declared open by the crier in a short ceremony, the final phrase of which invokes the grace of God. Again, there are such manifestations in our military forces, where those of our citizens who are under the restrictions of military service wish to engage in voluntary worship. Indeed, only last year an official survey of the country indicated that 64% of our people have church membership. . . . while less than 3% profess no religion whatever. . . . It can be truly said, therefore, that today, as in the beginning, our national life reflects a religious people who, in the words of Madison are "earnestly praying, as . . . in duty bound, that the Supreme Lawgiver of the Universe . . . guide them into every measure which may be worthy of His [blessing. . . .]"

Almost a hundred years ago in *Minor* v. *Board of Education of Cincinnati*, Judge Alphonzo Taft, father of the revered Chief Justice, in an unpublished opinion stated the ideal of our people as to religious freedom as one of:

> absolute equality before the law of all religious opinions and sects. . . . The government is neutral, and while protecting all, it prefers none, and it *disparages* none. . . .

The wholesome "neutrality" of which this Court's cases speak thus stems from a recognition of the teachings of history that powerful sects or groups might bring about a fusion or a concert of dependency of one upon the other to the end that official support of the State or Federal Government would be placed behind the tenets of one or of all orthodoxies. This the Establishment Clause prohibits. And a further reason for neutrality is found in the Free Exercise Clause, which recognizes the value of religious training, teaching and observance and, more particularly, the right of every person to freely choose his own course with reference thereto, free of any compulsion from the state. This the Free Exercise Clause guarantees. Thus, as we have seen, the two clauses may overlap. As we have indicated, the Establishment Clause has been directly considered by this Court eight times in the past score of years and, with only one Justice dissenting on the point, it has consistently held that the clause withdrew all legislative power respecting religious belief or the exercise thereof. The test may be stated as follows: what are the purpose and primary effect of the enactment? If either is the advancement or inhibition of religion then the enactment exceeds the scope of legislative power as circumscribed by the Constitution. That is to say that to withstand the strictures of the Establishment Clause there must be a secular legislative purpose and a primary effect that neither advances nor inhibits religion. . . . The Free Exercise Clause, likewise considered many times here, withdraws from legislative power, state and federal, the exertion of any restraint on the free exercise of religion. Its purpose is to secure religious liberty in the individual by prohibiting any invasions thereof by civil authority.

Hence it is necessary in a free exercise case for one to show the coercive effect of the enactment as it operates against him in the practice of his religion. The distinction between the two clauses is apparent—a violation of the Free Exercise Clause is predicated on coercion while the Establishment Clause violation need not be so attended.

Applying the Establishment Clause principles to the cases at bar we find that the States are requiring the selection and reading at the opening of the school day of verses from the Holy Bible and the recitation of the Lord's Prayer by the students in unison. These exercises are prescribed as part of the curricular activities of students who are required by law to attend. They are held in the school buildings under the supervision and with the participation of teachers employed in those schools. None of these factors, other than compulsory school attendance, was present in the program upheld in *Zorach* v. *Clauson*. The trial court in [*Schempp*] has found that such an opening exercise is a religious ceremony and was intended by the State to be so. We agree with the trial court's finding as to the religious character of the exercises. Given that finding the exercises and the law requiring them are in violation of the Establishment Clause.

There is no such specific finding as to the religious character of the exercises in [*Murray*], and the state contends (as does the state in [*Schempp*]) that the program is an effort to extend its benefits to all public school children without regard to their religious belief. Included within its secular purposes, it says, are the promotion of moral values, the contradiction to the materialistic trends of our times, the perpetuation of our institutions and the teaching of literature. The case came up on demurrer, of course, to a petition which alleged that the uniform practice under the rule had been to read from the King James version of the Bible and that the exercise was sectarian. The short answer, therefore, is that the religious character of the exercise was admitted by the State. But even if its purpose is not strictly religious, it sought to be accomplished through readings, without comment, from the Bible. Surely the place of the Bible as an instrument of religion cannot be gainsaid, and the State's recognition of the pervading religious character of the ceremony is evident from the rule's specific permission of the alternative use of the Catholic Douay version as well as the recent amendment permitting nonattendance at the exercises. None of these factors is consistent with the contention that the Bible is here used either as an instrument for nonreligious moral consideration or as a reference for the teaching of secular subjects.

The conclusion follows that in both cases the laws require religious exercises and such exercises are being conducted in direct violation of the rights of the appellees and petitioners. Nor are these required exercises mitigated by the fact that individual students may absent themselves upon parental request, for that fact furnishes no defense to a claim of unconstitutionality under the Establishment Clause. . . . Further, it is no defense to urge that the religious practices here may be relatively minor encroachments on the First Amendment. The breach of neutrality that is today a trickling stream may all too soon become a raging torrent and, in the words of Madison, "it is proper to take alarm at the first experiment on our liberties.". . .

It is insisted that unless these religious exercises are permitted a "religion of secularism" is established in the schools. We agree of course that the State may not establish a "religion of secularism" in the sense of affirmatively opposing or show-ing hostility to religion, thus "preferring those who believe no religion over those who do believe.". . . We do not agree, however, that this decision in any sense has that effect. In addition, it might well be said that one's education is not complete without a study of comparative religion or the history of religion and its relation-ship to the advancement of civilization. It certainly may be said that the Bible is worthy of study for its literary and historic qualities. Nothing we have said here indicates that such study of the Bible or of religion, when presented objectively as part of a secular program of education, may not be effected consistent with the First Amendment. But the exercises here do not fall into those categories. . . .

Finally, we cannot accept that the concept of neutrality, which does not permit a State to require a religious exercise even with the consent of the majority of those affected, collides with the majority's right to free exercise of religion. While the Free Exercise Clause clearly prohibits the use of state action to deny the rights of free exercise to *anyone*, it has never meant that a majority could use the machinery of the State to practice its beliefs. Such a contention was effectively answered by Mr. Justice Jackson for the Court in *West Virginia Board of Education* v. *Barnette,* 319 U.S. 624, 638, 63 S. Ct. 1178, 1185, 87 L. Ed. 1628, (1943):

> The very purpose of a Bill of Rights was to withdraw certain subjects from the vicissitudes of political controversy, to place them beyond the reach of majorities and officials and to establish them as legal principles to be applied by the courts. One's right to. . . freedom of worship. . . and other fundamental rights may not be submitted to vote; they depend on the outcome of no elections.

The place of religion in our society is an exalted one, achieved through a long tradition of reliance on the home, the church and the inviolable citadel of the individual heart and mind. We have come to recognize through bitter experience that it is not within the power of government to invade that citadel, whether its purpose or effect be to aid or oppose, to advance or retard. In the relationship between man and religion, the State is firmly committed to a position of neutral-ity. . . .

It is so ordered.

Judgment in [*Schempp*] affirmed; judgment in [*Murray*] reversed and case re-manded with directions.

[The concurring opinions of MR. JUSTICE DOUGLAS and MR. JUSTICE BRENNAN are not reprinted here.]

MR. JUSTICE STEWART, *dissenting.*

I think the records in the two cases before us are so fundamentally deficient as to make impossible an informed or responsible determination of the constitutional issues presented. Specifically, I cannot agree that on these records we can say that the Establishment Clause has necessarily been violated. But I think there exist serious questions under both that provision and the Free Exercise Clause. . . which require the remand of these cases for the taking of additional evidence.

. . .It is, I think, a fallacious oversimplification to regard these two provisions as establishing a single constitutional standard of "separation of church and state," which can be mechanically applied in every case to delineate the required boundaries between government and religion. We err in the first place if we do not recognize, as a matter of history and as a matter of the imperatives of our free society, that religion and government must necessarily interact in countless ways. Secondly, the fact is that while in many contexts the Establishment Clause and the Free Exercise Clause fully complement each other, there are areas in which a doctrinaire reading of the Establishment Clause leads to irreconcilable conflict with the Free Exercise Clause.

A single obvious example should suffice to make the point. Spending federal funds to employ chaplains for the armed forces might be said to violate the Establishment Clause. Yet a lonely soldier stationed at some faraway outpost could surely complain that a government which did not provide him the opportunity for pastoral guidance was affirmatively prohibiting the free exercise of religion. And such examples could readily be multiplied. The short of the matter is simply that the two relevant clauses of the First Amendment cannot accurately be reflected in a sterile metaphor which by its very nature may distort rather than illumine the problems involved in a particular case.

* * * * *

That the central value embodied in the First Amendment—and, more particularly, in the guarantee of "liberty" contained in the Fourteenth—is the safeguarding of an individual's right to free exercise of his religion has been consistently recognized. . . .

It is this concept of constitutional protection embodied in our decisions which makes the cases before us such difficult ones for me. For there is involved in these cases a substantial free exercise claim on the part of those who affirmatively desire to have their children's school day open with the reading of passages from the Bible.

* * * * *

It might also be argued that parents who want their children exposed to religious influences can adequately fulfill that wish off school property and outside school time. With all its surface persuasiveness, however, this argument seriously misconceives the basic constitutional justification for permitting the exercises at issue in these cases. For a compulsory state educational system so structures a child's life that if religious exercises are held to be an impermissible activity in schools, religion is placed at an artificial and state created disadvantage. Viewed in this light, permission of such exercises for those who want them is necessary if the schools are truly to be neutral in the matter of religion. And a refusal to permit religious exercises thus is seen, not as the realization of state neutrality, but rather as the establishment of a religion of secularism, or at the least, as government support of the beliefs of those who think that religious exercises should be conducted only in private.

What seems to me to be of paramount importance, then, is recognition of the fact that the claim advanced here in favor of Bible reading is sufficiently substantial to make simple reference to the constitutional phrase of "establishment of religion" as inadequate an analysis of the cases before us as the ritualistic invocation of the nonconstitutional phrase "separation of church and state." What these cases compel, rather, is an analysis of just what the "neutrality" is which is required by the interplay of the Establishment and Free Exercise Clauses of the First Amendment, as imbedded in the Fourteenth.

I have said that these provisions authorizing religious exercises are properly to be regarded as measures making possible the free exercise of religion. But it is important to stress that, strictly speaking, what is at issue here is a privilege rather than a right. In other words, the question presented is not whether exercises such as those at issue here are constitutionally compelled, but rather whether they are constitutionally invalid. And that issue, in my view, turns on the question of coercion.

It is clear that the dangers of coercion involved in the holding of religious exercises in a schoolroom differ qualitatively from those presented by the use of similar exercises or affirmations in ceremonies attended by adults. Even as to children, however, the duty laid upon government in connection with religious exercises in the public schools is that of refraining from so structuring the school environment as to put any kind of pressure on a child to participate in those exercises; it is not that of providing an atmosphere in which children are kept scrupulously insulated from any awareness that some of their fellows may want to open the school day with prayer, or of the fact that there exist in our pluralistic society differences of religious belief.

* * * * *

[I]t seems to me clear that certain types of exercises would present situations in which no possibility of coercion on the part of secular officials could be claimed to exist. Thus, if such exercises were held either before or after the official day, or if the school schedule were such that participation were merely one among a number of desirable alternatives, it could hardly be contended that the exercises did anything more than to provide an opportunity for the voluntary expression of religious belief. On the other hand, a law which provided for religious exercises during the school day and which contained no excusal provision would obviously be unconstitutionally coercive upon those who did not wish to participate. And even under a law containing an excusal provision, if the exercises were held during the school day, and no equally desirable alternative were provided by the school authorities, the likelihood that children might be under at least some psychological compulsion to participate would be great. In a case such as the latter, however, I think we would err if we assumed such coercion in the absence of any evidence.

Viewed in this light, it seems to me clear that the records in both of the cases before us are wholly inadequate to support an informed or responsible decision. Both cases involve provisions which explicitly permit any student who wishes, to be excused from participation in the exercises. There is no evidence in either case as to whether there would exist any coercion of any kind upon a student who did not want to participate. . . .

. . . It is conceivable that these school boards, or even all school boards, might eventually find it impossible to administer a system of religious exercises during school hours in such a way to meet this constitutional standard— in such a way as completely to free from any kind of official coercion those who do not affirmatively want to participate. But I think we must not assume that school boards so lack the qualities of inventiveness and good will as to make impossible the achievement of the goal.

I remand both cases for further hearings.

3. The Problem of State Religion, 1951

SOURCE: From John Courtney Murray, S.J., "The Problem of State Religion," *Theological Studies*, XII (1951):160-67. Copyright © 1951 by *Theological Studies*. Reprinted with permission.

What therefore the Church must seek, and has sought, in every age is such a vital application of her principles, such an institutional embodiment of them, as will make them operative in particular temporal contexts towards the permanent ends, human and supernatural, which she has always in view. The history of Church-State relations is the history of this manner of adaptive application. It records many compromises, but no ideal realizations.

The legal institution known as the state-church, and the later embodiment in the written constitutional law of territorial states of the concept of Catholicism as "the religion of the state," represent an application of Catholic principles (and of the medieval tradition, itself an adaptation) to the complex political, social, religious, and cultural conditions prevailing in the modern state, as it appeared on the dissolution of medieval Christendom, took form in the era of political absolutism, flourished in the era of "confessional absolutism" (to use Eder's phrase) under the royal governments in the "Catholic nations" of post-Reformation Europe, and sought reinstatement in the monarchic restorations of the nineteenth century. As a necessary adaptation of principle this legal institution was at first tolerated by the Church; later, in the circumstances of fixed religious divisions, it became the object of more positive acquiescence; still later, in the circumstances created by the French Revolution, it was defended against the laicizing monism of Continental Liberalism, which destroyed the institution of the state-church in consequence of its denial of the Catholic thesis of juridical and social dualism under the primacy of the spiritual, of which the institution was, however defectively, an expression. In the course of this defense the application of the thesis was identified with the thesis itself—an identification that was never canonized by the Church.

Since the institution of the state-church was an adaptation to a particular historical context, it does not represent a permanent and unalterable exigence of Catholic principles, to be realized in any and all historical situations in which there is verified the general hypothesis of a "Catholic population." This legal institution need not be defended by Catholics as a sort of transtemporal "ideal," the single and only institutionalized form of Church-State relationships which can claim the support of principles, the unique "thesis" beside which all other solutions to the Church-State problem must be regarded as "hypothesis," provisional concessions to *force majeure.*

Where the conditions of its origin still more or less prevail, the institution of the state-church is still the object of defense. But the long history of the Church's adaptation of her permanent principles to perpetually changing political realities has not come to a climax and an end with this institution, in such wise that the only valid present effort must be in the direction of a restoration of what existed in a particular epoch of the past—the national state-church by law established, with legal disabilities for dissenters.

On the contrary, the Church can, if she will (and if Catholic thinkers clarify the way for her), consent to other institutionalizations of Church-State relationships and regard them as *aequo iure* valid, vital, and necessary adaptations of principle to legitimate political and social developments.

Such a development is presented by the democratic state. The term does not designate the special type of state which issued from French Revolutionary ideology and Continental Liberalism, which was merely another form of the absolutist state. The term refers to the political idea of the state derived from "the liberal tradition" of the West, which has been best preserved, though not guarded in its purity, in the Anglo-Saxon democratic tradition; Continental Liberalism was a deformation of the liberal tradition; it was in effect simply another form of absolutist state-monism, to which the liberal tradition stands in opposition.

Democracy today presents itself with all the force of an idea whose time has come. And there are two reasons why the present task of Catholics is to work toward the purification of the liberal tradition (which is their own real tradition) and of the democratic form of state in which it finds expression, by restoring both the idea and the institutions of democracy, to their proper Christian foundations. First, this form of state is presently man's best, and possibly last, hope of human freedom. Secondly, this form of state presently offers to the Church as a spiritual power as good a hope of freedom as she has ever had; it offers to the Church as the Christian people a means, through its free political institutions, of achieving harmony between law and social organization and the demands of their Christian conscience; finally, by reason of its aspirations towards an order of personal and associational freedom, political equality, civic friendship, social justice, and cultural advancement, it offers to the Church the kind of cooperation which she presently needs, and it merits in turn her cooperation in the realization of its own aspirations. . . .

With regard to the special problem of religious freedom one remark may be made. There would seem to be a valid analogy between the constitutional provision for religious freedom in the democratic state and the legal institution of the state-church in the post-Reformation monarchic states, in the sense that both represent an analogical adaptation to analogous situations. The latter institution was an adaptation to two facts: (1) the emergence of the modern state as a "person," as autonomous, with an autonomy that extended to state determination of the religion of the people; with this fact is allied the concept of "the people" as purely passive in the face of government, whose purposes are determined apart from consultation of the people; (2) the religious division of universal Christian society into separate and autonomous Catholic and Protestant nations and states. The former institution is an adaptation to two analogous facts: (1) the emergence of "the people" into active self-consciousness, into a spiritual autonomy that extends to a rejection of governmental determination or even tutelage of their religion; with this fact is allied the concept of "the state" as the instrument of the people for limited purposes sanctioned by the people; (2) the religious divisions within territorial states between persons of different religions. When they are viewed in this historical perspective, it is difficult to see why one institution is any less, or more, an adaptation of principle than the other, why one should be considered more valid and vital than the other, why one has a greater right to claim the support of principle than the other.

Actually, from the standpoint of principle the crucial point is not the fact of religious unity or disunity, with the former basing a "thesis" and the latter an "hypothesis"; for both situations are predicated on a disruption of Catholic unity in the proper sense. The crucial question is whether the concept of the state and the concept of the people that undergirds the legal institution of the state-church is any more rational than the concept of the state and the concept of the people that undergirds the legal institution of religious freedom. The answer would seem to be that the latter concepts are certainly more rational and better founded in Christian thought.

The foregoing propositions set forth, simply in outline, the major points of a theory of Church-State relationships which may, I think, be considered tenable in the light of the full Catholic tradition of thought and practice in the matter.

4. Shall Women Be Ordained?, 1955

SOURCE: From Hellen C. Woolson, "Shall Women Be Ordained?" *Outreach* (Aug.-Sept. 1955):199-200. Copyright © 1955 by *Outreach*. Reprinted with permission of *Horizons,* the magazine of Presbyterian women.

The matter seemed to center basically around four questions: What does the Bible say about it? What does the theology of the Presbyterian Church say about it? What bearing does the historical and traditional attitude of the Church have on it? What has the present-day sociological status of women to do with it?

It seemed, therefore, that any decision the committee might reach should be thoroughly grounded theologically and philosophically. The committee felt that it should study statements already published on the position of women in the Church and in the world, and further that additional studies by our own theologians were needed. Therefore, it asked two outstanding men to prepare statements—one on the Biblical basis and one on the theological basis for ordination of women. These statements were carefully studied as were others that delineated the historical and traditional position of women in the Church, the sociological status of women in the world, and the instances of increasing co-operation between the sexes, particularly in opportunities for service in many fields. Some of the findings that influenced the committee follow:

The Bible teaches us that in Christ Jesus *there is neither male nor female.* The New Testament certainly supports the view that before God men and women are equal—neither sex is inferior to the other in access to God's grace and gifts. Women did serve as deaconesses in the Apostolic Church and did hold other positions of authority. Old Testament writers tell of many women who were prophetesses—women clearly chosen and inspired by God. Acts 2:17 implies that at Pentecost women as well as men received the Spirit and prophesied or spoke with tongues. God has spoken and speaks today through both men and women.

If we interpreted the Bible literally, we would never have approved ordaining women as elders. For there is just as much and just as little basis for ordaining women as elders as there is for ordaining them as ministers! It is true that women were never mentioned as priests or bishops in the Old Testament or the New. But the fact that they were prophetesses brings up the crucial question whether prophecy may be regarded as a regular ministry of the Church, and opens up the whole field of our reformed understanding of the ministry. This leads to a consideration of the theological or reformed doctrinal view of the place of women in the Church.

Two major theological issues are involved: first, the relation between men and women from the point of view of their divine creation, their redemption in Christ, and their coexistence in the Christian faith and life; and, secondly, the whole doctrinal interpretation of the Church and the ministry. In its report to General Assembly the committee stated "that it is proper to speak of equality of status for men and women both in terms of their creation and their redemption; that it is proper to speak of equality of status for men and women in the Church and its ministry; that there is no theological ground for denying ordination to women simply because they are women . . . that there is no theological barrier against the ordination of women if ordination would contribute to the edification and nurturing of the Church in its witness to the Lord of the Church."

These are only some of the arguments and considerations that the committee studied—only one more may be mentioned here. The ministry is today becoming more and more diversified. Ordained ministers are working in many new fields, such as radio and television; in social agencies; as chaplains in industry; in psychotherapy; as counselors; as directors of Christian education. Plainly, to be a minister is not necessarily to be a preacher, and both men and women have varied and unique qualifications for varied and unique ministries.

Women may be doctors, lawyers, engineers, professors, architects, even ball players and bus drivers. If, then, God calls a woman to preach the gospel and chooses to speak through her, dare man or the Church question his choice? In Christ *there is neither male nor female.*

5. A Roman Catholic for President?, 1960

SOURCE: From J. C. Bennett, "A Roman Catholic for President?" *Christianity & Crisis* XX, no. 3 (Mar. 7, 1960):17-19. Copyright © 1960 by *Christianity & Crisis.* Reprinted with permission of *Christianity & Crisis.*

The issue raised by the possibility of a Roman Catholic candidate for the Presidency is the most significant immediate problem that grows out of the confrontation of Roman Catholicism with other religious communities in the United States. There are a great many Protestants of influence who are inclined to say that they would never vote for a Roman Catholic for President. Many of them refuse to say this with finality, but there is a strong trend in this direction. Our guess is that it may be stronger among the clergy and among official Protestant spokesmen than among the laity.

Aside from crude forms of prejudice and a reluctance to accept the fact that this is no longer a Protestant country, there are two considerations behind this position that have some substance. The first is that the traditional teaching of the Catholic Church is at variance with American conceptions of religious liberty and of church-state relations. There is a fear that a Catholic President might be used by a politically powerful Catholic Church to give that church the preferred position to which, according to its tradition, it believes itself entitled.

The other consideration is that there are a few specific issues on which there is a Catholic position, and, short of any basic change in our institutions, the nation's legislation and policy might be deflected by a Catholic President toward these known positions of his church. One example that is not often mentioned is the intransigent view of the problems of the cold war that was expressed in the American Catholic Bishops' statement late in 1959. (We would not vote for any man, Protestant or Catholic, who takes such a view.)

On matters of this kind most Catholics are more likely to be affected by the position taken by the authorities of their church than would a Protestant. Even though they may not agree with the bishops, it would be embarrassing to oppose them publicly. Catholic bishops do their debating privately; American Catholicism on the hierarchical level, therefore, gives the impression of a united front that no Protestant churches are able to give.

We want to direct three comments to those who take a negative view concerning a possible Roman Catholic President:

(1) If the American people should make it clear that a Catholic could never be elected President, this would be an affront to 39,500,000 of our fellow citizens, and it would suggest that full participation in American political life is denied to them as Catholics. This would be true even though Catholics are governors, senators, congressmen and Supreme Court justices. We believe that this situation would wound our common life and damage our institutions more grievously than it would be possible for a Catholic President to do even if he chose to. We are shocked that so many Protestants seem unwilling to give any weight to this.

(2) We are justified in ascertaining what view of church-state relations and of the basis of religious liberty a particular Catholic candidate holds. We may learn this without grilling him, for his record of public service and its implications would be an open book.

There are two main views of religious liberty that are held among Catholics. The traditional view regards as normative the idea of a Catholic state with the church in a privileged position and with at least a curtailment of the liberties of non-Catholics. This view is an inheritance from an earlier period of history, and many Catholic theologians and ecclesiastical leaders now reject it. They believe in religious liberty for non-Catholics on principle and not merely as a matter of pragmatic adjustment to the American situation.

This more liberal view is not limited to this country; it is held widely in stern Europe. It is one view held in Vatican circles. Those who hold this view believe that Pius XII was at least open to it, and they are even more sure that this is true of his generous-minded successor. . . .

(3) So far as the specific issues on which there is a known Catholic position are concerned, there are very few that come to the desk of the President. More of them are dealt with by mayors and governors, and the Republic has survived many Catholic mayors and governors. And on many issues within the purview of the President, the Catholic community is divided—even, for example, on the appointment of an ambassador to the Vatican. (It was a Baptist who made the latest appointment to the Vatican.) Furthermore, a President is subjected to so many pressures and counterpressures that he is less vulnerable to any one form of pressure than most other public servants.

There is the vexing problem of birth control. As a domestic problem it belongs chiefly to the states, and it is fortunate that many Catholics, while they do not reject their church's position on birth control in terms of morals and theology, do not believe there should be a civil law that imposes the Catholic moral teaching upon non-Catholics. . . .

We should like to add to these considerations a more positive note: a Catholic President who is well instructed in the moral teachings of his church would have certain assets. (It is chiefly in the areas of sex and medicine that the Protestant finds elements of an intolerable legalism in Catholic moral teaching.) If he is of an essentially liberal spirit he may absorb the best in the real humanism of Catholic thought.

A Catholic President might have a better perspective on the issue of social justice than many Protestants. He might be guided by the ethical inhibitions present in Catholic views of the just war so as to resist the temptation to make military necessity paramount in all matters of national strategy. He might have a wiser and more seasoned understanding of the claims of the person in relation to the community than many a one-sided Protestant individualist.

We are not now speaking of any particular Catholic candidate, and there are elements in Catholic moral doctrine that we reject. When these are interpreted by the narrower type of ecclesiastic, we often find them repellent. But Catholic teaching has its better and more humane side, and it is the repository of much wisdom that could stand a Catholic President in good stead.

6. Excerpt from "The Council Opens," 1963

SOURCE: Excerpts from "The Council Opens" from *Letters from Vatican City* by Xavier Rynne. Copyright © 1963, renewed 1991 by Farrar, Straus & Giroux, Inc. Reprinted by permission of Farrar, Straus and Giroux, LLC.

To anyone who had the good fortune to be standing in front of the bronze doors leading into the papal palace, on the side of St. Peter's Square, at eight o'clock on the morning of Thursday, October 11, 1962, there was suddenly revealed a dazzling spectacle. At that moment, two papal gendarmes, resplendent in parade uniform of white trousers and black topboots, coats, and busbies, slowly swung the great doors open, exposing to a portion of the crowd row upon row of bishops, clad in flowing white damask copes and mitres, descending Bernini's majestic *scala regia* from the papal apartments. As brilliant television floodlights were switched on along the stairway, the intense light brought to mind Henry Vaughan's lines:

> I saw Eternity the other night,
> Like a great ring of pure and endless light.

In rows of sixes, an apparently inexhaustible phalanx of prelates filed out of the Vatican palace, swung to their right across St. Peter's Square, then wheeled right again, to mount the ramplike steps leading into the basilica. Every now and then, this white mass was dotted with the black cassock, full beard, and round headdress of an oriental bishop, and here and there with the bulbous gold crown and crossed pectoral reliquaries of a bishop of the Byzantine rite. Toward the end came the scarlet ranks of the Sacred College of Cardinals. Finally, the pope appeared, carried, in deference to the wishes of his entourage, on the *sedia gestatoria*, and looking rather timid, perhaps even frightened—as he always does when first mounting this oriental contraption— but gradually warming to the mild acclamation of the overawed crowd, and gently smiling and quietly weeping as he was carried undulantly forward, blessing the onlookers. At the entrance to the Council hall in the basilica, the procession halted while the pope dismounted and walked the length of the nave to the Confession of St. Peter.

Before the high altar the pope had ordered the substitution of a simpler, more informal style of throne for the unwieldy, pretentious "doctoral" throne, with a red damask backdrop and canopy, that the organizers of the Council had devised. The significance of this was soon made clear by the pope's opening speech, which stressed the Council's pastoral, or ministering, role over the dogmatic, or condemnatory, approach. After the traditional hymn "Veni Creator Spiritus," a solemn mass of the Holy Spirit was celebrated, in which the Epistle and the Gospel were chanted in both Greek and Latin, to signify the unity of both parts of the Church, East and West. The celebrant was the elderly but vigorous Cardinal Tisserant, bearded dean of the College of Cardinals. A touch of Byzantine court ceremonial followed the mass, as the cardinals mounted the steps of the papal throne one by one, with their scarlet mantles trailing behind them, to make their obeisance to the See of Peter. After the bishops' solemn profession of faith in unison, recitation of the litany of the Saints, and more prayers from the Greek rite, Pope John began to deliver his sermon.

In clear and resonant tones that could be distinctly heard throughout the basilica, the pope, after a few introductory remarks, said that he was tired of listening to the prophets of doom among his advisers. "Though burning with zeal," he said, these men "are not endowed with very much sense of discretion or measure." They maintain that "our era, in comparisons with past eras, is getting worse, and they behave as though they had learned nothing from history, which is nevertheless the great teacher of life." They were, he said, under the illusion that "at the time of the former Councils, everything was a triumph for the Christian idea and way of life and for proper religious liberty," and he added, "We feel that we must disagree with these prophets of doom, who are always forecasting disaster, as though the end of the world were at hand," and continually warning him, "in the course of our pastoral office," that the modern world is "full of prevarication and ruin. . . ."

* * * * *

The pope then proceeded to outline, serenely and optimistically, what he expected of the Council and why he had summoned it. "Divine Providence," he said, "is leading us to a new order of human relations." It was imperative for the Church "to bring herself up to date where required," in order to spread her message "to all men throughout the world." While the Church must "never depart from the sacred patrimony of the truth received from the Fathers," she must "ever look to the present, to new conditions and new forms of life introduced into the modern world, which have opened new avenues to the Catholic apostolate."

Then came the phrases, so pregnant with meaning, that either alarmed or grati-fied his listeners, depending on their theological outlook. The pope said that he had not called the Council to discuss "one article or another of the fundamental doctrine of the Church . . . which is presumed to be well known and familiar to all; for this, a Council was not necessary." Thus were ruled out the hopes of those who had expected the Council to proclaim some new dogma, isolated from the rest of Christian doctrine, in the manner of the previous Ecumenical Council here, in 1869-70, which concentrated on the dogma of papal infallibility. No, said the pope; "the world expects a step forward toward doctrinal penetration and a forma-tion of consciences." This must be "in conformity with authentic doctrine," of course, but it "should be studied and expounded through the methods of research and through the literary forms of modern thought." In other words, doctrine was to be made more intelligible to contemporaries in the light of scholarship in bibli-cal, theological, philosophical, and historical disciplines.

He next touched on a subject that is almost taboo in traditionalist Catholic theological circles, saying, "The substance of the ancient doctrine of the *depositum fidei* is one thing; the way in which it is expressed is another." That is, Catholic doctrine remains the same in substance, but the formulations of it vary and are not to be regarded as unalterable ends in themselves. The task of the Council, he told the assembled prelates, was to find the best formulas for our time, without being too hidebound or showing a too slavish respect for those of the previous age. He further emphasized the pastoral, rather than the doctrinal, note by declaring, "Nowa-days, the bride of Christ [the Church] prefers to make use of the medicine of mercy rather than that of severity. She considers that she meets the needs of the present day by demonstrating the validity of her teaching rather than by condem-nation." This was an unmistakable disavowal of the inquisitorial and condemna-tory approach of the Holy Office. Finally, the pope turned his attention to the problem of Christian unity. "The entire Christian family has not yet fully attained the visible unity in truth" desired by Christ, he said, and the Catholic Church "therefore considers it her duty to work actively so that there may be fulfilled the great mystery of that unity." He said that the key to "the brotherly unity of all" — embracing not only Christians but "those who follow non-Christian religions" — is "the fullness of charity," or love. Thus Pope John put his seal on the methods and goals of Catholic participation in the ecumenical, or worldwide, movement for reunion.

This inaugural address to the Council, carefully worded and balanced, and de-livering a bold message of renewal and reform, marked the end of the closed men-tality that has characterized not a few Catholic bishops and theologians since the sixteenth century. Whether this message reached all the prelates to whom it was addressed, or will be heeded by all it did reach, is another matter; one does not cease being a prophet of doom overnight. But the Council as a whole received the pope's message gladly.

Essays

After World War II a sharp debate arose in the United States between Catholics on one hand, and Protestants and liberals on the other over the place of Catholicism in post-World War II American pluralism and democracy. In the first essay, Philip Gleason of the University of Notre Dame discusses the ambiguities of the concept of pluralism, and the tendency to treat democracy as a civil religion in the analysis of Catholic authoritarianism. In the second essay, Barbara Brown Zikmund of Hartford Seminary reviews the deliberations of Methodists, Presbyterians, Lutherans, and Episcopalians over their concerns about the ordination of women. The final essay, by Mark Silk of Trinity College (CT), analyzes the rise of the "New Evangelicalism" during World War II and its development through the early 1960s.

Pluralism, Democracy, and Catholicism in the Era of World War II

PHILIP GLEASON

SOURCE: From Philip Gleason, "Pluralism, Democracy, and Catholicism in the Era of World War II," *Review of Politics* 49 (1987):208-12, 214-17, 218-24. Copyright © by Notre Dame University. Reprinted with permission.

Background of the Catholic Issue

The 1928 election was, of course, the high point of anti-Catholic sentiment in the twentieth century. The extreme to which no-popery was carried aroused considerable sympathy for Catholics, however, and the next few years were marked by improved inter-religious feeling. The depression, which crowded cultural issues off center-stage, was basic to this development, but as an important element in the Democratic coalition, Catholics also benefited from Franklin D. Roosevelt's election. As president, Roosevelt appointed more Catholics to office than anyone ever had before. Catholics may also have benefited in a more diffuse way from the concern for improved intergroup relations that emerged in the context of New Deal liberalism.

After 1935 this mellowing was sharply offset by a series of developments that poisoned relations with liberals and Protestants. Concentrating first on the liberals (though recognizing that many Protestants were included in this group), we note that Father Coughlin's shift to an anti-New Deal position in 1935-36 alerted liberals to the fascistic tendencies of his activities. Thereafter his growing extremism on the menace of communism, his open anti-Semitism after 1938, and the sometimes violent behavior of his Christian Front followers contributed to the linkage between Catholicism and fascism which many American liberals took for granted by the end of the decade. In New York City, where much liberal opinion was formed, Catholic anti-Semitism (and Christian Front hooliganism) reflected not just the influence of Coughlin, but also Irish Catholic frustration over losses sustained in the 1930's to the growing political, economic, and cultural power of the city's Jewish community. . . .

The liberal case against the Catholic church was summed up in 1939 in George Seldes's *Catholic Crisis,* a book that one reviewer thought (incorrectly) might "become the *novissimum testamentum* of the rapidly growing American anti-Catholic reaction." To Seldes the Catholic church was clearly in league with fascism. Support for Franco was the centerpiece, but Vatican softness toward Germany and Italy, and opposition to liberalism and communism, buttressed his case. The domestic scene Seldes covered with a farrago of evidence ranging from Father Coughlin and anti-Semitism to Catholic ties with corrupt politicians (especially Boss Hague) and objectionable pressure-group tactics brought to bear on Congress, state legislatures, the press, the film industry, and private groups or individuals who espoused causes of which Catholics disapproved, such as birth control.

Seldes's indictment was comprehensive in its way, but it failed to bring out the point that the clash between Catholics and liberals was at bottom one of radically divergent worldviews. For Catholics, the great evil of the day was secularism—the exclusion of God from human life, personal and social—and against that evil they launched a vigorous campaign in the 1930's and 1940's. Essential to the campaign was a philosophical critique of the intellectual position underlying secularism; in carrying out that critique, Catholics became involved in harsh polemics with the thinkers they called "naturalists," the most prominent of whom was John Dewey. As pacesetters for American liberalism, thinkers like Dewey already had ample reason for annoyance at Catholics; the assault on their ideas, and the degree to which religious ideas seemed to be regaining intellectual respectability, aroused them to something like outrage.

The deepest source of bitterness was that Catholics and naturalists each accused the other of holding principles that furnished the intellectual foundation for totalitarianism. Underlying the mutual recrimination was a disagreement about how values are grounded. Catholics and other "absolutists," as they came to be known, held that there is an inherent structure of value in reality; that man can discern its basic pattern, and that he is obligated to take it as his guide in the social and political realm as well as in personal and family life. The naturalists, or "relativists," on the other hand, denied that reality exhibited any such inherent structure of value; they affirmed instead that man evolves his own values from social experience and imposes them on reality.

The relativist position dominated American intellectual life in the 1930's, but those who held it were profoundly discomfited by the charge that their own principles left them no grounds on which to object to Hitler because all he was doing was imposing on reality a set of values different from their own, but which they had no warrant for saying was evil. Moreover, the charge continued, by denying that values rested on everything more than human volition, the relativists had actually paved the intellectual way for Hitlerism. Unable to refute the charge as formulated, the relativists simply dismissed it and brought a *tu quoque* counter-charge against the absolutists. According to their etiology, totalitarianism in politics derived from authoritarianism in thought; that in turn was inseparable from the conviction that one could attain the truth about things in their very essence; hence Catholics and other absolutists were the real intellectual progenitors of totalitarianism.

This interpretation complemented the widely accepted linkage between Catholicism and fascism, and it was the majority view of American intellectuals. But the Catholic-absolutist critique had put secular intellectuals on the defensive for a time, and it would have required supernatural patience (to which, of course, they made no pretension) for them not to have felt anger as well as chagrin. By the time the war ended, they were thoroughly aroused on the subject of Catholic authoritarianism and prepared to respond vigorously to any further provocation.

Protestants too had had as much as they could take of Catholic "aggressiveness." Many of them were alienated in the late 1930's for reasons already mentioned. Yet the campaign for interreligious brotherhood being promoted by the National Conference of Christians and Jews provided a countercurrent of good will. In these circumstances, President Roosevelt's 1939 appointment of Myron C. Taylor as his "personal representative" to the Vatican constituted a significant turning point in the overall climate of Protestant feeling. Because it raised the church-state issue in highly visible form, and even more because it seemed to symbolize a new status for Catholics in the national community, the Taylor appointment aroused strong Protestant opposition from groups relatively untouched by the anti-Catholic feeling generated by issues like the Spanish Civil War.

The church-state issue was sharpened in 1940 by the appearance of a book restating the traditional teaching on the desirability of Catholicism's being the established religion of the state. Separation of church and state and religious freedom were, according to this teaching, merely expedients tolerable in situations where the Catholic faith could not, for practical reasons, be established as the religion of the state. This formulation was all the more shocking because its author was John A. Ryan, the outstanding American Catholic liberal of his generation. Naturally, no non-Catholic reader was satisfied with Ryan's bland reassurance that the possibility of establishing the Catholic religion in the United States was so remote that no sensible person need feel any concern about it. Indeed, the Ryan book seemed to give the lie to the protestations by American Catholic leaders that they were sincerely committed to the American principle of religious freedom and church-state separation.

The growing strength and assertiveness of American Catholics took on a more disquieting cast in the light of this revelation of what Protestants regarded as the ultimate intentions harbored by the Catholic church. Something else that heightened their anxieties was the conviction that the hierarchy was pursuing a carefully thought out plan to "take over" America and subvert the democratic ideals and values that were rooted in its Protestant heritage. The degree to which this conviction had established itself by the end of the war in the minds of the leaders of mainstream Protestantism—not just the radical fringe of traditional Catholic baiters—is made clear by an eight-part series entitled, "Can Catholicism Win America," which appeared in the *Christian Century* between 29 November 1944 and 17 January 1945. . . .

The Ambiguities of Pluralism

With this rough sketch of the background, and without attempting to treat the subject comprehensively, we turn now to the ambiguities of pluralism. Although Horace M. Kallen introduced the key term "cultural pluralism" in the twenties, it did not catch on until the end of the next decade and only came into general use in the wartime years and after. By that time it meant something quite different from what Kallen originally had in mind. Written in reaction to the one hundred per-cent Americanism of World War I, his original version of cultural pluralism was radically antiassimilationist. It envisaged American nationality, not as a distinctive something-in-itself, but as a collocation of autonomous ethnic nationalities, each of which had its own spiritual enclave, all somehow coexisting harmoniously within the political entity called the United States. When the term was taken up by the students of intergroup relations in the late thirties, however, cultural pluralism had lost its hard edge and become an enlightened form of Americanization theory. Although it laid verbal stress on diversity, its proponents acknowledged that it was "essentially a technique of social adjustment which will make possible the preser-vation of the best of all cultures" as contributors to the generic American culture. It was, in other words, a relaxed version of the classic melting-pot ideal, which was precisely what Kallen meant to discredit and overthrow.

The assimilationist version of cultural pluralism came into wider usage in the war years because it was ideally suited to the rhetorical requirements of the situa-tion—that is, it allowed the insistence on wartime unity to be couched in the language of tolerance and respect for diversity. We were, after all, fighting a brutal totalitarian regime based on an abhorrent doctrine of racial supremacy. What united us in this desperate struggle was our common commitment to a set of ideals, the ideals of democracy—indeed, of Western civilization—among which respect for the dignity of the individual, whatever his background, loomed very large. Sharing this common ground, our differences were unimportant. Of course, we had to live up to our ideals; hence the message of tolerance for diversity, respect for cultural pluralism, took on a certain urgency. But at bottom it assumed we were more alike than different because we were "Americans All." As Louis Adamic put the matter in 1940: by respecting diversity, "we will produce unity—automatically—and make it dynamic, bring[ing] out the basic sameness of people. . . ."

As this term that seemed to say one thing and mean another became ever more bland and innocuous, students of government complicated matters even more by applying the word "pluralism" to America's multigroup political system. Although it came out of a different intellectual tradition, this usage blended with pluralism as it was understood by commentators on intergroup relations, making the term more diffuse and generalized than ever.

Catholics were conventionally included among the minorities to be cherished in our pluralistic society and reducing religious prejudice was a time-honored goal of those committed to better intergroup relations. Catholics found the idea of pluralism congenial and were using the term freely by around 1950. By that date social scientists were also calling attention to the tendency for ethnic distinctiveness to fade into a broader social differentiation based on religion. This interpretation, fully elaborated in Herberg's triple-melting-pot thesis of 1955, suggested that cultural pluralism was resolving itself into religious pluralism, or at least that religion and race were the most basic elements in American pluralism.

That, of course, was how Catholics saw the matter. Being defined as a religious minority, they regarded respect for religious differences as the foundation stone of American pluralism, which they interpreted to mean that a religious minority was warranted in pursuing its own way of life so long as it did not thereby infringe on the rights of others. Hence they were shocked when Protestants and liberals denounced as "divisive" activities that Catholics believed were wholly legitimate expressions of American pluralism.

Although occasionally referred to in the twenties and thirties, divisiveness emerged as a leading issue only in the postwar era of religious controversy when it was closely associated with the school question. Not only were Catholic efforts to get public funds for their schools denounced as divisive, so also was the very existence of parochial schools, even if maintained by Catholics themselves on a fully voluntary basis. Nor could the charge always be dismissed as the work of Catholic-baiters like Paul Blanshard. It was also made by the prestigious president of Harvard University, James B. Conant. While disclaiming any thought of weakening America's prized diversity, he nevertheless characterized parochial schools as a threat to national unity. Indeed, Conant sounded like an old-fashioned advocate of the melting pot in praising the role played by the public school in assimilating immigrants.

Divisiveness was not, however, confined to the schools. Protestant observers had long warned that the hierarchy was mobilizing the Catholic faithful into religiously segregated associations as part of their campaign to take over American society. The tremendous array of institutions and societies Catholics had built up, along with the heavy stress laid on what was called "Catholic Action," lent plausibility to such fears. By 1951 the danger seemed so pressing that the *Christian Century* was moved to the extreme of repudiating pluralism itself. An editorial entitled "Pluralism—National Menace" made the warning explicit, linking it with an exposé of Catholic mobilization in the city of Buffalo which was described in an accompanying article. In the face of this kind of pluralism, the editors felt no embarrassment in calling universal public education "the *sine qua non* of a homogeneous society," and in urging "straightforward, uncompromising resistance to any efforts by any group to subvert the traditional American way of life."

Rejection of pluralism itself was highly anomalous, and quite unnecessary in view of the availability of "divisiveness" as a pejorative term. That is no doubt the reason the *Christian Century's* repudiation of pluralism had no impact on general usage. But it does call attention to the puzzling relationship of pluralism and divisiveness. Why was the former overwhelmingly acclaimed while the latter was universally deplored? Was it possible to be pluralized without being somehow divided? What made one kind of diversity good and another kind bad? For enlightenment of this perplexity we turn to Horace Kallen, the inventor of "cultural pluralism."

Kallen's *Cultural Pluralism and the American Idea* (1956) was his first major treatment of the subject in thirty years, and his ideas had changed dramatically. Pluralism was no longer primarily associated with ethnic cultures and their preservation; the vision of a federation of nationalities had vanished. Rather cultural pluralism had been extended to include the most "diverse utterance of diversities— regional, local, religious, ethnic, esthetic, industrial, sporting, and political. . . ." But Kallen was not prepared to embrace *every* kind of pluralism: absolutist or isolationist pluralism, a pluralism of noninteracting social monads, he rejected with something like indignation. . . .

Catholic Authoritarianism and the Civil Religion of Democracy

The role played by World War II in stimulating the development of democracy as a civil religion can hardly be overestimated. The need to mobilize the nation's spiritual resources in the desperate struggle against totalitarianism naturally brought about a terrific emphasis on democracy as the symbol of the values for which we fought. As a result, wartime nationalism assumed a highly ideological form, expressing itself in fervent reaffirmations of traditional democratic ideals, the four freedoms, and what Gunnar Myrdal called in 1944 "the American creed." Mention of Myrdal in this context calls to mind another aspect of the situation, already alluded to in passing, namely the point that emphasis on the universalistic values of democracy as the basis of wartime unity was what made possible the seemingly paradoxical celebration of pluralism. It was, to repeat, only because the nation was united on the ideology of democracy that it was committed to tolerating diversity—and could afford to do so.

All this was, in my opinion, not only understandable in the circumstances, but also necessary and proper. I do not, in other words, regard what has just been said as an unmasking of something cynical or manipulative. On the contrary, I cannot conceive of anything more appropriate for emphasis at the time than the traditions of democracy. But of course there were drawbacks as well. Like all developments, the emphasis on democracy was subject to its own distinctive excesses, labored under built-in difficulties, and carried negative potentialities.

The most obvious negative potentiality was realized in the semi-hysteria over subversion that developed in the Cold War years. Although deplorable, this kind of fixation on the danger of "un-American" tendencies was but the obverse side of wartime insistence on the democratic ideology as the touchstone of national unity.

The built-in difficulty that democracy is a highly abstract concept that means different things to different people tended to aggravate the impassioned confusion of the postwar years. Misunderstanding springing from this source led easily to suspicion of bad faith, for it is difficult not to question the honesty of an antagonist who claims to be devoted to a principle cherished by all, but who interprets it as justifying policies one believes to be perverse. While it was inherent in the situation, this difficulty was perhaps made worse by the tendency of secular liberals to think of democracy in "cultural" terms, that is, as a mode of behavior or "way of life" rather than as a set of institutional arrangements or the principles which those institutions were intended to embody.

The cultural definition of democracy appealed to the liberals because it enabled them to get around the claim of the absolutists that the good society had to be based on common assent to universally binding general principles. But it inevitably implied a behavioral test of true democracy. After all, if democracy is a way of life, only those who live that way are really democrats. To the extent that they accepted a cultural definition of democracy, liberals were thus inadvertently erecting behavioral conformity into the test of authentic Americanism.

The built-in difficulties and negative potentialities already mentioned were reinforced by what I consider the distinctive excess of the wartime emphasis on democracy—namely, the tendency to invest democracy with the aura of the sacred, to exalt it to the level of a civil religion. Given democracy's close association with the deepest values of Western civilization, this kind of tendency was natural enough at a time when those values were threatened with annihilation. More often than not, it was merely an implicit tendency—illustrated, for example, in the crisis-induced association of American values and the "Judeo-Christian tradition"—but it was occasionally formulated in more explicit terms. The article by Kallen referred to above is one of these explicit formulations, and it also illustrates how liberals sometimes insisted on conformity to their understanding of "the democratic way of life" as the test of true Americanism.

Kallen's article, which was popular in approach, appeared in the *Saturday Review of Literature* in July 1951. Defining religion in Deweyesque terms as that which a person invests with ultimate importance and "bets his life on," Kallen proceeded immediately to the assertion that science and democracy were a religion in this sense. They were one religion because science was democracy in the realm of ideas, while democracy was "the method of science" applied to human relations. This religion was also called "secularism," a designation that Kallen accepted despite the hackles it raised in some quarters.

The distinctive feature of this religion, according to Kallen, was that its "what" was a "how," by which he meant that its content was a process or method rather than a body of teachings. That method he described as "a free mobility, wherein majorities may become minorities without any loss of rights and minorities [may become] majorities without any accrual of privilege; where every majority guarantees all minorities equal liberty and equal justice and protects them from the dangers of coercion and injustice at its own hands." Attuned as it was to the cosmic flux of reality, this religion assured an "open society in which the entire miscellany of mankind may enter freely and move and have their beings in safety, all equally free to unite themselves with their fellows or to abandon one union and join another as their consciences direct, their needs prompt, and their understandings guide."

This religion—which was Kallen's midcentury version of pluralism seen from a different angle—might appear terribly vague, but it was not without practical implications. For true believers like Kallen, "the democratic faith" was "the religion *of* and *for* religions"—in other words, it was superior to all other religions and had the responsibility of seeing to it that they obeyed its principles. No "assumption of infallibility" on the part of a subordinate faith could be tolerated, for example, nor could any other practice "repugnant to the religious life" as that was defined by the religion of science and democracy. And since "free mobility" was the crucial "what/how" of the democratic faith, it was unacceptable for any subordinate religion to impede the free coming and going of its followers by attempting to keep them apart from other religionists.

From what has already been said, one might infer that the Roman Catholic church would have trouble adjusting itself to the regime of science-democracy-secularism as the religion of religions. Another area of incompatibility emerged from Kallen's discussion of ministry. Since it did not accept any "invidious distinction between the 'religious' and the other vocations of man," the democratic faith affirmed "the priesthood of all believers" and thereby consummated the liberation of the human conscience begun by the Protestant Reformation. Directly opposed to this democratic understanding of religious ministry was "clericalism," by which Kallen understood the pretension of a sacerdotal caste to special powers that were used to justify special privileges.

By this point in the article it was clear that Catholicism was incompatible with the religion of science and democracy. Kallen did not shrink from the duty this laid upon him of pointing out that fact, and of exploring its implications. Indeed, he devoted at least a fifth of his space to the peril to democracy posed by "the Roman Catholic hierarchy," which had become so "notably aggressive" in resisting the salutary processes of secularization that all non-Catholics were justifiably alarmed. He covered familiar ground in saying that the Church had "declared war" on church-state separation, denounced the Supreme Court, and demanded an ambassador to the Vatican. He was more original, however, in relating these offenses to a perverted interpretation of the American principle of freedom of religion.

According to the "sacerdotal argument" advanced by the Roman hierarchy, Kallen explained, freedom of religion was identified with "the liberty of a priestly craft [sic], calling themselves 'the teaching church,' to impose its authority willy-nilly." But that was, of course, wrong; freedom of religion was *not* intended to allow churches to conduct themselves in keeping with their own law, "such as the canon law." What freedom of religion really involved, Kallen declared as the exegete of the democratic faith, was "recognition by the state . . . of the liberty of the personal conscience . . . of the individual's right of private judgment which secures him from the aggressions and coercions of sacerdotal authority. . . ." In other words, it was the job of the state to make sure all the subordinate religions conducted themselves "democratically" in their dealings with their own communicants. And if they didn't, the state would presumably require them to do so.

As an illustration of this extraordinary interpretation of freedom of religion and separation of' church and state, Kallen pointed to the area of education. Consider the case, he said, of "an American parent believing in the Roman Catholic religion." Such a person had as much right as anyone else to send his children to the public school; but according to the law of the Catholic church, he could do so only under pain of sin. This amounted, in Kallen's view, to "suppression of the parent's right by clerical coercion," and it constituted "a violation of the Constitution." He failed to specify what should be done, but since it was unconstitutional and wrong, judicial and/or legislative relief would seem to be called for—court orders or laws spelling out what the Catholic church could and could not do in maintaining its own internal discipline. Theoretically, the church might be required to do away with the hierarchy as such, since that authoritarian structure was clearly the root of the offense against the religion of science, democracy, and secularism.

Even without drawing that inference, Kallen's article confirmed precisely the point Catholics were always urging against their secular-liberal critics—namely, that the secular-liberal position amounted to a religion in itself and one that claimed the privileged status of being normative for American society. Kallen's affirmation of his own sectarian version of democracy as a civil religion was not a momentary aberration; he repeated it in 1954 and 1965. Nor was he the only one to make such an affirmation in that era. J. Paul Williams, a professor of religion at Mount Holyoke, did the same, laying particular emphasis on the role of the public school in inculcating "the democratic ideal *as religion* [sic]." Williams spoke of the public school as "a veritable temple for the indoctrination of democracy," and prescribed as *"worship"* school exercises aimed at revitalizing democratic idealism. Will Herberg asserted in 1952 that "influential Jewish religious leaders" had been advocating essentially the same thing "for years."

This kind of talk was an embarrassment to public school spokesmen who endorsed strict separationism and insisted that secular education was in no way identifiable with religious or "metaphysical" instruction. In 1954, however, the prominent historian of American religion, Sidney E. Mead, chided the public for ignoring Williams's argument. Mead, who was to emerge in the 1960's as a leading apologist for American civil religion, all but explicitly endorsed Williams's dictum that "governmental agencies must teach the democratic ideal *as religion.*" This, he frankly admitted, "is essentially an appeal for a State Church in the United States, and . . . [the] arguments for it largely parallel those traditionally used to defend Establishments."

What Mead failed to explain was how such an establishment could get around the First Amendment, which proscribed establishments of religion without making an exception for the religion of democracy. Writers sympathetic to American civil religion do not address this problem very straightforwardly—at least not in the terms presented here. Perhaps the reason is that, for a writer like Kallen, the word *democracy* stood for the ultimate principles underlying human life, and the idea that the Constitution could really proscribe its being "established" as the common faith of Americans was simply incoherent. But this, of course, is merely to assume that the religion of democracy cannot be proscribed because it is *true*, while it is entirely proper for false religions to be proscribed—especially (Kallen at least would add) religions as antipathetic to "democracy" as Roman Catholicism was.

It was because of this tendency to absolutize democracy, to elevate it to religious status, that Catholics, who were themselves abused as authoritarians, responded in like terms, calling their secularist critics "totalitarians" who insisted that everyone else think and act as they did. While often shrill in defending themselves, Catholics were on solid ground in rejecting Kallen's "democratic faith" as the normative formulation of Americanism. At the same time, reasonable Catholics were deeply concerned to mitigate the controversies, and to correct the genuine abuses their critics pointed out. Most of all, Catholics were embarrassed by commitment to an outmoded ideal of church-state union. Hence it is no accident that a revitalized American Catholic liberalism was forged in the era of controversy, the most significant achievement of which was John Courtney Murray's working out of a persuasive Catholic rationale for religious freedom and separation of church and state.

But that is another story. The point of this one is that analysis of the controversies of the forties helps us to identify basic conceptual ambiguities that have persisted in more recent discussions of pluralism and democracy, religion and secular humanism.

Winning Ordination for Women in Mainstream Protestant Churches

BARBARA BROWN ZIKMUND

SOURCE: Excerpts from *Women and Religion in America, volume 3: 1900-1968* by Rosemary R. Ruether. Copyright © 1986 by Rosemary R. Ruether and Rosemary S. Keller. Reprinted by permission of HarperCollins Publishers, Inc.

From 1800 to 1860, American society was strongly influenced by a coalition of political and intellectual leaders rooted in (1) Congregational, Reformed, and Presbyterian traditions; (2) the legacy of Episcopalian and Lutheran state churches; and (3) indigenous evangelistic groups of Baptists, Disciples, and Methodists. This mix produced a so-called "evangelical consensus," which became known as "mainstream Protestantism." To be sure, "mainstream" sometimes stretched to include numerically marginal groups such as Quakers, Brethren, and Unitarians, but the common definition primarily included the above groups.

Mainstream Protestantism depends upon voluntarism. Local congregational life and denominational structures thrive on the volunteer energies of millions of church members. Through voluntary service these Christians launch missions, sustain local congregational life, and support clergy. For mainstream Protestant men and women, especially women, church work has great appeal. By the end of the nineteenth century, therefore, it was not surprising that women began to question some of the unexamined assumptions surrounding their membership and leadership in the churches. Women lacked equality of influence and opportunity. Eventually, this meant that women sought ordination.

Before examining the specific debates and arguments on ordination, it is important to note that the ordination of women is integrally connected to patterns of lay equality in the church. In most mainstream denominations no progress is made towards the recognition of women clergy until women gain significant power and influence as laity. The journey begins with basic citizenship rights in the local congregation. Are women allowed to speak up in church meetings? Do women have a vote? Eventually, the issue expands to deal with questions of lay leadership. Can women serve on the vestry, the session, the official board, the church council? Can women represent their church at regional, diocesan, or national meetings? Sometimes certain lay responsibilities call for "ordination" as deacon or ruling elder. Mainstream Protestant churches rarely take up the question of women's ordination (as clergy to preach and lead worship) until questions of lay leadership have been resolved.

Among Congregationalists, Baptists, and other denominations with congregational polity, most battles over lay citizenship were finished long before the twentieth century. If women served their churches as lay leaders, it was not difficult to support the idea of women as clergy. Most scholars believe that the first ordination of a woman in mainstream Protestantism was carried out by Congregationalists in 1853. The one exception in this pattern is the Disciples. They ordained a woman to preach long before there was general acceptance of female lay elders. This is because lay elders exercise important liturgical roles in the Christian Church (Disciples of Christ).

Denominations following presbyterian or episcopal polity went much slower. Some justification for women as ruling elders or members of the vestry was necessary before the question of women clergy became appropriate. Once that question was answered, however, the issue was more practical than theological. How could a married woman do it? What was the relationship of ordained ministry to mission and educational work? What if local churches did not want women pastors? Could anyone envision women bishops? Cautious church leaders did not want to take this step if it was impractical. In connectional churches, where clergy belong to a regional structure beyond their status in a local congregation, ordination was actually one step away from total equality. Methodist women could not rest until they had gained membership in annual conference.

Winning ordination in mainstream American white Protestantism, therefore, begins with basic lay suffrage in the local church and moves to full equality of opportunity for clergy throughout a denominational system. Many denominations with congregational polity progressed quickly through this cycle in the nineteenth century, even though legal equality did not always mean the end of injustice. Methodists, Presbyterians, Lutherans, and Episcopalians started the cycle later.

Therefore the struggle for women's ordination or equal clergy status in the twentieth century is most clearly documented by an examination of these four groups.

Methodists

In the 1880s several women were elected to the General Conference of the Methodist Episcopal Church (ME), North, but the Conference refused to seat them. Four years later, female delegates appeared again; this time they were seated. Also in 1880, two women, Anna Howard Shaw and Anna Oliver (who already held licenses to preach), came before the General Conference seeking ordination. The Conference refused to act. Furthermore, it rejected the unofficial practice of licensing women, declaring that "no member of the church shall preach without a license." Anna Howard Shaw left the Methodist Episcopalians to be ordained by the smaller and more progressive Methodist Protestant Church. Anna Oliver stayed to press her case, albeit unsuccessfully. The Methodist Episcopal Church, South also refused to license or ordain women.

From 1880 to 1920 the status of women evangelists and leaders in the ME Church, North was ambiguous. However, in 1920 the General Conference received a memorial from the Kansas conference supporting the licensing and ordination of women. The Conference voted to license women, but referred the question of ordination to a Commission for study. In 1924 Commission recommended that women be ordained as local preachers, but not admitted to membership in the annual conferences. Without conference membership, ordained women could only serve those churches left open after every male member had received his appointment. During the debate efforts were made to remove the word "local" from the recommendation, thereby giving women full status and equality as clergy. According to Madeline Southard, a licensed preacher and founder of a new ecumenical association for women preachers, the debate never dealt with ordination, but concerned itself with the practical ramifications of "conference membership."

At approximately the same time, the ME Church, South granted rights to women. This denomination never did license or ordain women until forced to do so by the reunion of Methodism in 1939.

Every four years, from 1924 to 1956, the General Conference of the Methodist Episcopal Church, North, and later, the reunited Methodist Church considered the question of full ecclesiastical standing for female ordained Methodist preachers. When the Methodist Church came into being in 1939, the three uniting churches struck a compromise on women's status: southern ME churches were forced to accept women as local preachers; northern ME churches retained ordination without conference membership; and Methodist Protestants, who ordained women and gave them conference membership, were given assurances that already ordained women would not lose their conference membership even though full status would no longer be available to women. It was a close vote, with only seven votes preventing the new Methodist Church from granting full ecclesiastical equality to women.

Finally, in 1956, prodded by two thousand memorials on the issue, the General Conference acted. The badly divided Committee recommended that women be admitted to conferences, but that "only unmarried women and widows may apply"; thereby they avoided the problem of appointments for married women. A strong minority report argued for no change at all. An amendment tried to reserve the decision to each annual conference. The debate was practical and administrative, not theological. In the end the General Conference acted decisively, rejecting the qualified recommendation of the Committee and voting full access to the "travelling ministry" (and conference membership) to all ordained Methodist women.

In 1968, the Methodist Church merged with the Evangelical United Brethren (EUB) Church. The EUB Church was itself a 1947 merger of two German Methodist bodies. One side of that union, the Church of the United Brethren in Christ, went back to eighteenth century. Beginning in 1841, it appears that the United Brethren licensed many women to preach at the local level. By 1889, the General Conference officially endorsed granting a license to a woman, "provided she complies with the usual conditions required of men." That same year a woman was ordained by the Central Illinois Conference.

The Evangelical Church and its predecessor bodies, however, never ordained women. During conversations leading up to the EUB union, "women's ordination" was rarely discussed. Yet in 1947, when the newly constituted EUB General Conference reviewed the policies of the new denomination worked out by the bishops, they discovered that the union would not take away "the ministerial status of any man or woman," but there would "be no ordination as ministers granted to women" in the EUB Church. As time went by, however, the question never became a controversial issue. Certain bishops continued to ordain women, but these "isolated instances neither provoked any recorded objections nor inspired any generally accepted practice." In 1968, the Methodist Church merged with the Evangelical United Brethren Church. It was clearly stated that women would have full ecclesiastical standing in the resulting United Methodist Church.

Presbyterians

Presbyterian concerns about the ordination of women relate even more closely to issues of lay status because Presbyterians commonly ordain lay deacons and ruling elders. In the early 1920s, overtures authorizing women to these lay offices came before the General Assembly of the Presbyterian Church in the USA (northern). In 1923, the decision was made to ordain women as deacons. This was also the time period when the strong independent women's organizations in the church were absorbed into a unified denominational structure through reorganization. Many women were dissatisfied with this development and raised questions about women's role in the church. By the late 1920s, northern Presbyterians were asked to vote whether women should be ordained as ruling elders (local lay leaders) and/ or teaching elders (clergy responsible for the ministry of word and sacrament). The General Assembly sent three overtures on women's status to the presbyteries. The first one was in support of total equality. The second and third approved women as ruling elders and licensed evangelists. Only the overture authorizing women to be ordained as ruling elders passed. By asking for full equity, which was not voted, women nevertheless gained increased power as lay leaders.

Eventually, however, pressure for a recognized status for women serving the church through professional ministries of mission, evangelism, and education mounted. To meet this need, in 1938 the General Assembly established a category of "commissioned church worker." It was clearly stated, however, that this status did not "confer any ministerial rights and privileges." Women could now prepare for full-time service in local congregations, but they remained unordained.

After the Second World War, the question of women clergy again confronted the General Assembly. Another overture approving the eligibility of women to the ordained ministry of Word and Sacrament was sent to the presbyteries, but it did not even receive majority support, let alone the required two-thirds vote. A *New York Times* article summarized the debate with tongue in cheek.

Finally, in 1953, the Presbytery of Rochester (New York) raised the issue again. A committee was appointed to study the question. By 1955, it recommended that women be ordained as teaching elders (clergy). This time it passed by an over-whelming majority. In the religious enthusiasm of the 1950s, women clergy were no longer a threat. Those who voted for women clergy, however, did not think that great numbers of women would seek ordination. Women would serve in educa-tion, in rural settings, in the urban crisis, and as assistants to established clergy. People refused to see women's ordination as an invitation to real equality.

Obviously, women's ordination could not be ignored in the conversations that led to the merger of the Presbyterian Church in the USA and the United Presbyte-rian Church of North America (UPNA) in 1958. The smaller, conservative UPNA had ordained women as deacons in 1906. However, United Presbyterians had never ordained women as ruling elders or ministers, although a number of women had served as recognized evangelists. In the new church it was decided that women would have full equality, at least in principle. But no one was enthusiastic. In spite of their commitment to principle, Presbyterian church leaders from all sides did little to break down the *de facto* inequality that continued.

The Presbyterian Church, US (southern) could not even affirm the principle, having never ordained women to any office even though women did serve on national committees and boards. In 1952, the issue was hotly debated at its Gen-eral Assembly with no action. In 1957, the assembly sent a measure to the presbyteries approving the ordination of women only as deacons and ruling elders. It was voted down. Finally, in 1964, almost a full decade after northern church action, southern Presbyterians approved women as deacons, elders, and ministers all at once.

Actually, the small Cumberland Presbyterian Church, which broke away from southern Presbyterianism on frontier issues in the early nineteenth century, led all other Presbyterian groups in its acceptance of women as lay elders and ministers. Not all Cumberland presbyteries applauded this openness, but in 1889 the Nolin

Presbytery (Kentucky) ordained the first Presbyterian woman to the full work of the gospel ministry.

Lutherans

Lutheranism in America began the cycle of concern about women's role in the church even later than the Presbyterians. During the first half of the twentieth century, American Lutheran church bodies remained fragmented and psychologically tied to their various European traditions. Women in American Lutheran churches organized into women's guilds and societies, but concern for equal lay leadership and clergy rights rarely developed before 1940. At that time, several things brought the issue forward. First of all, the incredible changes in women's role in American society could no longer be avoided. The isolation of first generation immigrants was breaking down. Lutheran women actively engaged in many aspects of political and social life.

Second, American Lutheranism was strongly influenced by European developments. In the aftermath of the Second World War, Lutheran churches in Scandinavia began to change. The Norwegian state church had the right to appoint women pastors in 1938. After the war there was great need for pastors; women were no longer attracted to the deaconess role; and, because many Lutheran churches were state churches, political movements for human rights had an impact upon church policies. In 1948, the Danish parliament opened ordination to women. By 1950, a Swedish church commission recommended ordination, but because of the controversy over church-state relationships and the ecumenical ramifications of such action the decision was delayed until 1958. Three Swedish women were finally ordained in 1960.

Changes in American practice began with the question of vote and voice for women at several levels of the church. In 1907, Augustana Lutherans decided that women could vote in their local churches and, in 1930, they were seated as delegates to judicatory meetings. In 1934 United Lutherans approved women as delegates, members of the church council, and members of boards and commissions. The American Lutheran Convention seated its first woman delegate in 1944.

Meanwhile, the Lutheran Church-Missouri Synod (LC-MS) delayed the question. Finally, in 1954, they authorized a study of "women's suffrage in the church," only refusing to grant local voting rights to women in 1956.

Lutherans were also very influenced by developments in biblical scholarship and the ecumenical agenda of the World Council of Churches. In the late 1950s, many Lutheran bodies were preoccupied with church union. In 1960, the American Lutheran Church (ALC) consolidated Midwestern Lutheranism. And in 1962, four other groups united to form another even larger Lutheran body, the Lutheran Church in America (LCA). Throughout this period the question of women's ordination was raised, but not resolved. Scholars debated the biblical, theological, practical, and ecumenical issues. Many concluded that there were no biblical or theological reasons against women's ordination. Missouri Synod Lutherans objected that the question was not being dealt with correctly. They published an

English translation of a German book on the subject to show that the ordination of women would be a "practical invalidation of the proclamation concerning woman's subordination." By the late 1960s, the three major American Lutheran churches (LCA, ALC, and LC-MS) held an Inter-Lutheran Consultation on the Ordination of Women. They agreed that it was possible (and even Lutheran) to disagree. It was only a matter of time before the LCA and ALC acted to ordain women. They argued that "although the Gospel does not change, conditions do. New situations, differing customs, continued research, the on-going work of God, and the promptings of the Spirit demand constant reconsideration of previous assumptions."

Episcopalians

The Protestant Episcopal Church in the United States sees itself in continuity with worldwide Anglicanism. Consequently, Episcopal efforts to deal with the question of women's ordination were strongly influenced by what happened in England and among other Anglicans.

In 1920, the Lambeth Conference (a regular meeting of all Anglican bishops held every ten years) declared that "the ordination of a deaconess confers upon her holy orders." But, by 1930, the bishops changed their interpretation. Ordination was only for male priests, deaconesses were appointed.

This confusion prompted one thoughtful Anglican scholar to write a book supporting the admission of women to full priesthood. As the Dean of Emmanuel College at Cambridge, he argued that "to perpetuate habits of mind and methods of organization suited to the period when women's subjugation was axiomatic is under the circumstances of today to invite failure; it is to prefer a stage coach in an era of motorcars and aeroplanes." The book was reprinted on this side of the Atlantic with an introduction on "The American Situation." Although ignored by Episcopalians, it was an inspiration to women in many denominations.

Most American Episcopalians became aware of questions surrounding women's role in the church in the 1940s. In 1947, the diocese of Vermont approved the election of women to local vestries. Many dioceses, however, continued to keep women off vestries and to question the validity of women delegates to the Triennial Convention. By 1950, reports from the World Council of Churches and a controversy caused when the Bishop of Hong Kong ordained a woman made many Episcopalians aware of the issue. Methodist and Presbyterian action in the mid-1950s exacerbated the situation.

Finally, in 1964, the General Convention changed the canon on deaconesses to "ordered" rather than "appointed." Within the year Bishop James Pike interpreted that to mean that an "ordered" deaconess had the authority of Holy Orders and could be in charge of a parish. The House of Bishops met in 1965 to deal with the furor and commissioned a study on the larger question of the role of women in ministry. The Committee reported a year later that the burden of proof was on the opposition to show "that the unique character of the ordained ministry makes that ministry a special case and justifies the exclusion of women from it."

The struggle for ordination in the Episcopal Church went well into the 1970s. Several times the House of Bishops voted in favor of women priests, only to have the vote defeated by laity in the House of Deputies. It was not resolved until unauthorized ordinations (1974) forced the church to deal with the issue after the fact. Even then, concerns for mutual recognition and ecumenical unity continued to undermine Episcopal commitments to full equality for women.

Mainstream Protestantism in Context

During all of these years of Methodist, Presbyterian, Lutheran, and Episcopalian activity, women in denominations that had ordained women many years earlier watched with interest. They began to ask each other why they failed to reap the benefits of their "equality." They asked their denominations to clarify long-standing practices concerning women. They pressed for better placement and representation for women clergy. Female seminary admission to master of Divinity programs rose as increasing numbers of women openly prepared themselves for pastoral ministry.

These same years also caused conservative Protestants to become more and more defensive. After the modernist-fundamentalist controversy, which raged during the first few decades of the twentieth century, hard-line conservative evangelical Protestantism withdrew from the mainstream. Relying upon a network of Bible colleges and independent nonsectarian mission organizations, conservative evangelicals ignored the question of women's ordination. From time to time, some zealous soul would write a small pamphlet deploring the changing role of women and defending "old time religion." All efforts to reinterpret scriptural admonitions against women speaking in church were dismissed as the work of the devil.

In the 1970s, however, this isolation began to crack. Ecumenical theological education made it difficult to do theology by "proof text." Neoevangelicals generated a spirit of self-criticism and concern for social justice. Electronic evangelism sought respectability. Biblical scholarship discovered that Jesus was a feminist. By the 1980s, the problem of women's ordination had become so relevant that the Southern Baptist Convention acted to condemn it.

The more important context for mainstream Protestantism was the ecumenical movement. By the 1940s and 1950s, any examination of women's ordination had to be approached with geographical and denominational sophistication. In some denominations the question concerned women preaching, in others it involved sacramental authority. It was not uncommon for younger mission churches to ordain women, in spite of the policies of parent denominations. Social and cultural differences raised questions about the authority of the Bible for all times and places. Theologians examined the nature of the church and called for a new appreciation of the laity. By 1964, the ordination of women was a major ecumenical issue.

Finally, important political, economic, and social factors influenced twentieth-century developments surrounding ordination for women in mainstream Protestantism. In 1920, the women's suffrage amendment was ratified and women became voting citizens. Church women began to wonder, If women can go to the polls to vote for the president and congress, why can't we vote and serve as leaders in our churches?

Economic patterns of supply and demand also had an impact upon the situation. During the 1920s, the economy was expanding and there were more pastorates than clergy. But during the depression and wartime, churches did not feel the same pressure to ordain women. Only in the postwar religious revival of the 1950s, did Methodists and Presbyterians finally grant equal ecclesiastical status to women. It is no accident that the periods of greatest advancement for women clergy in mainstream Protestantism always came when there was an undersupply of trained clergymen.

More than politics or economics, however, the social context of women's lives invited twentieth-century women to consider ministry. Compared with their grandmothers, women were living longer, staying healthier, benefiting from more education, and spending a major portion of their lives employed outside the home. It was only natural that these women, nourished by the Christian church, began responding to God's call in new ways.

But recognizing the call, and getting the ecclesiastical structures to honor and support that call, was only the beginning. It was true that women did seem to have an advantage in certain pastoral situations, especially in their ministry with and to other women. But the framework for their ministry was rarely supportive. Women were forced to make their own way without the social and institutional acceptance so readily available to men.

Winning ordination in mainstream Protestantism was and is a process, not an event. It began when women spoke up in their local churches and voted their concerns. It progressed when women accepted church leadership responsibilities at home and in denominational structures. It became more complicated when women felt God's call to serve in ordained ministries of Word and Sacrament. It was advanced when ecclesiastical bodies recognized the ministerial authority of women and men as equal. And it will be fully won when women find appropriate recognition and support for their theology and their ministries throughout church and society.

The Rise of the "New Evangelicalism": Shock and Adjustment
MARK SILK

SOURCE: From *Between the Times: The Travail of the Protestant Establishment, 1900-1960* by William R. Hutchison, ed. Copyright © Cambridge University Press 1989. Reprinted with the permission of Cambridge University Press.

"Sectarianism receives new lease on life," announced the *Christian Century's* May 19, 1943, editorial on the formation of the National Association of Evangelicals for United Action (NAE). The leaders of the new organization claimed that the great majority for whom the Federal Council of Churches "has presumed to speak" were misrepresented by the policies of that body. Nonsense, snapped the nondenominational weekly. "Every kind of conservatism" within the NAE could be found in bodies belonging to the Federal Council of Churches (FCC)—"and this not in suppressed minorities or in inarticulate and misrepresented majorities, as the 'evangelicals' say, but in the personnel of every part of the organizational structure from top to bottom." As the *Century* saw it, the NAE's founders clearly desired not representation within a united Protestantism but control of part of Protestantism's divided house.

Thus did the New Evangelicalism of Boston pastor Harold Ockenga and Chicago theologian Carl Henry first strike the Protestant establishment, whose chief preoccupation during and just after World War II was institutionalizing ecumenism, what with the Federal Council of Churches about to grow into the National Council (NCC) and the World Council aborning. Efforts on the part of disaffected conservatives to organize in opposition could hardly fail to raise establishment hackles.

The Antiestablishment Gauntlet

The National Association of Evangelicals was not the only such organizational undertaking. The year before, Carl McIntire, a preacher from Collingswood, New Jersey, had established the American Council of Christian Churches (ACCC). A student at Princeton Theological Seminary in the late twenties, McIntire had followed his teacher, the fundamentalist Presbyterian divine J. Gresham Machen, when the latter crossed into Pennsylvania to found Westminster Seminary. In McIntire, however, a native strain of American antiestablishmentarianism ran so pure that within a few years he broke with Machen and founded his own denomination. The American Council, too, manifested his radically oppositional character, becoming a kind of ecclesiastical *doppelgänger* to the establishment's ecumenical bodies; whithersoever they went to meet, there would the American Council go, compelling the Federal Council or National Council or World Council to issue warnings to press and public not to labor under any confusion about which was which and what was what. Living to vituperate and harass, McIntire and his fundamentalist followers classically embodied the paranoid style in American politics during the postwar period.

If the American Council represented the parodic termination of the fundamentalist-modernist battles of the twenties and early thirties, the National Association of Evangelicals expressed the ambition of the next generation. After the Scopes trial of 1925, the fundamentalist tide had ebbed swiftly from the mainline denominations: the Presbyterians and Northern Baptists, both of which had been threatened with takeover, extruded their fundamentalists. As far as could be told from within establishment citadels, fundamentalism had become a throwback, part of the folkways of those "upland primates" on whom Mencken had reported with such relish from Dayton, Tennessee. But the throwback survived and prospered, and not only in mountain hollows. Across the country alternative institutions—congregations, Bible schools, publishing houses—sprang into being outside the mainstream denominations. Anyone turning the radio dial in the thirties would come across many voices preaching fundamentalist faith.

By the forties, this world had produced a new breed of conservatives, anxious to wipe away the stigma of fundamentalism (they eschewed the term) but confident that their old-time religion represented a cure for whatever ailed America. This, however, would require cooperation, a coordination of effort, a united evangelical front. And already there was a divided house. As Carl Henry, the New Evangelicalism's preeminent theological voice, put it in 1947:

> The force of the redemptive message will not break with apostolic power upon the modern scene unless the American Council of Churches and the National Association of Evangelicals meet at some modern Antioch, and Peter and Paul are face to face in a spirit of mutual love and compassion. If, as is often remarked, the Federal Council of Churches is the voice of Protestant liberalism in America, Protestant evangelicalism too needs a single voice.

Was this more than pious rhetoric? Given McIntire's style, an amalgamation of the American Council and the National Association of Evangelicals would seem to have been neither possible nor desirable; the NAE was better positioned to counter the FCC on its own.

The seriousness of its threat to the establishment remained to be seen. In 1948, committees of both the Reformed Church in America and the United Presbyterian Church (not to be confused with the 1958 Presbyterian amalgamation of the same name) met to study the relative merits of remaining in the Federal Council or switching to the NAE. The same year, the question of membership in the FCC was put before presbyteries of the Presbyterian Church in the United States. Yet none of the three chose to run up different interdenominational colors, and it was soon plain that the NAE was not about to give mainline ecumenism a head-to-head run for its money. There were, however, other ways of doing battle.

In April of 1953, for example, as National Council panjandrum G. Bromley Oxnam, the Methodist bishop of Washington, prepared to defend himself against charges of Communist fellow-traveling before the House Un-American Activities Committee, the NAE annual convention passed a resolution supporting government investigations of ideologically suspect religious leaders. Day in and day out, the NCC was denounced as an ominous superchurch by *United Evangelical Action,* the official NAE organ, under the editorship of James DeForest Murch. But unlike the American Council the NAE did not seek to burn all bridges to the establishment. The *Christian Century* put it this way: "The [ACCC] insists that its members must not only repudiate and denounce apostasy (i.e., the National Council), but also separate from it. The NAE settles for repudiation and denunciation." The point was that the NAE sought the membership not only of whole denominations, but also of individuals, schools, missions, and congregations whose parent denominations belonged to the National Council; it was, in effect, bent on raiding behind

NCC lines and not least in the matter of fund-raising. In the mid-fifties, the Reverend J. Kenneth Miller, a Long Island minister who served on the United Presbyterian Church's World Service Committee, sent a couple of dunning letters he had received from NAE organizations to H. J. McKnight, a fellow committee member (and United Presbyterian representative to the NCC joint Department of Stewardship and Benevolence). Miller complained of the NAE's ethics in trying to siphon funds from a denomination that possessed its own benevolent and interchurch bodies. Ecclesiastical punctilio was not his only concern. "This N.A.E. outfit," he wrote of the World Evangelical Fellowship in 1956, "has influence in this Synod."

Yet it was not through such sallies or through denunciation or, for that matter, through the influence of its neofundamentalist theologians that the New Evangelicalism disturbed the course of the Protestant mainstream. Rather, the disturbance came through the reemergence on the national religious scene of urban mass revivalism. The man responsible, of course, was Billy Graham, the North Carolina farm boy who, by the mid-1950s, had become perhaps the most famous Protestant in the world. Nothing better displays the character of the Protestant establishment during the celebrated postwar religious revival than its divided response to Graham, and to the evangelism for which he stood.

The Headway of Billy Graham

Ever since his 1949 Los Angeles crusade Graham had basked in a glowing secular press; but cooler temperatures prevailed in the pages of the *Christian Century*. The *Century* duly noted Graham's presence at the NAE conventions of 1951, 1952, and 1953; it was decidedly noncommittal on the effects of his 1951 Seattle crusade. Certainly the journal did not share the enthusiasm that greeted Graham's speech before the 1952 Southern Baptist Convention—especially when "the most popular young evangelist of the day . . . mopped his brow and cried, 'When this convention voted earlier this week not to affiliate with any other group, I thanked God.'" The vote in question was to ratify a committee report that, among other things, attacked both the World and the National Council of Churches; it was, said the editorial correspondent, "the most perverse, unbrotherly and dangerous pronouncement made by any Southern Baptist Convention in many years." Yet barely two years later, with Graham playing to overflow houses across the Atlantic, came the following words:

> In London as in America, Billy Graham is revealing himself as extraordinarily teachable and humble, considering that he is surrounded with the fevered adulation of crowds so much of the time. He will learn a great deal in London, and will, if he keeps up the growth which has characterized his last three years, put what he learns to good use for Christ and the church.

How to explain the change of heart?

Only a month before, Graham had ventured into Union Theological Seminary and, after speaking in chapel for forty-five minutes and answering questions in the Social Room for another thirty, had come away with one of the greatest ovations in that institution's memory. News of the encounter may well have reached the *Century's* editors in Chicago; in any event, their new view of Graham mirrored what John Bennett had to say in "Billy Graham at Union," in the May issue of the *Union Seminary Quarterly Review.* To explain the applause, Union's dean of faculty pointed to Graham's evident sincerity and magnetism, his verbal adroitness, and the simple relief of his audience at finding him not as bad as they feared. Yet underneath it all, said Bennett, there was reason to think that Graham was "breaking the pattern" of the crude and mercenary evangelist: "Many of us gained the strong impression that he can be used for highly constructive Christian purposes in the churches and in the nation."

For Bennett, "breaking the pattern" meant that Graham understood the limits of mass evangelism and the importance of financial propriety. It also meant, at least he hoped it did, that Graham's grasp of "biblical truth" would be sufficient to correct his enthusiasm for America's "culture religion" (e.g., his inability to understand the laughter that greeted his pointing to the American Legion's back-to-God campaign as a sign of a national return to religion); and that his "ecumenical outlook and strategy" (the word "ecumenical" recurred often in his remarks) might "deliver him from the worst effects of Fundamentalism." In any case, Graham's use of the Bible did not represent a "hard Fundamentalism," and there was evidence that he was "growing" in his social outlook. "I am," Bennett concluded, "publishing this article with some hesitation":

> I do not like to set myself up as a judge of Billy Graham in this way and I do not want this record of my surprise to seem patronizing. It is a fact that until his visit to Union I had classed him as a fundamentalist and socially reactionary evangelist and had dismissed him as a possible constructive force in the American Church. On the other hand there is a chance that this article may be too optimistic and hence misleading. . . . When all is said, I believe that his coming to Union was a very good lesson for us. It may have helped us to realize more vividly, what we should have known from Church History, that God can work powerfully through men who do not meet all our specifications.

The Galahad of the New Evangelicalism had won a provisional seat at the establishment's Round Table. . . .

A case can be made that during the mid-fifties a kind of evangelical excitement took hold in mainline Protestantism that harked back to the days before Scopes, when "the evangelization of the world in this generation" was a goal establishmentarians could happily embrace. With liberalism (read: modernism) on the run in the loftiest theological circles, those who professed The Fundamentals were no longer so easily dismissed: by his classic revivalist's willingness to ignore doctrinal and institutional barriers in gathering his forces, Graham proved capable of enlisting the support of sophisticated clergy as well as layfolk throughout the mainline denominations. It was also the hour of the American Century (as proclaimed by Henry Luce, the China missionary's son), and the country was pleased to think of itself as on the march against dark, atheistic powers at loose in the world. Why not a return to the yoked advance of American power and American religion? I do not want to overstate the case. There were many in high Protestant places who wanted no part of revivalistic religion. But their very criticism of Graham stirred up an opposition that bore witness to a New Evangelical appeal within even the most forbidding bastions of the establishment.

Niebuhr versus Graham

The most important criticism issued from Reinhold Niebuhr, than whom no Protestant theologian was more thoroughly inoculated against the seductions of evangelistic enthusiasms. He fired first from his own journal, *Christianity and Crisis,* in a March 5, 1956, editorial responding to news that Billy Graham would be coming to New York. "We dread the prospect," he wrote:

> Billy Graham is a personable, modest and appealing young man who has wedded considerable dramatic and demagogic gifts with a rather obscurantist version of the Christian faith. His message is not completely irrelevant to the broader social issues of the day but it approaches irrelevance. For what it may be worth, we can be assured that his approach is free of the vulgarities which characterized the message of Billy Sunday, who intrigued the nation about a quarter century ago. We are grateful for this much "progress."

Niebuhr's central concern was that by "presenting Christianity as a series of simple answers to complex questions" Graham would only strengthen the modern inclination to dismiss the gospel as irrelevant to contemporary life.

Niebuhr's editorial "we," however, presumed too much, for two issues later a sharp rejoinder from editorial board member Henry P. Van Dusen, the president of Union Theological Seminary, appeared in the letters column. Calling his editor's opposition to Graham "thoroughly unscriptural" for ignoring apostolic recognition of "diversities of gifts" and "differences of operations," Van Dusen emphasized the need to present the masses with a "more readily digestible form" of the gospel than the "'strong meat' of a sophisticated interpretation":

> Dr. Niebuhr prefers Billy Graham to Billy Sunday. There are many, of whom I am one, who are not ashamed to testify that they would probably never have come within the sound of Dr. Niebuhr's voice or the influence of his mind if they had not been *first* touched by the message of the earlier Billy. Quite probably five or ten

years hence there may appear in the classrooms and churches of Billy Graham's severest critics not a few who will be glad to give parallel testimony to his role in *starting* them in that direction.

Niebuhr next carried the attack to the pages of the *Christian Century*, where in May he rather more gently took Graham to task for biblical literalism and pietistic moralism. In a mannerly reply, E. G. Homrighausen, dean of Princeton Seminary and head of the NCC's Department of Evangelism, charged Niebuhrian neo-orthodoxy with being "hesitant and weak in calling persons to a positive faith":

> I have, frankly, been disappointed in its inability to lead the way in the revival or rebirth or restoration of a relevant Protestantism in the local church. And if men like Graham have arisen and are being heard by the thousands, it may be that what he is and says in sincerity ought to be said in a better way by the neo-orthodox with all their accumulation of intelligence about the Bible and history and personality in our times.

Niebuhr came back, in August, with his "Proposal to Billy Graham," which, with Bennettian hopefulness, urged Graham to raise high the banner of racial justice and "become a vital force in the nation's moral and spiritual life." That drew "A Proposal to Reinhold Niebuhr" from the New Evangelical theologian E. J. Carnell; Carnell's proposal was that Niebuhr let his "Yes" to Billy Graham resound ("dialectically") as loudly as his "No." Niebuhr's increasingly moderated stance toward Graham had its institutional analogue. In the summer of 1956, Episcopal bishop John S. Higgins of Rhode Island, a member of the NCC's policy committee, sent a private letter to NAE president Paul Petticord exploring the possibility of rapprochement between the two umbrella organizations. Petticord had the bad taste to make Higgins's letter public, denouncing the feeler at a meeting of the World Evangelical Fellowship; but then, much to the approval of the *Christian Century*, Paul S. Rees, a past NAE president, cordially informed Bishop Higgins of his eagerness to participate in informal conversations to that end.

The importunate note that crept into establishmentarian discourse in 1955 and 1956 had to do, more than anything else, with the impending New York crusade: Preparations for it, according to the *Christian Century*, were "so extensive that they threaten to overrun every other church activity." Those raising questions were begging for "a diversified campaign so that a fuller, more accurate account of Protestant Christianity will be given the great community." Given that the big money would be withdrawn if Drs. Niebuhr, Tillich, or Bennett were featured "even in smaller tents" (!), might not Dr. Graham be "more explicit about his ecumenicity"? Conceivably it was not the gospel, but the establishment, that Graham threatened to render irrelevant in Gotham. In the event, the NCC's Department of Evangelism joined the bandwagon; H. H. McConnell, the deputy executive director, took on the responsibility of directing the follow-up program of "visitation evangelism." Yet even before Graham stood up to address his first Madison Square Garden crowd on May 15, 1957, the bloom was coming off the rose for McConnell's boss, Executive Director Berlyn Farris.

At the NCC General Board meeting on May 1 and 2, the Commission to Study Evangelism presented its report. Farris and members of his staff had served as consultants to the twenty-three-member commission, which included such diverse figures as Georgia Harkness, E. G. Homrighausen, and Norman Vincent Peale; but the report itself was largely the work of Robert Calhoun of Yale, a man of no great evangelical enthusiasm, and it embodied a barely disguised neo-orthodox critique of the whole American revivalist tradition. Thus: Original sin condemned society for all time to the status of "a living corporate web of wrong action and impulse that no human being can escape." The evils of the day were not faithlessness and bad morals but the idols of a modem civilization more complex than what went before. Evangelism was the business of God and the entire Church: although preachers possessed a special role, the itinerant exhortation of mass audiences was an uncertain thing:

> Such preaching is revivalism, a method that involves both possible values and very real perils for evangelism, to which it can at best make substantial contributions, of which at worst it can be a gross caricature, and with which in any event it is not to be identified. Revivalists can indeed, under God, be evangelists of power; but it is not their distinctive method that makes them so.

According to the minutes of the meeting, various suggestions were offered toward making the document more conventionally evangelical. One discussion group "asked for a more positive description of revivalism as it relates to evangelism"; in the final, printed version, the phrase "possible values and very real perils" was changed to "possible values and possible perils." Nowhere was there either the rallying cry or the institutional specifics that Farris had had in mind. A week later, in his report to the managers of his department, he bravely called the report "stimulating, challenging, and thought-provoking," adding, "It won't answer all the questions, but it will build fires under our thinking." A month later, citing the department's ongoing shortage of funds, he suddenly announced his resignation, effective July 1, to become director of district evangelism for the Board of Evangelism of the Methodist Church.

But the event that really turned the tide was the New York crusade itself. As even *Life* put it in its July 1 issue:

> Billy Graham opened his New York crusade in high hopes that it would "soon be like a mighty river through the city." But after 37 days of his 66-day stand in Madison Square Garden, the river has not been mighty. New Yorkers have talked

surprisingly little about Billy—unlike his smash hits in London and Los Angeles, where he was the talk of the town.

Graham was simply not as much a force to be reckoned with as had been hoped—or feared. Besides this, the manifest nature of the crusade, with its well-oiled mechanisms of conversion, its well-scrubbed and well-mannered audiences, inspired a new establishmentarian line on Graham, evident in the *Christian Century's* three stiff editorials on the crusade but most bluntly put in the piece contributed to *Life* by Reinhold Niebuhr:

> Graham is honest and describes the signers of his decision cards as "inquirers" rather than "converts." It would be interesting to know how many of those attracted by his evangelistic Christianity are attracted by the obvious fact that his new evangelism is much blander than the old. For it promises a new life, not through painful religious experience but merely by signing a decision card. Thus a miracle of regeneration is promised at a painless price by an obviously sincere evangelist. It is a bargain.

Graham had previously been charged with excessive acquiescence in America's culture-religion, and the long-term effects of his revivals had long been questioned. But in contrast, say, to Peale, he had always been credited with offering up a good strict version of traditional American Protestantism. Now he was merely another dispenser of postwar piety, purveying the things of the spirit on the cheap.

Graham himself turned the other cheek. "I have read nearly everything Mr. Niebuhr has written, and I feel inadequate before his brilliant mind and learning," he told journalist Noel Houston. He continued his pursuit of good but not overclose relations with the NCC. In December of 1957, for example, he wrote to General Secretary Roy G. Ross expressing thanks that his greetings had been extended to the NCC's General Assembly; apologizing for not being able to attend in person ("due to extensive dental work and one or two speaking commitments"), applauding the choice of Edwin T. Dahlberg as president ("I have admired him for many years"), and mentioning his recent collaboration with the Department of Evangelism's H. H. McConnell ("a very warm friend"). As far as the establishment was concerned, however, New York was Graham's high-water mark. After that, there were no more expectations that revivalism, Billy style, might really make a difference. The difference was to be sought elsewhere.

Beyond the Pale

In 1958, in what is surely one of the few *Life* articles ever regularly cited in scholarly footnotes, Henry P. Van Dusen identified a "Third Force" in Christianity (alongside Catholicism and Protestantism) composed of Adventists, Pentecostals, Jehovah's Witnesses, and other often-despised "fringe" groups; growing by leaps and bounds, it was no less than "the most extraordinary religious phenomenon of our time." Van Dusen had observed these churches firsthand during a three-month visit to the Caribbean three years before. Now he celebrated their "direct biblical message"; its promise of "an immediate, life transforming experience of the living-God-in-Christ" was, he said, "far more significant to many individuals than the version of it normally found in conventional churches." Van Dusen stressed, above all, that followers were expected to "practice an active, untiring, seven-day-a-week Christianity." Sympathetic enough to the New Evangelicalism to have served on Billy Graham's New York committee, he nonetheless drew no connection between the Third Force and the NAE, although five of the Third Force groups listed at the end of his article—the Assemblies of God, the Church of God (based in Cleveland, Tenn.), the International Church of the Foursquare Gospel, the Pentecostal Church of God in America, and the Pentecostal Holiness Church—in fact constituted nearly two-thirds of the NAE's total membership. It was as though the NAE *as such* had become too conventional, as though the vitality of the Third Force had to lie in its independence from any sort of religious consensus. In *The New Shape of American Religion* (1959), Martin Marty took more or less this tack. After blaming Billy Graham for his "failure to become unpopular with people outside the churches," he looked for help from the "protesting intransigents" of the Third Force: "The square pegs that do not fit the round holes of eroded religious expression might call us all to a higher witness."

Soon, however, new challenges were in the air, challenges that stifled all establishmentarian yearning after life-transforming religion on America's spiritual periphery, challenges that cast the New Evangelicals even further beyond the pale. On the evening of September 12, 1960, John Fitzgerald Kennedy stood up in the ballroom of the Rice Hotel in Houston to address that city's ministerial association. For months Kennedy had been trying to lay the issue of his Catholicism to rest, but to no avail; and it was clear whence the bulk of the opposition came. In April 1960 the NAE had resolved to oppose the election of any Roman Catholic as president of the United States. On September 4, a front-page article in the *New York Times* announced that "in Texas and throughout the South, the issue between the Southern Baptists and Senator Kennedy has been joined." On September 8, a new organization calling itself the National Conference of Citizens for Religious Freedom had charged that the Democratic candidate would be unable "to withstand the determined efforts of the hierarchy of his church . . . to breach the wall of separation between church and state." Although this group had as its putative leader Norman Vincent Peale (and also included Charles Clayton Morrison, the former editor of the *Christian Century*), it was preponderantly a New Evangelical affair starring founding father Harold Ockenga, the NAE's public affairs secretary Clyde W. Taylor, Daniel Poling of the *Christian Herald,* and L. Nelson Bell, an editor of *Christianity Today* and Billy Graham's father-in-law. Theirs was the constituency to whom Kennedy appealed when he went down to Houston.

"I believe," said the candidate, "in an America where the separation of church and state is absolute—where no Catholic prelate would tell the President (should he be Catholic) how to act, and no Protestant minister would tell his parishioners for whom to vote." For those who had followed his remarks on the religious issue, most of what he had to say was familiar, but there was one significant alteration of substance:

> If the time should ever come—and I do not concede any conflict to be remotely possible—when my office would require me to either violate my conscience, or violate the national interest, then I would resign the office, and I hope any other conscientious public servant would do likewise.

Significantly, one hundred Protestant, Catholic, and Jewish leaders had that very day issued their "Statement on Religious Liberty in Relation to the 1960 National Campaign," which covered, in a few more words, the identical ground:

> No citizen in public office dare be false either to his conscience or to his oath of office. Both his conscience and his oath impose responsibilities sacred under the law of God. If he cannot reconcile the responsibilities entailed by his oath with his conscience, then he must resign, lest he fail his nation and his God.

Here was the establishmentarian voice of America, joined in interfaith union to insist on the right of citizens of all faiths to run for the highest office in the land. Not, to be sure, that the Protestant establishment—engaged in running skirmishes with the Catholic Church throughout the postwar period—had been entirely unambivalent about this. Back in May, in *Look*, Bishop Oxnam and the current NCC president, Eugene Carson Blake, had expressed reservations about having a Roman Catholic in the White House. But by the fall, hostility to the *principle* of a Catholic president rested largely with the Protestant antiestablishment.

The hostility was not, at least in the establishment's eyes, merely a matter of anti-Catholic prejudice and *odium theologicum*. As John Bennett wrote a few days after Kennedy's Houston speech:

> Those who take the leadership in this Protestant attack on the Roman Church as a campaign issue are also persons who would not support a liberal Democrat no matter what his religion; . . . the opposition on the religious issue centers in that part of the country where the opposition is equally strong on the issue of civil rights and on the economic philosophy of Senator Kennedy and his platform.

Shades of Scopes: The evangelicals were now simply to be ranged among the forces of darkness in the South. The forces of light, meanwhile, were banding together.

In mid-January 1963, a conference was convened at Chicago's Edgewater Beach Hotel by the NCC's Department of Racial and Cultural Relations, the Social Action Commission of the Synagogue Council of America, and the Social Action Department of the National Catholic Welfare Conference. Six hundred and fifty-seven delegates from these and sixty-seven other religious and religiously affiliated groups turned out for four days of speeches and workshops. Marking the one hundredth anniversary of Lincoln's Emancipation Proclamation, the National Conference on Religion and Race was neither one more exercise in "interfaith dialogue" nor, like the National Conference of Christians and Jews, ecumenism in the breach. For the first time in American history, central bodies of Protestantism, Catholicism, and Judaism had joined together for the purpose of spearheading a nationwide social reform—specifically, "to increase the leadership of religion in ending racial discrimination in the United States." It was something very like a new American religious establishment.

And it did not need Billy Graham. In 1964, in response to an inquiry from a Mrs. H. J. Van Dort of Spring Valley, California, on the relations of Graham and the NCC, Executive Director Colin Williams stated tersely, "My understanding is that Dr. Graham has spoken at National Council of Churches gatherings but has not been officially involved in National Council activities. His denomination is not a member church of the National Council of Churches." Politics had become the heart of the matter. The following year, in a lead editorial tided "Demythologizing Neoevangelicalism," the *Christian Century* charged Graham with speaking "out of both sides of his mouth," at once repudiating socially activist Christians for "sidetracking the Gospel" and yet stressing the importance of taking stands on the issues of the day. The real issue was, said the editorial, *which stands?* In recent months the neo-evangelicals themselves had made it clear that their oft-professed reluctance to engage in secular politics was just a disguise for all the stands that were bad: capital punishment, right-to-work laws, "military maximalism," and so on. "Now that we are all admitting that we are playing the same game it will be possible to ask whose detail of ecumenical policy and whose program of social concern is more likely to be congruent with Christian norms, more productive of human good." Congruent? Imbued with the spirit of reform, the establishment was now prepared to see the evangelical opposition as arrayed on the side of reaction, and even as unchristian.

Some years before, in an article much taken to heart by NCC activists like Mississippian Will Campbell, the Louisiana Catholic writer Walker Percy had claimed that Southern society, for all its churchiness, was not really Christian; or at least that its upper-class leaders were not. They were, rather, citizens of the ancient Stoic type, who until recently had looked after Negroes as an act of *noblesse oblige,* and presided over a genteel community of manners based on their own self-esteem and the "extraordinary native courtesy and dignity" of the Negroes. But now, said Percy, that time was over; the Negro was demanding his rights and the Southern gentleman, joining a White Citizens Council or simply lapsing into silence, was happy to let him "taste the bitter fruits of his insolence." How different was the Christian scheme of things, where what the Stoic found intolerable simply became "the sacred right which must be accorded the individual, whether deemed insolent or not." Archbishop Rummel of New Orleans had declared segregation a sin (this was 1956); sooner or later Southerners would have to face up to their Christian heritage and answer him. "And the good pagan's answer is no longer good enough for the South. . . ."

In his famous "Letter from Birmingham Jail," Martin Luther King, Jr., wrote, "If today's church does not recapture the sacrificial spirit of the early church, it will lose its authenticity, forfeit the loyalty of millions, and be dismissed as an irrelevant social club with no meaning for the twentieth century." Yet even should the church fail, he stated, the civil rights struggle would triumph. "We will win our freedom because the sacred heritage of our nation and the eternal will of God are embodied in our echoing demands." The prophetic mission of America itself would carry the day. A few years later, William McLoughlin, who had earlier seen Billy Graham as the standard-bearer of a "Fourth Great Awakening," asserted that the evangelical Third Force had made little headway in winning over American Protestantism between 1957 and 1965, and he argued that any such possibility was now "extremely unlikely." The real "third force in Christendom," he said, was "the pietistic spirit of American culture itself—not only the American sense of mission which leads it into world leadership for the containment of Communist expansion in the name of democratic freedom for all men, and not only the sense of charity or stewardship which leads it into giving economic assistance in billions of dollars each year to help others to help themselves, but the sense of religious commitment and ideals that Americans inscribe [sic] to democracy and their way of life." The age of civil religion had (briefly) arrived.

Thus, from World War II to the war in Vietnam, the New Evangelicalism provided the establishment with a foil against which to define its concerns. It was The Other—first an antiecumenical other and then a spiritually conventional other, a politically reactionary other, and a disappearing unsecular other. Later, when the Protestant center stage came to be occupied by the likes of Jerry Falwell and Pat Robertson, establishmentarians would tend to see the evangelicals outside their ranks as a hegemonic other. For a short span of the postwar era, however, thought was given to the possibility that evangelicalism was not an adversary of the establishment but an ally. That may seem to have been the last hurrah of an earlier day, but if anything like a Protestant establishment is to survive, it is worth wondering whether it could not happen again.

Questions for Reflection and Discussion

1. What challenges to religious unity in the two decades after World War II are presented in the documents?

2. According to Philip Gleason, what were the obstacles to Catholicism's inclusion in America's religious culture after World War II? How did these obstacles create conflict in Catholicism's search for a consensus with non-Catholics?

3. How does Barbara Brown Zikmund's essay illustrate religious tension when several denominations addressed the issue of ordination for women?

4. Which of the four levels of religious tension are presented in Mark Silk's analysis of the rise of New Evangelicalism?

5. Does this chapter emphasize religious conflict or consensus in the post-World War II years? more inclusion or exclusion?

Additional Readings

Alley, Robert S. *The Supreme Court on Church and State.* New York: Oxford University Press, 1988.

Ammerman, Nancy. *Bible Believers: Fundamentalists in the Modern World.* Piscataway, NJ: Rutgers University Press 1987.

Cox, Harvey. *The Secular City: Secularization and Urbanization in Theological Perspective.* New York: Macmillan, 1966.

Eckhardt, A. Roy. *The Surge of Piety in America: An Appraisal.* New York: Association Press, 1958.

Gaspar, Louis. *The Fundamentalist Movement.* The Hague: Mouton, 1963.

Hardon, S.J., John A. *The Protestant Churches of America.* Westminster: Newman, 1956.

Herberg, Will. *Protestant, Catholic, and Jew: An Essay in American Religious Sociology.* Garden City, NY: Doubleday and Co., 1955.

Howlett, Duncan. *The Fourth American Faith.* New York: Harper and Row, 1964.

Kane, John J. *Catholic-Protestant Conflicts in America.* Chicago: Regnery, 1955.

Lotz, David W., Donald W. Shriver, Jr., and John F. Wilson, eds. *Altered Landscapes: Christianity in America, 1935-1985.* Grand Rapids, MI: Wm. B. Eerdmans, 1989.

Martin, William. *A Prophet with Honor: The Billy Graham Story.* New York: Wm. Morrow, 1991.

Marty, Martin. *Modern American Religion: Under God Indivisible, 1941-1960.* Chicago: University of Chicago Press, 1996.

McIntire, Carl. *Modern Tower of Babel.* Collingswood, NJ: Beacon Press, 1949.

Nash, Ronald. *The New Evangelicalism.* Grand Rapids: Zondervan Publishing House, 1963.

Roche, Douglas J. *The Catholic Revolution.* New York: David McKay Company, 1968.

Sittser, Gerald L. *A Cautious Patriotism: The American Churches and the Second World War.* Chapel Hill: University of North Carolina Press, 1997.

Stone, Jon R. *On the Boundaries of American Evangelicalism: The Postwar Evangelical Coalition.* New York: St. Martin's Press, 1997.

Chapter 15

Religion and the Civil Rights Movement

Issue

How did religion in America contribute to the rise of the civil rights movement?

The previous chapter examines several critical issues that reveal American religion in tension. The period from World War II to Vietnam, often characterized as a time of cultural consensus, in fact was rife with considerable unrest and conflict. No area of American life reflected this more clearly than the civil rights movement, spawned partly by World War II discriminatory treatment of African Americans, and by President Truman's bold move on behalf of civil rights in 1948, when he issued an executive order barring segregation in the armed forces. In 1954 *the* Brown v. Board of Education *decision put Americans on alert that change was in the wind. A centuries-old tension over matters of race was ripe for confrontation, and American religion was at its core.*

Social change often comes with "glacial slowness," and civil rights change was no different. "The collision between the hopes raised by the 1954 Brown *decision and the indignities of persistent discrimination and segregation sparked a new phase in the civil-rights movement." In their efforts to do away with the long-enduring hardships of Jim Crowism, African Americans, and particularly black religious leaders, established new organizations and implemented new tactics. No religious black leader did more to spark resistance to American racial duplicity than Martin Luther King, Jr., who as a twenty-seven-year-old minister in 1955 expressed the anger of Montgomery, Alabama, blacks as they initiated their year-long bus boycott. "There comes a time when people get tired, tired of being segregated and humiliated, tired of being kicked about by the brutal feet of oppression," King declared.*

In King the bus boycott gave the nation an African American leader who never retreated from the inherent tension and conflict of the new movement for racial justice. His role as an organizer of the Southern Christian Leadership Conference (SCLC) in 1957 eventually led to his incarceration in a Birmingham jail in 1963. The letter he wrote there to a group of antagonistic white clergy combined the spirit of evangelical Christianity with a nonviolent resistance strategy. In his letter he emphasized the tension produced by direct action. "Nonviolent direct action seeks to create such a crisis and establish such creative tension that a community that has constantly refused to negotiate is forced to confront the issue. . . . I have earnestly worked and preached against violent tension, but there is a type of constructive tension that is necessary for growth."

During the remainder of the decade the struggle for equality produced much tension—tension between blacks and whites, blacks and blacks, and whites and whites—and much of it in the name of religion. A spate of national and civil rights legislation in mid-decade emerged while America's streets hemorrhaged with lootings, burnings, and killings. Easy answers were not forthcoming when bewildered citizens of both races asked why such mayhem was happening just when African Americans were starting to achieve some of their goals. For some blacks and whites—and religious persons among them—the pace of change was too rapid; for others it was not rapid enough. This truth is revealed in the documents and essays that follow. What was the role of religion in the civil rights movement? Why were religious Americans of both races on both sides of this tension? Which of the four dimensions of religious tension are revealed in the civil rights movement?

Documents

Over a period of a decade and a half from the mid-1950s to the end of the 1960s numerous positions on the civil rights movement were staked out. Pitched battles were fought between blacks and whites and between members of each race. And clergy on both sides were deeply involved in the conflagration. In the first document, Ernest Q. Campbell and Thomas F. Pettigrew of Harvard University report on their study of the role of Little Rock's ministers in the showdown over the forced integration of the city's public schools in 1957, and reflect on the broader role of Southern clergy on matters of race in the South. For a century the African Americans' demand for equal justice had infuriated the Ku Klux Klan. During the decade following the Brown decision (1954) the quasi-religious organization increased its activity of intimidation and destruction. In the summer of 1964, soon after the bodies of three slain civil rights workers were found, the Klan in Mississippi issued a statement giving its side of the murders. The second selection is its account of the event. By the mid-1960s the spectrum of civil rights protests widened to include black nationalist organizations such as the Black Muslims. Founded in 1930 in the black ghetto of Detroit, the Black Muslims represented a more aggressive alternative to the King-led SCLC. In the third document, C. Eric Lincoln provides a brief overview of the organization, and then recounts the ten propositions of protest issued by the Muslims. In the midst of the civil rights movement, David Reimers authored his White Protestantism and the Negro *(1965) in which he argued that white Protestantism's historical treatment of African Americans was not better or worse than that of American society as a whole, including its attack on segregation into the 1960s. Reimers's argument is presented in the fourth selection. The fifth document is Martin Luther King, Jr.'s explanation of his theory of nonviolence on which his leadership in the civil rights movement was based. In the final selection, Albert B. Cleage, Jr. argues the importance of the Black Messiah to the black community during the civil rights movement.*

1. The Ministry and Integration: "The Greatest Threat to Segregation", 1959

SOURCE: Ernest Q. Campbell and Thomas F. Pettigrew, *Christians in Racial Crisis: A Study of Little Rock's Ministry* (Public Affairs Press, Washington, D.C., 1959), 1-4.

"In the South itself the 1954-57 period demonstrated that perhaps the greatest threat to the unity sought by organized segregationists came from the churches, themselves entangled in all but continuous debate."

—*Weldon James*

The white South today presents what appears to be a solid wall of resistance to racial desegregation. What sentiment there is to abide by the Supreme Court's rulings seems to be totally silenced—so silenced in fact that Hodding Carter, the editor of the *Delta Democrat-Times*, believes that "the First Amendment of our Constitution is probably in more danger in the South today than are our white and Negro children."

Enforced silence necessarily implies that the South may not be as solid as it would like to appear. Indeed, many influential southerners do not fully approve of their region's position. Neither martyrs nor moralists, they simply hold certain other values above the maintenance of segregation. The prominent businessman may not want integration, but he deeply fears the economic effects of community violence and disorder. The respected lawyer may have his doubts about the wisdom of the Supreme Court, but he firmly believes in the sanctity of the law. The dedicated educator may prefer separate schools, but he unhesitatingly chooses integration before the abolition of public instruction. And the popular newspaper editor may have reservations about the situation in his own locality, but he clearly sees the inevitability of desegregation in its national and international perspectives. Yet these ideas of the businessman, lawyer, educator, and newspaperman go largely unexpressed in the South at this time—in part because of the very involvements and commitments in the community that make these men influential.

One important group of southerners, however, has not been so easily silenced. Though by no means of one accord themselves, ministers provide "perhaps the greatest threat to the unity sought by organized segregationists." They have become a threat simply by voicing antisegregationist sentiments at a time when no other respected leaders dared.

While the relatively fundamentalist sects typically have favored segregation, practically every major denomination in the South has publicly advocated compliance with the federal courts. Though these pronouncements vary somewhat in firmness, they are strikingly similar in intent and wording. Thus the General Assembly of the U.S. Presbyterian Church (Southern) agreed in 1954: "The assembly commends the principle of the decision and . . . urges all our people to lend their assistance to those charged with the duty of implementing the decision." The Southern Baptist Convention announced in the same year: "We recognize that this Supreme Court decision is in harmony . . . with the Christian principles of equal justice and love for all men . . . We urge our people and all Christians to conduct themselves in this period of adjustment in the spirit of Christ." The Episcopalians followed in 1955: "The 58th General Convention of the Protestant Episcopal Church . . . now commends to all the clergy and people of this church that they accept and support this ruling of the Supreme Court. . . ." In 1956 the Methodist General Conference made their statement: "The decisions of the Supreme Court . . . relative to segregation make necessary far-reaching and often difficult readjustments throughout the nation. We call upon our people to effect these adjustments in all good faith, with brotherliness and patience. . . . Let these things, however, be done in love lest the cause of Christ suffer at our hands."

More recent pronouncements by these denominations have tended to be stronger and more detailed. In 1957, for instance, southern Presbyterians reinforced previous statements with a widely publicized declaration of particulars that specifically condemned discrimination in education, employment, religion, and politics, admonished their communicants against Klan or Citizens' Council membership, and firmly supported the debated Koinonia interracial community in Georgia. Passed by an overwhelming majority, this declaration leaves little doubt as to the Presbyterian position.

But it is a giant step from the lofty ideals of national and regional conventions to the realities of a segregationist congregation back home. In regard to the integration resolution of the Southern Baptists one observer remarked to Robert Penn Warren: "They were just a little bit exalted. When they got back with the home folks a lot of 'em wondered how they did it."

Much of the minister's ardor is dampened when he returns to his flock though this is not to say that he bends completely to their will. It is not without significance that some fairly strong announcements have been made on the local level. Witness the 1954 statement of the New Orleans Council of Churches: "We believe that this decision is consistent with the spirit and teachings of Jesus Christ. . . . We call upon the members of our state legislature to find just ways of implementing in our state the decision of the U.S. Supreme Court." Early in 1957 the Ministerial Association of Richmond, Virginia, issued a "Statement of Conviction" that indicted both the segregationist Governor and the General Assembly for their "exceedingly inept handling of the current racial situation." And in the spring of 1958, 300 white clergymen, representing 13 Protestant denominations in Dallas, Texas, took a firm position on the school integration question facing their city when they announced flatly that "enforced segregation is morally and spiritually wrong."

Keep in mind that such ministerial behavior has taken place in a milieu seething with dissent—a milieu in which outspoken pastors are censured by other members of the clergy and sometimes lose their positions. Yet, in spite of all of this, a few southern clergymen have ventured beyond the statement-issuing level into community action.

Roman Catholic authorities have integrated many of their educational facilities in the border and middle South. In 1947, seven years before the Supreme Court handed down its decision, Archbishop Ritter of St. Louis integrated all parochial elementary and secondary schools and sternly warned 700 parents that under Canon Law they would be "excommunicated if they presumed to interfere in the administrative office of their Bishop by having recourse to any authority outside the Church." Desegregation proceeded without incident. In a city that is 24 percent Catholic the Bishop's position was bound to have a marked effect on public school integration eight years later. It has been noted that a majority of the teachers in St. Louis attribute part of the success of their public school integration to the initial desegregation of the Catholic schools.

At the present time Archbishop Rummel of New Orleans is attempting similar action. Believing segregation to be "morally wrong and sinful," he recently announced that his large parochial school system would be integrated. In view of lay protest, however, he set no date.

The Protestant clergy is frequently involved when attempts at public school integration meet with violent opposition. For example, in 1956, when an organized segregationist protest in Henderson, Kentucky, led to a widespread student boycott and a mob of 200 white adults demonstrated before the school in question, the Henderson Ministerial Association went into action. Immediately, the Association issued newspaper and radio announcements urging the end of the boycott; these continued until the resistance movement crumbled.

Sometimes activity of this sort has been physically dangerous for clergymen. During the integration crisis in Mansfield, Texas, in September 1956, an Episcopal rector from Fort Worth had to be escorted through a mob by a State Ranger after pointedly discussing "the Christian merits of their demonstrations and of desegregation." Some months later the Baptist pastor of the largest church in Clinton, Tennessee, led nine Negro children to an integrated school during that community's disturbances. On his return from the school he was attacked by segregationists who inflicted face cuts on him. And Ku Klux Klan cross burnings in small Alabama towns have been aimed at intimidating white ministers. During the 1956 Christmas celebration to Opelika, a Baptist pastor invited a Negro high school delegation to hear his church perform *The Messiah*. As a warning against such "race mixing," a five-foot cross was burned in front of his home. Later, in Sylacauga, Alabama, threats against the families of two outspoken ministers were made after a Klan demonstration and cross burnings before their churches.

The importance of courageous ministerial action for desegregation is belittled by some observers of the southern scene who insist that such gestures have been ineffectual. To be sure, single incidents do not always reap immediate results. But when all of the ministerial protest are considered together they become of crucial significance for at least three fundamental reasons.

First, Protestant churches historically have profoundly affected the culture of the "Bible Belt." Second, ministers are in a unique position to attack one of the weakest links in segregationist armor—guilt over past treatment of the Negro. And, finally, these actions are important as publicized disruptions in what otherwise might appear to be complete southern unanimity on integration. . . .

2. The Mind of the Ku Klux Klan, 1964

SOURCE: From *Eyewitness* by William Loren Katz. P. 463. Copyright © 2000 by Ethrac Publications, Inc. Reprinted with permission.

Q.   What is your explanation of why there have been so many National Police Agents [F.B.I.?] involved in the case of the "missing civil rights workers?"

A.   First, I must correct you on your terms. Schwerner, Chaney and Goodman were not civil rights workers. They were Communist Revolutionaries, actively working to undermine and destroy Christian Civilization. The blatant and outlandish National Police activity surrounding their case merely points up the political overtones of the entire affair. . . .

Q.   By "political overtones" do you mean that the case has a bearing on the forthcoming elections?

A.   It is doubtful that the case itself will be made an issue in the election. However, the incumbent in the White House [Lyndon B. Johnson] is a communist sympathizer, as proven by his numerous acts of treason, and his sole chance of victory in the November election will depend upon his being able to hold his communist-liberal block together by continuing to support and protect all Domestic Communists. . . .

Q.   Isn't it unlikely that the Communists would do that [kill the three civil rights workers themselves] in this case? Schwerner was a valuable man?

A.   Not at all. The Communists never hesitate to murder one of their own if it will benefit the party. Communism is pure, refined, scientific Cannibalism in action. A case in point is the murdered Kennedy. Certainly, no President could have been a more willing tool to the Communists than was the late and unlamented "Red Jack." He cooperated with them at every turn. Yet . . . he was callously given up for execution by those whom he had served so well. . . .

Q.   Do the White Knights of the KU KLUX KLAN advocate or engage in unlawful violence?

A.   We are absolutely opposed to street riots and public demonstrations of all kinds. Our work is largely educational in nature. . . . All of our work is carried on in a dignified and reverent manner. . . . We are all *Americans* in the White Knights of the KU KLUX KLAN of Mississippi.

3. The Black Muslims as a Protest Movement, 1964
SOURCE: From *Assuring Freedom to the Free* by Arnold M. Rose, ed. Copyright © 1964 by Wayne State University Press. All rights reserved. Reprinted with permission.

The Black Muslims are a symbol and a product of social conflict. They represent a point at the extreme edge of a spectrum of protest organizations and movements which involves, directly or indirectly, probably every Negro in America. The spectrum of protest begins on the near side with the conservative churches, then shades progressively into the relatively more militant congregations, the Urban League, the NAACP, the SCLC, the SNCC, CORE, and finally the unknown number of black nationalist organizations of which the Black Muslim movement is the largest and the best known. The organizations mentioned do not exhaust the roster of protest by any means. Some of the protest movements have sizeable memberships in spirit of their amorphous character. Some have no more than ten or twelve members. Some do not even have names. . . .

The Black Muslims are among the best organized and most articulate of the protest movements. In terms of their immediate internal objectives, they have a highly effective leadership, some of which has been recruited from the Christian churches and retrained by Elijah Muhammad to serve the cause of Black Islam. Their newspapers and magazines are superior in layout and technical quality to much of the Negro press; and their financial support of the movement is probably higher in proportion to income than that of any similar group. Yet, the Black Muslims are not generally acceptable to the spirit of protest which has won universal respect and frequent admiration for some other members of the Negro's spectrum of protest. . . .

. . . Generally speaking, the movement has been a protest directed at the whole value-construct of the white Christian society of which the Black Muslims feel themselves (as Negroes) to be an isolated and unappreciated appendage. Hence, the burden of their protest is against their "retention" in a society where they are not wanted. This is the soft side of the "Armageddon complex" which looks to the removal of the source of their discomfiture rather than to going anywhere themselves. Mr. Muhammad teaches that "the white man's home is in Europe," and that "there will be no peace until every man is in his own country."

In a recent issue of the official Muslim newspaper, *Mr. Muhammad Speaks*, the Muslims stated their protest in the form of the following ten propositions:

1.   We want freedom. We want a full and complete freedom.

2.   We want justice. Equal justice under the law. We want justice applied equally to all, regardless of creed or class or color.

3.   We want equality of opportunity. We want equal membership in society with the best in civilized society.

4.   We want our people in America whose parents or grandparents were descendants from slaves, to be allowed to establish a separate state or territory of their own. . . .

5.   We want freedom for all Believers of Islam now held in federal prisons. We want freedom for all black men and women now under death sentence in innumerable prisons in the North as well as the South.
We want every black man and women to have the freedom to accept or reject being separated from the slave master's children and establish a land of their own. . . .

6.   We want an immediate end to the police brutality and mob attacks against the so-called Negro throughout the United States.

7.   As long as we are not allowed to establish a state or territory of our own, we demand not only equal justice under the laws of the United States, but equal employment opportunities—NOW! . . .

8.   We want the government of the United States to exempt our people from ALL taxation as long as we are deprived of equal justice under the laws of the land.

9.   We want equal education—but separate schools up to 16 for boys and 18 for girls on the condition that the girls be sent to women's colleges and universities. We want all black children educated, taught without hindrance or suppression.

10.   We believe that intermarriage or race mixing should be prohibited. We want the religion of Islam taught without hindrance or suppression.

These are some of the things that we, the Muslims, want for our people in North America.

4. White Protestantism and The Negro, 1965

SOURCE: From *White Protestantism and the Negro* by David M. Reimers, copyright by Oxford University Press, Inc. Used by permission of Oxford University Press, Inc.

In the article in the *Christian Century* in 1931, William E. B. DuBois declared, "The church, as a whole, insists on a divine mission and guidance and the indisputable possession of truth. Is there anything in the record of the church in America in regard to the Negro to prove this? There is not. If the treatment of the Negro by the Christian Church is called 'divine,' this is an attack on the conception of God more blasphemous than any which the church has always been so ready and eager to punish." DuBois's stricture had been made before, and it has certainly been made since. Some of the abolitionists had assailed the white churches as bulwarks of slavery, and in the early 1960's numerous church conferences produced speakers who attacked the churches for their race relations practices.

The critics of white Protestantism's treatment of the Negro had much evidence to support their strictures. But Protestantism's treatment of the Negro was no better and no worse than that of American society as a whole. Fundamental to an understanding of the race problem in Protestantism is the fact that the churches are social institutions that are shaped by the culture in which they exist. There were experiments in American history that attempted to build a holy society, but often these experiments were sharply modified by the very environment and people they sought to mold. This was especially true after the end of the colonial era.

Church members, whether in the pre-twentieth century days, when they represented only a minority of the community, or in the twentieth century, were also members of a variety of social groups and were pressured and influenced by many social forces. Hence, the attitudes and practices of white Protestant churches regarding the Negro were those of white America generally. . . .

In attacking segregation, Protestantism was in the mainstream of American life. It was no accident that the call for a "non-segregated church and a non-segregated society" came at about the same time as the threatened Negro march on Washington, Myrdal's *American Dilemma*, and President Truman's Commission on Civil Rights.

With the new goal, pronouncements covering almost every aspect of the race problem came from church conferences and religious leaders. But it is doubtful if many of the laity and even some of the leadership were fully aware of their denomination's position on the race problem. Thus the problem lay in implementation. Protestant churches are voluntary associations, and their social pronouncements are binding upon no individual or congregation. Rather, they serve as guideposts for social behavior.

By the early 1960's the white churches had made some progress in implementing their desire for truly interracial churches. Negroes were occupying leadership positions they had never filled before, church administration and church-related institutions were being desegregated, and even local congregations were becoming racially inclusive. At best, however, practice fell considerably short of preaching. Much of the desegregation within the churches stopped short of full integration. Southern seminaries, for example, admitted Negro students but did not hire Negro deans and faculty. Negroes became bishops, but their work was generally confined to Negro churches. Local white congregations admitted Negroes to membership but did not allow them to serve in the pulpits or in other leadership positions. Full integration, in which all phases of church life were open to all without regard to race and in which Negroes served in nonracial capacities, was far from being achieved by 1965. In 1959 Liston Pope of the Yale Divinity School wrote of Protestantism,

> Its record indicates clearly, however, that the church is the most segregated major institution in American society. It has lagged behind the Supreme Court as the conscience of the nation on questions of race, and it has fallen far behind trade unions, factories, schools, department stores, athletic gatherings, and most other

areas of human association as far as the achievement of integration in its own life is concerned.

Whether or not Pope's comment was entirely fair, the fact is that Protestantism had not been in the vanguard of integration. . . .

If the white churches on the whole were slow in climbing to the high plateau established by their own social pronouncements, many individual Protestants over the years were ahead of institutionalized religion. Some were in the antislavery movement or active during Reconstruction. Some protested against the churches' own segregationist and discriminatory practices. Some worked in associations such as the women's missionary groups or the National Council of Churches' Department of Race Relations. The distinction between the social institution and the individuals and groups within it is an important one, for these individuals and groups acted as the moral voice of the churches when the churches themselves practiced segregation and discrimination.

The individuals who fought slavery, segregation, and discrimination were often torn between conflicting loyalties. On the one hand, their Christian consciences drove them to seek justice, which at times meant denouncing the church for its racial practices. On the other hand, their roots and loyalties lay with the church, which for all its imperfections was still the carrier of the word of God. Some of these people were forced out of the church or left it voluntarily, as was the case with Will Alexander. Others remained within the church and formed such groups as the Episcopal Society for Cultural and Racial Unity to correct the faults of the church and to reconcile Negroes and whites.

Another contribution of the white churches to the development of a truly democratic society was made inadvertently. After the Civil War, they talked of evangelism and Christian education to uplift the American Negro. Although the educational programs of northern missionaries smacked of paternalism and Booker T. Washington's philosophy, they also propagated the Christian gospel. The churches and their schools talked long and loud of Christianity, and many Negro ministers absorbed these teachings. In the 1950's these Negro clergymen made themselves heard. Whether Ralph Abernathy or Martin Luther King, Jr., in the South, or James H. Robinson in the North, these Negro churchmen began to lead their people in demanding the fulfillment of the democratic and Christian ideals that white churches had taught them. It may well be that these Negro churchmen will yet teach the white Protestant churches the full meaning of the gospel of the brotherhood of man they espouse.

5. Martin Luther King Explains Nonviolent Resistance, 1967

SOURCE: From *Eyewitness* by William Loren Katz. Pp. 468-470. Copyright © 2000 by Ethrac Publications, Inc. Reprinted with permission.

During my freshman days in 1944 at Atlanta's Morehouse College I read Henry David Thoreau's essay *On Civil Disobedience* for the first time. Here, in this courageous New Englander's refusal to pay his taxes and his choice of jail rather than support a war that would spread slavery's territory into Mexico, I made my first contact with the theory of nonviolent resistance. Fascinated by Thoreau's idea of refusing to cooperate with an evil system, I was so deeply moved that I reread the work several times.

A few years later I heard a lecture by Dr. Mordecai Johnson, President of Howard University. Dr. Johnson had just returned from a trip to India and he spoke of the life and teachings of Mahatma Gandhi. His message was so profound and electrifying that I left the meeting and bought a half-dozen books on Gandhi's life and works.

Before reading Gandhi, I had believed that Jesus' "turn the other cheek" philosophy and the "love your enemies" philosophy could only be useful when individuals were in conflict with other individuals—when racial groups and nations were in conflict, a more realistic approach seemed necessary. But after reading Gandhi, I saw how utterly mistaken I was.

During the days of the Montgomery bus boycott, I came to see the power of nonviolence more and more. As I lived through the actual experience of this protest, nonviolence became more than a useful method; it became a way of life.

Nonresistance attacks the forces of evil rather than the persons who happen to be doing the evil. As I said to the people of Montgomery: "The tension in this city is not between white people and Negro people. The tension is at bottom, between justice and injustice, between the forces of light and the forces of darkness. And if there is a victory, it will be a victory not merely for fifty thousand Negroes but a victory for justice and the forces of light. We are out to defeat injustice and not white persons who may be unjust."

It must be emphasized that nonviolent resistance is not for cowards. *Nonviolent resistance does resist.* If one uses this method because he is afraid or merely because he lacks the weapons of violence, he is not truly nonviolent. That is why Gandhi often said that if cowardice is the only alternative to violence, it is better to fight. He made this statement knowing that there is always another choice we can make: There is the way of nonviolent resistance. No individual or group need submit to any wrong, nor need they use violence to right a wrong. This is ultimately the way of the strong man.

The nonviolent resistance of the early Christians shook the Roman Empire. The nonviolence of Mahatma Gandhi and his followers had muzzled the guns of the British Empire in India and freed more than three hundred and fifty million people from colonialism. It brought victory in the Montgomery bus boycott.

The phrase "passive resistance" often gives the false impression that this is a sort of "do-nothing method" in which the resister quietly and passively accepts evil. But nothing is further from the truth. For while the nonviolent resister is not physically aggressive toward his opponent, his mind and emotions are always active, constantly seeking to persuade his opponent that he is wrong—constantly seeking to open the eyes of blind prejudice. This is not passive nonresistance to evil, it is active nonviolent resistance to evil.

Nonviolence does not seek to defeat or humiliate the opponent, but to win his friendship and understanding. The nonviolent resister not only refuses to shoot his opponent but he also refuses to hate him. To strike back in the same way as his opponent would do nothing but increase the existence of hate in the universe. Along they way of life, someone must have sense enough and morality enough to cut off the chain of hate.

In the final analysis all life is interrelated. All humanity is involved in a single process, and all men are brothers. To the degree that I harm my brother, no matter what he is doing to me, to that extent I am harming myself. Why is this? Because men are brothers. If you harm me, you harm yourself.

6. The Black Messiah, 1968

SOURCE: From *The Black Messiah* by Albert B. Cleage, Jr. Pp. 3-9. Copyright © 1969 by Africa World Press. Reprinted with permission.

For nearly 500 years the illusion that Jesus was white dominated the world only because white Europeans dominated the world. Now, with the emergence of the nationalist movements of the world's colored majority, the historic truth is finally beginning to emerge—that Jesus was the non-white leader of a non-white people struggling for national liberation against the rule of a white nation, Rome. The intermingling of the races in Africa and the Mediterranean area is an established fact. The Nation Israel was a mixture of Chaldeans, Egyptians, Midianites, Ethiopians, Kushites, Babylonians and other dark peoples, all of whom were already mixed with the black people of Central Africa.

That white American continue to insist upon a white Christ in the face of all historical evidence to the contrary and despite the hundreds of shrines to Black Madonnas all over the world, is the crowning demonstration of their white supremacist conviction that all things good and valuable must be white. On the other hand, until black Christians are ready to challenge this lie, they have not freed themselves from their spiritual bondage to the white man nor established in their own minds their right to first-class citizenship in Christ's kingdom on earth. Black people cannot build dignity on their knees worshipping a white Christ. We must put down this white Jesus which the white man gave us in slavery and which has been tearing us to pieces.

Black Americans need to know that the historic Jesus was a leader who went about among the people of Israel, seeking to root out the individualism and the identification with their oppressor which had corrupted them, and to give them faith in their own power to rebuild the Nation. This was the real Jesus whose life is most accurately reported in the first three Gospels of the New Testament. On the other hand, there is the spiritualized Jesus, reconstructed many years later by the Apostle Paul who never knew Jesus and who modified his teachings to conform to the pagan philosophies of the white gentiles. Considering himself an apostle to the gentiles, Paul preached individual salvation and life after death. We, as black Christians suffering oppression in a white man's land, do note need the individualistic and otherworldly doctrines of Paul and the white man. We need to recapture the faith in our power as a *people* and the concept of Nation, which are the foundation of the Old Testament and the prophets, and upon which Jesus built all of his teachings 2,000 years ago.

Jesus was a revolutionary black leader, a Zealot, seeking to lead a Black Nation to freedom, so the Black Church must carefully define the nature of the revolution.

What do we mean when we speak of the Black Revolution? I can remember an incident at the beginning of the Harlem Rebellion only a few short years ago when a news reporter snapped an unforgettable picture of a black girl who was present when a black boy was brutally killed by a white apartment house caretaker. She stood there on the sidewalk, her face contorted with anger and frustration, tears streaming down her cheeks, and she screamed at the cops who had rushed to the scene to keep their kind of law and order, "Kill me too! Kill me too!"

This was the absolute in frustration. "The problem of being black in a white man's world is just too big. I don't know what to do with it. So just kill me too and get it over with." That was what she was saying.

Black brothers and sisters all over the country felt a spontaneous identification with that girl because every black person has felt just this kind of frustration. We feel it every day. At every meeting some young black man jumps to his feet screaming, "I can't stand it any longer. Let's take to the streets and get it over with!" We all know how he feels and why he feels that way. Sometimes we go home and say it was a very "nervous" meeting, and everyone knows what we are talking about because each of us has felt that same sense of powerlessness that makes us ache with helplessness and hopelessness and drives us to seek death as an easy way out. Those of use who cry out think of ourselves as revolutionists and participants in the Black Revolution. But a revolution seeks to change conditions. So each day we must decide. Either we are trying to achieve the power to change conditions or we have turned from the struggle and are seeking an heroic moment when we can die in the streets.

As black people, we have entered a revolution rather than the evolution or gradual change which white folks would like us to accept. We want to move fast enough to be able to see that we are moving. And four hundred years of standing still is a long time. We are trying to make the world over so that our children and our children's children can have power and live like human beings. We look at the world in which we live today and we are determined to turn the world upside down.

But when I hear cries of "Kill me too!" I know that that individual no longer has any hope. When he screams, "Let's get together and die in the streets," I know that in his desperate hopelessness this individual has put aside the revolution. Dying in the streets is not revolution. This is escapism. This is suicide. But it is *not* revolution. As long as there is the slightest possibility of victory, we are still engaged in a revolution. But when an individual sees no way to achieve power to change conditions, then the revolution is over. It doesn't make any difference how he spends his remaining time, singing hymns, getting drunk or buying guns. For him the revolution is over.

The Black Church has not always been revolutionary, but it has always been relevant to the everyday needs of black people. The old down-home black preacher who "shouted" his congregation on Sunday morning was realistically ministering to the needs of a black people who could not yet conceive of changing the conditions which oppressed them. If you can't solve your problems, you can at least escape from them! So we had Saturday night to escape in one way, and Sunday morning to pray for repentance and to escape in another way. The Church was performing a valuable and real function. However uneducated the old-time preacher was, he was relevant and significant. What he offered was an ingenious interpretation of a slave Christianity to meet the needs of an oppressed and suffering people. He took it and used it so that black people could go to church on Sunday morning and find the strength to endure white folks for another six days. You could go to church and "shout" and feel that God was just, even though the world in which you lived was unjust. Implicit in every ignorant black preacher's sermon was the faith that God must eventually shake white people over hell-fire, and that after death black people were going to heaven. White people were the oppressors. They were the sinners, they were guilty. Black people were innocent and suffered oppression through no fault of their own. Therefore, they were going to heaven and walk on golden streets, and white people were going to hell. There is still profound truth in this simple message of the primitive Black Church.

But today the Church must reinterpret its message in terms of the needs of a Black Revolution. We no longer feel helpless as black people. We do not feel that we must sit and wait for God to intervene and settle our problems for us. We waited for four hundred years and he didn't do much of anything, so for the next four hundred years we're going to be fighting to change conditions for ourselves. This is merely a new theological position. We have come to understand how God works in the world. Now we know that God is going to give us strength for our struggle. As black preachers we must tell our people that we are God's chosen people and that God is fighting with us as we fight. When we march, when we take it to the streets in open conflict, we must understand that in the stamping feet and the thunder of violence we can hear the voice of God. When the Black Church accepts its role in the Black Revolution, it is able to understand and interpret revolutionary Christianity, and the revolution becomes a part of our Christian faith. Every Sunday morning when we preach from the Old Testament, or when we preach about Jesus, we seek to help black people understand that the struggle in which we are engaged is a cosmic struggle, that the very universe struggles with us when we fight to throw off the oppression of white people. We want black people to understand that they are coming to church to get the strength and direction to go out and fight oppression all week. We don't pray for the strength to endure any more. We pray for the strength to fight heroically.

Basic to our struggle and the revitalization of the Black Church is the simple fact that we are building a totally new self-image. Our rediscovery of the Black Messiah is a part of our rediscovery of ourselves. We could not worship a Black Jesus until we had thrown off the shackles of self-hate. We could not follow a Black

Messiah in the tasks of building a Black Nation until we had found the courage to look back beyond the slave block and the slave ship without shame.

In recent years the contradiction inherent in the worship of a white Christ by black people oppressed by whites has become increasingly acute. In the Negro Renaissance after World War I the anguish of this contradiction was voiced by poet Countee Cullen in his famous lines:

> . . . My conversion came high-priced;
> I belong to Jesus Christ, . . .
> Lamb of God, although I speak
> With my mouth thus, in my heart
> Do I play a double part. . . .
> Wishing he I served were black. . . ?

The widespread repudiation by many black Americans of a white Christ has added to the attractiveness of the Black Muslim movement. But many more black Americans, race conscious enough to reject a white Christ, have been reluctant to embrace Islam in view of the role played by the Arabs in fostering and carrying on the slave trade in Africa. The result has been the self-exclusion of most black militants from any religious affiliations whatsoever.

The only black leader in this country to meet this problem head-on was Marcus Garvey who organized the African Orthodox Church with a black hierarchy, including a Black God, a Black Jesus, a Black Madonna, and black angels. Forty years ago black Americans apparently were not ready for Garvey's religious ideas, although to this day, in every major city, individual Garveyites continue to circulate portraits of a Black Jesus. In Africa, however, Garvey's religious ideas played a key role in founding the African Independent Churches which in many countries acted as the center of the liberation movement. As Roosevelt University professor and writer, St. Clair Drake, has pointed out, the Kenya Africans invited one of Garvey's bishops to train and ordain their preachers and to help form the African independent schools and churches out of which the Mau Mau eventually grew.

The Black Church in America has served as the heart and center of the life of black communities everywhere, but, for the most part, without a consciousness of its responsibility and potential power to give a lost people a sense of earthly purpose and direction. During the Black Revolt following the 1954 Supreme Court desegregation decision, the Southern Black Church found that involvement in the struggle of black people for freedom was inescapable. Without a theology to support its actions (actions almost in contradiction to its otherworldly preachings), it provided spokesmen and served as a meeting place and source of emotional inspiration. In the North, where the black man's problems at one time seemed less pressing, the Black Church has failed miserably to relate itself to the seething ghetto rebellions and therefore has practically cut itself off from vast segments of the black community. The Northern Church has been black on the outside only, borrowing its theology, its orientation and its social ideology largely from the white Church and the white power structure.

The present crisis, involving as it does the black man's struggle for survival in America, demands the resurrection of a Black Church with its own Black Messiah. Only this kind of a Black Christian Church can serve as the unifying center for the totality of the black man's life and struggle. Only this kind of a Black Christian Church can force each individual black man to decide where he will stand—united with his own people and laboring and sacrificing in the spirit of the Black Messiah, or individualistically seeking his own advancement and maintaining his slave identification with the white oppressor. . . .

Essays

That religion was the heart and soul of the civil rights movement has long been contended. The role of the National Council of Churches is a case in point. In the first essay, James F. Findlay, Jr. of the University of Rhode Island examines the importance of the Council in the early stages of the movement. At the center of the black church's revolutionary role in the movement was Martin Luther King, Jr. and the Southern Christian Leadership Conference (SCLC) which he helped to establish. Adam Fairclough of the University of East Anglia in North Norwich, (UK) describes the importance of the organization in the black community's quest for social change. In the final essay, Charles Marsh, of the University of Virginia, reminds the reader that not all religious participation in the civil rights movement was supportive. Marsh presents the story of a high priest of the anti-civil rights movement, Sam Bowers.

The Origins of Activism, 1950-1963
JAMES F. FINDLAY, JR.

SOURCE: From *Church People in the Struggle: The National Council of Churches and the Black Freedom Movement, 1950-1970* by James F. Findlay, Jr., copyright © 1993 by James F. Findlay, Jr. Used by permission of Oxford University Press, Inc.

On October 12, 1958, before 30,000 people, the President of the United States, Dwight Eisenhower, laid the cornerstone of the Interchurch Center, the permanent home of the National Council of Churches at 475 Riverside Drive in New York City. The outdoor ceremony, on land donated by John D. Rockefeller, Jr., directly across the street from the "Cathedral of Protestantism," Riverside Church, was a moment charged with symbolism, partly obvious, partly hidden. The presence and active participation of President Eisenhower suggested strongly the powerful cultural role the National Council and the Protestant churches it represented continued to play in American life. This moment was almost a classic manifestation of the "civil religion" of the nation in operation. A long procession of robed clerics and academicians, which formed at Riverside Church and then moved slowly to the construction site a block away, "read like a Who's Who of American Protestantism." At the back of the ceremonial platform fluttered large varicolored banners representing thirty-seven Protestant and Eastern Orthodox denominations, almost all members of the National Council of Churches. The presence of the ecumenical movement overarching those denominations seemed almost palpable. It was, one observer noted, "the largest gathering [to date] to pay tribute to the developing solidarity of Protestant and Orthodox churches in the United States."

There were grass-roots participants, too—a massed choir of 500 to sing to the president, bell-ringers from nearby churches, even several hundred of the construction workers building the Interchurch Center joined the procession to the construction site. Perhaps these people served as an unconscious counterbalancing image to the suprachurch connotations the National Council of Churches could never avoid entirely. Finally and appropriately, the benediction was rendered by Harry Emerson Fosdick, pastor emeritus of Riverside Church and since the 1920s a key leader and personal symbol of the forces of liberal Protestantism that underlay and animated the celebration. Looking back one might surmise that for many of the participants the celebration itself and the permanent, material reminder of the day—the growing steel shell of national Protestant headquarters in Morningside Heights—left them with a sense of self-satisfaction, faith in the continuing institutional success of key religious bodies of the nation, and even some feelings of cultural triumphalism.

Indeed, the historical record that remains of mainline Protestantism in the 1950s seems tinged with similar attitudes and feelings. The National Council of Churches again provides reminders of those tendencies. From the time of Harry Truman on, leaders from the two major political parties regularly addressed the biennial (after 1954 triennial) general assemblies and other special convocations of the National Council. These were opportunities for policymakers in Washington, especially those in the executive branch and the State Department, to utilize a relatively neutral but sympathetic platform to explain and defend their programs. Conversely, these appearances usually provided politicians and government officials with an implicit sense of support from a powerful and important opinion-shaping portion of the general public. John Foster Dulles was directly involved in the work of both the Federal Council of Churches and the National Council before becoming Secretary of State in 1953. Arthur Flemming, Eisenhower's appointment as first head of the Department of Health, Education, and Welfare, was also deeply involved in the activities of the council in both the fifties and the sixties. All these events provided further confirmation of the many informal ways church and state reinforced each other and that in the 1950s mainstream Protestantism was still a part of the informal national religious "establishment."

Even the seemingly uninspired fact of the publication of a new edition of the Bible highlighted the mainstream Protestants who produced it. The Revised Standard Version of the Bible, published in 1952, was the product of fifteen years of scholarly endeavor and the first comprehensive update of the scriptures in half a century. Clearly this was an ecumenical effort widely acclaimed throughout a nation historically deeply attached to Bible study and Bible-related religious faiths. Eventually, in 1963, the "RSV" was accepted, with minor additions, as the official Roman Catholic Bible, a further ecumenical triumph. The National Council of Churches, representing the Protestant denominations who made the scholarly re-evaluation possible, held the copyright. Inevitably this meant a continuous windfall of publicity (and profits) for ecumenical and mainstream Protestantism from the moment the first copy of the new Bible, bound in Moroccan leather, was presented to President Truman in the Oval Office on September 26, 1952.

The widespread Protestant sense of well-being in the fifties also rested on a set of statistics that conveyed very positive images. These were the numbers, published on an annual basis, that established precise levels of church membership, church benevolences, monies invested in new church buildings, even Sunday School enrollments. Throughout the fifties all of these data produced a steadily upward curve that delighted church leaders and were widely publicized. By 1960 the official estimate was that over 63 percent of the American public were church members, a fourteen-point increase in twenty years. Over 35 percent were Protestants, by far the largest religious grouping.

The increase in church membership in the decade was sufficiently dramatic to cause church publicists to proclaim the presence of a widespread "religious revival." There were questions, though, to be raised about these claims. Looking closely at the relevant long-term data, one quickly noticed that church membership as a percentage of the total population increased 8 percent in the decade of the forties versus 6 percent in the fifties, yet no one talked about a "religious revival" occurring in the earlier ten-year period. Even more serious questions were raised by people wondering how deep and lasting the so-called revival was (a perennial issue in previous revivals in this country, extending back to the colonial era). In late 1956 members of the news staff of the National Council of Churches circulated a questionnaire to "a representative cross-section of the nation's leadership in religious and civic affairs," which asked "Is there a religious revival?," and then printed many of the replies. Liston Pope, Dean of Yale Divinity School and a specialist in race relations and social ethics, forcefully expressed the concerns of some of the doubters:

> At this time of the greatest need, the influence of religion on human affairs appears to be indirect and, all told, rather minimal. . . . The religious agencies [have not] been of very much importance in bridging over the gaps between economic classes and racial groups; indeed the churches and other Christian bodies have largely adapted themselves to these divisions. Even with respect to the values by which men live and judge their social institutions, religious forces for the most part have been relegated to the sidelines and secular values are elevated to positions of supreme importance.

Pope's early life as a southerner and the fact that professionally he was a close student of the intractable racial puzzles of this county probably helped to endow him with a strong streak of realism. And our study of the National Council of Churches—one of those "other Christian bodies" to which Pope so delicately referred—and its work in race relations in the 1950s make his generalizations even more apropos. Perhaps, then, our initial description of the fifties are wrong. Better to say that the churches possessed *disparate* tendencies—not just the triumphant mood that so many church people sensed and spoke about, but other attitudes and practices that conveyed less dynamic and positive images.

Throughout the 1950s the National Council of Churches expressed itself on racial matters primarily in two ways. First, by means of resolutions adopted by the key governing bodies of the council—some in the large general assembly meetings held every two or three years, but most at sessions of the General Board, a much smaller but representative "executive committee" that was the true policymaking organ of the council. Second, the Department of Racial and Cultural Relations was responsible for the creation and implementation of ongoing programs designed as specific, tangible expressions of the National Council's broad public statements regarding racial prejudice and segregation. Because of the far-reaching impact of race on American life, other agencies of the council (for example, the migrant ministry program, the Department of Town and Country, or the Division of Christian Education) occasionally directly, and sometimes indirectly, also dealt with racial issues. But over the years the council's thought and action on race were revealed most clearly in the general policy resolutions mentioned above and in the work of the Department of Racial and Cultural Relations.

Between 1950 and 1958 the National Council adopted as official policy two dozen resolutions on racial issues connected to broad societal concerns and specific historical events. Probably the most important of these was the "Statement on the Churches and Segregation" adopted by the General Board in June 1952. The resolution was important for several reasons. First, it reasserted an official policy regarding racial discrimination that had been announced by the Federal Council of Churches in March 1946, which had influenced a number of Protestant denominations to pass similar resolutions in the intervening years. Second, it focused specifically on the churches, made clear their deep complicity in the nation's practice of racial discrimination and segregation, and stated that because "the pattern of segregation is diametrically opposed to what Christians believe about the worth of men," "we must take our stand against it." The statement then went on to suggest specific ways in which the churches at all levels could begin to end their own and the larger society's discriminatory practices, to work for a "a non-segregated church and a non-segregated community." . . .

Between 1960 and 1963 a rapidly ascending curve of major challenges to the national racial status quo occurred, principally in the southern states, to which in one way or another the churches were going to have to respond. There had been a number of unheralded local demonstrations in different parts of the South prior to 1960, but the famous college student sit-ins at five-and-ten-cent stores, beginning in the spring of 1960 in Charlotte, North Carolina, and quickly spreading throughout the upper South and the Border States, signaled national recognition of sit-ins and boycotts as a new pressure tactic being used by the black community. This was in addition to action through the courts, initiated chiefly by the NAACP, which had begun the process of school desegregation in the middle and late 1950s. The student sit-ins were soon followed by CORE-sponsored "Freedom Rides" on interstate buses into the Deep South in May 1961, which resulted in severe violence in Alabama and Mississippi. These events also forced the Kennedy administration to intervene, rather hesitantly, for the first time in the escalating crisis.

In 1962 mass demonstrations and legal tests of segregation in the Deep South continued, especially at Albany, Georgia, and at the University of Mississippi. (The campaign in Albany began in November 1961 and lasted almost a year; the crisis at Ole Miss occurred chiefly in the fall of 1962.) The demonstration in "Albenny" ultimately failed and constituted a major defeat for Martin Luther King, Jr., and the Southern Christian Leadership Conference, which sponsored them. But Albany was the first spot where predominant northern white church people (principally ministers) marched with the SCLC. Although Will Campbell had reservations about this particular church activity, it was a sign of stirrings in the mainline churches, which would soon lead to much deeper and more direct involvement of the National Council of Churches, and other denominations, in the racial struggle.

Other pressures for direct action by the churches were developing. In January 1963 a national Conference on Religion and Race convened in Chicago. It represented the first major ecumenical effort—Protestants, Catholics, and Jews joining together—to focus attention on the racial crisis. The three-day gathering attracted several hundred religious leaders, but rhetoric still outweighed the ability to mount concrete programs of action. A "continuing" office of the conference was established in New York City following the meeting in Chicago, but proper funding, broad church support, and imaginative leadership failed to materialize and the office closed within a year. Thus the leaders of the Conference on Religion and Race failed in an ambitious effort to become major ecumenical spokesmen on matters of race. But the gathering in Chicago and subsequent efforts to maintain the enthusiasms generated there pointed to growing sentiments among church people that more should be done nationally to help African American citizens secure long-denied basic rights.

The National Council of Churches through the Department of Racial and Cultural Relations was an official sponsor and financial supporter of the Conference on Religion and Race, but its top leadership never endorsed enthusiastically the idea of the continuing office of the conference. It created another layer of bureaucracy and increased the babble of voices striving to offer some form of national religious leadership on racial matters. There was too much of a tinge of established policies and procedures there. J. Oscar Lee and his followers were the voice of the National Council in this instance, in the eyes of some following tradition too much and possessing too limited a vision.

In any case, the aftermath of the Conference on Religion and Race did not clarify leadership problems in the mainline churches about racial issues. Indeed, individual denominations under the National Council's umbrella seemed readier than the ecumenical organization to adopt an activist stance. On May 20, 1963, the General Assembly of the United Presbyterian Church, U.S.A., established a Commission on Religion and Race to address racial problems in the denomination and in the country at large. The Presbyterians also voted to fund their commission with a hefty budget of $150,000 for the remaining six months of 1963.

The Conference on Religion and Race also highlighted the increasingly significant impact that Martin Luther King, Jr., was making on the predominantly white churches. He was a member of the steering committee that planned the conference, and he delivered one of the major speeches there. In the 1950s religious leaders from the black community other than King had frequently addressed groups in the mainline churches. Two of them were Howard Thurman, dean of the chapel at Boston University during and after the time King was a student there, and Benjamin Mays, president of Morehouse College and a close friend of the King family. Both men were urbane, sophisticated speakers and preachers.

King, however, represented a younger generation of black clergy whose direct action tactics were transforming the civil rights struggle. In the late fifties and early sixties he also engaged in a busy schedule of speech making throughout the country, much of it before white church groups. He made a major speech to the triennial General Assembly of the National Council of Churches in 1957 and wrote the sermon for Race Relations Sunday that same year. King's willingness to engage in direct action and to preach powerfully to white congregations about the consequences was immensely compelling. Clearly by 1963 he was the leading African American interpreter of the black freedom struggle, in all its moral urgency, to white church people nationwide.

On April 3, 1963, two and a half months after the close of the conference in Chicago, King launched his now-famous campaign to desegregate the tough, deep-south city of Birmingham, Alabama. The intense white opposition there to mass marches and demonstrations eventually caught the attention of the nation and the world and landed King in jail. From that jail in Birmingham the young black minister penned his famous *Letter*, addressed to the white clergy of the city (and of the nation). It was King's most powerful indictment of the white churches for their lack of involvement in the black struggle for freedom. It was also very widely read in the white religious community, being published first in its entirety in *The Christian Century*, probably the best-known ecumenical weekly in Protestantism. From behind bars King wrote:

> In the midst of a mighty struggle to rid our nation of racial and economic injustice I have heard many ministers say, "Those are social issues with which the gospel has

no real concern," and I have watched many churches commit themselves to a completely otherworldly religion which makes a strange, unbiblical distinction between body and soul, between the sacred and the secular. . . . But the judgment of God is upon the church as never before. If today's church does not recapture the sacrificial spirit of the early church it will lose its authenticity, forfeit the loyalty of millions, and be dismissed as an irrelevant social club with no meaning for the 20th century.

Passages like these, coupled with his activism, made King a personal model for many younger clergy. In a Birmingham jail he offered not only a powerful rebuke to the continuing inactivism of most white religious leaders, but also words that could help create, finally, the *kairos.* . . .

The twelve-story Interchurch center, now completed and fully occupied, also facilitated the interchange of ideas. The Presbyterians and the Methodists, especially, housed several important national divisions and boards in the building. There was a constant circulation of information, plans, and personal support among these groups. The Episcopalians and the United Church of Christ had their national offices elsewhere in the city, but it was not hard to join deliberations at the Interchurch Center or to share ideas by phone or informal get-togethers. For example, the National Board of Missions of the United Presbyterian Church, U.S.A., notably activist and liberal in the programs it advanced throughout the sixties, occupied offices at "475." Regier, a Presbyterian, received strong support from several of the staff of the National Board of Missions, including the director, Kenneth Neigh, and his two principal assistants, David Ramage and Bryant George. Ramage, Neigh, and Regier started their careers in the Midwest, they and George were contemporaries of one another, either as students or faculty, at McCormick Seminary in Chicago, and all had become experts in interracial ministries in inner city areas of the Windy City before coming to New York. Bryant George, one of the few African Americans on *any* national denominational staff, representing the small but not insignificant African American constituency of the United Presbyterian Church, had known Ramage since they were teenage leaders of national Presbyterian youth groups. These men were politically savvy, tough minded ("steely-eyed" one secular coworker later dubbed them), and deeply committed to supporting change in national racial practices. Neigh was a member of the General Board of the National Council and was an influential spokesperson there. These men helped Regier draft the documents establishing the Commission on Religion and Race, supported also by people like Arthur Walmsley, an Episcopalian from downtown, and Truman Douglass, head of the Board of Homeland Ministries of the United Church of Christ and, as previously mentioned, mentor of Bob Spike. When the United Presbyterians established *their* commission on race in May 1963, that group, too, established its offices in "the Godbox" on Riverside Drive. Its director, Gayraud Wilmore, and his staff worked closely with Spike's people, and this added another yeasty ingredient to the mix at the Interchurch Center.

Union Theological Seminary played a similar role to that of the Presbyterians in providing recruits who helped shape the activist programs at the Interchurch Center. The center and the seminary were on opposite sides of the same street corner, which symbolized their interconnections. Two recent graduates of Union, Bruce Hanson and John Pratt, joined the staff of the Commission on Religion and Race. Although Reinhold Niebuhr was ill and did not participate directly in any of these developments, his spirit seemed to hover over much of what was transpiring. Younger members of the seminary faculty, like Roger Shinn, helped to plan programs instituted by the National Council, such as the Student Interracial Ministry (a series of summer interracial pulpit "exchanges" begun in 1960), and joined demonstrations in the South and elsewhere that often were the result of these activities.

There was a sense of irony about all this. High-level church leaders, often thought of as plodding and unimaginative bureaucrats, had become program innovators, moving out ahead of a largely culture-bound church to try to lead American mainline Protestantism toward some broad realization of deeply rooted biblical concerns for the poor and dispossessed and for a society of near equals, especially regarding race. This was risky business, for these people at the Interchurch Center and in various denominational headquarters in New York City and elsewhere in the country were a distinct minority, a small elite within the churches. They possessed considerable decision-making power and had access, through denominational gift giving and endowments, to substantial financial resources. For a time at least, given the national focus on racial matters and the powerful pressures for change emanating from both religious and secular allies in the African American community, they might carry their vast local constituencies with them. But a constant though unspoken problem was that they might move too rapidly, or too far out ahead of their cautious lay constituencies, tethered so much to local parishes and often to parochial visions of life. These bureaucrat-leaders were also very middle-class, too exclusively white, and almost entirely male—the epitome of the leadership throughout the mainline churches. By the end of the 1960s the bursting forth of feminism, the national furies unleashed by the Vietnam War, continuing racial antagonisms, and the emergence of a militant young black leadership within the churches as well as in the larger society challenged at many points all previous leadership groups in the National Council and the denominations. The council then struggled painfully to change, but it was not enough to avoid setbacks and reversals everywhere.

But that was all in the future. In 1963 opportunity beckoned to the "new breed" of church leader in the National Council of Churches and in the denominations served by the council. These people sought to forge a new public stance for the mainstream churches regarding racial issues, to involve the churches directly in support of the demands of black Americans that the latter be given long-denied political and economic rights and be admitted fully into the mainstream of American life. *Kairos* seemed about to be made manifest. And in a sense these national church leaders also signaled a return to the Social Gospel of the early twentieth century, but to focus now much more directly on racial concerns, which was a less frequent interest of the earlier church activists.

Certainly the work of these church people was a major realization of the attitudes embodied in Colin Williams's *Where in the World.* The publication of that little book coincided almost exactly with the creation of the National Council of Churches' Commission on Religion and Race. Excitedly Williams noted at the end of his essay "that a responsible Church body has officially broken free from its own internal machinery, in response to God's urgent call from the needs of the world" and has offered "to allow itself" to shape its servant-missionary role "around this worldly need." Such action, exclaimed Williams, "is a miracle of grace!" In this flush of enthusiasm Williams perhaps overstated the theological and historical significance of what had transpired. But he was sufficiently clear-eyed to conclude with a troubling thought: "The big question now is, will the churches be free enough to support the necessary action when it lies outside their ordered forms?" . . .

The Civil Rights Movement and the Soul of America
ADAM FAIRCLOUGH

SOURCE: From *To Redeem the Soul of America: The Southern Christian Leadership Conference and Martin Luther King, Jr.,* by Adam Fairclough. Copyright © 1987 by the University of Georgia Press. Reprinted with permission of the publisher.

"The most wonderful thing has happened right here in Montgomery, Alabama," wrote Virginia Durr, one of that city's handful of white radicals, on December 7, 1955. For the second day, blacks had boycotted local buses as a protest against their unfair treatment under the segregation laws. "It is almost 100 per cent effective," Durr told a friend, "and they are carrying it on in the most orderly and disciplined way and with the utmost determination."

The Montgomery bus boycott was not the first of its kind. Two years earlier, in Baton Rouge, Louisiana, blacks had also boycotted city buses, and by means of economic pressure, assisted by a willingness to compromise by both white and black, succeeded in establishing the principle of "first come, first served" segregated seating. Under this arrangement white passengers took seats from the front of the bus towards the rear, while blacks seated themselves from the back towards the front. It eliminated the more objectionable features of bus segregation: the need for blacks having to surrender their places to whites, or being compelled to stand while reserved "white" seats remained empty. While the boycott lasted, the blacks, led by the Reverend T. J. Jemison, utilized 150 cars and taxis to provide free lifts. Virtually no blacks rode the buses.

Blacks in Montgomery did not expect their own boycott to last long; after all, they were not seeking the abolition of segregation, merely equality of treatment within the existing system. They were not aware of the events in Baton Rouge, but they did know that other cities in the Deep South, notably Mobile and Atlanta, had already conceded the "first come, first served" principle. They would need only to stay off the buses for a week or two to achieve this eminently reasonable demand. In Baton Rouge, it had taken precisely seven days.

If white officials in Montgomery had shown the same degree of flexibility as those in Baton Rouge, they could have both ended the boycott within days and preserved segregated seating. Their intransigence, however, prolonged the boycott and persuaded blacks that there could be no just solution within the framework of segregation. When negotiations with the city and the bus company broke down, the organizers of the boycott confronted the stark choice of pressing on with protest or backing down. If popular support had ebbed or crumbled, the latter would have been the only realistic alternative. As it was, the degree of black optimism and solidarity made an admission of defeat unthinkable. "The people are just as enthusiastic now as they were in the beginning of the protest," wrote the leader of the boycott, Martin Luther King, Jr., in September 1956. "They are determined never to return to jim crow buses. The mass meetings are still jammed and packed and above all else the buses are still empty."

By then, another bus boycott was underway, in Tallahassee, Florida. When this protest began, whites of influence instinctively turned to the black leaders they knew best, the teachers, who had traditionally deferred to white sensibilities and pandered to white paternalism with the tact and finesse of seasoned diplomats. In an attempt to mediate, the editor of the *Tallahassee Democrat,* Malcolm Johnson, asked a respected high school principal to select five or six "responsible" Negroes with whom the city and the bus company could do business—with the understanding, of course, that the principle of segregation was not negotiable. To his shock and discomfiture, however, Johnson found himself confronted by a roomful of angry blacks who resisted the usual evasive courtesies and insisted upon pressing their demands. The figures with whom white officialdom preferred to deal could not stop the boycott: blacks were not only rejecting the status quo, they were also following new leaders. And the latter refused to observe the old rules: they were not interested in paternalism, they regarded deference as demeaning, and, above all, they were uncompromising in their opposition to segregation. The relationship between black and white had been transformed, Johnson recalled some two decades later. "The preachers took over from the teachers."

The bus boycotts in Baton Rouge, Montgomery, and Tallahassee were led by ministers and organized through the black church. The Tallahassee boycott movement, the Inter-Civic Council, numbered six clergymen among its nine officers and was led by the Reverend C. K. Steele. The boycott organization in Montgomery, the Montgomery Improvement Association, was similarly top-heavy with men of the cloth, with two dozen ministers helping Martin Luther King keep the protest in motion. When the state of Alabama outlawed the National Association for the Advancement of Colored People, a clergyman, Fred Shuttlesworth, organized an alternative organization in Birmingham. Preachers were indeed moving into the vanguard of black protest in the South.

White leaders, dumbfounded by the sudden emergence of hitherto obscure clerics, refused to acknowledge their legitimacy. These new men, they reasoned, must be radicals, Communists, outsiders—self-seeking parvenus whose hold over their followers rested on a clever combination of duress, demagogy, and deceit. But however much whites ignored, denigrated, or persecuted them, the new leaders won respect and support from ordinary blacks and became forces to be reckoned with. And out of these church-led protest movements came a new civil rights organization, the Southern Christian Leadership Conference, founded in 1957. SCLC was an unusual, unorthodox, and in some ways even bizarre outfit. After a faltering start, however, SCLC became a dynamic force within the civil rights movement and one of the most effective political pressure groups in American history. It has left an indelible mark on the South.

The formation and importance of SCLC mirrored a basic fact about the leadership in the Southern black movement of the 1950s and 1960s: ministers wielded influence out of all proportion to their numbers. Such prominence reflected the economic facts of life in the South. Most blacks, educated or not, middle-class or working-class, depended on a white landlord or employer; they could ill afford to be identified as "troublemakers." To oppose segregation was to invite eviction, loss of livelihood, loss of credit. Teachers were particularly vulnerable to economic retaliation: in some Southern states they could be fired merely for advocating integration or belonging to the NAACP. College teachers were more difficult to get rid of, but they, too, might be squeezed out of their posts for challenging the status quo. On the other hand, churches were owned and controlled by blacks themselves; ministers could be fired by their congregations alone. With a high degree of economic independence, preachers enjoyed a freedom of speech and action denied to the majority of blacks. This vital connection between economic safety and black leadership is also evident in the occupations of laymen who became prominent in the civil rights movement: many, if not most, were self-employed businessmen and professionals whose clientele was wholly or mainly blacks—doctors, dentists, lawyers, undertakers, store owners. Like ministers, they enjoyed economic security which gave them the latitude to defy white opinion. It was ironic that segregation, by helping to create a self-sufficient black middle class, inadvertently nurtured its leading adversaries. The most effective opponents of segregation were often its principal black beneficiaries.

The appearance of church leadership in movements against segregation reflected a shift in black attitudes rather than a bold initiative by preachers; the relationship between clergy and community was one of symbiosis rather than leaders and led. Churchmen had always functioned as leaders and spokesmen, but they had usually accommodated to the racial mores of the time; indeed, generations of black activists and intellectuals had excoriated the church for is conservatism and lack of social and political awareness. It would be unrealistic, however, to suppose that ministers were completely out of step with their parishioners. In Myrdal's blunt words, "If the preachers have been timid and pussyfooting, it is because Negroes in general have condoned such a policy and would have feared more radical leaders." There had always been exceptions, of course, but in the 1930s segregation seemed unassailable and few black ministers saw much sense in hitting their heads against this particular brick wall. It was a period in which preachers reached the nadir of their prestige; black businessmen and professionals were far more active in supporting trade unions and civil rights organizations.

The Second World War engendered a fundamental reorientation of black expectations and attitudes. Servicemen returned home with broader mental horizons, increased confidence, and greater self-esteem. They had fought and defeated the racist tyranny of the Axis; they were in no mood to readapt passively to the South's humiliating caste system. The injustices of segregation rankled more than ever, and clashes over the "color line," especially in buses and streetcars, became increasingly common during and after the war. Fewer blacks now accepted the system without question or regarded it as inevitable; why should they when the federal government itself was beginning to openly oppose it? Roosevelt's Fair Employment Practices Committee, the Democrats' civil rights plank in 1948, Truman's decision to integrate the armed forces, and Eisenhower's support for desegregation in the District of Columbia—all these pointed to the conclusion that white supremacy, in its formal-legal expression at least, was doomed.

Political involvement fostered rising expectations. In 1944 the Supreme Court outlawed the "white primary," the complex of rules which had excluded blacks from the Democratic party and barred them from voting in the all-important Democratic primary elections. This epochal decision marked the reentry of Southern blacks into political life (although it took another quarter of a century to complete the process). Throughout most of the rural South, as well as in cities like Birmingham and New Orleans, the vast majority of the black population was still disfranchised. But in many cities some, if not all, of the obstacles to black voting came down. Taking the South as a whole, the proportion of black adults who were registered voters increased from 5 percent in 1944 to 20 percent in 1952. By the early 1950s blacks were beginning to exert a palpable political influence in parts of the South. Blacks were elected to city councils in the North Carolina cities of Winston-Salem (1947) and Greensboro (1951); in 1952 a black candidate won a public election in Georgia. However circumscribed, political leverage encouraged blacks to agitate for pay parity with white teachers, the appointment of black policemen, a more equitable share of municipal services, and "first come, first served" segregated bus seating. Such campaigns were often successful, and a growing number of black Southerners confidently looked forward to fairer treatment, better conditions, and improved opportunities.

Thus the impulse which led to the civil rights movement came from outside the church and was nurtured by politics. In Montgomery, in the period before the bus boycott, the leading black activists were E. D. Nixon, a railroad porter and trade union official; Rufus Lewis, a businessman; and Jo Ann Robinson, a college teacher. All three headed political clubs which, in the early 1950s became increasingly vociferous in articulating black grievances and demands. One issue which they repeatedly raised was that of segregation on the city buses: between 1953 and 1955 they met city and bus company officials on at least four occasions to complain about abusive drivers and about company policies which made blacks stand over empty seats or surrender their places to whites. Mrs. Robinson's group, the Women's Political Council, took the lead in these meetings, and the conviction that a united black vote had helped to elect one of the city commissioners encouraged it to adopt an increasingly forthright stand. The bus boycott was no bolt from the blue.

The inception of the boycott underlined the fact that the original dynamic came from without the black church, not from ministers but from lay people. The contribution of Rosa Parks should not be underestimated. Her decision to choose arrest rather than humiliation when driver J. F. Blake ordered her to give up her seat on December 1, 1955, was more than the impulsive gesture of a seamstress with sore feet. Although shy and unassuming, Rosa Parks held strong and well-developed views about the iniquities of segregation. Long active in the NAACP, she had served as secretary of the local branch. In the summer of 1953 she spent two weeks at Highlander Folk School in Monteagle, Tennessee, an institution which assiduously encouraged interracial amity. Founded and run by Myles Horton, Highlander flouted the local segregation laws and gave black and white Southerners a virtually unique opportunity to meet and mingle on equal terms. Rosa Parks's protest on the Cleveland Avenue bus was the purposeful act of a politically aware person. It was also part of a groundswell of discontent among Montgomery's black population. The arrest of fifteen-year-old Claudette Colvin earlier in 1955 had had the makings of a cause célèbre, but when the girl became pregnant the case was dropped. But as Virginia Durr explained, Rosa Parks was known throughout the community as a woman of unblemished character: "So as the Negroes said, 'when they messed with her they messed with the WRONG ONE,' and the whole Negro community united overnight."

Plans for a mass protest were well advanced by the time the church entered the picture, with the Women's Political Council again taking the initiative. Upon learning of the Parks arrest, Jo Ann Robinson immediately suggested a boycott and spread word of the plan through the women's club; she also ran off forty thousand handbills from a mimeograph machine at Alabama State College. The black ministers who met on the evening of December 2 to discuss the boycott were confronted with a fait accompli. And it was not until December 5 that Martin Luther King became president of the boycott organization; by the time he made his first speech as leader, blacks had been off the buses for a day. The ministers took over the leadership of the boycott with obvious reluctance: the protest would never have got off the ground but for E. D. Nixon, lawyer Fred Gray, and the Women's Political Council. The fact that they selected King, a newcomer to Montgomery, to be their spokesman is perhaps the most revealing comment on the timidity of the local clergy. As one of the woman activists put it, "The ministers who didn't want the presidency of the MIA . . . were just chicken, passing the buck to Dr. King." Nevertheless, the formation of the Montgomery Improvement Association brought the preachers into the forefront of the protest, and they remained there for the duration.

Why did the leadership of the boycott pass so swiftly to clergymen? Their economic independence was obviously important: as Professor Lawrence D. Reddick of Alabama State put it, the more vulnerable teachers like himself and Jo Ann Robinson were obliged to remain "discreetly in the background." Equally impor- tant, ministers were pushed to the forefront because the principal activists, Robinson, Nixon, and Lewis, realized that blacks could be far more effectively mobilized for mass action through the church than through secular organizations. The existing political clubs were small and disproportionately middle-class. They were also, quite often, at loggerheads. As Rufus Lewis put it, "It was a small group working over here for this reason and another small group working over there for that rea- son. . . . They were not thinking of bringing in the mass of the folks." E. D. Nixon agreed with this assessment: the established leadership had been fragmented, cliquish, and quarrelsome. The church, by contrast, extended throughout the community, bridging political factions and spanning political classes. As an organizational tool it was second to none. In a city with neither a black radio station nor a widely read black newspaper, the church provided the information network. It also provided the meeting places, the fundraising machinery, and the means of organizing an alternative transportation system.

The church also possessed unique prestige. It was the oldest and most respected institution in the black South. Central to their culture, the symbol of their histori- cal experience, the expression of their sublimated hopes and aspirations, the church gave blacks solidarity, self-identity, and self-respect. When it came to arousing and manipulating an audience, the black preacher knew few rivals. "I had never truly understood the term 'collective experience,'" wrote sociologist John Dollard in 1937, "until participating in a well-planned Negro revival service." Through the church, the boycott harnessed the emotionalism and theatricality of black religion. The morale-boosting mass meetings, with their hymns, sermons, and "pep talks," provided entertainment and a sense of involvement. "With the help of those preach- ers who could preach and those other folks who could pray," remembered the Reverend S. S. Seay, "we kept the churches filled." Its links with the church gave the boycott coherence, respectability, and religious fervor.

It might still be wondered why the black ministers of Montgomery, with their record of political passivity, accepted the leadership that was thrust upon them in this way. They did so, in part, because they did not anticipate the herculean task that lay before them. Most, King included, were skeptical about the boycott's chances of success. Had the first day proved a flop, they doubtless would have quietly but quickly disengaged themselves. But with the buses practically empty and support for the protest solid, they had little choice but to continue. The obstinacy of the white officials and the enthusiasm of the black population trapped the ministers in their leadership role: if they dropped out now they would be branded as cowards and traitors.

As the boycott went from strength to strength, the ministers began to enjoy their new role. By early 1956 the protest was attracting national and international publicity. Although many of the news stories focused on King—a fact which caused some jealousy and resentment—the other leaders shared in the limelight; initially cagey about revealing their identities, they now enjoyed the prestige conferred by media coverage. As the authorities resorted to repression, the MIA's leaders won the respect and affection of the black population: when the city indicted them under Alabama's rusty antiboycott law, they did not wait to be arrested but gave themselves up. They were "laughing and slapping each other" as they turned themselves in, wrote Virginia Durr, "and saying, 'Man, man, where you bin, must have slept late,' and then all dying laughing." Arresting the leaders had been precisely the thing needed to make the protest more united and determined. At a packed church meeting after the arrests, about two thousand blacks vowed "by thundering stamping applause" to continue the boycott. Each repressive act by white officialdom tightened the bonds of pride and trust between the preachers and the people. . . .

The inauguration of King's birthday as a national holiday in 1986 prompts the obvious question: what did King and SCLC achieve? Their outstanding victory, the Voting Rights Act, has wrought a remarkable change in the South's political landscape. Between 1964 and 1975, the black electorate increased from 2 million to 3.8 million. In Alabama, black registration increased from 19.3 to 58.1 percent; in Georgia, from 27.4 to 56.3 percent; and in Mississippi, from 6.7 to 67.4 percent. By 1976, black registration across the South stood at 63.1 percent, only five percentage points below the white level. The number of black elected officials had climbed to 1,913, a larger total than the rest of the nation put together. In the cities and in parts of the Black Belt, some striking political changes have occurred: the election of a black sheriff in Lowndes County and a black mayor in Birmingham testify to the success of the civil rights movement.

But that success is a limited one. Blacks are still grossly underrepresented in the halls of government. By 1980, the number of black elected officials had risen to 2,458, yet blacks still held a mere 3 percent of the South's elective offices while constituting one-fifth of the South's population. The Voting Rights Act survived the Nixon administration's attempt to weaken its scope; indeed, in several important respects it has been strengthened. In 1975, moreover, a majority of Southern congressmen voted to renew the act for a further seven years. Nevertheless, there is convincing evidence that whites have persevered in their attempts to minimize the impact of the black vote. Although the barriers to black registration have all but disappeared, new obstacles to fair representation crop up in the guise of "at-large" city and county elections, multimember legislative districts, gerrymandered political boundaries, and a host of other more or less sophisticated methods of nullifying or diluting the black vote. Only section 5 of the Voting Rights Act, enforced by a vigilant federal judiciary, inhibits the widespread adoption of such discriminatory devices. Legislation cannot, however, eliminate individual prejudice. There is ample reason to believe that white racism continues to restrict black representation, by and large, to areas with black majorities or near majorities. This appears to be equally true, moreover, in the North. Taking the United States as a whole, the 5,606 blacks who held elective office in 1983 comprised a little over one percent of all elected officials. Yet blacks make up fully 12 percent of the total population.

The relatively small number of black elected officials, however, understates the influence of the emergent black vote in the South. Even when they lack the numbers to elect a member of their own race, black voters can frequently defeat white candidates or, conversely, supply their margin of victory. Had the racial polarization of the 1960s become the dominant characteristic of Southern politics, then blacks would be an impotent and isolated minority. Indeed, the "lily-white" strategy pursued by nascent Republican organizations in Georgia, South Carolina, and elsewhere seemed to presage a partisan realignment in which whites deserted the Democratic party en masse in order to reestablish their racial and political dominance. Should such a party switch occur, political scientist Numan V. Bartley predicted in 1970, "the Second Reconstruction would be followed by the rule of Bourbon Democrats, this time calling themselves Republicans."

The vigor of party competition, however, has prevented this kind of clear-cut realignment, giving blacks more room for political maneuver. The resilience of the Democratic party did not, it is true, necessarily benefit blacks. White Democrats often responded to the Republican challenge by stressing their segregationist credentials and pointedly ignoring black voters. Thus many contests witnessed two candidates, both equally conservative, attempting to outflank each other on the race issue. In Alabama, the Wallace organization proved so successful in beating off challenges from the Right that, as Alexander P. Lamis noted, it could control the Democratic nominations and steamroller the Republican opposition without any black support.

By the early 1970s it was nevertheless apparent that the kind of one-party domination that characterized Alabama was becoming exceptional. Elsewhere, party competition made the black vote too pivotal to be discounted or deliberately alienated. The lessening of overt racial tensions, moreover, slowed the white exodus from the Democratic party and paved the way for tacit but effective black-white electoral alliances. As Lamis has written, "skilful Democratic party leaders" in South Carolina and elsewhere "were quick to make a quiet accommodation with blacks," while retaining enough white support to give them winning majorities. Governors elected by this type of coalition—Jimmy Carter of Georgia, Reuben Askew of Florida, John West of South Carolina, Cliff Finch of Mississippi, Edwin Edwards of Louisiana, and many others—eschewed appeals to white prejudice, openly courted black voters, and accepted desegregation as a fait accompli. Even George Wallace, finding himself dependent on black support in his effort to recapture the governorship in 1982, played down his segregationist past and actively sought black allies. As Andrew Young put it, "It used to be Southern politics was just 'nigger' politics—a question of which candidate could 'outnigger' the other. . . . [But] now that we've got 50, 60, 70 percent of the black votes registered, everybody's proud to be associated with their black brothers and sisters." The Voting Rights Act has brought about a striking transformation in the climate, at least, of political debate.

But the kind of political realignment envisaged by SCLC's strategists has thus far failed to materialize. Although the racist demagogy that polluted political discourse during the era of the civil rights movement has largely vanished, the egalitarian rhetoric which succeeded it did not imply any commitment to radical, or even mildly redistributionist, economic policies. The nonsegregationist Democrats who assembled biracial coalitions rarely campaigned as liberals, sometimes made coded gestures to racist sentiment, and usually avoided the kind of policies that might be offensive to their conservative white supporters. The black-white coalitions of the contemporary South are therefore unstable alliances between two groups whose political views and objectives are in many respects fundamentally opposed. While blacks have consistently favored social and economic liberalism, whites of all classes have become increasingly disenchanted with federal programs which, in their eyes, benefit blacks at the expense of white taxpayers. "The low status whites are . . . Georgia's most politically conservative people," wrote Numan V. Bartley in 1970; the idea that blacks and whites would unite across class lines behind economic and social reform was "ludicrous." In 1975 Bartley and his collaborator, Hugh D. Graham, extended this conclusion to the entire South after a comprehensive survey of political trends. Whites might have conceded defeat on the segregation issue, they argued, "but . . . underlying the region's newly found racial moderation was a continuing commitment to social conservatism."

Neither the expansion of the black electorate nor the emergence of a two-party system have made the South markedly more receptive to the kind of economic radicalism espoused by SCLC. Despite—or perhaps because of—the dynamic economic growth of the "Sun Belt," the South remains the region where local taxation is most regressive, where trade unions are most feeble (every state has an anti-union "right-to-work" law), and where a disproportionate share of the nation's poor reside. The South's two-party system, Lamis concluded in 1984, had not yet provided blacks with a political structure appropriate to the "sustained promotion of their interests."

The relative political isolation of blacks becomes more apparent in the context of presidential voting. In every election since 1964, blacks found themselves allied with a minority of the white voters. With the exception of 1976, moreover, the solid Democratic vote delivered by blacks failed to offset the decline in Democratic support among whites. Blacks are thus yoked to a minority political party, and a declining minority party to boot. Far from strengthening and radicalizing the Democrats, the civil rights movement hastened the disintegration of the New Deal coalition, as both Southern whites and Northern "ethnics" abandoned their traditional allegiance to embrace the social and economic conservatism of the Republican party.

The electoral success of the Reagan-led "New Right," and the subsequent dismantling of many Great Society programs, highlight the failure of SCLC's efforts to put democratic socialism on the political agenda. The decline of organized labor—trade union membership plummeted between 1970 and 1980—effectively undermined Bayard Rustin's strategy of constructing a political majority on the basis of a Negro-labor-liberal alliance. And the likelihood of an assertive movement of the poor, of the kind King tried to initiate in 1967-68, seems remote in light of the political apathy that became increasingly characteristic of the poor during the 1970s. Voter turnouts, even in presidential elections, slumped, and "disproportionate numbers of minority, low-wage, young and female voters [have] become permanent abstentionists." In the Carter-Ford race, the national turnout dipped to 54 percent; four years later, barely 53 percent of the electorate bothered to cast ballots. Although voter turnout in the South has risen to approach the national average, there is evidence that in the South, too, an increasing number of blacks are ceasing to participate in the electoral process. From a peak of 63 percent of those eligible in 1976, black voter registration declined to 57 percent in 1980. White registration, on the other hand, continued to rise, reaching 72 percent at the time of the Carter-Reagan contest. Black political influence appears to have reached a plateau, and might even be on the wane. King's lament that "our political leaders are bereft of influence in the councils of political power" needs to be qualified, but it is still broadly accurate.

Black advances in the economic sphere have been limited and precarious. True, nonwhite workers in stable, full-time employment increased their median income from 66 percent of the white average in 1960 to 79 percent in 1978. But the high rate of irregular and part-time employment among nonwhites meant that the overall income of nonwhite male workers remained, on average, only 64 percent of the white level. Black unemployment, 15 percent in 1985, remains more than twice the rate among whites. In 1985 the median income of black families stood at only 56 percent of the white level—little improvement over the rate obtained twenty years earlier. Over a third of all black families are still classified as "poor" according to the restrictive federal definition. Dependent upon low-wage jobs and federal income-support programs, most blacks remain on the margins of the economy.

Concentrated in the declining central cities, blacks are peculiarly ill-placed to take advantage of new employment opportunities. In the suburbs of Chicago, for example, the number of jobs increased by 71 percent during the 1960s; in Chicago itself, on the other hand, total employment fell by 12 percent, although the city's population diminished by only 5 percent. With the acceleration of "white flight" and the extension of the ghetto, the quality of housing enjoyed by Chicago's blacks has markedly improved. But the racism that SCLC dramatized in 1966 still segregates the population, excluding even affluent blacks from the suburbs. The high-sounding promises of the Chicago Summit Agreement turned out to be worthless. Faced with a 1969 court order requiring it to locate new public housing outside the ghetto, the Chicago Housing Authority refused to build any accommodation at all until another court order, in 1973, compelled it to do so. Black marches through Marquette Park in 1976 evoked the same kind of hostility that greeted SCLC ten years earlier. In Chicago, as in other cities, the impact of the 1968 Civil Rights Act has been negligible. Housing segregation "persists on a massive scale," writes one authority, "virtually unaffected by racial changes in other realms."

In the sphere of foreign policy, SCLC's influence has been equally evanescent. The view that SCLC helped to end the war in Vietnam is hard to sustain. America's withdrawal from Vietnam, moreover, disproved the notion that resources previously devoted to war and defense would be transferred to nonmilitary use. Military spending and rearmament has carried on apace; the money "saved" on Vietnam did not help blacks and poor people. As Bayard Rustin put it, "The peace windfall never materialized." The Carter administration promised a new approach to world affairs, stressing the value of nonintervention, human rights, and disarmament. Within two years, however, it reverted to traditional Cold War policies. With the election of Ronald Reagan, defense spending escalated sharply and foreign policy regressed to the dogmatic antiradicalism of the Truman-Eisenhower years.

It might be argued that blacks in the South destroyed segregation only to discover what blacks in the North already knew: that laws against discrimination represented an unfulfilled promise, not a representation of fact. A dispassionate analysis might also conclude that in abolishing segregated public accommodations, the civil right movement, to quote Bayard Rustin, "affected institutions which are relatively peripheral to the American socio-economic order and to the fundamental conditions of life of the Negro people." Indeed, Rustin contended that the halfhearted white resistance to desegregation reflected the fact that Jim Crow was anachronistic and economically redundant: the structure of segregation was "imposing but hollow."

There is a danger, however, of slighting SCLC's achievements by underestimating the depth and duration of the white opposition to desegregation. It is true that many of SCLC's battles concerned issues that were mainly symbolic: the humiliation involved in being confined to the back of the bus, being addressed by one's given name, continually seeing signs stating "white only." Yet the tenacity with which whites defended these symbols of domination suggest that in attacking segregation, the civil rights movement struck at the heart of the Southern caste system. Desegregation and universal suffrage did not end discrimination or eliminate poverty, but they did knock away the two main props of white supremacy—and the destruction of institutionalized white supremacy was the essential precondition for black advancement.

Blacks achieved dignity as a people not only in removing the South's racist totems, but also in the means whereby they attained that goal. Although few shared King's total commitment to nonviolence, the examples of Lebanon and Northern Ireland point to the logic and validity of his philosophy. It would be facile to suppose that nonviolence can be utilized at will, in any given situation. The violence of a Northern Ireland stems from deeply rooted nationalisms, and it was precisely the *absence* of a strong nationalistic tradition among Southern blacks that made nonviolence a feasible strategy. SCLC did not impose an alien philosophy upon a puzzled and skeptical people, but skillfully attuned its methods and its message to the idealism of the black church. Its articulation of the Exodus myth drew upon a folk tradition that went back to slavery days. SCLC worked with the grain of Southern black history and culture, not against it.

No one understood that history and culture, nor expressed the aspirations of black Southerners, better than Martin Luther King, Jr. SCLC itself was far more than King, but his death revealed how completely he dominated it through intellect, personality, moral example, and organizational skill. King raised at least half of SCLC's funds virtually single-handed. Only he could move and influence such a variety and number of Americans. None of his colleagues matched the depth of his commitment to nonviolence. King's courage, dedication, and idealism have often been noted. But he also possessed more subtle qualities of leadership. He had the ability to use people—not in a manipulative or exploitative manner, but in the sense of utilizing their talents to further an ideal. Unrelentingly self-critical himself, he tolerated weakness, frailty, and error in his colleagues for the sake of harnessing their strengths. He was also willing to let other people use him if he thought it served a constructive purpose. Young and others thought King irritatingly indecisive, but his fondness for consultation and debate strengthened his decision making. Aware that people were constantly seeking to influence and manipulate him, he sought out different opinions. He took few steps without being advised of the possible consequences. He therefore blamed no one for his mistakes but himself.

Why did SCLC fail to acquire the solidity and stability of the NAACP? Ella Baker thought that it started out one the wrong footing with its King-centered structure. Levison believed that SCLC should have recruited a dues-paying mass membership, thus freeing it from its precarious dependence upon white contributors. According to Wachtel, SCLC ought to have stayed in the South, to consolidate and fully exploit its victories there. Rustin blamed SCLC's decline on, among other things, the absence of a democratic framework within the organization. King's advisers all agreed that the decision to go to Chicago was a costly and avoidable error.

Yet the people who designed and built SCLC had been less interested in constructing an organization than in structuring a nascent movement. Rustin, Levison, and Baker viewed organization as a means to an end, not an end in itself. During their long careers as political activists they had worked with or through a variety of organizations and movements, including labor unions, pacifist groups, the NAACP—and, yes, the Communist party—in their quest for radical change. King viewed SCLC in the same pragmatic light. If SCLC ceased to serve as a vehicle for reform, he believed, it would lose its purpose. Time after time, he placed organizational self-interest and self-preservation after the pursuit of his ideals; "If I lose the fight," he one said, "then SCLC will die anyway." SCLC did not fail: it may have lost the struggle for economic justice, but it won its original battle against white supremacy. Indeed, by opening up avenues of political advancement it became, to some extent, a victim of its own success. Nothing was more natural than SCLC's decline, for it derived its strength from an insurgency which it shaped and guided but did not create. Without the power of marching feet behind it, SCLC lost its dynamism. "We are a movement," said one of its staff, "not an organization."

High Priest of the Anti-Civil Rights Movement:
The Calling of Sam Bowers

CHARLES MARSH

SOURCE:Marsh, Charles, *God's Long Summer: Stories of Faith and Civil Rights.* Copyright © 1997 by Princeton University Press. Reprinted by permission of Princeton University Press.

The Making of a Christian Militant

When Sam Bowers surveyed America's social landscape from his beloved Mississippi in early 1964, he did not simply lament the changing South—the desecration of "sovereign" southern states, their time-honored practices attacked by liberal politicians, northern media elites, and civil rights workers. The world Bowers saw was more menacing and full of dangers greater than even these assaults on caste and custom. Right before his eyes, on the alluvial soil of the very heart of the Confederacy, appeared all the signs of a two-thousand-year war between the idolatrous agents of Baal and the soldiers of the one true God, the "Galilean Jesus Christ."

As Imperial Wizard of the White Knights of Ku Klux Klan, Bowers ruled over a four-year campaign of pervasive white terrorism during which he was suspected of orchestrating at least nine murders, seventy-five bombings of black churches, and three hundred assaults, bombings, and beatings. From 1964 until his conviction in 1967 on federal civil rights violations in the triple murder of Michael Schwerner, James Chaney, and Andrew Goodman, Bowers was the animating force behind white Mississippi's journey into the heart of militant rage, the Kurtz at the heart of darkness of the anti-civil rights movement. Standing before what he considered a world-historical moment, Bowers believed he was called by God to accomplish the urgent task of eliminating the "heretics." He described the moment in a recruiting poster that appeared on telephone poles, church bulletin boards, café windows, and front porches throughout the state:

> The administration of our National Government is now under the actual control of atheists who are Bolsheviks by nature. As dedicated agents of Satan, they are absolutely determined to destroy Christian Civilization and all Christians. . . . [Our] members are Christians who are anxious to preserve not only their souls for all Eternity, but who are MILITANTLY DETERMINED, God willing, to save their lives, and the Life of this Nation, in order that their descendants shall enjoy the same, full, God-given blessings of True Liberty that we have been permitted to enjoy up to now.
>
> We do not accept Jews, because they reject Christ, and through the machinations of their International Banking Cartel, are at the root-center of what we call "Communism" today.
>
> We do not accept Papists, because they bow to a Roman dictator, in direct violation of the First Commandment and the True American Spirit of Responsible, Individual Liberty.
>
> We do not accept Turks, Mongols, Tarters, Orientals, Negroes, nor any other person who native background of culture is foreign to the Anglo-Saxon system of Government by responsible, FREE, Individual Citizens.
>
> If you are a Christian, American Anglo-Saxon who can understand the simple

Truth of this Philosophy, you belong in the White Knights of the Ku Klux Klan of Mississippi. We need your help right away. Get your Bible out and Pray! You will hear from us.

When Bowers described the deluge of civil rights workers and federal law enforcement agents in the summer of 1964 as a "crucifixion" of the "innocent people" of God, the stage was set for a holy crusade to purge the land of those who had betrayed his Lord. Bowers resurrected the Klan's Christian identity with a fanatic's zeal and, as journalist Wyn Craig Wade wrote, "restored to the hackneyed word *crusade* its thirteenth-century purpose of murdering the infidels." He was determined to fight the battle until the bitter end.

Sam Holloway Bowers, Jr., was born in New Orleans on August 6, 1924. His biography defies stereotypes of klansmen as backwoods, semi-literate rednecks. His father was a salesman from Gulfport. His mother, the former Evangeline Payton, was the daughter of a wealthy planter. Bowers was supremely proud of his family pedigree. His grandfather, Eaton J. Bowers, was a prominent Mississippi attorney who had been admitted to the bar at the age of nineteen and served three terms in the United States Congress from 1903 to 1911; he was the most revered male figure in Bowers's life. Bowers also claimed to be a direct descendent of "the first president of the first constituted legislative assembly on this continent, the Virginia House of Burgesses." For three generations, the Bowers family were practicing Methodists; Dr. Charles Betts Galloway, (the father of the well-loved Methodist bishop of Mississippi from 1886-1909, Charles Betts Galloway, Jr.) And Bowers's great-grandfather, Eaton Jackson Bowers, Sr., married the sisters Adelaide and Sallie Lee Dinkins. The grandfather Eaton J. Bowers had been a trustee and steward in his Methodist church in Bay St. Louis, Mississippi. In fact, Sam Bowers himself might have gone on to Millsaps College and become "a great Methodist man" had he not early suspected that even the most benign authorities posed grave personal dangers to him. Baptist theology and polity, with its happy distrust of creeds and hierarchy, better fit his anti-clerical bent. In 1966 Bowers joined the Hillcrest Baptist Church in Laurel, Mississippi, where he taught (and continues to teach) an adult Sunday school class.

Bowers's parents were divorced when he was fourteen. After a series of short stays with his father in Florida, the Mississippi Gulf Coast, and New Orleans, he moved to Jackson, Mississippi, in the summer of 1939. His mother Evangeline took a secretarial job at the Agricultural and Industrial Board and later at the Department of Motor Vehicles. In Jackson, Bowers and his mother lived in an apartment on North West Street near the state capitol, a few blocks away from Jackson's largest churches, including the Capitol Street Methodist church and First Baptist Church. In the nearby Belhaven neighborhood, Ross Barnett, the successful attorney who would later become governor as a die-hard segregationist, lived in a house on Fairview Street; as did William Simmons, the man who later ruled over the Citizens' Council of Mississippi. On Pinehurst Street, Eudora Welty had settled into her brilliant writing life, have returned from New York in the early 1930s to live in the neighborhood of her childhood.

Bowers's mother was a woman of strict discipline and deliberate erudition, who insisted he learn from her example. He would mind his manners and his language. Certain forms of civility would be expected of the boy at all times: polite forms of address, eloquence in conversation, refined tastes—nothing less would be suitable to his upbringing and lineage. Should an ungrammatical phrase or sentence pass from his mouth, it would not be tolerated without punishment. Evangeline believed that eloquence and skillful rhetoric made a child virtuous; "purify a young man's speech, and his heart and mind will follow," Bowers recalls his mother saying. Yet he believed that her discipline was tempered with genuine affection. She wanted her son to seek learning not solely out of a sense of duty but for the sake of a higher principle. Although she was adamant that the boy abstain from reading trash books and dime-store novels, it was the "majesty of language" that fueled her demands. "She did not dogmatically state her views, but would say things like, 'you would be so much better off reading the classics.' She had a gentle way about her. She was a master psychologist in this manner." With the same persuasion she attempted to keep her son interested in his school life. "I know you aren't terribly interested in school," she would say, "but please try to do better. These years will pass soon enough." Yet notwithstanding his mother's admonitions and lofty expectations, he found it impossible to treat his school teachers with the respect they demanded.

By the time Bowers entered Jackson's Central High School, he had begun to feel threatened by the "adult world" of his teachers, refusing to conform to their standards of appropriate behavior. In fact, he took "secret pleasure" in performing poorly in school; he enjoyed thwarting his teachers' efforts to instruct. They tried to reassure Evangeline that her son had "so much potential if he'd just apply himself"; nonetheless, it gave him "some sense of power" to confound and aggravate intrusive adult authority. He would skip school and race boxcars on a hilly road near Millsaps College. He defied anyone to take measures of discipline against him. "The adult authorities could not socially stigmatize me because I succeeded in frustrating the adult world," he said. And this was crucial, especially at a time when he was feeling "almost fully powerless and at the mercy of stronger personalities"—feeling intruded upon, as though outsiders were interfering with his "childhood mission." His mission, even in these early years, was to preserve innocence before the crushing blows of nihilistic authority; to defy the authority of those who were "bent on making impositions" on him. "Many great men, like Douglas MacArthur, were really just mama's boys," Bowers once said. "They were children to the end."

Yet, as he soon discovered, a child "cannot take too much overlooking or imposition before he must rage out against those powers which are seeking to tear him away from his equanimity." By age fifteen Bowers was deeply resentful of all authority figures, whose degeneracy he claims to have felt with a visceral intensity. He exhibited his anger and frustration in a kind of hyperactivity that sometimes gave way to temper tantrums and other times to wild and exaggerated humor. "The adult authorities were bent on making impositions on my childhood, and I despised them for it." Bowers abruptly returned to New Orleans in the fall of his senior year—at his father's insistence—and attended Fortier High School. But he was so furious for having been taken away from Jackson that by the middle of the fall semester he dropped out of high school and joined the Navy—even against his mother's wishes—shortly after Pearl Harbor in December of 1941.

Bowers would later understand his childhood abhorrence of adult imposition— or "outside agitation"—as a "predestined formation," which prepared him well for future battles with "the alien prophets of Baal." However, he had to undergo a series of formative religious experiences before his militant vocation became clear to him—before he was able to understand that God had singled him out for a high and holy calling. The first took place just after V-J Day, in August of 1945. Having been stationed with the Navy in the Pacific, Bowers had discovered that the discipline imposed by the military was able to accommodate his visceral rage against outside agitation and put that rage (at least temporarily) to positive, mostly patriotic, use. Discipline or authority did not necessarily signal conformity and self-disintegration, rather it could channel hostility toward the elimination of specific, justifiable targets. Whereas the adult, "academic" authorities seemed to persecute Bowers "for the sake of their own gratuitous pleasure and gratification," the Navy gave him a reason to accept discipline—for "the country's honor and health were at stake." On this day after the news of the Japanese surrender and the end of World War II, Bowers got off duty and climbed to the top of the ship's deck. It was a clear, blue morning, he remembers—the sea had never looked so beautiful. Recalling the immense sacrifice his countrymen had made for the sake of freedom, and his comrades who had died in combat, tears came to his eyes. Full of sadness, yet deeply grateful for his privilege to stand before this moment, Bowers uttered the prayer: "I thank you Lord. There were many better men than I who perished in this war. I don't know why you spared my life, but I appreciate it. And for the rest of my life I'll seek to understand the purpose of your mercy, and to live accordingly." He sensed the great, incomprehensible mystery of God's sovereign plan, and the growing recognition of his unique role in it. He was ready to pursue an immense destiny, marked by the Almighty God himself.

Bowers was honorably discharged as Machinist Mate First Class in December 1945. For the next two years he studied engineering at Tulane University and the University of Southern California (although he did not receive a bachelor's degree until his incarceration in the mid-1970s at McNeil Island federal penitentiary in Washington state, when he completed formal theological studies through Pacific Lutheran University's prison program.) In the late 1940s Bowers returned to Laurel from the West Coast, where he tried his hand without much success in various business ventures before setting up a vending machine operation called the Sambo Amusement Company. He began reading Nazi and racist philosophy and the novels of Thomas Dixon, which he later required his fellow klansmen to read. Such Dixon novels as *The Leopard's Spots* and *The Clansmen*—which D. W. Griffith would make into his epochal film, *The Birth of a Nation*—offered depictions of "African barbarism" and black sexual degeneracy in contrast to "God's first law of life," the "white man's instinct of racial purity."

Even friends who shared Bowers's interests and genuinely enjoyed his company found him alternately eccentric and frightening. Stockpiled in his living quarters were original manuscripts on religion and political philosophy, racing car paraphernalia, guns and ammunition, a collection of masks (large rubber caricatures of presidents, movie stars and blacks) and his wardrobe of fashionable suits and ties. One acquaintance described his habit of wearing a swastika armband and of clicking his heels in front of his dog, saluting the canine with a "Heil Hitler!" Bowers's unpredictable capacity for anger always kept other men at a distance, even at times his roommate and best friend, Robert Larson, who accompanied him to Laurel from California and shared his living quarters in the back of the company's clapboard building. When Bowers was angry, a former colleague noted, he would "stalk rapidly back and forth, fists clenched, countenance . . . fierce enough to make any target of his rage quickly back off."

The second formative experience in the development of Bowers's priestly self-consciousness proved more specifically religious, and more commanding than the earlier. In 1955, he was arrested for illegal possession of liquor—a demeaning ordeal for a man who took pride in his aristocratic lineage. He pleaded guilty and was fined one hundred dollars. Bowers's arrest, combined with the collapse of another business venture, brought him to the brink of self-destruction. He felt unraveled and desperate. Family memories haunted him. The brilliant victory at war was now darkened by his own disjointed past and an unpromising future—unfinished degrees at two universities, job failures, career uncertainties, personal fears, and an arrest. "Sam had failed me totally—economically, personally, ethically, and in every real way," he recalled. "I felt totally crushed by life, and wanted to destroy everything, including myself." He looked on God "with absolute antipathy."

But all that changed in an experience of "overwhelming grace." Like Paul's conversion on the Damascus road or Martin Luther's encounter with his St. Ann while walking along an empty road during a thunderstorm, Bowers was also on a journey. On a drive along a two-lane highway on a late summer afternoon in south Mississippi, contemplating suicide and equipped for the task, Bowers felt suddenly transported by a power greater than he had ever before experienced. In a moment of mystical intensity, God spoke to him the words, "Don't be afraid; everything is all right." Bowers explained, "The living God made himself real to me even when I did not deserve it." It was not a vision he beheld; there was no blinding light or appearance of a holy personage. Rather, his was an "ecstatic realization." Although moments earlier he had wanted to destroy everything including himself, he now felt his whole identity melt into divine bliss. His inner anguish vanished; hope was renewed and energy restored in an experience of "unmerited grace." The effect was not to leave him blinded or in any way incapacitated. God "used his blackjack on Paul a lot more vigorously than he did on Sam," he insisted. Yet like Paul with his vision of dazzling light, strange voices, and terrifying blindness, Bowers received the clear and overwhelming conviction on which his life would be forever after based: that he had seen and witnessed the living God, that this God knew his name and had called him for a special purpose. "To be saved one must go to the point of insanity," Bowers said. One must realize there is nothing left to do but throw oneself into the hands of divine mercy, perform any task, fulfill any demand for the saving God.

Behind the wheel of his pickup truck that summer evening, Bowers discovered that God's love was wholly unmerited; that "all the horrible experiences of [his] life could be redeemed by the unbounded goodness of the one true God." He felt "on air for three days," his thoughts about suicide having given way to the new perspective his life had been given. "Sam Bowers," he resolved, "I'm going to live the rest of my life with you, but don't expect me to take you quite so seriously again. Your life is no longer your own: it is God's." With the world around him reconfigured and full of sense, he gave himself to his work, his friends, and the nurturing of his divine call.

Soon thereafter Bowers's religious identity acquired its decisive Christian character, when a young friend prevailed upon him to take a more active role in the study of Scripture. He is Bowers's account: "A boy was working with me in one of my side occupations. We supplied cigarettes to the cigarette machines around town. We would wake up early Monday mornings and make the rounds refilling the machines. This boy was always fresh from his Sunday sermon, which he always found inspiring and invigorating. In his presence, I restricted my anti-clerical venom, which I often spewed out on friends, even though I took my spirituality very seriously. We would sometimes debate certain topics, like the infallibility of Scripture, or the authorship of the New Testament books. The boy's knowledge of the Bible, though a naive one I thought, was very much alive to him. As a result of these discussions, I decided I needed to get more familiar with the Bible, so I purchased a King James Bible at the local Baptist book store. When I read the epistolary dedicatory, I realized that these guys were speaking truth—and, of course, I've always been interested in the majesty of language."

The embracing sense of divine peace that Bowers had experienced on the deck of the naval vessel and in his pickup truck epiphany he now discovered in the words of Scripture, particularly in the Elizabethan eloquence of the King James Bible. A magnificent new world opened up to him; it was as if the *sensus literalis* of Scripture gave Bowers a new way of seeing the realities of his own distinctive geographical and spiritual place. An indissoluble link with the prophets and the fiery convert Paul was forged in his religious self-understanding. These biblical writers seemed to speak directly to him. As he gave himself to the study of Scripture, Bowers began to realize that his rage (which at times dissipated only to return with new intensity) could be put in service to the work of the Lord. His anger found a religious energy and thus a warrant to the career awaiting him. No one less than Jesus Christ himself was calling him to the priestly task of preserving the purity of his blood and soil. To his education in the literature of racial superiority and cultural nationalism, Bowers added a disciplined study of the Bible. He would never stray from the conviction that he had been called according to God's high purpose. . . .

Questions for Reflection and Discussion

1. What evidence do the documents provide of the religious tension present in the civil rights movement?

2. According to James F. Findlay, Jr., what critical role did the National Council of Churches play in the early stages of the civil rights movement?

3. Adam Fairclough makes the case that Martin Luther King, Jr., and the Southern Christian Leadership Conference were important in the black community's quest for social change. On what bases does he make this argument?

4. As described by Charles Marsh, what influences prepared Sam Bowers to become a high priest of the anti-civil rights movement?

5. Were any of the four dimensions of religious tension *not* present in the civil rights movement?

Additional Readings

Branch, Taylor. *Parting the Waters: America in the King Years, 1954-63.* New York: Simon and Schuster, 1988.

_____. *Pillar of Fire: America in the King Years, 1963-65.* New York: Simon and Schuster, 1998.

Cone, James. *Martin and Malcolm and America: A Dream or a Nightmare.* Maryknoll, NY: Orbis Books, 1991.

Davis, Cyprian. *The History of Black Catholics in the United States.* New York: Crossroad, 1990.

Garrow, David. *Bearing the Cross: Martin Luther King and the Southern Christian Leadership Conference.* New York: William Morrow and Company, Inc., 1986.

_____. "Martin Luther King, Jr., and the Spirit of Leadership," *Journal of American History* 74 (Sept. 1987): 438-47.

Haley, Alex. *The Autobiography of Malcolm X.* New York: Grove Press, Inc., 1965.

Lincoln, C. Eric, ed. *The Black Experience in Religion.* New York: Anchor Books, 1974.

_____. *The Negro Pilgrimage in America: The Coming of Age of the Blackamericans.* New York: Frederick A. Praeger, Publishers, 1969.

Lischer, Richard. *The Preacher King: Martin Luther King, Jr., and the Word that Moved America.* New York: Oxford University Press, 1995.

McGreevy, John T., "Radical Justice and the People of God," *Religion and American Culture* 4 (Summer 1994): 221-54.

Nelsen, Hart M., Raytha L. Yokley, and Anne K. Nelsen. *The Black Church in America*. New York: Basic Books, Inc, Publishers, 1971.

Ochs, Stephen. *Desegregating the Altar: The Josephites and the Struggle for Black Priests*. Baton Rouge: Louisiana State University Press, 1990.

Sernett, Milton C., ed. *Afro-American Religious History: A Documentary Witness*. Durham, NC: Duke University Press, 1985.

Weisbrot, Robert. *Father Divine*. New York: Chelsea House, 1992.

Wilmore, Gayraud. *Black Religion and Black Radicalism*. Garden City, NY: Doubleday, 1972.

Chapter 16

By the early 1970s the search for American stability revealed an incomplete ecumenism filled with rancor and strife. American culture started coming apart at the seams in the previous decade, and any prior notion of a cultural consensus was now only an illusion. For religion in America it was not much different. New alliances formed across the three primary faiths in America to engage in the struggle over the meaning of America—what has come to be known as "the culture wars."

Religion and the Search for American Stability

Issue

How was American religion restructured at the close of the millennium?

"*Christian fundamentalists, Orthodox Jews, and conservative Catholics have joined forces in a fierce battle against their progressive counterparts—secularists, reform Jews, liberal Catholics and Protestants,*" remarks James Davison Hunter in Culture Wars*(1991), "as each side struggles to gain control over such fields of conflict as the family, art, education, law, and politics.*"

Indeed, the meaning of America was at the heart of nearly every discussion over American culture at the close of the millennium, as it had been for all of the final third of the twentieth century. As historian Martin Marty notes in Under God, Indivisible, 1941-1960 *(1996), the choice of many Americans in the 1950s was "centripetalism, interfaith and ecumenical activity, the common life, and consensus.*" But by 1965, American society plunged into chaos due to assassinations, burnings, and war. The consensus to which many Americans aspired in 1960 was only superficial a decade later. "*The centrifugal pattern reappeared with a vengeance after the mid-sixties,*" writes Marty.

What did all this mean for religion in America? Would common bonds and symbols of a reborn civil religion be an adequate reminder of successful, worn paths of America past? For that matter, did Americans—even religious Americans—care or wish to give attention to the past?

What is clear is that mainline Protestant churches declined in membership and attendance, and a smaller percentage of Roman Catholics attended mass, during the final decades of the twentieth century. At the same time, it was equally clear that America was not less religious at the start of the twenty-first century. Conservative evangelicalism realized new growth, and increased interest abounded in sects, the occult, and a variety of nontraditional approaches to Christianity. With the rise of individualism during the late twentieth century, the search for American stability in the midst of a declining sense of community presented the nation with an enormous challenge. For the culture wars included sharp and protracted skirmishes over the place of racial minorities, women, homosexuals, and nontraditional religious practitioners within the ever-broadening scope of American religion.

If it seems that the critical issues of American religion at the outset of the twenty-first century are a mirror reflection of the critical issues at the start of the American odyssey in the seventeenth century, it is probably more truth than imagination. To be sure, the four interrelated dimensions of religious tension in America's early religious experience are still with us today.

Documents

In the first document, the California Supreme Court ruled in the case People v. Woody *that Navajo Indians who used peyote in their religious rites were not in violation of the state's narcotics laws. The second selection introduces some of the basic precepts of Zen Buddhism, which had the greatest appeal of all Oriental religions in America during the 1970s. In the third selection, church history professor Richard F. Lovelace addresses the subject of active homosexuality within religious diversity in the late twentieth century. Lawrence N. Jones of Harvard University's school of religion discusses in the fourth document a new agenda for black churches for the 1980s and beyond. Excommunicated Mormon Sonia Johnson responds in the fifth document to the summons to trial in Virginia following her open support for the Equal Rights Amendment. In the sixth selection, Chicano priest Frank Ponce calls upon the Catholic Church to be more inclusive—"enculturation," he calls it. The final document reveals the tension over inclusion of women in the Orthodox Jewish community.*

1. The Native American Church, Peyote, and *People* v. *Woody,* 1964

SOURCE: *People* v. *Woody* 394 P.2d 813, 1964.

The plant Lophophora williamsii, a small, spineless cactus, found in the Rio Grande Valley of Texas and northern Mexico, produces peyote, which grows in small buttons on the top of the cactus. Peyote's principal constituent is mescaline. When taken internally by chewing the buttons or drinking a derivative tea, peyote produces several types of hallucinations, depending primarily upon the user. In most subjects it causes extraordinary vision marked by bright and kaleidoscopic colors, geometric patterns, or scenes involving humans or animals. In others it engenders hallucinatory symptoms similar to those produced in cases of schizophrenia, dementia praecox, or paranoia. Beyond its hallucinatory effect, peyote renders for most users a heightened sense of comprehension; it fosters a feeling of friendliness toward other persons.

Peyote, as we shall see, plays a central role in the ceremony and practice of the Native American Church, a religious organization of Indians. Although the church claims no official prerequisites to membership, no written membership rolls, and no recorded theology, estimates of its membership range from 30,000 to 250,000, the wide variance deriving from differing definitions of a "member." As the anthropologists have ascertained through conversations with members, the theology of the church combines certain Christian teachings with the belief that peyote embodies the Holy Spirit and that those who partake of peyote enter into direct contact with God.

Peyotism discloses a long history. A reference to the religious use of peyote in Mexico appears in Spanish historical sources as early as 1560. Peyotism spread from Mexico to the United States and Canada; American anthropologists describe it as well established in this country during the latter part of the nineteenth century. Today, Indians of many tribes practice Peyotism. Despite the absence of recorded dogma, the several tribes follow surprisingly similar ritual and theology; the practices of Navajo members in Arizona practically parallel those of adherents in California, Montana, Oklahoma, Wisconsin, and Saskatchewan.

The "meeting," a ceremony marked by the sacramental use of peyote, composes the cornerstone of the peyote religion. The meeting convenes in an enclosure and continues from sundown Saturday to sunrise Sunday. To give thanks for the past good fortune or find guidance for future conduct, a member will "sponsor" a meeting and supply to those who attend both the peyote and the next morning's breakfast. The "sponsor," usually but not always the "leader," takes charge of the meeting; he decides the order of events and the amount of peyote to be consumed. Although the individual leader exercises an absolute control of the meeting, anthropologists report a striking uniformity of its ritual.

A meeting connotes a solemn and special occasion. Whole families attend together, although children and young women participate only by their presence. Adherents don their finest clothing, usually suits for men and fancy dresses for the women, but sometimes ceremonial Indian costumes. At the meeting the members pray, sing, and make ritual use of drum, fan, eagle bone, whistle, rattle and prayer cigarette, the symbolic emblems of their faith. The central event, of course, consists of the use of peyote in quantities sufficient to produce an hallucinatory state.

At an early but fixed stage in the ritual the members pass around a ceremonial bag of peyote buttons. Each adult may take four, the customary number, or take none. The participants chew the buttons, usually with some difficulty because of extreme bitterness; later, at a set time in the ceremony any member may ask for more peyote; occasionally a member may take as many as four more buttons. At sunrise on Sunday the ritual ends; after a brief outdoor prayer, the host and his family serve breakfast. Then the members depart. By morning the effects of the peyote disappear; the users suffer no aftereffects.

Although peyote serves as a sacramental symbol similar to bread and wine in certain Christian churches, it is more than a sacrament. Peyote constitutes in itself an object of worship; prayers are directed to it much as prayers are devoted to the Holy Ghost. On the other hand, to use peyote for nonreligious purposes is sacrilegious. Members of the church regard peyote also as a "teacher" because it induces a feeling of brotherhood with other members; indeed, it enables the participant to experience the Deity. Finally, devotees treat peyote as a "protector." Much as a Catholic carries his medallion, an Indian G.I. often wears around his neck a beautifully beaded pouch containing one large peyote button.

The record thus establishes that the application of the statutory prohibition of the use of peyote results in a virtual inhibition of the practice of defendants' religion. To forbid the use of peyote is to remove the theological heart of Peyotism.

We have weighted the competing values represented in this case on the symbolic scale of constitutionality. On the one side we have placed the weight of freedom of religion as protected by the First Amendment; on the other, the weight of the state's "compelling interest." Since the use of peyote incorporates the essence of the religious expression, the first weight is heavy. Yet the use of peyote presents only slight danger to the state and to the enforcement of its laws; the second weight is relatively light. The scale tips in favor of the constitutional protection.

We know that some will urge that it is more important to subserve the rigorous enforcement of the narcotic laws than to carve out of them an exception for a few believers in a strange faith. They will say that the exception may produce problems of enforcement and that the dictate of the state must overcome the beliefs of a minority of Indians. But the problems of enforcement here do not inherently differ from those of other situations which call for the detection of fraud. On the other hand, the right to free religious expression embodies a precious heritage of our history. In a mass society, which presses at every point toward conformity, the protection of a self-expression, however unique, of the individual and the group becomes ever more important. The varying currents of the subcultures that flow into the mainstream of our national life give it depth and beauty. We preserve a greater value than an ancient tradition when we protect the rights of the Indians who honestly practiced an old religion in using peyote one night at a meeting in a desert hogan near Needles, California.

The judgment is reversed.

2. Zen Buddhism in America, 1976

SOURCE: By Gary Snyder, from *The Real Work: Interviews & Talks, 1964-1979,* copyright © 1980 by Gary Snyder. Reprinted by permission of New Directions Publishing Corp.

. . . I stay with Zen, because sitting, doing zazen, is a primary factor. Sitting is the act of looking-in. Meditation is fundamental, you can't subtract anything from that. It's so fundamental that it's been with us for forty or fifty thousand years in one form or another. It's not even something that is specifically Buddhist. It's as fundamental a human activity as taking naps is to wolves, or soaring in circles is to hawks and eagles. It's how you contact the basics and the base of yourself. And Zen has cut away a lot of frills, to keep that foremost.

Now the completion of this is understood very clearly in the Tibetan tradition when they speak of the three mysteries: body, speech, and mind. This is fundamental Buddhism to me; it's fundamental to existence itself, and Buddhism is about existence. The three things that are closest to us—our bodies, our minds, and our language—are the three things we know least about, that we pay least attention to, that we use as our tools throughout our lifetimes to various relatively limited ends, including survival, but there's very little attention to the fact of existence of this in its own right. A simple message of the teaching is that much of the pain, suffering, confusion, and contradiction you encounter in your own life is simply caused by not paying attention to what you have closest to you from the beginning and then using it well: body, speech, and mind. The three practices are then: sitting meditation, for exploring the mind; singing or chantings or poetry or mantras, for exploring speech and voice; and yoga, or dance, or hoeing the garden and gathering firewood, for the exploration of the body. We all do all these things, so all that needs to be added to that is a real awareness and attention in the doing, and a realization of the marvelousness, the mysteriousness, of all these simple acts, which again comes back to the sitting meditation, because it's at that point that you can really nurture and contact the marvelousness — and also the tiresomeness [in your life]. . . .

For myself personally all I would add to that are some very ancient and to me beautiful and useful ways of handling things: attention to place; gratitude to the physical universe and to all the other beings for what they exchange with you; good health, good luck, good crops. Basic old-style religion.

3. Homosexuality and the Church, 1978

SOURCE: From *Homosexuality and the Church* by Richard F. Lovelace. Pp. 10-13. Copyright © 1979 by Fleming H. Revell Company, a division of Baker Book House. Used by permission.

. . . it is not a confession of theological bankruptcy to make a careful study of the arguments defending active homosexuality which are being commended to the church. The church is periodically responsible to examine any new data—medical, psychological, exegetical, or theological—which seem to call her previous understanding into question, and to give them a fresh and fair evaluation. As a Roman Catholic bishop engaged in this kind of study remarked, "To listen is not necessarily to approve, to report is not necessarily to endorse, to study is not necessarily to change, but not to consult is to fail."

Recent developments both in our society and in the church make it apparent that the laity and Christian leaders must face this issue and deal with it. The struggle for gay civil rights which has been escalating since the 1960s triggered a continuing national controversy in the aftermath of Anita Bryant's campaign in Dade County, Florida, in the spring of 1977. The church needs to assess its response to Miss Bryant's Christian motivation and her strategy. A whole new denomination of active homosexuals who profess to be Evangelical and Pentecostal in their theology, the Metropolitan Community Church, has gathered congregations in every major city in America. Its missionary outreach has been met with an amazing numerical response within the gay community. How is the church to regard this phenomenon? Should it condemn this ministry as the effect of a false gospel, or learn to expand its own ministry by observing the eager response of gay persons to those who are presenting a partial Gospel but are reaching out in compassion? Virginia Mollenkott and Letha Scanzoni, two writers who profess to be Evangelical in outlook and who have done important work in developing biblical arguments in support of feminism, have published a book advocating homosexual marriage. Should the church regard this approach as a representative Evangelical position? How will Evangelicals themselves respond to leaders among them who elect to follow this approach?

But the examination of this issue may not only be necessary for the church; it may be advantageous. Costly and unsettling as it is, this study may produce as many incidental benefits as the space program. Like the indulgence issue in the time of Luther, the problem of homosexuality touches the nerve of many crucial spiritual and theological questions. It also grips the attention of the laity and threatens the economic base of clergy and administrators. Thus it is possible that reformation and renewal of many aspects of the church's life and thought can develop around the consultations considering this issue. Approval of the ordination of active homosexuals is only the logical outcome of trends in the church's theology, biblical understanding, and sexual mores which have been developing over a long period with little close scrutiny among the mass of the laity. This issue sharply dramatizes the direction of these trends and makes their outcome clearly visible. Thus the church is being forced to face up to the full implications of many shifting theological currents to which it has adjusted during this century and come up with clear answers to questions like the following:

• Is the Bible still the supreme guide to Christian faith and practice? What is the role in ethical guidance of reason, experience, and the Holy Spirit? How shall we respond to new methods of interpreting the Bible which contradict our previous understanding of its teaching, or which urge us to strike out alone and put aside that teaching?

- Are all men accepted by God because of the love and grace of Jesus Christ, regardless of their attitudes toward Him and their actions among men? Or must an individual turn to God in a response of repentant faith in Christ, leading to continued growth in holiness, in order to accept the offer of God's forgiveness and enter the sphere of real Christianity?

- Is situation ethics an adequate guide to the meaning of repentance and the fulfillment of God's will? Should the church's sexual ethic in the late twentieth century endorse all behavior which seems loving, whether or not it occurs within the traditional limits of gender, marriage, and the family?

- Can the church tolerate a diversity of convictions and life-styles in its sexual morality? Or is it responsible to call for some degree of uniformity?

If the leadership and laity of the church are motivated by the present struggle to ask these questions seriously, the degree of spiritual and theological awakening which results will more than compensate for the expense and the uneasiness involved in the study process. And there will be other dimensions in which the church will be awakened and renewed. Most importantly, it will discover that its own unconscious fear and hatred of gay persons has led it to join our society's unchristian rejection of homosexuals and therefore to neglect mission and ministry to the gay community. As new ministries involving openly repentant homosexual leaders emerge, the conventional self-righteousness of respectable parishioners will be transformed into the fellowship of forgiven sinners who are broken in the awareness of their own needs, and thus sensitive and compassionate in reaching out to help the needs of others. As different groups of Christians in the church are forced into conversation about the homosexual issue, they will be forced to face honestly the theological diversity within the large denominations. They will be led out of pluralism-in-isolation toward a healthier condition to pluralism-in-dialogue, speaking the truth to one another in love, and seeking the unity of the Spirit in mutual apprehension of the mind of Christ. Old theological battle lines will break down, leading to the establishment of a new theological consensus in the church, a consensus which will be more sensitively committed both to biblical revelation and to the need for redemptive transformation both of individuals and society. Crisis and conflict over the ordination of homosexuals will turn out to be grains of sand which produce pearls in the church's life and experience. The homosexual issue is a problem which God has set before the church, the solution of which must involve a thorough-going tune-up of theology, spirituality, ministry, and mission. . . .

4. The Black Churches: A New Agenda, 1979

SOURCE: Copyright 1979 Christian Century Foundation. Reprinted with permission from the April 19, 1979, issue of *Christian Century*.

As Bishop John Hurst Adams of the African Methodist Episcopal Church observed recently, black churches are operating essentially on the agenda given to them by their founders. The first agenda of early black American congregations and then of emergent denominations included (1) the proclamation of the gospel,

(2) benevolences, (3) education and, by the mid-19th century, (4) foreign missions. (Of course, in the antebellum period a concern for the eradication of slavery was also central.) That these items continue to dominate the churches' mission priorities and stewardship planning may be attributed in part to the continuing marginality and relative powerlessness of blacks in American society. It is due also to the fact that religious institutions in black communities have not been sufficiently cognizant of the radical implications which the changing political, economic and social realities have for their life. Bishop Adams's antidote for this institutional inertia is "zero-based" mission planning–an imaginative and valid suggestion.

I

Some early black congregations began as benevolent societies, and all of them were concerned for the welfare of the sick, the widowed and the orphaned. Most congregations continue to maintain benevolent funds, but they are no longer accorded high priority. It is obvious in the light of massive need that the churches' impact in this area can be only palliative. The social welfare programs sponsored by the government and by community and private agencies are far better resourced and programmatically more comprehensive than those that individual churches can sustain. The churches' task in the area of benevolence has become that of ensuring that persons gain access to the benefits for which they are eligible.

The churches' historic concern for education initially focused on efforts to compensate for the exclusion of blacks from access to elementary education. After emancipation, the most pressing concern became that of establishing and supporting secondary schools and colleges. By 1900 the churches had compiled an impressive record: black Baptist associations were supporting some 80 elementary schools and 18 academies and colleges; the African Methodist Episcopal churches were underwriting 32 secondary and collegiate institutions; and the smaller AME Zion denomination was supporting eight. The denomination now named the Christian Methodist Episcopal Church, only 30 years old in 1900, had established five schools. Blacks now have broad access to public secondary and higher education, and the need for church-related institutions to fill an educational vacuum has lessened considerably. The question as to whether there is a qualitative difference in the education being offered in church-sponsored colleges as over against state-supported institutions is a matter that has to be debated in the zero-based mission planning that Bishop Adams suggests.

Blacks have traditionally directed their modest foreign mission efforts to the Caribbean islands and to Africa. The institutional forms of these missions have not differed significantly from those of the majority churches; they have focused on church development, health-care institutions and education. (It may be observed that black churches have established hospitals in Africa but none in America.) The need for such missionary services is diminishing and will doubtless decline more rapidly as independent African and Caribbean nations preempt these areas of responsibility for the state.

If the traditional concerns for education, benevolences and foreign missions need to be carefully scrutinized and their priority status evaluated, the first priority in the life of the churches does not require such rethinking. The *raison d'être* of black churches has not differed from that of churches of any age. They have been the bearers of the good news that God cares about, affirms, forgives and redeems human beings to whom he has given life, and that he acts in their history. This message of divine concern has enabled black believers to survive humanely in inhumane circumstances. The communities of faith have been the social matrixes within which individual significance and worth have been given concrete embodiment and a sense of belonging has been conferred. The form in which this message is conveyed may change, but its essential content will remain the same.

Though not a part of the formal agenda of the churches, church buildings have been crucial community assets. From the earliest times they were the only assembly halls to which the black community had access. They housed schools, dramatic productions, cultural events, social welfare programs, rallies and benefits of all sorts, and civil and human rights activities. The requirements in these areas are less critical today. But if the need for meeting space has declined, the claims placed on church members by movements for social, political and economic justice have not diminished. W.E.B. DuBois once remarked that the NAACP could not have survived without the support of black churches and their members. This is still the case. Though many social organizations and unions give support to such movements, church members form an indispensable segment of their constituencies, as the recent financial crisis involving the NAACP in Mississippi made clear. The churches continue to have access to the largest audience that can be gathered in black communities. . . .

IV

As we look toward the future, the agenda for black churches is a complex one. The existence of the churches is not in jeopardy; they are and will continue to be for large numbers of persons the only accessible institutions that will meet their need to be affirmed in their identity and sense of belonging in both a human and a divine dimension. What is in jeopardy is the capacity of the churches to attract urban dwellers in large numbers while church programs are geared to a 19th century rural ethos.

The most significant phenomenon to impact black churches in this century has been migration to the cities. Urban churches grew and prospered as a result of that population movement, but the rural ethos continued to be reflected in worship, organization and mission priorities. There are now persons in the pews who were born in the city, who are secular in their outlook, who are keenly aware of the ways in which their lives are shaped by structures which they do not control, and who are concerned that their religious institutions should be active agents of social change. This new constituency requires programs of Christian nurture that address the consciousness, realities and urgencies of contemporary urban life. In this connection the church must become bilingual: it must understand the language of the world and translate the gospel into the idioms and symbols of that language. Christian nurture must also be bifocal. It must keep its eye on heaven, but it must not fail to see the world at hand and seek to enable persons to wrest meaning and significance from their lives in it.

Perhaps the central agenda of the black churches in the years ahead is accurately to assess their corporate potential for impacting the quality of life available to their constituencies. This task will require, as a matter of first priority, careful determination of mission priorities and the mobilization of resources for the implementation. These activities must be carried out in recognition of the fact that many of the problems affecting the lives of individuals in negative ways are systemic, and can be dealt with only at that level. This effort will inevitably involve individual congregations in difficult decisions concerning the allocation of resources formerly committed to the traditional mission agenda. Local autonomy will have to yield to functional ecumenism for the sake of faithfulness in pursuing God's will and purpose that justice and peace shall prevail among human beings.

Historically, black churches have been clergy-dominated. This situation must change if religious institutions are to continue to attract gifted persons to their company. It is imperative that the talents of church members be increasingly utilized on behalf of the mission of the church. An important byproduct of the involvement of laity in mission is that better-trained lay and clergy leadership be required. Warm evangelicalism will not compensate for naive understanding of the powers and principalities of the world.

It has frequently been observed that the quality of life in inner-city communities is deteriorating at alarming rates, and that part of this deterioration is attributable to the erosion of moral and humane values. Churches must not ignore these phenomenon. They must be concerned that large numbers of young people never come within the sphere of their teaching or influence. While it is widely agreed that the causes for the morbidity of communities in urban centers are traceable to diverse factors, churches cannot be quiescent in the face of them. Family structures must be reinforced, and churches must be active agents and participants in organizations seeking to help communities improve themselves.

Missionary conventions and church boards face an important period of self-examination. They must ask themselves what the increasing sense of self-identity in the Third World has to say to missionary structures. What does the indigenization of churches mean for black missionaries in black countries? Black church missions early reflected the "redemption of Africa" theme. What does that term connote at a time when cultural Christianity is undergoing rigorous scrutiny? What does it mean to affirm indigenous religion while proclaiming the gospel of Jesus Christ? In the light of Third World realities, have the terms "missions" and "missionary" become anachronistic?

Another entry that must be prominent on the agenda of black churches is the nature of worship. Is the "old-time religion" good enough for contemporary urbanites? How can churches respond to the desire of individuals for spontaneity in worship so that form is not mistaken for substance? Can churches devise means for accommodating a genuine desire to abandon outmoded forms without derogating from the claims of the gospel and the truth that worship is the service of God? The ability to sing a gospel song with feeling is not to be equated with transformation of one's life nor with continued commitment to the One who is Lord.

Black churches must begin to examine the economic realities of their existence, not in the light of their individual or denominational budgets alone, but in view of their tremendous possibilities to effect social change by utilizing the considerable resources that pass through their hands. In a city with 300 churches, it is fair to assume conservatively that the average Sunday offering would amount to $300 per church or nearly $100,000 for all churches. If this sum were put in a single bank, considerable leverage would be generated to influence that bank's loan policy in regard to urban neighborhoods. Churches need to consider what cooperative buying of goods and services might mean in savings, influence on the employment practices of vendors, and overall economic impact.

It will be noted that an agenda has been suggested for black churches irrespective of their denominational affiliation. I offer no apology for this lack of differentiation since the situation of one black church is, in large measure, the situation of all black churches. All are addressing themselves to the needs of an oppressed people. One might even suggest that the agenda is appropriate for all churches that wish to take seriously the ministry of Christ in the world.

V

While the challenges facing black churches are difficult ones, there are important harbingers that bode well for the future. Modestly increasing numbers of bright young people from all denominations are seeking theological training. They are exerting increasing pressure on educational institutions to equip them to be resources to the communities in which they will serve, as well as competent leaders of religious institutions. There are also evidences that the denominational leadership of the church is becoming more aware of the changed context within which mission must be implemented. Another important sign is that church membership has been holding steady and that middle-class defections have not been as numerous as some had predicted.

At the local level laypersons are increasingly asserting their right to participate in the governance of the churches. Clergy serving churches with congregational polity are finding themselves to be governed by constitutions and by-laws in direct contrast to the monarchical clergy styles of a passing generation. Laypeople are also exerting pressure on their churches to demonstrate an authentic sense of social responsibility.

Another favorable index is the broadening effort to provide basic training for church leaders who are not formally qualified to pursue graduate theological education. This theological training which is both theoretical and practical will have significant impact on the churches and their ministries.

But the most significant development in recent years has been an increasing awareness among blacks not affiliated with the churches that religious institutions are as critical to the survival of Afro-Americans in the present as they have been in the past. Thus there is pressure from all quarters for the churches to actualize their potential as agents of social change without derogation of their traditional role as communities of faith. Black churches need not abandon their historic mission agendas but rather should consider them in the light of new realities in the world where [their] mission must be implemented.

5. A Mormon Response to the Equal Rights Amendment, 1979

SOURCE: From *From Housewife to Heretic* by Sonia Johnson. Pp. 276, 278-80. Copyright © by WildFire Books. Reprinted with permission of the author.

I read the letter again. This was Wednesday night [Nov. 14, 1979]—late by now. The trial was set for early Saturday morning. Slowly I began to understand the strategy behind it all. They were giving me only two days! Two days to prepare my defense, to prepare myself spiritually, psychologically, two days to find witnesses. *Only two days!* The cruelty of that and the already clear judgment it revealed that had been made about my guilt struck me like a heavy fist in the face. They did not intend to give me a real trial at all! They were not even going to give me a real chance to defend myself. I had been found guilty and now they were only going through the formalities. . . .

Press coverage of the trial had begun.

Thursday, November 15. I tried all day to reach Jeff [Willis]. Judy told me he was on jury duty (ironies never ceased) and could not be reached all day. Frantically, I explained to her that I had only two days before the trial and that I did not even know what the charges were. Would she please help me get in touch with Jeff. Finally, she made an appointment for me with him at 8 P.M. that night at the Sterling Park Ward chapel. One whole precious day wasted. In the end, I drove out to Sterling Park Ward alone, and at 8 P.M. sat for the last time alone with Jeff Willis in that office.

As I recall, the first question I asked him was, "Who is my accuser?" "I am," he answered. "Who is my judge, then?" "I am," he said again. "But how can you be both my accuser and my judge? For heaven's sake, Jeff, I've been an American too long to feel comfortable with that. I'm accustomed to at least the appearance of due process. If you've decided I'm guilty—and you must have, since you're willing to accuse me—how can you bring an impartial decision?" "Don't worry, Sonia," he assured me. "I will receive the correct decision through inspiration from our Heavenly Father. The courts of the church are courts of love." Ignoring the love nonsense, I asked, "How do you expect to be able to hear God's will over the roar of your own conviction that I'm guilty? What exactly do you expect him to do, Jeff? Hit you over the head with a lightning bolt? Knock you down on the road to Langley?"

I was not mollified. I was as prayerful a person as I had ever known (except for my mother), and I knew how hard it is to get answers. I had heard mission presidents say that they could not tell whether or not someone had negroid ancestry no matter how hard they prayed. I very much suspected that Jeff was more influenced by what his superiors told him *they* had heard from God than he was from what he had personally managed to glean. "Wait just a second, God. I have to check it out with the Big Boys." But I was determined not to view the situation as hopeless—though I know now that it was from the beginning.

"What are the charges against me, Jeff? Please write them down so we will each know this is what you said, and so I won't make a mistake when I tell my witnesses what they need to respond to."

He refused to write anything down. That's what comes of working for the CIA—deep distrust as a first response. So I asked him if he would dictate the charges to me. He agreed to do that. Perhaps because they were not in his handwriting, he could forever deny that they had come from him. I cannot imagine why else he refused to write them himself. These are his exact words as I took them down on the night of November 15, 1979:

> You have broken the covenants you made in the temple, specifically:
> 1. evil speaking of the Lord's anointed;
> 2. the law of consecration;
> 3. your general attitude and expression.

I protested. Where have I spoken evil of the Lord's anointed? I asked. In your APA speech, he answered. Show me the place, I demanded. "You call them chauvinistic," he shot back. "That's not evil; that's true!" I replied. "And what's this about the law of consecration?" You promised in the temple to give your time, your talents, all the Lord has blessed you with and all he may yet bless you with to the upbuilding of the church and to the establishment of Zion."

"Jeff, I pay a full tithing and have all my life. I'm the ward organist and spend many extra hours practicing alone and with the choir. I teach the cultural refinement lesson in Relief Society, I am a visiting teacher [in the Relief Society], I attend church, we hold family home evenings, I attend the temple. If you're going to excommunicate everybody in the ward who is doing this much or less, you won't have anybody left in the congregation when you're through!

"And tell me how I'm going to defend myself against your annoyance at my 'general attitude and expression.' What does that even mean? Just because men in the church don't like uppity women, does that mean we should all be *excommunicated*?" I thought but held my tongue: "Do we have to have an attitude of hero worship and awe even when our male leaders do little or nothing to deserve it? Why should we be in awe? Because you're *male*?"

6. Hispanics and the Catholic Church, 1980

SOURCE: Frank Ponce, in *New Catholic World* (July/August, 1980), 164-65. Copyright ©
1980 by Paulist Press. Reprinted with permission of Rev. John Lynch.

How has the Church responded to the challenge of enculturation? On the one
hand, the Church has responded ambiguously, in many ways out of a fear that
allowing cultural diversity would wound the Church's unity, and also because
applying the Gospel in a given culture is extremely complex. On the other hand,
there are hopeful signs that a greater consciousness regarding the demands of
enculturation is arising. But on the whole, the Church's failures have often been
more impressive than its successes.

For example, one need only look closely at the ethnic, racial, and cultural
make-up of our parishes. Especially in dioceses or regions where Blacks, Hispanics, American Indians, or other minorities predominate, we need to ask: How are
these groups represented—not merely in a token way—in parish councils, in
diocesan pastoral councils? And if parishes—the particular "local Churches"
imaging the universal Church—truly breed vocations, why are our seminaries
pathetically bereft of Blacks, Hispanics, or American Indians? (The seminaries
of religious orders fare better here than diocesan seminaries perhaps because of
the "missions" influence.) More importantly in their evangelizing efforts, do our
parishes continue to "save the saved," or are bold, creative efforts made to reach
out to the alienated, the disaffected, the marginal—most of them the very groups
excluded by our lack of cultural sensitivity? How we answer these questions as
Church will help us gauge our efforts at enculturation.

The picture becomes clearer—or muddier, depending on one's perspective—
when we look at the Church's national leadership. To be sure, there are now eight
Hispanic bishops, when in 1970 there was only one. And to be sure, there are
now five Black bishops, when ten years ago there were none. Yet, given the centuries-old presence of these two groups in the United States (and that there are
approximately 320 bishops), is not the record rather dismal? And what of the
(lack of) presence of American Indians? They have a saint, Kateri Tekakwitha,
but it is odd that the mystery of episcopal divine election has not yet alighted on
any American Indian for the bishop's office. Now one should not dwell on the
"numbers game," but statistics do tell us part of the problem and gives us part of
the solution.

As one who participated in the Detroit "Call to Action" in 1976, 1 could not
help but be gratified by the number of racial, cultural, and ethnic groups there
represented. I was not inspired, however, by the lack of similar representation at
the "Call to Action" follow-up, "To Do the Work of Justice," held in Washington, D.C., this past March. This national workshop asked bishops to send their
diocesan personnel to learn skills enabling them to carry out the mandate of the
Detroit meeting. The conclusion: few dioceses have—or are willing to involve—
Blacks, Hispanics, American Indians, Asian Americans, or other minorities in
responsible, diocesan decision-making positions.

We trumpet loudly the importance of a Catholic press in forming and informing our faithful. Yet I could not help swallowing hard when the excellent paper, *Impact,* published by the National Organization of Black Catholics (NOBC) reported in its December 1978 issue that only two Black journalists work in the Catholic press, which has 470 publications. Certainly these figures are little better among Hispanics, American Indians, or Asian Americans.

On everyone's lips these days, especially after the tragic Jonestown events, is the meteoric rise of cults. One of these, the so-called "Moonies," is alive and well among Hispanics. In Brooklyn the "Moonies" have bought a large storefront building, offered various health services, staffed their offices with bilingual personnel (the director is a Cuban ex-priest), and provided food for families. Hispanics flock there by the hundreds. How many are converted is unknown. But this much is known: Hispanics are respected, they are served cheerfully—and in *their own language.* How many Catholic schools, churches, and agencies can boast the same? Of course I could recount numerous stories about Hispanic services being relegated to Church basements, Blacks discriminated against in numerous seminaries, derision of American Indian religious beliefs in Catholic publications, perduring stereotypes of "inscrutable Eastern" orientals and such. But you get the idea: we've a long way to go making enculturation a fact, not a fiction, in our Catholic Church.

7. Feminism and Traditional Judaism, 1981

SOURCE: From *On Women and Judaism: A View from Tradition* by Blu Greenberg. Pp. 21-22, 25-26, 27-29. Copyright © 1981 by Jewish Publication Society of America. Reprinted with permission.

I was born into a strongly traditional family. With all the structure this entails, it was quite natural to be socialized early into the proper roles. I knew my place and I like it—the warmth, the rituals, the solid, tight parameters. I never gave a thought as to what responsibilities I did or didn't have as a female growing up in the Orthodox Jewish community. It was just the way things were—the most natural order in the world.

My friends and I shared the same world of expectation. I remember the year of the bar mitzvahs of our eighth-grade male friends. We girls sat up in the women's section of the synagogue and took great pride in "our boys." If we thought about ourselves at all, it was along the lines of "thank God we are females and don't have to go through the public ordeal." Quite remarkably, there never was any envy of what the boys were doing, never a thought of "why not us?" Perhaps it was because we knew that our big moment would come: as proper young ladies growing up in the modern Orthodox community in the 1950s, *our* puberty rite was the Sweet Sixteen.

My short-lived encounter with daily prayer ended when I was fourteen. I had graduated from a local yeshiva in Far Rockaway, New York, and had begun commuting to a girls' yeshiva high school in Brooklyn. This meant getting up an hour earlier to catch the 7:18 Long Island train, so prayer was the first thing to go. I had it down to a science: if I laid out my clothes in exactly the right order the night before, I could set the alarm for 6:52, get up, wash, dress, eat the hot breakfast without which, my mother insisted, a person could not face the world each day, and still have time to walk briskly to the train. I would reserve a four-seater in the same car each day. Just as the train started to pull out, my friends who were attending the boys' yeshiva would come dashing down the platform and fling themselves onto the slowly moving train. I knew that they had been up since six o'clock to allow enough time for *shaharit*, the mandatory morning prayers. There they were, a little bleary-eyed, already spent at 7:18, with just a package of Sen-Sen for breakfast. Those were wonderful, funny trips. Though I laughed with the boys each morning, I certainly didn't envy their more rigorous regimen. . . .

After my marriage in the late 1950s, my feelings of contentment and fulfillment were enhanced rather than diminished. The ways of a traditional Jewish woman suited me just fine. All those platitudes about building a faithful Jewish home were not nearly as pleasant as the real thing itself. Moreover, none of those obligations ruled out graduate studies and plans for a career. It was a time of peaceful coexistence between the traditional roles and the initial stirrings of self-actualization for women. I considered myself very lucky to have a husband to care for me and I for him—a man, moreover, who encouraged me to expand my own horizons.

The religious role of a married woman was also perfect in my eyes. I found the clear division of labor, and its nonnegotiable quality, most satisfying. It never crossed my mind that experiencing certain mitzvot vicariously was anything less than the real thing. Quite the reverse. When my husband had to be away on the Sabbath, the act of my reciting the blessings over the wine and the bread for our small children only served to heighten my sense of loneliness for him.

The real thing, then, was for him to perform his mitzvot and for me to attend to mine. I wasn't looking for anything more than I had, certainly not in the way of religious obligations or rights. On those bitter cold Sabbath mornings I was absolutely delighted to linger an hour longer in a nice warm bed and play with the kids rather than to have to brave the elements. I could choose to go to the synagogue when I wanted or pray at home when I wanted; for my husband there was no choice.

The *mehitzah* separating men from women in the synagogue served to symbolize the dividing line. Although there were certain things about sitting behind the *mehitzah* that I didn't exactly appreciate, none seemed an attack on my womanhood. No only did I not perceive the *mehitzah* to be a denigration of women in the synagogue, but I couldn't understand why some Jews felt that way. At some level, to me the *mehitzah* symbolized the ancient, natural, immutable order of male and female. One didn't question such things. . . .

And then came feminism. In 1963, I read Betty Friedan's *Feminine Mystique*, still the classic text of the women's movement. I was a little intimidated by its force and had trouble with what seemed to me a portent of friction between the sexes, but the essential idea, equality of women, was exciting, and mind-boggling, and very just. Still, correct or not, it didn't mean me, nor did it apply to women in

Judaism. On that score I was defensive, resistant, and probably just plain frightened. It must have threatened my status quo.

And yet . . . Once I had tasted of the fruit of the tree of knowledge, there was no going back. The basic idea had found a resting spot somewhere inside me. Little by little, and with a good deal of prodding from my husband, I became sensitized to issues and situations that previously had made no impression on me. Some of my complacency was eroded; my placidity churned up. In place of blind acceptance, I slowly began to ask questions, not really sure if I wanted to hear the answers. Because I was so satisfied, because I had no sense of injustice, some of the new thinking, including my own, came to me as a shock. Things that had run right past me before I now had to grab hold of, for a still moment, to examine under the white light of equality.

I began to think not just about the idea, but about myself as a woman—in relation to people, to a place in the larger society, to a career, and finally to Judaism. I did not look back over my past and say it was bad. In fact I knew it was very good. What I did begin to say was that perhaps it could have been better. Again, it was not a case of closing my eyes and thinking hard. Instead, it was a series of incidents, encounters, a matter of timing; it was also memories and recollections, a review in which isolated incidents began to emerge as part of a pattern. This pattern now had to be tested against a new value framework.

It was almost ten years before I began systematically to apply the new categories to my Jewishness. As I reviewed my education, one fact emerged—a fact so obvious that I was stunned more by my unresponsiveness to it over the years than by the fact itself. It was this: the study of Talmud, which was a primary goal in my family and community, consistently was close off to me. Beginning with elementary school, the girls studied Israeli folk dancing while the boys studied Talmud. In the yeshiva high school, the girls' branch had no course of study in Talmud; the boys' branch had three hours a day. In Israel, in the Jewish studies seminar, all of the classes were coeducational except Talmud. The girls studied laws and customs on one day and enjoyed a free period the other four days.

And then there was my father. The great love of his life, beyond his family, was not his business; it was his study of the Talmud. Every day, before he left for work, he would spend an hour studying Talmud with a rabbi friend. In fact, he had not missed a day of study in his life, even during family vacations or times of stress. Yet although he reviewed religious texts regularly with his daughters, it was never Talmud. He even would collar my dates, while I was getting ready, for a few minutes of Talmud discussion. That we didn't participate in those years more directly in our father's passion for Talmud study was not a willful denial on his part; he simply was following custom. As a result of all this, when I began to study rabbinic literature in graduate school in my late twenties, I realized that my male fellow students all had the edge of fifteen or twenty years of Talmud study behind them.

Gradually, too, I became aware of the power of conditioning and how early in life it takes place. On the last Sabbath that my husband served as rabbi of a congregation, the children and I decided to surprise him. Moshe, then ten and a half, prepared the haftarah reading, David, nine, the *An'im Zemirot* prayer, and J.J., six, the *Adon Olam.* It was a real treat for their father and for the entire congregation; it seemed to the boys as if the whole world was proud of them. On the following Sunday morning, their grandparents visited and gave each of the boys two dollars for doing such a fine job. When the boys told Deborah, then eight, that they each had been given two dollars, she complained that it wasn't fair. At which point Moshe retorted, with the biting honesty of a ten year old: "Well, so what, you can't even do anything in the synagogue!" Click, click, I thought to myself, another woman radicalized.

Oddly enough, until that moment it never occurred to me that it could or should be otherwise, that perhaps it wasn't "fair" to a little girl. Even more astounding was the fact that with all the weeks of practice, all the fuss I had made over the boys beforehand, and all the compliments they received afterward, Deborah never once had complained. It was only the two dollars that finally got to her; to everything else she had already been conditioned . . . to expect nothing.

Essays

In the first essay, Sydney E. Ahlstrom, late of Yale University, describes the 1960s and 1970s as the Traumatic Years. He discusses five issues that produced private and collective unrest, and the impact they had on American religion. In the second essay, Robert Wuthnow of Princeton University argues that new religious alignments formed from the mid-1970s to the mid-1980s following a decade of religious upheaval in the 1960s. In the final essay, Thomas C. Reeves of the University of Wisconsin-Parkside describes reasons for and evidence of the malaise of mainline Protestant liberalism during the final years of the twentieth century.

The Traumatic Years:
American Religion and Culture in the '60s and '70s
SYDNEY E. AHLSTROM

SOURCE: From Sydney Ahlstrom, "The Traumatic Years: American Religion and Culture in the '60's and '70's," *Theology Today* 36 (1980):504-5, 505-7, 507-9, 510-11, 511-16, 519-22. Copyright © 1980 by *Theology Today.* Reprinted with permission.

American Civilization was founded in an epoch of divisive religious ferment. During the nineteenth century, amid numerous denominational schisms, countless indigenous sects and cults arose. Even new religions were founded. The later twentieth century has experienced yet another explosion of spiritual unrest, and now the newest immigration, from across the Pacific, is deepening the nation's pluralism. It is hardly surprising that even the efforts of scholars to describe an American character have foundered, one after the other, on the rocks of ethnic, racial, cultural, and religious diversity.

The first necessity is to frame an inclusive religious category, for otherwise one would be tempted either to lose oneself in a welter of details or to overemphasize that minority of Americans who are formally affiliated with the institutions of the Judaeo-Christian tradition. One must see religion as a virtually universal aspect of being human. Integrated personhood intrinsically consists of a felt relation of the environing world, a more or less ordered structure of values, some sense of the transcendent, and at least a rudimentary notion of personal or collective destiny or purpose. One can hardly imagine a person, either now or in times past, whose religious commitments could not be described if serious conversations could be arranged or personal records studied. . . .

In England, to be sure, the fabric of English life was considerably restored, but in America a truly glorious revolution was slowly carried out. Bernard Bailyn can justly claim that by the 1730s substantially all of the liberties to be demanded in 1776 were practical realities of American life, except that legal guarantees were lacking. Intrinsic to the entire accomplishment, moreover, was the way in which Puritan piety and ethics undergirded and animated the new social order. As the nation grew prosperous, the larger Protestant churches brought strong and persistent theological support to this ideology. Gradually this blending of religion, social ethics, and politics became a unified gestalt or value configuration. Americans not only likened themselves to Old Israel but insisted that their country was God's New Israel. Timothy Dwight in his anthem for the new nation in 1777 knew no restraint. He hailed Columbia as "queen of the world and child of the skies." Its reign was to be "the last and the noblest of time." The founding fathers themselves showed the same confidence. "Heaven smiles upon our undertakings," says the national seal: NOVUS ORDO SECLORUM. A generation later Lyman Beecher would declare that "the Mosaic institute more resembled our own than any government on earth ever did or does." Gathering all of these ideas together in a way that brought peculiar satisfaction to the people was Francis Samuel Smith's hymn, "My Country 'Tis of Thee," written hurriedly in 1832. Through all vicissitudes this tradition maintained itself. Julia Ward Howe's "Mine eyes have seen the glory" survived the Civil War and became a national song. Fifty million immigrants aroused nativist responses, yet the newcomers in the long run strengthened the impulse, and Irving Berlin's "God Bless America" is appropriately the last (so far) to win wide popular acceptance.

One thing, therefore, remains certain: that the essentially religious notion of this country as an Elect Nation with a Manifest Destiny is an overwhelmingly important factor that any study of recent decades must ponder. For the vast majority of Americans, the Union has always been an object of veneration with rites and symbols of its own. It has been apprehended as a source of moral norms, which, if not absolute, nevertheless transcend individual desires. Only very rarely, moreover, have even the strictest ecclesiastical authorities or other critics denounced these tendencies as idolatrous or illicit. It was amid the massive social, moral, and economic dislocations of the Gilded Age, however, that something like a continuous movement of dissent began to emerge. Not until the Great Crash of 1929 and the depression which followed did the magnitude of public policy changes become sufficiently great to effect changes in the public orthodoxy. By the end of World War II a moderate form of the "welfare state" had won widespread popular acceptance. With these developments in mind we proceed to a consideration of the last decade and a half of the republic's second century, remembering that it was while it was approaching the Bicentennial that the nation's sense of purpose fell to its lowest ebb.

That we may better understand the rude transitions that brought us to this condition it is useful to revisit a time when a quite different spirit pervaded the country, and for this purpose the Eisenhower years may serve very well. In the nostalgic memories of most it was a halcyon time. The decade's most sensational corruption scandal involved a Columbia professor and a popular television quiz show, unless it was the vicuña coat that led to the resignation of the president's chief adviser. College students of the sixties remembered those years as a time of bobbysoxers in pleated skirts; whereas those of the seventies who read Will Herberg's well-received study, *Protestant Catholic Jew* (1955), find that world so remote from their own experience that they confuse it with the world of Tolkien's *Lord of the Rings*. Some reflection on the fifties, therefore, may sharpen our perceptions of what the next fifteen years would do.

I

At the risk of oversimplification one may say that the Truman administration was primarily concerned with the gargantuan tasks of postwar reconstruction and that it was the good fortune of President Dwight David Eisenhower to ride the crest of a postwar boom. Fulfilling a campaign promise, the victorious general's first deed was to negotiate a treaty that ended the enormously divisive war in Korea. The gates of the temple of Janus were closed, and Americans, as the pundits so often said, had the father figure they wanted. In tune with the trend of the times, Eisenhower was also permissive—even to the length of giving the country's most unprincipled demagogue, Senator Joseph McCarthy, enough rope to hang himself in 1954, thus ending a rampage that had begun in 1950. His basic role was to be an indulgent guardian of a nation bent on getting and spending. . . .

. . . the distinctive spiritual tone of the decade unfolded. Because "normalcy" was again in vogue much of the country's traditional religious life went on in its customary way, though television was now reaching new and receptive audiences. Yet gradually the "Eisenhower Revival" took on a character of its own. Most pronounced was a general heightening of religious interest in forms which were discontinuous with the more familiar types of American revivalism. To some degree this was even true of the Billy Graham Evangelistic Association, which was incorporated in 1950. Though harkening back in many respects to the techniques that Charles G. Finney had developed before the Civil War and which Dwight L. Moody and Billy Sunday had continued to use, Graham's crusades were different. Television seems to have reshaped the message. There was now a far larger use of public-relations techniques, a more studied avoidance of controversial topics, and an absence of doctrinal specificity which antagonized many of the more strict fundamentalist leaders.

More important than Graham's influence was a surprising and almost unsolicited increase in church membership that affected almost all denominations, whether liberal or conservative. At least in statistical terms this trend brought an end to the extended "religious depression" which had set in during the 1920s. This growth took place chiefly in the sprawling reaches of suburbia, where former denizens of American cities were now adjusting to new modes of living. So marked was the trend that Gibson Winter would speak of *The Suburban Captivity of the Churches* (1951).

For many people the resort to the churches may not have been profoundly motivated, but it was, nevertheless, a very reasonable effort to break through the anonymity of suburban living and to search for friends, a phenomenon which contemporary critics often derided as a lust for togetherness. Marshall Sklare, in an important study, found these social conditions conducive to the rise of Judaic "Conservatism" as a middle tradition between Orthodoxy and Reform. Will Herberg, on the other hand, probably with primary concern for the Jewish experience, emphasized the degree to which church-going provided a means for "third-generation immigrants" to reclaim their religious heritage. He pointed to the Triple Melting Pot, where each of his three main groups established their identity as Americans by means of religious participation. He thus attributed the increased popularity of American religion chiefly to a desire to celebrate the American Way of Life. Like so many Americans of the period, he paid little attention to the momentous changes going on in the great migrations of black Americans which were then going on; but there is little doubt that he touched on a very prominent feature of the times. Even the American Legion sponsored a widely advertised Back-to-God hour. President Eisenhower himself was baptized in a private ceremony; and in a famous public statement he insisted that "our government makes no sense unless it is founded on a deeply felt religious faith—and I don't care what it is." In a like spirit, prayer breakfasts and other religious meetings were often held in quasi-governmental contexts. More official were the acts of Congress which declared IN GOD WE TRUST to be the national motto and amended the Pledge of Allegiance to include the words "under God."

Behind all these developments was a growing recognition that the nation's new affluence entailed increasingly urban modes of living that had profound implications for the personal composure and social relations of very many Americans. Two works of social analysis found particular acceptance during these years. Perhaps most widely quoted was *The Lonely Crowd* (1935) by David Riesman, Nathan Glazer, and Reuel Denny, which described the "other-directed" conformists who predominated in the newly competitive American scene. William Whyte's *The Organization Man* (1956) dealt with rapidly growing numbers of middle-class Americans "who have left home spiritually as well as physically to take the vows of organization life." He was referring to those who work in and belong to "the great organized enterprises" that "will set the American temper." One of his more forcefully made points was that the trends being set were extinguishing the Protestant ethic. His final counsel was to "fight the Organization." Needless to say, the fight never got off the ground, nor did many seek to gain the "autonomy" that Riesman *et al.* had rather unrealistically prescribed for the Lonely Crowd. Instead one beheld an unexpected increase of new forms of middle-class alienation.

Nobody knows just what all of these people did for their uneasiness of spirit, but many of them, no doubt, helped swell the church rolls. More certain is it that millions of them turned to the consolatory literature that Americans had been producing in ever greater abundance since the Gilded Age, when many authors and movements responded to the public's growing need for harmonious inspiration. The first great postwar best-seller in this field was *Peace of Mind* (1946) by Rabbi Joshua Loth Liebman of Boston, whose thoughtful blending of religious counsel and Freudian insights make the book something of a landmark in the field. Enormously more popular, however, were the efforts of the Reverend Norman Vincent Peale, whose *Guide to Confident Living* (1948) and *The Power of Positive Thinking* (1952) broke all records for the genre and for many other genres as well. Peale in fact made himself into a multimedia institution with his endlessly repeated formulae designed to put people on the road to composure and success. To what extent he deepened the anxiety of a status-conscious people can only be guessed. . . .

In fact, one sees in these attitudes and interests of the fifties a premonitory sign of the secularizing theologies of the sixties. And in President Eisenhower's expression of alarm over the growing power of "the military-industrial complex" one may see an intimation of the next decade's radical protest. Yet there can be no mistaking the prevailing complacency with which moral and religious trends were being viewed. Because a nation does not oblige historians by changing sharply at ten-year intervals, the same judgment would have to be applied to the Camelot years, when John F. Kennedy sought to rejuvenate the nation's aspirations. In unexpected ways, however, his short term of office marked the onset of a new time of calamities that included his own assassination.

II

The late Richard Hofstadter declared that if he ever undertook to write a history of the United States during the 1960s he would entitle it "The Age of Rubbish." It is understandable why a professor who experienced the tumults at Columbia University would be led to that judgment, and he no doubt could have found many collaborators from other universities. But it might well have been a parochial book— and it is probably fortunate that he never wrote it. Every decade, to be sure, has its share of rubbish; but the dominant concerns of the sixties were of momentous import.

The turbulent period to be assayed is that which lies between the election of John F. Kennedy in 1960 to those days in April 1975 when an unelected President inaugurated the Bicentennial Era at Lexington and Concord while news of the collapsing American regime in Vietnam poured in upon him. Nobody is likely to deny that these years were tumultuous, troubled, and traumatic, and that the fifties by comparison were serene. In the realm of religion and ethics one could justify the adjective "revolutionary." Never before in the country's history have so many Americans expressed revolutionary intentions and actively participated in efforts to alter the shape of American civilization in almost every imaginable aspect—from diet to diplomacy, from art to the economic disorder. . . .

Moral shock, the sudden discovery that dry rot has weakened the supporting members of a very comfortable structure of values, is a traumatic experience often followed by religious doubt which then yields, gradually or suddenly, to a new religious and ethical outlook. For a great many Americans the era was traumatic in just this sense. That is why it may be understood as a Great Awakening even though it was a time of fear and trembling for many Americans. The issues which occasioned all this private and collective consternation were very numerous, and each of them could be subdivided. There were at least five, however, that gained massive public attention, and it is hard to see one as more important than the others.

They can be briefly listed: (1) race and racism, (2) war and imperialism, (3) sex and sexism, (4) exploitation and environmentalism, and (5) government and the misuse of power. Underlying all of these was the fundamental question of Justice, which is the first virtue of any society. Because young people took such an unprecedented role among those who were active in these interconnected moral campaigns, the nature and function of educational institutions also became prime objects of concern—and sometimes of overt assault. Serious contention of some of these questions is as old as the Judaeo-Christian tradition, others (notably 3 and 4) had emerged much more recently. But all of them were revived with great urgency during the era under discussion. If these several protest and reform movements are seen as a whole they constitute a full-scale critique of the American way of life: both the social injustices of the system itself and the ideological, philosophical, and theological assumptions that have justified and legitimated the existing social order. In this "nation with the soul of a church" these injustices and assumptions are so deeply implicated in the nexus of religion and the moral life that they must be seen as essential to this essay. Most immediate and direct in their impact were those movements which brought the churches and their members—especially the clergy—into active participation, often at the price of alienating large portions of the constituency as a whole.

III

In this category the civil-rights movement is by all odds first and most important. It might even be said to have been initiated in the churches during the Great Awakening and the British evangelical revival; in America it was spurred by the Revolution, but it was not really effective until the great antislavery revivals of the 1830s. After the Civil War it was the Radical Republicans who led the struggle until the Grand Old Party's chieftains bade farewell to the Bloody Shirt in the 1890s. The Supreme Court decision of 1954 was the decisive twentieth-century event, but it was only with the Montgomery boycott of 1956 and the voice of Martin Luther King that a nationwide interracial movement became a sustained reality; and during the ensuing decade no one person contributed more than King to the nation's moral dignity.

The movement peaked at Selma in 1964. Then followed the time of burning cities and finally the emergence of Black Power in 1966 after the shooting of James Meredith turned his march from Memphis to Jackson into an ambulating conference of the movement's black leadership. By the time of King's assassination the old civil-rights movement had come to an end, but not without having precipitated a crisis of conscience in white America and an awakening of self-consciousness in black America. Nothing quite like it had happened anywhere else in the world.

The anti-Vietnam War movement began gathering strength as a direct response to President Johnson's drastic escalation of the war during the spring of 1965 with the sense of betrayed campaign promises adding to its bitterness. An outmoded and unfair conscription added further grounds for anger. Many others saw the war as a disastrous abandonment of the civil-rights movement. And gradually, among youth especially, there developed an intensity of feeling that is probably unique in the country's history; by 1968 it had so grown in volume and intensity as seriously to challenge the country's sense of public order. It was accompanied by a deep animosity for persons, agencies, and institutions that in any way supported the military effort. Finally in 1968, after Senator Eugene McCarthy had impressively challenged the war policy, a proud, ambitious, and stubborn President decided not to run for a second term. The agitations continued, however, for yet another half decade, with domestic atrocities such as those at Kent State University in the spring of 1970 increasing their tempo and intensity. The lack of a military or political settlement meanwhile continued to widen the dissenting constituency. Finally, after the traumas of Watergate and the resignation of President Nixon, the American regime in Vietnam simply collapsed. The objective of the long protest was finally gained, but in a context and for reasons that led to confusion rather than to hope.

Compared to the violence and divisiveness of the struggle for racial justice and antiwar agitation, the new feminist movement, often dated from Betty Friedan's *The Feminine Mystique* (1963), and the environmental awakening, similarly linked to Rachel Carson's *Silent Spring* (1962), were relatively peaceful in their outward aspect. Both of them, however, owed much of the provocations and questioning of American values that arose out of the civil rights and antiwar movements. These two issues, on the other hand, raised questions that challenge the most fundamental assumptions and most basic institutions of Western (or for that matter world) civilization. They lead, moreover, to reorientations of attitude and behavior that make serious assessment of the entire biblical tradition almost inescapable. One might say, indeed, that the aims of neither could be attained without basic revisions, both personal and collective, of the most time-honored American attitudes toward religion and morality.

It was the wide range of questions dealing with sexual attitudes and practices that aroused the deepest consternation and the most controversy. Before long most of the state legislatures, all levels of the judicial system including the Supreme Court, and nearly all of the churches were in one way or another wrestling with questions of birth control, sterilization, abortion, divorce laws, homosexuality, pornography, and the immensely difficult and controversial problem of defining and then establishing the rights of women. Underlying and complicating these issues are four particular problems: the deep theological, psychological, and social roots of male chauvinism in Western culture; the effects of changing attitudes on the family, as well as the needs and rights of children; the adaptation or adjustment of men and women who are seriously threatened by this social revolution; and finally, the difficulty of accepting personal responsibility for choices caused by the precipitous loss of the churches' moral authority and the manifest incapacity of "experts" to agree in their counsel. It is this last consideration, incidentally, that reveals the difficulty if not the folly of making sharp distinctions between the "religious" and the "secular."

In the long run it is probably the ecological issue, including problems of resource depletion and energy shortages, that will require the most excruciating policy decisions and personal adaptations in the world's most technologically advanced nations. When Robert L. Heilbroner describes *The Decline of Business Civilization,* he is not writing a scenario of social revolution but of the stark necessity for modifying exploitative attitudes and practices; and the same contention is present in Michael Harrington's *The Twilight of Capitalism,* though Harrington places more emphasis on the incapacity of the present system to achieve social justice and a reasonable level of equality. Quite aside from these inescapable demands for reform, however, one can only marvel at the degree to which less immediate environmental concerns for water, air, noise, ugliness, and natural open spaces have entered the American consciousness, changed ways of living, and motivated the foundations of countless reform organizations—nearly all of this in a fifteen-year period.

As for the whole long crisis of confidence in American government that began with the infamous credibility gap of the Johnson administration and continued on down through the Pentagon Papers affair to the collapse of the Nixon administration and the final Vietnam debacle, it was somehow the ultimate trauma of the era under discussion. The era was marked throughout by a steady deterioration of national trust of a dozen different kinds depending on as many grounds of dissatisfaction. Inequities in the military conscription system, racial discrimination, the impersonality of big government, the venality of small government, corruption in high office, desolated cities, the harshness of the police, and official dishonesty about the war—all of these played their part. And everyone over the age of thirty years remembers the disenchantment they created. Because deep suspicions remain, reformist zeal and political concern is replaced by self-seeking and privatization, even though the need for reform and political activism is greater than ever. From the vantage point of the later seventies, however, the most important result is a profound alteration of the American "civil religion." Ideological confusion and disbelief have taken its place. This circumstance in turn leads toward a consideration of traditional religious institutions whose situation reflects many of the same characteristics.

IV

The obvious place to open our consideration of instituted religion in America is with the nearly simultaneous election of America's first Roman Catholic President and the election of Pope John XXIII. The impact of these two events was immense, and it would be intensified three years later when the young man who had so utterly belied the idea of a "Catholic peril" was assassinated. Almost at once the old Know-Nothing syndrome faded away, and in 1964 the Republican Party, despite its nativist heritage, nominated a Catholic for Vice President. By this time the effects of Pope John's revolution began to enter into the life of the world, partly because of his own charismatic qualities but also because he summoned an ecumenical council which even in its first session brought the Counter Reformation to an end and set the church to the manifold intellectual and institutional tasks of aggiornamento. Protestants, Jews, and Communists alike were affected by the kinds of dialogue that ensued. Very soon there was hardly a city or village in America that had not experienced a drastic change in religious relationships.

For Roman Catholic Americans, the combined effects of Vatican II and rapid changes in their social situation had created grounds for extreme forms of disorientation. The classic Catholic ethos forged after the Reformation at the Council of Trent evaporated. The old defensive stance of the "immigration era" was replaced by a new sense of responsibility for American policy. Catholic scholars, meanwhile, led an assault upon the "ghetto mentality" created by the church-controlled educational system. At the same time came sudden transformations of the Mass, the passing of many traditional forms of catechetics, devotion, and obedience—even fish on Friday. More troubling still were changes in theology and moral philosophy. At precisely the time when the country was being deeply agitated by a wide range of "sexual" questions, a new emphasis on the individual conscience gained importance. Long-suppressed dissatisfactions of the clergy and other religious also came into the open, and many reforms in seminaries and religious orders were instituted, though even these measures did not prevent innumerable demissions of priests, nuns, monks, and even bishops.

Accompanying these trends was a marked decline of interest in entering religious vocations, and hence the closing of seminaries and convents as well as the secularizing of schools and colleges. All of these changes, meanwhile, were made even more confusing by the reactionary pronouncements and encyclicals of Pope Paul VI, whose *Humanae Vitae* (1968) against birth control has been judged by some to be the most fateful encyclical since Pope Leo X's excommunication of Martin Luther. One need not agree with Malachi Martin's sensational prediction that "well before the year 2000 there will no longer be a religious institution recognizable as the Roman Catholic Church of today," but one can confidently say that no part of the American population has had to accommodate itself to more drastic changes in the realm of theology, morals, and customary practice than "the Catholic quarter." And to make matters more difficult, the values of Protestantism, which so many Catholics were viewing with newly deepened respect, were themselves being drastically challenged. . . .

VI

An inflowing tide of new and non-traditional religion, along with a corresponding emergence of countercultural lifestyles, was another major expression of the disenchantment and disorientation which Americans experienced during the Traumatic Era. To some degree, the new religions were also part of a radical critique of the moral and theological attitudes of the Judaeo-Christian tradition.

One might even say that the protest movement as a whole, including a vast peripheral group that was sympathetic but not actively engaged, was held together by a set of attitudes and enthusiasms that marked it off as a distinct religious phenomenon. It existed for a brief but memorable period between the early sixties and early seventies. At once joyous and angry, serious and critical, it was shaped by disaffection with conventional America and pervaded by a strong awareness of a generation gap. Most of its adherents were under the age of thirty years. Rage and disappointment led some to violence, but interpersonal warmth and affection and a desire for authentic personal relationships were everywhere apparent. Wide sympathy for the poor and the abused and hopes for a new America were widespread. It was the age of the guitar. This whole generation was animated by a new popular music that was in diverse ways deeply ideological. The incredible Beatles almost defined the movement's time-span, but Bob Dylan, Joan Baez, Peter, Paul & Mary, Simon and Garfunkel, and many, many others provided a meaningful hymnody. Woodstock was a mount of transfiguration for the fortunate thousands who could say that they were there. And the elegy for this "generation lost in space" was *American Pie,* released by Don McLean in 1971.

In the midst of this decade of turmoil, however, many particular religious commitments were formed and new religions adopted. Many of the religions to which people turned were in at least two respects not new. Some of them had maintained a lively existence since ancient times. Even in America the fascination with Eastern religions dates back to Emerson, Thoreau, and the Transcendentalists, who found it a welcome and rational alternative to both the "pale negations of Boston Unitarianism" and the doctrinaire theology of New England orthodoxy. Along with this turning to the religions of India and the East, and for similar reasons, came a more esoteric revival of gnosticism, kabalism, astrology, theosophy, and "heretical" forms of mysticism, some of which had been organized movements in America since the Gilded Age. Among black Americans an "Islamic" movement had been discernible since the 1920s, though it was only in the 1960s that the Black Muslims, chiefly because of Malcolm X, made their greatest impact on the social order. . . .

In the midst of this fermenting situation, the place of conservative evangelicalism is somewhat ambiguous in that large parts of its scattered constituency are themselves, and by overt profession, a religiously and socially deviant subculture, which in some of its manifestations takes on almost the character of a new and radically charismatic religion. Some evangelical youth movements, for example, share many organizational and ideological characteristics of Mr. Moon's much-criticized Unification Church. When seen in a full perspective, therefore, the phenomenon of America's new religions becomes so valuable an index of the elements of change in the moral and religious realm that it is worthwhile to attempt a brief summary statement.

1. Extreme diversity of religious belief and of correspondingly distinctive ways of life have from the earliest times been a characteristic feature of the American experience. A growing commitment to libertarian individualism encouraged this tendency even in later centuries even after governmental intervention in the social order had become necessary. Denominational schisms, as well as the founding of sects, cults, and new religions, became prominent aspects of American life.

2. Immigration, migration across the continent, and very diverse forms of rapid social change led to the formation of innumerable large and small subcultures whose life situations and religious traditions varied accordingly. In these myriad contexts, charismatic religious leaders could and did attract followings of extremely diverse types.

3. The new industrial revolution that followed World War II created still other grounds for religious discontent as older forms of *Gemeinschaft* yielded to more impersonal forms of living together, and these tendencies to alienation accelerated during the 1960s. In the antitechnocratic countercultural ethos that then emerged, neither the moral attitudes nor the traditional theology of the major denominations had much appeal. The religious establishment was apprehended as both conventional and authoritarian.

4. The positive result of mounting dissatisfaction was a widespread and highly variegated turn toward other-minded religious movements according to principles of elective affinity, and usually in ways that, if not formally communal, were at least responsive to a pervasive desire to share and express a meaningful structure of moral and religious values.

5. Amid the shocks and disappointments of the 1970s, the militancy of American dissent waned, but in almost no ways had it led to a rebirth of confidence or hope. As a result, new religions continue to multiply and flourish. American dissent has waned, but there is little or no evidence of a rebirth of confidence, and the future is more uncertain than ever. As a result the new religions continue to subdivide and flourish. As usual their diversity was extreme, ranging from Satanism to disciplined forms of Zen. Most nearly traditional is a noticeable attraction to evangelical groups, which have always encouraged meaningful small-group relationships, and which are themselves in a broad sense countercultural in outlook. By and large, therefore, the new religions tend to exhibit an untraditional tendency: opposition to dogmatism and code morality; a strong disapprobation of the exploitative mentality, pollution of the biosphere, and the wasting of natural resources whether by industry or through the country's endemic gluttony. They tend to feel and express a sense of oneness with the natural world which is conducive to a mystical approach to reality that may verge on pantheism or on the esoteric. A discountenancing of racist and sexist stereotypes and behavior is almost everywhere apparent, as is a strong emphasis on warm and authentic personal relationships. When seen as a whole, the new religions in many ways perpetuate the aims and ideals of the older counterculture. They do not, by and large, reinforce

the social attitudes engendered by the Puritan ethic. They try to ameliorate the ways in which monolithic institutions and materialistic striving tend to dehumanize the social order. If this analysis is to any considerable degree accurate, therefore, one may say that the new religions in concrete and very intense ways embody, or at least suggest, the less intense but nevertheless pervasive and enduring impact of the Traumatic Era on American attitudes and behavior.

VII

If we take a broader view of the years since President John F. Kennedy issued his spirited summons to the nation, the overwhelming fact is that the entire religious realm—moral, spiritual, and attitudinal—has been so fundamentally altered that we confront a "new America" in the 1980s. A new and comprehensive agenda of expectations and reform has gradually taken shape. Yet the evaluations and priorities placed on these new goals for the republic are very diverse. For many people, especially those with long memories, John Donne's sense of "all coherence gone" is the dominant reaction. A well-behaved America has passed away, and with it the certitudes that had always shaped the nation's well-being and sense of destiny. For many others, and especially those who in various ways had supported the movements of protest and reform which made the era memorable, the sense of disorientation is far less deeply felt. For most of them urban decay, high levels of crime, gross inequalities, and malfunctioning institutions are simply constitutive of the American way of life. Rapid social change and shifting mores are the normal conditions of existence. Even among the more thoughtful elements of this latter constituency, however, there is neither exultation nor a feeling of triumph, but rather widespread doubts as to the possibilities for significant institutional change or of any basic shifts of power in the economic order. For this constituency as well as for the other, America has a clouded future. Because such a convergence of views is indeed new for America, the legacy of the Traumatic Years can be interpreted only as at once both momentous and unresolved.

Toward Religious Realignment

ROBERT WUTHNOW

SOURCE: Wuthnow, Robert, *The Restructuring of American Religion: Society and Faith since World War II.* Copyright © 1988 by Princeton University Press. Reprinted by permission of Princeton University Press.

Consolidation and Deepening Division

If the 1960s was a decade of social and religious upheaval, the period from about 1973 through the mid-1980s was a time of consolidation—of continuity in the major educational and religious patterns established in the 1960s—and of deepening division between religious liberals and religious conservatives. Continuities can be seen in this period both in religion itself and in the relations between religion and the educational system.

Within conventional religion, aggregate indices of religious strength remained virtually constant during this period. Church membership fell from 62 percent of the total population in 1974 to 61 percent in 1975 and remained there for the next decade. In 1980, 2,055 new religious books were published, representing 4.8 percent of all new books, compared with 5.0 percent in 1970. Sales of religious books actually made up a slightly larger share of the total in 1980 (10.3 percent) than in 1970 (9.2 percent). Religious contributions remained constant throughout the decade at 1.0 percent of personal income. And church attendance during a typical week hovered around 40 percent or 41 percent from 1971 on.

Measures of religious beliefs and attitudes also pointed toward a leveling out in the 1970s and 1980s, after the dramatic slumps of the late 1960s. Whereas only 14 percent of the public thought religion's influence was increasing in 1970, this figure rose to 31 percent by 1974, climbed further to 44 percent in 1976, hit 44 percent again in 1983 after having sagged somewhat in the late 1970s, and then rose to 48 percent in 1985. Between 1973 and 1985 the proportion who indicated a great deal or a lot of confidence in the churches or organized religion held virtually steady, varying between 64 percent and 66 percent. The number who felt religion could answer all or most of today's problems was 61 percent in 1985, compared with 62 percent in 1974. And the number who said religion was very important to them held steady at around 55 percent, after having declined from 70 percent in 1965 and 75 percent in 1952.

During this period, Americans also continued to register exceptionally strong levels of commitment to relatively simple aspects of religious belief and practice, although some of the more specific tenets of religious belief showed the lasting effects of erosion occurring in the 1960s. By the mid-1980s, for example, approximately nine of every ten adults in the United States still claimed to pray—a third of these saying they prayed at least twice a day—a figure that was about the same as that in national polls dating back to the late 1940s. Seven in ten said they believed in the divinity of Jesus, in life after death, and in heaven, all figures that had scarcely changed at all from the early 1950s. On the other hand, belief in a tenet that was to become a kind of shibboleth in the division between religious liberals and religious conservatives—whether the Bible is literally true—had fallen below 40 percent by the early 1970s, after having been recorded at 65 percent in 1963, and remained at this low level through the mid-1980s. And despite the fact that a majority of the public believed in the divinity of Jesus, considerably fewer now believed it necessary to accept Jesus in order to be saved (38 percent in 1981, compared with 51 percent in 1964). Similarly, most people still claimed some belief in God, but fewer now held this belief with certainty than in the past (62 percent said they had no doubts about God's existence in 1981, compared with 77 percent in 1964).

A few denominational mergers and sectarian reactions to these mergers appeared in the 1970s and 1980s, but by and large the period was quieter than the 1960s in these respects. One of the most publicized movements in the 1970s was the formation of the Association of Evangelical Lutheran Churches, a theologically liberal denomination involving 245 local congregations, which emerged in 1976 after a conservative faction captured control of the Lutheran Church-Missouri Synod and forced a number of the denomination's liberal seminary professors to resign their positions. Other significant mergers that were finally effected in the 1980s after years of negotiations were those uniting the northern and southern branches of the Presbyterian church and bringing together the American Lutheran Church and the Lutheran Church in America. As before, some of these mergers were accompanied by the emergence of splinter groups. But generally, the degree of schismatic activity fell considerably below that of the 1960s. For example, only 12 new sectarian groups came into existence in the 1970s, compared with 57 in the 1960s.

Most of the new religious movements still in existence by the 1980s had been founded sometime prior to 1972. One source lists 111 new religious organizations as coming into existence in the 1970s, but most of these were founded in 1970 or 1971, and even the total figure is well below that listed for the 1960s (184). After the mass suicide of more than 900 cult members at Jonestown, Guyana, in 1978, and the emergence of a more vigorous anticult movement, many of the new religious movements adopted a lower profile. Consequently, evidence on the extent of their memberships and activities became more difficult to obtain. Available evidence, though, suggests that new religious experimentation by no means died out; but it probably did not grow after the early 1970s either. National surveys conducted during that decade, for example, showed little change in participation rates between the mid-1970s and the end of the decade. About 1 percent of the public claimed to be involved in Eastern religions, about 4 percent said they practiced TM, and about 3 percent claimed they were involved in yoga. Given the small percentages, these figures were, of course, subject to considerable variation from sampling error. More recent estimates have come from less systematic sources. They also suggest that participation in new religious movements is quite small relative to the larger population. Yet, in absolute terms, the numbers are scarcely inconsiderable. A relatively complete estimate of the numbers involved in one kind of new religious activity or another in the greater Philadelphia area, for example, indicates approximately 90,000 participants (out of a total population of more than 3 million). Followup research on people who were involved in new religions in the late 1960s and early 1970s also suggests that a very high proportion still pursue some kind of nonconventional religious philosophy, although actual membership in organized groups and in communal living arrangements has dropped off sharply.

The fate of specific kinds of new religions has varied markedly since the early 1970s, depending greatly on leadership style and dominant beliefs. Many of the more authoritarian movements either fled the country or declined considerably as a result of litigation, public suspicion, or financial difficulties. Movements like the Children of God and Divine Light, for example, relocated many of their members in other countries, while the leadership of the Rajneesh community in Oregon fled the United States, and some of the leaders of movements like Synanon and the Unification Church were jailed. Many of the democratically led movements have fared better, although some of the more idealistic of these groups have found it difficult to sustain the levels of sacrifice required over long periods of time. The

Farm, a highly successful communal movement in Tennessee, which was organized by lecturer Steve Gaskin in 1971, for example, underwent a massive internal reorganization in 1983 after nearly half its members defected. Today, its economic and political structure comes much closer to that of the larger society than was initially the case. The most viable movements, however, have been ones such as TM, yoga, *est,* and various self-help groups that offer therapy, meditation techniques, and other kinds of courses on a relatively short-term basis without demanding total involvement or intensive changes in life style. Indeed, the proliferation of health food stores, esoteric book stores, meditation centers, and organizations offering courses on a for-pay basis suggests that new religious orientations may be increasingly organized as a commercial offshoot of the broader religious establishment.

The fact that new religious movements gradually ceased to attract the wider publicity they enjoyed in the early 1970s has also meant that they will play a less vital symbolic role in American religion. The division between religious liberals and religious conservatives is to some extent reflected in publicized reactions to the new religions. Conservative religious periodicals occasionally run feature stories warning readers of the heresies of new religions (a favorite target being the so-called "New Age Movement") and study guides for anticult classes can be found in conservative bookstores. Liberal churches and liberal religious periodicals, in contrast, have been much more likely to ask what can be learned from the new religions. Taking a more tolerant attitude toward other religions in general, their response has often been to suggest ways in which to incorporate insights about meditation, mystical experience, holistic health, therapy, massage, and so on, into Christianity. For the most part, however, the new religions have played a much less prominent role in the religious tensions of the 1980s than in the early 1970s.

More visible by far have been the various movements on the religious right. Groups like Moral Majority, as well as the prominent role played by religious television, have become the controversial issues of the 1980s. These, to a much greater extent than any of the movements in the 1960s, have contributed to the polarization evident between religious liberals and religious conservatives. . . .

While many of the tendencies in the larger religious organizations reflect continuities with the changes initiated in the 1960s, a more detailed breakdown of how different segments of the population stand with respect to these tendencies again requires a look at broader developments. The continued promotion of science and technology and the consolidation of educational divisions as a major source of social differentiation still constitute an important part of this larger picture. By 1980, 32 percent of the adult population (over age 25) had completed at least some college education, compared with only 21 percent in 1970. Total enrollments in higher education rose from 8.6 million in 1970 to 12.1 million in 1980. The proportion of young people age 18 to 24 who were in school rose from 35 percent to 40 percent. And expenditures on higher education from all sources increased from $23.4 billion in 1970 to $50.7 billion in 1980. Two-thirds of U.S. exports were still in high-technology industries and increasing attention was being devoted to developing these industries since they were the principal areas in which the country enjoyed in the 1970s rose by 22.3 percent after inflation and an increasing share of these expenditures was being borne by the private sector. The new class, it appeared, was destined to play an ever greater role in American society. . . .

The "education gap" in social attitudes and in religion that was becoming evident by 1970 became even more pronounced during the following decade. Those with college educations were considerably more likely to espouse religious views which in one way or another had come to be regarded as liberal orientations. The better educated were more likely in their own minds to identify themselves as religious liberals. And their views on church matters, social and moral questions, and political issues all tended to set them off from religious conservatives. Those without college educations, on the other hand, were much more likely to identify themselves as religious conservatives, to hold more traditional religious views, and to espouse a wide range of social and political attitudes that reflected a conservative orientation.

In a 1981 survey, for example, approximately half of the college educated American public identified themselves as "religiously liberal." In comparison, only one person in seven among those who had only grade school educations identified themselves this way. Views of the Bible, as noted earlier, were one of the issues on which the better and less educated divided most sharply. More than half of the grade school educated thought the Bible should be regarded as the literal word of God. Only a fifth of the college educated felt this way. People from different educational strata also took radically different positions on issues confronting the church. For example, 47 percent of the college educated thought it acceptable for homosexuals to be hired as clergy, compared with only 17 percent of those with grade school educations In an earlier survey devoted to issues confronting the Roman Catholic church, huge differences had also been evident between the different educational strata. Among college educated Roman Catholics, for instance, 48 percent said they approved of women being ordained as priests, compared with only 28 percent of the non-college groups. Similarly, three-quarters of the former said they approved of the changes in the church since the Second Vatican Council, compared with about half of the latter.

Polls conducted in the mid-1980s have documented even more clearly the role of educational differences in the current divide between religious liberals and religious conservatives. . . . Of all the social background questions in the study, education was the factor that most clearly discriminated between religious liberals and religious conservatives.

Judging from other results, it is understandable why persons with different educational levels hold these different views about their religious orientations. Among college graduates, only one person in three thinks the Bible is absolutely true (contains no errors); among persons who have only attended high school the figure is closer to two-thirds. Of all college graduates, only a quarter say they have been "born again." The figure is approximately half among persons with high school educations. Half of the less educated sector says reading the Bible is very important to them, compared with only a quarter of college graduates.

In more subtle ways, educational differences also add up to quite divergent styles of religious expression. For example, college graduates are about three times more likely than persons without college education to put the Second Commandment (loving your neighbor) ahead of the First Commandment (loving God). The better educated are also about three times as likely to think it possible to be a true Christian without believing in the divinity of Christ. Those with low levels of education, in contrast, are about twice as likely as college graduates to believe that being baptized is necessary in order truly to know God. The two groups also view Jesus and God in quite different ways. For instance, college graduates are about twice as likely as those without college educations to be most impressed by Jesus' compassion and forgiveness. The less educated, in comparison, are more likely to be impressed by Jesus' healings, miracles, and goodness. Those with higher levels of education are considerably more likely to attribute androgenous characteristics to God; those with lower levels of education, to emphasize the masculinity of God.

More generally, persons with different levels of education also differ on a wide variety of social, political, and moral issues. For example, most of the polls that have asked about legalized abortion show nearly twice as much support among those with college educations than in the noncollege sector. On civil liberties items, such as allowing an atheist to teach, only a quarter of those who have graduated from college express disapproval, compared with 60 percent of those who do not hold a college degree. On national defense, more than four in ten college degree holders say the country is spending too much, compared with only a quarter of those without college degrees. Differences of similar magnitude exist on most survey questions about pornography, homosexuality, and abiding by strict moral standards. To the extent that religious organizations have generally regarded these as important issues to discuss, therefore, it is not surprising that a major division has emerged in these organizations between persons with high and low levels of education.

In addition to dividing people on social issues and on religious attitudes, the role of higher education can also be seen in some of the longer range trends that have been mentioned. It was suggested earlier, for instance, that religious participation rates declined more rapidly in the 1960s among the better educated than in the rest of the population. The full extent of these changes can be seen more clearly in light of additional evidence from the 1980s. Between 1958 and 1982, the most serious declines in regular church attendance came about among younger people with at least some college education. Specifically, there was a 19 percentage point difference between the two periods among college educated persons between the ages of 25 and 34. And there was a 21 point difference among college educated persons between the ages of 35 and 44. In none of the other categories were the differences this great. In other words, being a younger, better educated person in the 1980s was associated with relatively modest levels of religious participation, whereas the same kind of person in the late 1950s was likely to be much more active in religious involvement. Not only were there considerably more people

with college educations by the 1980s, but these people were now less conventionally religious than their counterparts had been a generation earlier. Again, education
seemed to have become associated with a kind of "gap" in religious commitment
that had not been there prior to the 1960s.

If the better educated were no longer as actively involved in religious organizations as they once were, their growing numbers nevertheless had become a significant influence in most denominations. By the 1980s, a majority—or very substantial
minorities—of the members of most denominations carried college educations as
part of their personal experience and brought with them many of the more liberal
outlooks that went along with this experience. According to polls conducted in
1984, for example, 68 percent of all Episcopalians had been to college, as had an
equal proportion of Jews. Among Presbyterians, six in ten had been to college. And
better than four in ten had been to college in each of the following: American
Lutheran Church, Lutheran Church-Missouri Synod, United Methodist, United
Church of Christ, and Roman Catholic. Of the large established denominations,
only Baptists continued to be comprised primarily of persons without college educations. And even among Baptists the percentage who had been to college was by
no means inconsiderable: 29 percent among American Baptists, 30 percent among
Southern Baptists.

As the religiously active public became better educated, there was some denominational switching along educational lines as well. When people changed
denominations, they tended to move toward denominations that most closely reflected their own levels of education. Among all denominational switchers, for
example, 43 percent of those who had not been to college shifted either to one of
the Baptist denominations or to a religious sect. In contrast, only 28 percent of the
college educated switchers shifted to one of these groups. And on the other side of
the scale, those who had been reared in one of these denominations were likely to
"move up" to one of the better educated denominations if they themselves were
better educated. For instance, 16 percent of the switchers who had been raised as
Baptists but who had college educations became Episcopalians or Presbyterians.
The comparable figure for former Baptists without college educations was 7 percent. Among former members of Protestant sects, the differences were even more
pronounced: 31 percent of the college educated became Episcopalians or Presbyterians, compared with 8 percent of those without college educations. And the same
was true among people reared in denominations with an ample mixture of different educational levels. Among former Methodists, 21 percent of the college educated became Presbyterians or Episcopalians, compared with only 10 percent of
the non-college educated.

Were these patterns to continue on any sizable scale, they would of course result
in the division of denominations along educational lines. The better educated denominations would increasingly become the refuge of college graduates; denominations with large numbers of persons without college educations would attract
even larger numbers of the same kind of people. This does not appear to be happening, however . . . the major denominations are becoming more similar to one

another in educational composition rather than less similar. Several reasons explain why. One is that large numbers of church members still stay put rather than switching denominations at all. A second is that little switching seems to occur from better educated denominations to less educated denominations among those who themselves have lower levels of education. A third factor is that a sizable number of the better educated who switch denominations cease to affiliate with any denomination, rather than joining the better educated denominations. For instance, 16 percent of all former Methodists who switch and who have been to college list their current affiliation as "none." And 19 percent of the former Baptists with college educations do so. Consequently, the better educated denominations, such as the Episcopal and Presbyterian churches, have not grown in overall membership, even though the general population is becoming more highly educated. . . . it appears that average education levels have grown faster among members of denominations that previously had the lowest education levels, perhaps simply because they had more "room to grow." The upshot, then, is that most denominations have substantial numbers of both the better educated and the less educated.

To the extent that rising levels of education have carried with them more liberal orientations, these views are now much more prominently represented in the major denominations than they have been in the past. Liberal theological orientations are more prevalent. Support for interdenominational cooperation is stronger. And reinforcement for liberal clergy who favor social activism, egalitarianism, and tolerant positions on issues such as pornography, homosexuality, ordination of women, and so on, is likely to be more pronounced. Often these shifts remain subtle, especially when they are clouded by the statements of powerful leaders at the top of these denominations. In other cases, the changes have been clear and decisive. Among United Methodists, for example, the proportion of laity who regarded individual salvation as the chief goal for the church to pursue dropped from 63 percent in 1958 to 55 percent in 1975 to 31 percent in 1983—with comparable shifts being evident in church policies as well. Similarly, among Southern Baptists, rapidly rising education levels among pastors and members alike during the 1970s, as well as broader changes taking place in the South, led to wholesale questioning of the denomination's traditional stand on biblical inerrancy—which only in the 1980s came to be resisted by an even more powerful movement among conservatives in the denomination. Again, education was a decisive factor in shaping the ways in which Southern Baptists aligned themselves on these issues.

Over the past quarter century, therefore, a noticeable move to the left has taken place in many sectors of American religion. In contrast with the solid centrism evident in the 1950s, many denominations have undergone a high degree of turbulence surrounding the civil rights movement, the anti-war protests, the counterculture, and a more general upgrading of educational levels with corresponding shifts in social values and religious orientations. At the same time, these shifts have not been so sweeping as to merely carry the day. They have generated countermovements and have been resisted by a strong enough constituency to have resulted more in polarization between the right and the left rather than a clear victory for either side. . . .

Confused and Helpless

THOMAS C. REEVES

SOURCE: Reprinted with the permission of The Free Press, a Division of Simon & Schuster, Inc., from *The Empty Church: The Suicide of Liberal Christianity* by Thomas C. Reeves. Copyright © 1996 by Thomas C. Reeves.

. . . A major reason for the numerical decline of the mainline churches is their failure to retain their own children once they have reached the age of decision. Presbyterians, Methodists, and Episcopalians lose nearly half their young people for good. Indeed, fully 48 percent of Presbyterian youth drop out of churchgoing altogether. This alienation and indifference is revealed on the college level by the difficulty students today often have even spelling "Presbyterian" and "Episcopalian." Denominational history and theology interest my students about as much as baroque opera or the insects of Paraguay.

The mainline membership is graying rapidly. By 1983, nearly half of all mainliners were 50 years of age or older. In 1994, 61.4 percent of the laity in the United Methodist Church were 50 years or older. (In the general population, 25.5 percent were over 50.) Conservative Protestants are younger than liberal Protestants in part because they are more successful in keeping their children in church.

Few observers anticipate a dramatic resurgence in mainline membership. The Methodist theologian Stanley Hauerwas of Duke Divinity School said in 1993, "God is killing mainline Protestantism in America, and we goddam well deserve it."

Giving as a percentage of annual income decreased in Protestant churches between 1968 and 1993, from 3.35 percent to 2.97 percent in eight denominations affiliated with the National Council of Churches. Indeed, a study of eleven denominations between 1921 and 1993 reported that per member giving as a percentage of income was lower in 1992 than in 1921, and even lower than in 1933, the depth of the Great Depression.

Giving to overseas Protestant ministries based in the United States was $2 billion in 1992—less than what Americans spent on guns ($2.48 billion) in 1994. This figure looks even worse when compared with consumer expenditures for illegal drugs (an estimated $49 billion in 1993); alcohol ($44 billion in 1992), legal gambling (nearly $40 billion annually), leisure travel (an estimated $40 billion in 1992), and cosmetics ($20 billion in 1992). This plus the decline in membership have caused serious financial problem in the mainline denominations.

The Presbyterian Church (USA), faced with a $5 million budget deficit in 1993, sacked more than 200 national staff members. In 1994, a top official at the Presbyterian Center in Louisville said, "We see the need to trim our budget by about 5 percent a year." The Evangelical Lutheran Church in America, created out of a merger of three smaller Lutheran groups in 1988, racked up more than $21 million in deficits in its first three years and cut some twenty positions from its national offices. Between 1991 and 1995, the Episcopal Church cut its national office staff by about one-third, and its budget declined more than $3.6 million between 1994 and 1995. The budget was cut $2.45 million for 1995-96. At the National Council of Churches, created and maintained largely by the mainline churches, contributions from members dropped 50 percent between 1975 and the late 1980s, and the fulltime staff was cut to 61, down from 187 two decades earlier.

Morale throughout the mainline ranks is low. One major study concluded that "The liberal Protestant community is mired in a depression, one that is far more serious and deeper than it has suffered at any time in this century." A Gallup poll revealed that only 27 percent of Protestants gave their church an excellent rating. The Methodists, scoring the highest among the mainline bodies, reported 25 percent; the Presbyterians, 18 percent; and the Episcopalians, 9 percent.

Missionary zeal has been almost lost. Gallup reports, "Invitation and evangelism are virtually ignored by the mainline churches." In 1985 a third of the nation's Methodist churches had performed no baptisms; almost two-thirds offered no membership training or confirmation classes; and nearly one-half lacked a list of potential new members. The Episcopal Church in 1996 sponsored just 25 overseas missionaries worldwide (one was in England), down from 59 in 1989.

Colleges and universities founded by mainline churches have in large part become either secular, largely secular, or obscure. In 1990, the presidents of 69 Presbyterian colleges and universities issued a manifesto that discussed "the demise of Protestant hegemony, the decline of mainline churches and the importance of denominationalism" and concluded that "The Presbyterian Church could be close to the point where its involvement in higher education might be lost forever."

Mainline church headquarters, conventions, organizations, and agencies seem almost inevitably to fall under the control of liberals—a generic, albeit at times slippery term for those on the left. Thus official pronouncements and actions often disturb people in the pews, who by and large are more moderate or conservative. (In 1994, more than 40 percent of mainline church members were Republicans, while about 25 percent were Democrats. According to an exit poll taken that fall, only 11 percent of the nation's voters called themselves liberal, while 12 percent said they were "somewhat liberal". In 1992, 43 percent of mainliners voted for Bush and 34 percent for Clinton.) Two Methodist professors of religion have declared, "it seems inconceivable that an agency of any mainline, Protestant denomination should espouse some social position unlike that of the most liberal Democrats. The church is the dull exponent of conventional secular political ideas with a vaguely religious tint."

In 1992, the Presbyterian Church (USA) elected The Rev. John H. Fife to its top post. Fife had been arrested in the 1960s for picketing in front of the suburban homes of central-city landlords, and during the same years counseled draft resisters and marched in Selma and Birmingham, Alabama. In 1986 he was found guilty of federal charges of conspiracy and two counts of aiding the transportation of an illegal alien. While running for office in the Presbyterian's annual convention, he favored a committee report supporting abortion rights. Fife's election made him "symbolic leader of the church for the year."

That same year, the United Church of Christ moved its headquarters from New York City to Cleveland, Ohio, in an attempt to counter charges that East Coast liberals were running the show. Not long after the furniture arrived, denominational leaders began alienating locals by attacking Chief Wahoo, the Cleveland Indians' popular logo, as offensive to Native Americans.

In 1995, the largest church lobby in Washington, D.C., was the United Methodist Board for Church and Society. With a staff of nearly forty, the board was spending $2.5 million a year. On what? Mark Tooley of the Institute for Religion and Democracy observed in a trenchant report on the Board:

> Like fossils trapped in amber, directors and staffers embraced yesterday's causes by calling for an unlimited welfare state, praising Fidel Castro's Cuba, urging global U.S. military withdrawal, bemoaning the revival of free market economics, and affirming, of all things, the sexual revolution.

The obvious question is, Why do liberals dominate? As we have seen, liberals have long been prominent in the mainline. But there is also an important principle of group dynamics involved here: moderate, otherwise busy people are no match for zealous, ideological interest groups eager to attain power. This is as true for churches as it is for any other institution. . . .

Some on the right view the plight of the mainline churches as a byproduct of a massive and deliberate assault by left-wing secularists, often called secular humanists, upon the whole of the Christian faith and the American way of life. Concerned Women for America, the nation's largest women's organization (much larger than the heralded National Organization for Women), has claimed that "the secular humanists, who deny God and traditional moral values, have almost gained total control of our public policies, our schools, even our lawmaking institutions and courts—in just one or two generations." The historian James Hitchcock contends that secular humanism "has a keen sense of being locked into a continuous philosophical and social struggle with religious belief, in which the ultimate stakes are nothing less than the moral foundations of society." Many conservatives like Hitchcock fail to be distressed by the deterioration of liberal churches, seeing them as collaborators with forces determined to de-Christianize our civilization.

Other observers see the mainline churches as mere victims, casualties of such modern phenomena as urbanism, industrialism, rising educational levels, prosperity, social mobility, the changing nature of the family, and so on. It is true, for example, that liberal Protestants, being higher in the social structure, have lower fertility rates than conservative Protestants, and this has had an impact on the decrease in young members.

One interpretation of the mainline malaise, posited in 1972 by Dean M. Kelley, an official of the National Council of Churches, has warranted frequent commentary. In *Why Conservative Churches Are Growing,* Kelley argued that successful churches make strict demands, both of faith and practice, on their members. The "business" of religion, he contended, was "to explain the ultimate meaning of life" and "the quality which makes one system of ultimate meaning more convincing than another is not its content but its seriousness/strictness/costliness/bindingness." By this standard, then, the mainline churches, light on questions of eternal importance, lacking a distinctive identity, and permissive to the bone, seem doomed.

Two liberal professors of religion, Wade Clark Roof and William McKinney, concluded in 1987 that Kelley's thesis had in general proved sound. "Careful analysis of membership trends shows that the churches hardest hit were those highest in socioeconomic status, those stressing individualism and pluralism in belief, and those most affirming of American culture." The sociologists Roger Finke and Rodney Stark agreed, concluding in 1992, "to the degree that denominations rejected traditional doctrines and ceased to make serious demands on their followers, they ceased to prosper. The churching of America was accomplished by aggressive churches committed to vivid otherworldliness."

In 1994, a major study conducted by the Catholic University sociologist Dean R. Hoge and three others concluded that members of theologically conservative churches that stress financial sacrifice, personal piety, and personal salvation are the most generous givers.

In contrast to the mainline denominations, many conservative evangelical churches have been prospering. (Evangelicals stress personal conversion and such classical Protestant beliefs as the allsufficient authority of Scripture. Fundamentalists, who in general defend biblical inerrancy and reject modern ideas and values, are the right wing of the movement and represent about a third of all evangelicals. A recent study showed evangelical Protestants making up more than 20 percent of the nation's population.) An official of the Southern Baptist Convention, for example, could boast in 1994, "We're still growing at the rate of 750 members and five churches a week." Between 1965 and 1989 the Assemblies of God grew 121 percent, the Seventh Day Adventists grew 92 percent, the Church of God (Cleveland, Tennessee) grew 183 percent, and the Church of the Nazarene grew 63 percent. The major metropolitan areas abound in large and affluent nondenominational churches that seem especially successful in appealing to youth.

The success of these bodies, as suggested above, may be due to their rejection of the secular spirit of the age. The sociologist Daniel V. A. Olson argues that conservative churches prosper because their members are united in basic, orthodox Christian beliefs and values that are distinctive from mainstream American culture. . . .

Questions for Reflection and Discussion

1. How do the documents demonstrate the reappearance of a centrifugal pattern in American religion in the final third of the twentieth century?

2. What evidence does Sydney Ahlstrom provide in support of his thesis that the 1960s and 1970s were characterized by religious tension and unrest?

3. On what grounds does Robert Wuthnow contend that the early 1970s through the mid-1980s was a time of consolidation and of deepening division between religious liberals and religious conservatives?

4. Discuss Thomas Reeves's argument that mainline Protestant liberalism experienced a malaise during the final years of the twentieth century.

5. What influence did American religion have on the search for American stability during the later twentieth century?

6. Which of the four dimensions of religious tension were in evidence during the final quarter of the twentieth century?

Additional Readings

Bellah, Robert, et al. *Habits of the Heart: Individualism and Commitment in American Life*. New York: Harper and Row 1985.

Bloesch, Donald G. *The Future of Evangelical Christianity: A Call for Unity and Diversity*. Colorado Springs: Helmers and Howard, 1988.

Colaianni, James. *The Catholic Left: The Crisis of Radicalism Within the Church*. Philadelphia: Chilton Book Company, 1968.

Daly, Mary. *The Church and the Second Sex: With a New Feminist Postchristian Introduction*. New York: Harper, 1975.

Dolan, Jay P., et al. *Transforming Parish Ministry: The Changing Roles of Catholic Clergy, Laity, and Women Religious*. New York: Crossroad, 1989.

Ellwood, Robert S., Jr. *Alternative Altars: Unconventional and Eastern Spirituality in America*. Chicago: University of Chicago Press, 1979.

Furlong, Monica. *Zen Effects: The Life of Alan Watts*. New York: Houghton Mifflin Co., 1986.

Goldy, Robert G. *The Emergence of Jewish Theology in America*. Bloomington: Indiana University Press, 1990.

Greeley, Andrew M. *Religious Change in America*. Cambridge: Harvard University Press, 1989.

Hitchcock, James. *Catholicism and Modernity: Confrontation or Capitulation*. New York: Seabury Press, 1979.

Hunter, James Davison. *Culture Wars: The Struggle to Define America*. New York: HarperCollins, 1990.

Kelley, Dean. *Why Conservative Churches are Growing*. New York: Harper and Row, 1972.

McGreevey, John T. "Racial Justice and the People of God: The Second Vatican Council, the Civil Rights Movement, and American Catholics." *Religion and American Culture* 4 (Summer 1994):221-254.

Redmont, Jane. *Generous Lives: American Catholic Women Today*. New York: William Morrow, 1992.

Roof, Wade Clark. *A Generation of Seekers: The Spiritual Journeys of the Baby Boom Generation*. San Francisco: Harper San Francisco, 1993.

_____. *American Mainline Religion: Its Changing Shape of the Religious Establishment*. Piscataway, NJ: Rutgers University Press, 1987.

_____. *Spiritual Marketplace: Baby Boomers and the Remaking of American Religion*. Princeton: Princeton University Press, 1999.

Sarna, Jonathan D., ed. *Minority Faiths and the American Protestant Mainstream*. Champaign: University of Illinois Press, 1997.

Webber, Robert E. *Ancient-Future Faith: Rethinking Evangelicalism for a Postmodern World*. Grand Rapids: Baker Book House, 1999.

Additional Resources

Reference Works

Burgess, Stanley M., and Gary B. McGee, eds. *Dictionary of Pentecostal and Charismatic Movements.* Grand Rapids, MI: Zondervan Publishing House, 1988.

Burr, Nelson R., ed. A *Critical Bibliography of Religion in America.* 2 vols. Princeton, NJ: Princeton University Press, 1961.

Douglas, J. D., ed. *Twentieth-Century Dictionary of Christian Biography.* Grand Rapids, MI: Baker Book House, 1995.

Encyclopedia of American Catholic History. Collegeville, MN: The Liturgical Press, 1997.

Fraker, Anne T. *Religion and American Life: Resources.* Urbana: University of Illinois Press, 1989.

Gaustad, Edwin. *Historical Atlas of Religion in America.* New York: Harper and Row, 1962.

Hill, Samuel S., ed. *Encyclopedia of Religion in the South.* Macon, GA: Mercer University Press, 1984.

Lippy, Charles, and Peter Williams, eds. *Encyclopedia of American Religious Experience.* 3 vols. New York: Simon & Schuster, 1988.

Lippy, Charles H., ed. *Twentieth-Century Shapers of American Popular History.* Westport, CT: Greenwood Press, 1989.

Mead, Frank S., rev. by Samuel S. Hill. *Handbook of Denominations in the United States.* New Tenth Ed. Nashville: Abingdon Press, 1995.

Melton, J. Gordon. *Biographical Dictionary of American Cult and Sect Leaders.* New York: Garland Publishing, Inc., 1986.

_____. *Dictionary of Religious Organizations in the United States.* Third Ed. Detroit: Gale Research, Inc., 1993.

_____. *Encyclopedia of American Religion*. Fourth Ed. Detroit: Gale Research, Inc., 1993.

Meyer, F. E. *The Religious Bodies of America*. Fourth Rev. Ed. St. Louis: Concordia Publishing House, 1961.

Noll, Mark A., et al, eds. *Eerdman's Handbook to Christianity in America*. Grand Rapids, MI: Wm. B. Eerdmans Publishing Company, 1983.

Reid, Daniel G., et al, eds. *Dictionary of Christianity in America*. Downers Grove, IL: InterVarsity Press, 1990.

Swatos, William H., Jr., ed. *Encyclopedia of Religion and Society*. Walnut Creek, CA: AltaMira Press, 1998.

Williamson, William B., ed. *An Encyclopedia of Religion in the United States*. New York: Crossroad Publishing Company, 1992.

Internet Sites

American Religion Links
http://are.as.wvu.edu/

American Studies Crossroads
www.georgetown.edu/crossroads/

Center for the Study of American Religion and Culture at Indiana University-Purdue University at Indianapolis
www.iupui.edu/~raac/html/bibliographies.html

Center for the Study of Religion at Princeton University
www.princeton.edu/~csrel/

Center for the Study of Religion in Public Life–Religious History Project (Trinity College, Hartford, CT)
http://www.trincoll.edu/depts/csrpl/lilly_rel_history.htm

Church of Jesus Christ of Latter-Day Saints
www.lds.org/site_main_menu/frameset-global-mem_res.html

Cotton Mather Home Page
www.gty.org/~phil/mather.htm

Cushwa Center for the Study of American Catholicism
www.nd.edu/~cushwa/

Institute for the Study of American Evangelicals
www.wheaton.edu/isae/

Material History of American Religion Project
http://www.materialreligion.org/

North American Religions Section of the American Academy of Religion
www.columbia.edu/~jw40/nar.html

North Star
//religion@materialreligion.org/participants/weisenfeld.html

Religion and the Founding of the American Republic (Library of Congress Exhibition)
http://lcweb.loc.gov/exhibits/religion/

Religion Image Database
http://metalab.unc.edu.religion/

Religion Website Database
http://metalab.unc.edu/religionwww/index.html

Organizations

American Academy of Religion
American Catholic Historical Association
American Catholic Historical Society
American Jewish Historical Society
American Society of Church History
Conference on Faith and History
Evangelical and Reformed Historical Society
Friends Historical Association
Historical Commission of the Southern Baptist Convention
Historical Committee of the Mennonite Church
Historical Society of the United Methodist Church
Institute for the Study of American Evangelicals
Lutheran Historical Conference
Mormon Historical Association
Presbyterian Historical Society
Unitarian Universalist Historical Society